11E THE ART OF PUBLIC SPEAKING

STEPHEN E. LUCAS
UNIVERSITY OF WISCONSIN-MADISON

WITH ADDITIONAL COURSE MATERIALS FROM

COMMUNICATING AT WORK

Principles and Practices for Business and the Professions

Tenth Edition

RONALD B. ADLER
SANTA BARBARA CITY COLLEGE, EMERITUS

JEANNE MARQUARDT ELMHORST
CENTRAL NEW MEXICO COMMUNITY COLLEGE

McGraw Hill Learning Solutions

Boston Burr Ridge, IL Dubuque, IA New York San Francisco
St. Louis Bangkok Bogotá Caracas Lisbon London Madrid
Mexico City Milan New Delhi Seoul Singapore Sydney Taipei Toronto

The McGraw-Hill Companies

THE ART OF PUBLIC SPEAKING, Eleventh Edition
with additional course materials

This book is a McGraw-Hill Learning Solutions textbook and contains selected materials from the following sources:
The Art of Public Speaking, Eleventh Edition by Stephen E. Lucas. Copyright © 2012, 2009, 2007, 2004, 2001, 1998, 1995, 1992, 1989, 1986, 1983 by The McGraw-Hill Companies, Inc. Reprinted with permission of the publisher.
Communicating at Work: Principles and Practices for Business and the Professions, Tenth Edition by Ronald B. Adler and Jeanne Marquardt Elmhorst. Copyright © 2010, 2008, 2005, 2002, 1999, 1996, 1993, 1989, 1986, 1983 by The McGraw-Hill Companies, Inc. Reprinted with permission of the publisher.
Many custom published texts are modified versions or adaptations of our best-selling textbooks. Some adaptations are printed in black and white to keep prices at a minimum, while others are in color.

6 7 8 9 0 KNG KNG 16 15 14

ISBN-13: 978-0-07-762949-6
ISBN-10: 0-07-762949-3
part of
ISBN-13: 978-0-07-762948-9
ISBN-10: 0-07-762948-5

Learning Solutions Consultant: Melani Theis
Learning Solutions Representative: Nada Mraovic
Production Editor: Carrie Braun
Cover Image: 87831773.tif © Jupiterimages Corporation

About the Author

Stephen E. Lucas is Professor of Communication Arts and Evjue-Bascom Professor in the Humanities at the University of Wisconsin-Madison. He received his bachelor's degree from the University of California, Santa Barbara, and his master's and doctorate degrees from Penn State University.

Professor Lucas has been recognized for his work as both a scholar and a teacher. His first book, *Portents of Rebellion: Rhetoric and Revolution in Philadelphia, 1765–1776,* received the Golden Anniversary Award of the National Communication Association and was nominated for a Pulitzer Prize. His major articles include "The Schism in Rhetorical Scholarship" (1981), "The Renaissance of American Public Address: Text and Context in Rhetorical Criticism" (1988), "The Stylistic Artistry of the Declaration of Independence" (1990), and "The Rhetorical Ancestry of the Declaration of Independence" (1998), for which he received the Golden Anniversary Monograph Award of the National Communication Association. His most recent book is *Words of a Century: The Top 100 American Speeches, 1900–1999* (2009).

Professor Lucas has received a number of teaching awards, including the Chancellor's Award for Excellence in Teaching at the University of Wisconsin and the National Communication Association's Donald Ecroyd Award for Outstanding Teaching in Higher Education. His lecture course on "The Rhetoric of Campaigns and Revolutions" is among the most popular on campus and has twice been selected for statewide broadcast in its entirety by Wisconsin Public Radio. Professor Lucas is featured in the Educational Video Group's program on the history of American public address, and he has appeared on the History Channel's documentary on the Declaration of Independence.

Professor Lucas has directed the introductory public speaking course at the University of Wisconsin-Madison since 1973. Over the years he has been responsible for numerous teaching innovations and has supervised the training of hundreds of graduate assistants. In addition to participating in public speaking workshops and colloquia at schools throughout the United States, he has served as a judge for the major national English-language public speaking competitions in China, has lectured at numerous Chinese universities, and has conducted workshops for Chinese instructors on teaching public speaking. *The Art of Public Speaking* has been published in China both in translation and in English editions.

Stephen Lucas and his wife, Patty, live in Madison, Wisconsin, and have two sons, Jeff and Ryan. His interests include travel, sports, art, and photography.

Contents in Brief

Contents

HUNTER
The City University of New York

Chapter 13 Delivery 239

Chapter 14 Using Visual Aids 259

PART FIVE VARIETIES OF PUBLIC SPEAKING

Appendix Speeches for Analysis and Discussion A1

SPEECHES

SPEECHES BY GENRE

INTRODUCTORY SPEECHES

Self-Introduction

Introducing a Classmate

INFORMATIVE SPEECHES

from Adler, *Communicating at Work;*
Principles and Practices for Business and the Professions, 10 Edition

Chapter 2 Communication, Culture, and Work 34

Chapter 4 Verbal and Nonverbal Messages 90

A Note from the Author

The Art of Public Speaking will pass its 30th anniversary in the course of this edition. When I wrote the first edition, I could not have imagined the extraordinary response the book would receive. I am deeply appreciative of the students and teachers who have made it the leading work on its subject at colleges and universities across the United States and around the world.

In preparing this edition, I have retained what readers have identified as the main strengths of the book. *The Art of Public Speaking* is informed by classical and contemporary theories of rhetoric, but it does not present theory for its own sake. Keeping a steady eye on the practical skills of public speaking, it offers full coverage of all major aspects of speech preparation and presentation.

It also follows David Hume's advice that one "who would teach eloquence must do it chiefly by examples." Whenever possible, I have tried to *show* the principles of public speaking in action in addition to describing them. Thus you will find in the book a large number of narratives, speech excerpts, and full sample speeches that illustrate the principles of effective public speaking.

Because the immediate task facing students is to present speeches in the classroom, I rely heavily on examples that relate directly to students' classroom needs and experiences. The speech classroom, however, is a training ground where students develop skills that will serve them throughout life. Therefore, I also include a large number of illustrations drawn from the kinds of speaking experiences students will face after they graduate from college.

Because speeches are performative acts, students need to be able to view speakers in action as well as read their words on the printed page. *The Art of Public Speaking* has an extensive video program that is available both on DVD and on *Connect Public Speaking,* the book's innovative online learning platform. The video program includes 27 full student speeches, plus more than 60 speech excerpts. Nine of the full speeches and more than 25 of the excerpts are new to this edition.

Connect also provides a wide range of teaching and learning resources in addition to the speech videos. These resources include hands-on study tools, critical-thinking exercises, speech analysis questions, worksheets, assessment forms, and more. Taken together, the book and *Connect* provide an interactive public speaking program that meets the needs of students and teachers alike.

The Art of Public Speaking has changed over the years in response to changes in technology, student demographics, and instructional needs. But it has never lost sight of the fact that the most important part of speaking is thinking. The ability to think critically is vital to a world in which personality and image too often substitute for thought and substance. While helping students become capable, responsible speakers, *The Art of Public Speaking* also seeks to help them become capable, responsible thinkers.

Preface

FEATURES OF THE ELEVENTH EDITION

The eleventh edition of *The Art of Public Speaking* builds on its predecessors with expanded coverage in key areas that students find most challenging—plunging into the first speech, avoiding fallacies, using supporting materials properly, citing sources orally, developing and presenting visual aids, and taking public speaking from classroom to career.

These content revisions are combined with a thorough revision of *Connect Public Speaking,* the pathbreaking online learning platform for *The Art of Public Speaking* at www.mcgraw-hillconnect.com. The book, *Connect,* and the other resources available with *The Art of Public Speaking* are all designed to work hand in hand. They provide an integrated teaching and learning system that is without parallel among public speaking textbooks.

Helping students make the leap from principles to performance

THE ART OF PUBLIC SPEAKING CONNECTS STUDENTS TO THE PRACTICE OF PUBLIC SPEAKING.

Clear, consistent coverage and a friendly, authoritative voice that speaks personably to students and gives them the principles they need to create and deliver dynamic public speeches.

Print and video examples show the principles of public speaking in action rather than just describing them. NEW

- NEW Every chapter of *The Art of Public Speaking* has been thoroughly revised to present relevant, easy-to-grasp real-world models that speak to the newest generation of students.
- NEW Student speeches on DVD and on *Connect* provide models of major speech genres. There are a total of 27 full student speeches (9 new to this edition), including 5 "Needs Improvement" versions. There are also more than 60 videos (27 new to this edition) that illustrate specific skills and concepts from the book. Icons in the margins of the main text direct readers to the appropriate videos.
- Written and narrated by Stephen E. Lucas, *Introductions, Conclusions, and Visual Aids* utilizes the principles of visual learning

to reinforce key concepts from the book. Part One of this 30-minute DVD uses excerpts from a wide range of student speeches to illustrate the principles of effective introductions and conclusions. Part Two contains examples of speakers using a variety of visual aids and presentation media.

NEW **LearnSmart, *Connect's* adaptive diagnostic study tool, helps students absorb and internalize key ideas from the text.** LearnSmart adapts to individual students and, based on their responses, identifies strengths and weaknesses in their grasp of course content. By tracking student responses, instructors can use class time to focus on subjects that students find most challenging.

Helping students apply principles discussed in the text to the creation of their own speeches

THE ART OF PUBLIC SPEAKING CONNECTS STUDENTS TO CONFIDENCE IN PUBLIC SPEAKING.

NEW **Improved coverage of persuasive speaking.** Chapter 16, "Speaking to Persuade," includes many new examples, including a new full speech with commentary. Chapter 17, "Methods of Persuasion," has a revised discussion of reasoning, plus expanded coverage of fallacies and a new sample speech with commentary.

A full chapter on "Giving Your First Speech" (Chapter 4). This chapter gives students the support they need to present their first speeches at the start of the term—long before most of the principles of public speaking have been covered in class. Two new sample speeches with commentary provide models of introductory presentations. NEW

More on supporting ideas and source citation. In response to requests from instructors, Chapter 8 provides expanded coverage of how to use supporting materials and how to cite sources orally. Chapter 7 takes account of new developments in online research and provides criteria for assessing information gleaned from the Internet. NEW

Revised chapter on visual aids (Chapter 14). Among other changes, the popular PowerPoint appendix has been integrated into the main chapter, providing more streamlined and up-to-date coverage of visual aids. NEW

Interactive assignments and activities in *Connect* take online pedagogy to a new level. The latest version of *Connect* offers a wide range of assignable and assessable online activities. These include exercises for critical thinking, speech videos with questions for analysis, scrambled outline exercises, chapter study questions, key-term diagnostics, and speech checklists and worksheets. NEW

Strong connection between public speaking principles and real-world application. "Using Public Speaking in Your Career" activities place students in realistic, professional scenarios and help them make the leap from classroom to career. NEW

Comprehensive chapter-ending pedagogy builds critical thinking skills. Each chapter contains review questions and exercises for critical thinking. The exercises require students to work with—and to think about—skills and concepts covered in the chapter. They are vital to the integrated teaching and learning system that has helped make *The Art of Public Speaking* so successful.

Student Workbook. This popular supplement contains exercises, checklists, worksheets, evaluation forms, and other materials designed to help students master the principles of effective speechmaking presented in the text.

Helping novices gain practice time and become effective public speakers

THE ART OF PUBLIC SPEAKING CONNECTS STUDENTS TO SUCCESS IN PUBLIC SPEAKING.

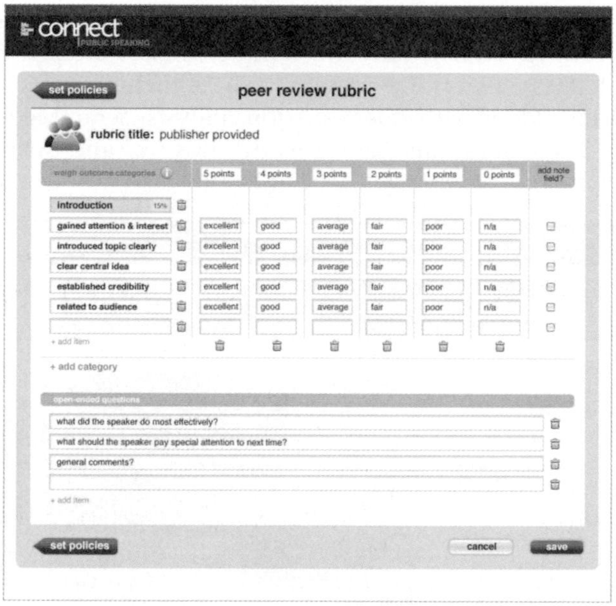

NEW **Speech Capture.** This cutting-edge tool lets instructors evaluate speeches live, using a fully customizable rubric. Instructors can also upload speech videos on behalf of students, as well as create and manage peer review assignments. Students can upload their own videos for self-review and/or peer review.

NEW **Outline Tool, with enhanced user interface.** The Outline Tool guides students systematically through the process of organizing and outlining their speeches. Instructors can customize parts of the outliner, and also turn it off if they don't want their students to use it.

NEW **Topic Helper, as well as access to EasyBib and Survey Monkey online tools.** The Topic Helper helps students select a topic for speech assignments. EasyBib is a Web-based tool that automates the formatting of citations and bibliographies. Survey Monkey, also a Web-based tool, helps students create and manage audience-analysis questionnaires.

RESOURCES FOR INSTRUCTORS

The Art of Public Speaking has an exceptional set of instructional resources that provide a fully integrated, comprehensive teaching and learning program for instructors of all experience levels.

Easier online course management through *Connect*-Blackboard CMS integration. McGraw-Hill's partnership with Blackboard allows for full integration of McGraw-Hill content and digital tools into Blackboard, featuring single sign-on capability for students and faculty. NEW

Annotated Instructor's Edition. The *Annotated Instructor's Edition* provides a wealth of teaching aids for each chapter in the book. It is also cross-referenced with *Connect,* the *Instructor's Manual,* the Instructor's Resource CD-ROM, and other supplements that accompany *The Art of Public Speaking.*

Instructor's Manual. This comprehensive guide to teaching from *The Art of Public Speaking* contains suggested course outlines and speaking assignments; chapter outlines; supplementary exercises and classroom activities; feedback for all exercises and activities; and 45 additional speeches for discussion and analysis.

The *Instructor's Manual,* Test Bank, and PowerPoint slides are available on *Connect,* the Online Learning Center, and the Instructor's Resource CD-ROM.

Test Bank. The *Test Bank* furnishes 2,600 examination questions based on *The Art of Public Speaking.*

PowerPoint Slides with Video Clips. Fully revised for this edition, more than 400 PowerPoint slides include text, photographs, illustrations, and video clips, and can be customized by instructors for lecture or discussion.

Online Learning Center. The *Art of Public Speaking* Online Learning Center, located at www.mhhe.com/lucas11e, enables teachers to download the full roster of teaching resources:

- *Instructor's Manual*
- *Test Bank* (Microsoft Word files, as well as computerized EZTest versions)
- PowerPoint slides
- *Teaching Public Speaking*
- *Teaching Public Speaking Online,* fully revised for the eleventh edition by Jennifer Cochrane of Indiana University and Purdue University at Indianapolis
- *Handbook for Teachers of Non-Native Speakers of English*

Instructor's Resource CD-ROM. The *Instructor's Manual, Test Bank,* PowerPoint slides, and other items in the Online Learning Center are also available on this CD-ROM.

ACKNOWLEDGMENTS

"'Tis the good reader," said Ralph Waldo Emerson, "that makes the good book." I have been fortunate to have very good readers indeed, and I would like to thank the reviewers, symposium and focus-group participants, and contributors whose names appear on pages xxiii–xxv for their expertise and helpful comments and suggestions.

In addition, I would like to express my gratitude both to the students at the University of Wisconsin whose speeches provided the material for many of the examples in the book and to members of the Communication Arts 100 teaching staff who helped me by collecting sample speeches and by offering feedback on the tenth edition. I am especially grateful to Sarah Jedd, assistant director of Communication Arts 100, for her splendid work in that capacity and for her many contributions to the book.

Thanks go as well to Margaret Procario for her work on the *Instructor's Manual* and the *Test Bank;* to Jennifer Cochrane for her supplement on using *The Art of Public Speaking* in an online course; and to Ashley Hinck, who helped with the research for this edition. Above all, I am indebted to Paul Stob, who worked with me on the book and supplements throughout the preparation of this edition. His contributions were indispensable.

I also owe thanks to *The Art of Public Speaking* team at McGraw-Hill. David Patterson, Susan Gouijnstook, Mikola De Roo, Suzie Flores, and Jamie Daron joined the book this edition, and they have continued its tradition of excellence. Now in her fourth edition as marketing manager, Leslie Oberhuber continues to prove why she is one of the best in the business. Mike Ryan, Steve Debow, and Ed Stanford all provided executive support and direction.

In this day and age, publishing a textbook involves much more than the book itself. Working with the editorial team, Janet Byrne Smith and Adam Dweck skillfully managed the new version of *Connect.* Other members of the *Connect* team included Vicki Splaine, Debabrata Acharya, Pravarna Besa, Manish Gupta, Irina Reznick, Sanjay Shinde, Sujoy Banerjee, John Brady, Priscila Depano, Nidhi Kumari, and Suzy Cho. Meghan Campbell coordinated the addition of LearnSmart to the online resources.

As production editor for the book, Carey Eisner handled a thousand details with skill and aplomb. Preston Thomas oversaw the creation of a new design and cover. Natalia Peschiera coordinated the photo program, and Jennifer Blankenship located a wealth of images on a tight schedule. Vicki Malinee helped steer the supplements through production.

As always, my biggest debt is to my wife, Patty, whose love and support have sustained me through the years.

Stephen E. Lucas
Madison, Wisconsin

REVIEWERS, SYMPOSIUM AND FOCUS-GROUP PARTICIPANTS, AND CONTRIBUTORS

Main-Text Reviewers

Bob Alexander, *Bossier Parish Community College*
Barbara Armentrout, *Central Piedmont Community College*
Richard Armstrong, *Wichita State University*
Gretchen Arthur, *International Academy of Technology and Design*
Leonard Assante, *Volunteer State Community College*
Jennifer Becker, *University of Missouri–Columbia*
Kimberly Berry, *Ozarks Technical Community College*
Patrick Breslin, *Santa Fe Community College*
Christa Brown, *Minnesota State University–Mankato*
Ferald J. Bryan, *Northern Illinois University*
Jack Byer, *Bucks County Community College*
Richard Capp, *Hill College*
Nick Carty, *Dalton State University*
Mary Carver, *University of Central Oklahoma*
Crystal Church, *Cisco Junior College*
Jennifer Cochrane, *Indiana University–Purdue University, Indianapolis*
Shirley Lerch Crum, *Coastal Carolina Community College*
Karen Dwyer, *University of Nebraska–Omaha*
Tracy Fairless, *University of Central Oklahoma*
Rick Falvo, *College of Lake County*
Bryan Fisher, *Francis Marion University*
Bonnie Gabel, *McHenry County College*
Paul Gaustad, *Georgia Perimeter College*
Kevin Gillen, *Indiana University*
Donna Gotch, *California State University, San Bernardino*
Catherine Gragg, *San Jacinto College*
JoAnna Grant, *California State University, San Bernardino*
Neva Kay Gronert, *Arapahoe Community College*
Omar Guevara, *Weber State University*
Karen Hamburg, *Camden Community College*
Tina M. Harris, *University of Georgia*
Daria Heinemann, *Keiser University*
Marcia Hotchkiss, *Tennessee State University*
Delwyn Jones, *Moraine Valley Community College*
Susan Kilgard, *Anne Arundel Community College*
Amy King, *Central Piedmont Community College*
Patricia King, *McHenry County College*
Linda Kurz, *University of Missouri–Kansas City*
Jerri Lynn Kyle, *Missouri State University*
Kathleen LeBesco, *Marymount Manhattan College*
Mark Lewis, *Riverside Community College*
Sujanet Mason, *Luzerne County Community College*
Peg McCree, *Middle Tennessee State University*
Nicki L. Michalski, *Lamar University*
Marjorie Keeshan Nadler, *Miami University*
Ronn Norfleet, *Kentucky Community and Technical College System–Jefferson Community and Technical College*
Kekeli Nuviadenu, *Bethune-Cookman College*
Holly Payne, *Western Kentucky University*
Theodore Petersen, *Helmick Johnson Community College*
Jeff Peterson, *Washington State University–Pullman*
James (Tim) Pierce, *Northern Illinois University*
Jean R. Powers, *Holmes Community College*
Barry Poyner, *Truman State University*
William Price, *Georgia Perimeter College*
James E. Putz, *University of Wisconsin–La Crosse*
Jennifer Reem, *Nova Southeastern University*
Belinda Russell, *Northeast Mississippi Community College*
Diane Ryan, *Tidewater Community College*
Rhona Rye, *California State Polytechnic University, Pomona*
Cara Schollenberger, *Bucks County Community College*
Jay Self, *Truman State University*
Michael J. Shannon, *Moraine Valley Community College*
Gale Sharpe, *San Jacinto College*
Richard Sisson, *Georgia Perimeter College*
Amy R. Slagell, *Iowa State University*
Katherine Taylor, *University of Louisville*
Cindu Thomas-George, *College of Lake County*
Joseph Valenzano, *University of Nevada, Las Vegas*
Jill Voran, *Anne Arundel Community College*
Linda J. White, *Central Piedmont Community College*
Theresa White, *Faulkner State Community College*
Alan Winson, *John Jay College of Criminal Justice*
Carleen Yokotake, *Leeward Community College*

Symposia and Regional Focus-Group Participants

Donna Acerra, *Northampton Community College*
Krista Appelquist, *Moraine Valley Community College*
Vera Barkus, *Kennedy-King College*
Barbara Baron, *Brookdale Community College*
Mardia Bishop, *University of Illinois–Champaign*
Audrey Bourne, *North Idaho College*
Karen Braselton, *Vincennes University*
Melissa Broeckelman-Post, *California State University–Los Angeles*
Cynthia Brown El, *Macomb Community College, Center Campus*
Kristin Bruss, *University of Kansas–Lawrence*
Bobette Bushnell, *Oregon State University*
Pamela Cannamore, *Kennedy-King College*
Helen Chester, *Milwaukee Area Technical College–Milwaukee*
Jennifer Cochrane, *Indiana University–Purdue University, Indianapolis*
Jennifer Del Quadro, *Northampton Community College*
Amber Erickson, *University of Cincinnati*
Kris Galyen, *University of Cincinnati*
Joan Geller, *Johnson & Wales University*
Ava Good, *San Jacinto College*
JoAnna Grant, *California State University, San Bernardino*
Delwyn Jones, *Moraine Valley Community College*
Amy King, *Central Piedmont Community College*
Bryan Kirby, *Ivy Technical Community College, Indiana*
Steven Lebeau, *Indiana University–Purdue University, Indianapolis*
Cindy Leonard, *Bluegrass Community and Technical College, Main Campus*
Tobi Mackler, *Montgomery County Community College*
Molly Mayer, *University of Cincinnati*
James McCoy, *College of Southern Nevada–Henderson*

Peg McCree, *Middle Tennessee State University*
Libby McGlone, *Columbus State Community College*
Delois Medhin, *Milwaukee Area Technical College–Milwaukee*
Stanley Moore, *Henry Ford Community College*
Marjorie Keeshan Nadler, *Miami University*
John Nash, *Moraine Valley Community College*
Ronn Norfleet, *Kentucky Community and Technical College System–Jefferson Community and Technical College*
Edward Panetta, *University of Georgia*
Alexander Papp, *Cuyahoga Community College*
Tim Pierce, *Northern Illinois University*
Sunnye Pruden, *Lone Star College, CyFair*
Jeff Przybylo, *William Rainey Harper College*
Shawn Queeney, *Bucks County Community College*
David Schneider, *Saginaw Valley State University*
Mike Shannon, *Moraine Valley Community College*
Amy R. Slagell, *Iowa State University*
Karen Slawter, *Northern Kentucky University*
Rick Soller, *College of Lake County*
Cindu Thomas-George, *College of Lake County*
Patrice Whitten, *William Rainey Harper College*
Julie Williams, *San Jacinto College*
Josie Wood, *Chemeketa Community College*
Henry Young, *Cuyahoga Community College*

Connect Board of Advisors

Sam Arenivar, *MiraCosta College*
Katherine Castle, *University of Nebraska–Lincoln*
Jennifer Cochrane, *Indiana University–Purdue University, Indianapolis*
Rich Jones, *Eastern Illinois University*
Bryan Kirby, *Ivy Technical Community College, Indiana*
Christine Lemesianou, *Montclair State University*
Maria Luskay, *Pace University*
Jeff Przybylo, *William Rainey Harper College*
Mike Shannon, *Moraine Valley Community College*
Julie Williams, *San Jacinto College*

LearnSmart Contributors

Mary Carver, *University of Central Oklahoma*
Jennifer Cochrane, *Indiana University–Purdue University, Indianapolis*
Ava Good, *San Jacinto College*
Amy King, *Central Piedmont Community College*
Marjorie Keeshan Nadler, *Miami University, Lead Subject Matter Expert*

Connect and LearnSmart Reviewers

Brent Adrian, *Central Community College–Grand Island campus*
Richard N. Armstrong, *Wichita State University*
Frank Barnhart, *Columbus State Community College*
Kimberly Berry, *Ozarks Technical Community College*
Annette Bever, *Vernon College*
Justin Braxton-Brown, *Hopkinsville Community College*
Melissa Broeckelman-Post, *California State University–Los Angeles*
Drew Butler, *Middle Tennessee State University*
Nick Carty, *Dalton State*
Leslie Collins, *Modesto Junior College*
Paige Davis, *Lone Star College, CyFair*
Denise Elmer, *Southeast Community College–Beatrice*
Pam Glasnapp, *University of Central Missouri*
JoAnna Grant, *California State University, San Bernardino*
Stacy B. Gresell, *Lone Star College, CyFair*
Jill Hall, *Jefferson Community and Technical College, Downtown*
Daria Heinemann, *Keiser University*
Richard Jones, *Eastern Illinois University*
Patti Keeling, *Chabot College*
Tressa Kelly, *University of West Florida*
Darren Linvill, *Clemson University*
Natonya Listach, *Middle Tennessee State University*
Jodie Mandel, *College of Southern Nevada–Henderson*
James McCoy, *College of Southern Nevada–Henderson*
Peg McCree, *Middle Tennessee State University*
Libby McGlone, *Columbus State Community College*
Terri Metzger, *California State University, San Bernardino*
John Nash, *Moraine Valley Community College*
Maria Parnell, *Brevard Community College–Melbourne*
Jean Perry, *Glendale Community College*
Tim Pierce, *Northern Illinois University*
William Price, *Georgia Perimeter College*
Greg Rickert, *Bluegrass Community and Technical College*
Thomas Sabetta, *University of Kentucky*
Jay Self, *Truman State University*
Michael Shannon, *Moraine Valley Community College*
Susan Silcott, *Ohio University Lancaster*
Richard (Kim) Sisson, *Georgia Perimeter College*
Katherine Taylor, *University of Louisville*
Alice Veksler, *University of Connecticut–Storrs*
Ann Marie Whyte, *Penn State University–Harrisburg*
Julie Williams, *San Jacinto College*

Design Reviewers

Barbara Baron, *Brookdale Community College*
Elizabeth Jill Coker, *Itawamba Community College–Tupelo*
Ferald J. Bryan, *Northern Illinois University*
Jack Byer, *Bucks County Community College*
Terri Helmick, *Johnson County Community College*
Steven King, *Ivy Technical Community College, Indiana*
Elizabeth Rumschlag, *Baker College, Auburn Hills*
David Simon, *Northern Illinois University*
Katherine Taylor, *University of Louisville*
Kristi Whitehill, *Ivy Technical Community College, Indiana*

Public-Speaking Survey Participants

Bob Alexander, *Bossier Parish Community College*
Barbara Armentrout, *Central Piedmont Community College*
Richard N. Armstrong, *Brevard Community College–Titusville*
Barbara Baron, *Brookdale Community College*
Kimberly Berry, *Ozarks Technical Community College*
Laura Berry, *Pearl River Community College*
Molly Brown, *Clinton Community College*
Ferald J. Bryan, *Northern Illinois University*
Jack Byer, *Bucks County Community College*
Rebecca Carlton, *Indiana University Southeast*
Mary Carver, *University of Central Oklahoma*
Helen Chester, *Milwaukee Area Technical College*

Cerbrina Chou, *Chemeketa Community College*
Melissa Click, *University of Missouri–Columbia*
Ron Compton, *Triton College*
Audrey Deterding, *Indiana University Southeast*
Kelly Driskell, *Trinity Valley Community College*
James Duncan, *Anderson University*
Karen Dwyer, *University of Nebraska, Omaha*
Rick Falvo, *College of Lake County*
Tori Forncrook, *Georgia Perimeter College*
Rebecca J. Franco, *Indiana University Southeast*
Meredith Frank, *La Salle University*
Bonnie Gabel, *McHenry County College*
Jodi Gaete, *Suffolk County Community College*
Colleen Garside, *Weber State University*
Paul Gaustad, *Georgia Perimeter College*
Jeffrey Gentry, *Rogers State University*
Pamela M. Glasnapp, *University of Central Missouri*
Robert Glenn, III, *Kentucky Community and Technical College System–Owensboro Community and Technical College*
Ava Good, *San Jacinto College*
Thomas Green, *Faulkner State Community College*
Neva Kay Gronert, *Arapahoe Community College*
William F. Harlow, *University of Texas–Permian Basin*
Kate Harris, *Loyola University–Chicago; Roosevelt University*
Tina Harris, *University of Georgia*
Terri Helmick, *Johnson County Community College*
Marcia Hotchkiss, *Tennessee State University*
Dr. David Johnson, *University of Maryland Eastern Shore*
Brenda Jones, *Franklin University*
Kate Kane, *Northeastern Illinois University*
Amy King, *Central Piedmont Community College*
Patricia King, *McHenry County College*
Sandy King, *Anne Arundel Community College*
Vijay Krishna, *College of the Canyons*
Linda Kurz, *University of Missouri–Kansas City*
Abby Lackey, *Jackson State Community College*
Victoria Leonard, *Cape Fear Community College*
Sujanet Mason, *Luzerne County Community College*
Wolfgang Mcaninch-Runzi, *University of Texas–Permian Basin*
Alison McCrowell Lietzenmayer, *Old Dominion University*
Nicki Michalski, *Lamar University–Beaumont*
Diane Miller, *Finlandia University; Michigan Technological University*
Holly Miller, *University of Nebraska–Omaha*
Stanley Moore, *Henry Ford Community College*
David Moss, *Mt. San Jacinto College–Menifee*
Heidi Murphy, *Central New Mexico Community College*
Ulysses Newkirk, *Kentucky Community and Technical College System–Owensboro Community and Technical College*
Ronn Norfleet, *Kentucky Community and Technical College System*
Dr. Lisa M. Orick-Martinez, *Central New Mexico Community College*
Maria Parnell, *Brevard Community College–Melbourne*
Jeff Przybylo, *William Rainey Harper College*
Jason Andrew Ramsey, *Indiana University Southeast*
Pamela J. Reid, *Copiah-Lincoln Community College*
Cynthia Robinson-Moore, *University of Nebraska–Omaha*
Rhona Rye, *California State Polytechnic University, Pomona*
Thomas J. Sabetta, *Cape Fear Community College*
Jay Self, *Truman State University*
Alisa Shubb, *University of California, Davis*
James Spurrier, *Vincennes University*
Katherine Taylor, *University of Louisville*
Lisa Turowski, *Towson University*
Alice Veksler, *University of Connecticut–Storrs*
Tom Vickers, *Embry Riddle Aero University–Daytona Beach*
Janice M. Vierk, *Metropolitan Community College–Omaha*
Myra H. Walters, *Edison State College*
Stephanie Webster, *University of Florida, Gainesville*
Linda J. White, *Central Piedmont Community College*
Theresa White, *Faulkner State Community College*
Cicely Wilson, *Victory University (formerly Crichton College)*
Alan Winson, *John Jay College of Criminal Justice*
Josie Wood, *Chemeketa Community College*
Tina Zagara, *Georgia Perimeter College*

The Art of Public Speaking

Harl

1

Speaking in Public

- The Power of Public Speaking
- The Tradition of Public Speaking
- Similarities Between Public Speaking and Conversation
- Differences Between Public Speaking and Conversation
- Developing Confidence: Your Speech Class
- Public Speaking and Critical Thinking
- The Speech Communication Process
- Public Speaking in a Multicultural World

Growing up in a tough neighborhood in the South Bronx, Geoffrey Canada had no intention of becoming a public speaker. A good student, he went to college at Bowdoin and then to graduate school at Harvard, where he earned a master's degree in education. After teaching in New Hampshire and Boston, he returned to New York City, where in 1990 he founded the Harlem Children's Zone.

Called "one of the biggest social experiments of our time" by the *New York Times Magazine,* the Harlem Children's Zone seeks not just to educate children, but to develop a community system that addresses issues such as health care, violence, substance abuse, and job training. Over the years, Canada has raised more than $100 million for the project, and he has helped change the lives of thousands of kids and families.

How has Canada achieved all this? Partly through his education, his commitment to children, and his seemingly limitless energy. But just as important is his ability to communicate with people through public speaking, which has been a primary vehicle for spreading his message. He has been described as a "charismatic, passionate, eloquent" speaker who leaves his audiences "awed."

If you had asked Geoffrey Canada early in his life, "Do you see yourself as a major public speaker?" he probably would have laughed at the idea. Yet today he gives more than 100 presentations a year. Along the way, he has spoken at the White House, has lectured at Harvard and Princeton, and has addressed the Aspen Institute and the Google International Zeitgeist. He has also appeared on *60 Minutes* and is featured in the film *Waiting for Superman*.

The Power of Public Speaking

Throughout history people have used public speaking as a vital means of communication. What the Greek leader Pericles said more than 2,500 years ago is still true today: "One who forms a judgment on any point but cannot explain" it clearly "might as well never have thought at all on the subject."[1] Public speaking, as its name implies, is a way of making your ideas public—of sharing them with other people and of influencing other people.

connect

View John F. Kennedy, Martin Luther King, Ronald Reagan, Barbara Jordan, and other speakers in the online Media Library for this chapter (Video 1.1)

During modern times, many women and men around the globe have spread their ideas and influence through public speaking. In the United States, the list includes Franklin Roosevelt, Billy Graham, Cesar Chavez, Barbara Jordan, Ronald Reagan, Martin Luther King, Hillary Clinton, and Barack Obama. In other countries, we see the power of public speaking employed by such people as former British Prime Minister Margaret Thatcher, South African leader Nelson Mandela, Burmese democracy champion Aung San Suu Kyi, and Kenyan environmentalist and Nobel Prize winner Wangari Maathai.

As you read these names, you may think to yourself, "That's fine. Good for them. But what does that have to do with me? I don't plan to be a president or a preacher or a crusader for any cause." Nevertheless, the need for public speaking will almost certainly touch you sometime in your life—maybe tomorrow, maybe not for five years. Can you imagine yourself in any of these situations?

You are one of seven management trainees in a large corporation. One of you will get the lower-management job that has just opened. There is to be a large staff meeting at which each of the trainees will discuss the project he or she has been developing. One by one your colleagues make their presentations. They have no experience in public speaking and are intimidated by the higher-ranking managers present. Their speeches are stumbling and awkward. You, however, call upon all the skills you learned in your public speaking course. You deliver an informative talk that is clear, well reasoned, and articulate. You get the job.

One of your children has a learning disability. You hear that your local school board has decided, for budget reasons, to eliminate the special teacher who has been helping your child. At an open meeting of the school board, you stand up and deliver a thoughtful, compelling speech on the necessity for keeping the special teacher. The school board changes its mind.

You are the assistant manager in a branch office of a national company. Your immediate superior, the branch manager, is about to retire, and there will be a retirement dinner. All the executives from the home office will attend. As his close working associate, you are asked to give a farewell toast at the party. You prepare and deliver a speech that is both witty and touching—a perfect tribute to your boss. After the speech, everyone applauds enthusiastically, and a few people have tears in their eyes. The following week you are named branch manager.

Fantasies? Not really. Any of these situations could occur. In a recent survey of more than 300 business leaders, the ability to communicate effectively—including public speaking—was ranked first among the skills of college graduates sought by employers. In another survey, the American Management Association asked 2,000 managers and executives to rank the skills most essential in today's workplace. What was at the top of their list? Communication skills.[2]

The importance of such skills is true across the board—for accountants and architects, teachers and technicians, scientists and stockbrokers. Even in highly specialized fields such as civil and mechanical engineering, employers consistently rank the ability to communicate above technical knowledge when deciding whom to hire and whom to promote.

Businesses are also asking people to give more speeches in the early stages of their careers, and many young professionals are using public speaking as a way to stand out in today's highly competitive job market.[3] In fact, the ability to speak effectively is so prized that college graduates are increasingly being asked to give a presentation as part of their job interview.

Nor has the growth of the Internet and other new technologies reduced the need for public speaking. In this age of e-mail and Twitter, businesses are concerned that college graduates are losing the ability to talk in a professional way. As career expert Lindsey Pollak states, "It's so rare to find somebody who has that combination of really good technical skills and really good verbal communication skills. You will be head and shoulders above your colleagues if you can combine those two."[4]

The same is true in community life. Public speaking is a vital means of civic engagement. It is a way to express your ideas and to have an impact on issues that matter in society. As a form of empowerment, it can—and often does—make a difference in things people care about very much. The key phrase here is "make a difference." This is what most of us want to do in life—to make a difference, to change the world in some small way. Public speaking offers you an opportunity to make a difference in something you care about very much.

The Tradition of Public Speaking

Given the importance of public speaking, it's not surprising that it has been taught and studied around the globe for thousands of years. Almost all cultures have an equivalent of the English word "orator" to designate someone with special skills in public speaking. The oldest known handbook on effective speech was written on papyrus in Egypt some 4,500 years ago. Eloquence was highly prized in ancient India, Africa, and China, as well as among the Aztecs and other pre-European cultures of North and South America.[5]

In classical Greece and Rome, public speaking played a central role in education and civic life. It was also studied extensively. Aristotle's *Rhetoric*, composed during the third century B.C., is still considered the most important work on its subject, and many of its principles are followed by speakers (and writers) today. The great Roman leader Cicero used his speeches to defend liberty and wrote several works about oratory in general.

Over the centuries, many other notable thinkers have dealt with issues of rhetoric, speech, and language—including the Roman educator Quintilian, the Christian preacher St. Augustine, the medieval writer Christine de Pizan, the British philosopher Francis Bacon, and the American critic Kenneth Burke. In recent years, communication researchers have provided an increasingly scientific basis for understanding the methods and strategies of effective speech.

Your immediate objective is to apply those methods and strategies in your classroom speeches. What you learn, however, will be applicable long after you leave college. The principles of public speaking are derived from a long tradition and have been confirmed by a substantial body of research. The more you know about those principles, the more effective you will be in your own speeches—and the more effective you will be in listening to the speeches of other people.

Similarities Between Public Speaking and Conversation

How much time do you spend each day talking to other people? The average adult spends about 30 percent of her or his waking hours in conversation. By the time you read this book, you will have spent much of your life perfecting the art of conversation. You may not realize it, but you already employ a wide range of skills when talking to people. These skills include the following:

1. *Organizing your thoughts logically.* Suppose you were giving someone directions to get to your house. You wouldn't do it this way:

> When you turn off the highway, you'll see a big diner on the left. But before that, stay on the highway to Exit 67. Usually a couple of the neighbors' dogs are in the street, so go slow after you turn at the blinking light. Coming from your house you get on the highway through Maple Street. If you pass the taco stand, you've gone too far. The house is blue.

Instead, you would take your listener systematically, step by step, from his or her house to your house. You would organize your message.

2. *Tailoring your message to your audience.* You are a geology major. Two people ask you how pearls are formed. One is your roommate; the other is your nine-year-old niece. You answer as follows:

> To your roommate: "When any irritant, say a grain of sand, gets inside the oyster's shell, the oyster automatically secretes a substance called nacre, which is principally calcium carbonate and is the same material that lines the oyster's shell. The nacre accumulates in layers around the irritant core to form the pearl."

> To your niece: "Imagine you're an oyster on the ocean floor. A grain of sand gets inside your shell and makes you uncomfortable. So you decide to cover it up. You cover it with a material called mother-of-pearl. The covering builds up around the grain of sand to make a pearl."

Many skills used in conversation also apply in public speaking. As you learn to speak more effectively, you may also learn to communicate more effectively in other situations.

3. *Telling a story for maximum impact.* Suppose you are telling a friend about a funny incident at last week's football game. You don't begin with the punch line ("Keisha fell out of the stands right onto the field. Here's how it started. . . ."). Instead, you carefully build up your story, adjusting your words and tone of voice to get the best effect.

4. *Adapting to listener feedback.* Whenever you talk with someone, you are aware of that person's verbal, facial, and physical reactions. For example:

You are explaining an interesting point that came up in biology class. Your listener begins to look confused, puts up a hand as though to stop you, and says "Huh?" You go back and explain more clearly.

A friend has asked you to listen while she practices a speech. At the end you tell her, "There's just one part I really don't like—that quotation from the attorney general." Your friend looks very hurt and says, "That was my favorite part!" So you say, "But if you just worked the quotation in a little differently, it would be wonderful."

Each day, in casual conversation, you do all these things many times without thinking about them. You already possess these communication skills. And these are among the most important skills you will need for public speaking.

To illustrate, let's return briefly to one of the hypothetical situations at the beginning of this chapter. When addressing the school board about the need for a special teacher:

- You *organize* your ideas to present them in the most persuasive manner. You steadily build up a compelling case about how the teacher benefits the school.
- You *tailor your message* to your audience. This is no time to launch an impassioned defense of special education in the United States. You must show how the issue is important to the people in that very room—to their children and to the school.

- You *tell your story* for maximum impact. Perhaps you relate an anecdote to demonstrate how much your child has improved. You also have statistics to show how many other children have been helped.
- You *adapt to listener feedback.* When you mention the cost of the special teacher, you notice sour looks on the faces of the school board members. So you patiently explain how small that cost is in relation to the overall school budget.

In many ways, then, public speaking requires the same skills used in ordinary conversation. Most people who communicate well in daily talk can learn to communicate just as well in public speaking. By the same token, training in public speaking can make you a more adept communicator in a variety of situations, such as conversations, classroom discussions, business meetings, and interviews.

Differences Between Public Speaking and Conversation

Despite their similarities, public speaking and everyday conversation are not identical. Imagine that you are telling a story to a friend. Then imagine yourself telling the story to a group of seven or eight friends. Now imagine telling the same story to 20 or 30 people. As the size of your audience grows, you will find yourself adapting to three major differences between conversation and public speaking:

1. *Public speaking is more highly structured.* It usually imposes strict time limitations on the speaker. In most cases, the situation does not allow listeners to interrupt with questions or commentary. The speaker must accomplish her or his purpose in the speech itself. In preparing the speech, the speaker must anticipate questions that might arise in the minds of listeners and answer them. Consequently, public speaking demands much more detailed planning and preparation than ordinary conversation.

2. *Public speaking requires more formal language.* Slang, jargon, and bad grammar have little place in public speeches. As committed as he is to improving the quality of education in urban schools, when Geoffrey Canada speaks to a legislative committee, he doesn't say, "We've got to get every damn incompetent teacher out of the classroom!" Listeners usually react negatively to speakers who do not elevate and polish their language when addressing an audience. A speech should be "special."

3. *Public speaking requires a different method of delivery.* When conversing informally, most people talk quietly, interject stock phrases such as "like" and "you know," adopt a casual posture, and use what are called vocalized pauses ("uh," "er," "um"). Effective public speakers, however, adjust their voices to be heard clearly throughout the audience. They assume a more erect posture. They avoid distracting mannerisms and verbal habits.

With study and practice, you will be able to master these differences and expand your conversational skills into speechmaking. Your speech class will provide the opportunity for this study and practice.

Developing Confidence: Your Speech Class

One of the major concerns of students in any speech class is stage fright. We may as well face the issue squarely. Many people who converse easily in all kinds of everyday situations become frightened at the idea of standing up before a group to make a speech.

If you are worried about stage fright, you may feel better knowing that you are not alone. A 2001 Gallup Poll asked Americans to list their greatest fears. Forty percent identified speaking before a group as their top fear, exceeded only by the 51 percent who said they were afraid of snakes. A 2005 survey produced similar results, with 42 percent of respondents being terrified by the prospect of speaking in public. In comparison, only 28 percent said they were afraid of dying.[6]

stage fright

Anxiety over the prospect of giving a speech in front of an audience.

in a different study, researchers concentrated on social situations and, again, asked their subjects to list their greatest fears. More than 9,000 people were interviewed. Here is the ranking of their answers:[7]

Greatest Fear

Public speaking

Speaking up in a meeting or class

Meeting new people

Talking to people in authority

Important examination or interview

Going to parties

Talking with strangers

Again, speechmaking is at the top in provoking anxiety.

NERVOUSNESS IS NORMAL

If you feel nervous about giving a speech, you are in very good company. Some of the greatest public speakers in history have suffered from stage fright, including Abraham Lincoln, Margaret Sanger, and Winston Churchill. The famous Roman orator Cicero said, "I turn pale at the outset of a speech and quake in every limb and in my soul."[8]

Oprah Winfrey, Conan O'Brien, and Jay Leno all report being anxious about speaking in public. Early in his career, Leonardo DiCaprio was so nervous about giving an acceptance speech that he hoped he would not win the Academy Award for which he had been nominated. Eighty-one percent of business executives say public speaking is the most nerve-wracking experience they face.[9] What comedian Jerry Seinfeld said in jest sometimes seems literally true: "Given a choice, at a funeral most of us would rather be the one in the coffin than the one giving the eulogy."

Actually, most people tend to be anxious before doing something important in public. Actors are nervous before a play, politicians are nervous before a campaign speech, athletes are nervous before a big game. The ones who succeed have learned to use their nervousness to their advantage. Listen to tennis star Rafael Nadal speaking after his 2010 Wimbledon title match against Tomas Berdych. "I was a little bit more nervous than usual," he admitted. "But if you are not nervous in the finals of Wimbledon, you are not human!" Putting his butterflies to good use, Nadal beat Berdych in straight sets to claim his second Wimbledon championship.

Much the same thing happens in speechmaking. Most experienced speakers have stage fright before taking the floor, but their nervousness is a healthy sign that they are getting "psyched up" for a good effort. Novelist and lecturer I. A. R. Wylie once said: "After many years of practice I am, I suppose, really a 'practiced speaker.' But I rarely rise to my feet without a throat constricted with terror and a furiously thumping heart. When, for some reason, I *am* cool and self-assured, the speech is always a failure."

adrenaline

A hormone released into the bloodstream in response to physical or mental stress.

In other words, it is perfectly normal—even desirable—to be nervous at the start of a speech. Your body is responding as it would to any stressful situation—by producing extra *adrenaline*.

This sudden shot of adrenaline is what makes your heart race, your hands shake, your knees knock, and your skin perspire. Every public speaker experiences all these reactions to some extent. The question is: How can you control your nervousness and make it work for you rather than against you?

DEALING WITH NERVOUSNESS

positive nervousness

Controlled nervousness that helps energize a speaker for her or his presentation.

Rather than trying to eliminate every trace of stage fright, you should aim at transforming it from a negative force into what one expert calls *positive nervousness*—"a zesty, enthusiastic, lively feeling with a slight edge to it. . . . It's still nervousness, but it feels different. You're no longer victimized by it; instead, you're vitalized by it. You're in control of it."[10]

Don't think of yourself as having stage fright. Instead, think of it as "stage excitement" or "stage enthusiasm."[11] It can help you get focused and energized in the same way that it helps athletes, musicians, and others get primed for a game or a concert. Actress Jane Lynch, talking about her gig hosting *Saturday Night Live*, said that she got through it with "that perfect cocktail of nervousness and excitement." Think of that cocktail as a normal part of giving a successful speech.

Here are six time-tested ways you can turn your nervousness from a negative force into a positive one.

Acquire Speaking Experience

You have already taken the first step. You are enrolled in a public speaking course, where you will learn about speechmaking and gain speaking experience. Think back to your first day at kindergarten, your first date, your first day at a new job. You were probably nervous in each situation because you were facing something new and unknown. Once you became accustomed to the situation, it was no longer threatening. So it is with public speaking. For most students, the biggest part of stage fright is fear of the unknown. The more you learn about public speaking and the more speeches you give, the less threatening speechmaking will become.

Of course, the road to confidence will sometimes be bumpy. Learning to give a speech is not much different from learning any other skill—it proceeds by trial and error. The purpose of your speech class is to shorten the process, to minimize the errors, to give you a nonthreatening arena—a sort of laboratory—in which to undertake the "trial."

The need for public speaking arises in many situations. Here Dr. John Holcomb updates the media on the condition of U.S. Representative Gabrielle Giffords after she was shot at a meeting in Tucson, Arizona.

Your teacher recognizes that you are a novice and is trained to give the kind of guidance you need to get started. In your fellow students you have a highly sympathetic audience who will provide valuable feedback to help you improve your speaking skills. As the class goes on, your fears about public speaking will gradually recede until they are replaced by only a healthy nervousness before you rise to speak.[12]

Prepare, Prepare, Prepare

Another key to gaining confidence is to pick speech topics you truly care about—and then to prepare your speeches so thoroughly that you cannot help but be successful. Here's how one student combined enthusiasm for his topic with thorough preparation to score a triumph in speech class:

> Jesse Young was concerned about taking a speech class. Not having any experience as a public speaker, he got butterflies in his stomach just thinking about talking in front of an audience. But when the time came for Jesse's first speech, he was determined to make it a success.
>
> Jesse chose Habitat for Humanity as the topic for his speech. He had been a volunteer for three years, and he believed deeply in the organization and its mission. The purpose of his speech was to explain the origins, philosophy, and activities of Habitat for Humanity.
>
> As Jesse spoke, it became clear that he was enthusiastic about his subject and genuinely wanted his classmates to share his enthusiasm. Because he was intent on communicating with his audience, he forgot to be nervous. He spoke clearly, fluently, and dynamically. Soon the entire class was engrossed in his speech.
>
> Afterward, Jesse admitted that he had surprised even himself. "It was amazing," he said. "Once I passed the first minute or so, all I thought about were those people out there listening. I could tell that I was really getting through to them."

How much time should you devote to preparing your speeches? A standard rule of thumb is that each minute of speaking time requires one to two hours of preparation time—perhaps more, depending on the amount of research needed for the speech. This may seem like a lot of time, but the rewards are well worth it. One professional speech consultant estimates that proper preparation can reduce stage fright by up to 75 percent.[13]

If you follow the techniques suggested by your teacher and in the rest of this book, you will stand up for every speech fully prepared. Imagine that the day for your first speech has arrived. You have studied your audience and selected a topic you know will interest them. You have researched the speech thoroughly and practiced it several times until it feels absolutely comfortable. You have even tried it out before two or three trusted friends. How can you help but be confident of success?

Think Positively

Confidence is mostly the well-known power of positive thinking. If you think you can do it, you usually can. On the other hand, if you predict disaster and doom, that is almost always what you will get. This is especially true when it comes to public speaking. Speakers who think negatively about themselves and the speech experience are much more likely to be overcome by stage fright than are speakers who think positively. Here are some ways you can transform negative thoughts into positive ones as you work on your speeches:

Negative Thought	Positive Thought
I wish I didn't have to give this speech.	This speech is a chance for me to share my ideas and gain experience as a speaker.
I'm not a great public speaker.	No one's perfect, but I'm getting better with each speech I give.
I'm always nervous when I give a speech.	Everyone's nervous. If other people can handle it, I can too.
No one will be interested in what I have to say.	I have a good topic and I'm fully prepared. Of course they'll be interested.

Many psychologists believe that the ratio of positive to negative thoughts in regard to stressful activities such as speechmaking should be at least five to one. That is, for each negative thought, you should counter with a minimum of five positive ones. Doing so will not make your nerves go away completely, but it will help keep them under control so you can concentrate on communicating your ideas rather than on brooding about your fears and anxieties.

Use the Power of Visualization

Visualization is closely related to positive thinking. It is used by athletes, musicians, actors, speakers, and others to enhance their performance in stressful situations. How does it work? Listen to long-distance runner Vicki Huber:

> Right before a big race, I'll picture myself running, and I will try and put all of the other competitors in the race into my mind. Then I will try and imagine

every possible situation I might find myself in . . . behind someone, being boxed in, pushed, shoved or cajoled, different positions on the track, laps to go, and, of course, the final stretch. And I always picture myself winning the race, no matter what happens during the event.

Of course, Huber doesn't win every race she runs, but research has shown that the kind of mental imaging she describes can significantly increase athletic performance.[14] It has also shown that visualization can help speakers control their stage fright.[15]

The key to visualization is creating a vivid mental blueprint in which you see yourself succeeding in your speech. Picture yourself in your classroom rising to speak. See yourself at the lectern, poised and self-assured, making eye contact with your audience and delivering your introduction in a firm, clear voice. Feel your confidence growing as your listeners get more and more caught up in what you are saying. Imagine your sense of achievement as you conclude the speech knowing you have done your very best.

visualization

Mental imaging in which a speaker vividly pictures himself or herself giving a successful presentation.

As you create these images in your mind's eye, be realistic but stay focused on the positive aspects of your speech. Don't allow negative images to eclipse the positive ones. Acknowledge your nervousness, but picture yourself overcoming it to give a vibrant, articulate presentation. If one part of the speech always seems to give you trouble, visualize yourself getting through it without any hitches. And be specific. The more lucid your mental pictures, the more successful you are likely to be.

As with your physical rehearsal of the speech, this kind of mental rehearsal should be repeated several times in the days before you speak. It doesn't guarantee that every speech will turn out exactly the way you envision it—and it certainly is no substitute for thorough preparation. But used in conjunction with the other methods of combating stage fright, it is a proven way to help control your nerves and to craft a successful presentation.

Know That Most Nervousness Is Not Visible

Many novice speakers are worried about appearing nervous to the audience. It's hard to speak with poise and assurance if you think you look tense and insecure. One of the most valuable lessons you will learn as your speech class proceeds is that only a fraction of the turmoil you feel inside is visible on the outside. "Your nervous system may be giving you a thousand shocks," says one experienced speaker, "but the viewer can see only a few of them."[16]

Even though your palms are sweating and your heart is pounding, your listeners probably won't realize how tense you are—especially if you do your best to act cool and confident on the outside. Most of the time when students confess after a speech, "I was so nervous I thought I was going to die," their classmates are surprised. To them the speaker looked calm and assured.

Knowing this should make it easier for you to face your listeners with confidence. As one student stated after watching a videotape of her first classroom speech, "I was amazed at how calm I looked. I assumed everyone would be able to see how scared I was, but now that I know they can't, I won't be nearly so nervous in the future. It really helps to know that you look in control even though you may not feel that way."

Don't Expect Perfection

It may also help to know that there is no such thing as a perfect speech. At some point in every presentation, every speaker says or does something that

Like many well-known public figures, Conan O'Brien often experiences stage fright before a speech. Most speakers report that their nervousness drops significantly after the first 30 to 60 seconds of a presentation.

does not come across exactly as he or she had planned. Fortunately, such moments are usually not evident to the audience. Why? Because the audience does not know what the speaker *plans* to say. It hears only what the speaker *does* say. If you momentarily lose your place, reverse the order of a couple statements, or forget to pause at a certain spot, no one need be the wiser. When such moments occur, just proceed as if nothing happened.

Even if you do make an obvious mistake during a speech, that is no catastrophe. If you have ever listened to Martin Luther King's "I Have a Dream," you may recall that he stumbles twice during the speech. Most likely, however, you don't remember. Why? Because you were focusing on King's message, rather than on the fine points of his delivery.

One of the biggest reasons people are concerned about making a mistake in a speech is that they view speechmaking as a performance rather than an act of communication. They feel the audience is judging them against a scale of absolute perfection in which every misstated word or awkward gesture will count against them. But speech audiences are not like judges in a violin recital or an ice-skating contest. They are not looking for a virtuoso performance, but for a well-thought-out address that communicates the speaker's ideas clearly and directly. Sometimes an error or two can actually enhance a speaker's appeal by making her or him seem more human.[17]

As you work on your speeches, make sure you prepare thoroughly and do all you can to get your message across to your listeners. But don't panic about being perfect or about what will happen if you make a mistake. Once you free your mind of these burdens, you will find it much easier to approach your speeches with confidence and even with enthusiasm.

Besides stressing the six points just discussed, your teacher will probably give you several tips for dealing with nervousness in your first speeches. They may include:

- Be at your best physically and mentally. It's not a good idea to stay up until 3:00 A.M. partying with friends or cramming for an exam the night before your speech. A good night's sleep will serve you better.
- As you are waiting to speak, quietly tighten and relax your leg muscles, or squeeze your hands together and then release them. Such actions help reduce tension by providing an outlet for your extra adrenaline.
- Take a couple slow, deep breaths before you start to speak. When they are tense, most people take short, shallow breaths, which only reinforces their anxiety. Deep breathing breaks this cycle of tension and helps calm your nerves.
- Work especially hard on your introduction. Research has shown that a speaker's anxiety level begins to drop significantly after the first 30 to 60 seconds of a presentation.[18] Once you get through the introduction, you should find smoother sailing the rest of the way.
- Make eye contact with members of your audience. Remember that they are individual people, not a blur of faces. And they are your friends.
- Concentrate on communicating with your audience rather than on worrying about your stage fright. If you get caught up in your speech, your audience will too.
- Use visual aids. They create interest, draw attention away from you, and make you feel less self-conscious.

checklist

Speaking with Confidence

YES	NO	
☐	☐	1. Am I enthusiastic about my speech topic?
☐	☐	2. Have I thoroughly developed the content of my speech?
☐	☐	3. Have I worked on the introduction so my speech will get off to a good start?
☐	☐	4. Have I worked on the conclusion so my speech will end on a strong note?
☐	☐	5. Have I rehearsed my speech orally until I am confident about its delivery?
☐	☐	6. Have I worked on turning negative thoughts about my speech into positive ones?
☐	☐	7. Do I realize that nervousness is normal, even among experienced speakers?
☐	☐	8. Do I understand that most nervousness is not visible to the audience?
☐	☐	9. Am I focused on communicating with my audience, rather than on worrying about my nerves?
☐	☐	10. Have I visualized myself speaking confidently and getting a positive response from the audience?

If you are like most students, you will find your speech class to be a very positive experience. As one student wrote on her course evaluation at the end of the class:

> I was really dreading this class. The idea of giving all those speeches scared me half to death. But I'm glad now that I stuck with it. It's a small class, and I got to know a lot of the students. Besides, this is one class in which I got to express *my* ideas, instead of spending the whole time listening to the teacher talk. I even came to enjoy giving the speeches. I could tell at times that the audience was really with me, and that's a great feeling.

Over the years, thousands of students have developed confidence in their speechmaking abilities. As your confidence grows, you will be better able to stand before other people and tell them what you think and feel and know—and to make them think and feel and know those same things. The best part about confidence is that it nurtures itself. After you score your first triumph, you will be that much more confident the next time. And as you become a more confident public speaker, you will likely become more confident in other areas of your life as well.

Public Speaking and Critical Thinking

That guy at the party last night really owned me when we were talking about the economy. I know my information is right, and I'm sure his argument didn't make sense, but I can't put my finger on the problem.

I worked really hard on my term paper, but it's just not right. It doesn't seem to hang together, and I can't figure out what's wrong.

Political speeches are so one-sided. The candidates sound good, but they all talk in slogans and generalities. It's really hard to decide who has the best stands on the issues.

critical thinking

Focused, organized thinking about such things as the logical relationships among ideas, the soundness of evidence, and the differences between fact and opinion.

Have you ever found yourself in similar situations? If so, you may find help in your speech class. Besides building confidence, a course in public speaking can develop your skills as a critical thinker. Those skills can make the difference between the articulate debater and the pushover, the A student and the C student, the thoughtful voter and the coin tosser.

What is critical thinking? To some extent, it's a matter of logic—of being able to spot weaknesses in other people's arguments and to avoid them in your own. It also involves related skills such as distinguishing fact from opinion, judging the credibility of statements, and assessing the soundness of evidence. In the broadest sense, critical thinking is focused, organized thinking—the ability to see clearly the relationships among ideas.[19]

If you are wondering what this has to do with your public speaking class, the answer is quite a lot. As the class proceeds, you will probably spend a good deal of time organizing your speeches. While this may seem like a purely mechanical exercise, it is closely interwoven with critical thinking. If the structure of your speech is disjointed and confused, odds are that your thinking is also disjointed and confused. If, on the other hand, the structure is clear and cohesive, there is a good chance your thinking is too. Organizing a speech is not just a matter of arranging the ideas you already have. Rather, it is an important part of shaping the ideas themselves.

What is true of organization is true of many aspects of public speaking. The skills you learn in your speech class can help you become a more effective thinker in a number of ways. As you work on expressing your ideas in clear, accurate language, you will enhance your ability to think clearly and accurately. As you study the role of evidence and reasoning in speechmaking, you will see how they can be used in other forms of communication as well. As you learn to listen critically to speeches in class, you will be better able to assess the ideas of speakers (and writers) in a variety of situations.

To return to the examples at the beginning of this section:

The guy at the party last night—would well-honed critical thinking skills help you find the holes in his argument?

The term paper—would better organization and a clear outline help pull it together?

Political speeches—once you get past the slogans, are the candidates drawing valid conclusions from sound evidence?

If you take full advantage of your speech class, you will be able to enhance your skills as a critical thinker in many circumstances. This is one reason public speaking has been regarded as a vital part of education since the days of ancient Greece.

Using public speaking in your CAREER

It's been three years since you graduated from college. After gaining experience as an administrative assistant at a major office equipment manufacturer, you've just been promoted to marketing manager for office copiers. Though you have occasionally given brief reports to other members of your work team, you're now facing your first speech to a large audience. At your company's annual sales meeting, you will address the sales force about the company's new multifunction printer/copiers, and how to sell them to dealers such as Office Depot and OfficeMax.

You're pleased to have this opportunity and you know it shows the company's faith in your abilities. Yet the closer you get to the day of the speech, the harder it is to control the butterflies in your stomach. There will be 200 people in your audience, including all the sales managers and regional managers, in addition to the sales force. All eyes will be on you. It's important that you come across as confident and well informed, but you're afraid your stage fright will send the opposite message. What strategies will you use to control your nerves and make them work for you?

The Speech Communication Process

As you begin your first speeches, you may find it helpful to understand what goes on when one person talks to another. Regardless of the kind of speech communication involved, there are seven elements—speaker, message, channel, listener, feedback, interference, and situation. Here we focus on how these elements interact when a public speaker addresses an audience.

SPEAKER

speaker

The person who is presenting an oral message to a listener.

Speech communication begins with a speaker. If you pick up the telephone and call a friend, you are acting as a speaker. (Of course, you will also act as a listener when your friend is talking.) In public speaking, you will usually present your entire speech without interruption.

Your success as a speaker depends on *you*—on your personal credibility, your knowledge of the subject, your preparation of the speech, your manner of speaking, your sensitivity to the audience and the occasion. But successful speaking also requires enthusiasm.

You can't expect people to be interested in what you say unless you are interested yourself. If you are truly excited about your subject, your audience is almost sure to get excited along with you. You can learn all the techniques of effective speechmaking, but before they can be of much use, you must first have something to say—something that sparks your own enthusiasm.

MESSAGE

message

Whatever a speaker communicates to someone else.

The message is whatever a speaker communicates to someone else. If you are calling a friend, you might say, "I'll be a little late picking you up tonight." That is the message. But it may not be the only message. Perhaps there is a certain tone in your voice that suggests reluctance, hesitation. The underlying message might be "I really don't want to go to that party. You talked me into it, but I'm going to put it off as long as I can."

Your goal in public speaking is to have your *intended* message be the message that is *actually* communicated. Achieving this depends both on what you say (the verbal message) and on how you say it (the nonverbal message).

Getting the verbal message just right requires work. You must narrow your topic down to something you can discuss adequately in the time allowed for the speech. You must do research and choose supporting details to make your ideas clear and convincing. You must organize your ideas so listeners can follow them without getting lost. And you must express your message in words that are accurate, clear, vivid, and appropriate.

Besides the message you send with words, you send a message with your tone of voice, appearance, gestures, facial expression, and eye contact. Imagine that one of your classmates gets up to speak about student loans. Throughout her speech she slumps behind the lectern, takes long pauses to remember what she wants to say, stares at the ceiling, and fumbles with her visual aids.

Her intended message is "We must make more money available for student loans." But the message she actually communicates is "I haven't prepared very well for this speech." One of your jobs as a speaker is to make sure your nonverbal message does not distract from your verbal message.

The powers of critical thinking you develop in researching and organizing your speeches can be applied in many forms of communication, including meetings and group projects.

CHANNEL

The channel is the means by which a message is communicated. When you pick up the phone to call a friend, the telephone is the channel. Public speakers may use one or more of several channels, each of which will affect the message received by the audience.

Consider a speech to Congress by the President of the United States. The speech is carried to the nation by the channels of radio and television. For the radio audience the message is conveyed entirely by the President's voice. For the television audience the message is conveyed by both the President's voice and the televised image. The people in Congress have a more direct channel. They not only hear the President's voice as amplified through a microphone, but they also see him and the setting firsthand.

In a public speaking class, your channel is the most direct of all. Your classmates will see you and hear you without any electronic intervention.

channel

The means by which a message is communicated.

LISTENER

The listener is the person who receives the communicated message. Without a listener, there is no communication. When you talk to a friend on the phone, you have one listener. In public speaking you will have many listeners.

Everything a speaker says is filtered through a listener's *frame of reference*—the total of his or her knowledge, experience, goals, values, and attitudes. Because a speaker and a listener are different people, they can never have exactly the same frame of reference. And because a listener's frame of reference can never be exactly the same as a speaker's, the meaning of a message will never be exactly the same to a listener as to a speaker.

You can easily test the impact of different frames of reference. Ask each of your classmates to describe a chair. If you have 20 classmates, you'll probably get 20 different descriptions. One student might picture a large, overstuffed

listener

The person who receives the speaker's message.

frame of reference

The sum of a person's knowledge, experience, goals, values, and attitudes. No two people can have exactly the same frame of reference.

easy chair, another an elegant straight-backed chair, yet another an office chair, a fourth a rocking chair, and so on.

Even if two or more envision the same general type—say, a rocking chair—their mental images of the chair could still be different. One might be thinking of an early American rocker, another of a modern Scandinavian rocker—the possibilities are unlimited. And "chair" is a fairly simple concept. What about "patriotism" or "freedom"?

Because people have different frames of reference, a public speaker must take great care to adapt the message to the particular audience being addressed. To be an effective speaker, you must be *audience-centered.* You will quickly lose your listeners' attention if your presentation is either too basic or too sophisticated. You will also lose your audience if you do not relate to their experience, interests, knowledge, and values. When you make a speech that causes listeners to say "That is important to *me,*" you will almost always be successful.

FEEDBACK

feedback

The messages, usually nonverbal, sent from a listener to a speaker.

When the President addresses the nation on television, he is engaged in one-way communication. You can talk back to the television set, but the President won't hear you. Most situations, however, involve *two-way* communication. Your listeners don't simply absorb your message like human sponges. They send back messages of their own. These messages are called feedback.

In public speaking there is plenty of feedback to let you know how your message is being received. Do your listeners lean forward in their seats, as if paying close attention? Do they have quizzical looks on their faces? Do they shuffle their feet and gaze at the clock? The message sent by these reactions could be "I am fascinated," "I am bored," "I agree with you," "I don't agree with you," or any number of others. As a speaker, you need to be alert to these reactions and adjust your message accordingly.

Like any kind of communication, feedback is affected by one's frame of reference. How would you feel if, immediately after your speech, all your classmates started to rap their knuckles on the desks? Would you run out of the room in despair? Not if you were in a European university. In many parts of Europe, students rap their knuckles on their desks to show admiration for a classroom lecture. You must understand the feedback to be able to deal with it.

INTERFERENCE

interference

Anything that impedes the communication of a message. Interference can be external or internal to listeners.

Interference is anything that impedes the communication of a message. When you talk on the telephone, sometimes there is static, or wires get crossed so that two different conversations are going on at once. That is a kind of interference.

In public speaking there are two kinds of interference. One, like the static or crossed wires in a phone conversation, is *external* to the audience. Many classrooms are subject to this kind of interference—from traffic outside the building, the clatter of a radiator, students conversing in the hall, a room that is stifling hot or freezing cold. Any of these can distract listeners from what you are saying.

A second kind of interference is *internal* and comes from within your audience. Perhaps one of your listeners has a toothache. She may be so distracted by the pain that she doesn't pay attention to your speech. Another listener could be worrying about a test in the next class period. Yet another could be brooding about an argument with his girlfriend.

FIGURE 1.1

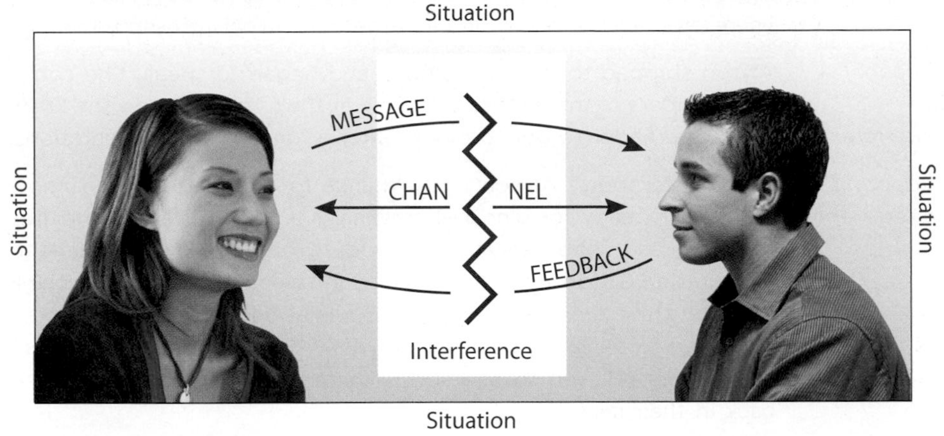

As a speaker, you must try to hold your listeners' attention despite these various kinds of interference. In the chapters that follow you will find many ways to do this.

SITUATION

The situation is the time and place in which speech communication occurs. Conversation always takes place in a certain situation. Sometimes the situation helps—as when you propose marriage over an intimate candlelight dinner. Other times it may hurt—as when you try to speak words of love in competition with a blaring stereo. When you have to talk with someone about a touchy issue, you usually wait until the situation is just right.

situation

The time and place in which speech communication occurs.

Public speakers must also be alert to the situation. Certain occasions—funerals, church services, graduation ceremonies—require certain kinds of speeches. Physical setting is also important. It makes a great deal of difference whether a speech is presented indoors or out, in a small classroom or in a gymnasium, to a densely packed crowd or to a handful of scattered souls. When you adjust to the situation of a public speech, you are only doing on a larger scale what you do every day in conversation.

(For a complete model of the speech communication process, see Figure 1.1 above.[20])

THE SPEECH COMMUNICATION PROCESS: EXAMPLE WITH COMMENTARY

The following example shows how the various components of the speech communication process interact:

Situation It was 5:15 P.M., and the fall sales conference of OmniBrands, Inc., had been going on all day. A series of new-product presentations to buyers from the company's largest customers had taken much longer than expected.

Speaker Alyson Kaufman was worried. As a marketing manager for fragrances, she was the last speaker of the day. When Alyson rose to address the audience, she knew she faced a difficult situation. She had been allotted 45 minutes to introduce her products, and the meeting was scheduled to end in 15 minutes. What's more, holiday sales of her entire product line depended in large part on this presentation.

Channel Alyson stepped to the microphone and began to speak. She could see members of the audience looking at their watches, and she knew

Interference they were eager to get to dinner after a long day of presentations.

Adapting to Interference "Good afternoon," Alyson said, "thanks for your attention. I know everyone is ready for dinner—I certainly am. I was given 45 minutes for my presentation—okay, everybody groan—but with your kind cooperation, I'll do my best to finish in under half an hour. I think you'll find the time well worth your while, because the products I am going to tell you about will seriously boost your holiday sales." Alyson was relieved to see several people smiling as they settled back in their seats.

Message Now that she had the audience's attention, Alyson presented each new product as briefly as she could. She streamlined her planned presentation to emphasize the features that would be most appealing to the buyers and the ones they would be most likely to remember. She ended by handing out samples of the products and promising to contact anyone who needed more information. She quickly added her e-mail address to her PowerPoint slides and was encouraged to see people writing it down.

Feedback As promised, Alyson finished in under half an hour. "And that wraps it up!" she concluded. "Let's eat!" Later, the marketing director complimented Alyson on dealing so well with a tough situation. "You did a great job," the marketing director said. "Next year, we'll try to make all the presentations as concise and efficient as yours."

Public Speaking in a Multicultural World

CULTURAL DIVERSITY IN THE MODERN WORLD

The United States has always been a diverse society. By the middle of the 19th century, it contained so many people from so many lands that novelist Herman Melville exclaimed, "You cannot spill a drop of American blood without spilling the blood of the whole world."[21]

One can only imagine what Melville would say today! The United States is the most diverse society on earth. That diversity can be seen in cities and towns, schools and businesses, community groups, and houses of worship all across the land. Consider the following:

- There are 195 nations in the world, and every one of them has someone living in the United States.
- Nearly 50 percent of the people in Miami were born outside the United States.
- More than 55 million people in the United States speak a language other than English at home.

These kinds of developments are not limited to the United States. We live in an age of international multiculturalism. The Internet allows for instant communication around the world. CNN is broadcast to more than 1 billion people globally. Social media connect people across ancient boundaries. Despite political, social, and religious differences, all nations are becoming part of a vast global network. For example:

- There are 82,000 transnational corporations around the world, and they account for one-third of the world's economic output.
- McDonald's sells twice as many hamburgers and French fries abroad than it does in the United States; Nike makes 63 percent of its sales through exports.
- France has as many Muslims as practicing Catholics; radio CHIN in Toronto, Canada, broadcasts in 31 languages.

CULTURAL DIVERSITY AND PUBLIC SPEAKING

Speechmaking becomes more complex as cultural diversity increases. Part of the complexity stems from the differences in language from culture to culture. Nothing separates one culture from another more than language. Language and culture are so closely bound that "we communicate the way we do because we are raised in a particular culture and learn its language, rules, and norms."[22]

The meanings attached to gestures, facial expressions, and other nonverbal signals also vary from culture to culture. Even the gestures for such basic messages as "hello" and "goodbye" are culturally based. The North American "goodbye" wave is interpreted in many parts of Europe and South America as the motion for "no," while the Italian and Greek gesture for "goodbye" is the same as the U.S. signal for "come here."[23]

Public speaking is a vital mode of communication in most cultures around the world. Here journalist Roxana Saberi, who was imprisoned in Iran for more than 100 days, speaks at a forum on media freedom held in Doha, Qatar.

Many stories have been told about the fate of public speakers who fail to take into account cultural differences between themselves and their audiences. Consider the following scenario:[24]

The sales manager of a U.S. electronics firm is in Brazil to negotiate a large purchase of computers by a South American corporation. After three days of negotiations, the sales manager holds a gala reception for all the major executives to build goodwill between the companies.

As is the custom on such occasions, time is set aside during the reception for an exchange of toasts. When it is the sales manager's turn to speak, he praises the Brazilian firm for its many achievements and talks eloquently of his respect for its president and other executives. The words are perfect, and the sales manager can see his audience smiling in approval.

And then—disaster. As the sales manager closes his speech, he raises his hand and flashes the classic U.S. "OK" sign to signal his pleasure at the progress of the negotiations. Instantly the festive mood is replaced with stony silence; smiles turn to icy stares. The sales manager has given his Brazilian audience a gesture with roughly the same meaning as an extended middle finger in the United States.

The next day, the Brazilian firm announces that it will buy its computers from another company.

As this story illustrates, public speakers can ill afford to overlook their listeners' cultural values and customs. The methods of effective speech explained throughout this book will be helpful to you when addressing culturally diverse audiences. Here we need to stress the importance of avoiding the ethnocentrism that often blocks communication between speakers and listeners of different cultural backgrounds.

AVOIDING ETHNOCENTRISM

ethnocentrism

The belief that one's own group or culture is superior to all other groups or cultures.

Ethnocentrism is the belief that our own group or culture—whatever it may be—is superior to all other groups or cultures. Because of ethnocentrism, we identify with our group or culture and see its values, beliefs, and customs as "right" or "natural"—in comparison to the values, beliefs, and customs of other groups or cultures, which we tend to think of as "wrong" or "unnatural."[25]

Ethnocentrism is part of every culture, and it can play a positive role in creating group pride and loyalty. But it can also lead to prejudice and hostility toward different racial, ethnic, religious, or cultural groups. To be an effective public speaker in a multicultural world, you need to keep in mind that all people have their special beliefs and customs.

Avoiding ethnocentrism does not mean that you must agree with the values and practices of all groups and cultures. At times you might try to convince people of different cultures to change their traditional ways of doing things—as speakers from the United Nations seek to persuade farmers in Africa to adopt more productive methods of agriculture, or as delegates from the United States and China attempt to influence the other country's trade policies.

If such speakers are to be successful, however, they must show respect for the cultures of the people they address. They need to adapt their messages to the values and expectations of their listeners.

When you work on your speeches, be alert to how cultural factors might affect how listeners respond. As we shall see in Chapter 6, for classroom speeches you can use audience-analysis questionnaires to learn about the backgrounds and opinions of your classmates. For speeches outside the classroom, the person who invites you to speak can usually provide information about the audience.

Once you know about any cultural factors that might affect your listeners' response, try to put yourself in their place and to hear your message through their ears. If there is a language difference, avoid words or phrases that might cause misunderstanding. When researching the speech, keep an eye out for visual aids and other materials that will relate to a wide range of listeners. When delivering the speech, be alert to feedback that might indicate the audience is having trouble grasping your ideas.

It is also important to avoid ethnocentrism when listening to speeches. When you listen to a speaker from a different cultural background, be on guard against the temptation to judge the speaker on the basis of his or her appearance or manner of delivery. No matter what the cultural background of the speaker, you should listen to her or him as attentively as you would want your audience to listen to you.[26]

Summary

Public speaking has been a vital means of personal empowerment and civic engagement throughout history. The need for effective public speaking will almost certainly touch you sometime in your life. Your speech class will give you training in researching topics, organizing your ideas, and presenting yourself skillfully. This training is invaluable for every type of communication.

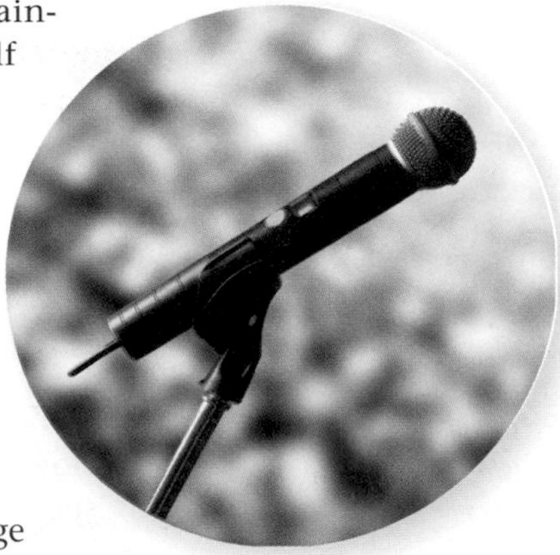

There are many similarities between public speaking and daily conversation, but public speaking is also different from conversation. First, it usually imposes strict time limitations and requires more detailed preparation than does ordinary conversation. Second, it requires more formal language. Listeners react negatively to speeches loaded with slang, jargon, and bad grammar. Third, public speaking demands a different method of delivery. Effective speakers adjust their voices to the larger audience and work at avoiding distracting physical mannerisms and verbal habits.

One of the major concerns of students in any speech class is stage fright. Your class will give you an opportunity to gain confidence and make your nervousness work for you rather than against you. You will take a big step toward overcoming stage fright if you think positively, prepare thoroughly, visualize yourself giving a successful speech, keep in mind that most nervousness is not visible to the audience, and think of your speech as communication rather than as a performance in which you must do everything perfectly.

A course in public speaking can also help develop your skills as a critical thinker. Critical thinking helps you organize your ideas, spot weaknesses in other people's reasoning, and avoid them in your own.

The speech communication process includes seven elements—speaker, message, channel, listener, feedback, interference, and situation. The speaker is the person who initiates a speech transaction. Whatever the speaker communicates is the message, which is sent by means of a particular channel. The listener receives the communicated message and provides feedback to the speaker. Interference is anything that impedes the communication of a message, and the situation is the time and place in which speech communication occurs. The interaction of these seven elements determines the outcome in any instance of speech communication.

Because of the diversity of modern life, many—perhaps most—of the audiences you address will include people of different cultural backgrounds. When you work on your speeches, be alert to how such factors might affect the responses of your listeners and adapt your message accordingly. Above all, avoid the ethnocentric belief that your own culture or group is superior to all others. Also keep in mind the importance of avoiding ethnocentrism when listening to speeches. Accord every speaker the same courtesy and attentiveness you would want from your listeners.

Key Terms

stage fright *(9)*
adrenaline *(10)*
positive nervousness *(10)*
visualization *(13)*
critical thinking *(16)*
speaker *(18)*
message *(18)*
channel *(19)*
listener *(19)*
frame of reference *(19)*
feedback *(20)*
interference *(20)*
situation *(21)*
ethnocentrism *(24)*

Review Questions

After reading this chapter, you should be able to answer the following questions:

1. In what ways is public speaking likely to make a difference in your life?
2. How is public speaking similar to everyday conversation?
3. How is public speaking different from everyday conversation?
4. Why is it normal—even desirable—to be nervous at the start of a speech?
5. How can you control your nervousness and make it work for you in your speeches?
6. What are the seven elements of the speech communication process? How do they interact to determine the success or failure of a speech?
7. What is ethnocentrism? Why do public speakers need to avoid ethnocentrism when addressing audiences with diverse cultural, racial, or ethnic backgrounds?

connect

For further review, go to the LearnSmart study module for this chapter.

Exercises for Critical Thinking

1. Think back on an important conversation you had recently in which you wanted to achieve a particular result. (*Examples:* asking your employer to change your work schedule; explaining to a friend how to change the oil and filter in a car; attempting to talk your spouse or partner into buying the computer you like rather than the one he or she prefers.) Work up a brief analysis of the conversation.

In your analysis, explain the following: (1) your purpose in the conversation and the message strategy you chose to achieve your purpose; (2) the communication channels used during the conversation and how they affected the outcome; (3) the interference—internal or external—you encountered during the conversation; (4) the steps you took to adjust to feedback; (5) the strategic changes you would make in preparing for and carrying out the conversation if you had it to do over again.

2. Divide a sheet of paper into two columns. Label one column "Characteristics of an Effective Public Speaker." Label the other column "Characteristics of an Ineffective Public Speaker." In the columns, list and briefly explain what you believe to be the five most important characteristics of effective and ineffective speakers. Be prepared to discuss your ideas in class.
3. On the basis of the lists you developed for Exercise 2, candidly evaluate your own strengths and weaknesses as a speaker. Identify the three primary aspects of speechmaking you most want to improve.

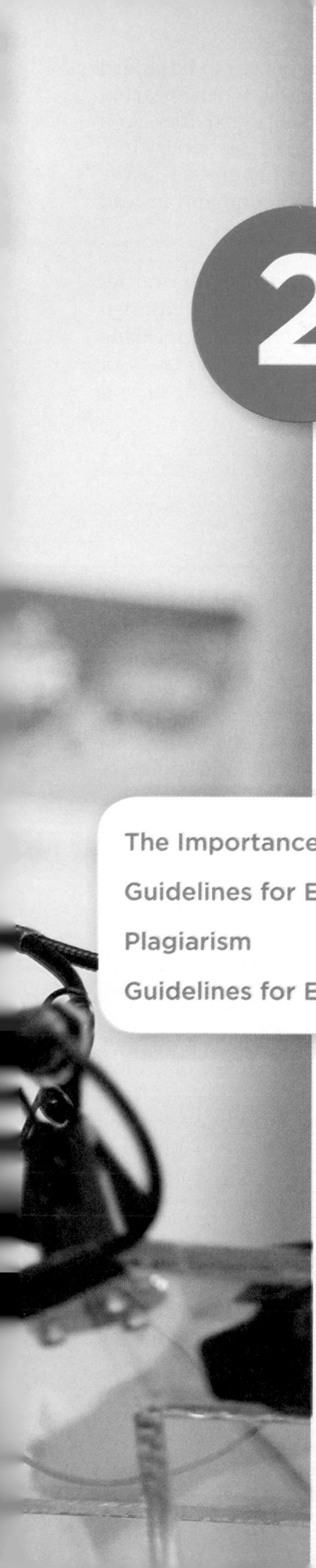

2

Ethics and Public Speaking

The Importance of Ethics

Guidelines for Ethical Speaking

Plagiarism

Guidelines for Ethical Listening

When the rumors started, Brian Pertzborn, chief financial officer for a prominent charity in the southwest United States, called a press conference. Dozens of reporters showed up. Brian looked directly into the cameras and said, "I assure you that no one at this charity has taken money away from the children and families we work so hard to serve. Embezzlement is illegal and a serious breach of trust. I would never let either happen."

Brian's presentation was highly convincing, and for a time it quieted the rumors. Unfortunately, his statements were false. Two months later, he was indicted by the federal government for stealing more than $2.5 million from the charity.

At the trial, it became clear that Brian was guilty as charged. It also came out that on the very day of his press conference, he had tried to cover his tracks by transferring some of the embezzled money to an overseas bank account.

When the judge sentenced Brian to a stiff prison sentence, she made it clear that she was influenced partly by Brian's lies at the press conference. Had he told the truth, his pleas for leniency might have been better received.

This is not a happy story, but it shows why public speaking needs to be guided by a strong sense of integrity. Brian Pertzborn was persuasive when speaking to the press, but he was unethical in lying to cover his illegal activities. As a result, he hurt people who relied on the charity, destroyed his reputation, and ended up with a long jail sentence. Perhaps if he had confessed before the cameras that day, he would have received a fine and a reprimand instead of the harshest sentence the judge could impose.

The goal of public speaking is to gain a desired response from listeners—but not at any cost. Speechmaking is a form of power and therefore carries with it heavy ethical responsibilities. As the Roman rhetorician Quintilian stated 2,000 years ago, the ideal of speechmaking is the good person speaking well. In this chapter, we explore that ideal by looking at the importance of ethics in public speaking, the ethical obligations of speakers and listeners, and the practical problem of plagiarism and how to avoid it.

The Importance of Ethics

ethics

The branch of philosophy that deals with issues of right and wrong in human affairs.

Ethics is the branch of philosophy that deals with issues of right and wrong in human affairs. Questions of ethics arise whenever we ask whether a course of action is moral or immoral, fair or unfair, just or unjust, honest or dishonest.

We face such questions daily in almost every part of our lives. The parent must decide how to deal with a child who has been sent home from school for unruly behavior. The researcher must decide whether to shade her data "just a bit" in order to gain credit for an important scientific breakthrough. The shopper must decide what to do with the $5 extra change mistakenly given by the clerk at the grocery store. The student must decide whether to say anything about a friend he has seen cheating on a final exam.

Questions of ethics also come into play whenever a public speaker faces an audience. In an ideal world, as the Greek philosopher Plato noted, all public speakers would be truthful and devoted to the good of society. Yet history tells us that the power of speech is often abused—sometimes with disastrous results. Adolf Hitler was unquestionably a persuasive speaker. His oratory galvanized the German people, but his aims were horrifying and his tactics despicable. He remains to this day the ultimate example of why the power of the spoken word needs to be guided by a strong sense of ethical integrity.

As a public speaker, you will face ethical issues at every stage of the speechmaking process—from the initial decision to speak through the final presentation of the message. And the answers will not always be easy. Consider the following example:

> Felicia Robinson is running for school board in a large eastern city. Her opponent is conducting what Felicia regards as a highly unethical campaign. In addition to twisting the facts about school taxes, the opponent is pandering to racial prejudice by raising resentment against African Americans and recently arrived immigrants.
>
> Five days before the election, Felicia, who is slightly behind in the polls, learns that the district attorney is preparing to indict her opponent for shady business practices. But the indictment will not be formally issued until after the election.

Nor can it be taken as evidence that her opponent is guilty—like all citizens, he has the right to be presumed innocent until proven otherwise.

Still, news of the indictment could be enough to throw the election Felicia's way, and her advisers urge her to make it an issue in her remaining campaign speeches. Should Felicia follow their advice?

There are creditable arguments to be made on both sides of the ethical dilemma faced by Felicia Robinson. She has tried to run an honest campaign, and she is troubled by the possibility of unfairly attacking her opponent—despite the fact that he has shown no such scruples himself. Yet she knows that the impending indictment may be her last chance to win the election, and she is convinced that a victory for her opponent will spell disaster for the city's school system. Torn between her commitment to fair play, her desire to be elected, and her concern for the good of the community, she faces the age-old ethical dilemma of whether the ends justify the means.

"So," you may be asking yourself, "what is the answer to Felicia Robinson's dilemma?" But in complex cases such as hers there are no cut-and-dried answers. As the leading book on communication ethics states, "We should formulate meaningful ethical guidelines, not inflexible rules."[1] Your ethical decisions will be guided by your values, your conscience, your sense of right and wrong.

ethical decisions

Sound ethical decisions involve weighing a potential course of action against a set of ethical standards or guidelines.

But this does not mean such decisions are simply a matter of personal whim or fancy. Sound ethical decisions involve weighing a potential course of action against a set of ethical standards or guidelines. Just as there are guidelines for ethical behavior in other areas of life, so there are guidelines for ethical conduct in public speaking. These guidelines will not automatically solve every ethical quandary you face as a speaker, but knowing them will provide a reliable compass to help you find your way.

Guidelines for Ethical Speaking

MAKE SURE YOUR GOALS ARE ETHICALLY SOUND

Not long ago, I spoke with a former student—we'll call her Melissa—who had turned down a job in the public relations department of the American Tobacco Institute. Why? Because the job would have required her to lobby on behalf of the cigarette industry. Melissa did not believe she could ethically promote a product that she saw as responsible for thousands of deaths and illnesses each year.

Given Melissa's view of the dangers of cigarette smoking, there can be no doubt that she made an ethically informed decision. On the other side of the coin, someone with a different view of cigarette smoking could make an ethically informed decision to *take* the job. The point of this example is not to judge the rightness or wrongness of Melissa's decision (or of cigarette smoking), but to illustrate how ethical considerations can affect a speaker's choice of goals.

Your first responsibility as a speaker is to ask whether your goals are ethically sound. During World War II, Hitler stirred the German people to condone war, invasion, and genocide. More recently, we have seen politicians who betray the public trust for personal gain, business leaders who defraud investors of millions of dollars, preachers who lead lavish lifestyles at the expense of their religious duties. There can be no doubt that these are not worthy goals.

But think back for a moment to the examples of speechmaking given in Chapter 1. What do the speakers hope to accomplish? Improve the quality of education. Report on a business project. Pay tribute to a fellow worker. Support Habitat for Humanity. Few people would question that these goals are ethically sound.

As with other ethical issues, there can be gray areas when it comes to assessing a speaker's goals—areas in which reasonable people with well-defined standards of right and wrong can legitimately disagree. But this is not a reason to avoid asking ethical questions. If you are to be a responsible public speaker, you cannot escape assessing the ethical soundness of your goals.

BE FULLY PREPARED FOR EACH SPEECH

"A speech," as Jenkin Lloyd Jones states, "is a solemn responsibility." You have an obligation—to yourself and to your listeners—to prepare fully every time you stand in front of an audience. The obligation to yourself is obvious: The better you prepare, the better your speech will be. But the obligation to your listeners is no less important. Think of it this way: The person who makes a bad 30-minute speech to an audience of 200 people wastes only a half hour of her or his own time. But that same speaker wastes 100 hours of the audience's time—more than four full days. This, Jones exclaimed, "should be a hanging offense!"

At this stage of your speaking career, of course, you will probably not be facing many audiences of 200 people. And you will probably not be giving many speeches in which the audience has come for the sole purpose of listening to you. But neither the size nor the composition of your audience changes your ethical responsibility to be fully prepared. Your speech classmates are as worthy of your best effort as if you were addressing a jury or a business meeting, a union conference or a church congregation, the local Rotary club or even the United States Senate.

Being prepared for a speech involves everything from analyzing your audience to creating visual aids, organizing your ideas to rehearsing your delivery. Most crucial from an ethical standpoint, though, is being fully informed about your subject. Why is this so important? Consider the following story:

> Victoria Nuñez, a student at a large state university, gave a classroom speech on suicide prevention. Victoria had learned about the topic from her mother, a volunteer on a suicide-prevention hotline, but she also consulted her psychology textbook, read several magazine articles on the warning signs of suicide, and interviewed a crisis-intervention counselor at the campus health service.
>
> In addition to her research, Victoria gave a lot of thought to planning and delivering her speech. She created a handout for the class listing signs that a person might attempt suicide and providing contact information for local mental-health resources. On the day of her speech, Victoria was thoroughly prepared—and she gave an excellent presentation.
>
> Only a few days later, one of Victoria's classmates, Paul Nichols, had a conversation with his roommate that raised a warning flag about whether the roommate might be depressed and in danger of suicide. Based on the information in Victoria's speech, Paul spoke to his roommate, got him to talk about his worries, and convinced him to seek counseling. Paul might have saved his roommate's life, thanks to Victoria's speech.

Among current public speakers, United Nations Secretary General Ban Ki-moon is well regarded for his ethically sound goals and public speaking skills.

This is an especially dramatic case, but it demonstrates how your speeches can have a genuine impact on your listeners. As a speaker, you have an ethical responsibility to consider that impact and to make sure you prepare fully so as not to communicate erroneous information or misleading advice. If Victoria had not done such a thorough job researching her speech, she might have given her classmates faulty information—information that might have had tragic results.

No matter what the topic, no matter who the audience, you need to explore your speech topic as thoroughly as possible. Investigate the whole story; learn about all sides of an issue; seek out competing viewpoints; get the facts right. Not only will you give a better speech, you will also fulfill one of your major ethical obligations.

BE HONEST IN WHAT YOU SAY

Nothing is more important to ethical speechmaking than honesty. Public speaking rests on the unspoken assumption that "words can be trusted and people will be truthful."[2] Without this assumption, there is no basis for communication, no reason for one person to believe anything that another person says.

Does this mean *every* speaker must *always* tell "the truth, the whole truth, and nothing but the truth"? We can all think of situations in which this is impossible (because we do not know the whole truth) or inadvisable (because it would be tactless or imprudent). Consider a parent who tells his two-year-old daughter that her screeching violin solo is "beautiful." Or a speaker who tells a falsehood in circumstances when disclosing the truth might touch off mob violence. Few people would find these actions unethical.[3]

In contrast, think back to the case of Brian Pertzborn at the start of this chapter. Brian knew he had embezzled money from the charity. Yet he denied that he had done so, even as he was profiting at the expense of people who depended on the charity's services. There is no way to excuse Brian's behavior.

Such blatant contempt for the truth is one kind of dishonesty in public speaking. But more subtle forms of dishonesty are just as unethical. They include juggling statistics, quoting out of context, misrepresenting sources, painting tentative findings as firm conclusions, citing unusual cases as typical examples, and substituting innuendo and half-truths for evidence and proof. All of these violate the speaker's duty to be accurate and fair in presenting information.

While on the subject of honesty in speechmaking, we should also note that ethically responsible speakers do not present other people's words as their own. They do not plagiarize their speeches. This subject is so important that we devote a separate section to it later in this chapter.

AVOID NAME-CALLING AND OTHER FORMS OF ABUSIVE LANGUAGE

"Sticks and stones can break my bones, but words can never hurt me." This popular children's chant could not be more wrong. Words may not literally break people's bones, but they can leave psychological scars as surely as sticks and stones can leave physical scars. As one writer explains, "Our identities, who and what we are, how others see us, are greatly affected by the names we are called and the words with which we are labeled."[4] This is why almost all communication ethicists warn public speakers to avoid name-calling and other forms of abusive language.

Name-Calling and Personal Dignity

name-calling

The use of language to defame, demean, or degrade individuals or groups.

Name-calling is the use of language to defame, demean, or degrade individuals or groups. When applied to various groups in America, it includes such epithets as "fag," "kike," "nigger," "honkey," "wop," "jap," "chink," and "spic." Such terms have been used to debase people because of their sexual orientation, religious beliefs, or ethnic background. These words dehumanize the groups they are directed against and imply that they do not deserve to be treated with dignity and respect.

In Chapter 12, we will look at ways you can avoid biased language in your speeches. For now, the point to remember is that, contrary to what some people claim, avoiding racist, sexist, and other kinds of abusive language is not simply a matter of political correctness. Such language is ethically suspect because it devalues and stereotypes the people in question.

Such language is also a destructive social force. When used repeatedly and systematically over time, it helps reinforce attitudes that encourage prejudice, hate crimes, and civil rights violations.[5] The issue is not one of politics, but of respecting the dignity of the diverse groups in contemporary society.

Name-Calling and Free Speech

Name-calling and abusive language also pose ethical problems in public speaking when they are used to silence opposing voices. A democratic society depends upon the free and open expression of ideas. In the United States, all citizens have the right to join in the never-ending dialogue of democracy. As a public speaker, you have an ethical obligation to help preserve that right by avoiding tactics such as name-calling that inherently impugn the accuracy or respectability of public statements made by groups or individuals who voice opinions different from yours.

This obligation is the same regardless of whether you are black or white, Christian or Muslim, male or female, gay or straight, liberal or conservative. A pro-union public employee who castigates everyone opposed to her ideas as an "enemy of the middle class" is on as thin ice ethically as a politician who labels all his adversaries "tax-and-spend liberals."

Like other ethical questions in public speaking, name-calling raises some thorny issues. Although name-calling can be hazardous to free speech, it is still protected under the free-speech clause of the Bill of Rights. This is why the American Civil Liberties Union, a major defender of constitutional rights, has opposed broadly worded codes against abusive speech on college campuses. To date, such codes have not survived legal challenges, and many schools are developing more sharply focused regulations that they hope will stand up in court.[6]

Bill of Rights

The first 10 amendments to the United States Constitution.

But whatever the legal outcome may be, it will not alter the ethical responsibility of public speakers—on or off campus—to avoid name-calling and other kinds of abusive language. Legality and ethics, though related, are not identical. There is nothing illegal about falsifying statistics in a speech, but there is no doubt that it is unethical. The same is true of name-calling. It may not be illegal to cast racial, sexual, or religious slurs at people in a speech, but it is still unethical. Not only does it demean the dignity of the groups or individuals being attacked, but it undermines the right of all groups in the United States to be fairly heard.

PUT ETHICAL PRINCIPLES INTO PRACTICE

It is easy to pay lip service to the importance of ethics. It is much harder to act ethically. Yet that is just what a responsible public speaker must do. As one popular book on ethics states, "Being ethical means behaving ethically *all the time*—not only when it's convenient."[7]

Questions of ethics arise whenever a speaker faces an audience. Here former soldier Melissa Stockwell, who was injured in the line of duty, talks at the annual Paralympic Military Sports Camp.

As you work on your speeches, you will ask yourself such questions as "Is my choice of topic suitable for the audience?" "Are my supporting materials clear and convincing?" "How can I phrase my ideas to give them more punch?" These are *strategic* questions. As you answer them, you will try to make your speech as informative, as persuasive, or as entertaining as possible.

But you will also face moments of *ethical* decision—similar, perhaps, to those faced by Brian Pertzborn, Felicia Robinson, and other speakers in this chapter. When those moments arrive, don't simply brush them aside and go on your way. Keep in mind the guidelines for ethical speechmaking we have discussed and do your best to follow them through thick and thin. Make sure you can answer yes to all the questions on the Checklist for Ethical Public Speaking below.[8]

checklist

Ethical Public Speaking

YES	NO	
☐	☐	1. Have I examined my goals to make sure they are ethically sound? a. Can I defend my goals on ethical grounds if they are questioned or challenged? b. Would I want other people to know my true motives in presenting this speech?
☐	☐	2. Have I fulfilled my ethical obligation to prepare fully for the speech? a. Have I done a thorough job of studying and researching the topic? b. Have I prepared diligently so as not to communicate erroneous or misleading information to my listeners?
☐	☐	3. Is the speech free of plagiarism? a. Can I vouch that the speech represents my own work, my own thinking, my own language? b. Do I cite the sources of all quotations and paraphrases?
☐	☐	4. Am I honest in what I say in the speech? a. Is the speech free of any false or deliberately deceptive statements? b. Does the speech present statistics, testimony, and other kinds of evidence fairly and accurately? c. Does the speech contain valid reasoning? d. If the speech includes visual aids, do they present facts honestly and reliably?
☐	☐	5. Do I use the power of language ethically? a. Do I avoid name-calling and other forms of abusive language? b. Does my language show respect for the right of free speech and expression?
☐	☐	6. All in all, have I made a conscious effort to put ethical principles into practice in preparing my speech?

Plagiarism

"Plagiarism" comes from *plagiarius,* the Latin word for kidnapper. To plagiarize means to present another person's language or ideas as your own—to give the impression you have written or thought something yourself when you have actually taken it from someone else.[9] We often think of plagiarism as an ethical issue in the classroom, but it can have repercussions in other situations:

plagiarism

Presenting another person's language or ideas as one's own.

Joanne Calabro was in her second year as school superintendent in the northern New Jersey town of Fort Lee. In the spring, she spoke at a ceremony for students being inducted into the National Honor Society. It was a brief speech—only six minutes—but the repercussions would last much, much longer.

One of the students at the ceremony recognized some of Calabro's passages and decided to check them online. He discovered that she had lifted the entire speech from a sample induction address posted on About.com. Further evidence came from a videotape of Calabro delivering the speech.

When confronted with the facts, Calabro admitted to an error in judgment but insisted she had done nothing illegal. In fact, the speech on About.com was protected by copyright law, and Calabro might have been liable to legal action had the Web firm been so inclined. What she could not escape were the ethical consequences. Facing severe criticism within the school district and from the press, she had little choice but to resign her post as superintendent.[10]

As this story shows, plagiarism is a serious matter. If you are caught plagiarizing a speech in class, the punishment can range from a failing grade to expulsion from school. If you are caught plagiarizing outside the classroom, you stand to forfeit your good name, to damage your career, or, if you are sued, to lose a large amount of money. It is worth your while, then, to make sure you know what plagiarism is and how to avoid it.

GLOBAL PLAGIARISM

Global plagiarism is stealing your speech entirely from another source and passing it off as your own. The most blatant—and unforgivable—kind of plagiarism, it is grossly unethical.

global plagiarism

Stealing a speech entirely from a single source and passing it off as one's own.

Global plagiarism in a college classroom usually occurs because a student puts off the assignment until the last minute. Then, in an act of desperation, the student downloads a speech from the Internet or gets one written by a friend and delivers it as his or her own.

The best way to avoid this, of course, is not to leave your speech until the last minute. Most teachers explain speech assignments far enough in advance that you should have no trouble getting an early start. By starting early, you will give yourself plenty of time to prepare a first-rate speech—a speech of your own.

If, for some reason, you fail to get your speech ready on time, do not succumb to the lure of plagiarism. Whatever penalty you suffer from being late will pale in comparison with the consequences if you are caught plagiarizing.

PATCHWORK PLAGIARISM

patchwork plagiarism

Stealing ideas or language from two or three sources and passing them off as one's own.

Unlike global plagiarism, in which a speaker pirates an entire speech from a single source, patchwork plagiarism occurs when a speaker pilfers from two or three sources. Here's an example:

Daniel Fine chose "Recent Discoveries About Dinosaurs" as the topic for his informative speech. In his research, Daniel found three especially helpful sources. The first was a printed guide to a recent museum exhibition about new dinosaur discoveries in North and South America. The second was Wikipedia, and the third was Montana State University's Web site about its dinosaur research program.

Unfortunately, instead of using these materials creatively to write a speech in his own words, Daniel lifted long passages from the museum guide, Wikipedia, and the university Web site and patched them together with a few transitions. When he was finished, he had a speech that was composed almost entirely of other people's words.

When Daniel's teacher read his speech outline, it did not sound authentic to her. So she plugged several phrases from the outline into Google. In less than a minute, she had found both the Wikipedia article and the Montana State University Web site. Soon after, she found an online version of the museum guide. Daniel was caught red-handed.

This story illustrates an important point about plagiarism. Daniel did not take his speech from a single source. He even did a little research. But copying from a few sources is no less plagiarism than is copying from a single source. When you give a speech, you declare that it is your work—the product of your thinking, your beliefs, your language. Daniel's speech did not contain any of these. Instead, it was cut and pasted wholly from other people's words.

"But," you may be thinking, "not many students are experts on their speech topics. Why should they be expected to come up with new ideas that even the experts haven't thought of?"

The answer is they aren't. The key is not whether you have something absolutely original to say, but whether you do enough research and thinking to come up with your own slant on the topic.

As with global plagiarism, one key to averting patchwork plagiarism is to start working on your speech as soon as possible. The longer you work on it, the more apt you are to come up with your own approach. It is also vital to consult a large number of sources in your research. If you have only two or three sources, you are far more likely to fall into the trap of patchwork plagiarism than if you consult a wide range of research materials.

INCREMENTAL PLAGIARISM

incremental plagiarism

Failing to give credit for particular parts of a speech that are borrowed from other people.

In global plagiarism and patchwork plagiarism, the entire speech is cribbed more or less verbatim from a single source or a few sources. But plagiarism can exist even when the speech as a whole is not pirated. This is called incremental plagiarism. It occurs when the speaker fails to give credit for particular parts—increments—of the speech that are borrowed from other people. The most important of these increments are quotations and paraphrases.

Speakers who begin work on their speeches early and consult a wide range of sources are less likely to fall into the trap of plagiarism than are speakers who procrastinate and rely on a limited number of sources.

Quotations

Whenever you quote someone directly, you must attribute the words to that person. Suppose you are giving a speech on Malcolm X, the famous African-American leader of the 1960s. While doing your research, you run across the following passage from Bruce Perry's acclaimed biography, *Malcolm: The Life of the Man Who Changed Black America:*

> Malcolm X fathered no legislation. He engineered no stunning Supreme Court victories or political campaigns. He scored no major electoral triumphs. Yet because of the way he articulated his followers' grievances and anger, the impact he had upon the body politic was enormous.[11]

This is a fine quotation that summarizes the nature and importance of Malcolm's impact on American politics. It would make a strong addition to your speech—as long as you acknowledge Perry as the author. The way to avoid plagiarism in this instance is to introduce Perry's statement by saying something like:

> In *Malcolm: The Life of the Man Who Changed Black America,* historian Bruce Perry says the following about Malcolm's impact on American politics: . . .

Or,

> According to historian Bruce Perry in his book *Malcolm: The Life of the Man Who Changed Black America,* . . .

Now you have clearly identified Perry and given him credit for his words rather than presenting them as your own.

Paraphrases

paraphrase

To restate or summarize an author's ideas in one's own words.

When you paraphrase an author, you restate or summarize her or his ideas in your own words. Suppose, once again, that your topic is Malcolm X. But this time you decide to paraphrase the statement from Bruce Perry's biography rather than quoting it. You might say:

> Malcolm X was not a politician. He did not pass any laws, or win any Supreme Court victories, or get elected to any office. But he stated the grievances and anger of his followers so powerfully that the whole nation took notice.

Even though you do not quote Perry directly, you still appropriate the structure of his ideas and a fair amount of his language. Thus you still need to give him credit—just as if you were repeating his words verbatim.

It is especially important in this case to acknowledge Perry because you are borrowing his opinion—his judgment—about Malcolm X. If you simply recount basic facts about Malcolm's life—he was born in Omaha, Nebraska, converted to the Nation of Islam while in prison, traveled to Mecca toward the end of his life, was assassinated in February 1965—you do not have to report the source of your information. These facts are well known and can be found in any standard reference work.

On the other hand, there is still considerable debate about Malcolm's views of other African-American leaders, the circumstances surrounding his death, and what he might have done had he lived. If you were to cite Perry's views on any of these matters—regardless of whether you quoted or paraphrased—you would need to acknowledge him as your source.

As more than one speaker (and writer) has discovered, it is possible to commit incremental plagiarism quite by accident. This is less offensive than deliberate plagiarism, but it is plagiarism nonetheless. There are two ways to guard against incremental plagiarism. The first is to be careful when taking research notes to distinguish among direct quotations, paraphrased material, and your own comments. (See Chapter 7 for a full discussion of research methods.) The second way to avoid incremental plagiarism is to err on the side of caution. In other words, when in doubt, cite your source.

PLAGIARISM AND THE INTERNET

When it comes to plagiarism, no subject poses more confusion—or more temptation—than the Internet. Because it's so easy to copy information from the Web, many people are not aware of the need to cite sources when they use Internet materials in their speeches. If you don't cite Internet sources, you are just as guilty of plagiarism as if you take information from print sources without proper citation.

One way to avoid patchwork plagiarism or incremental plagiarism when working with the Internet is to take careful research notes. Make sure you keep a record of the following: (1) the title of the Internet document, (2) the author or organization responsible for the document, (3) the date on which the document was last updated, (4) the date on which you accessed the site. You will need all this information for your speech bibliography.

You will also need to identify your Internet sources when you present the speech. It's not enough to say "As I found on the Web" or "According to the Internet." You need to specify the author and the Web site. In Chapter 8,

Using public speaking in your CAREER

Having graduated with a degree in public administration and hoping to pursue a career in politics, you have been fortunate to receive a staff position with one of the leading senators in your state legislature. Since your arrival two months ago, you have answered phones, ordered lunch, made copies, stapled mailings, and stuffed envelopes. Finally you have been asked to look over a speech the senator will deliver at your alma mater. Surely, you think, this will be the first of many important assignments once your value is recognized.

After reading the speech, however, your enthusiasm is dampened. You agree wholeheartedly with its support of a bill to fund scholarships for low-income students, but you're dismayed by its attack on opponents of the bill as "elitist bigots who would deny a college education to those who need it most." You haven't been asked to comment on the ethics of the speech, and you certainly don't want to jeopardize your position on the senator's staff. At the same time, you think his use of name-calling may actually arouse sympathy for the opposition.

The senator would like your comments in two hours. What will you tell him?

we'll look more closely at how to cite Internet documents. For now, keep in mind that providing such citations is one of your ethical responsibilities as a public speaker.

Another problem with regard to the Internet is the large number of Web sites that sell entire speeches or papers. In addition to being highly unethical, using material from one of these sites is extremely risky. The same technology that makes it easy to plagiarize from the Web makes it easy for teachers to locate material that has been plagiarized and the exact source from which it has been taken.

You should also know that almost all the speeches (and papers) offered for sale on the Web are of very low quality. If you are ever tempted to purchase one, keep in mind there is a good chance you will waste your money and get caught in the process. Here, as in other aspects of life, honesty is the best policy.

Guidelines for Ethical Listening

So far in this chapter we have focused on the ethical duties of public speakers. But speechmaking is not a one-way street. Listeners also have ethical obligations. They are (1) to listen courteously and attentively; (2) to avoid prejudging the speaker; and (3) to maintain the free and open expression of ideas. Let us look at each.

BE COURTEOUS AND ATTENTIVE

Imagine that you are giving your first classroom speech. You have put a great deal of time into writing the speech, and you have practiced your delivery until you are confident you can do well—especially once you get over the initial rush of stage fright.

You have worked hard on your introduction, and your speech gets off to a fine start. Most of your classmates are paying close attention, but some are not. One appears to be doing homework for another class. Another keeps sneaking glances at his cell phone. Two or three are gazing out the window, and one is leaning back in his chair with his eyes shut!

You try to block them out of your mind—especially since the rest of the class seems interested in what you are saying—but the longer you speak, the more concerned you become. "What am I doing wrong?" you wonder to yourself. "How can I get these people to pay attention?" The more you think about this, the more your confidence and concentration waver.

When you momentarily lose your place halfway through the speech, you start to panic. Your nerves, which you have held in check so far, take the upper hand. Your major thought now becomes "How can I get this over as fast as possible?" Flustered and distracted, you rush through the rest of your speech and sit down.

Just as public speakers have an ethical obligation to prepare fully for each speech, so listeners have a responsibility to be courteous and attentive during the speech. This responsibility—which is a matter of civility in any circumstance—is especially important in speech class. You and your classmates are in a learning situation in which you need to support one another.

When you listen to speeches in class, give your fellow students the same courtesy and attention you want from them. Come to class prepared to listen to—and to learn from—your classmates' speeches. As you listen, be conscious of the feedback you are sending the speaker. Sit up in your chair rather than slouching; maintain eye contact with the speaker; show support and encouragement in your facial expressions. Keep in mind the power you have as a listener over the speaker's confidence and composure, and exercise that power with a strong sense of ethical responsibility.

AVOID PREJUDGING THE SPEAKER

We have all heard that you can't judge a book by its cover. The same is true of speeches. You can't judge a speech by the name, race, lifestyle, appearance, or reputation of the speaker. As the National Communication Association states in its Credo for Ethical Communication, listeners should "strive to understand and respect" speakers "before evaluating and responding to their messages."[12]

This does not mean you must agree with every speaker you hear. Your aim is to listen carefully to the speaker's ideas, to assess the evidence and reasoning offered in support of those ideas, and to reach an intelligent judgment about the speech. In Chapter 3, we will discuss specific steps you can take to improve your listening skills. For now, it is enough to know that if you prejudge a speaker—either positively or negatively—you will fail in one of your ethical responsibilities as a listener.

MAINTAIN THE FREE AND OPEN EXPRESSION OF IDEAS

As we saw earlier in this chapter, a democratic society depends on the free and open expression of ideas. The right of free expression is so important that it is protected by the First Amendment to the U.S. Constitution, which declares, in part, that "Congress shall make no law . . . abridging the freedom

It is vital for a democratic society to maintain the free and open expression of ideas. Here Rabbi Greg Marx addresses an assembly in Philadelphia devoted to promoting religious tolerance.

of speech." Just as public speakers need to avoid name-calling and other tactics that can undermine free speech, so listeners have an obligation to maintain the right of speakers to be heard.

As with other ethical issues, the extent of this obligation is open to debate. Disputes over the meaning and scope of the First Amendment arise almost daily in connection with issues such as terrorism, pornography, and hate speech. The question underlying such disputes is whether *all* speakers have a right to be heard.

There are some kinds of speech that are not protected under the First Amendment—including defamatory falsehoods that destroy a person's reputation, threats against the life of the President, and inciting an audience to illegal action in circumstances where the audience is likely to carry out the action. Otherwise, the Supreme Court has held—and most experts in communication ethics have agreed—that public speakers have an almost unlimited right of free expression.

In contrast to this view, it has been argued that some ideas are so dangerous, so misguided, or so offensive that society has a duty to suppress them. But who is to determine which ideas are too dangerous, misguided, or offensive to be uttered? Who is to decide which speakers are to be heard and which are to be silenced?

No matter how well intentioned they may be, efforts to "protect" society by restricting free speech usually end up repressing minority viewpoints and unpopular opinions. In U.S. history, such efforts were used to keep women off the public platform until the 1840s, to muzzle labor organizers during the 1890s, and to impede civil rights leaders in the 1960s. Imagine what American society might be like if these speakers had been silenced!

It is important to keep in mind that ensuring a person's freedom to express her or his ideas does not imply agreement with those ideas. You can disagree entirely with the message but still support the speaker's right to express it. As the National Communication Association states in its Credo for Ethical Communication, "freedom of expression, diversity of perspective, and tolerance of dissent" are vital to "the informed decision making fundamental to a civil society."[13]

Summary

Because public speaking is a form of power, it carries with it heavy ethical responsibilities. Today, as for the past 2,000 years, the good person speaking well remains the ideal of commendable speechmaking.

There are five basic guidelines for ethical public speaking. The first is to make sure your goals are ethically sound—that they are consistent with the welfare of society and your audience. The second is to be fully prepared for each speech. The third is to be honest in what you say. The fourth is to avoid name-calling and other forms of abusive language. The final guideline is to put ethical principles into practice at all times.

Of all the ethical lapses a speaker can commit, few are more serious than plagiarism. Global plagiarism is lifting a speech entirely from a single source. Patchwork plagiarism involves stitching a speech together by copying from a few sources. Incremental plagiarism occurs when a speaker fails to give credit for specific quotations and paraphrases that are borrowed from other people.

In addition to your ethical responsibilities as a speaker, you have ethical obligations as a listener. The first is to listen courteously and attentively. The second is to avoid prejudging the speaker. The third is to support the free and open expression of ideas. In all these ways, your speech class will offer a good testing ground for questions of ethical responsibility.

Key Terms

ethics *(30)*
ethical decisions *(31)*
name-calling *(34)*
Bill of Rights *(35)*
plagiarism *(37)*
global plagiarism *(37)*
patchwork plagiarism *(38)*
incremental plagiarism *(38)*
paraphrase *(40)*

Review Questions

After reading this chapter, you should be able to answer the following questions:

1. What is ethics? Why is a strong sense of ethical responsibility vital for public speakers?
2. What are the five guidelines for ethical speechmaking discussed in this chapter?
3. What is the difference between global plagiarism and patchwork plagiarism? What are the best ways to avoid these two kinds of plagiarism?

connect™

For further review, go to the LearnSmart study module for this chapter.

4. What is incremental plagiarism? How can you steer clear of it when dealing with quotations and paraphrases?
5. What are the three guidelines for ethical listening discussed in this chapter?

Exercises for Critical Thinking

1. Look back at the story of Felicia Robinson on pages 30–31. Evaluate her dilemma in light of the guidelines for ethical speechmaking presented in this chapter. Explain what you believe would be the most ethical course of action in her case.
2. The issue of insulting and abusive speech—especially slurs directed against people on the basis of race, religion, gender, or sexual orientation—is extremely controversial. Do you believe society should punish such speech with criminal penalties? To what degree are colleges and universities justified in trying to discipline students who engage in such speech? Do you feel it is proper to place any boundaries on free expression in order to prohibit insulting and abusive speech? Why or why not? Be prepared to explain your ideas in class.
3. All of the following situations could arise in your speech class. Identify the ethical issues in each and explain what, as a responsible speaker or listener, your course of action would be.
   a. You are speaking on the topic of prison reform. In your research, you run across two public opinion polls. One of them, an independent survey by the Gallup Organization, shows that a majority of people in your state oppose your position. The other poll, suspect in its methods and conducted by a partisan organization, says a majority of people in your state support your position. Which poll do you cite in your speech? If you cite the second poll, do you point out its shortcomings?
   b. When listening to an informative speech by one of your classmates, you realize that much of it is plagiarized from a Web site you visited a couple weeks earlier. What do you do? Do you say something when your instructor asks for comments about the speech? Do you mention your concern to the instructor after class? Do you talk with the speaker? Do you remain silent?
   c. While researching your persuasive speech, you find a quotation from an article by a highly respected expert that will nail down one of your most important points. But as you read the rest of the article, you realize that the author does not in fact support the policy you are advocating. Do you still include the quotation in your speech?

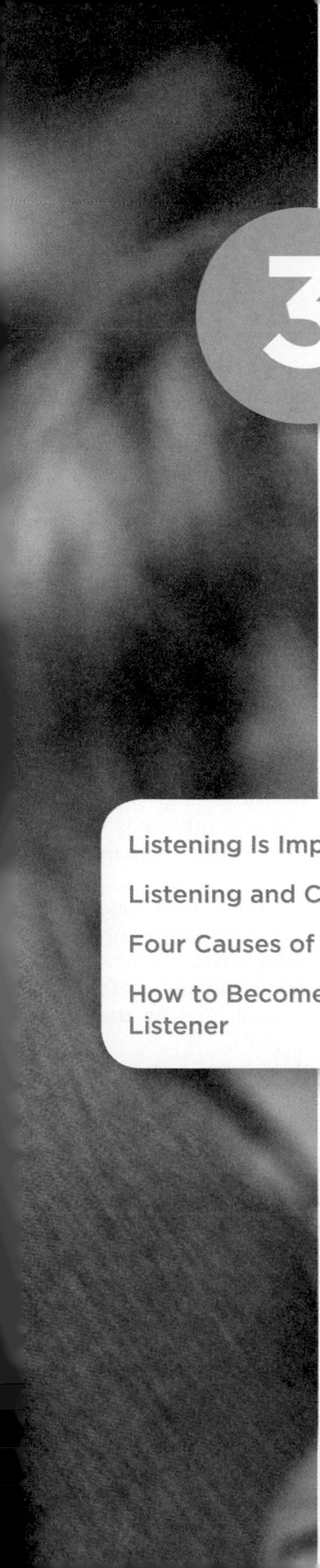

3

Listening

- Listening Is Important
- Listening and Critical Thinking
- Four Causes of Poor Listening
- How to Become a Better Listener

It had been a long day at the office. By the time Jason Whitehawk pulled his late-model car into the driveway at home, he was exhausted. As he trudged into the house, he routinely asked his wife, "How did things go with you at work today?"

"Oh, pretty well," she replied, "except for the terrorist attack in the morning and the outbreak of bubonic plague in the afternoon."

Jason nodded his head as he made his way to the sofa. "That's nice," he said. "At least someone had a good day."

This story illustrates what one research study after another has revealed—most people are shockingly poor listeners. We fake paying attention. We can look right at someone, appear interested in what that person says, even nod our head or smile at the appropriate moments—all without really listening.

Not listening doesn't mean we don't hear. *Hearing* is a physiological process, involving the vibration of sound waves on our eardrums and the firing of electrochemical impulses from the inner ear to the central auditory

hearing

The vibration of sound waves on the eardrums and the firing of electrochemical impulses in the brain.

system of the brain. But *listening* involves paying close attention to, and making sense of, what we hear. Even when we think we are listening carefully, we usually grasp only 50 percent of what we hear. After 24 hours we can remember only 10 percent of the original message.[1] It's little wonder that listening has been called a lost art.[2]

Listening Is Important

listening

Paying close attention to, and making sense of, what we hear.

Although most people listen poorly, there are exceptions. Top-flight business executives, successful politicians, brilliant teachers—nearly all are excellent listeners.[3] So much of what they do depends on absorbing information that is given verbally—and absorbing it quickly and accurately. If you had an interview with the president of a major corporation, you might be shocked (and flattered) to see how closely that person listened to your words.

In our communication-oriented age, listening is more important than ever. According to one study, more than 60 percent of errors made in business come from poor listening.[4] Replacing poor listening with good listening improves efficiency, sales, customer satisfaction, and employee morale. This is why, in most companies, effective listeners hold higher positions and are promoted more often than ineffective listeners. When business managers are asked to rank-order the communication skills most crucial to their jobs, they usually rank listening number one.[5]

Even if you don't plan to be a corporate executive, the art of listening can be helpful in almost every part of your life. This is not surprising when you realize that people spend more time listening than in any other communicative activity—more than reading, more than writing, more even than speaking.

Think for a moment about your own life as a college student. Most class time in U.S. colleges and universities is spent listening to discussions and lectures. A number of studies have shown a strong correlation between listening and academic success. Students with the highest grades are usually those with the strongest listening skills. The reverse is also true—students with the lowest grades are usually those with the weakest listening skills.[6]

There is plenty of reason, then, to take listening seriously. Employers and employees, parents and children, wives and husbands, doctors and patients, students and teachers—all depend on the apparently simple skill of listening. Regardless of your profession or walk of life, you never escape the need for a well-trained ear.

Listening is also important to you as a speaker. It is probably the way you get most of your ideas and information—from television, radio, conversation, and lectures. If you do not listen well, you will not understand what you hear and may pass along your misunderstanding to others.

Besides, in class—as in life—you will listen to many more speeches than you give. It is only fair to pay close attention to your classmates' speeches; after all, you want them to listen carefully to *your* speeches. An excellent way to improve your own speeches is to listen attentively to the speeches of other people. Over and over, teachers find that the best speakers are usually the best listeners.

A side benefit of your speech class is that it offers an ideal opportunity to work on the art of listening. During the 95 percent of the time when you are not speaking, you have nothing else to do but listen and learn. You can sit there like a stone—or you can use the time profitably to master a skill that will serve you in a thousand ways.

Listening and Critical Thinking

One of the ways listening can serve you is by enhancing your skills as a critical thinker. We can identify four kinds of listening:[7]

- *Appreciative listening*—listening for pleasure or enjoyment, as when we listen to music, to a comedy routine, or to an entertaining speech.
- *Empathic listening*—listening to provide emotional support for the speaker, as when a psychiatrist listens to a patient or when we lend a sympathetic ear to a friend in distress.
- *Comprehensive listening*—listening to understand the message of a speaker, as when we attend a classroom lecture or listen to directions for finding a friend's house.
- *Critical listening*—listening to evaluate a message for purposes of accepting or rejecting it, as when we listen to the sales pitch of a car salesperson or the campaign speech of a political candidate.

appreciative listening

Listening for pleasure or enjoyment.

empathic listening

Listening to provide emotional support for a speaker.

comprehensive listening

Listening to understand the message of a speaker.

critical listening

Listening to evaluate a message for purposes of accepting or rejecting it.

Although all four kinds of listening are important, this chapter deals primarily with comprehensive listening and critical listening. They are the kinds of listening you will use most often when listening to speeches in class, when taking lecture notes in other courses, when communicating at work, and when responding to the barrage of commercials, political messages, and other persuasive appeals you face every day. They are also the kinds of listening that are most closely tied to critical thinking.

As we saw in Chapter 1, critical thinking involves a number of skills. Some of those skills—summarizing information, recalling facts, distinguishing main points from minor points—are central to comprehensive listening. Other skills of critical thinking—separating fact from opinion, spotting weaknesses in reasoning, judging the soundness of evidence—are especially important in critical listening.

When you engage in comprehensive listening or critical listening, you must use your mind as well as your ears. When your mind is not actively involved, you may be hearing, but you are not *listening*. In fact, listening and critical thinking are so closely allied that training in listening is also training in how to think.

At the end of this chapter, we'll discuss steps you can take to improve your skills in comprehensive and critical listening. If you follow these steps, you may also become a better critical thinker.

Four Causes of Poor Listening

NOT CONCENTRATING

The brain is incredibly efficient. Although we talk at a rate of 120 to 150 words a minute, the brain can process 400 to 800 words a minute.[8] This would seem to make listening very easy, but actually it has the opposite effect. Because we can process a speaker's words and still have plenty of spare "brain time," we are tempted to interrupt our listening by thinking about other things. Here's what happens:

spare "brain time"

The difference between the rate at which most people talk (120 to 150 words a minute) and the rate at which the brain can process language (400 to 800 words a minute).

Elena Kim works in the public communications department of a large insurance company. She attends regular staff meetings with the communications director. The meetings provide necessary information, but sometimes they seem to drag on forever.

This morning the director is talking about the company's new executive vice president, who has just moved to headquarters from a regional firm in Florida. "Mr. Fernandez has never worked in a company this size, but his experience in Florida . . ."

"Florida," Elena dreams. "Sun, endless beaches, and the club scene in South Beach. Maybe I can snatch a few days' vacation in January. . . ."

Sternly, Elena pulls her attention back to the meeting. The communications director is now discussing the company's latest plan for public-service announcements. Elena is not involved in the plan, and her attention wanders once more.

That morning she had another argument with her roommate about cleaning the kitchen and taking out the garbage. Maybe it's time to decide if she can afford to live without a roommate. It sure would make for fewer hassles.

". . . an area Elena has researched extensively," the director is saying. Uh oh! *What* area does the director mean? Everyone looks at Elena, as she frantically tries to recall the last words said at the meeting.

It's not that Elena *meant* to lose track of the discussion. But there comes a point at which it's so easy to let your thoughts wander rather than to concentrate on what is being said. After all, concentrating is hard work. Louis Nizer, the famous trial lawyer, says, "So complete is this concentration that at the end of a court day in which I have only listened, I find myself wringing wet despite a calm and casual manner."[9]

Later in this chapter, we will look at some things you can do to concentrate better on what you hear.

LISTENING TOO HARD

Until now we have been talking about not paying close attention to what we hear. But sometimes we listen *too* hard. We turn into human sponges, soaking up a speaker's every word as if every word were equally important. We try to remember all the names, all the dates, all the places. In the process we often miss the speaker's main point. What is worse, we may end up confusing the facts as well.

Shortly after graduating from college, Carlos Molina landed an excellent job as a Web developer. Knowing he had never been good at budgeting his money, he signed up for a financial planning workshop.

People spend more time listening than in any other communicative activity. One benefit of your speech class is that it can improve your listening skills in a variety of situations.

The first session was about retirement planning. Simone Fisher, who was conducting the workshop, explained that 7 in 10 Americans between the ages of 22 and 35 do not have a monthly budget or a savings plan. Carlos wrote down every number Simone mentioned.

"To have a retirement income equal to 75 percent of your current salary," Simone continued, "you will need to invest at least 6 percent of your present earnings. You also need to account for inflation over time. This afternoon, we will meet with each of you personally to calculate your individual savings needs. In the meantime, I want to stress that the most important thing is to start saving now."

Carlos zealously typed each statistic into his laptop. When Simone opened the floor for questions, Carlos raised his hand and said, "I have two questions. When should I start saving for retirement? And how do I figure out how to account for future inflation?"

This is a typical example of losing the speaker's point by concentrating on details. Carlos had fixed his mind on remembering all the statistics in Simone's presentation, but he blocked out the main message—that it is best to start saving now and that he would get help developing an individual plan.

Rather than trying to remember everything a speaker says, efficient listeners usually concentrate on main points and evidence. We'll discuss these things more thoroughly later in the chapter.

JUMPING TO CONCLUSIONS

Kiah Lee, a recent college graduate, took a job as an editorial assistant in the research department of a regional magazine. Shortly after Kiah arrived, the editor in charge of the research department left the magazine for another job. For the next two months, Kiah struggled to handle the work of the research department by herself. She often felt in over her head, but she knew this was a good opportunity to learn, and she hated to give up her new responsibilities.

One day Derek Perkins, the editor in chief of the magazine, comes into Kiah's office to talk. The following conversation takes place:

Derek: You've done a great job these last two months, Kiah. But you know we really need a new editor. So we've decided to make some changes.

Kiah: I'm not surprised. I know I've made my share of mistakes.

Derek: Everyone makes mistakes when they're starting out. And you've been carrying a lot of responsibility. That's why . . .

Kiah: I know I'm inexperienced, and this is an important department.

Derek: Yes, it is. And it's not an easy job. We really need an editor and an assistant to handle all the work. That's why I wanted to tell you . . .

Kiah: I understand. I knew all along that I was just filling in.

Derek: Kiah, you're not listening.

Kiah: Yes, I am. You're trying to be nice, but you're here to tell me that you've hired a new editor and I'll be going back to my old job.

Derek: No, that's not it at all. I think you've done a fine job under difficult circumstances. You've proved yourself, and I intend to make *you* the editor. But I think you'll need an assistant to help you.

Why is there so much confusion here? Clearly, Kiah is unsure about her future at the magazine. So when Derek starts to talk about making some changes, Kiah jumps to a conclusion and assumes the worst. The misunderstanding could have been avoided if, when Derek had said, "We've decided to make some changes," Kiah had asked, "What changes?"—and then *listened.*

This is one form of jumping to conclusions—putting words into a speaker's mouth. It is one reason why we sometimes communicate so poorly with people we are closest to. Because we're so sure we know what they mean, we don't listen to what they actually say.

Another way of jumping to conclusions is prematurely rejecting a speaker's ideas as boring or misguided. That would be a mistake. Let's say the announced topic is "Architecture and History." It sounds dull. So you tune out—and miss a fascinating discussion filled with human-interest stories about buildings and other structures from the ancient pyramids to the latest skyscrapers.

Nearly every speech has something to offer you—whether it be information, point of view, or technique. You are cheating yourself if you prejudge and choose not to listen.

FOCUSING ON DELIVERY AND PERSONAL APPEARANCE

Avid readers of American history, Greg and Marissa were thrilled when they saw a poster at their local bookstore advertising a lecture by the author of a new book on the Battle of Gettysburg. The book had received good reviews, and Greg and Marissa made plans to attend the lecture.

Arriving at the bookstore, they took their seats and listened while the speaker discussed his research and major findings. "That was great," Marissa exclaimed when they got back to the car. But Greg was scowling. "What's wrong?" Marissa asked.

"I know you're going to think this is stupid," Greg began. "The guy was a decent speaker, and he seemed to know his stuff. But did you see the sport coat he was wearing? It's so retro—and his tie was atrocious. No matter how I tried, I kept thinking that he hadn't gone shopping since the 1980s."

This story illustrates a common problem. Sometimes we judge people by the way they look or speak and don't listen to what they say. It's easy to become distracted by a speaker's accent, personal appearance, or vocal mannerisms and lose sight of the message. Focusing on a speaker's delivery or personal appearance is one of the major sources of interference in the speech communication process, and it is something we always need to guard against.

How to Become a Better Listener

TAKE LISTENING SERIOUSLY

The first step toward becoming a better listener is to accord listening the seriousness it deserves. Good listeners are not born that way. They have *worked* at learning how to listen effectively. Good listening does not go hand in hand with intelligence, education, or social standing. Like any other skill, it comes from practice and self-discipline. Check your current skills as a listener by completing the Listening Self-Evaluation Worksheet on page 54.[10] Once you have identified your shortcomings as a listener, make a serious effort to overcome them.

BE AN ACTIVE LISTENER

So many aspects of modern life encourage us to listen passively. We listen to our iPods while studying. Parents listen to their children while fixing dinner. Television reporters listen to a politician's speech while walking around the auditorium looking for their next interview.

This type of passive listening is a habit—but so is active listening. Active listeners give their undivided attention to the speaker in a genuine effort to understand his or her point of view. In conversation, they do not interrupt the speaker or finish his or her sentences. When listening to a speech, they do not allow themselves to be distracted by internal or external interference, and they do not prejudge the speaker. They take listening seriously and do the best they can to stay focused on the speaker and his or her message.

active listening

Giving undivided attention to a speaker in a genuine effort to understand the speaker's point of view.

There are a number of steps you can take to improve your skills of active listening. They include resisting distractions, not allowing yourself to be diverted by a speaker's appearance or delivery, suspending judgment until you have heard the speaker out, focusing your listening, and developing note-taking skills. We'll discuss each of these in turn.

LISTENING SELF-EVALUATION

How often do you indulge in the following bad listening habits? Check yourself carefully in each one.

HABIT	FREQUENCY					SCORE
	Almost Always	Usually	Sometimes	Seldom	Almost Never	
1. Giving in to mental distractions	______	______	______	______	______	______
2. Giving in to physical distractions	______	______	______	______	______	______
3. Trying to recall everything a speaker says	______	______	______	______	______	______
4. Rejecting a topic as uninteresting before hearing the speaker	______	______	______	______	______	______
5. Faking paying attention	______	______	______	______	______	______
6. Jumping to conclusions about a speaker's meaning	______	______	______	______	______	______
7. Deciding a speaker is wrong before hearing everything she or he has to say	______	______	______	______	______	______
8. Judging a speaker on personal appearance	______	______	______	______	______	______
9. Not paying attention to a speaker's evidence	______	______	______	______	______	______
10. Focusing on delivery rather than on what the speaker says	______	______	______	______	______	______
					TOTAL	______

How to score:

For every "almost always" checked, give yourself a score of	2
For every "usually" checked, give yourself a score of	4
For every "sometimes" checked, give yourself a score of	6
For every "seldom" checked, give yourself a score of	8
For every "almost never" checked, give yourself a score of	10

Total score interpretation:		
	Below 70	You need lots of training in listening.
	From 71–90	You listen well.
	Above 90	You listen exceptionally well.

Effective listeners take their task seriously. If you approach listening as an active process, you will significantly sharpen your powers of concentration and comprehension.

RESIST DISTRACTIONS

In an ideal world, we could eliminate all physical and mental distractions. In the real world, however, we cannot. Because we think so much faster than a speaker can talk, it's easy to let our attention wander. Sometimes it's very easy—when the room is too hot, when construction machinery is operating right outside the window, when the speaker is tedious. But our attention can stray even in the best of circumstances—if for no other reason than a failure to stay alert and make ourselves concentrate.

Whenever you find this happening, make a conscious effort to pull your mind back to what the speaker is saying. Then force it to stay there. One way to do this is to think ahead of the speaker—try to anticipate what will come next. This is not the same as jumping to conclusions. When you jump to conclusions, you put words into the speaker's mouth and don't listen to what is said. In this case you *will* listen—and measure what the speaker says against what you had anticipated.

Another way to keep your mind on a speech is to review mentally what the speaker has already said and make sure you understand it. Yet another is to listen between the lines and assess what a speaker implies verbally or says nonverbally with body language. Suppose a speaker is introducing someone to an audience. The speaker says, "It gives me great pleasure to present to you my very dear friend, Ashley Hauser." But the speaker doesn't shake hands with Ashley. He doesn't even look at her—just turns his back and leaves the podium. Is Ashley really his "very dear friend"? Certainly not.

Attentive listeners can pick up all kinds of clues to a speaker's real message. At first you may find it difficult to listen so intently. If you work at it, however, your concentration is bound to improve.

DON'T BE DIVERTED BY APPEARANCE OR DELIVERY

If you had attended Abraham Lincoln's momentous Cooper Union speech of 1860, this is what you would have seen:

> The long, ungainly figure upon which hung clothes that, while new for this trip, were evidently the work of an unskilled tailor; the large feet and clumsy hands, of which, at the outset, at least, the orator seemed to be unduly conscious; the long, gaunt head, capped by a shock of hair that seemed not to have been thoroughly brushed out, made a picture which did not fit in with New York's conception of a finished statesman.[11]

But although he seemed awkward and uncultivated, Lincoln had a powerful message about the moral evils of slavery. Fortunately, the audience at Cooper Union did not let his appearance stand in the way of his words.

Similarly, you must be willing to set aside preconceived judgments based on a person's looks or manner of speech. Gandhi was an unimpressive-looking man who often spoke dressed in a simple white cotton cloth. Renowned physicist Stephen Hawking is severely disabled and can speak only with the aid of a voice synthesizer. Yet imagine how much poorer the world would be if no one listened to them. Even though it may tax your tolerance, patience, and concentration, don't let negative feelings about a speaker's appearance or delivery keep you from listening to the message.

On the other hand, try not to be misled if the speaker has an unusually attractive appearance. It's all too easy to assume that because someone is good-looking and has a polished delivery, he or she is speaking eloquently. Some of the most unscrupulous speakers in history have been handsome people with hypnotic delivery skills. Again, be sure you respond to the message, not to the package it comes in.

SUSPEND JUDGMENT

Unless we listen only to people who think exactly as we do, we are going to hear things with which we disagree. When this happens, our natural inclination is to argue mentally with the speaker or to dismiss everything she or he says. But neither response is fair, and in both cases we blot out any chance of learning or being persuaded.

Does this mean you must agree with everything you hear? Not at all. It means you should hear people out *before* reaching a final judgment. Try to understand their point of view. Listen to their ideas, examine their evidence, assess their reasoning. *Then* make up your mind. The aim of active listening is to set aside "one's own prejudices, frames of reference, and desires so as to experience as far as possible the speaker's world from the inside."[12] It has been said more than once that a closed mind is an empty mind.

FOCUS YOUR LISTENING

As we have seen, skilled listeners do not try to absorb a speaker's every word. Rather, they focus on specific things in a speech. Here are three suggestions to help you focus your listening.

Listen for Main Points

Most speeches contain from two to four main points. Here, for example, are the main points of a recent speech by Jack Hayes, director of the U.S. National Weather Service:[13]

1. The past 50 years have witnessed a number of pioneering innovations in meteorology.
2. Today, meteorologists can provide better weather warnings than at any time in history.
3. Future advances in meteorology will require visionary ideas and economic resources.

These three main points are the heart of Hayes's message. As with any speech, they are the most important things to listen for.

Unless a speaker is terribly scatterbrained, you should be able to detect his or her main points with little difficulty. Often a speaker will give some idea at the outset of the main points to be discussed in the speech. For example, at the end of his introduction, Hayes said he was going to reflect on "where we were, where we are, and . . . where we go from here." As the speech progressed, Hayes moved from point to point with signposts such as "Let's take a brief look at how far we've come" and "What's on the horizon for us?" After this, only the most inattentive of listeners could have missed his main points.

Listen for Evidence

Identifying a speaker's main points, however, is not enough. You must also listen for supporting evidence. By themselves, Hayes's main points are only assertions. You may be inclined to believe them just because they come from an important meteorologist. Yet a careful listener will be concerned about evidence no matter who is speaking. Had you been listening to Hayes's speech, you would have heard him support his claims with a mass of verifiable evidence. Here is an excerpt:

> Over the past 20 years, advances in science and technology have enabled us to increase public preparation for flash floods from 10 minutes to an hour and 10 minutes, a seven-fold improvement.
>
> We've improved accuracy in hurricane-track forecasting. In 1970, 48-hour track error was about 250 nautical miles. In 2009, it was less than 100 nautical miles. In fact, our current average error at 96 hours is better than our 48-hour forecast was in 1970, giving coastal residents and businesses two more days to prepare for the likes of a hurricane Katrina.

There are four basic questions to ask about a speaker's evidence:

Is it *accurate*?

Is it taken from *objective* sources?

Is it *relevant* to the speaker's claims?

Is it *sufficient* to support the speaker's point?

In Hayes's case, the answer to each question is yes. His figures about meteorological advances are well established in the public record and can be verified by independent sources. The figures are clearly relevant to Hayes's claim that improvements in meteorology are saving lives and money, and they are sufficient to support that claim. If Hayes's evidence were inaccurate, biased, irrelevant, or insufficient, you should be wary of accepting his claim.

We shall discuss these—and other—tests of evidence in detail in Chapters 8 and 17. For now, it's enough to know that you should be on guard against unfounded assertions and sweeping generalizations. Keep an eye out for the speaker's evidence and for its accuracy, objectivity, relevance, and sufficiency.

Listen for Technique

We said earlier that you should not let a speaker's delivery distract you from the message, and this is true. However, if you want to become an effective speaker, you should study the methods other people use to speak effectively.

Analyze the introduction: What methods does the speaker use to gain attention, to relate to the audience, to establish credibility and goodwill? Assess the organization of the speech: Is it clear and easy to follow? Can you pick out the speaker's main points? Can you follow when the speaker moves from one point to another?

Study the speaker's language: Is it accurate, clear, vivid, appropriate? Does the speaker adapt well to the audience and occasion? Finally, diagnose the speaker's delivery: Is it fluent, dynamic, convincing? Does it strengthen or weaken the impact of the speaker's ideas? How well does the speaker use eye contact, gestures, and visual aids?

As you listen, focus on the speaker's strengths and weaknesses. If the speaker is not effective, try to determine why. If he or she is effective, try to pick out techniques you can use in your own speeches. If you listen in this way, you will be surprised by how much you can learn about successful speaking.

DEVELOP NOTE-TAKING SKILLS

Speech students are often amazed at how easily their teacher can pick out a speaker's main points, evidence, and techniques. Of course, the teacher knows what to listen for and has had plenty of practice. But the next time you get an opportunity, watch your teacher during a speech. Chances are she or he will be listening with a laptop or pen and paper. When note taking is done properly, it is a surefire way to improve your concentration and keep track of a speaker's ideas.

The key words here are *when done properly*. Unfortunately, many people don't take notes effectively. Some try to take down everything a speaker says. They view the enterprise as a race that pits their note-taking speed against the speaker's rate of speech. As the speaker starts to talk, the note taker starts to write or type. But soon the speaker is winning the race. In a desperate effort to keep up, the note taker tries to go faster and faster. But even this is not enough. The speaker pulls so far ahead that the note taker can never catch up.[14]

Some people go to the opposite extreme. They arrive armed with pen, laptop, and the best of intentions. They know they can't write down everything, so they wait for the speaker to say something that grabs their attention.

Research confirms that listening carefully and taking effective notes are vital skills for success in college. They will also benefit you in countless situations throughout life.

Every once in a while the speaker rewards them with a joke, a dramatic story, or a startling fact. Then the note taker records a few words and leans back to await the next fascinating tidbit. By the end of the lecture, the note taker has a set of tidbits—and little or no record of the speaker's important ideas.

As these examples illustrate, most inefficient note takers suffer from one or both of two problems: They don't know *what* to listen for, and they don't know *how* to record what they do listen for.[15] The solution to the first problem is to focus on a speaker's main points and evidence. But once you know what to listen for, you still need a sound method of note taking.

Although there are a number of systems, most students find the *key-word outline* best for listening to classroom lectures and formal speeches. As its name suggests, this method briefly notes a speaker's main points and supporting evidence in rough outline form. Suppose a speaker says:

key-word outline

An outline that briefly notes a speaker's main points and supporting evidence in rough outline form.

Hospitals in the United States are facing a serious shortage of nurses. According to the American Hospital Association, the nurse shortage nationwide has reached an alarming total of 135,000. What's worse, a recent article in *Health Affairs* projects that the shortage will reach 260,000 by 2025. Hospitals in major cities such as New York, Los Angeles, and Miami have had to reduce services because of a lack of nurses.

There are four major causes for this shortage of nurses. One cause is that there are not enough faculty members at nursing schools to train the number of nurses needed by hospitals. A second cause is that nurses can find employment at medical facilities other than hospitals. A third cause is that many nurses are reluctant to stay on the job because of poor working hours that include nights, holidays, and weekends. A fourth cause is that nurses are burdened with excessive paperwork.

A key-word note taker would record something like this:

Serious nurse shortage
- Total of 135,000
- 260,000 by 2025
- Reduced services at hospitals

Four major causes
- Low faculty at nursing schools
- Employment available beyond hospitals
- Poor working hours
- Excessive paperwork

Notice how brief the notes are. Yet they accurately summarize the speaker's ideas. They are also very clear. By separating main points from subpoints and evidence, the outline format shows the relationships among the speaker's ideas.

Perfecting this—or any other—system of note taking requires practice. But with a little effort you should see results soon. As you become a better note taker, you will become a better listener. There is also a good chance you will become a better student. Research confirms that students who take effective notes usually receive higher grades than those who do not.[16]

Summary

Most people are poor listeners. Even when we think we are listening carefully, we usually grasp only half of what we hear, and we retain even less. Improving your listening skills can be helpful in every part of your life, including speechmaking.

The most important cause of poor listening is giving in to distractions and letting our thoughts wander. Sometimes, however, we listen too hard. We try to remember every word a speaker says, and we lose the main message by concentrating on details. In other situations, we may jump to conclusions and prejudge a speaker without hearing out the message. Finally, we often judge people by their appearance or speaking manner instead of listening to what they say.

You can overcome these poor listening habits by taking several steps. First, take listening seriously and commit yourself to becoming a better listener. Second, work at being an active listener. Give your undivided attention to the speaker in a genuine effort to understand her or his ideas. Third, resist distractions. Make a conscious effort to keep your mind on what the speaker is saying. Fourth, try not to be diverted by appearance or delivery. Set aside preconceived judgments based on a person's looks or manner of speech.

Fifth, suspend judgment until you have heard the speaker's entire message. Sixth, focus your listening by paying attention to main points, to evidence, and to the speaker's techniques. Finally, develop your note-taking skills. When done properly, note taking is an excellent way to improve your concentration and to keep track of a speaker's ideas.

Key Terms

hearing *(48)*
listening *(48)*
appreciative listening *(49)*
empathic listening *(49)*
comprehensive listening *(49)*
critical listening *(49)*
spare "brain time" *(50)*
active listening *(53)*
key-word outline *(59)*

Review Questions

After reading this chapter, you should be able to answer the following questions:

1. What is the difference between hearing and listening?
2. How is listening connected with critical thinking?
3. Why is it important to develop strong listening skills?
4. What are the four main causes of poor listening?
5. What are seven ways to become a better listener?

connect

For further review, go to the LearnSmart study module for this chapter.

Exercises for Critical Thinking

1. Which of the four causes of poor listening discussed in this chapter do you consider the most important? Choose a specific case of poor listening in which you were involved. Explain what went wrong.
2. Using the Listening Self-Evaluation Worksheet on page 54, undertake a candid evaluation of your major strengths and weaknesses as a listener. Explain what steps you need to take to become a better listener.
3. Watch the lead story this week on *60 Minutes, Dateline,* or *20/20.* Using the key-word outline method of note taking, record the main ideas of the story.
4. Choose a lecture in one of your other classes. Analyze what the lecturer does most effectively. Identify three things the lecturer could do better to help students keep track of the lecture.

4

Giving Your First Speech

- Preparing Your Speech
- Delivering Your Speech
- Sample Speeches with Commentary

You may be surprised to learn that one of the first assignments in your class is to give a speech. You say to yourself, "What am I going to do? I have barely started this course, yet I'm supposed to stand up in front of everyone and give a speech! I've only read a few pages in the textbook, and I don't know much about public speaking. Where do I begin?"

If these are your thoughts, you aren't alone. Most beginning speech students have a similar reaction. Fortunately, giving your first speech sounds a lot harder than it is. The purpose of this chapter is to help you get started on preparing and delivering your speech. Later chapters will expand on the subjects discussed here and will apply them to different kinds of speeches.

Preparing Your Speech

ice breaker speech

A speech early in the term designed to get students speaking in front of the class as soon as possible.

Usually a brief, simple presentation, the first assignment is often called an ice breaker speech because it is designed to "break the ice" by getting students up in front of the class as soon as possible. This is an important step because much of the anxiety associated with public speaking comes from lack of experience giving speeches. Once you have broken the ice by giving a speech, you will feel less anxious and will have taken the first step on the road to confidence.

DEVELOPING THE SPEECH

There are a number of possible assignments for the first speech. One is a speech of self-introduction that provides insight into the speaker's background, personality, beliefs, or goals. In other cases, students are asked to introduce a classmate, rather than themselves. Some instructors require yet a different kind of speech. Make sure you understand exactly what your instructor requires.

Focusing Your Topic

No matter what kind of introductory speech you are assigned, be sure to focus your presentation sharply so it conforms to the assigned time limit. One of the most common mistakes students make on their first speech is trying to cover too much.

It would be impossible, for example, to tell your audience everything about your life in a two- or three-minute speech. A better approach would be to focus on one or two events that have helped define who you are—competing in the state track meet, tutoring disadvantaged children, getting your first job, and the like. This allows you to make a few well-developed points about a clearly defined subject.

On the other hand, avoid the temptation to narrow the focus of your topic too much. Few listeners would be pleased to hear a two- or three-minute discussion of advanced trumpet-playing techniques. Such a speech would be too specialized for most classroom audiences.

Developing Your Topic

Once you have a topic for your speech, be creative in developing it. Think of ways to structure the speech so it will be interesting and meaningful to your audience. Look, for example, at the sample speeches with commentary at the end of this chapter. The first speaker explains aspects of his personality by referring to three of the apps on his cell phone. The second speaker uses the notion of a fork in the road when introducing one of her classmates. In both cases, the speakers found a creative way to frame their information.

Another possibility is to think of ways you can make your presentation mysterious or suspenseful. Suppose you are telling the audience about meeting a celebrity, visiting a famous place, or participating in a newsworthy event. Rather than identifying the celebrity at the outset, you might save his or her name for the end of your speech. As your story unfolds, tantalize your classmates with clues about your celebrity's gender, physical characteristics, special talents, and the like, but keep the name secret until the last moment.

Audiences are also interested in dangerous situations, adventure, and drama. If your task is to introduce a fellow student, find out if she or he has ever been in danger. Suppose your classmate was caught in a flood or spent

Your first speech provides a foundation for speeches you will give later. As you develop your skills, you will find yourself able to speak confidently and with strong eye contact in class and out.

a year in Africa with the Peace Corps. The details would make excellent material for a speech.

If you think about it, every person has faced risk, done the unusual, or triumphed over hardship. Try to find ways to include such fascinating experiences in your speech.

You can also make your speech interesting by using colorful, descriptive language. One speaker used this technique when introducing a fellow student, named Alexa, to the class. The speaker began by saying:

> The spotlight shines. The music blares. The crowd cheers. The colors, bright and vibrant, bleed together as Alexa and her partner sail around the dance floor. Her partner touches her hand and her waist, but only briefly. He then spins her away, and she glides across the floor in what seems like a single motion. Alexa has worked many weeks for this moment. Alexa, you see, is a championship ballroom dancer.

connect

View the introduction from "Gotta Dance" in the online Media Library for this chapter (Video 4.1).

The speaker could have said, "Alexa is a terrific ballroom dancer and finds it quite thrilling." Instead, the speaker painted a word picture so listeners could visualize the dance floor, the brilliant colors of the costumes, and the excitement of the competition as Alexa and her partner perform in perfect symmetry. Colorful and concrete illustrations like this are always more interesting than dull language and abstract generalizations.

You might wonder whether you should use humor to make your first speech entertaining. Audiences love witty remarks, jokes, and funny situations, but like anything else, humor is effective only when done well. It should flow naturally out of the speech content rather than being contrived. If you are not normally a funny person, you are better off giving a sincere, enthusiastic speech and leaving out the jokes. In no case should you include humor that involves obscenity, embarrasses individuals, or negatively stereotypes groups of people. The best kind of humor gently pokes fun at ourselves or at universal human foibles.

ORGANIZING THE SPEECH

Regardless of your topic, a speech usually has three main parts—an introduction, a body, and a conclusion. In Chapter 10, we will discuss each of these parts in detail. Here we focus on what you need to know about them as you prepare your introductory speech.

Introduction

introduction

The opening section of a speech.

Your first job in the introduction is to get the attention and interest of the audience. You can do this by posing a question, telling a story, making a startling statement, or opening with a quotation. The purpose of all these methods is to create a dramatic, colorful opening that will make your audience want to hear more.

For an example, look at the speech excerpt on Video 4.2 in the online Media Library for this chapter. The speaker's assignment was to present a narrative about a significant experience in his life. This is how he began:

connect

View the beginning of "The Secret" in the online Media Library for this chapter (Video 4.2).

> I never knew the secret until I took a year off from school, traveled halfway around the world, and lived for a year in Thailand. I was there to teach English, but the trip ended up being much more than a job. It was a voyage of discovery. I didn't know exactly what I would find, but I came home with a truly valuable secret.

After this introduction, the audience was eager to hear more about the speaker's secret.

In addition to gaining attention and interest, the introduction should orient your listeners toward the subject matter of your speech. In the longer speeches you will give later in the term, you will usually need to provide an explicit preview statement that identifies the main points to be discussed in the body of your speech. (For example, "Today I will inform you about the symptoms, causes, and treatment of sleep apnea.")

Because your introductory speech is so short, you may not need a detailed preview statement. But you still need to give your audience a clear sense of your topic and purpose. (Be sure to check with your instructor to see what kind of preview statement he or she prefers for the introductory speech.)

Body

body

The main section of a speech.

After getting the audience's attention and revealing your topic, you are ready to move into the body of your speech. In some speeches, the body seems to organize itself. If you are telling a story about a significant experience in your life, you will relate the events chronologically, in the order they occurred.

chronological order

A method of speech organization in which the main points follow a time pattern.

But not all speeches follow such a format. Suppose you have been asked to give a presentation introducing a classmate. You could organize the most important biographical facts about your subject in chronological order, but this might result in a dull, superficial speech: "Maria was born in Los Angeles in 1993, attended elementary school from 1998 to 2005, and graduated from high school in 2011."

topical order

A method of speech organization in which the main points divide the topic into logical and consistent subtopics.

A better way of structuring your remarks might be to discuss three of the most important aspects of Maria's life, such as hobbies, career goals, and family. This is called the topical method of organization, which subdivides the speech topic into its natural, logical, or conventional parts. Although there are many other ways to organize a speech, your first presentation will probably use either chronological or topical order.

Regardless of the method of organization you use, remember to limit the number of main points in the body of your speech. In a two-minute presentation, you won't have time to develop more than two or three main points.

Once you have selected those points, make sure each one focuses on a single aspect of the topic. For example, if your first point concerns your classmate's hometown, don't introduce irrelevant information about her job or favorite music. Save this material for a separate point, or cut it.

main points

The major points developed in the body of a speech.

Try to make your main points stand out by introducing each with a transition statement. In a speech about a classmate, you might begin the first main point by saying:

> Rico's family moved a great deal throughout his childhood.

transition

A word or phrase that indicates when a speaker has finished one thought and is moving on to another.

When you reach the second point, you might introduce it like this:

> Moving a lot led to Rico's outgoing nature and confidence in making friends. In fact, he has friends all around the world with whom he corresponds regularly over Facebook.

You have now let your audience know that the first main point is over and that you are starting the second one. The third main point might begin as follows:

> Corresponding with people all over the world is more than just a hobby for Rico, since he is majoring in international relations.

Transitions such as these will help your audience keep track of your main points.

Conclusion

When you finish discussing your final point, you will be ready to move into your conclusion. You need to accomplish two tasks in this part of the speech: let the audience know you are about to finish and reinforce your central idea.

conclusion

The final section of a speech.

If possible, end on a dramatic, clever, or thought-provoking note. For example, when talking about his "secret" in the speech mentioned earlier, the student devoted the body of his presentation to explaining his experiences in Thailand and how they opened his eyes to the universality of human experience. Then, in his conclusion, he wrapped up by saying:

> I needed to be in an entirely different culture to learn the secret—that despite differences in ancestry, language, history, and religion, human beings are pretty much the same wherever they might be. I thought I was going to meet people who were totally alien to me. Instead, I found that family, friendship, kindness, and community are as important on one side of the world as on the other.

connect™

View the ending of "The Secret" in the online Media Library for this chapter (Video 4.3).

The final lines end the speech on a strong note and underscore why the speaker's time in Thailand was so important.

Delivering Your Speech

Once you have selected a subject and organized the content into a clear structure, it is time to work on the delivery of your speech. Because this is your first speech of the term, no one expects you to give a perfectly polished

When developing your first speech, plan what you want to say, organize the material clearly, practice thoroughly, and use the extemporaneous method of delivery. You may be surprised at how much you enjoy the experience.

presentation. Your aim is to do as well as possible while laying a foundation you can build upon in later speeches. With this is mind, we'll look briefly at the extemporaneous method of speech delivery, the importance of rehearsing your speech, and some of the major factors to consider when speech day arrives.

SPEAKING EXTEMPORANEOUSLY

extemporaneous speech

A carefully prepared and rehearsed speech that is presented from a brief set of notes.

You might be inclined, as are many beginning speakers, to write out your speech like an essay and read it word for word to your listeners. The other extreme is to prepare very little for the speech—to wing it by trusting to your wits and the inspiration of the moment. Neither approach is appropriate.

Most experts recommend speaking extemporaneously, which combines the careful preparation and structure of a manuscript presentation with the spontaneity and enthusiasm of an unrehearsed talk. Your aim in an extemporaneous speech is to plan your major points and supporting material without trying to memorize the precise language you will use on the day of the speech.

The extemporaneous method requires you to know the content of your speech quite well. In fact, when you use this method properly, you become so familiar with the substance of your talk that you need only a few brief notes to remind you of the points you intend to cover. The notes should consist of key words or phrases, rather than complete sentences and paragraphs. This way, when you are in front of the audience, you will tell them what you know about the topic in your own words.

Prepare your notes by writing or printing key terms and phrases on index cards or sheets of paper. Some instructors require students to use index cards because they are small and unobtrusive, don't rustle or flop over, and can be held in one hand, which allows the speaker to gesture more easily. Other teachers recommend sheets of paper because you can get more information on them and because it is easier to print out computer files on paper. If you are unsure what your instructor prefers, ask well before your speech is due.

Whether you use index cards or sheets of paper, your notes should be large enough to read clearly at arm's length. Many experienced speakers double- or triple-space their notes because this makes them easier to see at a glance. Write or print on only one side of the index card or paper, and use the fewest notes you can manage and still present the speech fluently and confidently.

connect™

View an excerpt from "A Heart Worn on My Hand" in the online Media Library for this chapter (Video 4.4).

You can see an example of extemporaneous delivery on Video 4.4 in the online Media Library for this chapter. The student is giving a speech of self-introduction using a personal object—in this case, a softball glove—to explain something important about herself. As you view the excerpt, notice that even though the speaker's points are well planned, she is not tied to a manuscript. When talking about her glove, she sets down her notes and points to things on the glove that reflect different aspects of her life. All the while, she speaks directly to her classmates and makes strong eye contact with them.

At first, it may seem very demanding to deliver a speech extemporaneously. In fact, though, you use the extemporaneous method in everyday conversation. Do you read from a manuscript when you tell your friends an amusing story? Of course not. You recall the essential details of your story and tell the tale to different friends, on different occasions, using somewhat different language each time. You feel relaxed and confident with your friends, so you just tell them what is on your mind in a conversational tone. Try to do the same thing in your speech.

REHEARSING THE SPEECH

When you watch a truly effective extemporaneous speaker, the speech comes out so smoothly that it seems almost effortless. In fact, that smooth delivery is the result of a great deal of practice. As your speech course progresses, you will gain more experience and will become more comfortable delivering your speeches extemporaneously.

The first time you rehearse your introductory speech, however, you will probably struggle. Words may not come easily, and you may forget some things you planned to say. Don't become discouraged. Keep going and complete the speech as well as you can. Concentrate on gaining control of the ideas rather than on trying to learn the speech word for word. You will improve every time you practice.

For this approach to work, you must rehearse the speech out loud. Looking silently over your notes is not enough. Speaking the words aloud will help you master the content of your talk. Once you have a fairly good grasp of the speech, ask friends or family members to listen and to give constructive feedback. Don't be shy about asking. Most people love to give their opinion about something, and it's crucial that you rehearse with a live audience before presenting the speech in class.

As you practice, time your speech to make sure it is neither too long nor too short. Because of nerves, most people talk faster during their first speech than when they practice it. When you rehearse at home, make certain your speech runs slightly longer than the minimum time limit. That way, if your speaking rate increases when you get in front of your classmates, your speech won't end up being too short.

PRESENTING THE SPEECH

Delivering your first speech can be a nerve-wracking experience. As your class proceeds and you gain more experience, your confidence (and skill) will grow by leaps and bounds. We will take a detailed look at speech delivery in Chapter 13, but here are a few things to concentrate on in your first presentation.

Starting Your Speech

When it is your turn to speak, move to the front of the room and face the audience. Assume a relaxed but upright posture. Plant your feet a bit less than shoulder-width apart and allow your arms to hang loosely by your side. Arrange your notes before you start to speak. Then take a moment to look over your audience and to smile. This will help you establish rapport with your classmates from the start.

Gestures

gestures

Motions of a speaker's hands or arms during a speech.

Once you are into the speech, feel free to use your hands to gesture, but don't try to plan all your gestures ahead of time. If you don't normally use your hands expressively during informal conversation, you shouldn't feel compelled to gesture a lot during your speech. Whatever gestures you do use should flow naturally from your feelings.

Above all, don't let your gestures or bodily actions distract listeners from your message. Do your best to avoid nervous mannerisms such as twisting your hair, wringing your hands, shifting your weight from one foot to the other, rocking back and forth, or tapping your fingers on the lectern. No matter how nervous you feel, try to appear calm and relaxed.

Eye Contact

eye contact

Direct visual contact with the eyes of another person.

During your talk, look at your classmates as often as you can. One of the major reasons for speaking extemporaneously is to maintain eye contact with your audience. In your own experience, you know how much more impressive a speaker is when she or he looks at the audience while speaking.

If you have practiced the extemporaneous method of delivery and prepared your notes properly, you should be able to maintain eye contact with your audience most of the time. Be sure to look to the left and right of the room, as well as to the center, and avoid the temptation to speak exclusively to one or two sympathetic individuals.

If you are too nervous to look your classmates directly in the eye, try looking just to the side of each person, or just above his or her head. In this way, you will convey a sense of eye contact while easing your nerves.

Voice

Try to use your voice as expressively as you would in normal conversation. Concentrate on projecting to the back of the room and, despite your nerves, fight the temptation to race through your speech. If you make a conscious effort to speak up, slow down, and project clearly, you will be on the right track to an effective presentation.

Look, for example, at Video 4.5 in the online Media Library for this chapter, which presents excerpts from two ice breaker speeches. Neither speaker had taken a public speaking class before, yet both rose to the occasion by focusing on the basic elements of delivery we have just discussed. As you watch the video, notice how both—despite their nervousness—convey a sense of poise and confidence, establish strong eye contact with their classmates, and use the extemporaneous method of delivery. Work on doing the same in your first speech.

connect™

View excerpts from "Rhymes with Orange" and "My Life from Toe to Head" in the online Media Library for this chapter (Video 4.5).

Dealing with Nerves

As we saw in Chapter 1, it's normal to be nervous before delivering a speech of any kind. By applying the tips presented in that chapter for managing stage fright, you can stand up for your speech primed for success.

If you have butterflies in your stomach while you wait to go to the lectern, sit quietly in your chair and take several slow, deep breaths. You can also help reduce your tension by tightening and relaxing your leg muscles, or by squeezing your hands together and then releasing them. Keep in mind that while you may be anxious about giving your speech, usually your nervousness will not be visible to your audience.

All the topics discussed in this chapter are developed in much more detail in the rest of this book. For now, keep your introductory assignment in perspective. Remember that neither your audience nor your instructor expects perfection. You are not a professional speaker, and this is the first speech of the class. Do your best on the assignment and have fun with it. Plan what you want to say, organize the material clearly, practice thoroughly, and use the extemporaneous method of delivery. You may be surprised by how much you enjoy giving your first speech.

Sample Speeches with Commentary

The following presentations were prepared by students in beginning speech classes at the University of Wisconsin. The first is a speech of self-introduction; the second is a speech introducing a classmate. As you read the speeches, notice how clearly they are organized and how creatively they are developed. You can watch the delivery of both speeches in the online Media Library for this chapter.

connect™

View "There's an App for That" and "Fork in the Road" in the online Media Library for this chapter (Videos 4.6 and 4.7).

There's an App for That

COMMENTARY

The introduction captures attention and reveals the topic. By answering questions with the phrase "There's an app for that," the speaker provides a creative touch that runs through the entire speech. He ends the introduction by previewing the points he will discuss in the body.

Each main point in the body is clearly stated and discussed. As you can see from the online video, the speaker communicates sincerely and with good eye contact. His wry sense of humor about his family adds a nice touch.

As the speech proceeds, notice how the speaker uses his favorite apps to provide insight into his life, rather than to talk about the apps themselves.

The speaker completes the body by explaining his love of music. Information about activities and hobbies is often included in a speech of self-introduction.

The conclusion summarizes the speaker's main points. It then ties the entire speech together by returning to the question asked in the introduction and answering it with one last refrain of "There's an app for that."

SPEECH

A Portuguese dictionary? There's an app for that. How to cook so she's impressed? Yeah, there's an app for that. A game to play when class gets boring? There's an app for that, too. But is there an app for me, Michael Taylor? I'd like to think there are a few. Some of the things that make me who I am can be found by looking at the Photobucket, ESPN, and Pandora apps on my iPhone.

The first app you'd find would be Photobucket, which my little sister made me download. It holds the newest photos of life back home and allows my sister to share her photography talents with me. My family is warm and caring, and half the time they drive me nuts, but what is family for anyway? I know I can turn to them for anything, and I feel very lucky to have grown up in a family where there was always someone to support me.

Because I'm an athlete, I'd be lost without my ESPN ScoreCenter app. It gives me up-to-the-minute scores on any sport. I played football, baseball, and basketball in high school, and I would rather be on a team than compete by myself. Through sports, I have learned the importance of being part of something bigger than myself. I've also learned how to lose with dignity and how to win with class.

Finally, there's the Pandora app, which makes it super easy to explore new songs and groups. I've been involved with music ever since I started playing piano as a kid. Now I play jazz guitar, and I sing. While in high school, I performed with a couple of groups around the Twin Cities, and I really enjoyed it. As for here in Madison, I'm still looking for opportunities to showcase my talents.

So, through the Photobucket, ESPN, and Pandora apps I can answer my initial question: Is there really an app for Michael Taylor? Yeah, there's an app for that.

Fork in the Road

COMMENTARY

This paragraph is the speaker's introduction. The opening quotation gains attention, while the next sentence relates the quotation to the speaker's audience. Then the speaker identifies the central idea by noting that her classmate Bethany is facing her own fork in the road.

The body of this speech contains two main points, each of which deals with a possible direction for Bethany's life. The first focuses on her passion for art. As is evident from the online video, the speaker presents her ideas extemporaneously. She has strong eye contact, excellent vocal variety, and a personable manner of delivery.

The second main point deals with Bethany's passion for medicine. The story of J.C. explains why Bethany is so interested in medicine as a possible career. When well delivered, stories are an excellent way to make ideas concrete and to get listeners involved in a speech.

The speaker concludes by restating the central theme of her speech. Echoing language from the introduction gives the speech a strong sense of unity. The final words end on a positive note by stating that whichever path Bethany chooses, it will be "a road to success."

SPEECH

Inspirational speaker Liz Murray once said, a "fork in the road happens over a hundred times a day, and the choices you make will determine the shape of your life." At one point or another, we all come to that fork in the road, when we are forced to choose between two paths, not sure where either will lead. Our classmate Bethany is now at that point, forced to decide between her two passions: art and medicine.

From an early age, Bethany has been passionate about art. She has been drawing since the age of three and has continued to improve her skills ever since. Over the years, she has won many awards for her drawings, including the Wisconsin Scholastic Art Award. Bethany draws people, places, and things that she sees on a daily basis in the world around her. Drawing allows her to relax and to escape from the stress of life. And now, because of her passion, she is considering making art her career.

In addition to art, however, Bethany is also passionate about medicine. She dreams about one day doing medical mission work in Africa. She is motivated in part by her friend J.C., a Rwanda refugee whose leg was severely injured in an explosion about ten years ago. For eight years, J.C. lived with bomb-shell fragments in his lower leg. It was only two years ago, when he and his mother moved to the United States, that he was finally able to have surgery. Bethany's friendship with J.C. has inspired her to help those who lack sufficient medical care and to make her think that a career in medicine is right for her.

It can be said that Bethany has reached her fork in the road. She has a passion for drawing and a passion for medicine. Will she choose to follow her love for art and pursue a career as an artist? Or will she choose to follow her love for medical mission work and pursue a career as a doctor? It's hard to know right now, but either path Bethany chooses will surely be a road to success.

Summary

The purpose of this chapter is to help you get ready for your ice breaker speech. Later chapters will look more closely at all the aspects of speech preparation and delivery discussed here.

Once you know the exact assignment for your ice breaker speech, you can start working out your ideas. Focus on a limited number of main points and develop them creatively. Your speech will have three parts—introduction, body, and conclusion. Use transition statements to help the audience keep track of your points as the speech progresses.

Your teacher will probably ask you to deliver the speech extemporaneously. This means that the speech is carefully prepared in advance, but the exact language is chosen at the moment of delivery. To be successful, you will need to rehearse the speech multiple times to make sure you have full command of it.

When speech day comes, you will almost surely have butterflies in your stomach. Remember that nervousness is normal. Concentrate on communicating with your audience, rather than on worrying about your nerves. Try to appear calm and relaxed on the outside, no matter how you feel on the inside. Establish eye contact with the audience, use your voice expressively, and make sure your gestures and mannerisms do not distract from your message.

Key Terms

ice breaker speech *(64)*
introduction *(66)*
body *(66)*
chronological order *(66)*
topical order *(66)*
main points *(67)*
transition *(67)*
conclusion *(67)*
extemporaneous speech *(68)*
gestures *(70)*
eye contact *(70)*

Review Questions

After reading this chapter, you should be able to answer the following questions:

1. What two major steps are discussed in this chapter for developing your introductory speech?
2. When organizing your introductory speech, you should divide it into what three sections?
3. What method of delivery does this chapter recommend for your introductory speech?
4. What steps should you take when rehearsing your first speech?
5. What five elements of speech delivery are discussed in this chapter with regard to presenting your first speech?

connect

For further review, go to the LearnSmart study module for this chapter.

Exercises for Critical Thinking

1. Examine the two sample speeches with commentary on pages 72–73. Choose one, and answer the following questions about it.
   a. How does the opening paragraph gain the attention of the audience, introduce the subject of the speech, and preview the main points to be discussed in the body?
   b. How clearly is the body of the speech organized? What does the speaker do to help listeners follow the progression of ideas?
   c. How does the speaker conclude? Does the conclusion reinforce the central theme of the speech?
2. Are there occasions outside the classroom on which you might give a speech of self-introduction? Identify such an occasion and explain how you might apply the principles of introductory speeches discussed in this chapter.

5

Selecting a Topic and a Purpose

As you read through this book, you will find examples of hundreds of speeches that were delivered in classrooms, in the political arena, in community and business situations. Here is a very small sample of the topics they cover:

acupuncture	Native American casinos
breast cancer	obsessive-compulsive disorder
Cesar Chavez	phony pharmaceuticals
Everglades	Québec
free trade	Ramadan
Great Wall	school vouchers
Habitat for Humanity	Underground Railroad
identity theft	women's gymnastics
Jerusalem	x-rays
laser surgery	Yellowstone
Martin Luther King	zoos

Undoubtedly you noticed that the list runs from A to Z. This array of topics wasn't planned. It happened naturally in the course of presenting many different kinds of speeches. The list is given here to show you that there are literally endless possibilities for speech topics—from A to Z.

Choosing a Topic

The first step in speechmaking is choosing a topic. For speeches outside the classroom this is seldom a problem. Usually the speech topic is determined by the occasion, the audience, and the speaker's qualifications. When Bill Clinton lectures at a college campus, he often speaks about global citizenship. Christine Amanpour will discuss women and journalism. Stephen Colbert might share his views on current events. The same is true of ordinary citizens. The doctor is asked to inform high-school athletes and their parents about sports injuries, the head of a neighborhood coalition speaks about zoning regulations, the florist discusses how to grow thriving houseplants.

topic

The subject of a speech.

In a public speaking class, the situation is different. Students generally have great leeway in selecting topics. This would appear to be an advantage, since it allows you to talk about matters of personal interest. Yet there may be no facet of speech preparation that causes more gnashing of teeth than selecting a topic.

It is a constant source of amazement to teachers that students who regularly chat with their friends about almost any subject under the sun become mentally paralyzed when faced with the task of deciding what to talk about in their speech class. Fortunately, once you get over this initial paralysis, you should have little trouble choosing a good topic.

There are two broad categories of potential topics for your classroom speeches: (1) subjects you know a lot about and (2) subjects you want to know more about. Let's start with the first.

TOPICS YOU KNOW A LOT ABOUT

Most people speak best about subjects with which they are most familiar. When thinking about a topic, draw on your own knowledge and experience. Everyone knows things or has done things that can be used in a speech.

Think for a moment about unusual experiences you may have had or special expertise you may have acquired. One student, who grew up in Turkey, presented a fascinating speech about daily life in that country. Another used her knowledge as a jewelry store salesperson to prepare a speech on how to judge the value of cut diamonds. A third student, who had lived through a tornado, gave a gripping speech about that terrifying experience.

Too dramatic? Nothing in your life is as interesting? Yet another student, who described herself as "just a housewife who is returning to school to finish the education she started 20 years ago," delivered a witty speech on the adjustments she had to make in coming back to college—sitting in class with students young enough to be her children, balancing her academic work against her family commitments, and the satisfaction of completing the education she had begun years earlier.

When you look for a speech topic, keep in mind special expertise you may have or sports, hobbies, travel, and other personal experiences that would make for an interesting presentation.

Here are a few more examples of speech topics based largely on the students' personal knowledge and experience:

Interning at a Crime Lab

The Basics of Backpacking

Performing with the Native American Dance Troupe

How to Have a Successful Job Interview

TOPICS YOU WANT TO KNOW MORE ABOUT

On the other hand, you may decide to make your speech a learning experience for yourself as well as for your audience. You may choose a subject about which you already have some knowledge or expertise but not enough to prepare a speech without doing additional research. You may even select a topic that you want to explore for the first time. Say, for example, you've always been interested in Stonehenge but never knew much about it. This would be a perfect opportunity to research a fascinating subject and turn it into a fascinating speech.

Or suppose you run across a subject in one of your other classes that catches your fancy. Why not investigate it further for your speech class? One student used this approach to develop a speech on the subject of neuromarketing, which uses recent advancements in neuroscience to study the way people respond to products and promotions. After hearing about the subject in her marketing class, the student researched the topic further. In the process, she learned that neuromarketing is currently being used by some of the biggest corporations in the world. Using what she learned in her research, she put together a captivating speech that kept everyone's attention from beginning to end.

connect™

View an excerpt from "Neuromarketing: Whispers of the Brain" in the online Media Library for this chapter (Video 5.1).

Still another possibility—especially for persuasive speeches—is to think of subjects about which you hold strong opinions and beliefs. They may include national or international concerns such as gun control or climate change. Or perhaps you are closely involved in a local issue such as a school board election or a proposal to build a new student center. Not all such topics must be "political." They can deal with anything from graduation requirements to helping people with physical disabilities, from dormitory regulations to building a church recreation center.

BRAINSTORMING FOR TOPICS

brainstorming

A method of generating ideas for speech topics by free association of words and ideas.

After all this, you may still be thinking, "I *don't* care about neuromarketing. I've *never* been to Turkey. I'm *not* active in politics. WHAT am I going to talk about?" If you are having trouble selecting a topic, there are a number of brainstorming procedures you can follow to get started.

Personal Inventory

First, make a quick inventory of your experiences, interests, hobbies, skills, beliefs, and so forth. Jot down anything that comes to mind, no matter how silly or irrelevant it may seem. From this list may come a general subject area out of which you can fashion a specific topic. This method has worked for many students.

Clustering

If the first method doesn't work, try a technique called clustering. Take a sheet of paper and divide it into nine columns as follows: People, Places, Things, Events, Processes, Concepts, Natural Phenomena, Problems, and Plans and Policies. Then list in each column the first four or five items that come to mind. The result might look like this:

People	**Places**	**Things**
Barack Obama	Afghanistan	iPad
Hillary Clinton	Grand Canyon	Twitter
Sarah Palin	the moon	3-D TV
Lady Gaga	my hometown	movies

Events	**Processes**
graduation	learning CPR
Passover	cooking Indian food
Chinese New Year	avoiding credit-card debt
Cinco de Mayo	writing a job resumé

Concepts	**Natural Phenomena**
conservatism	asteroids
medical ethics	lightning
free-speech theories	tornadoes
Buddhism	earthquakes

Problems	Plans and Policies
national debt	offshore drilling
terrorism	charter schools
election fraud	domestic partner benefits
campus crime	immigration reform

Very likely, several items on your lists will strike you as potential topics. If not, take the items you find most intriguing and compose sublists for each. Try to free-associate. Write down a word or idea. What does that trigger in your mind? Whatever it is, write that down next, and keep going until you have four or five ideas on your list. For example, working from the lists printed above, one student composed sublists for movies, campus crime, and lightning:

connect

For an additional resource on speech topics, check the Topic Helper under the Library tab in Connect.

Movies	Campus Crime	Lightning
Academy Awards	police	thunder
prizes	fingerprints	noise
lotteries	hands	traffic
gambling	gloves	air pollution

Can you follow her trail of association? In the first column, movies made her think of the Academy Awards. The Academy Awards are prizes. Prizes reminded her of lotteries. Lotteries are a form of gambling. Suddenly, this student remembered an article she had read on the problem of gambling addiction in America. The idea clicked in her mind. After considerable research, she developed an excellent speech titled "Gambling Addiction: Why You Can't Beat the Odds."

That's a far cry from movies! If you started out free-associating from movies, you would doubtless end up somewhere completely different. This is what clustering is all about.

Internet Search

By clustering, most people come up with a topic rather quickly. But if you are still stymied, try an Internet search. Browse through a subject-based Web site, an online encyclopedia, or some other reference portal until you come across what might be a good topic. As an experiment, one student scanned the *Merriam-Webster Online Dictionary,* limiting herself to the letter *m*. Within 10 minutes, she had come up with these potential topics:

magic	minimum wage	Medal of Honor	middle ear
Madrid	moon	martial arts	muscular dystrophy
monarchy	meteorite	maple syrup	Mardi Gras
marriage	Marine Corps	mushroom	Mafia

Whatever the means you use for selecting a topic, *start early.* Pay attention to interesting subjects in conversation, on television and the Internet, in newspapers and magazines. Jot down ideas for topics as they occur to you.

Having an inventory of possible topics to choose from is much better than having to rack your brain for one at the last minute. If you get an early start on choosing a topic, you will have plenty of time to pick just the right one and prepare a first-rate speech.

Determining the General Purpose

Along with choosing a topic, you need to determine the general purpose of your speech. Usually it will fall into one of two overlapping categories—to inform or to persuade.

general purpose

The broad goal of a speech.

When your general purpose is to inform, you act as a teacher or lecturer. Your goal is to convey information clearly, accurately, and interestingly. If you describe how to lift weights, narrate the major events of the latest Middle East crisis, or report on your sorority's financial position, you are speaking to inform. Your aim is to enhance the knowledge and understanding of your listeners—to give them information they did not have before.

When your general purpose is to persuade, you act as an advocate or a partisan. You go beyond giving information to espousing a cause. You want to *change* or *structure* the attitudes or actions of your audience. If you try to convince your listeners that they should start a regular program of weight lifting, that the United States should modify its policy in the Middle East, or that your sorority should start a fund-raising drive to balance its budget, then you are speaking to persuade. In doing so, you cannot help but give information, but your primary goal is to win over your listeners to your point of view—to get them to believe something or do something as a result of your speech.

In speech classes, the general purpose is usually specified as part of the speech assignment. For speeches outside the classroom, however, you have to make sure of your general purpose yourself. Usually this is easy to do. Are you going to explain, report, or demonstrate something? Then your general purpose is to inform. Are you going to sell, advocate, or defend something? Then your general purpose is to persuade. But no matter what the situation, you must be certain of exactly what you hope to achieve by speaking.

Determining the Specific Purpose

specific purpose

A single infinitive phrase that states precisely what a speaker hopes to accomplish in his or her speech.

Once you have chosen a topic and a general purpose, you must narrow your choices to determine the specific purpose of your speech. The specific purpose should focus on one aspect of a topic. You should be able to state your specific purpose in a single infinitive phrase (to inform my audience about . . . ; to persuade my audience to . . .) that indicates *precisely* what you hope to accomplish with your speech.

For example, Duane Winfield, a student at a large state university, decided to give his first classroom speech on a topic from his personal experience. For the past two years, he had volunteered his time to perform music for patients in mental hospitals, nursing homes, and residences for disabled adults. He had seen how enthusiastically the patients responded to music, even when they remained unmoved by other kinds of stimuli. Duane's experience had given him a better understanding of the benefits of music therapy, and he wanted to share this understanding with his classmates. This gave him a topic and a general purpose, which he stated like this:

Topic: Music therapy

General Purpose: To inform

So far, so good. But what aspect of his topic would Duane discuss? The kinds of facilities in which he had worked? His specific role as a performer? The evidence that music therapy can improve patients' mental health? The needs of patients with different kinds of illnesses? He had to choose something interesting that he could cover in a six-minute speech. Finally, he settled on describing his most memorable experiences with patients to show how music therapy affected them. He stated his specific purpose this way:

Specific Purpose: To inform my audience about the benefits of music therapy for people with psychological or cognitive disabilities.

This turned out to be an excellent choice, and Duane's speech was among the best in the class.

Notice how clear the specific purpose statement is. Notice also how it relates the topic directly to the audience. That is, it states not only what the *speaker* wants to *say* but also what the speaker wants the *audience* to *know* as a result of the speech. This is very important, for it helps keep the audience at the center of your attention as you prepare your speech.

Using public speaking in your CAREER

Your communication degree has helped you land a job as spokesperson for the mayor of a medium-sized city on the West Coast. A year after starting the job, you are selected to organize an information campaign explaining the benefits of a new youth center proposed by the mayor.

To launch this campaign, you've decided to hold a news briefing at the end of the week. To open the briefing, you will present a short set of comments on the mayor's initiative. You decide to focus on four benefits of the youth center: (1) It will offer a range of activities—from sports to the arts—in a safe environment; (2) It will provide social networks for youths from all walks of life; (3) It will operate most hours of the day and night; (4) It will be free and open to everyone.

Following the format used in this chapter, state the general purpose, specific purpose, central idea, and main points of your comments.

Look what happens when the specific purpose statement does not include the audience.

Specific Purpose: To explain the benefits of music therapy for people with psychological or cognitive disabilities.

Explain to whom? To musicians? To medical students? To social workers? Those would be three different speeches. The musicians would want to know about the kinds of music Duane played. The medical students would want to hear about research on the benefits of music therapy. The social workers would want to learn how to implement a music program. Communicating effectively with each group would require preparing a different speech.

When the audience slips out of the specific purpose, it may slip out of the speaker's consciousness. You may begin to think that your task is the general one of preparing "an informative speech," when in fact your task is the specific one of informing a particular group of people. As we shall see in the next chapter, it is almost impossible to prepare a good speech without keeping constantly in mind the *people* for whom it is intended.

TIPS FOR FORMULATING THE SPECIFIC PURPOSE STATEMENT

Formulating a specific purpose is the most important early step in developing a successful speech. When writing your purpose statement, follow the general principles outlined on the following pages.

Write the Purpose Statement as a Full Infinitive Phrase, Not as a Fragment

Ineffective: 3-D technology.

More Effective: To inform my audience about the three major kinds of current 3-D technology.

The ineffective statement is adequate as an announcement of the speech topic, but it is not thought out fully enough to indicate the specific purpose.

Express Your Purpose as a Statement, Not as a Question

Ineffective: What is Día de los Muertos?

More Effective: To inform my audience about the history of Mexico's Día de los Muertos celebration.

The question might arouse the curiosity of an audience, but it is not effective as a specific purpose statement. It gives no indication about what direction the speech will take or what the speaker hopes to accomplish.

Avoid Figurative Language in Your Purpose Statement

Ineffective: To persuade my audience that the campus policy on student parking really stinks.

Choosing a topic is the first step in speech preparation. One way to come up with a good topic is to think about issues on which you hold strong opinions and beliefs.

More Effective: To persuade my audience that the campus policy on student parking should be revised to provide more spaces for students before 5 p.m.

Although the ineffective statement indicates something of the speaker's viewpoint, it does not state concisely what he or she hopes to achieve. Figurative language can reinforce ideas within a speech, but it is too ambiguous for a specific purpose statement.

Limit Your Purpose Statement to One Distinct Idea

Ineffective: To persuade my audience to become literacy tutors and to donate time to the Special Olympics.

This purpose statement expresses two unrelated ideas, either of which could be the subject of a speech. The easiest remedy is to select one or the other as a focus for your presentation.

More Effective: To persuade my audience to become literacy tutors.

Or:

More Effective: To persuade my audience to donate time to the Special Olympics.

Does this mean that you can never use the word "and" in your specific purpose statement? Not at all. Suppose your specific purpose is "To inform my audience about the causes and effects of epilepsy." In this case, "and" is appropriate because it connects two related parts of a unified topic. What you need to avoid is not simply the word "and," but a specific purpose statement that contains two unrelated ideas, either of which could be developed into a speech in its own right.

Make Sure Your Specific Purpose Is Not Too Vague or General

Ineffective: To persuade my audience that something should be done about unsafe school buses.

More Effective: To persuade my audience that the federal government should impose stronger safety standards for school buses in the United States.

The ineffective purpose statement falls into one of the most common traps—it is too broad and ill-defined. It gives no clues about what the speaker believes should be done about school buses. The more effective purpose statement is sharp and concise. It reveals clearly what the speaker plans to discuss.

The more precise your specific purpose, the easier it will be to prepare your speech. Consider this topic and specific purpose:

Topic: Hot-air balloons.

Specific Purpose: To inform my audience about hot-air balloons.

With such a hazy purpose, you have no systematic way of limiting your research or of deciding what to include in the speech and what to exclude. The origins of hot-air balloons, how they work, their current popularity—all could be equally relevant to a speech designed "to inform my audience about hot-air balloons."

In contrast, look at this topic and specific purpose:

Topic: Hot-air balloons.

Specific Purpose: To inform my audience about the scientific uses of hot-air balloons.

Now it is easy to decide what is germane and what is not. The origins of hot-air balloons, how they work, their popularity for recreation—all are interesting, but none is essential to the specific purpose of explaining "the scientific uses of hot-air balloons." Thus you need not worry about researching these matters or about explaining them in your speech. You can spend your preparation time efficiently.

QUESTIONS TO ASK ABOUT YOUR SPECIFIC PURPOSE

Sometimes you will arrive at your specific purpose almost immediately after choosing your topic. At other times you may do quite a bit of research before deciding on a specific purpose. Much will depend on how familiar you are with the topic, as well as on any special demands imposed by the assignment, the audience, or the occasion. But whenever you settle on your specific purpose, ask yourself the following questions about it.

Does My Purpose Meet the Assignment?

Students occasionally stumble over this question. Be sure you understand your assignment and shape your specific purpose to meet it. If you have questions, check with your instructor.

Can I Accomplish My Purpose in the Time Allotted?

Most classroom speeches are quite short, ranging from four to ten minutes. That may seem like a lot of time, but you will quickly find what generations of students have discovered—time flies when you are giving a speech!

Most people speak at an average rate of 120 to 150 words a minute. This means that a six-minute speech will consist of roughly 720 to 900 words. That is not long enough to develop a highly complex topic. Here are some specific purpose statements that would defy being handled well in the time normally allotted for classroom speeches:

> To inform my audience about the rise and fall of ancient Rome.
>
> To inform my audience about the role of technology in human history.
>
> To persuade my audience to convert to Buddhism.

You are much better off with a limited purpose that you have some reasonable hope of achieving in the short span of four to ten minutes.

Is the Purpose Relevant to My Audience?

The price of retirement homes in Palm Springs might be an engrossing topic for older citizens who are in the market for such dwellings. And the quality

checklist

Specific Purpose

YES	NO	
☐	☐	1. Is the specific purpose written as a full infinitive phrase?
☐	☐	2. Does the specific purpose include a reference to the audience?
☐	☐	3. Is the specific purpose phrased as a statement rather than a question?
☐	☐	4. Is the specific purpose free of figurative language?
☐	☐	5. Is the specific purpose limited to one distinct subject?
☐	☐	6. Does the specific purpose indicate precisely what I plan to accomplish in the speech?
☐	☐	7. Does the specific purpose meet the requirements of the assignment?
☐	☐	8. Can the specific purpose be accomplished in the time allotted for the speech?
☐	☐	9. Is the specific purpose relevant to my audience?
☐	☐	10. Does the specific purpose deal with a nontrivial subject?
☐	☐	11. Is the specific purpose suitable for a nontechnical audience?

of hot lunches in the elementary schools is of great concern to the students who eat them and the parents who pay for them. But neither subject has much relevance for an audience of college students. No matter how well you construct your speeches, they are likely to fall flat unless you speak about matters of interest to your listeners.

This is not to say you must select only topics that pertain directly to the college student's daily experience. Most students have wide-ranging backgrounds, interests, ideas, and values. And most of them are intellectually curious. They can get involved in an astonishing variety of subjects. Follow your common sense and make sure *you* are truly interested in the topic. Also, when speaking on a subject that is not obviously relevant to your listeners, find a way to tie it in with their goals, values, interests, and well-being. We'll discuss how to do this in the next chapter.

Is the Purpose Too Trivial for My Audience?

Just as you need to avoid speech topics that are too broad or complicated, so you need to steer clear of topics that are too superficial. How to build a fire without matches might absorb a group of Cub Scouts, but your classmates would probably consider it frivolous. Unfortunately, there is no absolute rule for determining what is trivial to an audience and what is not. Here are some examples of specific purposes that most people would find too trivial for classroom speeches:

To inform my audience about the parts of a backpack.

To inform my audience how to tie a bow tie.

To persuade my audience that espresso is better than cappuccino.

Is the Purpose Too Technical for My Audience?

Nothing puts an audience to sleep faster than a dry and technical speech. Beware of topics that are inherently technical and of treating ordinary subjects in a technical fashion. Although you may be familiar with the principles and vocabulary of international finance or clinical psychology, most of your classmates probably are not. There are aspects of these and similar subjects that can be treated clearly, with a minimum of jargon. But if you find that you can't fulfill your specific purpose without relying on technical words and concepts, you should reconsider your purpose.

Here are some examples of specific purposes that are overly technical for most classroom speeches:

To inform my audience about the solution to Fermat's Last Theorem.

To inform my audience about the principles of neutrino physics.

To inform my audience about the methods of encryption technology.

We will discuss the details of audience analysis and adaptation in Chapter 6. For the moment, remember to make sure that your specific purpose is appropriate for your listeners. If you have doubts, ask your instructor, or circulate a questionnaire among your classmates (see pages 111–113).

Phrasing the Central Idea

WHAT IS THE CENTRAL IDEA?

The specific purpose of a speech is what you hope to accomplish. The *central idea* is a concise statement of what you *expect to say*. Sometimes it is called the thesis statement, the subject sentence, or the major thought. Whatever the term, the central idea is usually expressed as a simple, declarative sentence that refines and sharpens the specific purpose statement.

central idea

A one-sentence statement that sums up or encapsulates the major ideas of a speech.

Imagine that you run into a friend on your way to speech class. She says, "I have to dash to my history lecture, but I hear you're giving a speech today. Can you tell me the gist of it in one sentence?" "Sure," you reply. "America's prison system suffers from three major problems—overcrowding of inmates, lack of effective rehabilitation programs, and high expense to taxpayers."

Your answer is the central idea of your speech. It is more precise than your topic (America's prison system) or your specific purpose statement ("To inform my audience of the three major problems facing America's prison system"). By stating exactly what the three major problems are, the central idea sums up your speech in a single sentence.

Another way to think of the central idea is as your *residual message*—what you want your audience to remember after they have forgotten everything else in the speech. Most of the time the central idea will encapsulate the main points to be developed in the body of the speech. To show how this works, let's take a few of the examples we saw earlier in this chapter and develop them from the topic, general purpose, and specific purpose to the central idea.

residual message

What a speaker wants the audience to remember after it has forgotten everything else in a speech.

We can start with the speech about music therapy.

Topic: Music therapy.

General Purpose: To inform.

Specific Purpose: To inform my audience about the benefits of music therapy for people with psychological or cognitive disabilities.

Central Idea: Music therapy developed as a formal mode of treatment during the twentieth century, utilizes a number of methods, and is explained by several theories that account for its success.

Look carefully at this example. It shows how the speaker might start with a broad subject (music therapy) that becomes narrower and narrower as the speaker moves from the general purpose to the specific purpose to the central idea. Notice also how much more the central idea suggests about the content of the speech. From it we can expect the speaker to address three main points—the first summarizing the development of music therapy, the second looking at methods of music therapy, and the third exploring theories that account for the success of music therapy.

connect

View the introduction from "The Benefits of Music Therapy" in the online Media Library for this chapter (Video 5.2).

This sharpening of focus as one proceeds to the central idea is crucial. Here is another example:

Topic: Día de los Muertos.

General Purpose: To inform.

Specific Purpose: To inform my audience about the history of Mexico's Día de los Muertos celebration.

Central Idea: Día de los Muertos can be traced to the Aztecs, was moved from summer to fall by Spanish priests, and today is celebrated in a number of ways in different regions of Mexico.

This central idea is especially well worded. We can assume from it that the body of the speech will contain three main points: (1) on the Aztec origins of Día de los Muertos, (2) on how it was changed by the Spanish, and (3) on the ways it is celebrated today.

Notice in each of these examples how much more the central idea reveals about the content of the speech than does the specific purpose. This is not accidental. Often you can settle on a specific purpose statement early in preparing your speech. The central idea, however, usually emerges later—after you have done your research and have decided on the main points of the speech. The process may work like this:

As an environmental science major, Marcia Esposito had learned that many experts fear the world may face a severe water shortage by the year 2025. She decided this would make a good topic for her informative speech. Tentatively, she adopted the following specific purpose statement: "To inform my audience about the seriousness of the growing international water crisis." Then Marcia started her research.

An article in *Time* magazine, which she located through LexisNexis, explained how the population in countries such as China, India, and Pakistan is outstripping the available supply of fresh water. According to the article, 400 million Chinese do not have access to suitable drinking water, and two-thirds of India's 1.1 billion people lack the water they need.

Next Marcia found a report on the United Nations Web site about the impact of pollution on the water supply. The report stated that in developing countries "more than 90 percent of sewage and 70 percent of industrial wastewater is dumped untreated into surface water."

Then Marcia hit upon the idea of interviewing one of her environmental science professors. In addition to confirming Marcia's research about the impact of population growth and pollution, the professor mentioned the problems caused by mismanagement of water supplies. Around the world, 65 to 70 percent of the water people use is lost to waste, evaporation, and other inefficiencies.

Marcia digested all this information. Now she was ready to formulate her central idea: "Population growth, pollution, and mismanagement are creating a serious shortage of fresh water in many parts of the world."

GUIDELINES FOR THE CENTRAL IDEA

What makes a well-worded central idea? Essentially the same things that make a well-worded specific purpose statement. The central idea (1) should be expressed in a full sentence, (2) should not be in the form of a question, (3) should avoid figurative language, and (4) should not be vague or overly general.

Here, for example, are four poorly written central ideas. See if you can identify the problem with each and figure out how each might be phrased more effectively:

Unlike the specific purpose, which you need to settle on early in the speech preparation process, the central idea usually takes shape later, as a result of your research and analysis of the topic.

Ineffective: Paying college athletes a monthly salary is a good idea.

Ineffective: Problems of fad diets.

Ineffective: What are nanorobots?

Ineffective: Mexico's Yucatán Peninsula is an awesome place for a vacation.

The first is too general. To say that paying college athletes a monthly salary is a "good idea" does not convey the speaker's viewpoint sharply and clearly. What does the speaker mean by a "good idea"? A revised central idea for this speech might be:

More Effective: Because college athletes in revenue-producing sports such as football and basketball generate millions of dollars in revenue for their schools, the NCAA should allow such athletes to receive a $300 monthly salary as part of their scholarships.

The second ineffective central idea is also too general, but it suffers further from not being written as a complete sentence. "Problems of fad diets" does not reveal enough about the content of the speech to serve as the central idea. It should be rewritten as a full sentence that identifies the problems of fad diets to be discussed in the speech:

More Effective: Although fad diets produce quick weight loss, they can lead to serious health problems by creating deficiencies in vitamins and minerals and by breaking down muscle tissue as well as fat.

checklist

Central Idea

YES	NO	
☐	☐	1. Is the central idea written as a complete sentence?
☐	☐	2. Is the central idea phrased as a statement rather than a question?
☐	☐	3. Is the central idea free of figurative language?
☐	☐	4. Does the central idea clearly encapsulate the main points to be discussed in the body of the speech?
☐	☐	5. Can the central idea be adequately discussed in the time allotted for the speech?
☐	☐	6. Is the central idea relevant to the audience?
☐	☐	7. Is the central idea appropriate for a nontechnical audience?

The third poorly written central idea is phrased as a question rather than as a full declarative sentence. Asking "What are nanorobots?" might be a good way to catch the attention of listeners, but it does not encapsulate the main points to be developed in the speech. A more effective central idea would be:

More Effective: Microscopic in size, nanorobots are being developed for use in medicine, weaponry, and daily life.

The final ineffective central idea is flawed by its use of figurative language. To say that the Yucatán Peninsula is an "awesome" place for a vacation does not indicate what characteristics of the Yucatán Peninsula the speaker intends to discuss. A better central idea might be:

More Effective: Mexico's Yucatán Peninsula has many attractions for vacationers, including a warm climate, excellent food, and extensive Mayan ruins.

Notice that in all these examples the more effective central idea sums up the main points of the speech in a single sentence. If you are having trouble phrasing your central idea, the reason may be that you do not yet have a firm grasp on the main points of your speech.

Do not worry too much about your central idea until after you have developed the body of your speech (see Chapter 9). If, at that point, you still can't come up with a clear, concise central idea, your speech itself may not be clear or concise. Keep working on the speech until you can compose a central idea that fits the criteria just discussed. The result will be a sharper central idea and a tighter, more coherent speech.

Summary

The first step in speechmaking is choosing a topic. For classroom speeches, you can choose a subject you know well or one you research especially for the speech. If you have trouble picking a topic, you can use one of three brainstorming procedures. First, make an inventory of your hobbies, interests, skills, beliefs, and so forth. Second, use clustering to list the first topics that come to mind in several categories. Third, use an Internet subject directory, encyclopedia, or similar reference site to help you scan possible topics.

The general purpose of your speech will usually be to inform or to persuade. When your general purpose is to inform, your goal is to communicate information clearly, accurately, and interestingly. When your general purpose is to persuade, your goal is to win listeners over to your point of view.

Once you know your topic and general purpose, you must focus on a specific purpose statement that indicates precisely what your speech seeks to achieve. The specific purpose statement should (1) be a full infinitive phrase; (2) be worded as a statement, not a question; (3) avoid figurative language; (4) concentrate on one distinct idea; (5) not be vague or general.

Keep several questions in mind as you formulate your specific purpose statement: Does my purpose meet the assignment? Can I accomplish my purpose in the time allotted? Is the purpose relevant to my audience? Is the purpose too trivial or too technical for my audience?

The central idea refines and sharpens your specific purpose. It is a concise statement of what you will say in your speech, and it usually crystallizes in your thinking after you have done your research and have decided on the main points of your speech. The central idea usually encapsulates the main points to be developed in the body of your speech.

Key Terms

topic *(78)*
brainstorming *(80)*
general purpose *(82)*
specific purpose *(82)*
central idea *(89)*
residual message *(89)*

Review Questions

After reading this chapter, you should be able to answer the following questions:

1. What three brainstorming methods can you follow if you are having trouble choosing a topic for your speech?
2. What are the two general purposes of most classroom speeches? How do they differ?

3. Why is determining the specific purpose such an important early step in speech preparation? Why is it important to include the audience in the specific purpose statement?
4. What are five tips for formulating your specific purpose?
5. What are five questions to ask about your specific purpose?
6. What is the difference between the specific purpose and the central idea of a speech? What are four guidelines for an effective central idea?

connect

For further review, go to the LearnSmart study module for this chapter.

Exercises for Critical Thinking

1. Using one of the brainstorming methods described in this chapter, come up with three topics you might like to deal with in your next classroom speech. For each topic, devise a specific purpose statement suitable for the speech assignment. Make sure your specific purpose statements fit the guidelines discussed in the chapter.
2. Here are several specific purpose statements for classroom speeches. Identify the problem (or problems) with each.

   To inform my audience how to sign up for Facebook.

   To persuade my audience that the U.S. government should increase funding for stem cell research and support the development of hydrogen-fuel vehicles.

   What is an individual retirement account?

   To inform my audience why square grooves are superior to U-shaped grooves on golf clubs.

   To inform my audience about New Zealand.

   Donate blood.

   To persuade my audience that something has to be done about the problem of antibiotic-resistant bacteria.
3. Below are three sets of main points for speeches. For each set, supply the general purpose, specific purpose, and central idea.

   General Purpose:

   Specific Purpose:

   Central Idea:

   Main Points:

   I. You should study abroad because it will enhance your personal development.

   II. You should study abroad because it will enhance your academic development.

   III. You should study abroad because it will enhance your career development.

General Purpose:

Specific Purpose:

Central Idea:

Main Points:

I. The first event in a triathlon is swimming.
II. The second event in a triathlon is cycling.
III. The third event in a triathlon is running.

General Purpose:

Specific Purpose:

Central Idea:

Main Points:

I. As a writer, Thomas Jefferson penned the Declaration of Independence and *Notes on the State of Virginia.*
II. As President, Thomas Jefferson negotiated the Louisiana Purchase and approved the Lewis and Clark expedition.
III. As an architect, Thomas Jefferson designed Monticello and the University of Virginia.

SIGILLVM

6

Analyzing the Audience

- Audience-Centeredness
- Your Classmates as an Audience
- The Psychology of Audiences
- Demographic Audience Analysis
- Situational Audience Analysis
- Getting Information About the Audience
- Adapting to the Audience

When President Barack Obama stepped to the lectern in Tucson, Arizona, on January 12, 2011, the eyes of the nation were upon him. Only four days earlier, 19 people had been gunned down at a grocery store during an open meeting for Congresswoman Gabrielle Giffords. Although Giffords survived, six people were killed. In the wake of this tragedy, Obama knew he had to reach multiple audiences, including families of the victims, residents of Arizona, and Americans in general.

He spent the first part of his speech eulogizing victims of the shooting. Then he turned to the need for reasoned public discourse that, instead of placing blame and pointing fingers, would remind Americans "of all the ways our hopes and dreams are bound together." He ended by referring to Christina Taylor Green, a nine-year-old girl who had been killed at the shooting. "I want our democracy to be as good as she imagined it," Obama stated. "All of us—we should do everything we can to make sure this country lives up to our children's expectations."

connect

View an excerpt from Barack Obama's Tucson speech of January 12, 2011, in the online Media Library for this chapter (Video 6.1).

The speech garnered almost universal praise. Historian Garry Wills called it "Obama's finest hour." Others deemed it "splendid," "inspirational," and a "remarkable display of oratory." Even Obama's critics praised the speech as "courageous," "genuine," and "pitch-perfect for the nation."

Audience-Centeredness

Obama's speech points up an important fact: Good public speakers are *audience-centered*. They know the primary purpose of speechmaking is not to browbeat the audience or to blow off steam. Rather, it is to gain a *desired response* from listeners.

Being audience-centered does not involve compromising your beliefs to get a favorable response. Nor does it mean using devious, unethical tactics to achieve your goal. As with Barack Obama, you can remain true to yourself and speak ethically while adapting your message to the goals, values, and attitudes of your audience.

audience-centeredness

Keeping the audience foremost in mind at every step of speech preparation and presentation.

To be audience-centered, you need to keep several questions in mind when you work on your speeches:

To whom am I speaking?

What do I want them to know, believe, or do as a result of my speech?

What is the most effective way of composing and presenting my speech to accomplish that aim?

The answers to these questions will influence every decision you make along the way—selecting a topic, determining a specific purpose, settling on your main points and supporting materials, organizing the message, and, finally, delivering the speech.

In many ways, adapting to an audience during a public speech is not much different from what you do in your daily social contacts. Few people would walk into a party and announce, "You know those people protesting at the administration building are way over the edge!"

People usually prefer to open controversial topics with a fairly noncommittal position. You might say, "What's going on at the administration building?" Then when you have heard and processed your companion's response, you can present your position accordingly. (You don't have to *agree* with a viewpoint different from your own, but neither do you have to hit your listeners over the head with your own opinion.)

identification

A process in which speakers seek to create a bond with the audience by emphasizing common values, goals, and experiences.

Effective speakers seek to create a bond with their listeners by emphasizing common values and experiences. Communication scholars call this process *identification*. Obama created identification with his audience by honoring the victims of the shooting and by showing how the nation could move forward in the wake of tragedy. "For all our imperfections," he said, "we are full of decency and goodness, and . . . the forces that divide us are not as strong as those that unite us."

When you make a speech, either in class or in some other forum, keep in mind the need to be audience-centered. Think in advance about your listeners' background and interests, about their level of knowledge regarding the speech topic, and about their attitudes regarding your stance on the topic. As you develop the speech, work on explaining your ideas so they will be clear, interesting, and persuasive to the audience.

At this point, you may be nodding your head and saying, "Of course, everyone knows that. It's only common sense." But knowing a precept and putting it into practice are two different matters. The aim of this chapter is to introduce the basic principles of audience analysis and adaption. Chapters 15 and 16 will deal with those features of audience analysis unique to informative and persuasive speaking.

Your Classmates as an Audience

There is a tendency—among students and teachers alike—to view the classroom as an artificial speaking situation. In a way, it is. Your speech class is a testing ground where you can develop your communication skills before applying them outside the classroom. The most serious measure of success or failure is your grade, and that is determined ultimately by your teacher.

Because of this, it is easy to lose sight of your fellow students as an authentic audience. But each of your classmates is a real person with real ideas, attitudes, and feelings. Your speech class offers an enormous opportunity to inform and persuade other people. As one student wrote on her evaluation form at the end of her speech class, "I thought the speeches would all be phony, but they weren't. I've not only learned a lot about speaking—I've learned a lot about other things from listening to the speeches in class."

The best classroom speeches are those that take the classroom audience as seriously as a lawyer, a politician, a minister, or an advertiser takes an audience. You should consider every audience—inside the classroom and out—as worthy of your best efforts to communicate your knowledge or convictions. At the least you show respect for your listeners. At the most you could make a real difference in their lives. The following story demonstrates the latter:

> Crystal Watkins gave an informative speech on the subject of small claims court, where ordinary people can press lawsuits involving up to $5,000 without lawyers. Part of her speech went like this: "It's two weeks after you have moved into a new apartment. A letter arrives from your old landlord. Expecting to get back your $800 security deposit, you joyfully tear open the envelope. Inside is a form letter explaining why your security deposit is not being refunded. What can you do about it? Nothing, right? Wrong! You can file a claim in small claims court."
>
> Lee Callaway, one of Crystal's classmates, paid close attention. At the end of the previous term, he had run into a situation just like the one Crystal described. Not having money to hire a lawyer, he assumed he would have to forfeit his security deposit. But now, as he listened to Crystal's speech, Lee decided he would try to get his money back in small claims court. He filed suit the next week, and within a month he had his money back—thanks in part to his classmate's speech!

Most of your classroom speeches won't have this much immediate impact. Nevertheless, any topic that you handle conscientiously can influence your listeners—can enrich their experience, broaden their knowledge, perhaps change their views about something important.[1]

The Psychology of Audiences

What do you do when you listen to a speech? Sometimes you pay close attention; at other times you let your thoughts wander. People may be compelled to attend a speech, but no one can make them listen. The speaker must make the audience *choose* to pay attention.

Even when people do pay attention, they don't process a speaker's message exactly as the speaker intends. Auditory perception is always selective. Every speech contains two messages—the one sent by the speaker and the one received by the listener.

As we saw in Chapter 1, what a speaker says is filtered through a listener's frame of reference—the sum of her or his needs, interests, expectations, knowledge, and experience. As a result, we listen and respond to speeches not as they are, but as we are. Or, to borrow from Paul Simon's classic song "The Boxer," people hear what they want to hear and disregard the rest.

egocentrism

The tendency of people to be concerned above all with their own values, beliefs, and well-being.

What do people want to hear? Very simply, they usually want to hear about things that are meaningful to them. People are *egocentric*. They pay closest attention to messages that affect their own values, beliefs, and well-being. Listeners approach speeches with one question uppermost in mind: "Why is this important to *me*?" As Harry Emerson Fosdick, the great preacher, once said: "There is nothing that people are so interested in as themselves, their own problems, and the way to solve them. That fact is . . . the primary starting point of all successful public speaking."

What do these psychological principles mean to you as a speaker? First, they mean your listeners will hear and judge what you say on the basis of what they already know and believe. Second, they mean you must relate your message to your listeners—show how it pertains to them, explain why they should care about it as much as you do. Here's an example:

> Mika Nakamura is a nutritionist who frequently gives presentations to different groups about making good food choices. Sometimes she speaks to groups of schoolchildren and their parents, sometimes to adult clubs and community organizations. Although her basic message—eat fresh, eat local—never varies, she has learned how important it is to tailor the message to her specific audience.
>
> When Mika speaks to children, her presentations are very hands-on. With the children's help, she typically prepares a nutritious and delicious shake for them to drink. Rather than telling them to eat more fruits and vegetables, she shows them a way to do it. She has learned from experience that children respond well to concrete learning.
>
> When her audience consists of working parents, Mika focuses on ways to prepare healthful food quickly and easily. For older adults with more free time, she presents more elaborate techniques and emphasizes the importance of good nutrition for healthy aging. When asked to speak to a gourmet club, she tells them about local sources of grass-fed meats and fresh fruits and vegetables.

As Mika's experience shows, you need some grasp of what your listeners know, believe, and care about. Saul Alinsky, the noted community organizer, advises, "People only understand things in terms of their experience," which means that to communicate with them, "you must get inside their experience."[2]

Good speakers are audience-centered. Whether speaking formally or informally, they look for creative ways to communicate their ideas and keep their audience's attention.

Of course, you can't actually get inside another person's experience. But you can learn enough about your audience to know what you should do to make your ideas clear and meaningful. How you can do this is our next topic.

Demographic Audience Analysis

One of the ways speakers analyze audiences is by looking at demographic traits such as age; gender; religion; sexual orientation; group membership; racial, ethnic, or cultural background; and the like. This is called *demographic audience analysis*. It consists of two steps: (1) identifying the general demographic features of your audience, and (2) gauging the importance of those features to a particular speaking situation.

demographic audience analysis

Audience analysis that focuses on demographic factors such as age, gender, religion, sexual orientation, group membership, and racial, ethnic, or cultural background.

While demographic audience analysis can be a useful tool in understanding your audience, like all tools, it can be used improperly. When analyzing demographic information about your audience, it is essential that you avoid stereotyping. Stereotyping involves creating an oversimplified image of a particular group of people, usually by assuming that all members of the group are alike. Examples of stereotyping include the erroneous notions that all African Americans are athletic or that all Asians excel in science. Looking at demographic factors can provide important clues about your audience, but you must use those factors prudently and responsibly.

stereotyping

Creating an oversimplified image of a particular group of people, usually by assuming that all members of the group are alike.

In addition, as we shall see later in this chapter, you should always combine your demographic audience analysis with situational audience analysis.

The importance of any given demographic factor will vary from audience to audience depending on the occasion and the speech topic. If you keep this in mind, demographic analysis can be a valuable starting point in gauging your audience's background, interests, values, and beliefs. Here are a few of the major demographic factors you should consider.

AGE

As Aristotle noted almost 2,500 years ago and as researchers have confirmed many times since, few things affect a person's outlook more than his or her age. Of course, no age group is monolithic. There is no generation in which everyone thinks alike, buys the same products, or votes for the same political candidates. Yet each generation has more or less common values and experiences that set it apart from other generations. Whatever your age, you are a product of your world.

You can see what this means for your speeches. Suppose you address an audience of older people. If you refer to Kanye West, Ke$ha, or Rihanna, your audience may have no idea who you mean. Similarly, if you speak to an audience of young adults and casually mention Watergate, they may not know what you are talking about. Even if younger listeners do recognize the name, it will not produce the same emotional associations as in people who lived through the Watergate break-in and the subsequent resignation of President Richard Nixon.

Depending on the composition of your speech class, you may face an audience that is mostly in their late teens and early twenties. If so, you can assume a common level of age experience. On the other hand, 40 percent of college students today are age 25 or older, and some classrooms include students in their thirties, forties, and beyond. You may then have to tackle two or three generations. This will give you good practice for speeches outside the classroom, where age is usually a major factor in audience analysis.

GENDER

Question: What do you call a female doctor?
Answer: A doctor.

This probably strikes you as a strange question. Few Americans in the second decade of the 21st century identify their doctor by gender. Yet as recently as 1970, only 8 percent of doctors in the United States were women, and the phrase "female doctor" was often heard. Today, 30 percent of American doctors—and 50 percent of medical-school students—are women. The phrase "female doctor" has become extinct.

As in medicine, vocational distinctions between the sexes have been eroding for many years. Women work in construction trades, run corporations, enlist in the armed forces, and serve as college athletic directors. Men work as receptionists, nurses, flight attendants, and day-care attendants.

In addition, the "typical" composition of audiences has changed. At one time, for example, civic groups such as Kiwanis and Rotary clubs were all-male. Today most have sizable contingents of women. Parent associations, which were once composed almost solely of women, now include plenty of interested fathers. Here, as in other areas, the old stereotypes no longer apply.

What does this have to do with public speaking? Speakers who fail to take account of current gender attitudes and practices are almost certain to provoke negative reactions among some listeners, male and female alike. If you're delivering a speech about small businesses, for example, and you refer to business owners generically as "he," or to all shoppers as "she," your word choice will doubtless lead some listeners to squirm in their seats.

At the same time, it is important to recognize that men and women are not alike in all their values and beliefs. When it comes to politics, for instance, American women tend to be more concerned about issues such as education, health care, and social justice, whereas men tend to stress economics and national security. But keep in mind that these are generalizations. There are lots of women who believe that national security comes first, just as there are plenty of men who give priority to social issues. An astute speaker will be equally attuned to the differences *and* the similarities between the sexes.[3]

RELIGION

Current events around the world demonstrate that religious views are among the most emotionally charged and passionately defended of all human concerns. Even your small speech class might include a wide range of faiths, as well as atheists and agnostics. You cannot assume that your views on religion—whatever they may be—are shared by your listeners.

As the United States has become more diverse culturally, it has also become more diverse religiously. The traditional mix of Protestantism, Catholicism, and Judaism has been enriched by growing numbers of Buddhists, Muslims, Hindus, Sikhs, Russian Orthodox, and others. One leading scholar on the subject says the United States is "the most religiously diverse nation in the world."[4]

Demographic audience analysis is vital to successful public speaking in any situation. Here Tibetan Buddhists gather at a ceremony celebrating the 900th anniversary of the birth of spiritual leader Gyalwang Karmapa.

There is also great diversity within different faiths. You cannot assume that all Catholics support the official view of their church on birth control or women in the priesthood, that all Baptists are being born-again, or that all Muslims favor a subservient status for women. In matters of religion, the United States is truly a nation of many faiths, many voices, many views.

Whenever you speak on a topic with religious dimensions, be sure to consider the religious orientations of your listeners. Doing so can help you avoid potentially embarrassing pitfalls. In some cases, it may make the difference between an unsuccessful speech and a successful one.

SEXUAL ORIENTATION

Philip Ward, president of a major engineering firm, was hosting his annual awards banquet to recognize outstanding employees. After presenting all the plaques and checks, he said: "Now that we have honored these fine people for their career and community accomplishments, I would like to take a moment to recognize the spouses and partners who have supported their exceptional efforts." The room filled with applause.

After the ceremony, Ward made his way around the room shaking hands and chatting with award winners. "I want to congratulate you again on your superior design for the Houston water project," he said to Joanne Fitzpatrick.

"Thank you for the award," Joanne replied. "And I want to thank you for being sensitive to the fact that many of us are supported by partners as well as by spouses. It really meant a lot to Julie and me to feel recognized and included."

As an experienced speaker and a successful businessperson, Philip Ward is aware of the need to adapt to his audience on the basis of sexual orientation. By mentioning "partners" as well as "spouses," he took an inclusive stance acknowledging that couples can be same-sex or opposite-sex, married or unmarried.

When you work on your speeches, keep an eye out for language, examples, and other elements that may unintentionally exclude listeners with same-sex partners. The word "homosexual," for example, is considered derogatory by lesbians and gay men. So are references to a gay or lesbian "lifestyle." As there is no single heterosexual lifestyle, there is no single lesbian or gay lifestyle.

Just as audiences often include people of varying occupations, ages, races, and religions, so too do they contain people of different sexual orientations. Effective public speakers take all these demographic factors into account when preparing their remarks.

RACIAL, ETHNIC, AND CULTURAL BACKGROUND

As we saw in Chapter 1, the United States has long been a multicultural society. Populated originally by Native Americans and then by immigrants from all over the world, it is today a multiracial, multiethnic country of unmatched diversity. The majority of Americans support this diversity as a positive development in today's globalized world. Attitudes about race and ethnicity are quite different from what they were even a few decades ago.

These new attitudes are especially evident among Americans born from 1981 to 2000, often referred to as the Millennial Generation. The most racially and ethnically diverse generation in U.S. history, it is also the most tolerant of racial and ethnic differences. As time goes by, this tolerance may continue to grow as the nation becomes even more diverse.

Yet even if you are speaking to an audience composed primarily of members of the Millennial Generation, you must be sensitive to issues of race, ethnicity, and cultural background. Despite their similarities as Americans, people of European descent, blacks, Latinos, Asians, and many others have different customs and beliefs that may bear upon your speech topic.

Because we live in an age of globalization, you may also find yourself addressing listeners from countries other than your own. Not only does the United States contain a substantial percentage of people born in other lands, but more than 5 million Americans (not including those in military service) live abroad. If all those Americans were placed in one state, it would be the 20th largest state in the Union. This is one reason why employers identify the ability to communicate effectively with people of different cultural backgrounds as one of the most desirable skills for current college graduates.

Regardless of where you are speaking, be aware that some of your listeners may have racial, ethnic, or cultural perspectives that will affect their attitudes toward your speech topic. Try to gauge what those perspectives are and how they are likely to affect the audience's response to your message. Adjust your remarks so they will be as clear, suitable, and convincing as possible.

GROUP MEMBERSHIP

"Tell me thy company," says Don Quixote, "and I'll tell thee what thou art." For all our talk about rugged individualism, Americans are very group-oriented. Workers belong to unions, businesspeople to chambers of commerce. Hunters join the National Rifle Association, environmentalists the Sierra Club, feminists the National Organization for Women. Doctors enroll in the American Medical Association, lawyers in the American Bar Association. There are thousands of such voluntary organizations in the United States.

Similar groups abound on campus. Some of your classmates may belong to fraternities or sororities, some to Campus Crusade for Christ, some to the Young Republicans, some to the film society, some to the ski club, and so forth. For speeches in the classroom, as well as for those outside the classroom, the group affiliations of your audience may provide excellent clues about your listeners' interests and attitudes.

Age; gender; religion; sexual orientation; racial, ethnic, and cultural background; group membership—these are just a few of the variables to consider in demographic audience analysis. Others include occupation, economic position, social standing, education, intelligence, and place of residence. Indeed, *anything* characteristic of a given audience is potentially important to a speaker addressing that audience. For your classroom speeches, you may want to learn about your classmates' academic majors, years in school, extracurricular activities, living arrangements, and job aspirations.

Perhaps the most important thing to keep in mind about demographic audience analysis is that it is not an end in itself. Your aim is not just to list the major traits of your listeners, but to find in those traits clues about how your listeners will respond to your speech. Once you have done that, you are ready to move on to the next stage of audience analysis.

Situational Audience Analysis

situational audience analysis

Audience analysis that focuses on situational factors such as the size of the audience, the physical setting for the speech, and the disposition of the audience toward the topic, the speaker, and the occasion.

Situational audience analysis usually builds on demographic analysis. It identifies traits of the audience unique to the speaking situation at hand. These traits include the size of the audience, the physical setting, and the disposition of the audience toward the subject, the speaker, and the occasion.

SIZE

Outside the classroom, the size of an audience can, with the aid of television and radio, range in the millions. Most speech classes, however, consist of between 20 and 30 people—a small- to medium-sized audience. This is a good size for beginning speakers, most of whom are terrified at the prospect of addressing a huge crowd. As you gain more experience, though, you may welcome the challenge of speaking to larger groups. Some speakers actually prefer a large audience to a small one.

No matter what size group you are addressing, bear in mind one basic principle: The larger the audience, the more formal your presentation must be. Audience size may also affect your language, choice of appeals, and use of visual aids.

PHYSICAL SETTING

Which of the following would you rather address?

> An audience assembled immediately after lunch, crammed into an overheated room with inadequate seating
>
> An audience assembled at 10:00 in the morning, comfortably seated in an airy, well-lighted room

Undoubtedly you chose the second option. Any of the adverse conditions listed in the first could seriously impair your audience's willingness to accept your ideas or even listen to you at all.

When you face any speaking situation, it is important to know in advance if there will be any difficulties with the physical setting. For classroom speeches, of course, you already do know. But speeches outside the classroom can present unpleasant surprises unless you do your homework beforehand.

When you are invited to speak, don't be shy about asking questions of the person who arranged the speech. If possible, look over the room a few days in advance, or else arrive early on the day of your speech to inspect the room. If it is too warm or too cold, see about adjusting the thermostat. Check the seating arrangements and the location of the lectern to be sure your audience can see you. In short, do everything you can to control the influence of physical setting on your audience.

What about circumstances you can't control? Your speech *is* scheduled directly after lunch or dinner. The room *is* too small for the audience expected. The heat *cannot* be regulated. Then you are simply going to have to work harder to adapt to these aspects of your listeners' discomfort.

Above all, don't be influenced *yourself* by the poor physical setting. If your audience sees that you are energetic, alert, and involved with your topic, chances are they will forget their discomfort and come right along with you.

DISPOSITION TOWARD THE TOPIC

As we saw in Chapter 5, you should keep your audience in mind when choosing a topic. Ideally, you will pick a topic that suits them as well as it suits you. Once you have your topic, however, you must consider in more detail their interest in the topic, knowledge about it, and attitudes toward it.

Interest

Outside the classroom, people do not often expend the time and effort to attend a speech unless they are interested in the topic. But the members of your speech class are a captive audience. Sometimes they will be deeply interested in your topic, particularly if it relates directly to them. Most of the time they will range from fairly interested to mildly curious to downright indifferent.

One of your tasks will be to assess their interest in advance and to adjust your speech accordingly. Most important, if your topic is not likely to generate great interest, you must take special steps to get your classmates involved. Here is a brief example of how to do this:

> Sharon wanted to persuade her classmates to vote on a regular basis. She started by saying: "Suppose a total stranger was responsible for making life-or-death decisions about your life. You'd want to have a say in who that person was, wouldn't you? Well, total strangers do make decisions that affect you every single day—those total strangers are called members of Congress, Senators, and the President. And you can help choose all those people by doing one simple thing—voting on election day."

connect™

View the beginning of "Make Your Voice Heard: Get Out and Vote" in the online Media Library for this chapter (Video 6.2).

In the chapters that follow, we'll look closely at all the ways you can develop interest in your topic—by an arresting introduction, provocative supporting materials, vivid language, dynamic delivery, visual aids, and so forth.

Knowledge

There is often a strong correlation between interest in a topic and knowledge about it. People tend to be interested in what they know about. Likewise, they are inclined to learn about subjects that interest them. But there are exceptions. Few students know much about handwriting analysis, yet most would find it an absorbing topic. On the other hand, almost all know a lot about checking books out of the library, but few would find it a fascinating subject for a speech.

Your listeners' knowledge about your topic will to a large extent determine what you can say in your speech. If your listeners know little about your topic—whether or not they find it interesting—you will have to talk at a more elementary level. If they are reasonably well informed, you can take a more technical and detailed approach.

Attitude

The attitude of your listeners toward your topic can be extremely important in determining how you handle the material. If you know in advance the prevailing attitude among members of your audience, you can adjust your speech to address their concerns or to answer their objections. Consider the experiences of the following two students—one who did not account for listener attitude and one who did:

attitude

A frame of mind in favor of or opposed to a person, policy, belief, institution, etc.

Jen Salerno spoke about family-leave policies in the workplace. On the basis of her research, she believed there was evidence that such policies unfairly benefited a few parents at the expense of other employees, such as single people and childless couples. Unfortunately, rather than citing her sources and acknowledging that her point of view was controversial, Jen presented her material as though it were general knowledge.

The speech was not well received. As one student commented, "You may be right in what you say, but I have trouble believing it. We've heard so much about the need for businesses to be family-friendly—can it all be wrong? I think you would have been more persuasive if you had looked at both sides of the issue rather than just your own."

Had Jen taken the skepticism of her audience into account and established the credibility of her sources, she might have made her arguments more convincing to her audience.

Compare the approach of Bryan Watts, who also espoused a controversial viewpoint:

connect™

View an excerpt from "The Internet and Our Future" in the online Media Library for this chapter (Video 6.3).

Concerned about the economic woes of his state, Bryan decided to give a persuasive speech calling for a sales tax on goods purchased over the Internet. After distributing an audience-analysis questionnaire among his classmates, Bryan found that 80 percent of them opposed his plan. They gave two major reasons. First, they believed they were taxed enough already. Second, they thought an Internet sales tax would be too difficult to implement.

Although Bryan disagreed with those beliefs, he realized he could neither ignore them nor insult his classmates for holding them. He knew he would have to discuss these points logically and with hard evidence if he were to have any chance of persuading his audience.

As it turned out, Bryan did convince some members of the class to reconsider their beliefs. He could not have done so without first investigating what those beliefs were and then adapting his message to them.[5]

DISPOSITION TOWARD THE SPEAKER

Let's return for a moment to Jen's speech about family leave. Jen was a first-year student with no special background in workplace issues. It's not surprising that her classmates took her statements with a large grain of salt. But suppose Jen had been a recognized expert who had conducted research on the impact of family leave on employee attitudes and business productivity. Then her listeners would have found her much more believable. Why? Because an audience's response to a message is invariably colored by their perception of the speaker.

The more competent listeners believe a speaker to be, the more likely they are to accept what he or she says. Likewise, the more listeners believe that a speaker has their best interests at heart, the more likely they are to respond positively to the speaker's message.

Situational audience analysis provides crucial information that a speaker can use when preparing the speech and when adapting to developments during the speech.

We will come back to this subject in detail when we deal with strategies for persuasive speaking in Chapter 17. For now, keep in mind that your listeners will always have *some* set of attitudes toward you as a speaker. Estimating what those attitudes are and how they will affect your speech is a crucial part of situational audience analysis.

DISPOSITION TOWARD THE OCCASION

It was graduation day at Valencia High School. The mood was festive as the valedictorian spoke eloquently about the special memories of the graduating class. There was laughter when the principal recounted a well-known prank from the class picnic.

Then, Russell Merritt, the mayor, rose to say a few words. "What a pleasure it is to be here," he said. "I'm so proud of you, the graduates, and you, the parents who raised such a terrific group of kids." He continued in this vein for a couple minutes, interrupted by applause as he heaped praise on the students, their parents, their teachers, and their community.

The listeners' enthusiasm faded as Merritt began talking about building a new library to replace the town's old one. This was a controversial issue, and it was going to be voted on in an upcoming referendum. The more the mayor talked about it, the more irritated his audience became. When he concluded, he was met with grudging applause and quite a few hostile glares.

On other occasions, Merritt's remarks would not have touched off such a negative response. But graduation day was understood by the audience to be a celebratory occasion that focused on the students and their achievements. The last thing anyone expected to hear was a political speech. What angered the audience was not what the mayor said, but that he exploited the occasion for his own purposes.

Using public speaking in your **CAREER**

As an economics professor, your research on the Social Security system has attracted media attention. Aware of your expertise, the local Rotary club has invited you to speak on the subject at the club's weekly meeting.

Having taken a public speaking class in college, you know how important it is to analyze the audience you will be addressing. To prepare for your speech, you have arranged a telephone interview with the club's president to find out more about your audience. List (1) the two most important questions you want to ask the president about the demographics of your audience, and (2) the two most important questions you want to ask about the situational traits of your audience. Be specific in your questions and be prepared, if necessary, to explain your choice of questions.

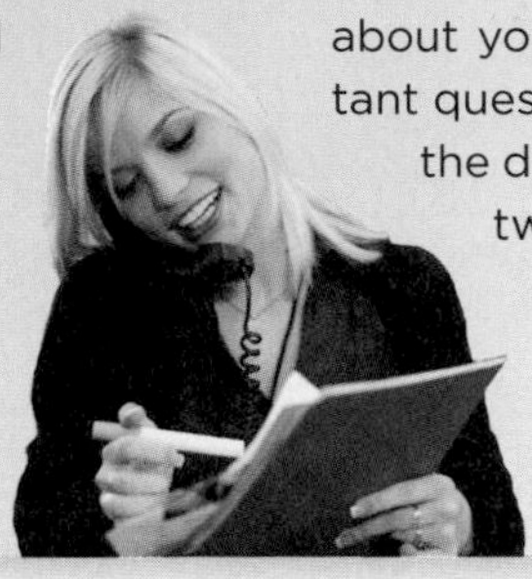

No matter what the situation, listeners have fairly definite ideas about the speeches they consider appropriate. Speakers who seriously violate those expectations can almost always count on infuriating the audience.

Perhaps most important, the occasion will dictate how long a speech should be. When you are invited to speak, the chairperson will usually say how much time you have for your talk. If not, be sure to ask.

Once you know, pare down your speech so it fits easily within the allotted time. Do not exceed that time under any circumstances, for you are likely to see your audience dwindle as you drone on. (This is one reason why most teachers insist that classroom speeches be kept within the designated time limit. It provides crucial training for speeches you will give outside the classroom.)

There are other audience expectations that apply to your classroom situation. One is that speeches will conform to the assignment. Another is that speakers will observe appropriate standards of taste and decorum. Failure to adhere to these expectations may disturb your classmates and will almost certainly damage your grade.

Getting Information About the Audience

Now that you know *what* to learn about an audience, the next question is, *how* do you learn it? A person running for political office can rely on hired professional pollsters. If, as is more likely, you are invited sometime to address a particular group—say a meeting of the local Rotary club—the person who invites you can usually provide a good sketch of the audience. Ask your contact where you can find out more about the group's history and mission. If you know someone who has spoken to the same group, be sure to sound out that person.

What about your classmates as an audience? You can learn a lot about them just by observation and conversation, but you may want to know more about their knowledge and attitudes on specific speech topics. Some teachers require students to do a formal audience-analysis questionnaire for at least one of their speeches. In addition to providing information about your classroom audience, such a questionnaire gives you practice in developing the skills of audience analysis you will need for speeches after your class is over.

There are three major types of questions to choose from when developing an audience-analysis questionnaire: fixed-alternative questions, scale questions, and open-ended questions.

Fixed-alternative questions, as their name implies, offer a fixed choice between two or more responses. For example:

fixed-alternative questions

Questions that offer a fixed choice between two or more alternatives.

Do you know what the insanity plea is in the U.S. legal system?

Yes ________________

No ________________

Not sure ________________

By limiting the possible responses, such questions produce clear, unambiguous answers. They also tend to yield superficial answers. Other techniques are needed to get beneath the surface.

Scale questions resemble fixed-alternative questions, but they allow more leeway in responding. For example:

scale questions

Questions that require responses at fixed intervals along a scale of answers.

How often do you believe the insanity plea is used in U.S. court cases?

Very seldom ——|——|——|——|—— Very often

Questions like these are especially useful for getting at the strength of a respondent's attitudes.

Open-ended questions give maximum leeway in responding. For example:

open-ended questions

Questions that allow respondents to answer however they want.

What is your opinion about the insanity plea in U.S. court cases?

Under what circumstances do you think the insanity plea is legitimate in a criminal trial?

Although open-ended questions invite more detailed responses than the other two types of questions, they also increase the likelihood of getting answers that do not give the kind of information you need.

Because each type of question has its advantages and disadvantages, many questionnaires contain all three types. Figure 6.1 (page 112) shows a questionnaire that was distributed before a classroom speech on volunteering. By using all three types of questions, the speaker did two things—elicited specific information about the audience and probed more deeply into their attitudes toward the speech topic. The results broke down as follows:

1. Roughly half of the class had not participated as a volunteer. Therefore, the speaker knew she would have to explain clearly what was involved in this kind of work.
2. Five students knew someone close to them who had benefited from volunteer work by a community, religious, or charitable organization; most

Two fixed-alternative questions establish the listeners' level of knowledge about and degree of involvement with the topic.

1. Have you ever engaged in volunteer work for a community, religious, or charitable organization?

   Yes ______________________
   No ______________________

2. Have you or anyone close to you ever benefited from the volunteer work of a community, religious, or charitable organization?

   Yes ______________________
   No ______________________
   Not sure ______________________

This scale question is designed to show the attitudes of listeners who have participated in volunteer work.

3. If you have engaged in volunteer work, how would you rate the experience?

   ☐ Very rewarding
   ☐ Somewhat rewarding
   ☐ Neutral
   ☐ Somewhat unrewarding
   ☐ Very unrewarding

Another scale question gauges the listeners' sense of social obligation.

4. Do you agree or disagree with the following statement? To the extent possible, people have an obligation to help those in less fortunate circumstances.

   ☐ Strongly agree
   ☐ Mildly agree
   ☐ Undecided
   ☐ Mildly disagree
   ☐ Strongly disagree

Two open-ended questions help gauge the listeners' disposition toward volunteer work. The last question is especially important. It probes the specific issues the speaker needs to address for listeners who have not engaged in volunteer work.

5. If you have worked as a volunteer, do you plan to do so again? Why or why not?

6. If you have not worked as a volunteer, what is your major reason for not doing so? Please explain.

FIGURE 6.1
Sample Questionnaire

said they were not sure. Thus the speaker could not depend on a high degree of personal involvement among the audience.

3. All but one of the students who had engaged in volunteer work rated it "very rewarding" or "somewhat rewarding." Not only would this portion of the audience be inclined to support the speaker's position, but the speaker could point to their attitude as proof that working as a volunteer is a rewarding experience.
4. Nearly 75 percent of the respondents either "strongly agreed" or "mildly agreed" that people have an obligation to help those in less fortunate circumstances. The speaker could therefore depend on an audience favorably inclined to the basic premise underlying volunteer work.

5. Answers to the fifth question—"If you have worked as a volunteer, do you plan to do so again? Why or why not?"—were interesting. All the respondents indicated that they planned to engage in volunteer work again, but most said they were not likely to do so while in college because they were too busy with other activities.
6. Nearly 90 percent of the students who had not engaged in volunteer work stated that their major reason for not doing so was a lack of time. In combination with the answers to question 5, these responses showed that the speaker would have to deal persuasively with the time issue if she were to be successful in convincing people to volunteer while they were enrolled in school.

connect

View how the speaker in Video 6.3 used an audience-analysis questionnaire in his speech (Video 6.4).

This questionnaire revealed a great deal about the listeners' knowledge, attitudes, and concerns. In putting together your own questionnaire, keep the following principles in mind:

1. Plan the questionnaire carefully to elicit precisely the information you need.
2. Use all three types of questions—fixed-alternative, scale, and open-ended.
3. Make sure the questions are clear and unambiguous.
4. Keep the questionnaire relatively brief.

Adapting to the Audience

Once you have completed the audience analysis, you should have a pretty clear picture of your listeners. But this does not guarantee a successful speech. The key is how well you *use* what you know in preparing and presenting the speech.

This point deserves special attention because it poses one of the hardest tasks facing novice speakers. Most people can identify the major characteristics of their audience, but many have trouble *adapting* their ideas to the audience. There are two major stages in the process of audience adaptation. The first occurs before the speech, as part of your preparation and rehearsal. The second occurs during the presentation of the speech itself.

AUDIENCE ADAPTATION BEFORE THE SPEECH

As we have seen, you must keep your audience in mind at every stage of speech preparation. This involves more than simply remembering who your listeners will be. Above all, it means two things: (1) assessing how your audience is likely to respond to what you say in your speech, and (2) adjusting what you say to make it as clear, appropriate, and convincing as possible.

This is not always easy to do. We are all so wrapped up in our own ideas and concerns that we have trouble seeing things from other people's perspective—especially if their perspective is different from ours. To step outside your own frame of reference and see things from another person's point of view is a real achievement.

Yet this is what a successful speaker eventually learns to do. You must submerge your own views so completely that you can adopt, temporarily, those of your listeners. When you do this, you will begin to hear your speech through the ears of your audience and to adjust it accordingly. Try to imagine what they will like, what they will dislike, where they will have doubts or questions, whether they will need more details here or fewer there, what will interest them and what will not.

At every point you must *anticipate* how your audience will respond. Put yourself in their place and respond to your speech as they would.

Here is how one student worked out his problems of audience adaptation:

Juan Ruiz, a junior geology major, decided to give an informative speech about how earthquakes occur. From his audience analysis, he learned that only a handful of his classmates knew much about geology. Juan realized that he would have to present his speech at an elementary level and with a minimum of scientific language.

As he prepared the speech, Juan kept asking himself, "How can I make this clear and meaningful to someone who knows nothing about earthquakes or geological principles?" Because he was speaking in the Midwest, he decided to begin by noting that the most severe earthquake in American history took place not in California, but at New Madrid, Missouri, in 1811. If such an earthquake happened today, it would be felt from the Rocky Mountains to the Atlantic Ocean and would flatten most of the cities in the Mississippi Valley. That, he figured, should get his classmates' attention.

Throughout the body of his speech, Juan dealt only with the basic mechanics of earthquakes and carefully avoided technical terms such as "asthenosphere," "lithosphere," and "subduction zones." He also prepared PowerPoint slides to illustrate his points.

To be absolutely safe, Juan asked his roommate—who was not a geology major—to listen to the speech. "Stop me," he said, "anytime I say something you don't understand." Juan's roommate stopped him four times, and at each spot Juan worked out a way to make his point more clearly. Finally, he had a speech that was interesting and perfectly understandable to his audience.

As you work on your speeches, try to keep your listeners constantly in mind. Anticipate how they will respond to your ideas. Be creative in thinking about ways to adapt your message to them. Like Juan, you will give a much better speech.

AUDIENCE ADAPTATION DURING THE SPEECH

No matter how hard you prepare ahead of time, things may not go exactly as planned on the day of your speech. For speeches in the classroom, you may find that the projector for your visual aids is not available or that another student has the same topic as you. For speeches outside the classroom, you might learn that the audience will be much larger (or smaller) than you had anticipated, or that the amount of time available for your speech has been cut in half because a previous speaker has droned on for too long.

If something like this happens to you, don't panic. Find another way to present your visual aids. Modify your introduction to mention the other student's speech on your topic. Adjust your delivery to the changed audience size. If you find that you have less time than you had planned, condense your speech to its most essential points and present them in the time available. Your listeners will sympathize with your predicament and will appreciate

In political campaigns, poll-taking helps the candidates keep track of public opinion. For classroom speeches, you can use an audience-analysis questionnaire to gauge the knowledge and opinions of your listeners.

your regard for their time. This will more than compensate for your lost speaking time.

Finally, be sure to keep an eye out during your speech for audience feedback. If your listeners are sitting forward in their chairs, looking at you with interest, and nodding their heads in approval, you can assume that things are going well. But suppose you find them frowning or responding with quizzical looks. Then you may need to back up and go over your point again, as in this example:

Brandi Michaels, an economics major, had worked diligently to make sure her speech on the U.S. trade deficit was not too technical for her classmates. She explained everything from the ground up, prepared two excellent visual aids, and practiced giving the speech to her best friend, a music major and self-confessed "economics imbecile."

On the day of Brandi's speech, everything went well until she got to her second main point, when she noticed that several of her classmates seemed puzzled by the relationship between international trade deficits and the U.S. cost of living. Knowing they would be lost for the rest of the speech if they didn't understand that relationship, Brandi paused and said, "I can see some of you are confused by my explanation. Let me try it again from a different angle."

As Brandi went through the material again, she could see her classmates nodding their heads in understanding. She could now go on with her speech, confident that her audience was ready to go with her.

Adapting to your audience is one of the most important keys to successful public speaking. Like other aspects of speechmaking, it is sometimes easier said than done. But once you master it, you'll see that it pays dividends in more personal facets of your life—when you adapt to an audience of one.

Summary

Good speakers are audience-centered. They know that the aim of speechmaking is to gain a desired response from listeners. When working on your speeches, keep three questions in mind: To whom am I speaking? What do I want them to know, believe, or do as a result of my speech? What is the most effective way of composing and presenting my speech to accomplish that aim?

To be an effective speaker, you should know something about the psychology of audiences. People are egocentric. They typically approach speeches with one question uppermost in mind: "Why is this important to *me*?" Therefore, you need to study your audience and adapt your speech to their beliefs and interests.

The first stage in learning about your audience is to identify demographic traits such as age, gender, religion, sexual orientation, group membership, and racial, ethnic, or cultural background. The second stage is identifying traits of the audience unique to the speaking situation. These traits include the size of the audience, attitudes influenced by the physical setting, and your listeners' disposition toward the topic, toward you as a speaker, and toward the occasion.

For speeches outside the classroom, you can best get information about the audience by asking the person who invites you to speak. For classroom speeches, you can learn about your audience by observation and conversation. You also can circulate an audience-analysis questionnaire.

Once you complete the audience analysis, you must adapt your speech so it will be clear and convincing to your listeners. Put yourself in their place. Try to hear the speech as they will. Anticipate questions and objections, and try to answer them in advance. When you deliver your speech, keep an eye out for audience feedback and adjust your remarks in response.

Key Terms

audience-centeredness *(98)*
identification *(98)*
egocentrism *(100)*
demographic audience analysis *(101)*
stereotyping *(101)*
situational audience analysis *(106)*
attitude *(108)*
fixed-alternative questions *(111)*
scale questions *(111)*
open-ended questions *(111)*

Review Questions

After reading this chapter, you should be able to answer the following questions:

1. Why must a public speaker be audience-centered?
2. What does it mean to say that people are egocentric? What implications does the egocentrism of audiences hold for you as a public speaker?
3. What are the six demographic traits of audiences discussed in this chapter? Why is each important to audience analysis?

4. What is situational audience analysis? What factors do you need to consider in situational audience analysis?
5. How can you get information about an audience?
6. What are the three kinds of questions used in questionnaires? Why is it a good idea to use all three in audience analysis?
7. What methods can you use to adapt your speech to your audience before the speech? During the speech?

connect

For further review, go to the LearnSmart study module for this chapter.

Exercises for Critical Thinking

1. Advertisers are usually very conscious of their audience. Choose an issue of a popular magazine such as *Time, Newsweek, Sports Illustrated, Vanity Fair, Rolling Stone,* or the like. From that issue select three advertisements to analyze. Try to determine the audience being appealed to in each advertisement, and analyze the appeals (verbal and visual) used to persuade buyers. How might the appeals differ if the ads were designed to persuade a different audience?
2. Below are three general speech topics and, for each, two hypothetical audiences to which a speech might be delivered. For each topic, write a brief paragraph explaining how you might adjust your specific purpose and message according to the demographic characteristics of the audience.

   a. Topic: "Data Encryption"

   Audience #1: 50% computer science majors, 30% physics majors, 20% fine arts majors

   Audience #2: 40% business majors, 40% history majors, 20% computer science majors

   b. Topic: "Sexual Assault: The Biggest Campus Crime"

   Audience #1: 80% female, 20% male

   Audience #2: 80% male, 20% female

   c. Topic: "The Fall of the Berlin Wall"

   Audience #1: Day class: 70% age 18 to 22, 30% age 23 and over

   Audience #2: Evening class: 50% age 35 and over, 30% age 23 to 34, 20% age 18 to 22

3. For your next speech, design and circulate among your classmates an audience-analysis questionnaire like that discussed on pages 111–113. Use all three kinds of questions explained in the text: fixed-alternative, scale, and open-ended. After you have tabulated the results of the questionnaire, write an analysis explaining what the questionnaire reveals about your audience and what steps you must take to adapt your speech to the audience.

7

Gathering Materials

- Using Your Own Knowledge and Experience
- Doing Library Research
- Searching the Internet
- Interviewing
- Tips for Doing Research

Suppose you are planning a trip to India. You want to know the major sites so you can work out an itinerary. You also need to know what things will cost, where the hostels are located, and how the train and bus systems work. How do you go about gathering all this information?

You can talk to people who have traveled in India and get ideas from them. You can consult guidebooks. You can search the Internet for information. If you have traveled to South Asia before, you can draw on that experience. Since you want your trip to be a success, you gather as much information as you can before you leave.

Gathering materials for a speech is like gathering information for any project. There are many resources available if you take advantage of them. You can interview people with specialized knowledge. You can do research on the Internet or in the library. Sometimes you can use yourself as a resource—whenever you have personal experience or above-average knowledge about a subject. Let's turn first to the resource of your own experience.

Using Your Own Knowledge and Experience

Everybody is an expert on something, whether it is video games, child care, or backpacking. As we saw in Chapter 5, we often speak best about subjects with which we are familiar. This is why many teachers encourage students to capitalize on their own knowledge and experience in developing speech topics.

When you choose a topic from your own experience, you may be tempted to depersonalize it by relying solely on facts and figures from books and the Internet. Such outside information is almost always necessary. But supplementing it with the personal touch can really bring your speeches to life.

One student, afflicted with diabetes, chose to explain how a person can live with the disease on a daily basis. He cited statistics on the incidence of diabetes in the United States, identified symptoms of the disease, and explained how it is treated. Along the way, he illustrated his points by talking about his personal experiences. Here is part of what he said:

> Being a diabetic presents a challenge one cannot afford to lose. On a personal note, I have tried not to let my diabetes affect my lifestyle. Last year, I spent nine months traveling in Central and South America. The trip was very memorable, but I had one particularly frightening experience that quickly makes you realize just how vulnerable a diabetic is. On the fifth day of a two-week excursion down the Amazon River, our canoe tipped, dumping everything into the water.
>
> Although I recovered my pack, part of its contents—including my insulin—were swallowed up by the river. Without insulin, I could not eat any food, for if I did, my blood sugar level would become too high and I could eventually go into convulsions, slip into a coma, and die. We returned back up the Amazon and traveled three days until we reached the first village and I could radio for more medicine. I was hot and hungry, but alive.

This speech has color and emotion. By drawing on his own experience, the speaker conveyed his point more meaningfully than he could have in any other way.

Even if your life stories are not that dramatic, you can still put them to work for you. By thinking over your past experiences—gathering material from yourself—you can find many supporting materials for your speeches.

Doing Library Research

Even in this age of the Internet, you will get some of the information for your speeches from the library. It contains many resources to help you find what you need, including librarians, the catalogue, reference works, and databases. We'll look at each in turn.

LIBRARIANS

Too often students waste their time wandering aimlessly in the library because they are afraid to ask for assistance. They don't want to appear stupid or to

FIGURE 7.1 Sample Catalogue Entry for a Book

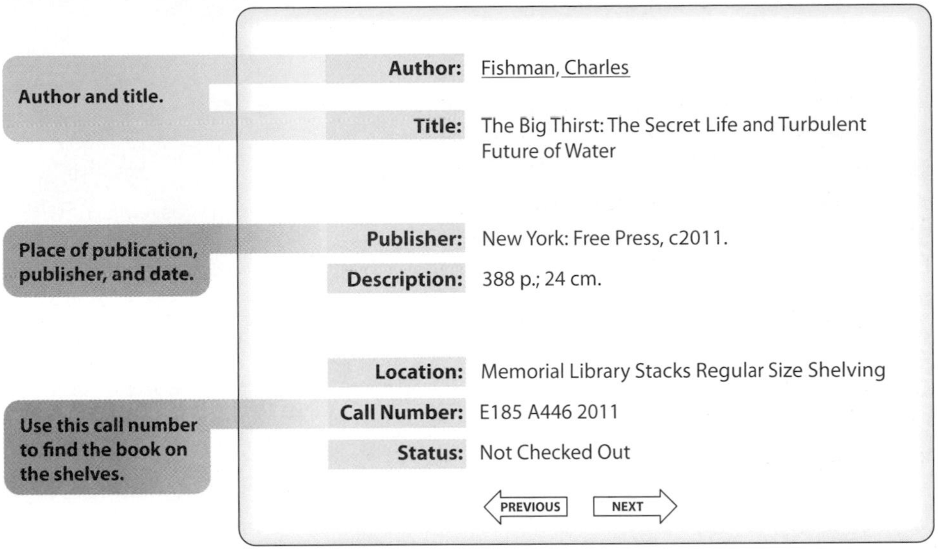

"bother" anyone. But would you be as sensitive about asking a doctor for help with a medical problem? Librarians are experts in their own field, trained in library use and research methods. If you have a question, don't hesitate to ask a librarian. He or she can help you find your way, locate sources, even track down a specific piece of information.

THE CATALOGUE

The catalogue lists all the books, periodicals, and other resources owned by the library. Although there are many different computer systems for library catalogues, most allow you to search for books by author, title, subject, or keyword. The catalogue also tells you whether the book you want is available or is already checked out.

Figure 7.1 above shows a sample catalogue entry for a book. The key to finding the book on the shelves is the *call number*. Once you have the call number, all you have to do is find the right section of the shelves (or stacks, as they are called in some libraries) and retrieve your book.

catalogue

A listing of all the books, periodicals, and other resources owned by a library.

call number

A number used in libraries to classify books and periodicals and to indicate where they can be found on the shelves.

REFERENCE WORKS

Reference works are usually kept in a part of the library called the reference section. The right reference work can save you hours of time by putting at your fingertips a wealth of information that might be difficult to locate through the library catalogue. The major kinds of reference works you are likely to use for your speeches are encyclopedias, yearbooks, quotation books, and biographical aids.

reference work

A work that synthesizes a large amount of related information for easy access by researchers.

Encyclopedias

We are all familiar with general encyclopedias such as the *Encyclopaedia Britannica*. But there are also special encyclopedias that cover their fields in more depth than do general encyclopedias. Some of the most frequently

Library research is vital for most speeches. Knowing the resources available in your library and how to use them efficiently will make the research process much more productive.

used special encyclopedias are the *African American Encyclopedia,* the *Encyclopedia of Religion,* and the *McGraw-Hill Encyclopedia of Science and Technology.*

Yearbooks

As the name implies, yearbooks are published annually. They contain an amazing amount of current information that would otherwise be all but impossible to track down. Two of the most valuable yearbooks are *Facts on File* and *World Almanac and Book of Facts.*

Quotation Books

The best-known collection of quotations is *Bartlett's Familiar Quotations.* With more than 25,000 quotations from historical and contemporary figures, it has long been regarded as an indispensable source for speakers and writers alike. Other excellent quotation books include the *Oxford Dictionary of Quotations, The New Quotable Woman,* and *Ancient Echoes: Native American Words of Wisdom.*

Biographical Aids

When you need information about people in the news, you can turn to one of the many reference works that contain brief life and career facts about contemporary men and women. The most popular biographical aids are published by Who's Who, which produces such titles as *International Who's Who* and *Who's Who in America.* More specialized biographical aids include *Contemporary Black Biography, Dictionary of Hispanic Biography,* and *Who's Who Among Asian Americans.*

newspaper and periodical database

A research aid that catalogues articles from a large number of magazines, journals, and newspapers.

NEWSPAPER AND PERIODICAL DATABASES

Newspaper and periodical databases allow you to locate articles in thousands of publications, including *Time, Atlantic,* the *New York Times,* and the *Wall*

Street Journal. Type a subject in your database's search box, and citations for articles on your subject will appear on screen.

In some cases, you may get an *abstract* of the article in addition to—or instead of—the full article. Keep in mind that the abstract is only a summary of the article. You should *never* cite an article in your speech on the basis of the abstract alone. Always consult the full article.

abstract

A summary of a magazine or journal article, written by someone other than the original author.

The exact databases you can use will depend on what is available through your library. Here are three major databases; odds are that your library will have at least one of them.

ProQuest. An excellent database that indexes thousands of periodicals and newspapers. Figure 7.2 below shows a sample screen from ProQuest with a magazine citation and abstract.

LexisNexis Academic. This database provides full-text access to more than 45,000 information sources, including magazines, legal documents, and television broadcast transcripts. LexisNexis also furnishes articles from more than 500 U.S. and international newspapers.

World News Connection. Provides full-text articles from more than 2,000 international sources, including newspapers, speeches, broadcasts, books, and reports.

ACADEMIC DATABASES

At colleges and universities around the world, experts are researching almost every aspect of the natural world and human society. Their work appears in respected, peer-reviewed journals. Academic databases make those journals available to you.

academic database

A database that catalogues articles from scholarly journals.

FIGURE 7.2 Sample Periodical Entry from ProQuest

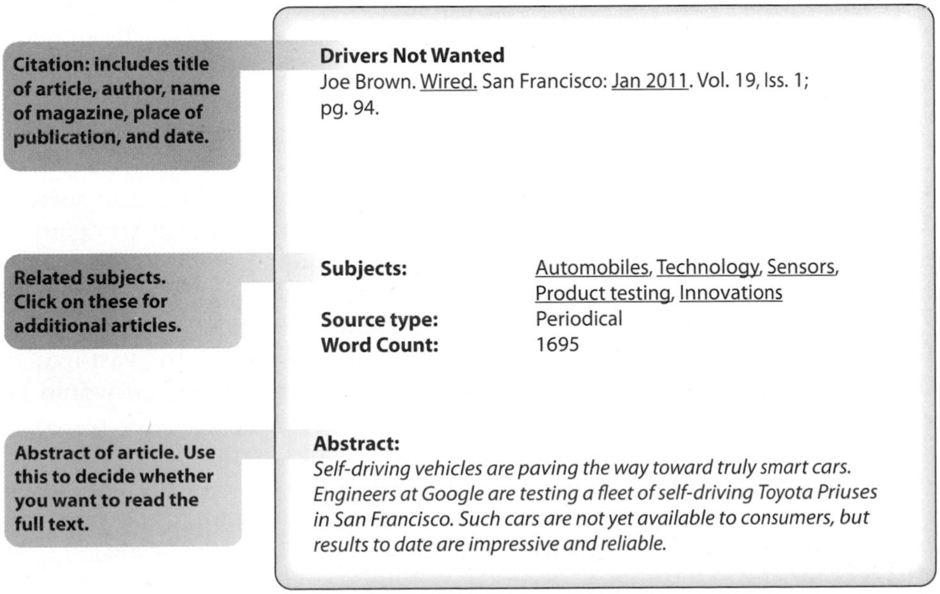

The best place to find scholarly research is in one of the following academic databases. Because each searches across different academic disciplines, you should be able to find what you need in one of the databases.

InfoTrac OneFile. Provides access to more than 100 million scholarly articles in areas from economics and sociology to science and medicine.

JSTOR. In addition to cataloguing more than 1,000 academic journals in various disciplines, JSTOR allows you to search images, letters, and other primary documents.

Google Scholar. A fast and easy way to search a broad range of scholarly literature. Advanced search tools let you narrow your search by author, publication, date, and subject matter.

Searching the Internet

The Internet has been called the world's biggest library. But unlike a library, the Internet has no central information desk, no librarians, no catalogue, and no reference section. Nor does it have a person or department in charge of determining whether materials are of high quality. You can unearth a great deal of information on the Internet, but you cannot always find the same range and depth as in a good library. This is why experts advise that you use the Internet to supplement, not to replace, library research.

In this section, we will look at ways you can go beyond browsing the Web and turn it into a powerful research tool for your speeches. After discussing search engines and other resources for conducting efficient, focused inquiries, we'll explain how to evaluate the reliability and objectivity of the research materials you find on the Web.

SEARCH ENGINES

Search engines are the key to finding materials on the Internet. There are numerous search engines, but the most widely used by far is Google. In addition to providing access to billions of Web pages, it has specialized search tools devoted to images, video, news, blogs, and finance.

The question is: How can you use Google and other search engines *systematically* to find what you need? The answer is: Develop a search strategy that will allow you to zero in precisely on the information required for your speech.

Suppose you are using Google to look for information about sports injuries among college cheerleaders. If you simply enter the word *cheerleading* in the search box, you will get a list of every document catalogued by Google that contains the word *cheerleading*—more than 45 million. Some will deal with sports injuries among college cheerleaders, but the vast majority will not. Scanning through everything to find what you need would be impossible.

How do you limit your search to get manageable results? If you type *college cheerleading* in Google's search box, you will still come up with 2.5 million citations. However, if you type "college cheerleading" in quotation marks, you will get only documents that contain the exact phrase "college cheerleading"—312,000 in all.

Research gives speakers facts and figures to support their ideas. Gary Locke, U.S. Ambassador to China, uses a wide range of supporting materials in his addresses to domestic and international audiences alike.

This is much better, but it's still too many to go through one by one. So you narrow your search still further. This time you type the following entry into Google's search box:

"college cheerleading" + "sports injury"

The + sign limits the search to items that contain both sets of keywords, "college cheerleading" and "sports injury." This time you get a list of 1,360 documents, all of which deal specifically with sports injuries among college cheerleaders. You won't be able to look through all 1,360, but usually you don't need to go past the first few pages of results. After that, you will run into lots of repetition and lower-quality sites.

Google also allows you to narrow your search by the kind of research source that will serve you best. Once your search terms are in the Google search box, you can click on *news* at the top of the page to explore recent news stories that mention "college cheerleading" and "sports injury." You can also click on *images, videos, blogs, scholar,* or *books* to search those kinds of resources. If nothing appears for "college cheerleading" and "sports injury" in these specialized categories, try removing the quotation marks and see what happens.

Of course, you will have to adjust your search terms depending on the kind of material you're looking for, but once you learn the basic principles for doing precise, pinpointed searches, you will greatly increase your odds of finding exactly what you need for your speeches.

SPECIALIZED RESEARCH RESOURCES

Search engines are extremely helpful, but they are not the only vehicles for finding information. The following specialized resources concentrate on sites that are most likely to be helpful as you work on your speeches.[1]

Virtual Libraries

Search engines help you find what's on the Internet, but they don't evaluate the quality of the sources they retrieve. Librarians and other information specialists are working to make it easier to locate reliable, high-quality Web resources. One result of their efforts is virtual libraries—search engines that combine Internet technology with traditional library methods of assessing data.

virtual library

A search engine that combines Internet technology with traditional library methods of cataloguing and assessing data.

The best virtual library on the Internet is a merger of two previous virtual libraries—Librarians' Internet Index and Internet Public Library. Now called ipl2 (www.ipl.org), this site has more than 20,000 entries organized into 12 main topics, including arts and humanities, education, and health and medical sciences (see Figure 7.3 below). In addition, ipl2 links to a large number of reference sites, as well as to a wide range of constantly evolving special collections.

Government Resources

One of the great strengths of the Internet as a research tool is the access it provides to government documents and publications. Whether you are looking for information from the federal government or from a state or local agency, chances are you can find it by starting your search at one of these Web sites:

USA.gov (www.usa.gov). One-stop shopping for all U.S. government information on the Internet. Provides links to more than 250 million Web pages from federal, state, local, and tribal governments.

Statistical Abstract (www.census.gov/compendia/statab). The standard reference source for numerical information on social, political, and economic aspects of American life. Compiled by the Census Bureau, its incredible array of facts are organized in table form.

World Factbook (www.cia.gov/library/publications/the-world-factbook). Published annually by the Central Intelligence Agency, the *World Factbook* is a rich compendium of information on every country in the world. Topics include people, government, economy, communication, transportation, and transnational issues.

FIGURE 7.3 Subject Screen from ipl2

The Special Case of Wikipedia

With more than 18 million articles, Wikipedia is the biggest encyclopedia in human history. Each month, some 400 million people access one or more of its articles, making it the seventh most visited Web site in the world.

But is Wikipedia a reliable source of information? Several years ago, it was not. Today, however, its reliability ratings are as high as those for print encyclopedias.[2] Major articles have been edited and refined over time to improve currency and accuracy. Articles still in development are flagged so readers know not to take their information at face value.

The most important thing to know about Wikipedia is that it can be a good place to *start* learning about a topic, but it is not a good place to end. Because of its convenience, Wikipedia is used by many people—including teachers and journalists—as a source of basic information. But experienced researchers know not to rely on it as their sole source of information.

One benefit of Wikipedia is that its major articles are followed by an extensive set of additional resources. Those resources include footnotes, a list of references, external links, and, in some cases, video and/or still images. If you take advantage of these resources, they will lead you to a vast amount of information beyond that in Wikipedia.

EVALUATING INTERNET DOCUMENTS

When you do research in a library, everything you find has been evaluated in one way or another before it gets to you. Books, magazines, and journals have editorial procedures to determine whether a given work should or should not be published. Once a work is published, it has to be approved by the acquisitions staff for inclusion in the library.

checklist

Evaluating Internet Documents

YES	NO	
☐	☐	1. Is the author of the document clearly identified?
☐	☐	2. If the author is identified, is he or she an expert on the topic?
☐	☐	3. If the author is not an expert, can his or her opinions be accepted as objective and unbiased?
☐	☐	4. If the author is not identified, can the sponsoring organization be determined?
☐	☐	5. Does the sponsoring organization have a reputation for expertise and objectivity?
☐	☐	6. Does the document include a copyright date, publication date, or date of last revision?
☐	☐	7. If a date is included, is the document recent enough to cite in my speech?

The Internet, of course, is a very different story. Anyone with a computer and access to the Internet can share his or her opinions with a discussion group, publish an electronic newsletter, or create a personal Web page. Never has the adage been more true than when applied to the Internet: "Don't believe everything you read."

In Chapter 8, we will discuss how to judge the soundness of supporting materials in general. Here we look at three criteria you can use to help distinguish between the jewels and the junk on the Internet.[3]

Authorship

Is the author of the Web document you are assessing clearly identified? If so, what are his or her qualifications? Is the author an expert on the topic? Can her or his data and opinions be accepted as objective and unbiased? Just as you should not cite a book or magazine article without identifying the author and his or her credentials, so you should not cite an electronic work in the absence of this information.

In a book or magazine article, information about the author is usually fairly easy to find. Too often, this is not true on the Internet. If you can't find information about the author in the document itself, look for a link to the author's homepage or to another site that explains the author's credentials.

Often you can learn about an author by typing his or her name in the Google search box. If the author is an accepted authority on the subject, there's a good chance Google will turn up information about his or her credentials, publications, and affiliation.

Sponsorship

Many Web documents are published by businesses, government agencies, public-interest groups, and the like rather than by individual authors. In such cases, you must judge whether the sponsoring organization is impartial enough to cite in your speech. Is the organization objective in its research and fair-minded in its statements? Is it economically unbiased with regard to the issue under discussion? Does it have a history of accuracy and nonpartisanship?

sponsoring organization

An organization that, in the absence of a clearly identified author, is responsible for the content of a document on the Internet.

Over the years, some organizations have developed strong reputations for their expertise and objectivity. Many of these are public-interest groups such as Consumers Union, Common Cause, and the American Cancer Society. Others include the National Archives, Centers for Disease Control, and similar government agencies. Private think tanks such as RAND, the Cato Institute, and the Brookings Institution often have definite political leanings but are usually well respected for the quality and substance of their research.

One way to gauge the credibility of an organization is to type its name into Google. If commentators have raised serious questions about an organization, those questions will usually surface in the first few pages of search results.

You can also check the *About* link on the organization's homepage. Often the resulting screen will identify the site's founders, purpose, or philosophy. If the homepage does not contain an *About* link, this may be a sign that the sponsoring organization is less than forthright and does not meet the necessary standards of objectivity and expertise.

What if you can't verify the credentials of an author or identify a credible sponsoring organization for an Internet document? The answer is easy: Don't use the document in your speech!

Using public speaking in your CAREER

After receiving your master's degree in education administration, you took a job at the state department of education. At the request of the governor, your section of the department has developed a new early childhood intervention program for children from impoverished households.

Now you have been asked to help publicize the program and to build support for it. You will be speaking to church groups, teachers' associations, family advocacy groups, and others with an interest in children's welfare. You want to prepare a talk that makes good use of statistics and expert testimony to demonstrate the value of early childhood education programs, especially for poor children.

As part of your research, you decide to look on the Web for supporting materials. List three reputable Web sites that provide useful statistics or testimony on the value of early childhood education. Explain why each Web site is reputable and list one statistic or expert quotation you obtain from each source.

Recency

One of the advantages of using the Internet for research is that it often has more recent information than you can find in print sources. But just because a document is on the Internet does not mean its facts and figures are up-to-the-minute.

The best way to determine the recency of an Internet document is to look for a copyright date, publication date, or date of last revision at the top or bottom of the document. If you are using a source located through a virtual library, you can usually be confident of its currency, as well as its objectivity and reliability. News, government, and academic sites also usually include the date on which a document was last updated.

Once you know the date of the document, you can determine whether it is current enough to use in your speech. This is especially important with regard to statistics, which you should never cite from an undated source, whether in print or on the Internet.

Of course, the date of a Web page is easy to change, so someone who wants to make information appear up-to-date can easily do so. But if you have already verified the credibility of the author and the sponsoring organization, you can usually assume that the date of the information is valid. If you can't find the date on which a Web document was created or last modified, search for another work whose recency you can verify.

Interviewing

Most people think of interviewing in terms of job interviews or conversations with celebrities. But there is another kind of interview—the research (or investigative) interview. Among journalists, it is a time-honored way to collect information. It is also an excellent way to gather materials for speeches.

When done well, interviewing (like many things) looks deceptively easy. In practice, it is a complex and demanding art. The principles of effective interviewing fall into three groups—what to do before the interview, what to do during the interview, and what to do after the interview.

To illustrate, we'll follow the entire interview process for a hypothetical speech about current issues in college athletics.

BEFORE THE INTERVIEW

research interview

An interview conducted to gather information for a speech.

The outcome of most interviews is decided by how well the interviewer prepares. Here are five steps you should take ahead of time to ensure a successful outcome.

Define the Purpose of the Interview

You have done Internet and library research about current issues in college athletics and have a good grasp of the major points of view. But you still have many questions about the situation at your school. You decide that the only way to get answers is to interview someone associated with the athletic program. In that decision you have begun to formulate a purpose for the interview.

Decide Whom to Interview

There are several possibilities, but you elect to start at the top—with the athletic director. That may seem a bit presumptuous, but in dealing with administrative organizations, it is usually best to go to the leaders first. They are likely to have a broad understanding of the issues. And if you need more specific information, they can get it for you or put you in touch with the right person.

Arrange the Interview

Because the athletic director is a busy person, you work out a plan for setting up the interview. Knowing that it's easier to brush off someone over e-mail or the telephone than in person, you go to the athletic office to request the interview. The athletic director agrees, and you set up the interview for three days later.

Decide Whether to Record the Interview

The major advantage of recording an interview is that it gives you an exact record you can check later for direct quotes and important facts. Even if you record the interview, however, you should still take notes by hand in case of technical malfunctions.

If the athletic director does not want the interview recorded, you will need to rely solely on your handwritten notes. Whatever you do, *never* record a conversation without the knowledge or consent of the person being interviewed. Not only is it unethical to do so, but the interviewee is bound to find out and you will only cause yourself trouble.

Prepare Your Questions

You now face the most important of your preinterview tasks—working out the questions you will ask. You should devise questions that are sensible, intelligent, and meaningful. Here are some types of questions to *avoid:*

- Questions you can answer without the interview. (How many sports does your school offer? What is the size of its athletic budget?) Queries like these just waste the subject's time and make you look foolish. Research this information before the interview.

- Leading questions. (Opinion polls show that most Americans believe athletics today have little relation to the academic purposes of a college education. You *do* think it's a problem, too, *don't you*?).
- Hostile, loaded questions. (I think it's disgraceful that many schools spend gobs of money on salaries for football and basketball coaches. Don't you think good teachers for all students are more important than coaches for a few athletes? What do you say to *that,* hmmm?)

You need not shy away from tough questions; just phrase them as neutrally as possible and save them until near the end of the interview. That way, if your interviewee becomes irritated or uncooperative, you'll still get most of the information you want.

Although some experienced journalists conduct interviews with only a few key-word notes on the areas to be covered, you want to be sure not to forget anything during the interview. So you arrange your questions in the order you want to ask them and take the list with you to the interview.

DURING THE INTERVIEW

Every interview is unique. Because the session will seldom go exactly as you plan, you need to be alert and flexible. Here are several steps you can take to make things proceed smoothly.

Dress Appropriately and Be on Time

The athletic director has a busy schedule and is doing you a favor by agreeing to an interview, so you show up on time. Since the interview is a special occasion, you dress appropriately. This is one way of confirming that you regard the interview as serious business.

Interviewing people with expertise on your speech topic can provide valuable information. When conducting an interview, be sure to listen attentively and to take accurate notes.

Repeat the Purpose of the Interview

The athletic director invites you into the office; you exchange a few introductory remarks. Now, before you plunge into your questions, you take a moment to restate the purpose of the interview. You are more likely to get clear, helpful answers if your subject knows why you are following a certain line of questioning.

Set Up the Recorder, if You Are Using One

If your subject has agreed to being recorded, keep one principle in mind: The recorder should be as casual and inconspicuous as possible. Most cell phones now offer applications for audio recording, giving you an easy way to capture the interview.

Keep the Interview on Track

Your goal in the interview is to get answers to the questions you have prepared. Suppose, however, that in answering one of your questions, the athletic director brings up an important point that is not covered on your list of questions. Rather than ignoring the point, you decide to pursue the new issue. You pose a couple questions about it, get helpful answers, then return to your prepared questions.

Throughout the interview, you pursue new leads when they appear, improvise follow-up questions when called for, then move on again in an orderly fashion. When the interview is over, you have answers to all your prepared questions—and a lot more.

Listen Carefully

During the interview, you listen attentively to the athletic director's answers. When you don't understand something, you ask for clarification. Chances are the athletic director will have been misquoted more than once in the press, so he or she will be happy to oblige.

Don't Overstay Your Welcome

Keep within the stipulated time period for the interview, unless your subject clearly wants to prolong the session. When the interview is over, you thank the athletic director for taking the time to talk with you.

AFTER THE INTERVIEW

Although the interview is over, the interviewing process is not. You must now review and transcribe your notes.

Review Your Notes as Soon as Possible

When you leave the athletic director's office, the interview is fresh in your mind. You know what the cryptic comments and scrawls in your notes mean. But as time passes, the details will become hazy. Don't let something like this true story happen to you:

> Years ago, a prominent woman—writer and diplomat—was being interviewed by a young reporter. Among other things, the reporter asked about hobbies and leisure activities. The woman replied that she enjoyed skeet shooting and raised Siamese cats. The reporter scribbled in her notes "shoots" and "cats"—but didn't

bother to put a comma or a dash between the words. The interview was published. And ever since, that prominent woman has been trying to live down the reputation that she "shoots cats."

In reviewing your notes, try to concentrate on two things—discovering the main points that emerged during the interview and pulling out specific information that might be useful in your speech.

Transcribe Your Notes

Once you settle on the most important ideas and information from the interview, you should transcribe that material so it is in the same format as the rest of your research notes (see pages 134–136). By putting all your research notes in a consistent format, you can arrange and rearrange them easily when you start to organize your speech.[4]

Tips for Doing Research

Few people regard doing research as one of life's great joys. But there are ways to make it less tedious and more productive. Here are four ways that are guaranteed to help.

START EARLY

The biggest mistake students make when faced with a research project is waiting too long to begin. The longer you wait, the more problems you will encounter. You may find that a vital book has been checked out of the library or that you no longer have time to arrange a crucial interview. No matter what kind of research you do, you can be sure of one thing: It will *always* take longer than you expect.

Starting early also gives you plenty of time to think about what you find. In researching, you will collect much more material than you will actually use. Preparing a speech is a little like constructing a jigsaw puzzle. Once you gather the pieces, you have to decide how they fit together. The more time you give yourself, the more likely you are to get the pieces to fit just right.

MAKE A PRELIMINARY BIBLIOGRAPHY

In your research, you will run across the titles of books, magazine articles, Internet documents, and so on that look as if they might contain helpful information about your speech topic. Enter *each* item you find in your preliminary bibliography, even though you don't know whether you will use it in your speech. As a result, you may have 15 or 20 works in your preliminary bibliography. But remember that you have not yet examined all those works. Of the 15 or 20 preliminary sources, only 7 or 8 are likely to be of much use. Those final sources will be listed on the bibliography you turn in with your speech outline (see Chapter 11, page 208).

preliminary bibliography

A list compiled early in the research process of works that look as if they might contain helpful information about a speech topic.

There are two major formats for citing documents in a bibliography. One comes from the Modern Language Association (MLA), the other from the

American Psychological Association (APA). Both are widely used by communication scholars; ask your instructor which he or she prefers.

Whichever format you adopt, make sure your bibliography is clear, accurate, and consistent. Figure 7.4 (page 135) lists sample MLA and APA citations for 10 kinds of sources that are cited most frequently in student speeches.

TAKE NOTES EFFICIENTLY

Asia Marshall started her speech preparation with the best of intentions. She was excited about her topic, "Great Women of Jazz," and she started research on the Internet the same day the assignment was announced. She found several interesting sources and took some notes about them. That evening, she checked out a fascinating book about Billie Holiday and read it straight through. She didn't bother taking notes because she was sure she'd remember it all. The next day, she looked through the *Encyclopedia of Jazz* and jotted a few notes on the back of her syllabus.

Then Asia remembered that she had a test in another class. Somewhat panicked, she put aside her speech research to study. When she got back to the speech, the deadline was only four days away. She dug out her notes, but what did they mean? One said, "Medford—*important!!!*" But who or what was Medford? Asia had thought she'd remember all about the Billie Holiday book, but without notes, it was mostly a blur by now. With a sense of doom, she faced up to the fact that she would have to start over—and finish in four days.

Sound familiar? This has happened to almost everyone at least once. But once is enough. There's a better way to take research notes. Here is a method that has worked well for many students:

Take Plenty of Notes

Few things are more aggravating than trying to recall some bit of information you ran across in your research but neglected to record. The moral of Asia Marshall's story is clear: If there is even an outside chance that you may need a piece of information, make a note of it. This will take a little extra time in the short run, but in the long run it can save you much grief.

Record Notes in a Consistent Format

You should use the same format for all your research notes, whether they come from Internet sources, library documents, or personal interviews. In each case, record the note, the source of the note, and a heading indicating the subject of the note (see Figure 7.5 on page 136).

The importance of the subject heading cannot be overemphasized. It is the first step to more efficient note taking. By telling you at a glance what each note is about, it will simplify the task of organizing your notes when you start to compose the speech. Once you start using subject headings, you'll see how helpful they can be.

Make a Separate Entry for Each Note

Many students try to record all the information from one source on a single note. This is not an effective procedure because it makes your notes almost

FIGURE 7.4 Sample Bibliography Formats

Book: Single author.	**MLA:**	Chua, Amy. *Battle Hymn of the Tiger Mother*. New York: Penguin, 2011. Print.
	APA:	Chua, A. (2011). *Battle hymn of the tiger mother.* New York, NY: Penguin.
Signed magazine article.	**MLA:**	Adler, Jerry. "The Growing Menace from Superweeds." *Scientific American* May 2011: 74–79. Print.
	APA:	Adler, J. (2011, May). The growing menace from superweeds. *Scientific American, 304*(5), 74–79.
Signed newspaper article.	**MLA:**	Tucker, Neely. "Your Novel Got Rejected? Join the E-Book Gold Rush!" *Washington Post* 8 May 2011: E1+. Print.
	APA:	Tucker, N. (2011, May 8). Your novel got rejected? Join the e-book gold rush! *The Washington Post,* pp. E1, E4.
Signed article in reference work.	**MLA:**	Emanuel, Kerry A. "Hurricanes." *Encyclopedia of Climate and Weather*. Ed. Stephen H. Schneider, Michael Mastrandrea, and Terry L. Root. 2nd ed. New York: Oxford University Press, 2011. Print.
	APA:	Emanuel, K. (2011). Hurricanes. In S. H. Schneider, M. Mastrandrea, & T. L. Root (Eds.), *Encyclopedia of climate and weather* 2nd ed., (pp. 138–141). New York, NY: Oxford University Press.
Personal interview.	**MLA:**	Hernandez, Claudia. Personal interview. 5 Oct. 2011.
	APA:	C. Hernandez (personal communication, October 5, 2011).
Speech or lecture.	**MLA:**	Chung, Cindy. "The Asian Diaspora." Asian American Studies 160: Asian American History. University of Wisconsin. 16 Sept. 2011. Lecture.
	APA:	Chung, C. (2011, September). *The Asian diaspora*. Lecture presented in Asian American Studies 160: Asian American History. University of Wisconsin.
Television program.	**MLA:**	"Lady Gaga and the Art of Fame." Narr. Anderson Cooper. *Sixty Minutes.* CBS. WUSA, Washington, 13 Feb. 2011. Television.
	APA:	Cooper, A. (Narrator). (2011). Lady Gaga and the art of fame [Television newsmagazine episode segment]. In J. Hamlin (Producer), *Sixty Minutes.* New York, NY: CBS News.
Online government publication.	**MLA:**	United States. Dept. of Labor. Bureau of Labor Statistics. "Women at Work." Mar. 2011. *BLS Spotlight on Statistics.* Web. 9 May 2011.
	APA:	U.S. Department of Labor, Bureau of Labor Statistics. (2011). Women at work. In *BLS spotlight on statistics*. Retrieved from http://www.bls.gov/spotlight/2011/women
Online newspaper article.	**MLA:**	Bowles, Scott. "Can 3-D Technology Save the Moviemaking Business?" *USA Today.* USA Today, 28 Mar. 2011. Web. 3 Apr. 2011.
	APA:	Bowles, S. (2011, March 28). Can 3-D technology save the moviemaking business? *USA Today*. Retrieved from http://www.usatoday.com
Online magazine article.	**MLA:**	Conley, Dalton. "Wired for Distraction: Kids and Social Media." *Time.* Time and Cable News Network, 19 Mar. 2011. Web. 3 May 2011.
	APA:	Conley, D. (2011, March 19). Wired for distraction: Kids and social media. *Time, 177*(7). Retrieved from http://www.time.com

FIGURE 7.5 Sample Research Note

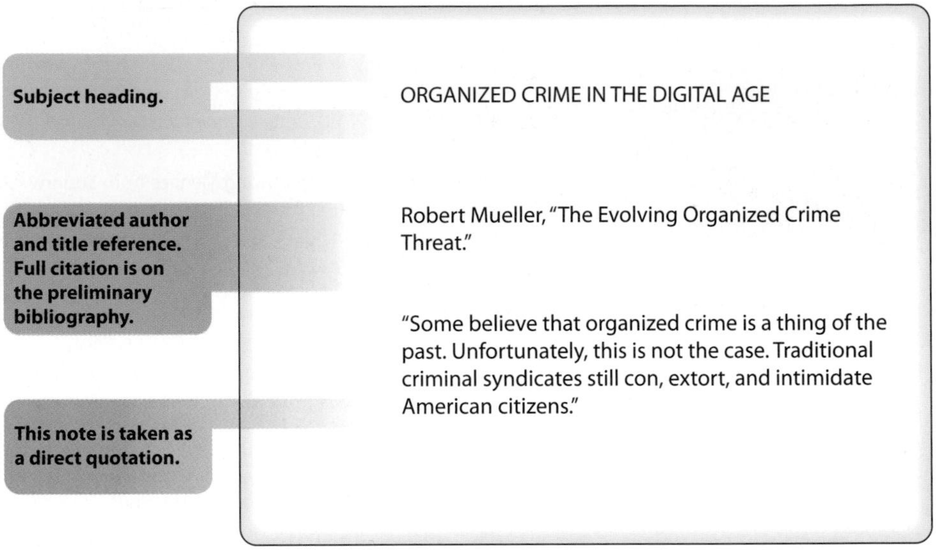

impossible to review and organize. A better approach is to make a separate note for *each* quotation or piece of information you record. Although you may end up with several notes from the same document, you will find that this approach allows you to keep better track of your research.

Distinguish Among Direct Quotations, Paraphrases, and Your Own Ideas

As we saw in Chapter 2, it's easy to plagiarize accidentally by not taking careful research notes. As you do research for your speeches, be sure to use quotation marks whenever you copy the exact words of a source. If you paraphrase, rather than quote verbatim, don't forget to include the source when you record the note.

By keeping track of quotations and paraphrases, you will be able to separate your own words and ideas from those of other people. This will help you avoid the trap of inadvertent plagiarism when you put your speech together.

THINK ABOUT YOUR MATERIALS AS YOU RESEARCH

Students often approach research as a mechanical routine that simply involves gathering the materials to be used in a speech or paper. But when done properly, research can be extremely creative.

If you *think about* what you are finding in your research, you will see your topic just a little bit differently with each note you take. You will find new relationships, develop new questions, explore new angles. You will, in short, begin to write the speech in your head even as you do the research. As you learn more about the topic, you will formulate a central idea, begin to sketch out main points and supporting points, experiment with ways of

To take research notes efficiently, record them in a consistent format; make a separate entry for each note; and distinguish among direct quotations, paraphrases, and your own ideas.

organizing your thoughts. You may even change your point of view, as did this student:

Francesca Lopez began her speech preparation with this central idea in mind: "Wild animals make more interesting pets than dogs and cats." She went about her research conscientiously, spending many hours online and in the library. In the process, she came upon some disturbing information about the capture of wild animals. She read that young chimpanzees and other apes were literally snatched out of their mothers' arms, and that the mothers were afterward heard to cry almost like humans. Back in her room that night, Francesca couldn't get her mind off the baby chimpanzees.

The next day, Francesca found some more disturbing material. One source told about the extraordinarily high death rate of wild animals during shipment to the United States. Again, that night Francesca brooded about the young animals dying of fear and cold in the cargo holds of airplanes.

By the time she finished her research, Francesca's central idea was completely different. When she spoke, her central idea was "The importation of wild animals for use as pets is inhumane."

This is an example of creative research—and of critical thinking. Francesca kept her mind open, read everything she could find about her topic, and thought seriously about what she found. Because of this thoughtful approach, she changed her mind.[5]

Your own speech preparation may not cause you to reverse your position, but it should give you new insights into your topic. If you approach research in this way, you may find that the time you spend researching is the most productive of all the time you devote to preparing your speech.

Summary

There are many resources you can use when gathering information for a speech. If you have personal experience or above-average knowledge about a topic, you can use yourself as a resource. Most of the time, however, you will need outside information, which you can get in the library, on the Internet, or by interviewing people with specialized information.

Finding what you need in the library is largely a matter of knowing how to search for information. The catalogue lists all the books, periodicals, and other resources owned by the library. Databases help you find articles in magazines, newspapers, and journals. The reference section includes encyclopedias, yearbooks, biographical aids, and books of quotations. If you have trouble finding something, don't hesitate to ask a librarian.

When looking for information online, you need a search strategy that will help you find exactly what you need. Given the lack of editorial review for most documents on the Web, it is especially important to evaluate the authorship, sponsoring organization, and recency of the research materials you find there.

You can also get information by conducting a personal interview. Before the interview, you should define its purpose, decide whom you are going to interview, and prepare the interview questions. Once the interview begins, be sure to listen attentively and to take accurate notes. Afterward, review and transcribe your notes as soon as possible.

No matter what sources you draw upon in gathering information, your research will be more effective if you start early and make a preliminary bibliography to keep track of all the books, articles, and Internet documents that look as if they might be helpful. By learning to take research notes effectively, you will save yourself time and energy every step of the way. And if you think about your materials as you research, you may find that gathering materials is the most creative part of your speech preparation.

Key Terms

catalogue *(121)*
call number *(121)*
reference work *(121)*
newspaper and periodical database *(122)*
abstract *(123)*
academic database *(123)*
virtual library *(126)*
sponsoring organization *(128)*
research interview *(130)*
preliminary bibliography *(133)*

Review Questions

After reading this chapter, you should be able to answer the following questions:

1. Why is it important to draw on your own knowledge and experience in gathering materials for your speeches?
2. What are five resources for finding what you need in the library?

3. What are three criteria for evaluating the soundness of research materials that you find on the Internet?
4. What are the three stages of a research interview? What should you do in each stage to help ensure a successful interview?
5. Why is it important to start your speech research early?
6. What is a preliminary bibliography? Why is it helpful to you in researching a speech?
7. What four things should you do to take research notes efficiently?

connect™

For further review, go to the LearnSmart study module for this chapter.

Exercises for Critical Thinking

1. Using one of the periodical and newspaper databases discussed on pages 122–123, find three magazine or newspaper articles on the topic of your next speech. Prepare a preliminary bibliography entry for each article. Read the full text of the articles and assess their value for your speech.
2. Using Google or another search engine, find three high-quality documents on the topic of your next speech. Prepare a preliminary bibliography entry for each document. Read the full text of the documents and assess them in light of the criteria for evaluating Internet documents discussed on pages 127–129.
3. Plan to conduct an interview for one of your classroom speeches. Be sure to follow the guidelines presented in this chapter for effective interviewing. Afterward, evaluate the interview. Did you prepare for it adequately? Did you get the information you needed? What would you do differently if you could conduct the interview again?

AFFORDABLE CA

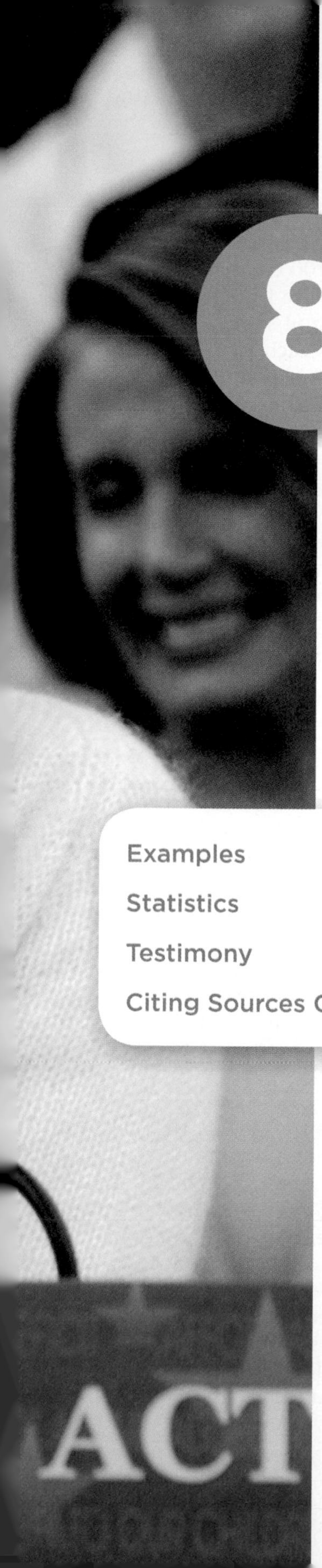

8

Supporting Your Ideas

- Examples
- Statistics
- Testimony
- Citing Sources Orally

An avid tea drinker, Laura Kramer decided to give her first classroom speech on the health benefits of tea. Part of her speech ran like this:

"If your family medical history shows that you are likely to develop heart disease, high cholesterol, circulatory problems, or Parkinson's disease, you need to be drinking more tea. Black tea and green tea have been proven to reduce the risk of many serious health problems. I've been drinking tea for years, and I am extremely healthy. If you start drinking tea, you can be healthy too."

After the speech, Laura's classmates were polite but skeptical. As one remarked, "Laura made some interesting points, but she's no doctor. I'd be more convinced if she had provided medical evidence to back up her opinion."

Good speeches are not composed of hot air and generalizations. They need strong supporting materials to bolster the speaker's point of view. In Laura's case, there is evidence that tea is helpful in treating some ailments, but most of the claims about its health benefits have yet to be verified by research. So Laura's listeners were right to be skeptical about her vague, unsupported generalizations.

The problem with generalizations is that they don't answer the three questions listeners always ask of a speaker: "What do you mean?" "Why should I believe you?" "So what?" Consider the following statements:

General	Less General	Specific
There are lots of community colleges in the United States.	Community colleges enroll a large number of students and play a vital role in American higher education.	According to the Department of Education, there are more than 1,100 community colleges in the United States. They enroll some 12 million students each year, which is 44 percent of all U.S. undergraduates.

Which statement do you find most interesting? Most convincing? Chances are you prefer that in the right-hand column. It is sharp and specific, clear and credible—just what a speech needs to come alive.

supporting materials

The materials used to support a speaker's ideas. The three major kinds of supporting materials are examples, statistics, and testimony.

The skillful use of supporting materials often makes the difference between a poor speech and a good one. In Chapters 15 and 17, we will look at special uses of supporting materials in informative and persuasive speeches. In this chapter, we focus on the basic kinds of supporting materials—examples, statistics, and testimony—and on general principles for using them effectively and responsibly.

Examples

The attack came after daybreak. The *Delta Ranger,* a cargo ship carrying bauxite, was steaming through the ink-blue Indian Ocean about 200 miles off Somalia's coast. A crewman on the bridge spied two speedboats zooming straight at the port side of his vessel. Moments later, bullets tore into the bridge, and vapor trails from rocket-propelled grenades streaked across the bow—pirates.

These lines are from the opening of an article in *Smithsonian* magazine about modern-day pirates that prey on international shipping. It illustrates a device well known to magazine writers—and public speakers: Get the audience involved.

example

A specific case used to illustrate or represent a group of people, ideas, conditions, experiences, or the like.

See how skillfully this example accomplishes the goal. It gives us a specific incident to focus on (the attack on the *Delta Ranger*). It sets the stage with details of time, place, color, and action. We can almost see ourselves on the bridge of the *Delta Ranger,* watching the pirates' speedboats and hearing their bullets tear into the ship. We would not be nearly as involved if the article had merely said, "Pirates are a serious menace to international shipping."

Research has shown that vivid, concrete examples have a strong impact on listeners' beliefs and actions.[1] Without examples, ideas often seem vague, impersonal, and lifeless. With examples, ideas become specific, personal, and lively. This is nowhere better illustrated than in the Bible and the Koran, both of which use all manner of stories, parables, and anecdotes to make abstract principles clear and compelling. There are several kinds of examples you may want to try in your speeches.

BRIEF EXAMPLES

Brief examples—also called specific instances—may be referred to in passing to illustrate a point. The following excerpt uses a brief example to illustrate the miraculous nature of recent advances in creating artificial limbs for accident victims:

brief example

A specific case referred to in passing to illustrate a point.

Changes in technology have made it possible for doctors to work wonders that once seemed impossible. Roger Charter, for example, lost both his feet when they were crushed in a truck accident. Now he has new feet—made of a springy plastic alloy that duplicates a normal arch. Not only can Roger walk normally, but he can run and play sports again!

Another way to use brief examples is to pile them one upon the other until you create the desired impression. Here is how one speaker used this technique to reinforce the point that Mexican Americans have made many valuable contributions to U.S. life:

Many of us are familiar with prominent Chicanos and Chicanas such as actress Jessica Alba, boxer Oscar De La Hoya, and guitarist Carlos Santana. But you may be less familiar with other Americans of Mexican origin who have made important contributions to U.S. society. Nancy Lopez played a crucial role in popularizing women's professional golf and won 48 tour championships. Dr. Ellen Ochoa is a former astronaut who logged more than 480 hours in space and invented several optical methods that greatly aid space exploration. Dr. Mario Molina won the 1995 Nobel Prize in Chemistry for his research on the formation and decomposition of the ozone layer.

connect™

View this excerpt from "Living in America" in the online Media Library for this chapter (Video 8.1).

EXTENDED EXAMPLES

Extended examples are often called narratives, illustrations, or anecdotes. By telling a story vividly and dramatically, they pull listeners into the speech. Here is such an example, from a speech by Sun Yan, a student at Fudan University in Shanghai, China. Participating in China's national English-language speech competition, Sun Yan used an extended example to illustrate the spirit of the Olympic Games:

extended example

A story, narrative, or anecdote developed at some length to illustrate a point.

In the history of the Olympic Games, there have been many shining stars. Among them was a European girl. With the lapse of time, her name has faded from memory, yet her unbending spirit shall never perish. It was she who highlighted the Olympic Creed.

In the lead though she had been, she stumbled near the terminus and her leg was injured. Competitors passed her from behind in succession until finally only her weak and lonely figure remained on the track. Doctors came and offered to take her away. Yet she refused. With the only strength left in her, she managed to get up and shuffled feebly to the endpoint with drops of blood along her trail.

But cheers broke out. Though she failed in the race, the girl won applause from people all over the world. It was she who elucidated the Olympic creed of participation. It was she who instilled perseverance in our minds.[2]

connect™

View this excerpt from "The Olympic Spirit" in the online Media Library for this chapter (Video 8.2).

This long example captures vividly the courage of the Olympic runner and her personification of the Olympic spirit. The speaker could merely have said,

"Olympic athletes often display great fortitude," but the story makes the point far more poignantly.

HYPOTHETICAL EXAMPLES

hypothetical example

An example that describes an imaginary or fictitious situation.

All the examples presented up to now have been factual; the incidents they refer to really happened. Sometimes, however, speakers will use a hypothetical example—one that describes an imaginary situation. Usually such examples are brief stories that relate a general principle.

Here is how one student used a hypothetical example to illustrate the use of honor codes to reduce cheating:

> Imagine this: You're taking your psychology exam when you notice the student sitting next to you is staring at your answers. You also see his open notebook under his desk. You feel your cheeks redden as you become angry that he may get a high score by cheating while you've worked hard to earn your grade. And you feel helpless because you think telling the professor will do nothing.
>
> But now imagine that you attend a school with an honors system. At the beginning of each exam, you sign a statement that says you will not cheat and that you accept the responsibility to report cheating. After the professor hands out the exam, she leaves the room. In this case, you have the power and the duty to report cheaters rather than feel robbed by them.
>
> Such a system has worked elsewhere and it can work at our school. Professor Donald McCabe, president of the Center for Academic Integrity, has surveyed more than 20,000 students at 70 colleges throughout the country, and his research shows that the level of cheating is significantly lower at schools with honor codes than at schools without them.

connect™

View this excerpt from "College Cheating: A National Epidemic" in the online Media Library for this chapter (Video 8.3).

This hypothetical example is especially effective. The speaker creates a realistic scenario, relates it directly to her listeners, and gets them involved in the speech. In addition, she uses figures from the president of the Center for Academic Integrity to show that honor codes help reduce the incidence of cheating on college campuses. Whenever you use a hypothetical example, it is a good idea to follow it with statistics or testimony to show that the example is not far-fetched.

TIPS FOR USING EXAMPLES

Use Examples to Clarify Your Ideas

You probably use clarifying examples all the time in everyday conversation. If you were explaining to a friend about different body types, you might say, "Look at Professor Shankar. He's a typical ectomorph—tall, thin, and bony." Examples are an excellent way to clarify unfamiliar or complex ideas. They put abstract ideas into concrete terms that listeners can easily understand.

This principle works exceptionally well in speeches. Suppose you are talking about suspension bridges. You could give a technical description:

> The suspension bridge has a roadway suspended by vertical cables attached to two or more main cables. The main cables are hung on two towers and have their ends anchored in concrete or bedrock.

If your audience were made up of people familiar with structural systems, they might be able to visualize what a suspension bridge looks like. But

No matter what the occasion, personal examples are an excellent way to clarify ideas and to build audience interest. To be most effective, they should be delivered sincerely and with strong eye contact.

for listeners lacking this background, you might want to add a simple example:

> Two well-known suspension bridges are the Golden Gate Bridge in San Francisco and the Brooklyn Bridge in New York.

Because almost everyone has at least seen a picture of the Golden Gate Bridge or the Brooklyn Bridge, using them as examples clarifies your meaning quickly and effectively.

Use Examples to Reinforce Your Ideas

In a speech titled "The Dangers of Cell Phones," one student dealt with the long-term health risks of cell phone use. She cited figures from the World Health Organization noting that people who use a cell phone for more than 10 years double their risk of developing brain tumors. She also discussed other problems associated with long-term exposure to cell phone radiation, including headaches, dizziness, circulatory problems, nausea, and cancer.

To reinforce her ideas, the speaker cited the example of Alan Marks, a father of three who developed a golf-ball-sized tumor in his brain from talking on his cell phone an hour a day for 23 years. She talked of Marks's health problems and of how he would have used his speakerphone or headset if he had known the perils of holding his phone next to his ear day after day, year after year.

connect

View this portion of "The Dangers of Cell Phones" in the online Media Library for this chapter (Video 8.4).

This example was very effective. It put the medical facts about the dangers of cell phones in vivid, human terms that everyone could understand. When you use such an example, make sure it is representative—that it does not deal with rare or exceptional cases. Your listeners are likely to feel betrayed if they suspect you have chosen an atypical example to prove a general point.

Use Examples to Personalize Your Ideas

People are interested in people. As social psychologist Elliot Aronson explains, "Most people are more deeply influenced by one clear, vivid, personal example than by an abundance of statistical data."[3] Whenever you talk to a general audience (such as your speech class), you can include examples that will add human interest to your speech. So far in this section, we have seen a number of such examples—the heroic Olympic runner, accident victim Roger Charter, and so on. The abstract becomes more meaningful when applied to a person. Which of the following would you be more likely to respond to?

> There are many hungry families in our community who could benefit from food donations.

Or:

> Let me tell you about Arturo. Arturo is four years old. He has big brown eyes and a mop of black hair and an empty belly. In all his four years on this earth, Arturo has never once enjoyed three square meals in a single day.

Try using examples with human interest in your speeches. You will soon discover why accomplished speakers consider them "the very life of the speech."[4]

Make Your Examples Vivid and Richly Textured

The richly textured example supplies everyday details that bring the example to life. Recall the example on page 143 of the Olympic runner. The speaker provided us with many details about the runner's bravery in the face of adverse conditions. The runner stumbles and injures her leg near the end of the race. She is passed by other competitors until she alone is left on the track. Doctors offer to help, but she refuses their assistance and shuffles to the finish line with drops of blood along her trail.

How much less compelling the example would have been if the speaker had merely said:

> One Olympic runner courageously completed her race despite being injured and exhausted.

Instead, the details let us *see* the runner as she battles through her pain and misfortune. She is much more likely to stay in our minds than a "brave runner who completed her race." The more vivid your examples, the more impact they are likely to have on your audience.

Practice Delivery to Enhance Your Extended Examples

An extended example is just like a story or narrative. Its impact depends as much on delivery as on content. Many students have discovered this the hard way. After spending much time and energy developing a splendid example, they have seen it fall flat because they did not make it vivid and gripping for listeners.

Look again at the speaker in Video 8.2. Notice how she uses her voice to increase the impact of her story about the Olympic runner. Like that speaker, you should think of yourself as a storyteller. Don't rush through your examples as though you were reading the newspaper. Use your voice to get listeners involved. Speak faster here to create a sense of action, slower there to

checklist

Using Examples

YES	NO	
☐	☐	1. Do I use examples to clarify my ideas?
☐	☐	2. Do I use examples to reinforce my ideas?
☐	☐	3. Do I use examples to personalize my ideas?
☐	☐	4. Are my examples representative of what they are supposed to illustrate or prove?
☐	☐	5. Do I reinforce my examples with statistics or testimony?
☐	☐	6. Are my extended examples vivid and richly textured?
☐	☐	7. Have I practiced the delivery of my extended examples to give them dramatic effect?

build suspense. Raise your voice in some places; lower it in others. Pause occasionally for dramatic effect.

Most important, maintain eye contact with your audience. The easiest way to ruin a fine example is to read it from your notes. As you practice the speech, "talk through" your extended examples without relying on your notes. By the day of your speech, you should be able to deliver your extended examples as naturally as if you were telling a story to a group of friends.

Statistics

We live in an age of statistics. Day in and day out we are bombarded with a staggering array of numbers: Keith Urban has sold more than 13 million albums. Drowsiness is a factor in 17 percent of U.S. traffic fatalities. Americans spend $60 billion a year on lottery tickets. The BP oil spill released more than 200 million gallons of oil into the Gulf of Mexico.

What do all these numbers mean? Most of us would be hard-pressed to say. Yet we feel more secure in our knowledge when we can express it numerically. According to Lord Kelvin, the 19th-century physicist, "When you can measure what you are speaking about, and express it in numbers, you know something about it. But when you cannot measure it, when you cannot express it in numbers, your knowledge is . . . meager and unsatisfactory." It is this widely shared belief that makes statistics, when used properly, such an effective way to clarify and support ideas.[5]

statistics

Numerical data.

Like brief examples, statistics are often cited in passing to clarify or strengthen a speaker's points. The following examples show how two students used statistics in their speeches:

To document the number of Chinese students in U.S. colleges and universities: "According to the Institute of International Education, nearly 130,000 Chinese students attended school in the United States last year—a 30 percent increase from the previous year."

To illustrate the dramatic increase in pay for professional athletes: "ESPN reports that just 20 years ago, the highest paid baseball player made $5 million. Today, the highest paid player makes more than $30 million a year."

Statistics can also be used in combination to show the magnitude or seriousness of an issue. We find a good instance of this technique in a student presentation about America's crowded roadways. To demonstrate his point that traffic congestion wastes massive amounts of time and money, the speaker cited the following figures:

connect™

View this excerpt from "Stuck in Traffic" in the online Media Library for this chapter (Video 8.5).

According to the Urban Mobility Report from Texas A&M University, Americans collectively spend 4.2 billion hours stuck in traffic each year. All told, traffic congestion results in more than $87 billion in wasted fuel and lost productivity. That number breaks down to about $750 per traveler each year. Clearly, we are wasting far too much time and money on traffic gridlock.

This is a well-supported argument. But what if the speaker had merely said:

Traffic jams are very costly for the United States.

This statement is neither as clear nor as convincing as the one containing statistics. Of course, the audience didn't remember all the numbers, but the purpose of presenting a series of figures is to create an *overall* impact on listeners. What the audience did recall is that an impressive array of statistics supported the speaker's position.

UNDERSTANDING STATISTICS

In his classic book *How to Lie with Statistics,* Darrell Huff exploded the notion that numbers don't lie. Strictly speaking, they don't. But they can be easily manipulated and distorted. For example, which of the following statements is true?

a. Enriched white bread is more nutritious than whole-wheat bread because it contains as much or more protein, calcium, niacin, thiamine, and riboflavin.

b. Whole-wheat bread is more nutritious than white bread because it contains seven times the amount of fiber, plus more iron, phosphorus, and potassium.

As you might expect, *both* statements are true. And you might hear either one of them, depending on who is trying to sell you the bread.

One can play with statistics in all kinds of areas. Which of these statements is true?

a. The cheetah, clocked at 70 miles per hour, is the fastest animal in the world.

b. The pronghorn antelope, clocked at 61 miles per hour, is the fastest animal in the world.

The cheetah, right? Not necessarily. The cheetah can go faster, but only for short sprints. The antelope can maintain its high speed over a much greater distance. So which is faster? It depends on what you're measuring. Put in

A speech that is supported by statistics is usually more persuasive than an undocumented presentation. Here California governor Jerry Brown uses economic data when discussing plans to reduce the state's budget deficit.

terms of human races, the cheetah would win the hundred-yard dash, but the antelope would win the marathon.

When you are dealing with money, statistics become even trickier. Consider the following facts:

a. In 1940, President Franklin D. Roosevelt earned a salary of $75,000.

b. In 1972, President Richard Nixon earned a salary of $200,000.

c. In 2010, President Barack Obama earned a salary of $400,000.

Which president was paid the most money? In purely mathematical terms, Obama is the highest earner. But a dollar today does not buy as much as it did in 1940, when Franklin Roosevelt was president. One measure of the inflation rate is the Consumer Price Index, which lets us gauge the value of the dollar in any given year against its purchasing power in 1972. If we apply the Consumer Price Index to the three presidents' salaries, we can see how much each earned in 1972 dollars:

a. In 1940, President Franklin D. Roosevelt earned a salary of $192,000.

b. In 1972, President Richard Nixon earned a salary of $200,000.

c. In 2010, President Barack Obama earned a salary of $78,000.

In other words, although Obama has the highest salary, the value of his $400,000 is less than half the value of Roosevelt's $75,000.

The point is that there is usually more to statistics than meets the eye.[6] When you track down statistics for your speeches, be sure to evaluate them in light of the following questions.

Are the Statistics Representative?

Say that on your way to class you choose ten students at random and ask them whether they favor or oppose banning recreational vehicles on public lands. Say also that six approve of such a ban and four do not. Would you then be accurate in claiming that 60 percent of the students on your campus favor banning recreational vehicles from public lands?

Of course not. Ten students is not a big enough sample. But even if it were, other problems would arise. Do the ten students interviewed accurately reflect your school's proportion of freshmen, sophomores, juniors, and seniors? Do they mirror the proportion of male and female students? Are the various majors accurately represented? What about part-time and full-time students? Students of different cultural and religious backgrounds?

In short, make sure your statistics are representative of what they claim to measure.

Are Statistical Measures Used Correctly?

Here are two groups of numbers:

Group A	Group B
7,500	5,400
6,300	5,400
5,000	5,000
4,400	2,300
4,400	1,700

mean

The average value of a group of numbers.

median

The middle number in a group of numbers arranged from highest to lowest.

mode

The number that occurs most frequently in a group of numbers.

Let us apply to each group three basic statistical measures—the mean, the median, and the mode.

The *mean*—popularly called the average—is determined by summing all the items in a group and dividing by the number of items. The mean for group A is 5,520. For group B it is 3,960.

The *median* is the middle figure in a group once the figures are put in order from highest to lowest. The median for both group A and group B is exactly the same—5,000.

The *mode* is the number that occurs most frequently in a group of numbers. The mode for group A is 4,400. For group B it is 5,400.

Notice the results:

	Group A	Group B
Mean	5,520	3,960
Median	5,000	5,000
Mode	4,400	5,400

All these measures have the same goal—to indicate what is typical or characteristic of a certain group of numbers. Yet see how different the results are, depending on which measure you use.

The differences among the various measures can be striking. For instance, the *mean* salary of local TV news anchorpersons is $75,100 a year. But the mean is inflated by the huge salaries (up to $1 million a year) paid to a few star anchors in media centers such as New York, Los Angeles, and Chicago. In contrast, the *median* salary of local news anchors is $59,000—not a sum to scoff at, but still $16,100 less than the mean.[7]

How might a speaker use these different measures? The owner of a television station would probably cite the *mean* ($75,100) to show that local news anchors are handsomely compensated for their work. An organization of news anchors might emphasize the *median* ($59,000) to demonstrate that salaries are not nearly as high as the station owner makes them out to be. Both speakers would be telling the truth, but neither would be completely honest unless she or he made clear the meaning of the statistics.

Are the Statistics from a Reliable Source?

Which is the more reliable estimate of the environmental dangers of toxic waste in a landfill—one from the U.S. Environmental Protection Agency or one compiled by the company that owns the landfill? Easy—the estimate by the EPA, which does not have a vested interest in what the figures look like. What about nutritional ratings for fast foods offered by Consumers Union (a highly respected nonprofit organization) or by Burger King? That's easy too—Consumers Union.

But now things get tougher. What about the competing statistics offered by groups for and against Medicare reform? Or the conflicting numbers tossed out by a governor and the public employee unions protesting against him? In these cases, the answer is not so clear, since both sides would present the facts according to their own partisan motives.

As a speaker, you must be aware of possible bias in the use of numbers. Since statistics can be interpreted so many ways and put to so many uses, you should seek figures gathered by objective, nonpartisan sources.

TIPS FOR USING STATISTICS

Use Statistics to Quantify Your Ideas

The main value of statistics is to give your ideas numerical precision. This can be especially important when you are trying to document the existence of a problem. Examples can bring the problem alive and dramatize it in personal terms, but your listeners may still wonder how many people the problem actually affects. In such a situation, you should turn to statistics. Research has shown that the impact of examples is enhanced when they are combined with statistics that show the examples to be typical.[8]

Suppose you are talking about the need for college students to avoid credit-card debt. Part of your speech deals with the large amount of debt the typical college student faces by the time he or she graduates. You give an example, you personalize the subject, you provide many details, as follows:

> Travis Blake left college a changed person. Not only had he earned his degree, but he had racked up almost $4,000 in credit-card debt. Travis was sure he would be able to pay off his debt once he got a full-time job. But when he received his first paycheck, he found that after paying his taxes and living expenses, he could make only the minimum monthly payment on his credit cards. Rather than getting rid of his debt, he would be paying it off for years.

Confronted with this example, a listener might think, "Poor Travis. But I'm not going to end up in his spot because I don't plan to leave college with a lot of credit-card debt." Anticipating just such a response, a sharp speaker would include figures to quantify the extent of credit-card debt among college students in general:

> According to an article last month in *USA Today,* the average credit-card debt of a graduating college student is $3,100, and new graduates spend almost 25 percent of their income on debt payments. If someone makes only the minimum monthly payment on his or her credit cards—which is what most people do—they will rack up more than $4,073 in interest charges alone before paying off their original $3,100 debt. Perhaps this explains why in the past few years

the number of people under 25 filing for bankruptcy has increased by more than 50 percent.

Now the audience is much more likely to agree that they need to keep a closer eye on their credit-card balance.

Use Statistics Sparingly

As helpful as statistics can be, nothing puts an audience to sleep faster than a speech cluttered with numbers from beginning to end. Insert statistics only when they are needed, and then make sure they are easy to grasp. Even the most attentive listener would have trouble sorting out this barrage of figures:

> According to the *World Factbook,* life expectancy in the United States ranks 50th in the world. The United States ranks 47th in the world in infant mortality. France ranks 9th. Americans spend more each year on health care than any other nation—$2.5 trillion dollars, or 17.6 percent of gross domestic product—yet the World Health Organization ranks the U.S. health care system 37th in overall performance among member nations.

Instead of drowning your audience in a sea of statistics, use only those that are most important. For example:

> According to the *World Factbook,* the United States has one of the lowest life expectancies among industrialized nations—plus one of the highest rates of infant mortality. Even though we spend more on health care than any other nation, the World Health Organization ranks 36 nations ahead of us on the overall performance of our health care system.

This second statement makes the same point as the first statement, but now the ideas are not lost in a torrent of numbers.

Identify the Sources of Your Statistics

As we have seen, figures are easy to manipulate. This is why careful listeners keep an ear out for the sources of a speaker's statistics. One student learned this by experience. In a speech titled "Tax Reform: Fact Versus Fiction," he claimed that the wealthiest 1 percent of U.S. taxpayers pay 38 percent of federal income taxes, even though they account for only 20 percent of all earned income. He also noted that the wealthiest 25 percent of Americans pay 86 percent of federal income taxes. These are startling statistics. But because the student did not say where he got them, his classmates were sure he must be wrong.

As it turned out, the figures were quite reliable. They had come from a study by the Internal Revenue Service reported in the *New York Times*. If the speaker had mentioned the source in his speech, he would have been more successful.[9]

Explain Your Statistics

Statistics don't speak for themselves. They need to be interpreted and related to your listeners. Notice how effectively one student did this in a speech about Chinese culture in the United States:

> Food is another aspect of Chinese culture that has become part of American life. According to Jennifer Lee's new book, *The Fortune Cookie Chronicles,* there

checklist

Using Statistics

YES	NO	
☐	☐	1. Do I use statistics to quantify my ideas?
☐	☐	2. Are my statistics representative of what they purport to measure?
☐	☐	3. Are my statistics from reliable sources?
☐	☐	4. Do I cite the sources of my statistics?
☐	☐	5. Do I use statistical measures (mean, median, mode) correctly?
☐	☐	6. Do I round off complicated statistics?
☐	☐	7. Do I use visual aids to clarify statistical trends?
☐	☐	8. Do I explain my statistics and relate them to the audience?

are some 43,000 Chinese restaurants in the United States. That's more than all the McDonalds, Burger Kings, and KFCs combined.

Explaining what statistics mean is particularly important when you deal with large numbers, since they are hard to visualize. How, for example, can we comprehend the size of the U.S. national debt, which is projected to hit $20 billion by 2015? We could explain that a trillion is a thousand billion and a billion is a thousand million. But millions and billions are almost as hard to visualize as trillions. Suppose, instead, we translate the huge numbers into terms a listener can relate to. Here is one speaker's solution:

How much money is a trillion dollars? Think of it this way. If you had $1 million and spent it at the rate of $1,000 a day, you would run out of money in less than three years. If you had $1 billion and spent it at the rate of $1,000 a day, you would not run out of money for almost 3,000 years. And if you had $1 trillion and spent it at the rate of $1,000 a day, you wouldn't run out of money for nearly 3 million years!

Whenever you use statistics in your speeches, think of how you can make them meaningful to your audience. Rather than simply reciting figures about, say, the continuing destruction of the world's rainforests, find a way to bring those figures home to your audience. You might say, as did one speaker:

connect

View this excerpt from "The Rainforests: Nature's Pharmacy" in the online Media Library for this chapter (Video 8.6).

According to the Rainforest Action Network, rainforest is disappearing at an alarming rate. Within the next second, we will lose an area of rainforest equal to two football fields. Within the next fifteen minutes, an area the size of this campus will be erased. By this time tomorrow, 214,000 acres, an area equivalent to the size of New York City, will be gone forever.

Be creative in thinking of ways to relate your statistics to your audience. This is probably the single most important step you can take to make statistics work in your speeches.

Round Off Complicated Statistics

Mount Kilimanjaro is 19,341 feet high; the official world land speed record is 763.065 miles per hour; the population of Libya is 6,461,454 people; the moon is 238,855 miles from earth.

These are intriguing figures, but they are too complicated to be readily understood by listeners. Unless there is an important reason to give exact numbers, you should round off most statistics. You might say that Mount Kilimanjaro is 19,300 feet high; the world land speed record is 763 miles per hour; the population of Libya is more than 6 million; and the moon is 239,000 miles from earth.

Use Visual Aids to Clarify Statistical Trends

Visual aids can save you a lot of time, as well as make your statistics easier to comprehend. Suppose you are discussing the declining purchasing power of the U.S. dollar over the past century. You could start by explaining that in 1913, before the United States entered World War I, the dollar was at an all-time high. It fell off during the war, but it regained value during the 1920s, and in 1933 it stood at 80 cents of its 1913 value. Beginning in the 1940s, however, the dollar started a long decline that has yet to end. By 2011, it was worth less than four cents compared to 1913.

These are interesting statistics, and you could build a good speech around them. But strung together in a few sentences they are hard to digest. Figure 8.1 shows how much more clearly the points can be made with a simple graph. We shall discuss visual aids in detail in Chapter 14. For the moment, keep in mind that they can be helpful in presenting statistical information.

FIGURE 8.1

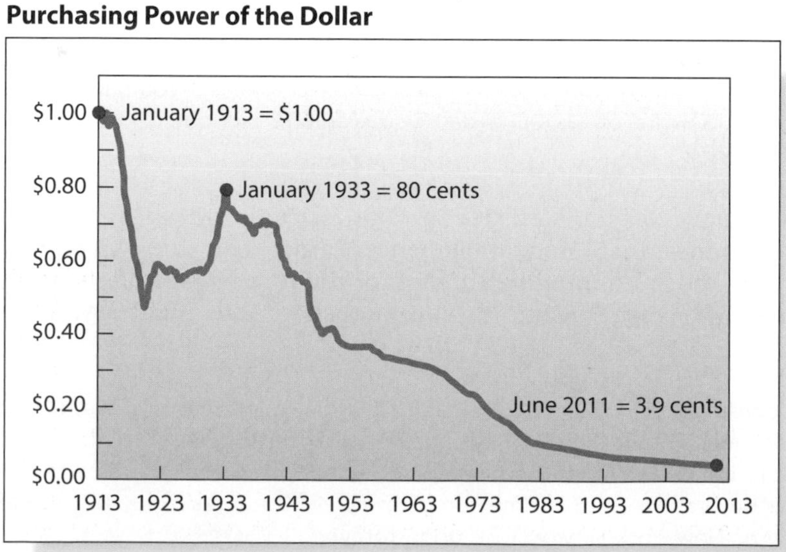

Testimony

Imagine that you are talking with a friend about the classes you plan to take next term. You are not sure whether to sign up for Psychology 230 or Accounting 181. Both are requirements; both meet at the same time of day. Your friend says, "I took those classes last year. They're both good, but Professor Hassam was excellent in Psych 230. If she's teaching it next term, I'd take it for sure." You check the timetable and find that Professor Hassam is indeed slated for Psychology 230. You sign up for her course.

As this story illustrates, we are often influenced by the *testimony* of other people. Just as you are likely to be swayed by your friend's recommendation about which class to take, so audiences tend to respect the opinions of people who have special knowledge or experience on the topic at hand. By quoting or paraphrasing such people, you can give your ideas greater strength and impact. The two major kinds of testimony are expert testimony and peer testimony.

testimony

Quotations or paraphrases used to support a point.

EXPERT TESTIMONY

In most speeches, you will probably rely on expert testimony—testimony from people who are acknowledged authorities in their fields. Citing the views of people who are experts is a good way to lend credibility to your speeches. It shows that you are not just mouthing your own opinions, but that your position is supported by people who are knowledgeable about the topic.[10]

expert testimony

Testimony from people who are recognized experts in their fields.

Expert testimony is even more important when a topic is controversial or when the audience is skeptical about a speaker's point of view. The following story explains how one student enlisted expert testimony for a speech on phony pharmaceuticals:

> The more Leah Giovanni researched her speech topic, the more she became convinced that the growth of fraudulent pharmaceuticals is a serious problem that requires action by the U.S. government. Yet Leah was not an expert on the subject. How could she convince her classmates to accept her ideas?
>
> Statistics helped, and so did examples. But that was not enough. To reinforce her credibility, Leah cited a wide range of experts who agreed with her—including investigative reporter Katherine Eban, author of a book on counterfeit medicines; Graham Jackson, editor of the *International Journal of Clinical Practice;* Tom Kubic, head of the Pharmaceutical Security Institute; and U.S. Representative Steve Israel of New York, who has sponsored legislation in Congress to deal with phony pharmaceuticals. By citing the views of these experts, Leah made her speech much more persuasive.

connect

View an excerpt from "Phony Pharmaceuticals" in the online Media Library for this chapter (Video 8.7).

PEER TESTIMONY

Another type of testimony often used in speeches is peer testimony—opinions of people like ourselves; not prominent figures, but ordinary citizens who have firsthand experience on the topic. This kind of testimony is especially valuable because it gives a more personal viewpoint on issues than can be gained from expert testimony.

peer testimony

Testimony from ordinary people with firsthand experience or insight on a topic.

For example, if you were speaking about the barriers faced by people with physical disabilities, you would surely include testimony from doctors and other medical authorities. But in this case, the expert testimony would be limited because it cannot communicate what it really means to have a physical disability. To communicate that, you need a statement from someone who can speak with the voice of genuine experience—as in the following case:

> Itzhak Perlman, the world-renowned violinist whose legs are paralyzed, once said: "When you are in a wheelchair, people don't talk to you. Perhaps they think it is contagious, or perhaps they think crippled legs mean a crippled mind. But whatever the reason, they treat you like a thing."

There is no way expert testimony could express these ideas with the same authenticity and emotional impact.

QUOTING VERSUS PARAPHRASING

direct quotation

Testimony that is presented word for word.

The statement from Itzhak Perlman is presented as a direct quotation. Testimony can also be presented by paraphrasing. Rather than quoting someone verbatim, you present the gist of that person's ideas in your own words—as did one student in her speech about America's potential water crisis:

> Writing in *Audubon* magazine, Dr. Peter Bourne, president of Global Water, a nonpartisan educational group in Washington, D.C., said most Americans do not yet realize the extent and urgency of the water problem. At the present rate, he says, we are headed for a crisis that will change the way we live in every part of the nation.

paraphrase

To restate or summarize a source's ideas in one's own words.

When should you use a direct quotation as opposed to paraphrasing? The standard rule is that quotations are most effective when they are brief, when they convey your meaning better than you can, and when they are particularly eloquent, witty, or compelling. If you find a quotation that fits these criteria, then recite the quotation word for word.

Paraphrasing is better than direct quotation in two situations: (1) when the wording of a quotation is obscure or cumbersome; (2) when a quotation is longer than two or three sentences. Audiences often tune out partway through lengthy quotations, which tend to interrupt the flow of a speaker's ideas. Since the rest of the speech is in your own words, you should put longer quotations in your own words as well.

TIPS FOR USING TESTIMONY

Quote or Paraphrase Accurately

quoting out of context

Quoting a statement in such a way as to distort its meaning by removing the statement from the words and phrases surrounding it.

Accurate quotation involves three things: making sure you do not misquote someone; making sure you do not violate the meaning of statements you paraphrase; making sure you do not quote out of context.

Of these, the last is the most subtle—and the most dangerous. By quoting out of context, you can twist someone's remarks so as to prove almost anything. Take movie advertisements. A critic pans a movie with these words:

> This movie is a colossal bore. From beginning to end it is a disaster. What is meant to be brilliant dialogue is about as fascinating as the stuff you clean out of your kitchen drain.

But when the movie is advertised in the newspapers, what appears in huge letters over the critic's name? "COLOSSAL! FROM BEGINNING TO END—BRILLIANT! FASCINATING!"

Citing expert testimony is an excellent way for students to lend credibility to their speeches. It shows that the speaker's views are shared by people who have special knowledge on the topic.

This is so flagrant as to be humorous. But quoting out of context can have serious consequences. Consider the following statement by a political candidate:

> Creating a national sales tax would provide needed revenue for programs such as education, health care, and national defense. Several European countries have such a tax, and it could work here. However, I do not support such a tax here—in fact, I don't support new taxes of any kind.

Now look what happens when the first part of that statement is quoted out of context by a competing candidate:

> Americans already pay too much in taxes. Yet my opponent in this election has stated—and I quote: "Creating a national sales tax would provide needed revenue for programs such as education, health care, and national defense. Several European countries have such a tax, and it could work here." Well, my opponent may think new taxes are good for Europe, but they're the last thing we need in the United States.

By quoting the original statement out of context, the competing candidate has created a false impression. Such behavior is highly unethical. Be sure, when you quote or paraphrase someone, that you represent their words and ideas with complete accuracy.

Use Testimony from Qualified Sources

We have all become accustomed to the celebrity testimonial in television and magazine advertising. The professional basketball player endorses a brand of athletic shoes. The movie star praises a hair spray or shampoo. So far, so good. These are the tools of the trade for the people who endorse them.

checklist

Using Testimony

YES	NO	
☐	☐	1. Do I use testimony to support my ideas?
☐	☐	2. Do I use testimony from qualified sources?
☐	☐	3. Do I use testimony from unbiased sources?
☐	☐	4. Do I distinguish between expert testimony and peer testimony?
☐	☐	5. Do I identify the sources of all testimony?
☐	☐	6. Do I quote and paraphrase all sources of testimony with complete accuracy?

But what happens when an Academy Award winner endorses a cell phone company? A tennis player represents a line of cameras? Do they know more about these products than you or I? Probably not.

Being a celebrity or an authority in one area does not make someone competent in other areas. Listeners will find your speeches much more credible if you use testimony from sources qualified *on the subject at hand.* As we have seen, this may include either recognized experts or ordinary citizens with special experience on the speech topic.

Use Testimony from Unbiased Sources

In a speech about the use of stun guns by police officers to subdue unruly students in public schools, a student said:

> Steve Tuttle, a spokesman for Taser International, said in a statement that "the Taser device has been shown to be medically safe when used on children" and that there is no reason to prohibit its use when necessary to maintain security in the public schools.

As you might expect, the students' classmates were not persuaded. After all, what would you expect someone at Taser International, the leading manufacturer of stun guns, to say—that its product is unsafe and should be banned?

Careful listeners are suspicious of testimony from biased or self-interested sources. Be sure to use testimony from credible, objective authorities.

Identify the People You Quote or Paraphrase

The usual way to identify your source is to name the person and sketch his or her qualifications before presenting the testimony. The following excerpt is from a speech arguing that excessive time spent at work is harming the quality of education for many American high-school students:

> In their book, *When Children Work,* psychology professors Ellen Greenberger of the University of California and Lawrence Steinberg of Temple University note

that intensive levels of work among youth tend to produce higher truancy and lower grades. According to Greenberger and Steinberg, one study after another has found that working more than a few hours a week has a negative impact on teenagers' academic performance.

Had the speaker not identified Greenberger and Steinberg, listeners would not have had the foggiest idea who they are or why their opinion should be heeded.

As we saw in Chapter 2, identifying the source of testimony is also an important ethical responsibility. If you use another person's words or ideas without giving credit to that person, you will be guilty of plagiarism. This is true whether you paraphrase the original source or quote it verbatim.

Citing Sources Orally

We have mentioned more than once in this chapter the importance of citing the sources of your supporting materials. Careful listeners are skeptical. They keep an ear out both for a speaker's information and for the sources of that information.

The bibliography in your speech outline should state the sources you used in constructing the speech (see Chapter 11, page 208). But listeners do not have access to your outline. You have to identify your sources orally, as you are speaking.

Unlike a written bibliography, oral source citations do not follow a standard format. What you include depends on your topic, your audience, the kind of supporting material you are using, and the claim you are making. The key is to tell your audience enough that they will know where you got your information and why they should accept it as qualified and credible. In most cases, you will need to identify some combination of the following:

- The book, magazine, newspaper, or Web document you are citing.
- The author or sponsoring organization of the document.
- The author's qualifications with regard to the topic.
- The date on which the document was published, posted, or updated.

Here is an example of a speech citation that includes all the above:

The power of earthquakes can be seen in more than just the damage they cause. Kenneth Chang, science reporter for the *New York Times*, reported in the paper's March 13, 2011, issue that the recent quake in Japan widened the country by 13 feet. It also tilted the earth's axis and shortened the day by a couple millionths of a second.

Because this speaker was citing statistics, she needed to show that they were up-to-date and came from a credible source. In the following example, the speaker is using testimony, but notice how he also establishes the credibility of his source and the recency of his information:

Human smuggling is big business, and the U.S. government has made little headway in stopping it. Just ask Scott Hatfield, chief of the Human Smuggling

checklist

Citing Sources Orally

YES	NO	
☐	☐	1. Do I identify all the print documents cited in my speech?
☐	☐	2. Do I identify all the Web documents cited in my speech?
☐	☐	3. Do I identify the authors or sponsoring organizations of the documents I cite?
☐	☐	4. Do I establish the authors' credentials with regard to the topic?
☐	☐	5. Do I use documents from sponsoring organizations with established expertise and objectivity?
☐	☐	6. Do I include the dates on which the documents were published, posted, or updated?
☐	☐	7. Do I use a variety of methods in citing my sources?

division at Immigration and Customs Enforcement, who was quoted last month in the *Houston Chronicle:* "Any time we shut down a smuggling organization, there's always somebody to take their place."

On the other hand, if you were quoting Abraham Lincoln's Gettysburg Address of November 19, 1863, about "government of the people, by the people, for the people," you would not need to explain Lincoln's qualifications (because he is so well known) or the date of his statement (because it does not affect the relevance of his words).

The same principles apply if you are citing online sources. It is not enough to say, "As I found on the Web," or "As the Internet states." On the other hand, it is not necessary to recite the entire address of the Web page. If you are citing a specific person, you should identify him or her and the name of the Web site on which you found the information—as in this example:

> In an article posted on MSNBC.com in March 2011, Harry Johns, president and chief executive of the Alzheimer's Association, states: "Alzheimer's disease doesn't just affect those with it. It invades families and the lives of everyone around them."

If you are citing an organization, rather than an individual, you need to provide the name of the organization:

> The U.S. Department of Agriculture explains on its Web site that providing nutritious meals and snacks to children in low-income areas during the summer months is critical to improving the health of America's kids.

Finally, notice how skillfully the speakers quoted above blend their citations into their speeches. They do not always say "According to . . ." or "As stated by. . . ." Nor do they use words like "quote . . . unquote." Usually you

FIGURE 8.2 Sample Oral Citations

Source	Sample oral citation
Book	William D. Schanbacher's 2010 book, *The Politics of Food*, explains that the Slow Food Movement was established "as an alternative to fast-paced life, specifically with respect to our eating habits, our knowledge of how food is produced, where it comes from, and how it affects the natural environment."
Newspaper	According to the *Los Angeles Times*, March 9, 2011, the Latino population of California is almost equal to that of the white population. Latinos make up 38 percent of the state's population, while whites compose 40 percent.
Magazine	The problems of the current kidney transplant system are explored by Amanda Glassman, director of Global Health Policy at the Center for Global Development, in last month's *Atlantic Monthly*. Glassman notes that while 87,000 Americans are on the waiting list, only 17,000 will receive a kidney transplant. More disturbing, 4,600 people will die this year because they don't receive a kidney in time.
Academic journal	A recent study published in the *Journal of Neuroscience* by researchers at Duke University demonstrates just how problematic sleep deprivation can be for compulsive gamblers. The less sleep a person has, the more he or she is willing to take big risks in the hope of a big score. And the result can be huge losses.
Organization or institution	The March 2011 report *Women in America*, prepared by the U.S. Department of Commerce and other government agencies, reveals that almost 40 percent of single women with children under the age of 18 live below the poverty line.
Interview	In an interview I conducted for this speech, Professor Lloyd Jasinski of the Political Science Department said that the impact of lobbyists has so corrupted the American political system that many people have lost their faith in government to serve the public good.
Television program	The October 10, 2010, episode of *60 Minutes* explains how much the stock exchange has changed in recent years. The majority of trades are no longer made by humans. In fact, almost 70 percent of trades are done by computers, which can buy and sell thousands of different stocks in the blink of an eye.
Web site	Overcrowding is particularly bad in the nation's community colleges. A February 9, 2011, article on *InsideHigherEd.com*, which is affiliated with the *Chronicle of Higher Education*, states that over 30 percent of community college students were not able to enroll in one or more of the classes they needed last semester because of overcrowding.

can modify your tone of voice or use brief pauses to let your listeners know when you are making a direct quotation.

In Figure 8.2 (on page 161), you will find more examples of how you can cite different kinds of sources in your speeches. Keep in mind, however, that the examples are just that—examples. They are presented to give you a fuller sense of the various methods of oral citation. You can use *any* of the methods with any of the sources. As with other aspects of public speaking, citing sources orally in your speeches is not a matter of following a rigid formula, but of adapting general principles to specific circumstances.

Summary

Good speeches need strong supporting materials to bolster the speaker's point of view. The three basic types of supporting materials are examples, statistics, and testimony.

In the course of a speech you may use brief examples—specific instances referred to in passing—and sometimes you may want to give several brief examples in a row to create a stronger impression. Extended examples are longer and more detailed. Hypothetical examples describe imaginary situations and can be quite effective for relating ideas to the audience. All three kinds of examples help clarify ideas, reinforce ideas, or personalize ideas. To be most effective, they should be vivid and richly textured.

Statistics can be extremely helpful in conveying your message as long as you use them sparingly and make them meaningful to your audience. Above all, you should understand your statistics and use them fairly. Make sure your figures are representative of what they claim to measure, that you use statistical measures correctly, and that you take statistics only from reliable sources.

Citing the testimony of experts is a good way to make your ideas more credible. You can also use peer testimony, from ordinary people who have firsthand experience on the topic. Regardless of the kind of testimony, you can either quote someone verbatim or paraphrase his or her words. Be sure to quote or paraphrase accurately and to use qualified, unbiased sources.

When citing sources in a speech, you need to let your audience know where you got your information and why they should accept it as qualified and credible. In most cases, this means identifying the document you are citing, its date of publication or posting, the author or sponsoring organization, and the author's credentials.

Key Terms

supporting materials *(142)*
example *(142)*
brief example *(143)*
extended example *(143)*
hypothetical example *(144)*
statistics *(147)*
mean *(150)*
median *(150)*
mode *(150)*
testimony *(155)*
expert testimony *(155)*
peer testimony *(155)*
direct quotation *(156)*
paraphrase *(156)*
quoting out of context *(156)*

Review Questions

After reading this chapter, you should be able to answer the following questions:

1. Why do you need supporting materials in your speeches?
2. What are the three kinds of examples discussed in this chapter? How might you use each kind to support your ideas?
3. What are five tips for using examples in your speeches?
4. Why is it so easy to lie with statistics? What three questions should you ask to judge the reliability of statistics?
5. What are six tips for using statistics in your speeches?
6. What is testimony? Explain the difference between expert testimony and peer testimony.
7. What are four tips for using testimony in your speeches?
8. What four pieces of information do you usually need to provide when making oral source citations in a speech?

connect™

For further review, go to the LearnSmart study module for this chapter.

Exercises for Critical Thinking

1. Each of the following statements violates at least one of the criteria for effective supporting materials discussed in this chapter. Identify the flaw (or flaws) in each statement.

   a. As Taylor Swift stated in a recent interview, U.S. policy toward North Korea should put more emphasis on bilateral negotiations.

   b. According to *The New York Times Almanac,* California has the largest Native American population of any state in the union—421,346. Arizona is second with 294,118 and Oklahoma is third with 287,124.

   c. I don't know why rental car companies don't like to rent to people under the age of 25. My friends and I all drive a lot, and none of us has been in an accident.

   d. In a random survey conducted last month among people visiting Las Vegas casinos, 96 percent of respondents opposed limitations on gambling in the United States. Clearly, then, the American people oppose such limitations.

   e. In the words of one expert, "The state education budget has been cut so much in recent years that any further cuts will do irreparable harm to our schools and the children they serve."

   f. Figures compiled by the Bureau of Labor Statistics show that the median salary for petroleum engineers in the U.S. is $108,910. This shows that petroleum engineers average almost $109,000 a year in salary.

   g. According to a study by American Airlines, passenger satisfaction among frequent fliers is growing each year.

2. Analyze "Bursting the Antibacterial Bubble" in the appendix of sample speeches following Chapter 19. Identify the main points of the speech and the supporting materials used for each. Evaluate the speaker's use of supporting materials in light of the criteria discussed in this chapter.

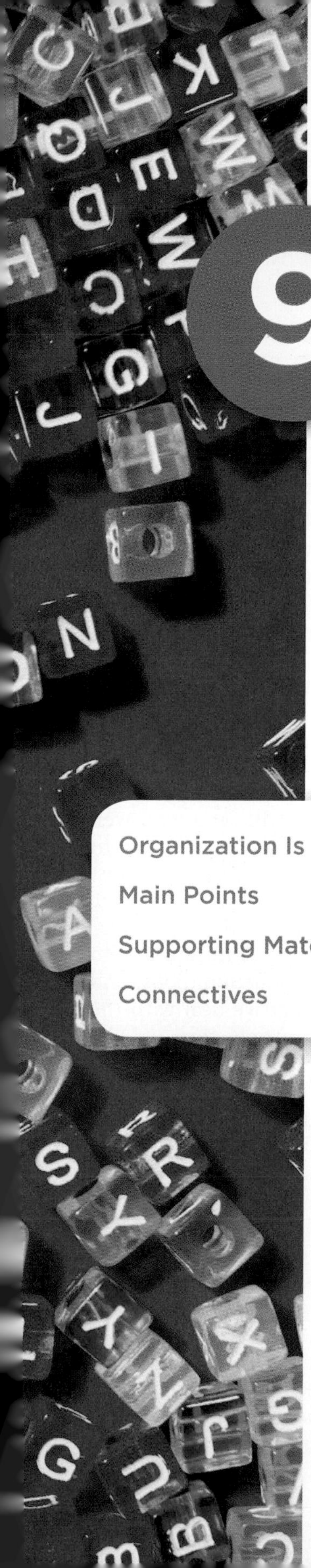

9

Organizing the Body of the Speech

- Organization Is Important
- Main Points
- Supporting Materials
- Connectives

Think about shopping in a store such as Ikea, Target, or Best Buy. Many of the items for sale are *organizers*—drawer organizers, desk organizers, closet organizers, kitchen organizers, bathroom organizers, office organizers, audio and video organizers.

Why all this quest for organization? Obviously, when the objects you possess are well organized, they serve you better. Organization allows you to see what you have and to put your hands immediately on the garment, the tool, the piece of paper, the DVD you want without a frenzied search.

Much the same is true of your speeches. If they are well organized, they will serve you better. Organization allows you—and your listeners—to see what ideas you have and to put mental "hands" on the most important ones.

Organization Is Important

In a classic study, a college professor took a well-organized speech and scrambled it by randomly changing the order of its sentences. He then had a speaker deliver the original version to one group of listeners and the scrambled version to another group. After the speeches, he gave a test to see how well each group understood what they had heard. Not surprisingly, the group that heard the original, unscrambled speech scored much higher than the other group.[1]

A few years later, two professors repeated the same experiment at another school. But instead of testing how well the listeners comprehended each speech, they tested to see what effects the speeches had on the listeners' attitudes toward the speakers. They found that people who heard the well-organized speech believed the speaker to be much more competent and trustworthy than did those who heard the scrambled speech.[2]

strategic organization

Putting a speech together in a particular way to achieve a particular result with a particular audience.

These are just two of many studies that show the importance of organization in effective speechmaking.[3] Listeners demand coherence. Unlike readers, they cannot flip back to a previous page if they have trouble grasping a speaker's ideas. In this respect a speech is much like a movie. Just as a director must be sure viewers can follow the plot of a film from beginning to end, so must a speaker be sure listeners can follow the progression of ideas in a speech from beginning to end. This requires that speeches be organized *strategically.* They should be put together in particular ways to achieve particular results with particular audiences.

Speech organization is important for other reasons as well. As we saw in Chapter 1, it is closely connected to critical thinking. When you work to organize your speeches, you gain practice in the general skill of establishing clear relationships among your ideas. This skill will serve you well throughout your college days and in almost any career you may choose. In addition, using a clear, specific method of speech organization can boost your confidence as a speaker and improve your ability to deliver a message fluently.

The first step in developing a strong sense of speech organization is to gain command of the three basic parts of a speech—introduction, body, and conclusion—and the strategic role of each. In this chapter we deal with the body of the speech. The next chapter will take up the introduction and the conclusion.

There are good reasons for talking first about the body of the speech. The body is the longest and most important part. Also, you will usually prepare the body first. It is easier to create an effective introduction after you know exactly what you will say in the body.

The process of organizing the body of a speech begins when you determine the main points.

Main Points

The main points are the central features of your speech. You should select them carefully, phrase them precisely, and arrange them strategically. Here are the main points of a student speech about the uses of hypnosis:

Specific Purpose: To inform my audience about some of the major uses of hypnosis.

Central Idea: Three major uses of hypnosis today are to control pain in surgery, to help people stop smoking, and to help students improve their academic performance.

Main Points:

I. Hypnosis is used in surgery as an adjunct to chemical anesthesia.

II. Hypnosis is used to help people stop smoking.

III. Hypnosis is used to help students improve their academic performance.

main points

The major points developed in the body of a speech. Most speeches contain from two to five main points.

These three main points form the skeleton of the body of the speech. If there are three major *uses* of hypnosis, then logically there can be three *main points* in the speech.

How do you choose your main points? Sometimes they will be evident from your specific purpose statement. Suppose your specific purpose is "To inform my audience about the development, technology, and benefits of hydrogen fuel cells." Obviously, your speech will have three main points. The first will deal with the development of hydrogen fuel cells, the second with the technology behind hydrogen fuel cells, the third with the benefits of hydrogen fuel cells. Written in outline form, the main points might be:

Specific Purpose: To inform my audience about the development, technology, and benefits of hydrogen fuel cells.

Central Idea: Developed as a highly efficient form of energy, hydrogen fuel cells use sophisticated technology and offer a number of economic and environmental benefits.

Main Points:

I. Hydrogen fuel cells were developed to provide a highly efficient form of energy.

II. Hydrogen fuel cells produce power through an electrochemical reaction involving hydrogen gas.

III. Hydrogen fuel cells provide an economically and environmentally superior method of powering motor vehicles.

Even if your main points are not stated expressly in your specific purpose, they may be easy to project from it. Let's say your specific purpose is "To inform my audience of the basic steps in making stained-glass windows." You know each of your main points will correspond to a step in the window-making process. They might look like this in outline form:

Specific Purpose: To inform my audience of the basic steps in making stained-glass windows.

Central Idea: There are four steps in making stained-glass windows.

Main Points:

I. The first step is designing the window.

II. The second step is cutting the glass to fit the design.

III. The third step is painting the glass.

IV. The fourth step is assembling the window.

You will not always settle on your main points so easily. Often they will emerge as you research the speech and evaluate your findings. Suppose your specific purpose is "To persuade my audience that our state should not approve proposals for online voting." You know that each main point in the speech will present a *reason* why online voting should not be instituted in your state. But you aren't sure how many main points there will be or what they will be. As you research and study the topic, you decide there are two reasons to support your view. Each of these reasons will become a main point in your speech. Written in outline form, they might be:

Specific Purpose: To persuade my audience that our state should not approve proposals for online voting.

Central Idea: Our state should not approve online voting because it will increase voter fraud and disfranchise people without Internet access.

Main Points:

I. Our state should not approve online voting because it will increase voter fraud.

II. Our state should not approve online voting because it will disfranchise people without access to the Internet.

NUMBER OF MAIN POINTS

You will not have time in your classroom speeches to develop more than four or five main points, and most speeches will contain only two or three. Regardless of how long a speech might run, if you have too many main points, the audience will have trouble sorting them out.

If, when you list your main points, you find that you have too many, you may be able to condense them into categories. Here is a set of main points for a speech about yoga:

Specific Purpose: To inform my audience about the practice of yoga.

Central Idea: Yoga is an ancient practice that involves the whole body.

Main Points:

I. Yoga breathing starts with deep inhalation.

II. Yoga breathing requires slow exhalation.

III. Yoga breathing includes prolonged pauses.

IV. Yoga breathing provides many benefits.

V. Yoga postures involve all parts of the body.

VI. Yoga postures increase flexibility.

VII. Yoga postures strengthen muscle tone.

VIII. Yoga postures demand precise movements.

connect™

View an excerpt from "Yoga: Uniting Mind, Body, and Spirit" in the online Media Library for this chapter (Video 9.1).

You have eight main points—which is too many. But if you look at the list, you see that the eight points fall into two broad categories: yoga breathing and yoga postures. You might, therefore, restate your main points this way:

I. One part of practicing yoga involves proper breathing.

II. Another part of yoga involves body postures.

Research studies confirm that clear organization is vital to effective public speaking. Listeners must be able to follow the progression of ideas in a speech from beginning to end.

STRATEGIC ORDER OF MAIN POINTS

Once you establish your main points, you need to decide the order in which you will present them. The most effective order depends on three things—your topic, your purpose, and your audience. Chapters 15 and 16 will cover special aspects of organizing informative speeches and persuasive speeches. Here we look briefly at the five basic patterns of organization used most often by public speakers.

Chronological Order

Speeches arranged chronologically follow a time pattern. They may narrate a series of events in the sequence in which they happened. For example:

chronological order

A method of speech organization in which the main points follow a time pattern.

Specific Purpose: To inform my audience how the Great Wall of China was built.

Central Idea: The Great Wall of China was built in three major stages.

Main Points:

I. Building of the Great Wall began during the Qin dynasty of 221–206 B.C.

II. New sections of the Great Wall were added during the Han dynasty of 206 B.C.–220 A.D.

III. The Great Wall was completed during the Ming dynasty of 1368–1644.

Chronological order is also used in speeches explaining a process or demonstrating how to do something. For example:

Specific Purpose: To inform my audience of the steps in laser-assisted corrective eye surgery.

Central Idea: There are three main steps in laser-assisted corrective eye surgery.

Main Points:

I. First, a thin layer is sliced off the surface of the eye to expose the cornea.

II. Second, an ultraviolet laser is used to reshape the cornea.

III. Third, the thin layer sliced off at the beginning of the surgery is reaffixed to the eye.

As this outline shows, chronological order is especially useful for informative speeches.

Spatial Order

spatial order

A method of speech organization in which the main points follow a directional pattern.

Speeches arranged in spatial order follow a directional pattern. That is, the main points proceed from top to bottom, left to right, front to back, inside to outside, east to west, or some other route. For example:

Specific Purpose: To inform my audience about the structure of a hurricane.

Central Idea: A hurricane is made up of three parts going from inside to outside.

Main Points:

I. At the center of a hurricane is the calm, cloud-free eye.

II. Surrounding the eye is the eyewall, a dense ring of clouds that produces the most intense wind and rainfall.

III. Rotating around the eyewall are large bands of clouds and precipitation called spiral rain bands.

connect™

View an excerpt from "The Wrath of Hurricanes" in the online Media Library for this chapter (Video 9.2).

Or:

Specific Purpose: To inform my audience about the three major regions in Italy.

Central Idea: Northern, central, and southern Italy have their own identities and attractions.

Main Points:

I. Northern Italy is home to Venice and its world-famous canals.

II. Central Italy is home to Rome and its historical treasures.

III. Southern Italy is home to Sicily and its culinary traditions.

Spatial order, like chronological order, is used most often in informative speeches.

Causal Order

causal order

A method of speech organization in which the main points show a cause-effect relationship.

Speeches arranged in causal order organize main points so as to show a cause-effect relationship. When you put your speech in causal order, you have two main points—one dealing with the causes of an event, the other dealing with its effects. Depending on your topic, you can devote your first main point to the causes and the second to the effects, or you can deal first with the effects and then with the causes.

Suppose your specific purpose is "To persuade my audience that a growing shortage of air-traffic controllers is a serious problem for U.S. aviation." Then you would begin with the causes of the shortage and work toward its effects:

Specific Purpose: To persuade my audience that a growing shortage of qualified air-traffic controllers is a serious problem for U.S. aviation.

The main points of a speech should be organized to communicate the speaker's message. Chronological order would work very well for a speech on the history of Mount Rushmore.

Central Idea:	The growing shortage of certified air-traffic controllers threatens the safety of air travel.
Main Points:	I. The U.S. aviation system faces a growing shortage of qualified air-traffic controllers.
	II. If this shortage continues, it will create serious problems for airline safety.

When the effects you are discussing have already occurred, you may want to reverse the order and talk first about the effects and then about their causes—as in this speech about the Mayan civilization of Central America:

Specific Purpose:	To inform my audience about the possible causes for the collapse of Mayan civilization.
Central Idea:	The causes for the collapse of Mayan civilization have not yet been fully explained.
Main Points:	I. Mayan civilization flourished for over a thousand years until 900 A.D., when it mysteriously began to disintegrate.
	II. Scientists have advanced three major explanations for the causes of this disintegration.

Because of its versatility, causal order can be used for both persuasive speeches and informative speeches.

Problem-Solution Order

Speeches arranged in problem-solution order are divided into two main parts. The first shows the existence and seriousness of a problem. The second presents a workable solution to the problem. For example:

Specific Purpose:	To persuade my audience that action is needed to combat the abuses of puppy mills.

Central Idea: Puppy mills are a serious problem that can be solved by a combination of legislation and individual initiative.

Main Points:

I. Puppy mills are a serious problem across the United States.

II. Solving the problem requires legislation and individual initiative.

connect

View an excerpt from "The Horrors of Puppy Mills" in the online Media Library for this chapter (Video 9.3).

Or:

Specific Purpose: To persuade my audience that the electoral college should be abolished.

Central Idea: Because the electoral college does not give equal weight to the vote of each citizen, it should be replaced with direct popular election of the President.

Main Points:

I. The electoral college is a serious problem in the U.S. political system because it does not give equal weight to each citizen's vote in electing the President.

II. The problem can be solved by abolishing the electoral college and electing the President by popular vote.

problem-solution order

A method of speech organization in which the first main point deals with the existence of a problem and the second main point presents a solution to the problem.

As these examples indicate, problem-solution order is most appropriate for persuasive speeches.

Topical Order

Topical order results when you divide the speech topic into *subtopics,* each of which becomes a main point in the speech.

Let's say your topic is Josephine Baker, an African-American entertainer and social activist in the middle of the 20th century. You could organize your speech chronologically—by discussing Baker's exploits during each decade of her career. On the other hand, you could arrange the speech topically—by dividing Baker's accomplishments into categories. Then your central idea and main points might be:

topical order

A method of speech organization in which the main points divide the topic into logical and consistent subtopics.

Specific Purpose: To inform my audience about the achievements of Josephine Baker.

Central Idea: Josephine Baker was a multitalented figure in the fight for racial justice.

Main Points:

I. As an entertainer, Baker captivated audiences in Europe and America.

II. As a spy, Baker gathered information on Nazi activities in France during World War II.

III. As a civil rights activist, Baker worked for racial equality on a variety of fronts.

Notice how the main points subdivide the speech topic logically and consistently. Each main point isolates one aspect of Baker's achievements. But suppose your main points look like this:

I. As an entertainer, Baker captivated audiences in Europe and America.

II. As a spy, Baker gathered information on Nazi activities in France during World War II.

III. During the 1950s, Baker expanded her activities and the scope of her influence.

This would *not* be a good topical order because main point III is inconsistent with the rest of the main points. It deals with a *time period* in Baker's life, whereas main points I and II deal with fields of achievement.

The Josephine Baker example refers to an informative speech. But topical order also works for persuasive speeches. Usually the topical subdivisions are the *reasons* why a speaker believes in a certain point of view. Here, for example, are the main points for a speech on why the United States should continue its program of space exploration:

Specific Purpose: To persuade my audience that the United States should continue its program of space exploration.

Central Idea: The United States should continue its program of space exploration because it produces scientific knowledge, generates technological breakthroughs, and opens access to natural resources.

Main Points:

I. The space program produces scientific knowledge about the nature of the solar system.

II. The space program generates technological breakthroughs that benefit many aspects of human life.

III. The space program opens access to natural resources that are in short supply on earth.

Because it is applicable to almost any subject and to any kind of speech, topical order is used more often than any other method of speech organization.

Using public speaking in your CAREER

You are the purchasing manager for a large jewelry manufacturer. The company's president sent you abroad to find new suppliers of base metals, including brass, copper, nickel, and aluminum. You were asked to evaluate each supplier based on the quality, availability, and cost of its products.

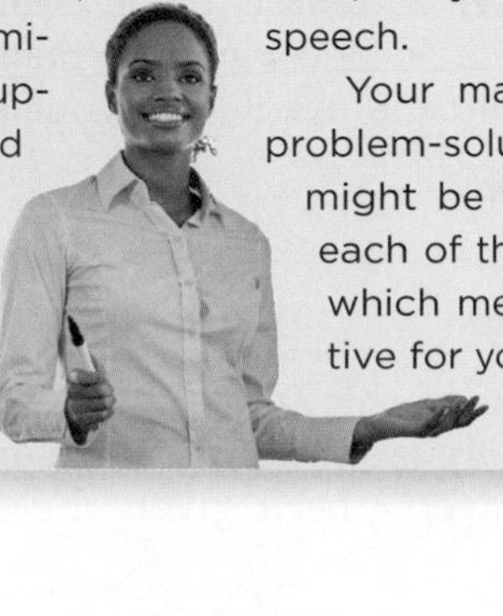

You have just returned from a 12-day trip to suppliers in Cambodia, China, South Korea, and the United Arab Emirates. You will present your findings and recommendations to the company's senior executives, but you're not sure how best to organize your speech.

Your major choices are chronological order, problem-solution order, and topical order. What might be the main points of your speech with each of these methods of organization? Explain which method you think would be most effective for your presentation.

TIPS FOR PREPARING MAIN POINTS

Keep Main Points Separate

Each main point in a speech should be clearly independent of the others. Compare these two sets of main points for a speech about the process of producing a Broadway play:

Ineffective	More Effective
I. The first step is choosing the play.	I. The first step is choosing the play.
II. The second step is selecting the cast.	II. The second step is selecting the cast.
III. The third step is conducting rehearsals and then performing the play.	III. The third step is conducting the rehearsals.
	IV. The fourth step is performing the play.

The problem with the left-hand list is that point III contains two main points. It should be divided, as shown in the right-hand list.

Try to Use the Same Pattern of Wording for Main Points

Consider the following main points for an informative speech about the benefits of karate:

Ineffective	More Effective
I. Karate gives you better mental discipline.	I. Karate improves your mental discipline.
II. You will become physically stronger through karate.	II. Karate increases your physical strength.
III. Taking karate lessons will teach you self-defense.	III. Karate teaches you self-defense.

The set of main points on the right follows a consistent pattern of wording throughout. Therefore, it is easier to understand and easier to remember than the set on the left.

You will find that it is not always possible to use this kind of parallel wording. Some speeches just don't lend themselves to such a tidy arrangement. But try to keep the wording parallel when you can, for it is a good way to make your main points stand out from the details surrounding them.

Balance the Amount of Time Devoted to Main Points

Because your main points are so important, you want to be sure they all receive enough emphasis to be clear and convincing. This means allowing sufficient time to develop each main point. Suppose you discover that the proportion of time devoted to your main points is something like this:

I. 85 percent
II. 10 percent
III. 5 percent

A breakdown of this sort indicates one of two things. Either points II and III aren't really *main* points and you have only one main point, or points II and III haven't been given the attention they need. If the latter, you should revise the body of the speech to bring the main points into better balance.

This is not to say that all main points must receive exactly equal emphasis, but only that they should be roughly balanced. For example, either of the following would be fine:

I. 30 percent	I. 20 percent
II. 40 percent	II. 30 percent
III. 30 percent	III. 50 percent

The amount of time spent on each main point depends on the amount and complexity of supporting materials for each point.

Supporting Materials

By themselves, main points are only assertions. As we saw in Chapter 8, listeners need supporting materials to accept what a speaker says. The outline below demonstrates how supporting materials can be integrated into the body of a speech. (In Chapter 11, we'll look at requirements for a complete speech outline. For now, concentrate on how the supporting materials relate to the main points.)

supporting materials

The materials used to support a speaker's ideas. The three major kinds of supporting materials are examples, statistics, and testimony.

I. Hypnosis is used in surgery as an adjunct to chemical anesthesia.
   A. Hypnosis reduces both the physical and psychological aspects of pain.
      1. Hypnosis can double a person's pain threshold.
      2. It also reduces the fear that intensifies physical pain.
   B. Hypnosis is most useful in cases when the patient is known to have problems with general anesthesia.
      1. Quotation from Dr. Harold Wain of the Mayo Clinic.
      2. Story of Linda Kuay.
      3. Statistics from *Psychology Today.*

II. Hypnosis is used to help people stop smoking.
   A. Many therapists utilize hypnosis to help people break their addiction to cigarettes.
      1. The U.S. Department of Health and Human Services considers hypnosis a safe and effective means of stopping smoking.
      2. Success rates are as high as 70 percent.
         a. Story of Alex Hamilton.
         b. Quotation from New York psychiatrist Dr. Herbert Spiegel.
   B. Hypnosis does not work for all smokers.
      1. A person must want to stop smoking for hypnosis to work.
      2. A person must also be responsive to hypnotic suggestion.

III. Hypnosis is used to help students improve their academic performance.
   A. Hypnosis enables people to use their minds more effectively.
      1. The conscious mind uses about 10 percent of a person's mental ability.
      2. Hypnosis allows people to tap more of their mental power.
   B. Studies show that hypnosis can help people overcome many obstacles to academic success.
      1. It improves ability to concentrate.
      2. It increases reading speed.
      3. It reduces test anxiety.

In Chapter 8, we discussed the major kinds of supporting materials and how to use them. Here, we need stress only the importance of *organizing* your supporting materials so they are directly relevant to the main points they are supposed to support. Misplaced supporting materials are confusing. Here's an example:

I. There are several reasons why people immigrate to the United States.
  A. Over the years, millions of people have immigrated to the United States.
  B. Many people immigrate in search of economic opportunity.
  C. Others immigrate to attain political freedom.
  D. Still others immigrate to escape religious persecution.

The main point deals with the reasons immigrants come to the United States, as do supporting points B, C, and D. Supporting point A ("Over the years, millions of people have immigrated to the United States") does not. It is out of place and should not be included with this main point.

If you find such a situation in your own speeches, try to reorganize your supporting points under appropriate main points, like this:

I. Over the years, millions of people have immigrated to the United States.
  A. Since the American Revolution, more than 90 million people have immigrated to the United States.

checklist

Main Points

YES	NO	
☐	☐	1. Does the body of my speech contain two to five main points?
☐	☐	2. Are my main points organized according to one of the following methods of organization? Chronological order Spatial order Causal order Topical order Problem-solution order
☐	☐	3. Are my main points clearly separate from one another?
☐	☐	4. As much as possible, have I used the same pattern of wording for all my main points?
☐	☐	5. Have I roughly balanced the amount of time devoted to each main point?
☐	☐	6. Is each main point backed up with strong, credible supporting materials?
☐	☐	7. Do I use connectives to make sure my audience knows when I am moving from one main point to another?

B. Today there are 38 million Americans who were born in other countries.

II. There are several reasons why people immigrate to the United States.
   A. Many people immigrate in search of economic opportunity.
   B. Others immigrate to attain political freedom.
   C. Still others immigrate to escape religious persecution.

Now you have two supporting points to back up your "millions of people" point and three supporting points to back up your "reasons" point.

Once you have organized your main points and supporting points, you must give attention to the third element in the body of a speech—connectives.

Connectives

Emily Chen was speaking to her class about the need for medical malpractice reform. She had rehearsed the speech several times, had a well-defined central idea, three sharp main points, and strong evidence to support her position. But when Emily delivered the speech, she said "All right" every time she moved from one thought to the next. After a while, her classmates started counting. By the end of the speech, most were too busy waiting for the next "All right" to pay attention to Emily's message. Afterward, Emily said, "I never even thought about saying 'All right.' I guess it just popped out when I didn't know what else to say."

We all have stock phrases that we use to fill the space between thoughts. In casual conversation they are seldom troublesome. But in speechmaking they distract listeners by calling attention to themselves.

connective

A word or phrase that connects the ideas of a speech and indicates the relationship between them.

What Emily's speech lacked were strong *connectives*—words or phrases that join one thought to another and indicate the relationship between them. Without connectives, a speech is disjointed and uncoordinated—much as a person would be without ligaments and tendons to join the bones and hold the organs in place. Four types of speech connectives are transitions, internal previews, internal summaries, and signposts.

TRANSITIONS

Transitions are words or phrases that indicate when a speaker has just completed one thought and is moving on to another. Technically, the transitions state both the idea the speaker is leaving and the idea she or he is coming up to. In the following examples, the transitional phrases are underlined:

transition

A word or phrase that indicates when a speaker has finished one thought and is moving on to another.

> Now that we have a clear understanding of the problem, let me share the solution with you.
>
> I have spoken so far of Cesar Chavez the community organizer, but it was his work as a labor leader that truly etched his name into American history.
>
> Keeping these points in mind about sign language, let's return to the sentence I started with and see if we can learn the signs for "You are my friend."

Notice how these phrases remind the listener of the thought just completed, as well as reveal the thought about to be developed.

INTERNAL PREVIEWS

internal preview

A statement in the body of the speech that lets the audience know what the speaker is going to discuss next.

Internal previews let the audience know what the speaker will take up next, but they are more detailed than transitions. In effect, an internal preview works just like the preview statement in a speech introduction, except that it comes in the body of the speech—usually as the speaker is starting to discuss a main point. For example:

> In discussing how Asian Americans have been stereotyped in the mass media, we'll look first at the origins of the problem and second at its continuing impact today.

After hearing this, the audience knows exactly what to listen for as the speaker develops the "problem" main point.

Internal previews are often combined with transitions. For example:

> [*Transition*]: Now that we have seen how serious the problem of faulty credit reports is, let's look at some solutions. [*Internal Preview*]: I will focus on three solutions—instituting tighter government regulation of credit bureaus, holding credit bureaus financially responsible for their errors, and giving individuals easier access to their credit reports.

You will seldom need an internal preview for each main point in your speech, but be sure to use one whenever you think it will help listeners keep track of your ideas.

INTERNAL SUMMARIES

internal summary

A statement in the body of the speech that summarizes the speaker's preceding point or points.

Internal summaries are the reverse of internal previews. Rather than letting listeners know what is coming up next, internal summaries remind listeners of what they have just heard. Such summaries are usually used when a speaker finishes a complicated or particularly important main point or set of main points. For example:

> In short, palm reading is an ancient art. Developed in China more than five thousand years ago, it was practiced in classical Greece and Rome, flourished during the Middle Ages, survived the Industrial Revolution, and remains popular today in many parts of the world.

Internal summaries are an excellent way to clarify and reinforce ideas. By combining them with transitions, you can also lead your audience smoothly into your next main point:

> [*Internal Summary*]: Let's pause for a moment to summarize what we have found so far. First, we have seen that firearm sales at gun shows too often put weapons in the hands of criminals. Second, we have seen that there is almost no accountability for gun-show dealers who sell to criminals. [*Transition*]: We are now in a position to see what can be done to close the gun-show loophole.

signpost

A very brief statement that indicates where a speaker is in the speech or that focuses attention on key ideas.

SIGNPOSTS

Signposts are very brief statements that indicate exactly where you are in the speech. Frequently they are just numbers. Here is how one student used

Experienced speakers include transitions and other connectives to help listeners keep track of their ideas. Here Adam Savage, co-host of *MythBusters*, addresses the media at the White Hose Science Fair.

simple numerical signposts to help her audience keep track of the major causes for the continuing problem of famine in Africa:

> <u>The first cause</u> of this problem is inefficient agricultural production.
>
> <u>The second cause</u> is recurrent drought in the affected countries.
>
> <u>The final cause</u> is mismanagement of available food resources by local leaders.

Another way to accomplish the same thing is to introduce your main points with a question, as did one student in his speech on mail-order fraud. His first main point showed that mail-order fraud continues to be a serious problem despite the growth of the Internet. He introduced it this way:

> So just how serious is the problem of mail-order fraud? Is it just a few isolated cases, or is it widespread enough to require serious measures to protect consumers?

His second main point dealt with ways to curb mail-order fraud. He introduced it by saying:

> So how can we solve this problem? Is there a way to protect the rights of legitimate mail-order companies while attacking the fraudulent ones?

Questions are particularly effective as signposts because they invite subliminal answers and thereby get the audience more involved with the speech.

Besides using signposts to indicate where you are in the speech, you can use them to focus attention on key ideas. You can do this with a simple phrase, as in the following example:

> <u>The most important thing to remember</u> about abstract art is that it is always based on forms in the natural world.

The underlined words alert the audience to the fact that an especially significant point is coming up. So do phrases such as these:

Be sure to keep this in mind . . .

This is crucial to understanding the rest of the speech . . .

Above all, you need to know . . .

Depending on the needs of your speech, you may want to use two, three, or even all four kinds of connectives in combination. You needn't worry too much about what they are called—whether this one is a signpost and that a transition. The important thing is to be aware of their functions. Properly applied, connectives can make your speeches more unified and coherent.

Summary

Clear organization is vital to speechmaking. Listeners demand coherence. They get only one chance to grasp a speaker's ideas, and they have little patience for speakers who ramble aimlessly from one idea to another. A well-organized speech will enhance your credibility and make it easier for the audience to understand your message.

The process of planning the body of a speech begins when you determine the main points. You should choose them carefully, phrase them precisely, and organize them strategically. Because listeners cannot keep track of a multitude of main points, most speeches should contain no more than two to five. Each should focus on a single idea, should be worded clearly, and should receive enough emphasis to be clear and convincing.

You can organize main points in various ways, depending on your topic, purpose, and audience. Chronological order follows a time pattern, whereas spatial order follows a directional pattern. In causal order, main points are organized according to their cause-effect relationship. Topical order results when you divide your main topic into subtopics. Problem-solution order breaks the body of the speech into two main parts—the first showing a problem, the second giving a solution.

Supporting materials are the backup ideas for your main points. When organizing supporting materials, make sure they are directly relevant to the main points they are supposed to support.

Connectives help tie a speech together. They are words or phrases that join one thought to another and indicate the relationship between them. The four major types of speech connectives are transitions, internal previews, internal summaries, and signposts. Using them effectively will make your speeches more unified and coherent.

Key Terms

strategic organization *(166)*
main points *(167)*
chronological order *(169)*
spatial order *(170)*
causal order *(170)*
problem-solution order *(172)*
topical order *(172)*
supporting materials *(175)*
connective *(177)*
transition *(177)*
internal preview *(178)*
internal summary *(178)*
signpost *(178)*

Review Questions

After reading this chapter, you should be able to answer the following questions:

1. Why is it important that speeches be organized clearly and coherently?
2. How many main points will your speeches usually contain? Why is it important to limit the number of main points in your speeches?
3. What are the five basic patterns of organizing main points in a speech? Which are appropriate for informative speeches? Which is most appropriate for persuasive speeches? Which is used most often?
4. What are three tips for preparing your main points?
5. What is the most important thing to remember when organizing supporting materials in the body of your speech?
6. What are the four kinds of speech connectives? What role does each play in a speech?

connect™

For further review, go to the LearnSmart study module for this chapter.

Exercises for Critical Thinking

1. What organizational method (or methods) might you use to arrange main points for speeches with the following specific purpose statements?

   To inform my audience of the causes and effects of Parkinson's disease.

   To inform my audience about the major kinds of symbols used in Native American art.

   To persuade my audience that the state legislature should enact tougher laws to curb the problem of predatory lending to college students.

   To inform my audience about the major stages of the civil rights movement from 1955 to 1970.

   To inform my audience about the educational philosophy of Jean Piaget.

   To inform my audience about the geographical regions of Brazil.

2. Turn to the outline of main points and supporting materials for the speech about hypnosis on page 167. Create appropriate transitions, internal previews, internal summaries, and signposts for the speech.
3. Identify the organizational method used in each of the following sets of main points.

I. Fraudulent charity fund-raising is a widespread national problem.
II. The problem can be solved by a combination of government regulation and individual awareness.

I. At the top of the rainforest is the emergent layer, where trees can be 200 feet tall.
II. Below the emergent layer is the canopy, where vegetation is so dense that it filters out 80 percent of the sunlight.
III. Beneath the canopy is the understory, where trees are less than 12 feet tall and grow large leaves to collect the small amount of sunlight.
IV. At the bottom is the forest floor, where there are almost no plants because of the lack of sunlight.

I. Sonia Sotomayor is best known as the first Hispanic justice of the U.S. Supreme Court.
II. Sonia Sotomayor is also an accomplished communicator who has given hundreds of public speeches.

I. Founded in 1948, NASCAR was limited primarily to the South through the 1950s and 1960s.
II. The modern era of NASCAR began in the 1970s with the development of the points system to crown a yearly champion.
III. Today NASCAR is one of the most popular spectator sports in America.

I. Caused by an antibiotic-resistant strain of staphylococcus bacteria, MRSA is prevalent among college students.
II. The effects of MRSA include skin infections, damage to internal organs, pneumonia, and, in some cases, death.

10

Beginning and Ending the Speech

The Introduction

The Conclusion

On the night of January 26, 1988, a conductor stepped to the podium at the Majestic Theatre in New York City, tapped his baton, raised his arms, and signaled the orchestra to play. Moments later, American theatergoers first heard the dramatic opening chords of *The Phantom of the Opera.* Today, this scene has been repeated more than 9,500 times and *Phantom* has become the longest-running musical in Broadway history.

Like most classic musicals, *Phantom of the Opera* begins with an overture—an orchestral introduction that captures the audience's attention and gives them a preview of the music they are going to hear. Without such an introduction—if the characters simply walked onstage and began singing or speaking—the beginning of the play would seem too abrupt, and the audience would not be suitably "primed" for the entertainment.

Similarly, most musicals end with a finale, when the whole cast is onstage, elements of the dramatic plot are resolved, portions of the principal songs are recalled, and the music is brought to a dramatic climax. If there were no such conclusion, if the actors merely stopped and walked offstage, the audience would be left unsatisfied.

Just as musical plays need appropriate beginnings and endings, so do speeches. The beginning, or introduction, prepares listeners for what is to come. The conclusion ties up the speech and alerts listeners that the speech is going to end. Ideally, it is a satisfying conclusion.

In this chapter, we explore the roles played by an introduction and a conclusion in speechmaking. We also discuss techniques aimed at fulfilling those roles. If you apply these techniques imaginatively, you will take a big step toward elevating your speeches from the ordinary to the splendid.

The Introduction

First impressions are important. A poor beginning may so distract or alienate listeners that the speaker can never fully recover. Moreover, getting off on the right foot is vital to a speaker's self-confidence. What could be more encouraging than watching your listeners' faces begin to register interest, attention, and pleasure? A good introduction, you will find, is an excellent confidence booster.

In most speech situations, the introduction has four objectives:

- Get the attention and interest of your audience.
- Reveal the topic of your speech.
- Establish your credibility and goodwill.
- Preview the body of the speech.

We'll look at each of these objectives in turn.

GET ATTENTION AND INTEREST

"Unless a speaker can interest his audience at once, his effort will be a failure." So said the great lawyer Clarence Darrow. If your topic is not one of extraordinary interest, your listeners are likely to say to themselves, "So what? Who cares?" A speaker can quickly lose an audience if she or he doesn't use the introduction to get their attention and quicken their interest.

Getting the initial attention of your audience is usually easy—even before you utter a single word. After you are introduced and step to the lectern, your audience will normally give you their attention. If they don't, wait patiently. Look directly at the audience without saying a word. In a few moments all talking and physical commotion will stop. Your listeners will be attentive. You will be ready to start speaking.

Keeping the attention of your audience once you start talking is more difficult. Here are the methods used most often. Employed individually or in combination, they will help get the audience caught up in your speech.

Relate the Topic to the Audience

People pay attention to things that affect them directly. If you can relate the topic to your listeners, they are much more likely to be interested in it.

Suppose, for example, one of your classmates begins her speech like this:

> Today I am going to talk about collecting postcards—a hobby that is both fascinating and financially rewarding. I would like to explain the basic kinds of collectible postcards, why they are so valuable, and how collectors buy and sell their cards.

A good introduction will get your speech off to a strong start. To be most effective, it should relate the topic to the audience and be delivered from a minimum of notes—as in this speech by British anthropologist Jane Goodall.

This is certainly a clear introduction, but it is not one to get you hooked on the speech. Now what if your classmate were to begin her speech this way—as one student actually did.

> It's Saturday morning, and you are helping clean out your grandmother's attic. After working a while, you stumble upon a trunk, open it, and discover hundreds of old postcards. Thinking about getting to the football game on time, you start tossing the cards into the trash can. Congratulations! You have just thrown away a year's tuition.

This time the speaker has used just the right bait. Chances are you will be hooked.

Even when you use other interest-arousing lures, you should *always* relate your topic to the audience. At times this will test your ingenuity, but it pays dividends. Here is an excellent example from a student speech about dreams. The speaker began by saying:

> You're being chased by an object of unspeakable horror, yet your legs can only move in slow motion. Each step takes unbearably long, and your frantic struggle to run faster is hopeless. Your pursuer gets closer, and your desperation turns to terror. You're completely helpless—eye to eye with death.
>
> Then you wake up, gasping for air, your heart pounding, your face clammy with sweat. It takes a few minutes for your heart and breathing to slow down. You reassure yourself that it was "just a dream." Soon you drift back to sleep.

connect

View the beginning of "In Your Dreams" in the online Media Library for this chapter (Video 10.1).

By using vivid language to describe something all his classmates had experienced, the speaker made sure of an attentive audience.

State the Importance of Your Topic

Presumably, you think your speech is important. Tell your audience why they should think so too. Here is how Judith Kaye, Chief Judge of the State of New York, used this method to involve her audience in a speech to the American Bar Association Center on Children and the Law:

> We know that a child is born into poverty in the United States every 36 seconds, and we see 12.8 million children living below the poverty line. . . . A child dies from neglect or abuse every six hours, a child is killed by gunfire almost every three hours, and the number of neglected or abused children each year would fill up the city of Detroit.[1]

These are striking statistics. By citing them in her introduction, Kaye emphasized the importance of her topic and captured the attention of her audience.

Clearly this technique is easy to use when discussing social and political issues such as child abuse, endangered species, terrorism, and stem cell research, but it is appropriate for other topics as well. Here is how one student handled it in a speech about starting a home aquarium:

> It is very hard to cuddle a fish. Fish won't roll over or fetch the morning paper. You won't find them curling up on your lap, chasing a ball of string, or rescuing a child from a burning building.
>
> Yet despite these shortcomings, 150 million tropical fish have found their way into 14 million American homes. Each year $60 million of tropical fish are sold in the United States, and they have earned a spot next to the all-American dog and the cuddly kitten in the hearts of millions of people. Today I would like to explain how you can start a home aquarium and discover the pleasures of owning tropical fish.

Whenever you discuss a topic whose importance may not be clear to the audience, you should think about ways to demonstrate its significance in the introduction.

Startle the Audience

One surefire way to arouse interest quickly is to startle your listeners with an arresting or intriguing statement. Everyone in the audience paid close attention after this speaker's introduction:

> Take a moment and think of the three women closest to you. Who comes to mind? Your mother? Your sister? Your girlfriend? Your wife? Your best friend? Now guess which one will be sexually assaulted during her lifetime. It's not a pleasant thought, but according to the U.S. Department of Justice, one of every three American women will be sexually assaulted sometime during her life.

Notice the buildup to the speaker's arresting statement, "Now guess which one will be sexually assaulted during her lifetime." This statement startles the audience—especially the men—and drives home at a personal level the problem of sexual assault against women.

This technique is highly effective and easy to use. Just be sure the startling introduction relates directly to the subject of your speech. If you choose a strong opening simply for its shock value and then go on to talk about something else, your audience will be confused and possibly annoyed.

Arouse the Curiosity of the Audience

People are curious. One way to draw them into your speech is with a series of statements that progressively whet their curiosity about the subject of the speech. For example:

> It is the most common chronic disease in the United States. Controllable but incurable, it is a symptomless disease. You can have it for years and never know until it kills you. Some 73 million Americans have this disease, and 300,000 will die from it before the year is out. Odds are that five of us in this class have it.
>
> What am I talking about? Not cancer. Not AIDS. Not heart disease. I am talking about hypertension—high blood pressure.

By building suspense about his subject, the speaker pulls his audience into the speech. Notice how much less effective the introduction would have been if he had simply said, "Today I am going to talk about high blood pressure."

Question the Audience

Asking a *rhetorical question* is another way to get your listeners thinking about your speech. Sometimes a single question will do:

> How would you respond if a loved one was the victim of terrorism?

> What would you think if you went to the doctor because you were ill and she told you to watch *Modern Family* as part of your treatment?

In other circumstances, you may want to pose a series of questions, each of which draws the audience deeper and deeper into the speech. Here is how one speaker used this method:

rhetorical question

A question that the audience answers mentally rather than out loud.

> Have you ever spent a sleepless night studying for an exam? Can you remember rushing to finish a term paper because you waited too long to start writing it? Do you often feel overwhelmed by all the things you have to get done at school? At work? At home?
>
> If so, you may be the victim of poor time management. Fortunately, there are proven strategies you can follow to use your time more effectively and to keep control of your life.

When using this technique, be sure to pause for just a moment after each question. This adds dramatic impact and gives the question time to sink in. The audience, of course, will answer mentally—not out loud.

Begin with a Quotation

Another way to arouse the interest of your audience is to start with an attention-getting quotation. You might choose your quotation from Shakespeare or Confucius, from the Bible or Talmud, from a poem, song, or film. Here is how one student used a humorous quotation to begin a speech about the need for political reform in the U.S. Congress:

> Mark Twain once said, "It could probably be shown by facts and figures that there is no distinctly American criminal class except Congress."

You need not use a famous quotation. The following made an effective introduction for a speech about bird watching:

"It is a moment I will never forget. I glimpsed a flash of color in the thicket, and then I saw it—a Bachman's Warbler, one of the rarest birds in all of America. I was so excited I could barely keep my binoculars from shaking."

This statement was made by my father. He is just one of the millions of people who have discovered the joys of bird-watching.

Notice that both of the quotations used here as examples are relatively short. Opening your speech with a lengthy quotation is a sure way to set your audience yawning.

Tell a Story

We all enjoy stories—especially if they are provocative, dramatic, or suspenseful. Consider the story one student told to open his remarks about the devastating earthquake and tsunami that struck Japan on March 11, 2011:

A young couple clutched their four-month-old baby girl as a tidal wave smashed into their home in northern Japan. The wave, caused by a massive 9.0 earthquake earlier in the day, was simply too powerful. It ripped the baby girl

checklist

Speech Introduction

YES	NO	
☐	☐	1. Do I gain the attention and interest of my audience by using one or more of the methods discussed in this chapter?
☐	☐	2. Do I relate the speech topic to my audience?
☐	☐	3. Do I clearly reveal the topic of my speech?
☐	☐	4. Do I establish my credibility to speak on this topic?
☐	☐	5. If my topic is controversial, do I take steps to establish my goodwill toward the audience?
☐	☐	6. Do I define any key terms that will be necessary for the audience to understand the rest of my speech?
☐	☐	7. Do I provide a preview statement of the main points to be covered in the body of the speech?
☐	☐	8. Is the introduction limited to 10–20 percent of my entire speech?
☐	☐	9. Have I worked out the language of my introduction in detail?
☐	☐	10. Have I practiced the delivery of my introduction so I can present it fluently, confidently, and with strong eye contact?

As you research your speeches, keep an eye out for quotations, stories, and other materials you can use to craft an introduction that will capture the attention of your listeners.

from the arms of her parents and carried her off amidst piles of debris. The parents could not stop weeping at the thought of their dead child.

Three days later, rescue workers were combing through mounds of wood, metal, and rock when they heard a faint cry. Working frantically, they pulled the lost baby out of the rubble—alive. "Her discovery put a new energy into the search," one of her rescuers told a local news crew in a story later reported by *Time* magazine.

Not everyone was as fortunate as that little girl—or as the parents who were reunited with her. But as Japan tried to overcome the devastation, any sign of hope was welcomed with open arms.

Like many good introductions, this one does a double job—it arouses the interest of the audience and gets listeners emotionally involved in the speech.

You can also use stories based on your personal experience. Here is how one pre-med student used such a story. She began by recounting the first time she observed doctors performing surgery in the operating room:

There I stood, wearing a surgical mask, in the middle of a large, brightly lit room. In the center of the room were five figures huddled over a table. I found it difficult to see since everything was draped in blue sheets, yet I didn't dare take a step toward the table.

Then one of the figures called to me, "Angela, get over here and take a closer look." My knees buckled as I walked through the sterile environment. But eventually I was there, standing over an unconscious body in the operating room.

connect

View the beginning of "Hoping to Heal" in the online Media Library for this chapter (Video 10.2).

The effectiveness of any story—especially a personal one—hinges on the speaker's delivery as well as on the content. As you can see from the excerpt of this speech on Video 10.2 in the online Media Library for this chapter, the speaker uses pauses, eye contact, and changes in her tone of voice to help draw her audience into the speech. See if you can do the same in your introduction.

The seven methods discussed above are the ones used most often by student speakers to gain attention and interest. Other methods include referring to the occasion, inviting audience participation, using audio equipment or visual aids, relating to a previous speaker, and beginning with humor. For any given speech, try to choose the method that is most suitable for the topic, the audience, and the occasion.

REVEAL THE TOPIC

In the process of gaining attention, be sure to state clearly the topic of your speech. If you do not, your listeners will be confused. And once they are confused, your chances of getting them absorbed in the speech are almost nil.

This is a basic point—so basic that it may hardly seem worth mentioning. Yet you would be surprised how many students need to be reminded of it. You may hear speeches in your own class in which the topic is not clear by the end of the introduction. So you will know what to avoid, here is such an introduction, presented in a public speaking class:

> Imagine taking a leisurely boat ride along a peaceful waterway. The sun is high in the sky, reflecting brightly off the ripples around you. The banks are lush with mangrove and cypress trees. You see a stately pelican resting on a low-lying branch. You grab your camera, snap a shot, and check the result. The picture is perfect. But will it be perfect in the future?

What is the topic of this speech? Nature photography? No. Birding? No. Tourism in the tropics? No. The student was talking about efforts to restore the natural beauty of the Florida Everglades. But she did not make that clear to her audience. Suppose, instead, she had begun her speech differently:

> Alligators, panthers, otters, brown pelicans—these and other creatures have lost 50 percent of their habitat in south Florida over the past few decades. Now, however, there is an $8 billion program to preserve their home in the Florida Everglades. The largest restoration effort in the history of the world, it will rejuvenate one of America's most diverse ecosystems and protect it for future generations.

This opening would have provided a way to get the audience's attention, but it also would have related directly to the speech topic. If you beat around the bush in your introduction, you may lose your listeners. Even if they already know your topic, you should restate it clearly and concisely at some point in the introduction.

ESTABLISH CREDIBILITY AND GOODWILL

Besides getting attention and revealing the topic, there is a third objective you may need to accomplish in your introduction—establishing your credibility and goodwill.

credibility

The audience's perception of whether a speaker is qualified to speak on a given topic.

Credibility is mostly a matter of being qualified to speak on a given topic—and of being *perceived* as qualified by your listeners. Here is how one student established her credibility on the subject of weight lifting without sounding like a braggart:

> Once seen as an exclusively male activity, weight lifting has crossed the gender barrier—and with good reason. Regardless of whether you are male or female, weight lifting can give you a sense of strength and power, enhance your self-esteem, and make you look and feel better.
>
> I started lifting weights when I was in high school, and I have kept at it for the past eight years. I have also taught weight lifting in several health clubs, and I am a certified instructor through the Aerobics and Fitness Association of America.

Telling a story is an excellent way to gain attention in a speech introduction. The story should be clearly relevant to the topic and should be delivered expressively with strong eye contact.

> Using some of my experience, I would like to explain the basic kinds of weights and how to use them properly.

Whether or not you lift weights, you will probably be more interested in the speech when you realize that the speaker knows what she is talking about.

Your credibility need not be based on firsthand knowledge and experience. It can come from reading, from classes, from interviews, from friends—as in these cases:

> I have been interested in the myth of Atlantis for several years, and I have read a number of books and articles about it.

> The information I am going to share with you today comes mostly from my biology class and an interview with Reyna Vasquez of the local Audubon Society.

Whatever the source of your expertise, be sure to let the audience know.

Establishing your *goodwill* is a slightly different challenge. It is often crucial outside the classroom, where speakers have well-established reputations and may be identified with causes that arouse hostility among listeners. In such a situation, the speaker must try to defuse that hostility right at the start of the speech.

goodwill

The audience's perception of whether the speaker has the best interests of the audience in mind.

Occasionally you may have to do the same thing in your classroom speeches. Suppose you advocate a potentially unpopular position. You will need to make a special effort to ensure that your classmates will consider your point of view. This is how one student tried to minimize her classmates' opposition in the introduction of a speech urging them to change the way they use their cell phones:

> Now, don't worry, I'm not going to try to persuade you to abandon your constant companion. I still use mine on a regular basis, and I probably always will. But I do hope to persuade you to make one simple change in the way you use your cell phone—a change that will protect your health and could even make the difference between a long life and premature death.

connect

View this portion of "The Dangers of Cell Phones" in the online Media Library for this chapter (Video 10.3).

The speaker was clear about her intentions and reasonable in her expectations. By the end of the introduction, the audience knew she had their best interests at heart.

PREVIEW THE BODY OF THE SPEECH

As we saw in Chapter 3, most people are poor listeners. Even good listeners need all the help they can get in sorting out a speaker's ideas. One way to help your listeners is to tell them in the introduction what they should listen for in the rest of the speech. Here is an excellent example, from a speech by U.S. Secretary of Defense Robert Gates at the U.S. Military Academy, West Point, on February 25, 2011:

preview statement

A statement in the introduction of a speech that identifies the main points to be discussed in the body.

> Today, I'd like to focus on three interrelated issues—the future of conflict and the implications for the Army; how best to institutionalize the diverse capabilities that will be required; and the kinds of officers the Army will need for the 21st century.[2]

After this introduction, there was no doubt about Gates's topic or the main points he would cover in his speech.

In some types of persuasive speeches, you may not want to reveal your central idea until later in the speech. But even in such a situation you must be sure your audience is not left guessing about the main points they should listen for as the speech unfolds. Nearly always, you should include a *preview statement* like the following:

connect™

View these preview statements from student speeches in the online Media Library for this chapter (Video 10.4).

> The goal of my speech today is to inform you about Ramadan—specifically its history and practices. In the end, I hope you'll have a better understanding of this sacred time for Muslims in the United States and around the globe.

> I am convinced that we need to take action to combat the problem of phony pharmaceuticals. Later in my speech, I'll share a plan with you for curbing the spread of these dangerous drugs. But let's start by taking a closer look at the problem.

Preview statements such as these serve another purpose as well. Because they usually come at the very end of the introduction, they provide a smooth lead-in to the body of the speech. They signal that the body of the speech is about to begin.

There is one other aspect you may want to cover in previewing your speech. You can use your introduction to give specialized information—definitions or background—that your listeners will need if they are to understand the rest of the speech. Often you can do this very quickly, as in the following example:

> A triathlon is a race made up of three different events completed in succession. The events are usually swimming, biking, and running, though canoeing is sometimes substituted for one of these.

In other circumstances, you may have to explain an important term in more detail. Here is how one student handled the problem in a speech about the Underground Railroad used by slaves to escape from the South before the Civil War:

The term "Underground Railroad" was first used about 1830. But in fact, the Underground Railroad was neither underground nor a railroad. It was an informal network that provided runaway slaves food, clothing, directions, and places to hide on their escape routes to the North and to Canada.

Why was it called the Underground Railroad? Because of its secrecy and because many of the people involved used railroad terms as code words. Hiding places, for example, were called "stations," and people who helped the slaves were called "conductors." Over the years, the Underground Railroad helped thousands of slaves make their way from bondage to freedom.

SAMPLE INTRODUCTION WITH COMMENTARY

So far we have seen many excerpts showing how to fulfill the various objectives of an introduction. Now here is a complete introduction from a student speech. The side comments indicate the principles used in developing the introduction.

connect

View this introduction in the online Media Library for this chapter (Video 10.5).

Surrounded by Stuff

COMMENTARY	SPEECH
The speaker uses a story to gain attention. This story works particularly well because it is richly detailed and is high in human interest. The frequent use of "you" helps relate the story to the audience.	For my Aunt Josefina, life can be empty, even though she's surrounded by tons of stuff. Walking into her living room, you'll see stacks of magazines and newspapers, piles of clean and dirty laundry, and boxes of collectible figurines. But you won't find a place to sit down. In her kitchen, you'll see towers of dishes, scores of empty two-liter bottles, and over a dozen trash bags. But you won't see a kitchen table.
Now the speaker reveals her topic and defines the meaning of hoarding. The way she gradually reveals Aunt Josefina's malady helps build the audience's interest. Her personal involvement with the topic increases her credibility and goodwill.	Some people say Aunt Josefina is lazy. Others say she's just dirty. But my family and I know the truth: Aunt Josefina suffers from a mental disorder known as Collyer's Syndrome, or disposophobia. But you probably know it by its most common name: compulsive hoarding. Those who suffer from compulsive hoarding can't bring themselves to get rid of anything. It doesn't matter if the things are valuable; it only matters that they hold on to them.
The speaker uses statistics to show the importance of her topic. Mentioning her research for the speech further bolsters her credibility.	Over the years, my family and I have become painfully aware of what life is like for a compulsive hoarder. But until researching the topic for this speech, I had no idea how widespread the disorder was. Gail Steketee and Randy Frost, authors of *Stuff: Compulsive Hoarding and the Meaning of Things,* report that anywhere from 6 million to 15 million Americans are compulsive hoarders.
The introduction ends with a clear preview of the main points to be discussed in the body.	Today I would like to introduce you to the world of compulsive hoarding. I will show you the seriousness of the problem, the impact it can have on individuals and families, and the ways it can be treated.

TIPS FOR THE INTRODUCTION

1. Keep the introduction relatively brief. Under normal circumstances it should not constitute more than 10 to 20 percent of your speech.

2. Be on the lookout for possible introductory materials as you do your research. File them with your notes so they will be handy when you are ready for them.

3. Be creative in devising your introduction. Experiment with two or three different openings and choose the one that seems most likely to get the audience interested in your speech.

4. Don't worry about the exact wording of your introduction until you have finished preparing the body of the speech. After you have determined your main points, it will be much easier to make final decisions about how to begin the speech.

5. Work out your introduction in detail. Some teachers recommend that you write it out word for word; others prefer that you outline it. Whichever method you use, practice the introduction over and over until you can deliver it smoothly from a minimum of notes and with strong eye contact.

6. When you present the speech, don't start talking too soon. Make sure the audience has quieted down and is focused on you before you begin. Establish eye contact with the audience, smile, and then launch into your opening words. Give yourself every chance to make sure your introduction has the desired impact.

The Conclusion

"Great is the art of beginning," said Longfellow, "but greater the art is of ending." Longfellow was thinking of poetry, but his insight is equally applicable to public speaking. Many a speaker has marred an otherwise fine speech by a long-winded, silly, or antagonistic conclusion. Your closing remarks are your last chance to drive home your ideas. Moreover, your final impression will probably linger in your listeners' minds. Thus you need to craft your conclusion with as much care as your introduction.

No matter what kind of speech you are giving, the conclusion has two major functions:

- To let the audience know you are ending the speech.
- To reinforce the audience's understanding of, or commitment to, the central idea.

Let us look at each.

SIGNAL THE END OF THE SPEECH

It may seem obvious that you should let your audience know you are going to stop soon. However, you will almost certainly hear speeches in your class in which the speaker concludes so abruptly that you are taken by surprise. Too sudden an ending leaves the audience puzzled and unfulfilled.

How do you let an audience know your speech is ending? One way is through what you say. "In conclusion," "My purpose has been," "Let me end by saying"—these are all brief cues that you are getting ready to stop.

You can also let your audience know the end is in sight by your manner of delivery. The conclusion is the climax of a speech. A speaker who has carefully built to a peak of interest and involvement will not need to say anything like "in conclusion." By use of the voice—its tone, pacing, intonation, and rhythm—a speaker can build the momentum of a speech so there is no doubt when it is over.

The conclusion is your last chance to drive home your ideas. Here Geena Davis concludes her keynote address at the Spark Summit rally at Hunter College in New York City.

One method of doing this has been likened to a musical crescendo. As in a symphony in which one instrument after another joins in until the entire orchestra is playing, the speech builds in force until it reaches a zenith of power and intensity.[3] (This does *not* mean simply getting louder and louder. It is a combination of many things, including vocal pitch, choice of words, dramatic content, gestures, pauses—and possibly loudness.)

A superb example of this method is the memorable conclusion to Martin Luther King's "I've Been to the Mountaintop," the speech he delivered the night before he was assassinated in April 1968. Speaking to an audience of 2,000 people in Memphis, Tennessee, he ended his speech with a stirring declaration that the civil rights movement would succeed despite the many threats on his life:

crescendo ending

A conclusion in which the speech builds to a zenith of power and intensity.

> Like anybody, I would like to live a long life. Longevity has its place, but I'm not concerned about that now. I just want to do God's will, and he's allowed me to go up to the mountain, and I've looked over and I've seen the Promised Land. I may not get there with you, but I want you to know tonight that we as a people will get to the Promised Land. So I'm happy tonight. I'm not worried about anything; I'm not fearing any man. Mine eyes have seen the glory of the coming of the Lord.

Another effective method might be compared to the dissolve ending of a concert song that evokes deep emotions: "The song seems to fade away while the light on the singer shrinks gradually to a smaller and smaller circle until it lights only the face, then the eyes. Finally, it is a pinpoint, and disappears with the last note of the song."[4] Here is a speech ending that does much the same thing. It is from General Douglas MacArthur's moving farewell to the cadets at the U.S. Military Academy:

connect™

View the ending of Martin Luther King's "I've Been to the Mountaintop" in the online Media Library for this chapter (Video 10.6).

> In my dreams I hear again the crash of guns, the rattle of musketry, the strange, mournful mutter of the battlefield. But in the evening of my memory always I come back to West Point. Always there echoes and re-echoes: duty, honor, country.
>
> Today marks my final roll call with you. But I want you to know that when I cross the river, my last conscious thoughts will be of the Corps, and the Corps, and the Corps.
>
> I bid you farewell.

Using public speaking in your CAREER

Your degree in civil engineering has served you well and you are now the chief city planner for a major metropolis. After studying the issue for more than a year, you and the planning commission have decided that the best way to relieve the city's growing traffic congestion is to build a new downtown freeway. Unfortunately, there is no way to build the freeway without knocking down a number of houses and businesses.

Not surprisingly, the neighborhood association that represents the area through which the new freeway will run has expressed a number of concerns about the proposal. Because of your excellent public speaking skills, you have been chosen to represent the city at a meeting of the neighborhood association. You know that if your speech is to be persuasive, you must use the introduction to establish your credibility and goodwill so your listeners will be willing to listen receptively to what you say in the body.

Write a draft of your introduction. Be sure to address all four functions of a speech introduction discussed in this chapter.

The final words fade like the spotlight, bringing the speech to an emotional close.

You may think that you couldn't possibly end a speech with that much pathos—and you'd be right. MacArthur was an eloquent speaker discussing a grave issue with extraordinary poignance. This combination rarely occurs. But that doesn't mean you can't use the dissolve ending effectively. One student used it with great effect in a speech about the immigrant experience in the United States. During the body of the speech, the student spoke about the numbers of immigrants and the challenges they faced. Then, in her conclusion, she created a moving dissolve ending by evoking the emotional images of her grandfather's arrival in the United States:

> On a recent trip to Ellis Island, where my grandfather first stepped on American soil, I saw his name etched into the wall along with the names of tens of thousands of other immigrants. I saw the entry hall where he lined up to process his forms. I saw the room where he underwent a physical examination. I sensed the fear and insecurity he must have felt. But I could also sense his excitement as he looked forward to life in a land of opportunity—a land he came to think of as home.

dissolve ending

A conclusion that generates emotional appeal by fading step by step to a dramatic final statement.

Both the crescendo and the dissolve endings must be worked out with great care. Practice until you get the words and the timing just right. The benefits will be well worth your time.

REINFORCE THE CENTRAL IDEA

The second major function of a conclusion is to reinforce the audience's understanding of, or commitment to, the central idea. There are many ways to do this. Here are the ones you are most likely to use.

Summarize Your Speech

Restating the main points is the easiest way to end a speech. One student used this technique effectively in his persuasive speech about the AIDS epidemic in Africa:

> In conclusion, we have seen that the AIDS epidemic is having a devastating effect on African society. An entire adult generation is slowly being wiped out. An entirely new generation of AIDS orphans is being created. Governments in the nations most afflicted have neither the resources nor the expertise to counter the epidemic. Many African economies are being crippled by the loss of people in the workplace.
>
> Before it's too late, the United Nations and developed countries need to increase their efforts to halt the epidemic and bring it under control. The lives and well-being of tens of millions of people hang in the balance.

connect™

View the conclusion of "AIDS in Africa: A World Crisis" in the online Media Library for this chapter (Video 10.7).

The value of a summary is that it explicitly restates the central idea and main points one last time. But as we shall see, there are more imaginative and compelling ways to end a speech. They can be used in combination with a summary or, at times, in place of it.

End with a Quotation

A quotation is one of the most common and effective devices to conclude a speech. Here is a fine example, from a speech on volunteering for Big Brothers or Big Sisters:

> None of us have the extra time that we'd like. But whatever time you can spare, you'll be making a world of difference in the life of an underprivileged child. In the words of the poet Henry Wadsworth Longfellow, "Give what you have. To someone, it may be better than you dare to think."

The closing quotation is particularly good because its urgency is exactly suited to the speech. When you run across a *brief* quotation that so perfectly captures your central idea, keep it in mind as a possible conclusion.

Make a Dramatic Statement

Rather than using a quotation to give your conclusion force and vitality, you may want to devise your own dramatic statement. Some speeches have become famous because of their powerful closing lines. One is Patrick Henry's legendary "Liberty or Death" oration. It takes its name from the final sentences Henry uttered on March 23, 1775, as he exhorted his audience to resist British tyranny:

> Is life so dear, or peace so sweet, as to be purchased at the price of chains and slavery? Forbid it, Almighty God! I know not what course others may take; but as for me, give me liberty, or give me death.

Although your classroom speeches are not likely to become famous, you can still rivet your listeners—as Henry did—with a dramatic concluding statement. What follows is a particularly striking example, from a speech on suicide prevention. Throughout the speech, the student referred to a friend

checklist

Speech Conclusion

YES	NO	
☐	☐	1. Do I signal that my speech is coming to an end?
☐	☐	2. Do I reinforce my central idea by: Summarizing the main points of my speech Ending with a quotation Making a dramatic statement Referring to the introduction
☐	☐	3. Is the conclusion limited to 5–10 percent of my entire speech?
☐	☐	4. Have I worked out the language of my conclusion in detail?
☐	☐	5. Have I practiced the delivery of my conclusion so I can present it fluently, confidently, and with strong eye contact?

who had tried to commit suicide the previous year. Then, in the conclusion, she said:

> My friend is back in school, participating in activities she never did before—and enjoying it. I'm happy and proud to say that she's still fighting for her life and even happier that she failed to kill herself. Otherwise, I wouldn't be here today trying to help you. You see, I am my "friend," and I'm more than glad to say I've made it.

As you can imagine, the audience was stunned. The closing lines brought the speech to a dramatic conclusion. The speaker made it even more effective by pausing just a moment before the last words and by using her voice to give them just the right inflection.

Refer to the Introduction

An excellent way to give your speech psychological unity is to conclude by referring to ideas in the introduction. Here is how one student used the method in her speech about carbon monoxide poisoning:

Introduction It was supposed to be a time of celebration. Five friends had gathered in a south Florida hotel room to celebrate a birthday. Juchen Martial, one of the five, was turning nineteen. But the day after the birthday party, a maid passing by the hotel room glanced through a window and saw five dead bodies. All five friends had been killed.

Their killer was silent, invisible, odorless, and tasteless. Their killer was carbon monoxide. The friends had left their car running in a carport directly beneath their hotel room. Carbon monoxide seeped into the room and took their lives—as it does the lives of 400 people a year in the United States.

In the body of her speech, the student looked in detail at the problem of carbon monoxide poisoning and explained ways to head off the problem. Then, in her closing words, she tied the whole speech together by returning to the story described in her introduction:

Conclusion Remember those five friends I mentioned in the introduction of my speech? Their deaths were tragic and unnecessary. I hope the information I have provided today will help you avoid their fate. By understanding where carbon monoxide comes from, by recognizing the warning signs of carbon monoxide poisoning, and by following the simple preventive steps I've discussed, you can make sure that you don't fall victim to the silent killer.

connect™

View the beginning and ending of "The Silent Killer" in the online Media Library for this chapter (Video 10.8).

Summarizing the speech, ending with a quotation, making a dramatic statement, referring to the introduction—all these techniques can be used separately. But you have probably noticed that speakers often combine two or more in their conclusions. Actually, all four techniques can be fused into one—for example, a dramatic quotation that summarizes the central idea while referring to the introduction.

One other concluding technique is making a direct appeal to your audience for action. This technique applies only to a particular type of persuasive speech, however, and will be discussed in Chapter 16. The four methods covered in this chapter are appropriate for all kinds of speeches and occasions.

SAMPLE CONCLUSION WITH COMMENTARY

How do you fit these methods together to make a conclusion? Here is an example, from the speech about compulsive hoarding whose introduction we looked at earlier (page 195).

connect™

View this conclusion in the online Media Library for this chapter (Video 10.9).

COMMENTARY	CONCLUSION
The speaker gives an excellent summary of her speech. This is particularly important when speaking to inform because it gives you one last chance to make sure the audience remembers your main points.	Today we have seen that compulsive hoarding is a serious mental disorder whose effects can be devastating for individuals and families. It's also difficult to treat, which means that millions of Americans are left living a life of clutter and chaos.
By referring to her Aunt Josefina, whom she had mentioned in her introduction, the speaker unifies the entire speech. The quotation from Aunt Josefina and the speaker's final sentence end the speech on a strong note.	My Aunt Josefina is one of those people. She says: "People look at my apartment and know I have a problem. I look at my apartment and know I have a problem. I'm trying to get it under control, but it's a really long road." For my Aunt Josefina and millions of others, the good news is that understanding the problem is the first step toward conquering all the stuff.

TIPS FOR THE CONCLUSION

1. As with the introduction, keep an eye out for possible concluding materials as you research and develop the speech.

2. Conclude with a bang, not a whimper. Be creative in devising a conclusion that hits the hearts and minds of your audience. Work on several possible endings, and select the one that seems likely to have the greatest impact.

3. Don't be long-winded. The conclusion will normally make up no more than 5 to 10 percent of your speech.

4. Don't leave anything in your conclusion to chance. Work it out in detail, and give yourself plenty of time to practice delivering it. Many students like to write out the conclusion word for word to guarantee it is just right. If you do this, make sure you can present it smoothly, confidently, and with feeling—without relying on your notes or sounding wooden. Make your last impression as forceful and as favorable as you can.

Summary

First impressions are important. So are final impressions. This is why speeches need strong introductions and conclusions.

In most speech situations you need to accomplish four objectives with your introduction—get the attention and interest of the audience, reveal the topic of your speech, establish your credibility and goodwill, and preview the body of the speech. Gaining attention and interest can be done in several ways. You can show the importance of your topic, especially as it relates to your audience. You can startle or question your audience or arouse their curiosity. You can begin with a quotation or a story.

Be sure to state the topic of your speech clearly in your introduction so the audience knows where the speech is going. Establishing credibility means that you tell the audience why you are qualified to speak on the topic at hand. Establishing goodwill may be necessary if your point of view is unpopular. Previewing the body of the speech helps the audience listen effectively and provides a smooth lead-in to the body of the speech.

The first objective of a speech conclusion is to let the audience know you are ending, which you can do by your words or by your manner of delivery. The second objective of a conclusion is to reinforce your central idea. You can accomplish this by summarizing the speech, ending with a quotation, making a dramatic statement, or referring to the introduction. Sometimes you may want to combine two or more of these techniques. Be creative in devising a vivid, forceful conclusion.

Key Terms

rhetorical question *(189)*
credibility *(192)*
goodwill *(193)*
preview statement *(194)*
crescendo ending *(197)*
dissolve ending *(198)*

Review Questions

After reading this chapter, you should be able to answer the following questions:

1. What are the four objectives of a speech introduction?
2. What are seven methods you can use in the introduction to get the attention and interest of your audience?
3. Why is it important to establish your credibility at the beginning of your speech?
4. What is a preview statement? Why should you nearly always include a preview statement in the introduction of your speech?
5. What are six tips for your introduction?
6. What are the major functions of a speech conclusion?
7. What are two ways you can signal the end of your speech?
8. What are four ways to reinforce the central idea when concluding your speech?
9. What are four tips for your conclusion?

connect™

For further review, go to the LearnSmart study module for this chapter.

Exercises for Critical Thinking

1. Here are six speech topics. Explain how you might relate each to your classmates in the introduction of a speech.

Social Security	laughter
coffee	steroids
illiteracy	blood donation

2. Think of a speech topic (preferably one for your next speech in class). Create an introduction for a speech dealing with any aspect of the topic you wish. In your introduction, be sure to gain the attention of the audience, to reveal the topic and relate it to the audience, to establish your credibility, and to preview the body of the speech.
3. Using the same topic as in Exercise 2, create a speech conclusion. Be sure to let your audience know the speech is ending, to reinforce the central idea, and to make the conclusion vivid and memorable.

11

Outlining the Speech

Think what might happen if you tried to build a house without a floor plan or an architect's blueprint. You install a cathedral ceiling so you can have big windows and a huge ceiling fan, but the roof is so high it blocks your bedroom window upstairs. You put in sliding doors to the yard, but they can't be opened because they're too close to the fireplace to slide back without hitting it. You think it's a wonderful idea to have almost no interior walls. But when the first snowfall comes, your (unsupported) roof collapses.

Plans and blueprints are essential to architecture. So, too, are outlines essential to effective speeches. An outline is like a blueprint for your speech. It allows you to see the full scope and content of your speech at a glance. By outlining, you can judge whether each part of the speech is fully developed, whether you have adequate supporting materials for your main points, and whether the main points are properly balanced. An outline helps you make sure that related items are together, that ideas flow from one to another, that the structure of your speech will "stand up"—and not collapse.

Probably you will use two kinds of outlines for your speeches—one very detailed, for the planning stage, and one very brief, for the delivery of the speech.

The Preparation Outline

The preparation outline is just what its name implies—an outline that helps you prepare the speech. Writing a preparation outline means putting your speech together—deciding what you will say in the introduction, how you will organize the main points and supporting materials in the body, and what you will say in the conclusion.

GUIDELINES FOR THE PREPARATION OUTLINE

preparation outline

A detailed outline developed during the process of speech preparation that includes the title, specific purpose, central idea, introduction, main points, subpoints, connectives, conclusion, and bibliography of a speech.

Over the years, a relatively uniform system for preparation outlines has developed. It is explained below and is exemplified in the sample outline on pages 211–213. You should check with your teacher to see exactly what format you are to follow.

State the Specific Purpose of Your Speech

The specific purpose statement should be a separate unit that comes before the outline itself. Including the specific purpose makes it easier to assess how well you have constructed the speech to accomplish your purpose.

Identify the Central Idea

Some teachers prefer that the central idea be given immediately after the purpose statement. Others prefer that it be given and identified in the text of the outline. Check to see which your teacher wants.

Label the Introduction, Body, and Conclusion

If you label the parts of your speech, you will be sure that you indeed *have* an introduction and conclusion and have accomplished the essential objectives of each. Usually the names of the speech parts are placed in the middle of the page or in the far left margin. They are technical labels only and are not included in the system of symbolization used to identify main points and supporting materials.

Use a Consistent Pattern of Symbolization and Indentation

In the most common system of outlining, main points are identified by Roman numerals and are indented equally so as to be aligned down the page. Subpoints (components of the main points) are identified by capital letters and are also indented equally so as to be aligned with each other.

Beyond this, there may be sub-subpoints and even sub-sub-subpoints. For example:

I. Main point
   A. Subpoint
   B. Subpoint
      1. Sub-subpoint
      2. Sub-subpoint
         a. Sub-sub-subpoint
         b. Sub-sub-subpoint

II. Main point
  A. Subpoint
    1. Sub-subpoint
    2. Sub-subpoint
  B. Subpoint
    1. Sub-subpoint
    2. Sub-subpoint

The clear *visual framework* of this outline immediately shows the relationships among the ideas of the speech. The most important ideas (main points) are farthest to the left. Less important ideas (subpoints, sub-subpoints, and so on) are progressively farther to the right. This pattern reveals the structure of your entire speech.

visual framework

The pattern of symbolization and indentation in a speech outline that shows the relationships among the speaker's ideas.

Once you have organized the body of your speech (see Chapter 9), you should have identified the main points. You need only flesh out your outline with subpoints and sub-subpoints, as necessary, to support the main points. But suppose, as sometimes happens, you find yourself with a list of statements and are not sure which are main points, which are subpoints, and so forth. Such a list might look like this:

> There were 13 people at the Last Supper—Jesus and his 12 disciples.
>
> Many superstitions revolve around numbers.
>
> In the United States, 13 is often omitted in the floor numbering of hotels and skyscrapers.
>
> The number 13 has meant bad luck as long as anyone can remember.

Which statement is the main point? The second statement ("Many superstitions revolve around numbers"), which is broader in scope than any of the other statements. This would be one of the main ideas of your speech. The fourth statement is the subpoint; it immediately supports the main point. The other two statements are sub-subpoints; they illustrate the subpoint. Rearranged properly, they look like this:

I. Many superstitions revolve around numbers.
  A. The number 13 has meant bad luck as long as anyone can remember.
    1. There were 13 people at the Last Supper—Jesus and his 12 disciples.
    2. In the United States, 13 is often omitted in the floor numbering of hotels and skyscrapers.

Above all, remember that all points at the same level should immediately support the point that is just above and one notch to the left in your outline.

State Main Points and Subpoints in Full Sentences

Below are two sets of main points and subpoints for the same speech on the life of Martin Luther King.

Ineffective	More Effective
I. Montgomery	I. King began his civil rights career in the Montgomery bus boycott of 1955–1956.
II. 1960s	II. King's greatest triumphs came during the early 1960s.
A. Birmingham	A. In 1963, he campaigned against segregation in Birmingham, Alabama.
B. March	B. Later that year, he participated in the famous march on Washington, D.C.
1. 200,000	1. More than 200,000 people took part.
2. "Dream"	2. King gave his "I Have a Dream" speech.
C. Prize	C. In 1964, he received the Nobel Peace Prize.
III. Final years	III. King faced great turmoil during his final years.
A. Criticized	A. He was criticized by more militant blacks for being nonviolent.
B. Vietnam	B. He protested against the war in Vietnam.
C. Assassination	C. He was assassinated in Memphis, Tennessee, on April 4, 1968.

connect

For help formatting your outlines, use the automated Outline Tool in the online Speech Tools for this chapter.

The sample at left might serve as a speaking outline, but it is virtually useless as a preparation outline. It gives only vague labels rather than distinct ideas. It does not indicate clearly the content of the main points and subpoints. Nor does it reveal whether the speaker has thought out his or her ideas. But there is no concern about any of these matters with the outline on the right.

In sum, a skimpy preparation outline is of little value. Stating your main points and subpoints in full sentences will ensure that you develop your ideas fully.

Label Transitions, Internal Summaries, and Internal Previews

One way to make sure you have strong transitions, internal summaries, and internal previews is to include them in the preparation outline. Usually they are not incorporated into the system of symbolization and indentation but are labeled separately and inserted in the outline where they will appear in the speech.

Attach a Bibliography

bibliography

A list of all the sources used in preparing a speech.

You should include with the outline a bibliography that shows all the books, magazines, newspapers, and Internet sources you consulted, as well as any interviews or field research you conducted.

The two major bibliographic formats are those developed by the Modern Language Association (MLA) and the American Psychological Association (APA). Both are widely used by communication scholars; ask your instructor which he or she prefers. No matter which format you adopt, make sure your statement of sources is clear, accurate, and consistent. For help, turn to page 135

As blueprints are essential to architecture, so outlines are essential to speechmaking. Developing an outline helps ensure that the structure of your speech is clear and coherent.

in Chapter 7, where you will find sample citations for the kinds of sources used most frequently in classroom speeches.

Give Your Speech a Title, if One Is Desired

In the classroom you probably do not need a title for your speech unless your teacher requires one. In some other situations, however, a speech title is necessary—as when the speech is publicized in advance or is going to be published. Whatever the reason, if you do decide to use a title, it should (1) be brief, (2) attract the attention of your audience, and (3) encapsulate the main thrust of your speech.

A good title need not have what Madison Avenue would call "sex appeal"—lots of glitter and pizzazz. By the same token, there is certainly nothing wrong with a catchy title—as long as it is germane to the speech. Here are two groups of titles. Those on the left are straightforward and descriptive. Those on the right are figurative alternatives to the ones on the left.

Group I	**Group II**
Gambling Addiction	Against All Odds
The Rage to Diet	The Art of Wishful Shrinking
Living with Deafness	The Sounds of Silence
Unsafe Drinking Water	Toxins on Tap

Which group do you prefer? There are advantages and disadvantages to both. Those in the first group clearly reveal the topic, but they are not as provocative as those in the second group. Those in the second group are sure to arouse interest, but they do not give as clear an idea of what the speeches are about.

There is one other kind of title you should consider—the question. Phrasing your title as a question can be both descriptive and provocative. Using

checklist

Preparation Outline

YES	NO	
☐	☐	1. Does my speech have a title, if one is required?
☐	☐	2. Do I state the specific purpose before the text of the outline itself?
☐	☐	3. Do I state the central idea before the text of the outline itself?
☐	☐	4. Are the introduction, body, and conclusion clearly labeled?
☐	☐	5. Are main points and subpoints written in full sentences?
☐	☐	6. Are transitions, internal summaries, and internal previews clearly labeled?
☐	☐	7. Does the outline follow a consistent pattern of symbolization and indentation?
☐	☐	8. Does the outline provide a clear visual framework that shows the relationships among the ideas of my speech?
☐	☐	9. Does the bibliography identify all the sources I consulted in preparing the outline?
☐	☐	10. Does the bibliography follow the format required by my instructor?

this method, we can construct a third set of titles combining the virtues of groups I and II:

Group III

Do You Really Think You Can Beat the Odds?

Diets: How Effective Are They?

Can You See What I'm Saying?

Is Your Water Safe to Drink?

Sometimes you will choose a title for your speech very early. At other times you may not find one you like until the last minute. Either way, try to be resourceful about creating titles for your speeches. Experiment with several and choose the one that seems most appropriate.

SAMPLE PREPARATION OUTLINE WITH COMMENTARY

The following outline for a six-minute informative speech illustrates the principles just discussed. The commentary explains the procedures used in organizing the speech and writing the outline. (Check with your teacher to see if she or he wants you to include a title with your outline.)

Service Dogs

COMMENTARY

Stating your specific purpose and central idea as separate units before the text of the outline makes it easier to judge how well you have constructed the outline to achieve your purpose and to communicate your central idea.

Labeling the introduction marks it as a distinct section that plays a special role in the speech.

The opening gets attention and, as it progresses, reveals the topic of the speech.

Here the speaker establishes his credibility and previews the main points to be discussed in the body.

Including transitions ensures that the speaker has worked out how to connect one idea to the next. Notice that the transition is not included in the system of symbolization and indentation used for the rest of the speech.

Labeling the body marks it as a distinct part of the speech.

Main point I is phrased as a full sentence. The two subpoints of main point I are shown by the capital letters A and B and are also written in full sentences to ensure that the speaker has thought them out fully.

The progressive indentation shows visually the relationships among main points, subpoints, and sub-subpoints.

OUTLINE

Specific Purpose: To inform my audience about three major kinds of service dogs.

Central Idea: Guide dogs, assistance dogs, and seizure-alert dogs make a huge difference in the lives of their owners.

Introduction

I. Most of us hardly think about simple tasks such as turning on the television or walking across the street.
   A. But for many Americans with disabilities, these tasks are anything but simple.
   B. They could not be accomplished without service dogs.

II. According to the Americans with Disabilities Act, a service dog is any dog specially trained to assist an individual with a disability.

III. In researching this speech, I learned how indispensable service dogs are for millions of Americans.

IV. Today I will introduce you to three types of service dogs—guide dogs, assistance dogs, and seizure-alert dogs.

(*Transition:* Let's start by looking at guide dogs.)

Body

I. Once referred to as Seeing Eye dogs, guide dogs help the visually impaired navigate their surroundings.
   A. As explained in the 2010 *Handbook on Animal-Assisted Therapy,* guide dogs receive intensive training.
      1. Professional training lasts at least 5 months.
      2. Another month of training occurs after a dog is assigned to its owner.
      3. The result is a dog worth from $15,000 to $50,000.
   B. Guide Dogs of America is a major trainer of U.S. guide dogs.
      1. Its Web site says the group provides 50 trained dogs free of charge each year.
      2. It also notes that there are 7,000 guide dogs currently working in the U.S.

The transition shows how the speaker will get from main point I to main point II.

Like main point I, main point II is phrased as a full sentence.

(*Transition:* Like guide dogs, assistance dogs are invaluable for those who need them.)

II. Assistance dogs perform routine tasks for people with physical disabilities.
  A. These dogs' skills are truly amazing.
    1. They help people put on clothes, unload the washing machine, and pick up items on the floor.
    2. They also open and close doors, gather the mail, and manipulate keys and cell phones.
    3. In fact, they can do almost anything that is needed to help their owners with daily tasks.
  B. Assistance dogs are invaluable to their owners.
    1. Dr. Alice Blue-McLendon, of the Texas A&M College of Veterinary Medicine, notes that these dogs help their owners achieve a new sense of freedom and independence.
    2. Phil Day, owner of a black Labrador provided by Dogs for the Disabled, says: "I wouldn't be without an assistance dog; they help on so many different levels."

Points below the level of subpoint are indicated by Arabic numerals and lowercase letters. Sometimes they are not written as full sentences. Check to see what your teacher prefers.

(*Transition:* Now that we have looked at guide dogs and assistance dogs, let's turn to seizure-alert dogs.)

The transition indicates that the speaker is moving to his next main point.

This main point, like the first two, is stated as a full sentence.

III. Seizure-alert dogs warn owners with epilepsy when a seizure is about to occur.
  A. These dogs can sense a seizure from several seconds to 45 minutes before it occurs, says John Ensminger, author of *Service and Therapy Dogs in American Society*.
  B. How seizure-alert dogs acquire this ability is a mystery.
    1. Dogs cannot be trained to anticipate seizures.
    2. Some are born with the power and some are not.
    3. There are two major theories to explain the dogs' power.
      a. One theory holds that dogs anticipate seizures through their sensitivity to slight changes in nonverbal behavior.
      b. Another theory says they detect minor chemical changes through their acute sense of smell.

Notice the pattern of subordination in this section. Subpoint B states that how seizure-alert dogs acquire their ability is a mystery. Sub-subpoint 3 notes that there are two major theories to explain the dogs' power. Because items a and b expand upon the theories point, they are subordinated to it.

Conclusion

Labeling the conclusion marks it as a distinct part of the speech.

Summarizing the main points is standard procedure in an informative speech. The speaker's final line reinforces his central idea.

I. As we have seen, service dogs provide vital support for people with physical disabilities.
II. I have focused on guide dogs, assistance dogs, and seizure-alert dogs.
III. For their owners, these dogs are much more than "man's best friend"—they are a new way of life.

This is the final bibliography. It lists the sources actually used in writing the speech and is shorter than the preliminary bibliography compiled in the early stages of research. (See Chapter 7 for a discussion of the preliminary bibliography.)

This bibliography follows the 2009 Modern Language Association (MLA) format. Check with your instructor to see what format you should use for your bibliography.

Bibliography

United States. Dept. of Justice. *Americans with Disabilities Act*. 14 Jan. 2008. Web. 15 Apr. 2011.

Dogs for the Disabled. Dogs for the Disabled, 2010. Web. 17 Apr. 2011.

Ensminger, John J. *Service and Therapy Dogs in American Society*. Springfield: Charles C. Thomas, 2010. Print.

Fine, Aubrey H., ed. *Handbook on Animal-Assisted Therapy*, 3rd ed. London: Academic Press, 2010. Print.

Guide Dogs of America. Guide Dogs of America, 2011. Web. 18 Apr. 2011.

Veterinary Medicine and Biomedical Sciences. "Assistance Dogs: Offering a New Sense of Freedom." *Pet Talk. Texas A&M News and Information Services*. Texas A&M University, 25 Feb. 2011. Web. 17 Apr. 2011.

The Speaking Outline

"I was never so excited by public speaking before in my life," wrote one listener in 1820 after listening to Daniel Webster. "Three or four times I thought my temples would burst with the gush of blood. . . . I was beside myself, and am so still."[1]

Such reactions were not unusual among Webster's audiences. He thrilled two generations of Americans with his masterful orations. Incredible as it seems today, he did so while speaking for several hours at a time, often without using any notes! A reporter once asked how he managed this. "It is my memory," Webster said. "I can prepare a speech, revise and correct it in my memory, then deliver the corrected speech exactly as finished."[2]

Few people have Webster's remarkable powers of memory. Fortunately, it is no longer customary to speak from memory. Today most people speak extemporaneously—which means the speech is carefully prepared and practiced in advance, but much of the exact wording is selected while the speech is being delivered (see Chapter 13). Your speeches will probably be of this type. You should know, then, about the *speaking outline*—the most widely recommended form of notes for extemporaneous speeches.

speaking outline

A brief outline used to jog a speaker's memory during the presentation of a speech.

The aim of a speaking outline is to help you remember what you want to say. In some ways, it is a condensed version of your preparation outline. It should contain key words or phrases to jog your memory, as well as essential statistics and quotations that you don't want to risk forgetting. But it should also include material *not* in your preparation outline—especially cues to direct and sharpen your delivery.

Most speakers develop their own variations on the speaking outline. As you acquire more experience, you, too, should feel free to experiment. But for now, your best bet is to follow the basic guidelines below and to use the sample speaking outline on pages 216–217 as your model.

GUIDELINES FOR THE SPEAKING OUTLINE

Follow the Visual Framework Used in the Preparation Outline

Your speaking outline should use the same visual framework—the same symbols and the same pattern of indentation—as your preparation outline. This will make it much easier to prepare the speaking outline. More important, it will allow you to see instantly where you are in the speech at any given moment while you are speaking. You will find this a great advantage. As you speak, you will look down at your outline periodically to make sure you are covering the right ideas in the right order.

Compare the following two versions of a partial speaking outline. They are from an informative speech about the history of the U.S. women's rights movement.

Ineffective

I. 1840–1860
A. World Anti-Slavery Convention
B. Seneca Falls convention
1. Lucretia Mott
2. Elizabeth Cady Stanton
3. Declaration of Sentiments
II. 1900–1920
A. National American Woman Suffrage Association
1. Founding
2. Objectives
B. Nineteenth Amendment
1. Campaign
2. Ratification

More Effective

I. 1840–1860
    A. World Anti-Slavery Convention
    B. Seneca Falls convention
        1. Lucretia Mott
        2. Elizabeth Cady Stanton
        3. Declaration of Sentiments
II. 1900–1920
    A. National American Woman Suffrage Association
        1. Founding
        2. Objectives
    B. Nineteenth Amendment
        1. Campaign
        2. Ratification

The wording of both outlines is exactly the same. But the visual framework of the one on the right makes it easier to take in at a glance and reduces the odds of the speaker losing her or his place.

As with personal finance expert Suze Orman, many experienced speakers are more comfortable with a brief set of notes, or no notes at all, which allows them to communicate directly with the audience.

Make Sure the Outline Is Legible

Your speaking outline is all but worthless unless it is instantly readable at a distance. When you make your outline, use large lettering, leave extra space between lines, provide ample margins, and write or type on only one side of the paper.

Some speakers put their notes on index cards. Most find the 3 × 5 size too cramped and prefer the 4 × 6 or 5 × 8 size instead. Other people write their speaking outlines on regular paper. Either practice is fine, as long as your notes are immediately legible to you while you are speaking.

Keep the Outline as Brief as Possible

If your notes are too detailed, you will have difficulty maintaining eye contact with your audience.

Using public speaking in your **CAREER**

As the defense attorney in a car theft case, you need to prepare your closing argument to the jury before it begins its deliberations. After reviewing evidence from the trial, you decide to stress the following points to demonstrate the innocence of your client:

a. The stolen car was found abandoned three hours after the theft with the engine still warm; at the time the car was found, your client was at the airport to meet the flight of a friend who was flying into town.

b. Lab analysis of muddy shoe prints on the floor mat of the car indicates that the prints came from a size 13 shoe; your client wears a size 10.

c. Lab analysis shows the presence of cigarette smoke in the car, but your client does not smoke.

d. The only eyewitness to the crime, who was 50 feet from the car, said the thief "looked like" your client; yet the eyewitness admitted that at the time of the theft she was not wearing her glasses, which had been prescribed for improving distance vision.

e. The car was stolen at about 1 P.M.; your client testified that he was in a small town 250 miles away at 11 A.M.

f. In a statement to police, the eyewitness described the thief as blond; your client has red hair.

As you work on the outline of your speech, you see that these points can be organized into three main points, each with two supporting points. Compose an outline that organizes the points in this manner.

A detailed outline will tempt you to look at it far too often, as one student discovered:

Angela Rossi was speaking about the benefits of Pilates. She had prepared the speech thoroughly and practiced it until it was nearly perfect. But when she delivered the speech in class, she referred constantly to her detailed notes. As a result, her delivery was choppy and strained. After the speech, Angela's classmates remarked on how often she had looked at her notes, and she was amazed. "I didn't even know I was doing it," she said. "Most of the time I wasn't even paying attention to the outline. I knew the speech cold."

Many students have had the same experience. "As long as I have plenty of notes," they feel, "disaster will not strike." In fact, most beginning speakers use too many notes. Like Angela, they don't need all of them to remember the speech, and they find that too many notes can actually interfere with good communication.

To guard against this, keep your speaking outline as brief as possible. It should contain key words or phrases to help you remember major points, subpoints, and connectives. If you are citing statistics, you will probably want to include them in your notes. Unless you are good at memorizing quotations, write them out fully as well. Finally, there may be two, three, or four key ideas whose wording is so important that you want to state them in simple complete sentences. The best rule is that your notes should be the *minimum* you need to jog your memory and keep you on track.

Give Yourself Cues for Delivering the Speech

A good speaking outline reminds you not only of *what* you want to say but also of *how* you want to say it. As you practice the speech, you will decide that certain ideas and phrases need special emphasis—that they should be spoken more loudly, softly, slowly, or rapidly than other parts of the speech. You will also determine how you want to pace the speech—how you will control its timing, rhythm, and momentum. But no matter how you work these things out ahead of time, no matter how often you practice, it is easy to forget them once you get in front of an audience.

delivery cues

Directions in a speaking outline to help a speaker remember how she or he wants to deliver key parts of the speech.

The solution is to include in your speaking outline *delivery cues*—directions for delivering the speech. One way to do this is by underlining or otherwise highlighting key ideas that you want to be sure to emphasize. Then, when you reach them in the outline, you will be reminded to stress them. Another way is to jot down on the outline explicit cues such as "pause," "repeat," "slow down," "louder," and so forth. Both techniques are good aids for beginning speakers, but they are also used by most experienced speakers.

SAMPLE SPEAKING OUTLINE WITH COMMENTARY

Below is a sample speaking outline for a six-minute informative talk about service dogs. By comparing it with the preparation outline for the same speech on pages 211–213, you can see how a detailed preparation outline is transformed into a concise speaking outline.

COMMENTARY	OUTLINE
These comments remind the speaker to establish eye contact and not to race through the speech.	*Eye Contact!!* *Slow Down*
Including the main points of the introduction helps keep the speaker on track at the start of the speech.	I. Don't think about simple tasks—tv, crossing street. A. Not simple for Americans with disabilities. B. Cannot be accomplished without service dogs. II. ADA: Service dog is specially trained to assist person with a disability. III. Researched speech; learned dogs indispensable. IV. Today—guide dogs, assistance dogs, seizure-alert dogs. (Let's start with guide dogs.)
It's usually a good idea to pause briefly before launching into the first main point. This is another way of signaling that you are moving from the introduction to the body.	*—Pause—*

Most speakers label the body of the speech in the speaking outline as well as in the preparation outline.

Throughout the outline, key words are used to jog the speaker's memory. Because the final wording of an extemporaneous speech is chosen at the moment of delivery, it will not be exactly the same as that in the preparation outline.

Inserting transitions makes sure the speaker doesn't forget them.

Underlining reminds the speaker to stress key words or ideas.

Quotations are usually written out in full in the speaking outline.

Sources of statistics or testimony should be included in the speaking outline to make sure the speaker identifies them in the speech.

Notice how the body of the speech follows the same visual format as the preparation outline. This makes the outline easy to read at a glance.

It's usually a good idea to pause before entering the conclusion.

Including key ideas and phrases from the conclusion jogs the speaker's memory and ensures that the speech will end as planned.

Body

I. Help visually impaired navigate surroundings.
   A. Training: 2010 *Handbook on Animal-Assisted Therapy.*
      1. Professional training—5 months.
      2. Another month—with owner.
      3. Dogs worth $15,000 to $50,000.
   B. Guide Dogs of America trains U.S. dogs.
      1. Web site: free of charge to 50 people a year.
      2. 7,000 guide dogs in U.S.

(Like guide dogs, assistance dogs invaluable.)

II. Routine tasks for people with physical disabilities.
   A. <u>Amazing</u> skills.
      1. Clothes, washing machine, items on floor.
      2. Doors, mail, keys, cell phones.
      3. <u>Almost anything</u> needed for daily tasks.
   B. Invaluable to owners.
      1. Dr. Alice Blue-McLendon, Texas A&M Veterinary Medicine: help owners achieve freedom and independence.
      2. Phil Day: black Lab owner: "I wouldn't be without an assistance dog; they help on <u>so many</u> different levels."

(Now turn to seizure-alert dogs.)

III. Warn owners with epilepsy before seizures occur.
   A. Several seconds to 45 minutes warning: John Ensminger, *Service and Therapy Dogs in American Society.*
   B. How dogs do this is a mystery.
      1. Cannot be trained to anticipate seizures.
      2. Some born with power and some not.
      3. Two major theories explaining power.
         a. Anticipate seizures through nonverbal behavior.
         b. Detect minor chemical changes through smell.

—*Pause*—

Conclusion

I. As we have seen, service dogs support people with physical disabilities.
II. Focused today on guide dogs, assistance dogs, and seizure-alert dogs.
III. Service dogs are more than "man's best friend"—they are a new way of life.

Summary

Outlines are essential to effective speeches. By outlining, you make sure that related ideas are together, that your thoughts flow from one to another, and that the structure of your speech is coherent. You will probably use two kinds of outlines for your speeches—the detailed preparation outline and the brief speaking outline.

In the preparation outline, you state your specific purpose and central idea; label the introduction, body, and conclusion; and designate transitions, internal summaries, and internal previews. You should identify main points, subpoints, and sub-subpoints by a consistent pattern of symbolization and indentation. Your teacher may require a bibliography with your preparation outline.

The speaking outline should contain key words or phrases to jog your memory, as well as essential statistics and quotations. Make sure your speaking outline is legible, follows the same visual framework as your preparation outline, and includes cues for delivering the speech.

Key Terms

preparation outline *(206)*
visual framework *(207)*
bibliography *(208)*
speaking outline *(213)*
delivery cues *(216)*

Review Questions

After reading this chapter, you should be able to answer the following questions:

1. Why is it important to outline your speeches?
2. What is a preparation outline? What are the eight guidelines discussed in this chapter for writing a preparation outline?
3. What is a speaking outline? What are four guidelines for your speaking outline?

connect™

For further review, go to the LearnSmart study module for this chapter.

Exercises for Critical Thinking

1. In the left-hand column on page 219 is a partially blank outline from a speech about the Golden Gate Bridge. In the right-hand column, arranged in random order, are the subpoints to fill in the outline. Choose the appropriate subpoint for each blank in the outline.

Outline

I. More than 20 years passed from the time the Golden Gate Bridge was proposed to the time it opened.

A.

B.

C.

D.

II. Now 75 years old, the Golden Gate Bridge remains a marvel of modern engineering.

A.

1.

2.

B.

1.

2.

Subpoints

Today, those towers make it the world's third tallest suspension bridge.

Construction finally began in 1933 and ended in 1937.

The span between its towers is 4,200 feet.

At the time it was built, the Golden Gate was also the longest suspension bridge in the world.

In 1923, the State of California passed legislation authorizing construction of the bridge.

Its two towers rise almost 750 feet above the waters of the Pacific Ocean.

Once construction of the bridge was authorized, it took ten years to approve the design and financing.

That span makes it the ninth longest suspension bridge in the world today.

At the time it was built, the Golden Gate was the tallest suspension bridge in the world.

The bridge was originally proposed in 1916 but faced years of legal hurdles.

2. From the preparation outline on the Golden Gate Bridge you constructed in Exercise 1, create a speaking outline that you might use in delivering the speech. Follow the guidelines for a speaking outline discussed in this chapter.

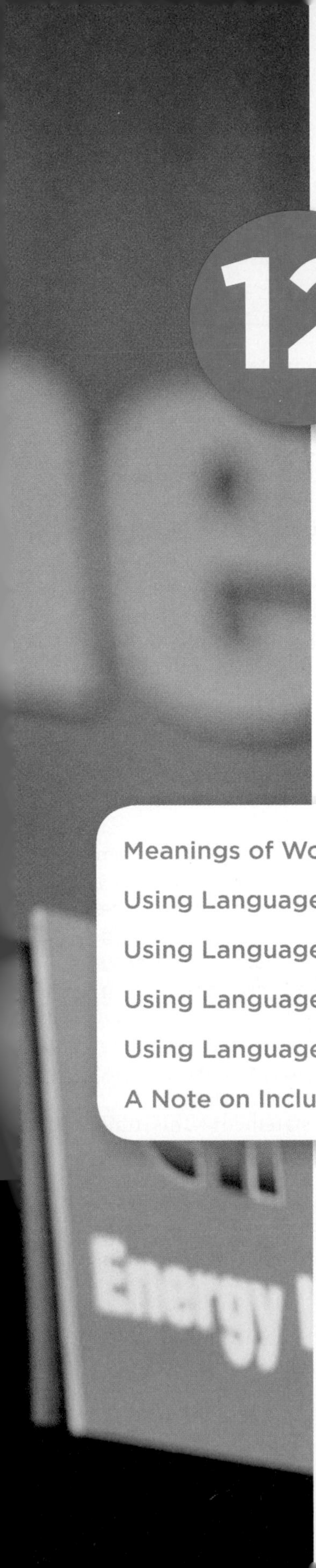

12

Using Language

Contrary to popular belief, language does not mirror reality. It does not simply describe the world as it is. Instead, language helps create our sense of reality by giving meaning to events. The words we use to label an event determine to a great extent how we respond to it.

For example, if you see the medical use of stem cells as "immoral," as "scientifically irresponsible," and as a "violation of human life," you will likely oppose it. But if you see the medical use of stem cells as "moral," as "scientifically responsible," and as a way to "alleviate pain and suffering," you will likely support it.

What separates these two viewpoints? Not the capabilities of modern medicine; not the conditions of people with genetic disorders; not the medical procedures of using stem cells. All those are the same for both sides. The difference is in the *meaning* given to them by the words that label them.[1]

Words are the tools of a speaker's craft. They have special uses, just like the tools of any other profession. Have you ever watched a carpenter at work? The job that would take you or me a couple of hours is done by the carpenter in 10 minutes—with the right tools. You can't drive a nail with a screwdriver or turn a screw with a hammer. It is the same with public speaking. You must choose the right words for the job you want to do.

Good speakers are aware of the meaning of words—both their obvious and their subtle meanings. They also know how to use language accurately, clearly, vividly, appropriately, and inclusively. This chapter will explore each of these areas.

Meanings of Words

denotative meaning

The literal or dictionary meaning of a word or phrase.

Words have two kinds of meanings—denotative and connotative. *Denotative* meaning is precise, literal, and objective. It describes the object, person, place, idea, or event to which the word refers. One way to think of a word's denotative meaning is as its dictionary definition. For example, denotatively, the noun "school" means "a place, institution, or building where instruction is given."

Connotative meaning is more variable, figurative, and subjective. The connotative meaning of a word is what the word suggests or implies. For instance, the connotative meaning of the word "school" includes all the feelings, associations, and emotions that the word touches off in different people. For some people, "school" might connote personal growth, childhood friends, and a special teacher. For others, it might connote frustration, discipline, and boring homework assignments.

connotative meaning

The meaning suggested by the associations or emotions triggered by a word or phrase.

Connotative meaning gives words their intensity and emotional power. It arouses in listeners feelings of anger, pity, love, fear, friendship, nostalgia, greed, guilt, and the like. Speakers, like poets, often use connotation to enrich their meaning. For example:

> <u>Terrorists</u> neither <u>listen to reason</u> nor engage in <u>reasoning</u> with others. Their aim is to generate <u>fear</u>—to <u>frighten</u> people into <u>submission</u>. They measure success by the magnitude of the <u>fear</u> they generate through <u>brutal, savage acts of violence</u>. <u>Terrorists</u> are prepared to <u>kill</u> to further whatever cause they claim to be pursuing. And the <u>heinousness</u> of these <u>murders</u> is accentuated by the fact that <u>terrorists murder without passion</u>. They <u>murder with cool deliberation and deliberate planning</u>. They are <u>utterly amoral</u>.

The underlined words in this passage have powerful connotations that are almost certain to produce a strong emotional revulsion to terrorism.

Here, in contrast, is another version of the same statement—this time using words with a different set of connotations:

> Terrorists do not seek to negotiate with their opponents. They seek victory by using political and psychological pressure, including acts of violence that may endanger the lives of some people. To the terrorist, ultimate objectives are more important than the means used to achieve them.

With the exception of "terrorist," the words in this statement are less likely to evoke an intensely negative response than those in the first statement.

Which statement is preferable? That depends on the audience, the occasion, and the speaker's purpose. Do you want to stir up your listeners' emotions, rally them to some cause? Then select words with more intense

Words are the tools of the speaker's craft. Good speakers use them accurately and correctly. They also use language that will be clear, vivid, and appropriate for their listeners.

connotative meanings. Or are you addressing a controversial issue and trying to seem completely impartial? Then stick with words that touch off less intense reactions. Choosing words skillfully for their denotative and connotative meanings is a crucial part of the speaker's craft.

Using Language Accurately

Using language accurately is as vital to a speaker as using numbers accurately is to an accountant. One student found this out the hard way. In a speech about America's criminal justice system, he referred several times to "criminal *persecution*." What he meant, of course, was "criminal *prosecution*." This one error virtually ruined his speech. As one of his classmates said, "How can I believe what you say about our courts when you don't even know the difference between prosecution and persecution?"

Fortunately, such outright blunders are relatively rare among college students. However, we all commit more subtle errors—especially using one word when another will capture our ideas more precisely. Every word has shades of meaning that distinguish it from every other word. As Mark Twain said, "The difference between the right word and the almost right word is the difference between lightning and the lightning bug."

If you look in a thesaurus, you'll find the following words given as synonyms:

thesaurus

A book of synonyms.

education knowledge expertise

All mean roughly the same thing—special grasp of a subject matter or skill. But all these words have different shades of meaning. See if you can fill in the best word to complete each of the sentences below:

1. Because he won a scholarship to a top university, Enrique received an excellent ____________.
2. Sophia acquired her ____________ of Chinese history by reading a number of books on the subject.
3. Ebony's ____________ as a business consultant comes from having worked with many clients over the years.

The best answers for the three statements are:

1. education   2. knowledge   3. expertise

Each of the words means something a little different from the others, and each says something special to listeners.

As you prepare your speeches, ask yourself constantly, "What do I *really* want to say? What do I *really* mean?" When in doubt, consult a dictionary or thesaurus to make sure you have the best words to express your ideas.

Using Language Clearly

People are different. What makes perfect sense to some may be gobbledygook to others. You cannot assume that what is clear to you is clear to your audience. Listeners, unlike readers, cannot turn to a dictionary or reread an author's words to discover their meaning. A speaker's meaning must be *immediately* comprehensible; it must be so clear that there is no chance of misunderstanding. You can ensure this by using familiar words, by choosing concrete words over abstract words, and by eliminating verbal clutter.

USE FAMILIAR WORDS

One of the biggest barriers to clear speech is using big, bloated words where short, sharp ones will do the job better.[2] This is especially true when it comes to technical language that may be familiar to the speaker but not to the audience. Yet, if you work at it, you will almost always be able to translate even the most specialized topic into clear, familiar language.

Here, for instance, are two passages explaining the devastating effects of a pregnant woman's drinking on her unborn child. The first passage is technically accurate, but it contains too many obscure words.

> The deleterious effects of alcohol on the unborn child are very serious. When a pregnant mother consumes alcohol, the ethanol in the bloodstream easily crosses the placenta from mother to child and invades the amniotic fluid. This can produce a number of abnormal birth syndromes, including central-nervous-system dysfunctions, growth deficiencies, a cluster of facial aberrations, and variable major and minor malformations.

Well-informed listeners can probably figure out "deleterious effects," "central-nervous-system dysfunctions," and "facial aberrations." But these terms don't create sharp mental images of what the speaker is trying to say.

Here, in contrast, is the second passage. It is utterly clear and shows what can be done with work, imagination, and a healthy respect for everyday words:

> When the expectant mother drinks, alcohol is absorbed into her bloodstream and distributed throughout her entire body. After a few beers or a couple of martinis, she begins to feel tipsy and decides to sober up. She grabs a cup of coffee, two aspirin, and takes a little nap. After a while she'll be fine.
>
> But while she sleeps, the fetus is surrounded by the same alcoholic content as its mother had. After being drowned in alcohol, the fetus begins to feel the

effect. But it can't sober up. It can't grab a cup of coffee. It can't grab a couple of aspirin. For the fetus's liver, the key organ in removing alcohol from the blood, is just not developed. The fetus is literally pickled in alcohol.[3]

This kind of plain talk is what listeners want. You cannot go wrong by following the advice of Winston Churchill to speak in "short, homely words of common usage." If you think big words (or a lot of words) are needed to impress listeners, bear in mind that the Gettysburg Address—considered the finest speech in the English language—contains 271 words, of which 251 have only one or two syllables.

CHOOSE CONCRETE WORDS

Concrete words refer to tangible objects—people, places, and things. They differ from abstract words, which refer to general concepts, qualities, or attributes. "Carrot," "pencil," "nose," and "door" are concrete words. "Humility," "science," "progress," and "philosophy" are abstract words.

concrete words

Words that refer to tangible objects.

Of course, few words are completely abstract or concrete. "Apple pie" is concrete, but in the United States, the phrase also has abstract values of patriotism and conventional morals. Usually, the more specific a word, the more concrete it is. Let us say you are talking about basketball. Here are several words and phrases you might use:

abstract words

Words that refer to ideas or concepts.

physical activity	↓	abstract/general
sports		
basketball		
professional basketball		
Kobe Bryant	↓	concrete/specific

As you move down the list, the words become less abstract and more concrete. You begin with a general concept (physical activity), descend to one type of activity (sports), to a particular sport (basketball), to a division of that sport (professional basketball), to one specific professional basketball player (Kobe Bryant).

Although abstract words are necessary to express certain kinds of ideas, they are much easier to misinterpret than are concrete words. Also, concrete words are much more likely to claim your listeners' attention. Suppose you make a speech about bed bugs, which are plaguing people from coast to coast. Here are two ways you could approach the subject—one featuring abstract words, the other concrete words:

Abstract Words

Bed bugs are highly newsworthy in the United States. They affect people regardless of social strata, demographic group, or region of the country. They are found in a wide range of social locations, some of which one might not expect. No matter where one lives, bed bugs are a growing problem.

Concrete Words

In recent months, bed bugs have made headlines across the country, affecting the rich and the poor, the clean and the dirty, the East Coast, the West Coast, and every place in between.

In New York City, bed bugs have been found in fancy hotels, crowded subways, even the Victoria's Secret store on Lexington Avenue. In Los Angeles, they have infiltrated public housing and posh Beverly Hills neighborhoods alike. In college towns, they are almost everywhere—dorm rooms, apartments, restaurants, movie theaters, bars, even sports arenas.

Bed bugs are becoming a pest of epidemic proportions.

connect

View this excerpt from "The Plague of Bed Bugs" in the online Media Library for this chapter (Video 12.1).

Notice how much more persuasive the second version is. A speech dominated by concrete words will almost always be clearer, more interesting, and easier to recall than one dominated by abstract words.

ELIMINATE CLUTTER

Cluttered speech has become a national epidemic. Whatever happened to such simple words as "before," "if," and "now"? When last seen they were being routed by their cluttered counterparts: "prior to," "in the eventuality of," and "at this point in time." By the same token, why can't politicians say, "We have a crisis," instead of saying, "We are facing a difficult crisis situation that will be troublesome to successfully resolve"?

This type of clutter forces listeners to hack through a tangle of words to discover the meaning. When you make a speech, keep your language lean and lively. Beware of using several words where one or two will do. Avoid flabby phrases. Let your ideas emerge sharply and firmly. Above all, watch out for redundant adjectives and adverbs. Inexperienced speakers (and writers) tend to string together two or three synonymous adjectives, such as "a learned and educated person" or "a hot, steamy, torrid day."

clutter

Discourse that takes many more words than are necessary to express an idea.

Here is part of a student speech that has been revised to eliminate clutter:

Sitting Bull was one of the most important ~~and significant of all~~ Native American leaders. He was born in ~~the year of~~ 1831 near Grand River, in ~~an area that is now part of the state of~~ *present-day* South Dakota. A fearless ~~and courageous~~ warrior, he ~~ended up being~~ *was* elected chief of the Hunkpapa Sioux in 1867. In the following years, he also attracted a large ~~and numerous~~ following among the ~~tribes of the~~ Cheyenne and Arapaho. He is best known ~~to people in this day and age~~ *today* for his ~~instrumental~~ role in ~~helping to lead the defeat of~~ *defeating* General Custer at the Battle of Little Big Horn in 1876. Although eventually ~~required against his will~~ *forced* to live ~~his life~~ on the Standing Rock Reservation in South Dakota, he never surrendered ~~to anyone~~ his dignity or his ~~personal~~ devotion to the Sioux way of life.

Notice how much cleaner and easier to follow the revised version is. No longer are the speaker's ideas hidden in a thicket of wasted words.

This kind of pruning is easy once you get the knack of it. The hardest part—and it is often very hard—is recognizing clutter and forcing yourself to

Even when discussing technical subjects, effective speakers such as Nobel Prize-winning economist Paul Krugman look for ways to communicate their ideas in clear, familiar language.

throw away the unnecessary words. Watch for clutter when you write your speech outlines. Be prepared to revise the outline until your ideas emerge clearly and crisply.

You can also help eliminate clutter by practicing your speeches with a digital recorder. As you play the speech back, keep an ear out not just for flabby phrases but for verbal fillers such as "you know," "like," and "really." Practice delivering the speech again, this time making a special effort to trim it of wasted or distracting words. This will not only make you a better public speaker, but it will also help you present ideas more effectively in meetings, conversations, and group discussions.[4]

Using Language Vividly

Just as you can be accurate without being clear, so you can be both accurate and clear without being interesting. Here, for example, is how Martin Luther King *might have* phrased part of his great "I Have a Dream" speech:

> Turning back is something we cannot do. We must continue to work against police brutality, segregated housing, disfranchisement, and alienation. Only when these problems are solved will we be satisfied.

Here is what King *actually* said:

> We cannot turn back. There are those who ask the devotees of civil rights, "When will you be satisfied?" We can never be satisfied as long as the Negro is the victim of the unspeakable horrors of police brutality. We can never be satisfied as long as our bodies, heavy with the fatigue of travel, cannot gain lodging in the motels of the highways and the hotels of the cities. . . . We cannot be satisfied as long as a Negro in Mississippi cannot vote and a Negro in New York believes he has nothing for which to vote.
>
> No, no, we are not satisfied, and we will not be satisfied until justice rolls down like waters and righteousness like a mighty stream.

Much more stirring, isn't it? If you want to move people with your speeches, use vivid, animated language. Although there are several ways to do this, two of the most important are imagery and rhythm.

IMAGERY

imagery

The use of vivid language to create mental images of objects, actions, or ideas.

One sign of a good novelist is the ability to create word pictures that let you "see" the haunted house, or "hear" the birds chirping on a warm spring morning, or "taste" the hot enchiladas at a Mexican restaurant.

Speakers can use imagery in much the same way to make their ideas come alive. Three ways to generate imagery are by using concrete words, simile, and metaphor.

Concrete Words

As we saw earlier in this chapter, choosing concrete words over abstract words is one way to enhance the clarity of your speeches. Concrete words are also the key to effective imagery. Consider the following excerpt from Ronald Reagan's famous address commemorating the 40th anniversary of D-Day. Speaking at the scene of the battle, Reagan dramatically recounted the heroism of the U.S. Rangers who scaled the cliffs at Pointe du Hoc to help free Europe from Hitler's stranglehold:

connect

View this excerpt from Ronald Reagan's speech at Pointe du Hoc in the online Media Library for this chapter (Video 12.2).

> We stand on a lonely, windswept point on the northern shore of France. The air is soft, but 40 years ago at this moment, the air was dense with smoke and the cries of men, and the air was filled with the crack of rifle fire and the roar of cannon.
>
> At dawn, on the morning of the 6th of June, 1944, 225 Rangers jumped off the British landing craft and ran to the bottom of these cliffs. . . . The Rangers looked up and saw the enemy soldiers—at the edge of the cliffs shooting down at them with machine guns and throwing grenades. And the American Rangers began to climb. They shot rope ladders over the face of these cliffs and began to pull themselves up.
>
> When one Ranger fell, another would take his place. When one rope was cut, a Ranger would grab another and begin his climb again. They climbed, shot back, and held their footing. Soon, one by one, the Rangers pulled themselves over the top, and in seizing the firm land at the top of these cliffs, they began to seize back the continent of Europe.

Concrete words call up mental impressions of sights, sounds, touch, smell, and taste. In Reagan's speech, we do not merely learn that the U.S. Rangers helped win the battle of D-Day. We visualize the Rangers landing at the foot of the cliffs. We see them fighting their way up the cliffs in the face of enemy grenades and machine guns. We hear the crack of rifle fire and the cries of the soldiers. The concrete words create images that pull us irresistibly into the speech.

Simile

simile

An explicit comparison, introduced with the word "like" or "as," between things that are essentially different yet have something in common.

Another way to create imagery is through the use of simile. Simile is an explicit comparison between things that are essentially different yet have something in common. It always contains the words "like" or "as." Here are some examples from student speeches:

> Walking into my grandparents' home when I was a child was like being wrapped in a giant security blanket.

Audience-oriented speakers put a premium on clear, vivid, uncluttered language. They give a great deal of thought to finding just the right words to express their ideas.

Air pollution is eating away at the monuments in Washington, D.C., like a giant Alka-Seltzer tablet.

These are bright, fresh similes that clarify and vitalize ideas. Some similes, however, have become stale through overuse. Here are a few:

fresh as a daisy	hungry as a bear
fit as a fiddle	busy as a bee
strong as an ox	happy as a lark

Such *clichés* are fine in everyday conversation, but you should avoid them in speechmaking. Otherwise, you are likely to be "dull as dishwater" and to find your audience "sleeping like a log"!

cliché

A trite or overused expression.

Metaphor

You can also use metaphor to create imagery in your speeches. Metaphor is an implicit comparison between things that are essentially different yet have something in common. Unlike simile, metaphor does not contain the words "like" or "as." For example:

America's cities are the windows through which the world looks at American society. (Henry Cisneros)

With globalization, the same sea washes all of humankind. We are all in the same boat. There are no safe islands. (Kofi Annan)

metaphor

An implicit comparison, not introduced with the word "like" or "as," between two things that are essentially different yet have something in common.

These are both brief metaphors. Sometimes, however, a speaker will develop a longer metaphor. Here is an excellent example, from Al Gore's speech accepting the Nobel Peace Prize for his efforts to help the world deal with climate change:

The earth has a fever. And the fever is rising. The experts have told us it is not a passing affliction that will heal by itself. We asked for a second opinion.

And a third. And a fourth. And the consistent conclusion, restated with increasing alarm, is that something basic is wrong.

When used effectively, metaphor—like simile—is an excellent way to bring color to a speech, to make abstract ideas concrete, to clarify the unknown, and to express feelings and emotions.[5]

RHYTHM

rhythm

The pattern of sound in a speech created by the choice and arrangement of words.

Language has a rhythm created by the choice and arrangement of words. Speakers, like poets, sometimes seek to exploit the rhythm of language to enhance the impact of their words. Winston Churchill was a master at this. Here is a passage from one of his famous speeches during World War II. To emphasize its cadence, the passage has been printed as if it were poetry rather than prose:

> We cannot tell what the course
> of this fell war will be. . . .
> We cannot yet see
> how deliverance will come,
> or when it will come.
> But nothing is more certain
> than that every trace of Hitler's footsteps,
> every stain of his infected and corroding fingers,
> will be sponged and purged
> and, if need be,
> blasted from the surface of the earth.

connect

View this excerpt from Winston Churchill's speech of June 12, 1941, in the online Media Library for this chapter (Video 12.3).

The impact of the passage was heightened by Churchill's superb delivery; but even by themselves the words take on an emphatic rhythm that reinforces the message. You can see why one observer said that Churchill "mobilized the English language and sent it into battle."[6]

A speech, however, is not a poem. You should never emphasize sound and rhythm at the expense of meaning. The aim is to think about ways you can use the rhythm and flow of language to enhance your meaning. Although you may never have paid much conscious attention to this subject, you can develop an ear for vocal rhythms by study and practice. What's more, you can easily begin now to use four basic stylistic devices employed by Churchill and other fine speakers to improve the rhythm of their prose.

Parallelism

parallelism

The similar arrangement of a pair or series of related words, phrases, or sentences.

The first device is parallelism—the similar arrangement of a pair or series of related words, phrases, or sentences. For example:

> *Rich and poor, intelligent and ignorant, wise and foolish, virtuous and vicious, man and woman*—it is ever the same, each soul must depend wholly on itself. (Elizabeth Cady Stanton)

The effects of parallelism are perhaps best illustrated by seeing what happens when it is absent. For instance, compare this statement:

> I speak as a Republican. I speak as a woman. I speak as a United States Senator. I speak as an American. (Margaret Chase Smith)

Using public speaking in your CAREER

Since graduating from college, you have developed a successful business that is located near the campus. As part of its plan to involve more alumni and community members in college affairs, the school has asked you to speak with new students during registration week for the fall term. In the opening section of your speech, you want the audience to feel what you felt the first few days you were on campus as a new student. The best strategy, you decide, is to present two or three similes that complete the sentence "Beginning college is like. . . ." Write your similes.

with this one:

I speak as a Republican. I speak as a woman. I speak as a United States Senator. And I am also addressing you as an American.

The first statement is clear, consistent, and compelling. The second is not. By violating the principle of parallel structure, its final sentence ("And I am also addressing you as an American") destroys the progression begun by the preceding three sentences. It turns a strong, lucid, harmonious statement into one that is fuzzy and jarring.

Repetition

Repetition means reiterating the same word or set of words at the beginning or end of successive clauses or sentences. For example:

repetition

Reiteration of the same word or set of words at the beginning or end of successive clauses or sentences.

If not now, when? *If not* us, who? *If not* together, how? (Gordon Brown)

We do not give up. *We do not* quit. *We do not* allow fear or division to break our spirit. (Barack Obama)

As you can see, repetition usually results in parallelism. In addition to building a strong cadence, it also unifies a sequence of ideas, emphasizes an idea by stating it more than once, and helps create a strong emotional effect.

Alliteration

The third device you can use to enhance the rhythm of your speeches is alliteration. The most common method of alliteration is repeating the initial consonant sound of close or adjoining words. For example:

alliteration

Repetition of the initial consonant sound of close or adjoining words.

*P*eace is essential for *p*rogress, but *p*rogress is no less essential for *p*eace. (Liaquat Ali Khan)

Nothing great is accomplished without *c*ooperation, *c*ompromise, and *c*ommon *c*ause. (Ban Ki-moon)

By highlighting the sounds of words, alliteration catches the attention of listeners and can make ideas easier to remember. Used sparingly, it is a marvelous way to spruce up your speeches. Used to excess, however, it can be laughable and draw too much attention, so that listeners get more involved in listening for the next alliteration than in absorbing the content of the speech.

Antithesis

antithesis

The juxtaposition of contrasting ideas, usually in parallel structure.

Finally, you might try using antithesis—the juxtaposition of contrasting ideas, usually in parallel structure. For example:

> Ask not what your country can do for you; ask what you can do for your country. (John F. Kennedy)
>
> Let us never negotiate out of fear. But let us never fear to negotiate. (John F. Kennedy)

It is no accident that both of these examples are from speeches by President Kennedy. Antithesis was one of his favorite language devices, and the one he used in his most memorable phrases. Because it nearly always produces a neatly turned phrase, it is a fine way to give your speeches a special touch of class.

You may be thinking that imagery and rhythm are too fancy for ordinary speeches like yours. This is not true. Take a look at the following excerpt from one student's speech about the Massachusetts 54th, the regiment of African-American soldiers during the Civil War featured in the movie *Glory:*

connect

View this excerpt from "The Massachusetts 54th" in the online Media Library for this chapter (Video 12.4).

> To join an army that didn't believe in you. To fight with an army who didn't like you. To die for an army that didn't respect you. This was the Massachusetts 54th. Today they lay where they died, on the beaches of South Carolina. Colonel Shaw and his men were piled together in a mass grave, which has since been covered by the shifting tides of the Atlantic. A small statue stands in Boston—a reminder of their sacrifice.
>
> Bravery, patriotism, and sacrifice. These are qualities of the Massachusetts 54th. With the help of their efforts, along with all the other black regiments that followed them, slavery did eventually come to an end.

This is vivid, moving language. The imagery is sharp and poignant, the rhythm strong and insistent. Think of how you can do similar things in your own speeches.

Using Language Appropriately

Here is part of a famous oration given by John Hancock in 1774, during the American Revolution. Speaking of the British soldiers who killed five Americans in the Boston Massacre, Hancock exclaimed:

> Ye dark designing knaves, ye murderers, parricides! How dare you tread upon the earth, which has drank in the blood of slaughtered innocents shed by your wicked hands? . . . Tell me, ye bloody butchers, ye villains high and low, ye wretches, do you not feel the goads and stings of conscious guilt pierce through your savage bosoms?

This is certainly vivid language—and Hancock's audience loved it. But can you imagine speaking the same way today? In addition to being accurate,

Language needs to be appropriate to a speaker's topic, as well as to the audience. A speech on Laser Radial sailing would use more action-oriented words than a speech about theories of psychology.

clear, and vivid, language should be appropriate—to the occasion, to the audience, to the topic, and to the speaker.

APPROPRIATENESS TO THE OCCASION

Language that is appropriate for some occasions may not be appropriate for others. As a simple example, a coach might address the football team as "you guys" (or worse!), whereas the speaker in a more formal situation would begin with "distinguished guests." Try reversing these two situations, and see how ridiculous it becomes. It's only common sense to adjust your language to different occasions.

APPROPRIATENESS TO THE AUDIENCE

Appropriateness also depends on the audience. If you keep this in mind, it will help you greatly when dealing with technical topics. When addressing an audience of physicians, you might use the word "parotitis" to refer to a viral disease marked by the swelling of the parotid glands. Your audience would know just what you meant. But when talking to a nonmedical audience, such as your classmates, the appropriate word would be "mumps."

You should be especially careful to avoid language that might offend your audience. Off-color humor or profanity might be appropriate in a comedy routine, but most listeners would find it offensive in a formal public speech. Remember, speakers are expected to elevate and polish their language when addressing an audience.

Of course, you cannot always be sure of how listeners will respond to what you say. When it comes to appropriateness, you will seldom go wrong by erring on the side of caution. (Put simply, "erring on the side of caution" means "when in doubt—don't.")

APPROPRIATENESS TO THE TOPIC

Language should also be appropriate to the topic. You would not use metaphor, antithesis, and alliteration when explaining how to change a bicycle tire. But you might use all three in a speech honoring U.S. soldiers who have died in defense of their country. The first topic calls for straightforward description and explanation. The second calls for special language skills to evoke emotion, admiration, and appreciation.

APPROPRIATENESS TO THE SPEAKER

No matter what the occasion, audience, or topic, language should also be appropriate to the speaker. Every public speaker develops his or her own language style.

"Terrific," you may be thinking. "I have my own style too. I feel more comfortable using abstract words, slang, and technical jargon. That's *my* way of speaking." But to say that language should be appropriate to the speaker does not justify ignoring the other needs for appropriateness. There is a difference between one's everyday style and one's *developed* style as a public speaker. Accomplished speakers have developed their speaking styles over many years of trial, error, and practice. They have *worked* at using language effectively.

You can do the same if you become language-conscious. One way to develop this consciousness is to read and listen to effective speakers. Study their techniques for achieving accuracy, clarity, and vividness, and try to adapt those techniques to your own speeches. But do not try to "become" someone else when you speak. Learn from other speakers, blend what you learn into your own language style, and seek to become the best possible you.

A Note on Inclusive Language

inclusive language

Language that does not stereotype, demean, or patronize people on the basis of gender, race, religion, disability, sexual orientation, or other factors.

As the United States has become more diverse, our language has evolved to reflect that diversity. Regardless of the situation, audiences expect public speakers to use inclusive language that is respectful of the different groups that make up American society. They also expect speakers to avoid stereotypes based on age, race, gender, disability, and other factors.

Today a number of principles for inclusive language have become so widespread that no aspiring speaker (or writer) can afford to ignore them. Here are a few of the most important.

Avoid the Generic "He"

generic "he"

The use of "he" to refer to both women and men.

Ineffective: Each time a surgeon walks into the operating room, *he* risks being sued for malpractice.

More Effective: Each time a surgeon walks into the operating room, *he or she* risks being sued for malpractice.

Often, a more graceful alternative is to pluralize. For example:

More Effective: Whenever surgeons walk into the operating room, *they* risk being sued for malpractice.

Avoid the Use of "Man" When Referring to Both Men and Women

Ineffective: If a large comet struck the Earth, it could destroy all of mankind.

More Effective: If a large comet struck the Earth, it could destroy all human life.

Avoid Stereotyping Jobs and Social Roles by Gender

Ineffective: Being a small businessman in the current economic climate is not easy.

More Effective: Being a small businessperson in the current economic climate is not easy.

Sometimes you can solve this problem with a simple twist in sentence construction. For example:

More Effective: Owning a small business is not easy in the current economic climate.

Use Names That Groups Use to Identify Themselves

One of the most fundamental ways of showing respect for others is to refer to them by the names they use to identify themselves and to avoid names they consider offensive.

Ineffective: Despite progress in recent years, homosexuals still face many forms of discrimination.

More Effective: Despite progress in recent years, lesbians and gay men still face many forms of discrimination.

Ineffective: The Paralympics show what handicapped people can accomplish in the athletic arena.

More Effective: The Paralympics show what people with disabilities can accomplish in the athletic arena.

Like many other aspects of American life, issues of inclusive language can sometimes be confusing. Language is alive and constantly evolving, so what is considered inclusive today may shift down the road. If you have questions in any particular case, check the Internet for the most up-to-date information. Using inclusive and respectful language is not a matter of political correctness, but it is a matter of P.C.—personal courtesy.[7]

Summary

Good speakers have respect for language and how it works. As a speaker, you should be aware of the meanings of words and know how to use language accurately, clearly, vividly, and appropriately.

Words have two kinds of meanings—denotative and connotative. Denotative meaning is precise, literal, and objective. Connotative meaning is more variable, figurative, and subjective. It includes all the feelings, associations, and emotions that a word touches off in different people.

Using language accurately is vital to a speaker. Never use a word unless you are sure of its meaning. If you are not sure, look up the word in a dictionary. As you prepare your speeches, ask yourself constantly, "What do I *really* want to say? What do I *really* mean?" Choose words that are precise and accurate.

Using language clearly allows listeners to grasp your meaning immediately. You can ensure this by using words that are known to the average person and require no specialized background, by choosing concrete words in preference to more abstract ones, and by eliminating verbal clutter.

Using language vividly helps bring your speech to life. One way to make your language more vivid is through imagery, which you can develop by using concrete language, simile, and metaphor. Another way to make your speeches vivid is by exploiting the rhythm of language with parallelism, repetition, alliteration, and antithesis.

Using language appropriately means adapting to the particular occasion, audience, and topic at hand. It also means developing your own language style instead of trying to copy someone else's.

The subject of inclusive language can be complex, but a number of inclusive usages have become so widely accepted that no aspiring speaker can afford to ignore them. They include avoiding the generic "he," dropping the use of "man" when referring to both men and women, refraining from stereotyping jobs and social roles by gender, and using names that groups use to identify themselves.

Key Terms

denotative meaning *(222)*
connotative meaning *(222)*
thesaurus *(223)*
concrete words *(225)*
abstract words *(225)*
clutter *(226)*
imagery *(228)*
simile *(228)*
cliché *(229)*
metaphor *(229)*
rhythm *(230)*
parallelism *(230)*
repetition *(231)*
alliteration *(231)*
antithesis *(232)*
inclusive language *(234)*
generic "he" *(234)*

Review Questions

After reading this chapter, you should be able to answer the following questions:

1. How does language help create our sense of reality?
2. What is the difference between denotative and connotative meaning? How might you use each to convey your message most effectively?
3. What are four criteria for using language effectively in your speeches?
4. What are three things you should do to use language clearly in your speeches?
5. What are two ways to bring your speeches to life with vivid, animated language?
6. What does it mean to say you should use language appropriately in your speeches?
7. Why is it important for a public speaker to use inclusive language? What four usages of inclusive language have become so widely accepted that no speaker can afford to ignore them?

connect™

For further review, go to the LearnSmart study module for this chapter.

Exercises for Critical Thinking

1. Arrange each of the sequences below in order, from the most abstract word to the most concrete word.

   a. housing complex, building, dining room, structure, apartment

   b. *Mona Lisa,* art, painting, creative activity, portrait

   c. automobile, vehicle, Ferrari, transportation, sports car

2. Rewrite each of the following sentences using clear, familiar words.

   a. My employment objective is to attain a position of maximum financial reward.

   b. All professors at this school are expected to achieve high standards of excellence in their instructional duties.

   c. In the eventuality of a fire, it is imperative that all persons evacuate the building without undue delay.

3. Each of the statements below uses one or more of the following stylistic devices: metaphor, simile, parallelism, repetition, alliteration, antithesis. Identify the device (or devices) used in each statement.

   a. "We are a people in a quandary about the present. We are a people in search of our future. We are a people in search of a national community." (Barbara Jordan)

   b. "The vice presidency is the sand trap of American politics. It's near the prize, and designed to be limiting." (Howard Fineman)

   c. "People the world over have always been more impressed by the power of our example than by the example of our power." (Bill Clinton)

   d. "America is not like a blanket—one piece of unbroken cloth, the same color, the same texture, the same size. America is more like a quilt—many patches, many sizes, and woven and held together by a common thread." (Jesse Jackson)

4. Analyze Martin Luther King's "I Have a Dream" in the appendix of sample speeches that follows Chapter 19. Identify the methods King uses to make his language clear, vivid, and appropriate. Look particularly at King's use of familiar words, concrete words, imagery, and rhythm.

californiaw

13

Delivery

- What Is Good Delivery?
- Methods of Delivery
- The Speaker's Voice
- The Speaker's Body
- Practicing Delivery
- Answering Audience Questions

If you were to record one of Conan O'Brien's comedy routines, memorize it word for word, and stand up before your friends to recite it, would you get the same response O'Brien does? Not very likely. And why not? Because you would not *deliver* the jokes as O'Brien does. Of course, the jokes are basically funny. But Conan O'Brien brings something extra to the jokes—his manner of presentation, his vocal inflections, his perfectly timed pauses, his facial expressions, his gestures. All these are part of an expert delivery. It would take you years of practice—as it took O'Brien—to duplicate his results.

No one expects your speech class to transform you into a multimillion-dollar talk show host. Still, this example demonstrates how important delivery can be to any public speaking situation. Even a mediocre speech will be more effective if it is presented well, whereas a wonderfully written speech can be ruined by poor delivery.

This does not mean dazzling delivery will turn a mindless string of nonsense into a triumphant oration. You cannot make a good speech without having something to say. But having something to say is not enough. You must also know *how* to say it.

nonverbal communication

Communication based on a person's use of voice and body, rather than on the use of words.

Speech delivery is a matter of *nonverbal communication.* It is based on how you use your voice and body to convey the message expressed by your words. There is a great deal of research showing that the impact of a speaker's words is powerfully influenced by his or her nonverbal communication. In this chapter, we will explain how you can use nonverbal communication to deliver your speeches effectively and to increase the impact of your verbal message.

What Is Good Delivery?

Wendell Phillips was a leader in the movement to abolish slavery in the United States during the 1800s. Some people considered him the greatest speaker of his time. The following story suggests one reason why:

> Shortly before the Civil War an Andover student, learning that Phillips was to lecture in Boston, made a 22-mile pilgrimage on foot to hear him. At first the trip seemed hardly worthwhile, for the student discovered that Phillips was not an orator in the grand manner, but spoke in an almost conversational style. He stood on the platform, one hand lightly resting on a table, talked for what seemed to be about 20 minutes, concluded, and sat down. When the student looked at his watch, he found to his astonishment that he had been listening for an hour and a half![1]

Good delivery does not call attention to itself. It conveys the speaker's ideas clearly, interestingly, and without distracting the audience. Most audiences prefer delivery that combines a certain degree of formality with the best attributes of good conversation—directness, spontaneity, animation, vocal and facial expressiveness, and a lively sense of communication.

Speech delivery is an art, not a science. What works for one speaker may fail for another. And what succeeds with today's audience may not with tomorrow's. You cannot become a skilled speaker just by following a set of rules in a textbook. In the long run, there is no substitute for experience. But take heart! A textbook *can* give you basic pointers to get you started in the right direction.

When you plan your first speech (or your second or third), you should concentrate on such basics as speaking intelligibly, avoiding distracting mannerisms, and establishing eye contact with your listeners. Once you get these elements under control and begin to feel fairly comfortable in front of an audience, you can work on polishing your delivery to enhance the impact of your ideas. Eventually, you may find yourself able to control the timing, rhythm, and momentum of a speech as skillfully as a conductor controls an orchestra.

Methods of Delivery

There are four basic methods of delivering a speech: (1) reading verbatim from a manuscript, (2) reciting a memorized text, (3) speaking impromptu, and (4) speaking extemporaneously. Let us look at each.

READING FROM A MANUSCRIPT

Certain speeches *must* be delivered word for word, according to a meticulously prepared manuscript. Examples include a Pope's religious proclamation, an engineer's report to a professional meeting, or a President's message to Congress. In such situations, absolute accuracy is essential. Every word of the speech will be analyzed by the press, by colleagues, perhaps by enemies. In the case of the President, a misstated phrase could cause an international incident.

manuscript speech

A speech that is written out word for word and read to the audience.

Although it looks easy, delivering a speech from manuscript requires great skill. Some people do it well. Their words "come alive as if coined on the spot."[2] Others ruin it every time. Instead of sounding vibrant and conversational, they come across as wooden and artificial. They falter over words, pause in the wrong places, read too quickly or too slowly, speak in a monotone, and march through the speech without even glancing at their audience. In short, they come across as *reading to* their listeners, rather than *talking with* them.

If you are in a situation where you must speak from a manuscript, practice aloud to make sure the speech sounds natural. Work on establishing eye contact with your listeners. Be certain the final manuscript is legible at a glance. Above all, reach out to your audience with the same directness and sincerity that you would if you were speaking extemporaneously.

RECITING FROM MEMORY

Among the feats of the legendary orators, none leaves us more in awe than their practice of presenting even the longest and most complex speeches entirely from memory. Nowadays it is no longer customary to memorize any but the shortest of speeches—toasts, congratulatory remarks, acceptance speeches, introductions, and the like.

If you are giving a speech of this kind and want to memorize it, by all means do so. However, be sure to memorize it so thoroughly that you will be able to concentrate on communicating with the audience, not on trying to remember the words. Speakers who gaze at the ceiling or stare out the window trying to recall what they have memorized are no better off than those who read dully from a manuscript.

SPEAKING IMPROMPTU

An impromptu speech is delivered with little or no immediate preparation. Few people choose to speak impromptu, but sometimes it cannot be avoided. In fact, many of the speeches you give in life will be impromptu. You might be called on suddenly to "say a few words" or, in the course of a class discussion, business meeting, or committee report, want to respond to a previous speaker.

impromptu speech

A speech delivered with little or no immediate preparation.

When such situations arise, don't panic. No one expects you to deliver a perfect speech on the spur of the moment. If you are in a meeting or discussion, pay close attention to what the other speakers say. Take notes of major points with which you agree or disagree. In the process, you will automatically begin to formulate what you will say when it is your turn to speak.

Whenever you are responding to a previous speaker, try to present your speech in four simple steps: First, state the point you are answering. Second, state the point you wish to make. Third, support your point with appropriate statistics, examples, or testimony. Fourth, summarize your point. This four-step method will help you organize your thoughts quickly and clearly.

If time allows, sketch a quick outline of your remarks on a piece of paper before you rise to speak. This will help you remember what you want to say and will keep you from rambling.

If the situation calls for you to speak from a lectern, walk to it calmly, take a deep breath or two (not a visible gasp), establish eye contact with your audience, and begin speaking. No matter how nervous you are inside, do your best to look calm and assured on the outside.

Once you begin speaking, maintain eye contact with the audience. Help the audience keep track of your ideas with signposts such as "My first point is . . . ; second, we can see that . . . ; in conclusion, I would like to say . . . ." By stating your points clearly and concisely, you will come across as organized and confident.

As with other kinds of public speaking, the best way to become a better impromptu speaker is to practice. You can do this on your own. Simply choose a topic on which you are already well informed, and give a one- or two-minute impromptu talk on some aspect of that topic. Any topic will do, no matter how serious or frivolous it may be. You don't even need an audience—you can speak to an empty room. Better yet, speak to a digital recorder and play it back to hear how you sound. The purpose is to gain experience in pulling your ideas together quickly and stating them succinctly.

SPEAKING EXTEMPORANEOUSLY

In popular usage, "extemporaneous" means the same as "impromptu." But technically the two are different. Unlike an impromptu speech, which is delivered off-the-cuff, an extemporaneous speech is carefully prepared and practiced in advance. In presenting the speech, the extemporaneous speaker uses only a brief set of notes or a speaking outline to jog the memory (see Chapter 11). The exact wording is chosen at the moment of delivery.

extemporaneous speech

A carefully prepared and rehearsed speech that is presented from a brief set of notes.

This is not as hard as it sounds. Once you have your outline (or notes) and know what topics you are going to cover and in what order, you can begin to practice the speech. Every time you run through it, the wording will be slightly different. As you practice the speech over and over, the best way to present each part will emerge and stick in your mind.

The extemporaneous method has several advantages. It gives more precise control over thought and language than does impromptu speaking; it offers greater spontaneity and directness than does speaking from memory or from a full manuscript; and it is adaptable to a wide range of situations. It also encourages the conversational quality audiences look for in speech delivery.

conversational quality

Presenting a speech so it sounds spontaneous no matter how many times it has been rehearsed.

"Conversational quality" means that no matter how many times a speech has been rehearsed, it still *sounds* spontaneous. When you speak extemporaneously—and have prepared properly—you have full control over your ideas, yet you are not tied to a manuscript. You are free to establish strong eye contact, to gesture naturally, and to concentrate on talking *with* the audience rather than declaiming *to* them.

For an example of extemporaneous delivery, look at Video 13.1 in the online Media Library for this chapter. The student is demonstrating how to breathe when doing yoga. She clearly has rehearsed a great deal, and she

Extemporaneous speeches are prepared ahead of time, but the exact words are chosen at the moment of presentation. This allows for more direct delivery than does reading from a manuscript.

knows what she wants to say, but she has not memorized the speech. She has a brief set of speaking notes in case she needs them, but she is not tied to the notes. Rather, she selects her words as she goes along, maintains strong eye contact with the audience, and has excellent conversational quality.

Like thousands of previous students, you can become adept at speaking extemporaneously by the end of the term. As one student commented in looking back at his class: "At the start, I never thought I'd be able to give my speeches without a ton of notes, but I'm amazed at how much progress I've made. It's one of the most valuable things I learned in the entire class."

connect

View an excerpt from "Yoga: Uniting Mind, Body, and Spirit" in the online Media Library for this chapter (Video 13.1).

Most experienced speakers prefer the extemporaneous method, and most teachers emphasize it. Later in this chapter (pages 251–252), we'll look at a step-by-step program for practicing your extemporaneous delivery.

The Speaker's Voice

What kind of voice do you have? Is it rich and resonant like Morgan Freeman's? Soft and alluring like Scarlett Johansson's? Loud and irritating like Dick Vitale's? Whatever the characteristics of your voice, you can be sure it is unique. Because no two people are exactly the same physically, no two people have identical voices.

A golden voice is certainly an asset for a public speaker, but some of the most famous speakers in history have had undistinguished voices. Abraham Lincoln had a harsh and penetrating voice; Winston Churchill suffered from a slight lisp and an awkward stammer. Like them, you can overcome natural disadvantages and use your voice to the best effect. Lincoln and Churchill learned to *control* their voices. You can do the same thing.

The aspects of voice you should work to control are volume, pitch, rate, pauses, vocal variety, pronunciation, articulation, and dialect.

VOLUME

volume

The loudness or softness of the speaker's voice.

At one time, a powerful voice was essential for an orator. Today, electronic amplification allows even a soft-spoken person to be heard in any setting. But in the classroom you will speak without a microphone. When you do, be sure to adjust your voice to the acoustics of the room, the size of the audience, and the level of background noise. If you speak too loudly, your listeners will think you boorish. If you speak too softly, they will not understand you.

Remember that your own voice always sounds louder to you than to a listener. Soon after beginning your speech, glance at the people farthest away from you. If they look puzzled, are leaning forward in their seats, or are otherwise straining to hear, you need to talk louder.

PITCH

pitch

The highness or lowness of the speaker's voice.

inflections

Changes in the pitch or tone of a speaker's voice.

monotone

A constant pitch or tone of voice.

Pitch is the highness or lowness of a speaker's voice. The faster sound waves vibrate, the higher their pitch; the slower they vibrate, the lower their pitch.

Changes in pitch are known as *inflections.* Inflection is what makes the difference between the "Aha!" triumphantly exclaimed by Sherlock Holmes upon discovering a seemingly decisive clue and the "Aha" he mutters when he learns the clue is not decisive after all. If you were to read the preceding sentence aloud, your voice would probably go up in pitch on the first "Aha" and down on the second.

In ordinary conversation, we instinctively use inflections to convey meaning and emotion. People who do not are said to speak in a *monotone,* a trait whose only known benefit is to cure insomnia in one's listeners.

Although few people speak in an absolute monotone, with no variation whatever in pitch, many fall into repetitious pitch patterns that are just as hypnotic. You can guard against this by recording your speeches as you practice them. If all your sentences end on the same inflection—either upward or downward—work on varying your pitch patterns to fit the meaning of your words.

RATE

rate

The speed at which a person speaks.

Rate refers to the speed at which a person talks. People in the United States usually speak at a rate between 120 and 150 words per minute, but there is no uniform rate for effective speechmaking. Franklin Roosevelt spoke at 110 words per minute, John Kennedy at 180. Martin Luther King opened his "I Have a Dream" speech at 92 words per minute and finished it at 145. The best rate of speech depends on several things—the vocal attributes of the speaker, the mood she or he is trying to create, the composition of the audience, and the nature of the occasion.

Two obvious faults to avoid are speaking so slowly that your listeners become bored or so quickly that they lose track of your ideas. Novice speakers are particularly prone to racing through their speeches at a frantic rate. Fortunately, this is usually an easy habit to break, as is the less common one of crawling through one's speech at a snail's pace.

The key in both cases is becoming aware of the problem and concentrating on solving it. Use a recording device to check how fast you speak. Pay special attention to rate when practicing your speech. Finally, be sure to include reminders about delivery on your speaking outline so you won't forget to make the adjustments when you give your speech in class.

PAUSES

Learning how and when to pause is a major challenge for most beginning speakers. Even a moment of silence can seem like an eternity. As you gain more poise and confidence, however, you will discover how useful the pause can be. It can signal the end of a thought unit, give an idea time to sink in, and lend dramatic impact to a statement. "The right word may be effective," said Mark Twain, "but no word was ever as effective as a rightly timed pause."

pause

A momentary break in the vocal delivery of a speech.

Developing a keen sense of timing is partly a matter of common sense, partly a matter of experience. You will not always get your pauses just right at first, but keep trying. Listen to accomplished speakers to see how they use pauses to modulate the rate and rhythm of their messages. Work on pauses when you practice your speeches.

Make sure you pause at the end of thought units and not in the middle. Otherwise, you may distract listeners from your ideas. Most important, do not fill the silence with "uh," "er," or "um." These *vocalized pauses* can create negative perceptions about a speaker's intelligence and often make a speaker appear deceptive.[3]

vocalized pause

A pause that occurs when a speaker fills the silence between words with vocalizations such as "uh," "er," and "um."

VOCAL VARIETY

Just as variety is the spice of life, so is it the spice of public speaking. A flat, listless, unchanging voice is as deadly to speechmaking as a flat, listless, unchanging routine is to daily life. When giving a speech, you should strive for vocal variety—changes in rate, pitch, and volume that will give your voice interest and expressiveness.

vocal variety

Changes in a speaker's rate, pitch, and volume that give the voice variety and expressiveness.

For an excellent example of vocal variety, look at Video 13.2 in the online Media Library for this chapter. The speaker, Sajjid Zahir Chinoy, was born and raised in Bombay, India, before coming to the United States to attend college at the University of Richmond. At the end of his senior year, Chinoy was selected as the student commencement speaker in a campus-wide competition. He spoke of the warm reception he received at Richmond and of how cultural differences can be overcome by attempting to understand other people.

The best rate of speech depends partly on the mood a speaker wants to create. To communicate the excitement of thoroughbred horse racing, you would probably speak at a faster-than-normal rate.

At the end of his speech, Chinoy received thunderous applause—partly because of what he said, but also because of how he said it. Addressing the audience of 3,000 people without notes, he spoke extemporaneously with strong eye contact and excellent vocal variety. The speech was so inspiring that the main speaker, Harvard psychiatrist Robert Coles, began his presentation by paying tribute to Chinoy. "I've been to a number of commencements," said Coles, "but I've never heard a speech quite like that!"

connect

View an excerpt from "Questions of Culture" in the online Media Library for this chapter (Video 13.2).

How can you develop a lively, expressive voice? Above all, by approaching every speech as Chinoy approached his—as an opportunity to share with your listeners ideas that are important to you. Your sense of conviction and your desire to communicate will give your voice the same spark it has in spontaneous conversation.

PRONUNCIATION

We all mispronounce words now and again. Here, for example, are four words with which you are probably familiar. Say each one aloud.

pronunciation

The accepted standard of sound and rhythm for words in a given language.

genuine	arctic
err	nuclear

Very likely you made a mistake on at least one, for they are among the most frequently mispronounced words in the English language. Let's see:

Word	Common Error	Correct Pronunciation
genuine	gen-u-wine	gen-u-win
arctic	ar-tic	arc-tic
nuclear	nu-cu-lar	nu-cle-ar
err	air	ur

Every word leads a triple life: it is read, written, and spoken. Most people recognize and understand many more words in reading than they use in ordinary writing, and about three times as many as occur in spontaneous speech.[4] This is why we occasionally stumble when speaking words that are part of our reading or writing vocabularies. In other cases, we may mispronounce the most commonplace words out of habit.

The problem is that we usually don't *know* when we are mispronouncing a word. If we are lucky, we learn the right pronunciation by hearing someone else say the word properly or by having someone gently correct us in private. If we are unlucky, we mispronounce the word in front of a roomful of people, who may raise their eyebrows, groan, or laugh.

All of this argues for practicing your speech in front of as many trusted friends and relatives as you can corner. If you have any doubts about the proper pronunciation of certain words, be sure to check a dictionary.

ARTICULATION

Articulation and pronunciation are not identical. Sloppy articulation is the failure to form particular speech sounds crisply and distinctly. It is one of several causes of mispronunciation, but you can articulate a word sharply and still mispronounce it. For example, if you say the "s" in "Illinois" or the "p" in "pneumonia," you are making a mistake in pronunciation, regardless of how precisely you articulate the sounds.

Among college students, poor articulation is more common than ignorance of correct pronunciation. We know that "let me" is not "lemme," that "going to" is not "gonna," that "did you" is not "didja," yet we persist in articulating these words improperly. Here are some other common errors in articulation you should work to avoid:

articulation

The physical production of particular speech sounds.

Word	Misarticulation
ought to	otta
didn't	dint
don't know	dunno
have to	hafta
want to	wanna
will you	wilya

If you have sloppy articulation, work on identifying and eliminating your most common errors. Like other bad habits, careless articulation can be broken only by persistent effort—but the results are well worth it. As Shakespeare advised, "Mend your speech a little, lest you may mar your fortunes."

DIALECT

Most languages have dialects, each with a distinctive accent, grammar, and vocabulary. Dialects are usually based on regional or ethnic speech patterns. The United States has four major regional dialects—Eastern, New England, Southern, and General American. We also have multiple ethnic dialects. As the nation has become more diverse culturally, it has also become more diverse linguistically.[5]

dialect

A variety of a language distinguished by variations of accent, grammar, or vocabulary.

Linguists have concluded that no dialect is inherently better or worse than another. Dialects are not linguistic badges of superiority or inferiority. They are usually shaped by our regional or ethnic background, and every dialect is "right" for the community of people who use it.

When is a given dialect appropriate in public speaking? The answer depends above all on the composition of your audience. Heavy use of any dialect—regional or ethnic—can be troublesome when the audience does not share that dialect. In such a situation, the dialect may cause listeners to make negative judgments about the speaker's personality, intelligence, and competence. This is why professional speakers have been known to invest large amounts of time (and money) to master the General American dialect used by most television news broadcasters.

Does this mean you must talk like a television news broadcaster if you want to be successful in your speeches? Not at all. Regional or ethnic dialects do not pose a problem as long as the audience is familiar with them and finds them appropriate. When speaking in the North, for example, a southern politician may avoid regional dialect. But when addressing audiences in the South, the same politician may intentionally include regional dialect as a way of creating common ground with listeners.

Although not strictly speaking a matter of dialect, the proficiency of non-native speakers of English often arises in the speech classroom. Fortunately, teachers and students alike usually go out of their way to be helpful and encouraging to international students and others for whom English is not the primary language. Over the years, many non-native speakers of English have found speech class a supportive environment in which to improve their proficiency in spoken English.[6]

The Speaker's Body

Imagine yourself at a party. During the evening you form impressions about the people around you. Jonte seems relaxed and even-tempered, Nicole tense and irritable. Kyndra seems open and straightforward, Bekah hostile and evasive. Amin seems happy to see you; Seth definitely is not.

How do you reach these conclusions? To a surprising extent, you reach them not on the basis of what people say with words, but because of what they say with their posture, gestures, eyes, and facial expressions. Suppose you are sitting next to Amin, and he says, "This is a great party. I'm really glad to be here with you." However, his body is turned slightly away from you, and he keeps looking at someone across the room. Despite what he says, you know he is *not* glad to be there with you.

Much the same thing happens in speechmaking. Posture, facial expression, gestures, eye contact—all affect the way listeners respond to a speaker. How we use these and other body motions to communicate is the subject of a fascinating area of study called kinesics. One of its founders, Ray Birdwhistell, estimated that more than 700,000 physical signals can be sent through bodily movement. Studies have shown that these signals have a significant impact on the meaning communicated by speakers.

kinesics

The study of body motions as a systematic mode of communication.

Research has also confirmed what the Greek historian Herodotus observed more than 2,400 years ago: "People trust their ears less than their eyes." When a speaker's body language is inconsistent with his or her words, listeners often believe the body language rather than the words.[7] Here are the major aspects of physical action that will affect the outcome of your speeches.

PERSONAL APPEARANCE

If you were Lady Gaga, you could show up to make an MTV Music Video Award presentation speech wearing a bizarre creation that left little to the imagination. If you were Albert Einstein, you could show up to address an international science conference wearing wrinkled trousers, a sweater, and tennis shoes. While the members of your audience would certainly comment on your attire, your reputation would not be harmed. In fact, it might be enhanced. You would be one of the few, the very few, who live outside the rules, who are expected to be unusual.

Now imagine what would happen if the president of a corporation showed up to address a stockholders' meeting attired like Lady Gaga, or if the President of the United States spoke on national television wearing wrinkled clothes and tennis shoes. Both presidents would soon be looking for work. Barring the occasional eccentric, every speaker is expected by her or

Good speakers use a lively voice to bring their ideas to life. They also use gestures, eye contact, and facial expressions to create a bond with their audience.

his audience to exhibit a personal appearance in keeping with the occasion of the speech.

Many studies have confirmed that personal appearance plays an important role in speechmaking.[8] Listeners always see you before they hear you. Just as you adapt your language to the audience and the occasion, so should you dress and groom appropriately. Although the force of your speech can sometimes overcome a poor impression created by personal appearance, the odds are against it. Regardless of the speaking situation, you should try to evoke a favorable first impression.

MOVEMENT

Novice speakers are often unsure about what to do with their body while giving a speech. Some pace back and forth across the podium, shift their weight from one foot to the other, fidget with their notes, or jingle coins in their pockets. Still others turn into statues, standing rigid and expressionless from beginning to end.

Such quirks usually stem from nervousness. If you are prone to distracting mannerisms, your teacher will identify them so you can work on controlling them. With a little concentration, these mannerisms should disappear as you become more comfortable speaking in front of an audience.

As important as how you act during the speech is what you do just *before* you begin and *after* you finish. As you rise to speak, try to appear calm, poised, and confident, despite the butterflies in your stomach. When you reach the lectern, don't lean on it, and don't rush into your speech. Give yourself time to get set. Arrange your notes just the way you want them. Stand quietly as you wait to make sure the audience is paying attention. Establish eye contact with your listeners. Then—and only then—should you start to talk.

When you reach the end of your speech, maintain eye contact for a few moments after you stop talking. This will give your closing line time to sink in. Unless you are staying at the lectern to answer questions, collect your notes and return to your seat. As you do so, maintain your cool, collected demeanor. Whatever you do, don't start to gather your notes before you have finished talking, and don't cap off your speech with a huge sigh of relief or some remark like, "Whew! Am I glad that's over!"

When practicing your speeches, spend a little time rehearsing how you will behave at the beginning and at the end. It is one of the easiest—and one of the most effective—things you can do to improve your image with an audience.

GESTURES

Few aspects of delivery cause students more anguish than deciding what to do with their hands. "Should I clasp them behind my back? Let them hang at my sides? Rest them on the lectern? And what about gesturing? When should I do that—and how?" Even people who use their hands expressively in everyday conversation seem to regard them as awkward appendages when speaking before an audience.

gestures

Motions of a speaker's hands or arms during a speech.

Over the years, more nonsense has been written about gesturing than any other aspect of speech delivery. Adroit gestures *can* add to the impact of a speech; but effective speakers do not need a vast repertoire of gestures. Some accomplished speakers gesture frequently, others hardly at all. The primary rule is this: Whatever gestures you make should not distract from your message. They should *appear* natural and spontaneous, help clarify or reinforce your ideas, and be suited to the audience and occasion.

Gesturing tends to work itself out as you acquire experience and confidence. For now, make sure your hands do not upstage your ideas. Avoid flailing them about, wringing them together, or toying with your rings. Once you have eliminated these distractions, forget about your hands. Think about communicating with your listeners, and your gestures will take care of themselves—just as they do in conversation.

EYE CONTACT

The eyes have been called "the windows of the soul." We look to them to help gauge a speaker's truthfulness, intelligence, attitudes, and feelings.

eye contact

Direct visual contact with the eyes of another person.

Although patterns of eye contact in everyday conversation vary from culture to culture, there is wide agreement across cultures on the importance of eye contact in public speaking. In most circumstances, one of the quickest ways to establish a communicative bond with your listeners is to look at them personally and pleasantly. Avoiding their gaze is one of the surest ways to lose them.

Speakers in the United States who fail to establish eye contact are perceived as tentative or ill at ease and may be seen as insincere or dishonest. It is no wonder, then, that teachers urge students to look at the audience 80 to 90 percent of the time they are talking. You may find this disconcerting at first. But after one or two speeches, you should be able to meet the gaze of your audience fairly comfortably.

It isn't enough just to look at your listeners; *how* you look at them also counts. Beware of the tendency to gaze intently at one part of the audience while ignoring the rest. In speech class, some students look only at the section of the room where the teacher is sitting. Others avoid looking anywhere near the teacher and focus on one or two sympathetic friends. You should try to establish eye contact with your whole audience.

When addressing a small audience such as your class, you can usually look briefly from one person to another. For a larger group, you can scan the

Research shows that eye contact is one of the most important elements in speech delivery. As with figure skating champion Michelle Kwan, you want your eyes to convey confidence, sincerity, and conviction.

audience rather than try to engage the eyes of each person individually. No matter what the size of your audience, you want your eyes to convey confidence, sincerity, and conviction.

Look at Video 13.3 in the online Media Library for this chapter to see a fine example of eye contact. The speaker is telling her classmates how they can become volunteers for the Special Olympics. Notice how she uses her eyes to connect with her listeners at a personal level. This is the kind of strong communication you should strive for in your speeches.[9]

Practicing Delivery

Popular wisdom promises that practice makes perfect. This is true, but only if we practice properly. You will do little to improve your speech delivery unless you practice the right things in the right ways. Here is a five-step method that has worked well for many students:

connect

View an excerpt from "Making a Difference Through the Special Olympics" in the online Media Library for this chapter (Video 13.3).

1. Go through your preparation outline *aloud* to check how what you have written translates into spoken discourse. Is it too long? Too short? Are the main points clear when you speak them? Are the supporting materials distinct, convincing, interesting? Do the introduction and conclusion come across well? As you answer these questions, revise the speech as needed.
2. Prepare your speaking outline. In doing so, be sure to follow the guidelines in Chapter 11. Use the same visual framework as in the preparation outline. Make sure the speaking outline is easy to read at a glance. Give yourself cues on the outline for delivering the speech.

3. Practice the speech aloud several times using only the speaking outline. Be sure to "talk through" all examples and to recite in full all quotations and statistics. If your speech includes visual aids, use them as you practice. The first couple of times, you will probably forget something or make a mistake, but don't worry. Keep going and complete the speech as well as you can. Concentrate on gaining control of the *ideas;* don't try to learn the speech word for word. After a few tries you should be able to get through the speech extemporaneously with surprising ease.
4. Now begin to polish and refine your delivery. Practice the speech in front of a mirror to check for eye contact and distracting mannerisms. Record the speech to gauge volume, pitch, rate, pauses, and vocal variety. Most important, try it out on friends, roommates, family members—anyone who will listen and give you an honest appraisal. Because your speech is designed for people rather than for mirrors or recorders, you need to find out ahead of time how it goes over with people.
5. Finally, give your speech a dress rehearsal under conditions as close as possible to those you will face in class. Some students like to try the speech a couple times in an empty classroom the day before the speech is due. No matter where you hold your last practice session, you should leave it feeling confident and looking forward to speaking in your class.

If this or any practice method is to work, you must start early. Don't wait until the night before your speech to begin working on delivery. A single practice session—no matter how long—is rarely enough. Allow yourself *at least* a couple of days, preferably more, to gain command of the speech and its presentation.

Answering Audience Questions

If you have ever watched a press conference or heard a speaker answer questions after a talk, you know the question-and-answer session can make or break a presentation. A speaker who handles questions well can strengthen the impact of his or her speech. On the other hand, a speaker who evades questions or shows annoyance will almost certainly create the opposite effect.

The question-and-answer session is a common part of public speaking, whether the occasion is a press conference, business presentation, public hearing, or classroom assignment. An answer to a question is often the final word an audience hears and is likely to leave a lasting impression.

PREPARING FOR THE QUESTION-AND-ANSWER SESSION

The first step to doing well in a question-and-answer session is to take it as seriously as the speech itself. The two major steps in preparing are working out answers to possible questions and practicing the delivery of those answers.

Formulate Answers to Possible Questions

Once you know that your presentation will include questions from the audience, you should be thinking about possible questions even as you are writing your speech. If you practice your speech in front of friends, family, or coworkers, ask them to jot down questions. Keep track of all the questions and formulate answers. Write your answers in full to make sure you have thought them through completely.

If you are giving a persuasive speech, be sure to work out answers to objections the audience may have to your proposal. No matter how careful you are to deal with those objections in your speech, you can be sure they will come up in the question-and-answer session.

If you are speaking on a topic with technical aspects, be ready to answer specialized inquiries about them, as well as questions that seek clarification, in nontechnical terms. You might even prepare a handout that you can distribute afterward for people who want more information.

Practice the Delivery of Your Answers

You would not present a speech to a room full of people without rehearsing. Neither should you go into a question-and-answer session without practicing the delivery of your answers.

One possibility is to have a friend or colleague listen to your presentation, ask questions, and critique your answers. This method is used by political candidates and business leaders before debates or press conferences. Another possibility is to record your answers to anticipated questions, play them back, and revise them until they are just right.

As you rehearse, work on making your answers brief and to the point. Many simple questions can be answered in 30 seconds, and even complex ones should usually be answered in a minute or two. If you practice answering questions beforehand, you will find it much easier to keep to these time limits.

Of course, there is no way to predict every question you will receive. But if you go into the question-and-answer period fully prepared, you will be able to adapt to whatever occurs.

MANAGING THE QUESTION-AND-ANSWER SESSION

If you have ever watched a skillful speaker field questions from the audience, you know there is an art to managing a question-and-answer session. Entire books have been written on this subject, but the following suggestions will help get you started on the right foot.

Using public speaking in your CAREER

Utilizing your business degree and computer savvy, you have made a success of the online marketing company you started after graduating from college. Now in its third year, the company has prepared a proposal to design the e-commerce site for a major sporting goods retailer. In your 30-minute presentation to the retailer's management team, you will review the homepage designs, site maps, and security protocols.

You notice on the agenda that another 30 minutes has been allotted after your presentation for questions and answers. Knowing from your previous experience with clients how important the Q&A session can be, you want to be sure you are ready for it. What steps will you take to prepare?

Approach Questions with a Positive Attitude

A positive attitude will help you answer questions graciously and respectfully. Try to view questions from the audience as signs of genuine interest and a desire to learn more about your subject. If someone asks about a point that seems clear to you, don't respond by saying, "I discussed that at the beginning of my talk," or "The answer seems obvious." Instead, use moments like these to reiterate or expand upon your ideas.

A speaker who adopts a sharp or defensive tone while answering questions will alienate many people in the audience. Even if you are asked a hostile question, keep your cool. Avoid the temptation to answer defensively, sarcastically, or argumentatively. Most people in the audience will respect you for trying to avoid a quarrel.

Listen Carefully

It's hard to answer a question well if you don't listen carefully to it. Give the questioner your full attention. When faced with an unclear or unwieldy question, try to rephrase it by saying something like, "If I understand your question, it seems to me that you are asking. . . ." Another option is simply to ask the audience member to repeat the question. Most people will restate it more succinctly and clearly.

Direct Answers to the Entire Audience

When you are being asked a question, look at the questioner. Direct your answer, however, to the entire audience. Make occasional eye contact with the questioner as you answer, but speak primarily to the audience as a whole. If you speak just to the questioner, the rest of your audience may drift off.

When speaking to a large audience, repeat or paraphrase each question after it is asked. This involves the entire audience and ensures that they know the question. In addition, repeating or paraphrasing the question gives you a moment to frame an answer before you respond.

Be Honest and Straightforward

If you don't know the answer to a question, say so. Don't apologize, don't evade, and most important, don't try to bluff. Do, however, let the questioner know that you take the question seriously. Offer to check into the answer as soon as possible after the speech. If a more knowledgeable person is at hand, ask if she or he knows the answer.

Stay on Track

It's easy to get diverted or lose control of time in a lively question-and-answer session. Unless there is a moderator, the speaker is responsible for keeping things on track. Allow one follow-up question from each person, and don't let yourself be dragged into a personal debate with any questioner. If someone attempts to ask more than two questions, respond graciously yet firmly by saying, "This is an interesting line of questioning, but we need to give other people a chance to ask questions."

Sometimes, a listener will launch into an extended monologue instead of posing a question. When this happens, you can retain control of the situation by saying something like, "Those are very interesting ideas, but do you have a specific question I can answer?" If the person persists, offer to talk individually with him or her after the session.

Question-and-answer sessions are an important part of public speaking around the globe. Here Mike Weightman of the International Atomic Energy Agency talks with reporters in Tokyo, Japan, about the nuclear power plant crippled in the 2011 earthquake and tsunami.

On some occasions, the length of the question-and-answer session is predetermined. On other occasions, it's up to the speaker. Make sure you allow enough time to get through issues of major importance, but don't let things drag on after the momentum of the session has started winding down. As the end approaches, offer to respond to another question or two. Then wrap things up by thanking the audience for its time and attention.[10]

Summary

Speech delivery is a matter of nonverbal communication. It is based on how you use your voice and body to convey the message expressed by your words. Rather than calling attention to itself, effective delivery conveys the speaker's ideas clearly, engagingly, and without distracting the audience.

There are four basic methods of delivering a speech: reading verbatim from a manuscript, reciting a memorized text, speaking impromptu, and speaking extemporaneously. When speaking extemporaneously, you will have a brief set of notes or a speaking outline and will choose the exact wording of your speech at the moment of delivery.

To use your voice effectively you should work on controlling your volume, pitch, rate, pauses, vocal variety, pronunciation, articulation, and dialect. Volume is the relative loudness of your voice, and pitch is the relative highness or lowness. Rate refers to the speed at which you talk. Pauses, when carefully timed, can add punch to your speech, but you should avoid vocalized pauses ("er," "um," and the like).

Vocal variety refers to changes in volume, pitch, rate, and pauses, and is crucial to making your voice lively and animated. You also need correct pronunciation and distinct articulation. Avoid heavy use of dialect in situations where the audience does not share the dialect or will find it inappropriate.

Posture, personal appearance, facial expression, gestures, and eye contact also affect the way listeners respond to speakers. Dress and groom appropriately, use gestures and bodily movement to enhance your message, and make eye contact with your listeners.

You should practice all these aspects of delivery along with the words of your speech. Start your practice sessions early so you will have plenty of time to gain command of the speech and its presentation.

If your speech includes a question-and-answer session, anticipate the most likely questions, prepare answers to them, and practice delivering those answers. During the question-and-answer period, listen carefully to the questions, approach them positively, and respond to them briefly, graciously, and straightforwardly. Direct your answers to the full audience, rather than to the questioner alone, and make sure to end the session in a timely fashion.

Key Terms

nonverbal communication *(240)*
manuscript speech *(241)*
impromptu speech *(241)*
extemporaneous speech *(242)*
conversational quality *(242)*
volume *(244)*
pitch *(244)*
inflections *(244)*
monotone *(244)*
rate *(244)*
pause *(245)*
vocalized pause *(245)*
vocal variety *(245)*
pronunciation *(246)*
articulation *(247)*
dialect *(247)*
kinesics *(248)*
gestures *(250)*
eye contact *(250)*

Review Questions

After reading this chapter, you should be able to answer the following questions:

1. What is nonverbal communication? Why is it important to effective public speaking?
2. What are the elements of good speech delivery?
3. What are the four methods of speech delivery?
4. What are the eight aspects of voice usage you should concentrate on in your speeches?
5. What are four aspects of bodily action you should concentrate on in your speeches?
6. What are the five steps you should follow when practicing your speech delivery?
7. What steps should you take when preparing for a question-and-answer session? What should you concentrate on when responding to questions during the session?

connect™

For further review, go to the LearnSmart study module for this chapter.

Exercises for Critical Thinking

1. An excellent way to improve your vocal variety is to read aloud selections from poetry that require emphasis and feeling. Choose one of your favorite poems that falls into this category, or find one by leafing through a poetry anthology.

   Practice reading the selection aloud. As you read, use your voice to make the poem come alive. Vary your volume, rate, and pitch. Find the appropriate places for pauses. Underline the key words or phrases you think should be stressed. Modulate your tone of voice; use inflections for emphasis and meaning.

   For this to work, you must overcome your fear of sounding affected or "dramatic." Most beginning speakers do better if they exaggerate changes in volume, rate, pitch, and expression. This will make you more aware of the ways you can use your voice to express a wide range of moods and meanings. Besides, what sounds overly "dramatic" to you usually does not sound that way to an audience. By adding luster, warmth, and enthusiasm to your voice, you will go a long way toward capturing and keeping the interest of your listeners.

   If possible, practice reading the selection into a digital recorder. Listen to the playback. If you are not satisfied with what you hear, practice the selection some more and record it again.

2. Watch a 10-minute segment of a television drama with the sound turned off. What do the characters say with their dress, gestures, facial expressions, and the like? Do the same with a television comedy. How do the nonverbal messages in the two shows differ? Be prepared to report your observations in class.

3. Attend a speech on campus. You may choose either a presentation by a guest speaker from outside the college or a class session by a professor who has a reputation as a good lecturer. Prepare a brief report on the speaker's delivery.

   In your report, first analyze the speaker's volume, pitch, rate, pauses, vocal variety, pronunciation, and articulation. Then evaluate the speaker's personal appearance, bodily action, gestures, and eye contact. Explain how the speaker's delivery added to or detracted from what the speaker said. Finally, note at least two techniques of delivery used by the speaker that you might want to try in your next speech.

verty

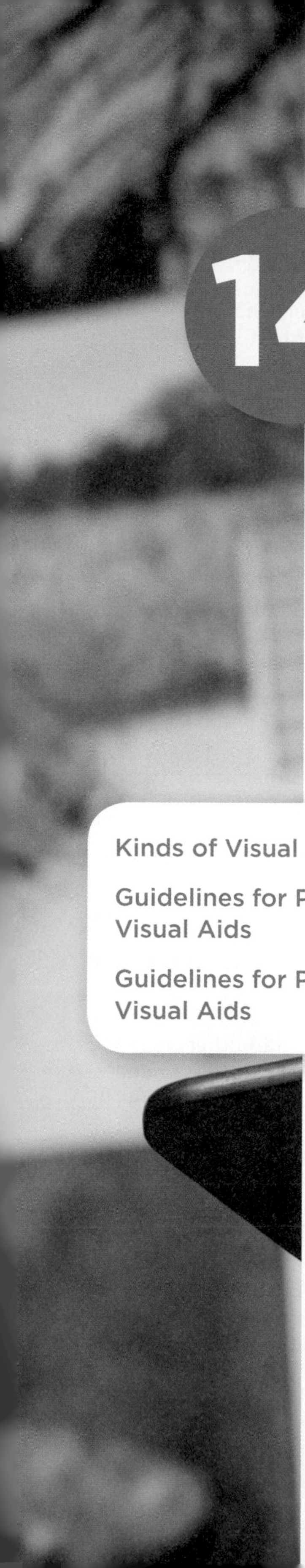

14

Using Visual Aids

Diagnosed with high blood pressure when he was in high school, Devin Marshall decided to give his persuasive speech on the excessive amount of salt in the American diet. On the day of his speech, he brought to class a large box, which he set on the table next to him. This immediately aroused the curiosity of his audience. Devin took from the box a container of Morton Salt, a measuring cup, and two plates. Then he began his speech.

First, he explained the monthly salt consumption recommended by the American Medical Association. To illustrate, he measured a cup of salt onto one plate and showed it to the audience. Next, he gave statistics about how much salt the average American consumes in a month. Again, as he spoke, he measured. When he was finished measuring, the second plate had three cups, almost two pounds of salt.

Finally, Devin said, "Now let's multiply that amount by 12 and see how much salt we eat over the course of a year." And he began taking out of the box one container of Morton Salt after another, until he had piled up a pyramid of 14 containers, or nearly 24 pounds of salt!

As the old saying tells us, one picture is worth a thousand words. Can you picture 2 pounds of salt? Or 24 pounds of salt? You could if you had watched Devin measure out the salt and stack up the Morton containers. This dramatic visual evidence brought home Devin's point more forcefully than would have been possible with words alone.

People find a speaker's message more interesting, grasp it more easily, and retain it longer when it is presented visually as well as verbally. In fact, when used properly, visual aids can enhance almost *every* aspect of a speech. An average speaker who uses visual aids will come across as better prepared, more credible, and more professional than a dynamic speaker who does not use visual aids. Visual aids can even help you combat stage fright. They heighten audience interest, shift attention away from the speaker, and give the speaker greater confidence in the presentation as a whole.[1]

For all these reasons, you will find visual aids of great value in your speeches. In this chapter, we will concentrate primarily on visual aids suitable for classroom speeches, but the same principles apply in all circumstances. For speeches outside the classroom—in business or community situations, for instance—you should have no difficulty if you follow the suggestions given here.

Let us look first at the kinds of visual aids you are most likely to use, then at guidelines for preparing visual aids, and finally at guidelines for using visual aids.

Kinds of Visual Aids

OBJECTS AND MODELS

Bringing the object of your speech to class can be an excellent way to clarify your ideas and give them dramatic impact. If your specific purpose is "To inform my audience how to choose the right ski equipment," why not bring the equipment to class to show your listeners? Or suppose you want to inform your classmates about the Peruvian art of doll making. You could bring several dolls to class and explain how they were made.

Some objects, however, cannot be used effectively in classroom speeches. Some are too big. Others are too small to be seen clearly. Still others may not be available to you. If you were speaking about a rare suit of armor in a local museum, you could, theoretically, transport it to class, but it is most unlikely that the museum would let you borrow it.

connect™

View an excerpt from "CPR" in the online Media Library for this chapter (Video 14.1).

If the object you want to discuss is too large, too small, or unavailable, you may be able to work with a model. For an example, check Video 14.1 in the online Media Library for this chapter. The speaker is talking about CPR, which he demonstrates on a training dummy he borrowed from the local Red Cross.

PHOTOGRAPHS AND DRAWINGS

In the absence of an object or a model, you may be able to use photographs or drawings. Neither, however, will work effectively unless they are large enough for the audience to see without straining. Normal-size photos are too small to be seen clearly without being passed around—which only diverts the

Photographs make excellent visual aids if they are large enough to be seen easily. Check Video 14.2 in the online Media Library for this chapter to see how one speaker used this photograph of the famous Incan ruins at Machu Picchu.

audience from what you are saying. The same is true of photographs and drawings in books.

The most effective way to show drawings and photographs is with PowerPoint. Notice, for example, how the speaker in Video 14.2 uses PowerPoint to present a photograph of the famous Incan ruins at Machu Picchu in Peru. No other method of showing the photograph would work as well.

For another example, take a look at Figure 14.1 (below), which shows a drawing used in a speech about the kinds of problems faced by people who have dyslexia. It allowed the speaker to translate complex ideas into visual terms the audience could grasp immediately.

connect

View an excerpt from "Machu Picchu: City of the Gods" in the online Media Library for this chapter (Video 14.2).

GRAPHS

Audiences often have trouble grasping a complex series of numbers. You can ease their difficulty by using graphs to show statistical trends and patterns.

graph

A visual aid used to show statistical trends and patterns.

FIGURE 14.1

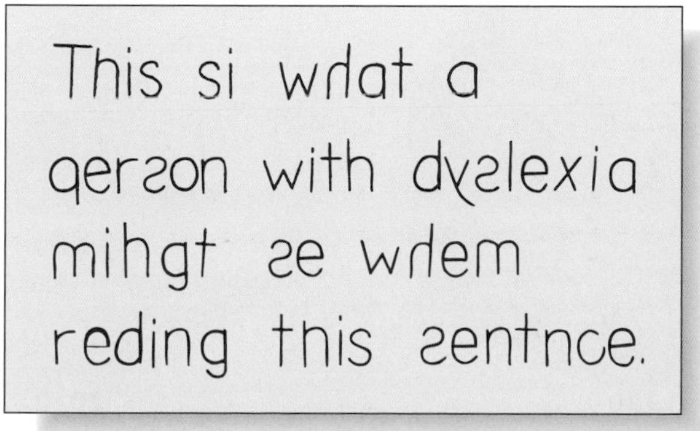

FIGURE 14.2

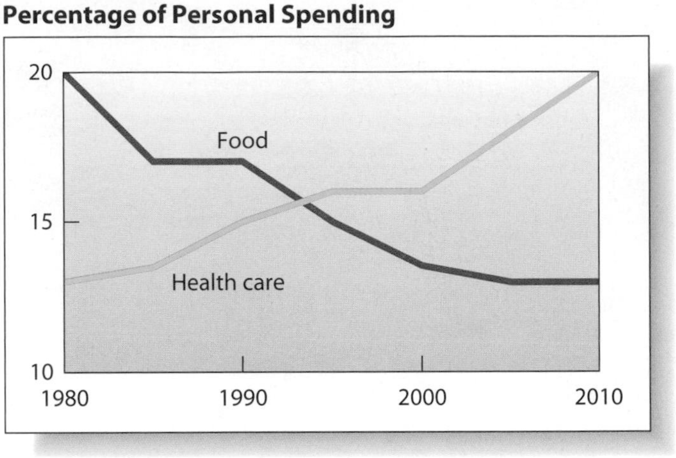

line graph

A graph that uses one or more lines to show changes in statistics over time or space.

The most common type is the *line graph*. Figure 14.2 (above) shows such a graph, used in a speech about the rising cost of health care. If you look at Video 14.3 in the online Media Library for this chapter, you can see how the speaker explained the graph. She said:

connect™

View the presentation of this graph in "America's Continuing Health Care Crisis" in the online Media Library for this chapter (Video 14.3).

> As you can see from this graph, based on figures from the U.S. government, health care continues to eat away at our budgets. Since 1980, it's risen from 13 percent of personal spending to 20 percent. Compare that to what we spend on food. In 1980, 20 percent of personal spending was on food; today it is 13 percent. That's right, over the past three decades health care has completely changed places with food as the largest category of personal expense.

The *pie graph* is best suited for illustrating simple distribution patterns. Figure 14.3 (below) shows how one speaker used a pie graph to help listeners

FIGURE 14.3

pie graph

A graph that highlights segments of a circle to show simple distribution patterns.

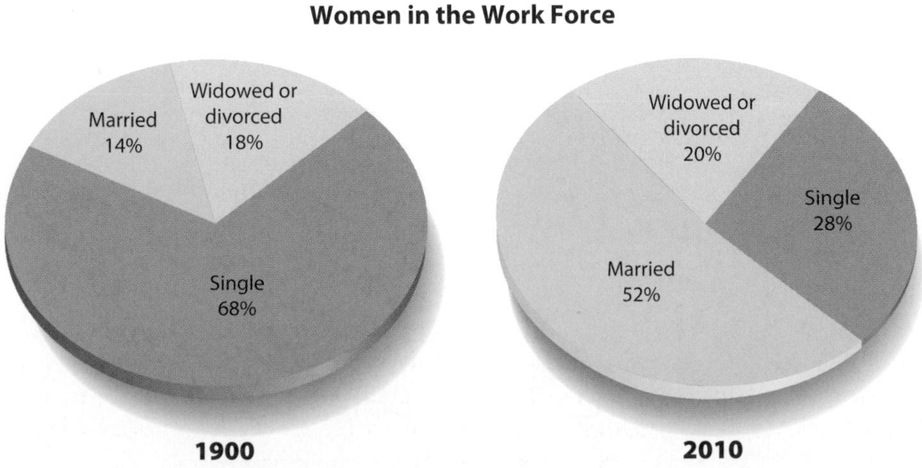

FIGURE 14.4

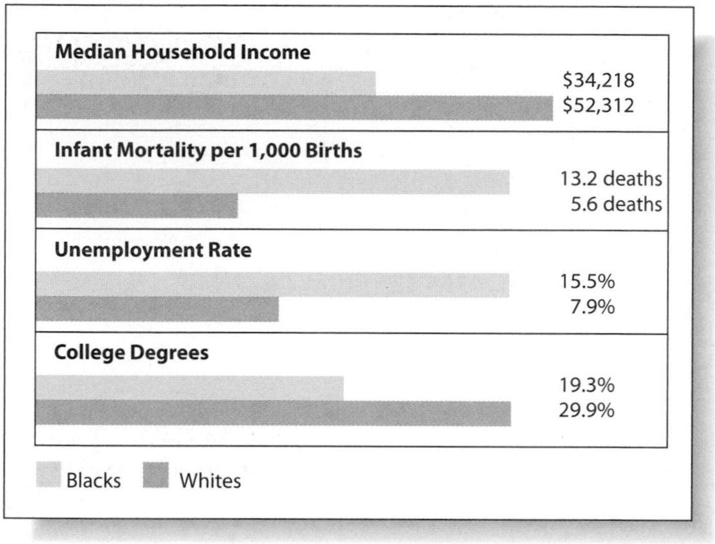

bar graph

A graph that uses vertical or horizontal bars to show comparisons among two or more items.

visualize changes in marital status among working women in the past century. The graph on the left shows the percentages of working women who were single, married, and widowed or divorced in 1900. The graph on the right shows percentages for the same groups in 2010.

Because a pie graph is used to dramatize relationships among the parts of a whole, you should keep the number of different segments in the graph as small as possible. A pie graph should ideally have from two to five segments; under no circumstances should it have more than eight.

The *bar graph* is a particularly good way to show comparisons among two or more items. It also has the advantage of being easy to understand, even by people who have no background in reading graphs.

Figure 14.4 (above) is an example of a bar graph from a speech titled "The Politics of Race in America." It shows visually the relative standing of whites and blacks with respect to median household income, infant mortality, unemployment, and college education. By using a bar graph, the speaker made her points more vividly than if she had just cited the numbers orally.[2]

CHARTS

Charts are particularly useful for summarizing large blocks of information. One student, in a speech titled "The United States: A Nation of Immigrants," used a chart to show the leading regions of the world for U.S. immigrants (Figure 14.5, page 264). These are too many categories to be conveyed in a pie graph. By listing them on a chart, the speaker made it easier for listeners to keep the information straight. Look at Video 14.4 in the online Media Library for this chapter to see how the student presented the chart during her speech.

connect™

View an excerpt from "The United States: A Nation of Immigrants" in the online Media Library for this chapter (Video 14.4).

The biggest mistake made by beginning speakers when using a chart is to include too much information. As we will discuss later, visual aids should be clear, simple, and uncluttered. Lists on a chart should rarely exceed seven or eight items, with generous spacing between items. If you cannot fit everything on a single chart, make a second one.

FIGURE 14.5

Region of Birth	Percent of U.S. Immigrants
Asia	36 percent
Mexico	14 percent
Europe	11 percent
Caribbean	11 percent
South America	10 percent
Africa	9 percent
Central America	5 percent
Other	4 percent

chart

A visual aid that summarizes a large block of information, usually in list form.

VIDEO

If you are talking about the impact caused by a low-speed automobile accident, what could be more effective than showing slow-motion video of crash tests? Or suppose you are explaining the different kinds of roller coasters found in amusement parks. Your best visual aid would be a video showing those coasters in action.

Despite its advantages, however, adding video to a speech can cause more harm than good if it is not done carefully and expertly. First, make sure the clip is not too long. While a 30-second video can illustrate your ideas in a memorable way, anything much longer will distract attention from the speech itself. Second, make sure the video is cued to start exactly where you want it. Third, if necessary, edit the video to the precise length you need so it will blend smoothly into your speech. Fourth, beware of low-resolution video that may look fine on a computer but is blurry and distorted when projected on a screen or monitor.

THE SPEAKER

Sometimes you can use your own body as a visual aid—by illustrating how a conductor directs an orchestra, by revealing the secrets behind magic tricks, by showing how to perform sign language, and so forth. In addition to clarifying a speaker's ideas, doing some kind of demonstration helps keep the audience involved. It also can reduce a speaker's nervousness by providing an outlet for extra adrenaline.

connect

View an excerpt from "Yoga: Uniting Body, Mind, and Spirit" in the online Media Library for this chapter (Video 14.5).

Doing a demonstration well requires special practice to coordinate your actions with your words and to control the timing of your speech. You can see an excellent example on Video 14.5 in the online Media Library for this chapter. After talking about the role of proper breathing in yoga, the speaker demonstrates three yoga poses. Notice how clearly she explains each pose, communicates directly with the audience, and maintains eye contact throughout her demonstration.

Special care is required if you are demonstrating a process that takes longer to complete than the time allotted for your speech. If you plan to show

Sometimes a speaker can use her or his body as a visual aid, as in this speech on yoga. Such a speech requires careful practice to coordinate the speaker's actions and words while maintaining eye contact with the audience.

a long process, you might borrow the techniques of television chefs. They work through most of the steps in making a perfect marinated chicken, but they have a second, finished chicken ready to show you at the last minute.

POWERPOINT

PowerPoint allows you to integrate a variety of visual aids—including charts, graphs, photographs, and video—in the same talk. Depending on the technological resources at your school, you may be able to use PowerPoint in your speech class. If so, it will provide training for speeches outside the classroom—especially in business settings, where PowerPoint presentations are made every day.

Later in this chapter, we will look at guidelines for preparing and presenting visual aids effectively. In the process, we'll pay special attention to what you can do to create and deliver high-quality PowerPoint slides. For now, consider the following factors when thinking about employing PowerPoint in your speeches.

Pluses and Minuses of PowerPoint

When used well, PowerPoint is a great boon to communication. Unfortunately, it is not always used well. Too often speakers allow it to dominate their presentations, wowing the audience with their technical proficiency while losing the message in a flurry of sounds and images. As technology expert Herb Lovelace states, it sometimes seems that "the fancier the PowerPoint presentation, the less valuable the ideas being presented."[3]

At the other extreme are speakers who throw their presentations together carelessly, assuming that using PowerPoint will magically produce a superb speech. Plodding through one poorly designed slide after another with little or no eye contact with the audience, these speakers would be better off if they had never heard of PowerPoint.

Another problem is that some speakers use PowerPoint to illustrate every point of their talk, so the speaker is virtually reading the speech to the audience as the words appear on screen. This is no more effective than reading dully from a manuscript, and it seldom produces genuine communication.

Planning to Use PowerPoint

If you are going to employ PowerPoint effectively, you need a clear idea of exactly why, how, and when to use it. Rather than putting everything you say on screen for the audience to read, you need to choose which aspects of your speech to illustrate. This requires careful planning.

connect™

View an excerpt from "The Horrors of Puppy Mills" in the online Media Library for this chapter (Video 14.6).

The first step is deciding where you can use PowerPoint to greatest advantage. After you have finished developing the speech, think about where you might employ PowerPoint to clarify or strengthen your ideas. Rather than using slides to illustrate every thought, look for spots where it will genuinely enhance your message.

One student, for example, used PowerPoint in a speech about puppy mills. After documenting the number of puppy mills in America and describing their cruelty, he said, "But you can see for yourself what the dogs have to endure." He then showed several photographs demonstrating the terrible conditions of dogs in puppy mills. The photographs provided powerful visual evidence to back up the speaker's claims.

connect™

View an excerpt from "Georges Seurat and the Art of Pointillism" in the online Media Library for this chapter (Video 14.7).

For another example, look at Video 14.7, in which the speaker discusses Georges Seurat's famous painting *Sunday Afternoon on the Island of la Grand Jatte*. The speaker uses a series of PowerPoint slides to show details of the painting that could not have been seen otherwise. He also does an excellent job of explaining each slide as he goes along.

As you plan your speeches, think how you can use PowerPoint to enhance your ideas. At the same time, remember that too many visuals—or poor visuals—can do more harm than good. Be creative and resourceful without allowing PowerPoint to overpower your entire speech.

Using public speaking in your CAREER

As a veterinarian and owner of a small-animal practice, you work closely with your local humane society to help control a growing population of unwanted dogs and cats. You and your staff devote many hours annually in free and reduced-cost medical services to animals adopted from the society. Now you have been asked to speak to the city council in support of legislation proposed by the society for stronger enforcement of animal licensing and leash laws.

In your speech, you plan to include statistics that (1) compare estimates of the city's dog population with the number of licenses issued during the past five years and (2) show the small number of citations given by local law enforcement for unleashed pets during the same period of time. Knowing from your college public speaking class how valuable visual aids can be in presenting statistics, you decide to illustrate one set of statistics with a chart and the other with a graph.

For which set of statistics will a chart be more appropriate? For which set will a graph be more appropriate? Of the three kinds of graphs discussed in this chapter—bar, line, pie—which will work best for your statistics, and why?

Guidelines for Preparing Visual Aids

Whether you are creating visual aids by hand or with PowerPoint, the following guidelines will help you design aids that are clear and visually appealing.

PREPARE VISUAL AIDS WELL IN ADVANCE

Preparing visual aids well in advance has two advantages. First, it means you will have the time and resources to devise creative, attractive aids. Second, it means you can use them while practicing your speech. Visual aids are effective only when they are integrated smoothly with the rest of the speech. If you lose your place, drop your aids, or otherwise stumble around when presenting them, you will distract your audience and shatter your concentration.

KEEP VISUAL AIDS SIMPLE

Visual aids should be simple, clear, and to the point. If you look back at the aids presented earlier in this chapter, you will see that all of them are clear and uncluttered. They contain enough information to communicate the speaker's point, but not so much as to confuse or distract the audience.[4]

When using PowerPoint, limit your slides to a manageable amount of information, and beware of the tendency to go overboard. It is possible to create a graphic that displays two charts, a photograph, and ten lines of text in five different typefaces with 250 colors. But who would be able to read it?

MAKE SURE VISUAL AIDS ARE LARGE ENOUGH

A visual aid is useless if no one can see it. Keep in mind the size of the room in which you will be speaking and make sure your aid is big enough to be seen easily by everyone. As you prepare the aid, check its visibility by moving to a point as far away from it as your most distant listener will be sitting.

If you are using PowerPoint, make sure your text and images are easy for everyone in your audience to see. By making sure your visual aid is large enough, you will avoid having to introduce it with the comment "I know some of you can't see this, but . . ."

What about using all capital letters? That might seem a great way to ensure that your print is large enough to be read easily. But research has shown that a long string of words in ALL CAPS is actually harder to read than is normal text. Reserve ALL CAPS for titles or for individual words that require special emphasis.

USE A LIMITED AMOUNT OF TEXT

When displaying text on visual aids, follow this general rule: Briefer is better. Succinct phrases containing only essential key words will help listeners grasp your basic point and process the information as you're speaking.

Brevity is especially important when using PowerPoint. One of the biggest mistakes people make with PowerPoint is putting too much text on a single

FIGURE 14.6

slide. A general rule for slides that contain only text is to include no more than a half-dozen lines of type. If you are combining text with images, you may need to limit yourself to fewer lines to keep the text from getting too small. If you have a number of important points to cover, spread them out over multiple slides.

Figure 14.6 (above) shows a slide from a speech about Easter Island, famous for its mysterious statues of unknown origin. Notice that the slide is not bogged down with information, presenting only an image of the statues, as well as a title and text identifying the location of Easter Island and the date it was discovered by Europeans. Because the slide is simple and clear, the speaker was able to present it succinctly and move to her next point.

USE FONTS EFFECTIVELY

font

A complete set of type of the same design.

Not all fonts are suitable for visual aids. For the most part, you should avoid decorative fonts such as those on the left in Figure 14.7 (page 269). Those on the right of the figure, however, will help make your aids audience-friendly.

Using fonts effectively can make a huge difference in your PowerPoint slides. In general, keep the following guidelines in mind when selecting fonts for your presentation:

- Choose fonts that are clear and easy to read.
- Avoid using ALL CAPS because they are difficult to read.
- Don't use more than two fonts on a single slide—one for the title or major heading and another for subtitles or other text.
- Use the same fonts on all your slides.
- Put titles and major headings in 44- to 36-point type; make subheads and other text 32- to 24-point.

FIGURE 14.7

Ineffective	More Effective
Blackmoor	Arial
Bradley Hand	Baskerville
Cracked	Cambria
ECCENTRIC	Courier
Handwriting	Gill Sans
ROSEWOOD	Optima
SchoolHouse	Times New Roman
Snell Roundhand	Verdana

If you use one of PowerPoint's built-in themes, you can be confident that the fonts, which have been preselected according to the design of the theme, are clear, legible, and consistent.

USE COLOR EFFECTIVELY

When used effectively, color can dramatically increase the impact of a visual aid. The key words, of course, are "when used effectively." Some colors do not work well together. Red and green are a tough combination for anyone to read, and they look the same to people who are color-blind. Many shades of blue and green are too close to each other to be easily differentiated—as are orange and red, blue and purple.

You can use either dark print on a light background or light print on a dark background, but in either case make sure there is enough contrast between the background and the text so listeners can see everything clearly. Avoid such colors as yellow on a white background or purple on a red background.

Also, stick to a limited number of colors and use them consistently. Use one color for background, one color for titles, and one color for other text throughout all your slides. This consistency will unify the slides and give your speech a professional appearance.

USE IMAGES STRATEGICALLY

One of the benefits of PowerPoint is the ease with which it allows you to include photographs, charts, graphs, and other images, including video. Unfortunately, some speakers are prone to adding images simply because it is easy, rather than because it is essential for communicating their message. You should *never* add images of any sort to a PowerPoint slide unless they are truly needed. There is a great deal of research showing that extraneous images distract listeners and reduce comprehension of the speaker's point.[4]

In addition to keeping your slides free of extraneous images, keep these guidelines in mind:

- Make sure images are large enough to be seen clearly.
- Choose high-resolution images that will project without blurring.
- Keep graphs and charts clear and simple.

- In most cases, include a title above charts and graphs so the audience knows what they are viewing.
- Edit video so it is integrated seamlessly into your slides.[5]

Guidelines for Presenting Visual Aids

No matter how well designed your visual aids may be, they will be of little value unless you display them properly, discuss them clearly, and integrate them effectively with the rest of your presentation. Here are seven guidelines that will help you get the maximum impact out of your visual aids.

DISPLAY VISUAL AIDS WHERE LISTENERS CAN SEE THEM

Check the speech room ahead of time to decide exactly where you will display your visual aids. If you are displaying an object or a model, be sure to place it where it can be seen easily by everyone in the room. If necessary, hold up the object or model while you are discussing it.

Once you have set the aid in the best location, don't undo all your preparation by standing where you block the audience's view of the aid. Stand to one side of the aid, and point with the arm nearest it. Using a pen, a ruler,

checklist

Preparing Visual Aids

YES	NO	
☐	☐	1. Have I prepared my visual aids well in advance?
☐	☐	2. Are my visual aids clear and easy to comprehend?
☐	☐	3. Does each visual aid contain only the information needed to make my point?
☐	☐	4. Are my visual aids large enough to be seen clearly by the entire audience?
☐	☐	5. Do the colors on my visual aids work well together?
☐	☐	6. Is there a clear contrast between the lettering and background on my charts, graphs, and drawings?
☐	☐	7. Do I use line graphs, pie graphs, and bar graphs correctly to show statistical trends and patterns?
☐	☐	8. Do I limit charts to no more than eight items?
☐	☐	9. Do I use fonts that are easy to read?
☐	☐	10. Do I use a limited number of fonts?

PowerPoint is an excellent way to show visual aids if it is used properly. Here linguist Steven Pinker uses PowerPoint during a lecture at the British Museum in London, England.

or some other pointer will allow you to stand farther away from the visual aid, thereby reducing the likelihood that you will obstruct the view.

If you are using a projection screen, check ahead of time to make sure it is not located where you will cast a shadow on it while you are speaking. If necessary, move the lectern to the side of the screen.

AVOID PASSING VISUAL AIDS AMONG THE AUDIENCE

Once visual aids get into the hands of your listeners, you are in trouble. At least three people will be paying more attention to the aid than to you—the person who has just had it, the person who has it now, and the person waiting to get it next. By the time the visual aid moves on, all three may have lost track of what you are saying.

Nor do you solve this problem by preparing a handout for every member of the audience. They are likely to spend a good part of the speech looking over the handout at their own pace, rather than listening to you. Although handouts can be valuable, they usually just create competition for beginning speakers.

Every once in a while, of course, you will want listeners to have copies of some material to take home. When such a situation arises, keep the copies until after you've finished talking and distribute them at the end. Keeping control of your visual aids is essential to keeping control of your speech.

DISPLAY VISUAL AIDS ONLY WHILE DISCUSSING THEM

Just as circulating visual aids distracts attention, so does displaying them throughout a speech. If you are using an object or a model, keep it out of sight until you are ready to discuss it. When you finish your discussion, place the object or model back out of sight.

The same principle applies to PowerPoint slides. They should be visible only while you are discussing them. You can accomplish this by adding blank slides as needed, so the audience's attention will not be diverted by the previous slide. It is also a good idea to add a blank slide at the end of your presentation, so your last content slide will not continue to be exposed after you have finished discussing it.

FIGURE 14.8

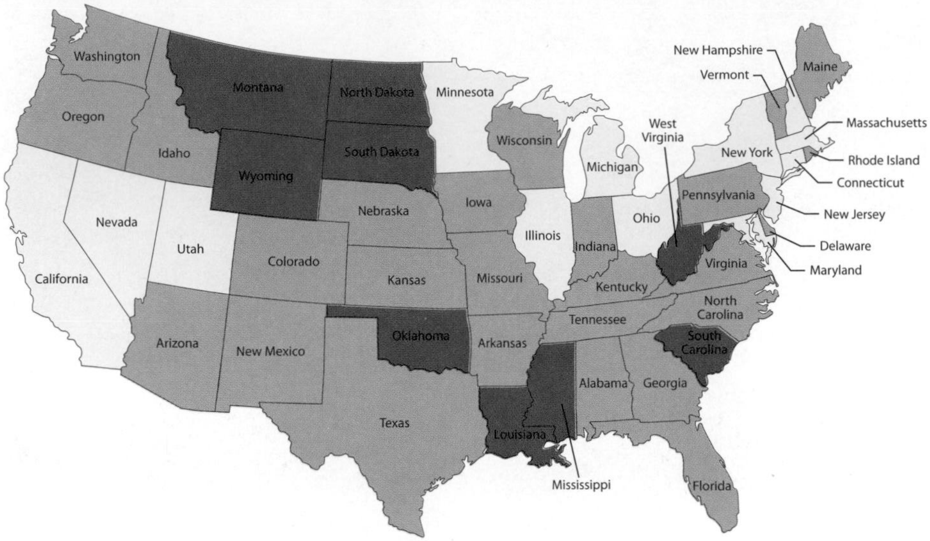

EXPLAIN VISUAL AIDS CLEARLY AND CONCISELY

Visual aids don't explain themselves. Like statistics, they need to be translated and related to the audience. For example, Figure 14.8 (above) is an excellent visual aid, but do you know what it represents? Probably not, unless you've kept up on the latest statistics of U.S. drunk-driving deaths. But even then, the full meaning of the map may not be clear until it is explained to you.

A visual aid can be of enormous benefit—but only if the viewer knows what to look for and why. Unfortunately, speakers often rush over their visual aids without explaining them clearly and concisely. Be sure to adapt your visual aids to the audience. Don't just say "As you can see . . ." and then pass quickly over the aid. Tell listeners what the aid means. Describe its major features. Spell out the meaning of charts and graphs. Interpret statistics and percentages. Remember, a visual aid is only as useful as the explanation that goes with it.

connect

View an excerpt from "The Tragedy of Drunk Driving" in the online Media Library for this chapter (Video 14.8).

As you can see from Video 14.8 in the online Media Library for this chapter, the speaker who used the map of drunk-driving deaths discussed above did an excellent job explaining how each color on the map corresponds to a different per-capita death rate. Having used the map during her practice sessions, she was able to integrate it into the speech smoothly and skillfully—and to maintain eye contact with the audience throughout her discussion of it. You should strive to do the same when you present visual aids in your speeches.

TALK TO YOUR AUDIENCE, NOT TO YOUR VISUAL AID

When explaining a visual aid, it is easy to break eye contact with your audience and speak to the aid. Of course, your listeners are looking primarily at the aid, and you will need to glance at it periodically as you talk. But if you keep your eyes fixed on the visual aid, you may lose your audience. By keeping eye contact with your listeners, you will also pick up feedback about how the visual aid and your explanation of it are coming across.

PRACTICE WITH YOUR VISUAL AIDS

This chapter has mentioned several times the need to practice with visual aids, but the point bears repeating. No matter what kind of visual aid you choose, be sure to employ it when you practice. Go through the speech multiple times, rehearsing how you will show your aids, the gestures you will make, and the timing of each move. In using visual aids, as in other aspects of speechmaking, there is no substitute for preparation.

If you are using PowerPoint, don't just click the mouse casually or rush quickly over your words when you practice. Make sure you know exactly when you want each slide to appear and disappear, and what you will say while each is on screen. Mark your speaking notes with cues that will remind you when to display each slide and when to remove it.

Rehearse with the mouse, keyboard, or iPad until you can use them without looking down for more than an instant when advancing your slides. Also concentrate on presenting the speech without looking back at the screen to see what is being projected. There is nothing wrong with glancing at the screen now and again as you explain your slides, but remember to address your remarks to the audience, not to the screen.

Given all the things you have to work on when practicing a speech with PowerPoint, you need to allow extra time for rehearsal. So get an early start and give yourself plenty of time to ensure that your delivery is as impressive as your slides.[6]

checklist

Presenting Visual Aids

YES	NO	
☐	☐	1. Have I checked the speech room to decide where I can display my visual aids most effectively?
☐	☐	2. Have I practiced presenting my visual aids so they will be clearly visible to everyone in the audience?
☐	☐	3. Have I practiced presenting my visual aids so they are perfectly timed with my words and actions?
☐	☐	4. Have I practiced keeping eye contact with my audience while presenting my visual aids?
☐	☐	5. Have I practiced explaining my visual aids clearly and concisely in terms my audience will understand?
☐	☐	6. If I am using handouts, have I planned to distribute them after the speech rather than during it?
☐	☐	7. Have I double-checked all equipment to make sure it works properly?
☐	☐	8. If I am using PowerPoint, do I have a backup of my slides that I can take to the speech with me?

CHECK THE ROOM AND EQUIPMENT

For classroom speeches, you will already be familiar with the room and equipment. If any of the technology fails, a technician can make the necessary adjustments. For speeches outside the classroom, however, the situation is very different. There is wide variation among computers and projectors, as well as among rooms equipped with multimedia connections. Even if you have used PowerPoint on previous occasions, you need to check the setup in the room where you will be speaking.

If possible, look at the room and equipment before the day of your speech. Hook up your computer to make sure everything works properly. If you are using a computer that is installed in the room, bring your slides on a flash drive so you can see how they work with that computer. If your presentation includes audio or video, double-check them using the room's audiovisual system. Arrange ahead of time to have a technician present so he or she can take care of any problems.

Sometimes, of course, it is not possible to visit the room before the day of your speech. In that case, plan to arrive an hour early to familiarize yourself with the equipment and to make sure it's working properly. Never assume that everything will be "just fine." Instead, assume that things will not be fine and that they need to be checked ahead of time. You will save yourself the embarrassment of having your speech delayed, cut short, or even canceled because of faulty equipment or unforeseen technical complications.

Finally, if you are using PowerPoint, *always* bring a backup of your slides on a flash drive even if you plan on using your own computer during the speech.

This may all seem like a lot of fuss and bother, but anyone who has given speeches with PowerPoint—or any other kind of visual aid—will tell you that it is absolutely essential.

Summary

There are many kinds of visual aids. Most obvious is the object about which you are speaking, or a model of it. Diagrams, sketches, and other kinds of drawings are valuable because you can design them to illustrate your points exactly. Photographs should be large enough to be seen clearly by all your listeners. Graphs are an excellent way to illustrate any subject dealing with numbers, while charts are used to summarize large blocks of information. Video can be useful as a visual aid, but it needs to be carefully edited and integrated into the speech. You can act as your own visual aid by performing actions that demonstrate processes or ideas.

If you use PowerPoint, plan carefully why, how, and when you will utilize it. Rather than putting everything you say on screen for your audience to read, use PowerPoint only when it will genuinely enhance your message.

No matter what kind of visual aid you use, you need to prepare it carefully. You will be most successful if you prepare your aids well in advance, keep them simple, make sure they are large enough to be seen clearly, and use a limited amount of text. If you are creating visual aids on a computer, use fonts, color, and images strategically and effectively.

In addition to being designed with care, visual aids need to be presented skillfully. Avoid passing visual aids among the audience. Display each aid only while you are talking about it, and be sure to place it where everyone can see it without straining. When presenting a visual aid, maintain eye contact with your listeners and explain the aid clearly and concisely. If you are using PowerPoint, make sure you check the room and equipment prior to the time of delivery. Above all, practice with your visual aids so they fit into your speech smoothly and expertly.

Key Terms

graph *(261)*
line graph *(262)*
pie graph *(262)*
bar graph *(263)*
chart *(264)*
font *(268)*

Review Questions

After reading this chapter, you should be able to answer the following questions:

1. What are the major advantages of using visual aids in your speeches?
2. What kinds of visual aids might you use in a speech?
3. What factors should you consider when planning to use PowerPoint in a speech?
4. What guidelines are given in the chapter for preparing visual aids?
5. What guidelines are given in the chapter for presenting visual aids?

connect

For further review, go to the LearnSmart study module for this chapter.

Exercises for Critical Thinking

1. Watch a how-to television program (a cooking show, for example) or the weather portion of a local newscast. Notice how the speaker uses visual aids to help communicate the message. What kinds of visual aids are used? How do they enhance the clarity, interest, and retainability of the speaker's message? What would the speaker have to do to communicate the message effectively without visual aids?
2. Consider how you might use visual aids to explain each of the following:
   a. How to perform the Heimlich maneuver to help a choking victim.
   b. The proportion of the electorate that votes in major national elections in the United States, France, Germany, England, and Japan, respectively.
   c. Where to obtain information about student loans.
   d. The wing patterns of various species of butterflies.
   e. The increase in the amount of money spent by Americans on health care since 1985.
   f. How to change a bicycle tire.
   g. The basic equipment and techniques of rock climbing.
3. Plan to use visual aids in at least one of your classroom speeches. Be creative in devising your aids, and be sure to follow the guidelines discussed in the chapter for using them. After the speech, analyze how effectively you employed your visual aids, what you learned about the use of visual aids from your experience, and what changes you would make in using visual aids if you were to deliver the speech again.

15

Speaking to Inform

Types of Informative Speeches: Analysis and Organization

Guidelines for Informative Speaking

Sample Speech with Commentary

Hayley Walden is the chief designer at a fast-growing company that creates and sells stylish, innovative knitwear. On a bright Tuesday in October, Hayley begins her workday by talking to a colleague from technical support about the computer problems she has been having. She demonstrates what goes wrong when she boots up and details the problems with the internal backup system.

Later that morning, Hayley has a long meeting with other members of her design team. They discuss their new line of products for the spring, going over everything from the manufacturing process to the marketing campaign. As the other staff members talk, Hayley takes careful notes and asks questions to make sure she understands every aspect of the spring product launch.

In the afternoon, Hayley rushes to a meeting with company executives, including the president, so she can report on what the design team discussed earlier in the day. She reviews the manufacturing process for the new knits, discusses the distribution chain for the company's goods, and explains different options for marketing a new line of spring jackets. Afterward, the president compliments Hayley for giving such a clear presentation. "Anyone who can communicate that well," the president says, "is going to go a long way in this company."

Hayley doesn't consider herself a "public speaker," but much of her job involves absorbing and communicating information clearly and effectively. Although Hayley is just a single person, her experience is not unusual. In one survey, graduates from five U.S. colleges were asked to rank the speech skills most important to their jobs. They rated informative speaking number one. In another survey, 62 percent of the respondents said they used informative speaking "almost constantly."[1]

Public speaking to inform occurs in a wide range of everyday situations. The business manager explains next year's budget. The architect reviews plans for a new building. The union leader informs members about a new contract. The church worker outlines plans for a fund drive. There are endless situations in which people need to inform others. Competence in this form of communication will prove valuable to you throughout your life.

informative speech

A speech designed to convey knowledge and understanding.

One of your first classroom assignments probably will be to deliver an informative speech in which you will act as a lecturer or teacher. You may describe an object, show how something works, report on an event, explain a concept. Your aim will be to convey knowledge and understanding—not to advocate a cause. Your speech will be judged in light of three general criteria:

Is the information communicated accurately?

Is the information communicated clearly?

Is the information made meaningful and interesting to the audience?

In this chapter, we will look at four types of informative speeches and the basic principles of informative speaking. Along the way, we will apply various general principles discussed in previous chapters.

Types of Informative Speeches: Analysis and Organization

There are many ways to classify informative speeches. Here we focus on the kinds you are most likely to give in your speech class: (1) speeches about objects, (2) speeches about processes, (3) speeches about events, and (4) speeches about concepts.

SPEECHES ABOUT OBJECTS

object

Anything that is visible, tangible, and stable in form.

As the word is used here, "objects" include anything that is visible, tangible, and stable in form. Objects may have moving parts or be alive; they may include places, structures, animals, even people. Here are examples of subjects for speeches about objects:

e-book readers	Susan B. Anthony
service dogs	titanium
human eye	Golden Gate Bridge

You will not have time to tell your classmates everything about any of these subjects. Instead, you will choose a specific purpose that focuses on one aspect of your subject. Working from the topics presented above, the following are examples of good specific purpose statements for informative speeches about objects:

To inform my audience about three major kinds of service dogs.

To inform my audience about the role of Susan B. Anthony in the U.S. women's rights movement.

To inform my audience what to look for when buying an e-book reader.

Notice how precise these statements are. As we saw in Chapter 5, you should select a specific purpose that is not too broad to achieve in the allotted time. "To inform my audience about Pablo Picasso" is far too general for a classroom speech. "To inform my audience about the major contributions of Pablo Picasso to modern art" is more precise and is a purpose you could reasonably hope to achieve in a brief talk.

If your specific purpose is to explain the history or evolution of your subject, you will put your speech in *chronological* order. For example:

Specific Purpose: To inform my audience about the major achievements of Frederick Douglass.

Central Idea: Although born in slavery, Frederick Douglass became one of the greatest figures in American history.

Main Points:

I. Douglass spent the first 20 years of his life as a slave in Maryland.

II. After escaping to the North, Douglass became a leader in the abolitionist movement to end slavery.

III. During the Civil War, Douglass helped establish black regiments in the Union Army.

IV. After the war, Douglass was a tireless champion of equal rights for his race.

If your specific purpose is to describe the main features of your subject, you may organize your speech in *spatial* order:

Specific Purpose: To inform my audience about the design of the St. Louis Arch.

Central Idea: The St. Louis Arch is divided into three sections, each with its own attractions.

Main Points:

I. The base of the St. Louis Arch houses a visitor's center with a museum, two movie theaters, and retail outlets.

II. The middle of the St. Louis Arch contains a high-speed tram that carries visitors from the base to the top.

III. The top of the St. Louis Arch has an observation deck 630 feet above the ground.

As often as not, you will find that speeches about objects fall into *topical* order. For example:

Specific Purpose: To inform my audience about the four major elements of a Japanese garden.

Central Idea: The four major elements of a Japanese garden are stones, sand, water, and plants.

Main Points:

I. The first element of a Japanese garden is stones, which symbolize mountains and islands.

II. The second element of a Japanese garden is sand, which symbolizes the sea or other vast areas.

III. The third element of a Japanese garden is water, which symbolizes purity and life.

IV. The fourth element of a Japanese garden is plants, which symbolize life and the changing seasons.

No matter which of these organizational methods you use—chronological, spatial, or topical—be sure to follow the guidelines discussed in Chapter 9: (1) limit your speech to between two and five main points; (2) keep main points separate; (3) try to use the same pattern of wording for all main points; (4) balance the amount of time devoted to each main point.

SPEECHES ABOUT PROCESSES

process

A systematic series of actions that leads to a specific result or product.

A process is a systematic series of actions that leads to a specific result or product. Speeches about processes explain how something is made, how something is done, or how something works. Here are examples of good specific purpose statements for speeches about processes:

To inform my audience how U.S. currency is made.

To inform my audience how to write an effective job resumé.

To inform my audience how hurricanes develop.

As these examples suggest, there are two kinds of informative speeches about processes. One kind explains a process so that listeners will *understand* it better. Your goal is to have your audience know the steps of the process and how they relate to one another. If your specific purpose is "To inform my audience how a nuclear power plant works," you will explain the basic procedures of a nuclear power plant. You will not instruct your listeners on how they can *operate* a nuclear power plant.

A second kind of speech explains a process so listeners will be better able to *perform* the process themselves. Your goal in this kind of speech is to have the audience learn a skill. Suppose your specific purpose is "To inform my audience how to take pictures like a professional photographer." You will present photographic techniques and show your listeners how they can utilize them. You want the audience to be able to *use* the techniques as a result of your speech.

Both kinds of speeches about processes may require visual aids. At the very least, you should prepare a chart outlining the steps or techniques of your process. In some cases you will need to demonstrate the steps or techniques by performing them in front of your audience. One student did sleight-of-hand magic tricks to show the techniques behind them. Another executed elementary tai chi maneuvers. In each case, the demonstration not only clarified the speaker's process, but captivated the audience as well. (If you are using visual aids of any kind, be sure to review Chapter 14.)

Informative speeches can be organized in many ways. A speech on the history of Renaissance art would likely be in chronological order, while a speech on techniques of painting would fall into topical order.

When informing about a process, you will usually arrange your speech in *chronological* order, explaining the process step by step from beginning to end. For example:

Specific Purpose: To inform my audience about the major rituals of a traditional Bengali wedding in India.

Central Idea: A traditional Bengali wedding consists of a series of rituals that take place before, during, and after the wedding ceremony.

Main Points:

I. Pre-wedding rituals include giving gifts to the bride and groom and dressing the bride in traditional fashion.

II. Rituals during the wedding ceremony include an exchange of garlands between the bride and groom, the chanting of mantras, and the giving away of the bride by her uncle.

III. Post-wedding rituals include a celebration at the home of the bride's family, a reception at the home of the groom's family, and the formal exit of the bride and groom.

Sometimes, rather than moving through a process step by step, you will focus on the major principles or techniques involved in performing the process. Then you will organize your speech in *topical* order. Each main point will deal with a separate principle or technique. For example:

Specific Purpose: To inform my audience of the common methods used by stage magicians to perform their tricks.

Central Idea: Stage magicians use two common methods to perform their tricks—mechanical devices and sleight of hand.

Main Points: I. Many magic tricks rely on mechanical devices that may require little skill by the magician.

II. Other magic tricks depend on the magician's skill in fooling people by sleight-of-hand manipulation.

Concise organization is especially important in speeches about processes. You must make sure each step is clear and easy to follow. If your process has more than four or five steps, group the steps into units to limit the number of main points. For example, in a speech explaining how to set up a home aquarium, a student presented the following main points:

I. First you must choose the size of your tank.
II. Then you must determine the shape of your tank.
III. You must also decide how much you can afford to pay for a tank.
IV. Once you have the tank, you need a filter system.
V. A heater is also absolutely necessary.
VI. You must also get an air pump.
VII. Once this is done, you need to choose gravel for the tank.
VIII. You will also need plants.
IX. Other decorations will round out the effects of your aquarium.
X. Now you are ready to add the fish.
XI. Freshwater fish are the most common.
XII. Saltwater fish are more expensive and require special care.

Not surprisingly, this was too much for the audience to follow. The speaker should have organized the points something like this:

I. The first step in establishing a home aquarium is choosing a tank.
  A. The size of the tank is important.
  B. The shape of the tank is important.
  C. The cost of the tank is important.
II. The second step in establishing a home aquarium is equipping the tank.
  A. You will need a filter system.
  B. You will need a heater.
  C. You will need an air pump.
  D. You will need gravel.
  E. You will need plants.
  F. You may also want other decorations.
III. The third step in establishing a home aquarium is adding the fish.
  A. Freshwater fish are the most common for home aquariums.
  B. Saltwater fish are more expensive and require special care.

The subpoints cover the same territory as the original twelve points, but three main points are much easier to understand and remember.

event

Anything that happens or is regarded as happening.

SPEECHES ABOUT EVENTS

The *Random House Dictionary* defines an event as "anything that happens or is regarded as happening." By this definition, the following are examples of suitable subjects for informative speeches about events:

Festival of the Sun	sleep deprivation
cyberterrorism	Battle of Little Big Horn
therapeutic massage	Olympic Games

As usual, you will need to narrow your focus and pick a specific purpose you can accomplish in a short speech. Here are examples of good specific purpose statements for informative speeches about events:

To inform my audience about the events at Peru's Festival of the Sun ceremony.

To inform my audience about the major types of therapeutic massage.

To inform my audience about what occurred at the Battle of Little Big Horn.

There are many ways to discuss events. If your specific purpose is to recount the history of an event, you will organize your speech in *chronological* order, relating the incidents one after another in the order they occurred. For example:

Specific Purpose: To inform my audience about the history of the Paralympics.

Central Idea: Olympic-style games for athletes with physical disabilities have made great strides since the first competition more than 60 years ago.

Main Points:

I. What would eventually become the Paralympics began in 1948 with a sports competition in Great Britain involving World War II veterans with spinal cord injuries.

II. In 1952, the event expanded when athletes from the Netherlands took part.

III. In 1960, the first Paralympic Games for international athletes took place in Rome.

IV. In 2001, an agreement was signed officially holding the Paralympic Games alongside the summer and winter Olympic Games.

You can approach an event from almost any angle or combination of angles—features, origins, implications, benefits, future developments, and so forth. In such cases, you will put your speech together in *topical* order. And you should make sure your main points subdivide the subject logically and consistently. For instance:

Specific Purpose: To inform my audience about three aspects of the Mardi Gras celebration in New Orleans.

Central Idea: The Mardi Gras celebration in New Orleans is renowned for its parades, costumes, and food.

Main Points:

I. The parades are lavish events that take place over the course of several weeks.

II. The costumes include disguises, medallions, and the official Mardi Gras colors of purple, green, and gold.

III. The food features Cajun and Creole dishes common to southern Louisiana.

SPEECHES ABOUT CONCEPTS

concept

A belief, theory, idea, notion, principle, or the like.

Concepts include beliefs, theories, ideas, principles, and the like. They are more abstract than objects, processes, or events. The following are examples of subjects for speeches about concepts:

Confucianism	nutritional theories
original-intent doctrine	philosophies of education
string theory	numerology

Taking a few of these general subjects, here are some specific purpose statements for speeches about concepts:

To inform my audience about the basic principles of Confucianism.

To inform my audience about the doctrine of original intent in constitutional interpretation.

To inform my audience about different philosophies of education in Asia and the United States.

Speeches about concepts are usually organized in *topical* order and focus on the main features or aspects of your concept. For example:

Specific Purpose: To inform my audience about the basic principles of nonviolent resistance.

Central Idea: The basic principles of nonviolent resistance stress using moral means to achieve social change, refusing to inflict violence on one's enemies, and using suffering as a social force.

Main Points:

I. The first major principle of nonviolent resistance is that social change must be achieved by moral means.

II. The second major principle of nonviolent resistance is that one should not inflict violence on one's enemies.

III. The third major principle of nonviolent resistance is that suffering can be a powerful social force.

Another approach is to define the concept you are dealing with, identify its major elements, and illustrate it with specific examples. An excellent instance of this came in a student speech about film theory:

Specific Purpose: To inform my audience about different approaches to film theory.

Central Idea: Approaches to film theory include auteur theory, structuralist theory, and genre theory.

The need to convey information effectively exists in all cultures. Here tea-servers dressed in traditional clothes learn the art of the tea ceremony in Sichuan Province, China.

Main Points:

I. Auteur theory focuses on the director's creative vision in the construction of a film.

II. Structuralist theory focuses on how film conveys meaning through the use of codes and conventions.

III. Genre theory focuses on patterns across major types of films such as drama, comedy, science fiction, and the like.

Speeches about concepts are often more complex than other kinds of informative speeches. When dealing with concepts, pay special attention to avoiding technical language, to defining terms clearly, and to using examples and comparisons to illustrate the concepts.

Look, for example, at Video 15.1 in the online Media Library for this chapter, which presents an excerpt from a student speech about the Chinese philosophy of Confucianism. Notice how the student defines Confucianism and then explains its unifying principle of *jen.* If you give an informative speech about a concept, give special thought to how you can make that concept clear and comprehensible to your listeners.

connect

View an excerpt from "Confucianism" in the online Media Library for this chapter (Video 15.1).

The lines dividing speeches about objects, processes, events, and concepts are not absolute. Some subjects could fit into more than one category, depending on how you develop the speech. For example, a speech about the destruction of ancient Pompeii by the eruption of Mount Vesuvius would probably deal with its subject as an event, but a speech on what causes volcanoes to erupt would most likely treat its subject as a process. The important step is to decide whether you will handle your subject as an object, a process, an event, or a concept. Once you do that, you can develop the speech accordingly.

Regardless of how you approach your topic, be sure to give listeners plenty of help in sorting out facts and ideas. One way is by using enough transitions, internal previews, internal summaries, and signposts (see Chapter 9). Another way is to follow the old maxim "Tell 'em what you're going to say; say it; then tell 'em what you've said." In other words, preview the main points of your speech in the introduction and summarize them in the conclusion. This will make your speech easier to understand and easier to remember.

Guidelines for Informative Speaking

All the previous chapters of this book relate to the principles of informative speaking. Selecting a topic and specific purpose, analyzing the audience, gathering materials, choosing supporting details, organizing the speech, using words to communicate meaning, delivering the speech—all must be done effectively if an informative speech is to be a success. Here we emphasize six additional points that will help make yours a success.

DON'T OVERESTIMATE WHAT THE AUDIENCE KNOWS

In a speech about meteorology, a student said, "If modern methods of weather forecasting had existed in 1900, the Galveston hurricane disaster would never have taken place." Then he was off to other matters, leaving his listeners to puzzle over what the Galveston hurricane was, when it happened, and what kind of destruction it wreaked.

The speaker assumed his audience already knew these things. But they were not experts on meteorology or on American history. Even those who had heard of the hurricane had only a fuzzy notion of it. Only the speaker knew that the hurricane, which killed more than 6,000 people when it unexpectedly struck on September 8, 1900, is still the deadliest natural disaster in American history.

As many speakers have discovered, it is easy to overestimate the audience's stock of information. In most informative speeches, your listeners will be only vaguely knowledgeable (at best) about the details of your topic. You cannot *assume* they will know what you mean. Rather, you must be *sure* to explain everything so thoroughly that they cannot help but understand. As you work on your speech, always consider whether it will be clear to someone who is hearing about the topic for the first time.

Suppose you are talking about bulletproof vests. Surely all of your classmates have heard of bulletproof vests, but most probably don't know how the vests work. How will you tell them? Here's one way:

> Ballistic vests, more commonly known as bulletproof vests, are pieces of personal body armor that protect human beings from damage incurred by explosively propelled projectiles. How? Intricately woven synthetic fibers such as Kevlar form a powerful mesh that laterally disperses a projectile's kinetic energy while at the same time deforming the projectile and stopping its momentum.

To someone who knows a lot about physics or textiles, this is probably perfectly clear. But someone who does not may get lost along the way. The tone of the statement is that of a speaker reviewing information already familiar to the audience—not of a speaker introducing new information.

Here, in contrast, is another explanation of bulletproof vests:

So how do bulletproof vests actually stop bullets? Let me explain with an example.

Imagine a police officer investigating a strange noise down a dark alley. He startles a drug dealer trying to make a sale, and before he knows it, bang! Luckily, the officer was wearing his bulletproof vest.

Instead of entering the officer's body, the bullet enters layer upon layer of strong, tightly woven fibers. Because of their strength and intricate pattern, the fibers begin to twist and deform the bullet. The fibers are so strong that they flatten the bullet out and absorb its energy. While the bullet may go through a couple layers of fabric, it stops well before going through the entire vest.

Thanks to these strong, tightly woven fibers, our police officer lives to put the drug dealer in cuffs.

This explanation is clear and simple. Its tone is that of a teacher unraveling a new subject.

Is it too simple? Not at all. The test of a good speaker is to communicate even the most complex ideas clearly and simply. Anyone can go to a book and find a learned-sounding definition of a bulletproof vest. But to say in plain English how a bulletproof vest works—that takes hard work and creative thinking.

Also, remember that readers can study a printed passage again and again until they extract its meaning, but listeners don't have that luxury. They must understand what you say in the time it takes you to say it. The more you assume they know about the topic, the greater your chances of being misunderstood.

RELATE THE SUBJECT DIRECTLY TO THE AUDIENCE

The British dramatist Oscar Wilde arrived at his club after the disastrous opening-night performance of his new play.

"Oscar, how did your play go?" asked a friend.

"Oh," Wilde quipped, "the play was a great success, but the audience was a failure."

Speakers have been known to give much the same answer in saving face after a dismal informative speech. "Oh," they say, "the speech was fine, but

In business as in other areas of life, effective informative speakers personalize their ideas and relate them directly to the audience.

the audience just wasn't interested." And they are at least partly right—the audience *wasn't* interested. But there is no such thing as a fine speech that puts people to sleep. It is the speaker's job to get listeners interested—and to keep them interested.

Informative speakers have one big hurdle to overcome. They must recognize that what is fascinating to them may not be fascinating to everybody. Once you have chosen a topic that could possibly be interesting to your listeners, you should take special steps to relate it to them. You should tie it in with their interests and concerns.

Start in the introduction. Instead of saying,

> I want to talk with you about chili peppers,

you could say:

connect

View this excerpt from "The Hidden World of Chili Peppers" in the online Media Library for this chapter (Video 15.2).

> Imagine your mouth burning like wildfire, your eyes squirting out uncontrollable tears, and your face red and sweating profusely. Are you sick? No. You just took a bite of a screaming hot chili pepper. Congratulations. You're partaking in a worldwide tradition that has been spicing up lives and diets for thousands of years.

But don't stop with the introduction. Whenever you can, put your listeners into the body of the speech. After all, nothing interests people more than themselves. Find ways to talk about your topic in terms of your listeners. Bring your material home to them. Get it as close to them as possible.

Here's an example. Let's say you are explaining how bed bugs spread from person to person and location to location. You have plenty of facts and could recite them like this:

> High-traffic areas provide ideal environmental conditions for bed bugs to spread. High-density locations such as dormitories, apartment buildings, and transportation terminals are among the most likely places to find bed bugs. Because bed bugs are attracted to items that allow them to hide, they often attach themselves to clothing, backpacks, purses, and the like. Bed bugs also thrive in cluttered locations that have a lot of items lying about.

This is valuable information, but it is not related to the audience. Let's try again:

connect

View this excerpt from "Don't Let the Bed Bugs Bite" in the online Media Library for this chapter (Video 15.3).

> Bed bugs spread most rapidly in places that have lots of people coming and going. If *you* live in the dorms or an apartment, if *you* travel through airports, train stations, and bus stations, or if *you* stay in hotels and motels, *you're* passing through prime breeding grounds for bed bugs.
>
> Bed bugs are like tiny hitchhikers. They'll insert themselves in *your* clothes, *your* luggage, *your* purse, *your* backpack, *your* coat—anything that has fabric and folds.
>
> Bed bugs are also drawn to locations where they can hide easily. So the more clutter *you* have in *your* environment, the more bed bugs will like to be *your* tiny companions.

Look at the frequent use of "you" and "your." The facts are the same, but now they are pointed directly at the audience. Research shows that using personal terms such as "you" and "your" in an informative speech significantly increases audience understanding of the speaker's ideas.[2]

DON'T BE TOO TECHNICAL

What does it mean to say that an informative speech is too technical? It may mean the subject matter is too specialized for the audience. Any subject can be popularized—but only up to a point. The important thing for a speaker to know is what can be explained to an ordinary audience and what cannot.

Say your subject is power amplifiers. It's no trick to demonstrate how to operate an amplifier (how to turn it on and off, adjust the volume, set the tone and balance controls). It's also relatively easy to explain what an amplifier does (it boosts the sound received from a DVD, iPod, or live performance). But to give a full scientific account of how an amplifier works cannot be done in any reasonable time unless the audience knows the principles of audio technology. The material is just too technical to be understood by a general audience.

Even when the subject matter is not technical, the language used to explain it may be. Every activity has its jargon, whether it be golf (bogey, wedge, match play); chemistry (colloid, glycogen, heavy water); or financial analysis (covered call, reverse bid, toehold acquisition). If you are talking to a group of specialists, you can use technical words and be understood. But you must do all you can to avoid technical words when informing a general audience such as your speech class.

Here, for instance, are two statements explaining stem cells and the roles they can play in the human body. The first is heavily laden with specialized language that would have little impact on ordinary listeners:

> Most multicellular organisms contain stem cells that reinvigorate themselves through the process of mitotic cellular division. Stem cells in early embryos represent basic units of life in higher organisms, while adult stem cells in somatic tissues

Using public speaking in your CAREER

As a financial planner at a local investment firm, you have been asked to speak to a group of recent college graduates about long-term financial planning. After considering what recent college graduates need to know about saving for their future, you decide to organize your presentation around four general stages of investing:

1. The early years of investing, which include putting aside small amounts of money that will grow over time.
2. The years of acquisition, which include balancing investments with large expenses such as raising children and paying a mortgage.
3. The years of accumulation, which include putting away as much money as possible in anticipation of retirement.
4. The retirement years, which include living off of savings and adjusting investments as needed.

As you look over these stages of investing, you think back to the public speaking course you took in college. You remember that informative speakers should relate their speech directly to the audience, should not be too technical, should not overestimate what the audience knows about the subject, and should be creative. How might each of these guidelines influence your presentation to recent college graduates? Be specific.

represent cellular stores capable of regenerating tissue and maintaining organ functions. Both are characterized by properties that permit accurate in vivo cell copying.

The second statement is perfectly understandable and shows how technical information can be made clear to the average person:

connect

View this excerpt from "The Promise of Stem Cells" in the online Media Library for this chapter (Video 15.4).

According to the National Institutes of Health, stem cells are general cells that have the potential to develop into any of the more than 200 different kinds of cells in the human body. Basically, they turn into a cell that has a specific job to do.

For example, stem cells might become muscle cells that help rebuild damaged tissue. They might become red blood cells that help deliver oxygen to different tissues. Or they might become brain cells that help the nervous system function. No matter what type of cells need assistance, stem cells can come to the rescue and replenish the cells our bodies need.

The Genetics Learning Center at the University of Utah explains it like this: Stem cells are like actors waiting for a casting call. Just as an actor waits to find out his or her next role, stem cells wait for signals from the body that tell them what to become. Once they get those signals, they begin to change into specific cells with specific jobs to do.

Much clearer, isn't it? The only specialized words in the whole passage are "stem cells." The rest of the language is straightforward, the ideas easy to grasp. This is what you should strive for in your informative speeches.

AVOID ABSTRACTIONS

"My task," said the novelist Joseph Conrad, "is, before all, to make you see." And make the reader see is just what Conrad did. Witness this passage, in which Conrad describes the aftermath of an explosion aboard a ship:

The first person I saw was Mahon, with eyes like saucers, his mouth open, and the long white hair standing straight on end round his head like a silver halo. . . . I stared at him in unbelief, and he stared at me with a queer kind of shocked curiosity. I did not know that I had no hair, no eyebrows, no eyelashes, that my young mustache was burnt off, that my face was black, one cheek laid open, my nose cut, and my chin bleeding.[3]

A speech is not a novel. Still, many informative speeches would be vastly improved by the novelist's bent for color, specificity, and detail.

description

A statement that depicts a person, event, idea, or the like with clarity and vividness.

One way to avoid abstractions is through *description*. When we think of description, we usually think of external events such as the explosion described by Conrad. But description is also used to communicate internal feelings. Here is how one student tried to convey to his audience the sensations he experienced when he first began sky diving:

As we wait for the plane to climb to the jump altitude of 12,000 feet, my mind races with a frenzied jumble of thoughts: "OK, this is the moment you've been waiting for. It's going to be great. Am I really going to jump out of an airplane from 12,000 feet? What if something goes wrong? Can I still back out? Come on now, don't worry. It'll be fine."

Even if we have not been sky diving, we have all had the same kinds of emotions on similar occasions. So what happened next?

Now it is time to jump. My palms are sweating and my heart is pounding so hard I think it may burst. "Get ready," yells the instructor. As I jump into the blue, I wonder, "What am I doing here?"

Yes—and then what?

The blast of air resistance blows me backward like a leaf at the mercy of an autumn wind. In about 10 seconds my body levels out and accelerates to a speed of 120 miles an hour. The air supports my body like an invisible flying carpet. There is no sound except for the wind rushing around my face. Any fears or doubts I had are gone in the exhilaration of free flight. Every nerve in my body is alive with sensation; yet I am overcome by a peaceful feeling and the sense that I am at one with the sky.

As we listen to the speaker we share his thoughts, feel his heart pound, and join his exhilaration as he floats effortlessly through the sky. The vivid description lends reality to the speech and draws us further in.

Another way to escape abstractions is with *comparisons* that put your subject in concrete, familiar terms. Do you want to convey what would happen if a comet or large asteroid struck the earth? You could say this:

comparison

A statement of the similarities among two or more people, events, ideas, etc.

If a comet or large asteroid struck the earth, the impact would be devastating.

True, but the statement is vague and abstract. It does not communicate your meaning clearly and concretely. Now suppose you add this:

To give you an idea how devastating the impact would be, it would be like all the nuclear bombs in the world going off at one spot.

Now you have made the abstract specific and given us a sharp new slant on things.

Like comparison, *contrast* can put an idea into concrete terms. Suppose you want to make the point that a person's chances of winning a state lottery are extremely low. You could say, "The odds, for example, of winning a state lottery are an astronomical 14 million to 1." The word "astronomical" suggests that you consider 14 million to 1 long odds, but long in comparison to what? One speaker offered this contrast:

contrast

A statement of the differences among two or more people, events, ideas, etc.

The odds of picking the correct six-digit sequence in a typical state lottery are 14 million to 1. In contrast, the odds of getting hit by lightning are only 700,000 to 1. The odds of dying in a car accident are 6,000 to 1. In other words, the odds are much stronger that you will get hit by lightning or be killed in a car crash than that you will win the jackpot in a state lottery.

This puts an abstract fact into meaningful perspective.

PERSONALIZE YOUR IDEAS

Listeners want to be entertained as they are being enlightened.[4] Nothing takes the edge off an informative speech more than an unbroken string of facts and figures. And nothing enlivens a speech more than personal illustrations. Whenever possible, you should try to *personalize* your ideas and dramatize them in human terms.

personalize

To present one's ideas in human terms that relate in some fashion to the experience of the audience.

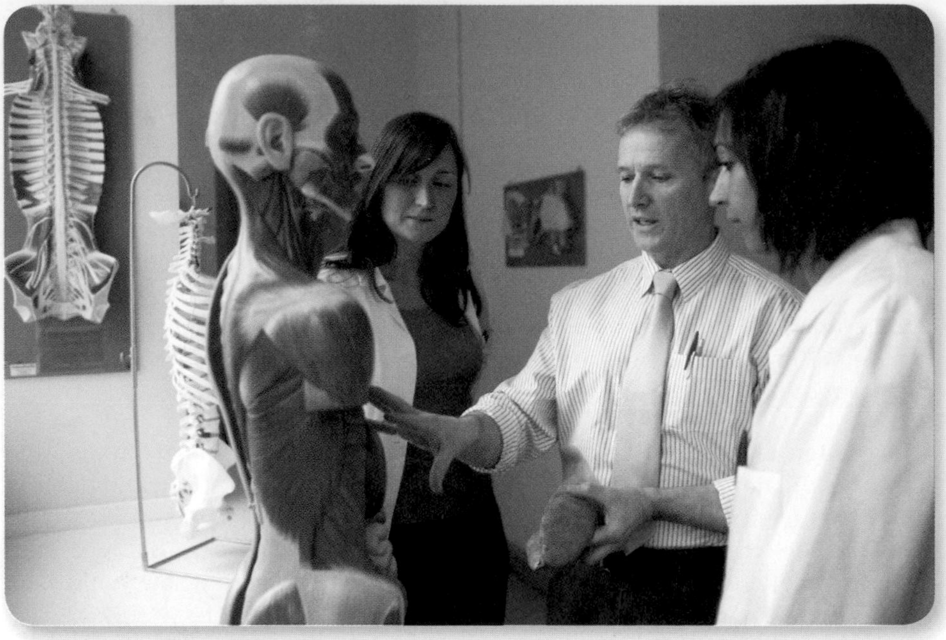

Informative speeches take place in a wide range of situations. Here a doctor explains a point about human anatomy to medical students.

Let's say you are talking about autism, the developmental disability marked by impaired communication and interaction skills. You would surely note that the condition affects 1 in every 500 children, occurs four times more frequently in males than in females, and is most prevalent among Caucasians. You would also note that the symptoms of autism include abnormal introversion, severely limited use of language, repetitive behaviors, avoidance of eye contact, loss of emotional control, and passive responses to affection.

But these are dry facts and figures. If you really want to get your audience involved, you will weave in some examples of children who suffer from autism. One speaker began by telling about Sam, her autistic nephew:

> My nephew Sam was the delight of our family when he was born, the first grandchild of my parents. He cooed and babbled, smiled at his mom and dad, grasped for the playthings around his crib. At family dinners on Sunday, we took turns holding him in our arms, feeding him, and singing him to sleep. He seemed like any normal infant in a secure and loving home.
>
> Then shortly before his second birthday we began to notice unusual behaviors. Sam avoided looking us in the eye, did not seem interested in learning words, played endlessly with the same toy, rocked back and forth in his chair for hours at a time, and was easily frustrated. My sister took him to a specialist, who gave the dreaded diagnosis: Sam was autistic.

During the body of the speech, the speaker mentioned Sam twice more to illustrate different aspects of autism. Then, at the end of the speech, she brought Sam's story to a hopeful conclusion:

> We have seen that autism is a very serious disorder whose causes are not well understood and whose effects on families and the lives of the children

themselves can be devastating. But we have also seen that early diagnosis and early intervention can help to modify and even turn around the symptoms of autism.

I am happy to say that Sam has benefited from such intervention. From the time he was two, he has been taught "normal" behavior patterns through aggressive therapy. Now he is able to participate in his class at the local school. He is also more responsive and affectionate at home. Sam continues to be our delight.

connect

View this excerpt from "Autism: Heartbreak and Hope" in the online Media Library for this chapter (Video 15.5).

It was a powerful ending. By putting a human face on a familiar topic, the speaker took autism out of the realm of statistics and medical jargon and brought it home in personal terms.

BE CREATIVE

Whether you are seeking alternatives to technical language, avoiding abstractions, personalizing ideas, or adapting to the audience's knowledge about the topic, you need to be creative in thinking about ways to achieve your objectives. A good informative speech is not an oral encyclopedia article. Like any other kind of speech, it requires a healthy dose of creativity.

If you look back at the examples on the previous few pages, you will see that all of them involve creative thinking by the speaker. As in these examples, creativity is often a matter of using language imaginatively and resourcefully. But creativity can involve *any* aspect of an informative speech, including visual aids—as can be seen in the speech on medical robots that is reprinted on pages 294–296.

Part of the speech deals with orderly robots, which transport medicine, food, and lab supplies around the hospital without a human by their side. The robots navigate by using "light whiskers"—invisible beams of sonar, infrared, and laser that constantly scan the environment to avoid collisions. Because the light whiskers are invisible, the speaker needed to find a way to make them visible for his audience. He did so by using a PowerPoint slide in which colored lines representing the light whiskers popped on screen in perfect coordination with the speaker's words. As you can see from Video 15.6, it was an effective—and creative—solution.

connect

View this excerpt from "Medical Robots: From Science Fiction to Science Fact" in the online Media Library for this chapter (Video 15.6).

If, like this speaker, you think creatively when constructing your informative speech, you are much more likely to be successful.

Sample Speech with Commentary

The following classroom speech provides an excellent example of how to apply the guidelines for informative speaking discussed in this chapter. Notice how the speaker takes what could be a dry, technical topic and makes it interesting. Also pay attention to how crisply the speech is organized and to how the speaker uses well-chosen supporting materials and visual aids to develop his ideas. You can view the speech in the online Media Library for this chapter.

connect

View "Medical Robots: From Science Fiction to Science Fact" in the online Media Library for this chapter (Video 15.7).

Medical Robots: From Science Fiction to Science Fact

COMMENTARY

SPEECH

The speaker starts with a richly detailed extended example that captures attention and interest.

Maureen Schrader lay on the operating table at Saint Barnabas Medical Center in Livingston, New Jersey. Four mechanical arms moved with precision over her abdomen. In one arm was a high-definition camera. The other three contained small surgical instruments that made a five-centimeter incision just below her ribcage. It was a tiny opening, but it was big enough to put a new kidney into Maureen's body.

As the speaker continues his opening example, he reveals that the mechanical arms mentioned in the first paragraph are actually robotic arms controlled by a surgeon.

At no point during the surgery did the surgeon actually touch Maureen. In fact, he sat several feet away peering into a monitor and holding what looked like video game controls. But the work of his hands was digitally recorded and sent to the robotic arms, which mimicked his every movement. The robot became an extension of the surgeon, and together they transplanted the kidney.

Here the speaker relates the topic to his audience, establishes his credibility, previews the main points to be discussed in the body of the speech, and provides a transition statement to the body.

Robots in the operating room are now a reality, and the next operation you or a family member undergoes may well involve a robot. But surgery is just one of the areas in which robots are changing modern medicine. As a pre-med student interested in becoming a surgeon, I've long been fascinated with medical robots. After researching the topic for this speech, I'd like to introduce you to the world of medical robots. We'll take a look at three kinds of robots in particular—orderly robots, remote-presence robots, and surgical robots. Let's begin with orderly robots.

Now the speaker moves into his first main point, dealing with orderly robots. He illustrates the point by focusing on the TUG robot.

Orderly robots help hospital staff accomplish routine tasks. Their primary function is to transport medicine, food, and lab supplies—and to do so without a human by their side. Here is one of the most popular orderly robots—the TUG, or tug robot—which, according to its manufacturer, can be found in more than 100 hospitals in the United States alone.

As you can see from the video of this speech, the speaker uses a creative visual aid to help his audience visualize the "light whiskers" used by TUG robots.

A September 2010 story in *Discovery News* explains how the robot works. Relying on a digital map of the hospital, the robot moves from room to room picking up and dropping off supplies. It senses people and obstacles by what are called "light whiskers"—invisible beams of sonar, infrared, and laser. These light whiskers are represented by the colored lines you see in this drawing. They constantly scan the environment to avoid collisions.

The speaker uses expert testimony to explain the benefits of orderly robots. Notice how he identifies the person he is quoting and his credentials before presenting the testimony.

TUG robots can also communicate with one another about the most efficient route to a location given current hallway conditions. They are highly efficient and make fewer delivery errors than people. Mark Weigel, director of food services at Bethesda Memorial Hospital in Maryland, notes that the TUG robot "never argues with patients, takes no breaks, is always polite and always on time."

The speaker moves into his second main point. He begins with a concise definition of remote-presence robots.

But orderly robots are not the only robots transforming modern medicine. Remote-presence robots allow a doctor to visit with a patient even when the doctor is not in the same room. "Remote presence" means that the doctor can be present with the patient even when the doctor is in a remote location.

The word "imagine" helps draw the audience further into the speech. A photograph shows exactly what a RP-7 remote-presence robot looks like.

Imagine you're sitting in a hospital room when in comes this—the RP-7. A 2009 story in *U.S. News & World Report* explains that physicians can pilot these robots from a laptop located anywhere in the hospital or in the world. A screen, camera, microphone, and speaker system—like the ones you see in this photograph—allow the doctor to interview the patient. Hospital staff can even attach medical devices such as electronic stethoscopes to the robot so the doctor can review a patient's vital signs.

Notice how the speaker identifies the source of his statistics and rounds off the numbers.

According to a 2010 article in *Hospital Management,* the RP-7 is used in more than 250 U.S. hospitals and has performed more than 100,000 clinic sessions. They are particularly useful in hospitals with a high patient-to-doctor ratio.

A transition at the beginning of this paragraph signals that the speaker is moving to his third main point. He again uses credible, well-chosen statistics to quantify his ideas.

In addition to orderly robots and remote-presence robots, a third kind of robot is transforming modern medicine. Surgical robots, like the kind I mentioned at the start of my speech, are increasingly being used in operating rooms around the world. Most popular is the one you see here—the da Vinci. According to a 2010 article in the *Miami Herald,* there are more than 1,400 da Vinci robots in hospitals worldwide, and they're used in more than 200,000 operations every year.

This paragraph provides an excellent example of how to explain visual aids and of how to communicate technical information in clear, nontechnical language.

How does da Vinci work? Intuitive Surgical, maker of da Vinci, explains that the surgeon controls the robot from a remote terminal. You can see the terminal in this photograph. Usually, the terminal is a few feet away, as in the photograph. But it can be as far as thousands of miles away, so a surgeon in San Francisco can operate on a patient in Miami. The surgeon controls the robot's arms utilizing an interactive 3-D imaging system. But make no mistake: Even though the robot is touching the patient, the surgeon is always in control.

Because the speaker is not a surgeon, he relies on expert testimony to explain the benefits of da Vinci surgical robots. As in other parts of the speech, his dynamic delivery creates a strong bond with his audience.

Doctors love da Vinci because it dramatically improves the quality of surgical procedures. Dr. Jeffrey Wolf, a head-and-neck surgeon at the University of Maryland Medical Center, states that da Vinci "gives us unprecedented access with really good 3-D visualization. . . . We're now able to perform intricate surgeries in a very small space with great dexterity." Da Vinci also reduces the risk of postsurgery complications, allows for faster healing, and helps patients leave the hospital sooner.

"In conclusion" signals that the speaker is coming to the end of his speech. He then summarizes the main points developed in the body.

In conclusion, we've seen that medical robots are playing an increasingly important role in modern medicine. Whether they're running errands for hospital employees, helping physicians connect with their patients, or acting as a surgeon's eyes and hands, medical robots have brought the future into the present.

The speaker ends on a strong note by stating that medical robots are now a matter of science fact, rather than of science fiction.

So the next time you find yourself at the hospital, keep your eyes peeled for the kind of technological marvels that used to exist only in science fiction. Medical robots are now a matter of science fact.

Summary

Speaking to inform occurs in a wide range of everyday situations. Improving your ability to convey knowledge effectively will be valuable to you throughout your life.

Informative speeches may be grouped into four categories—speeches about objects, speeches about processes, speeches about events, and speeches about concepts.

Objects include places, structures, animals, even people. Speeches about objects usually are organized in chronological, spatial, or topical order. A process is a series of actions that work together to produce a final result. Speeches about processes explain how something is made, how something is done, or how something works. The most common types of organization for speeches about processes are chronological and topical.

An event is anything that happens or is regarded as happening. Speeches about events are usually arranged in chronological or topical order. Concepts include beliefs, theories, ideas, and principles. Speeches. about concepts are often more complex than other kinds of informative speeches, and they typically follow a topical pattern of organization.

No matter what the subject of your informative speech, be careful not to overestimate what your audience knows about it. Explain everything so thoroughly that they can't help but understand. Avoid being too technical. Make sure your ideas and your language are fully comprehensible to someone who has no specialized knowledge about the topic.

Equally important, recognize that what is fascinating to you may not be fascinating to everybody. It is your job to make your informative speech interesting and meaningful to your audience. Find ways to talk about the topic in terms of your listeners. Avoid too many abstractions. Use description, comparison, and contrast to make your audience *see* what you are talking about. Try to personalize your ideas and dramatize them in human terms. Finally, be creative in thinking of ways to communicate your ideas.

Key Terms

informative speech *(278)*
object *(278)*
process *(280)*
event *(282)*
concept *(284)*
description *(290)*
comparison *(291)*
contrast *(291)*
personalize *(291)*

Review Questions

After reading this chapter, you should be able to answer the following questions:

1. What are the four types of informative speeches discussed in the chapter? Give an example of a good specific purpose statement for each type.
2. Why must informative speakers be careful not to overestimate what the audience knows about the topic? What can you do to make sure your ideas don't pass over the heads of your listeners?
3. What should you do as an informative speaker to relate your topic directly to the audience?
4. What two things should you watch out for in making sure your speech is not overly technical?
5. What are three methods you can use to avoid abstractions in your informative speech?
6. What does it mean to say that informative speakers should personalize their ideas?
7. Why is it important for informative speakers to be creative in thinking about ways to communicate their ideas?

connect™

For further review, go to the LearnSmart study module for this chapter.

Exercises for Critical Thinking

1. Below is a list of subjects for informative speeches. Your task is twofold: (a) Select four of the topics and prepare a specific purpose statement for an informative speech about each of the four. Make sure your four specific purpose statements include at least one that deals with its topic as an object, one that deals with its topic as a process, one that deals with its topic as an event, and one that deals with its topic as a concept. (b) Explain what method of organization you would most likely use in structuring a speech about each of your specific purpose statements.

hobbies	sports	education
animals	music	media
science	cultural customs	technology

2. Analyze "Ramadan" in the appendix of sample speeches that follows Chapter 19. Identify the specific purpose, central idea, main points, and method of organization. Evaluate the speech in light of the guidelines for informative speaking discussed in this chapter.

OCEANA

16

Speaking to Persuade

- The Importance of Persuasion
- Ethics and Persuasion
- The Psychology of Persuasion
- Persuasive Speeches on Questions of Fact
- Persuasive Speeches on Questions of Value
- Persuasive Speeches on Questions of Policy
- Sample Speech with Commentary

Ramon Trujillo started that particular school day by stopping at the library to return an overdue book. "Look," he explained to the librarian, "I know this book was due last week, but I was sick with the flu and couldn't even get out of bed. Do I still have to pay the fine? I can get you a note from the doctor if you need one." The librarian hemmed and hawed. Then he said, "Okay. You don't have a record of any other fines. Just this once."

With a sigh of relief, Ramon went on to his morning classes. At noon he was dashing across campus when a friend stopped him. "How about some lunch?" she asked. "I really can't," replied Ramon. "I have to stand at the table and get signatures on the tuition petition. I'll see you later, though."

During the afternoon, Ramon went to his job at a computer sales company. He arrived just in time for the weekly staff meeting, where he presented his ideas on how to increase customer satisfaction. "One thing I've noticed," he said, "is that most people don't realize they have only 14 days to return unopened merchandise for a full refund. Most stores have a 30-day return policy, and I know we've lost some customers because ours is shorter. Changing it might be inconvenient at first, but it will definitely help business in the long run." After listening to Ramon, the sales manager said, "I've always thought 14 days was plenty of time, but you've convinced me that we ought to change. Let's give it a try."

If you asked Ramon how he spent his day, he might say, "I returned a book, I went to class, I worked the tuition-petition table, I had a staff meeting at my job." In fact, he spent a large part of his day *persuading*—persuading people to do things they were reluctant to do or that had not occurred to them.

The Importance of Persuasion

Persuasion is the process of creating, reinforcing, or changing people's beliefs or actions.[1] The ability to speak (and write) persuasively will benefit you in every part of your life, from personal relations to community activities to career aspirations. When economists added up the number of people—lawyers, sales representatives, public relations specialists, counselors, administrators, and others—whose jobs depend largely on persuading people to adopt their point of view, they concluded that persuasion accounts for 26 percent of the U.S. gross domestic product![2]

persuasion

The process of creating, reinforcing, or changing people's beliefs or actions.

Understanding the principles of persuasion is also vital to being an informed citizen and consumer. By age 20, the average American has been exposed to 1 million television commercials—an average of 150 every day. Politicians and advertisers, salespeople and interest groups, fund-raisers and community activists—all vie for your attention, votes, money, time, and support. The more you know about persuasion, the more effective you can be in using your powers of critical thinking to assess the barrage of persuasive messages you are exposed to every day.

Although persuasion has been studied for more than 2,000 years, it is still the subject of lively debate among scholars. There are a number of scientific models of the persuasive process and a wide range of respected theories about how persuasion works. In this chapter and the next, we will explore the principles of persuasion as they apply to public speaking.

When you speak to persuade, you act as an advocate. Your job is to get listeners to agree with you and, perhaps, to act on that belief. Your goal may be to defend an idea, to refute an opponent, to sell a program, or to inspire people to action. Because persuasive speakers must communicate information clearly and concisely, you will need all the skills you used in speaking to inform. But you will also need new skills that take you from giving information to affecting your listeners' attitudes, beliefs, or actions.

Ethics and Persuasion

No matter what the speaking situation, you need to make sure your goals are ethically sound and that you use ethical methods to communicate your ideas. Meeting these obligations can be especially challenging when you speak to persuade. Would you be willing to shade the truth "just a bit" if it would guarantee a successful speech? How about juggling statistics, doctoring quotations, passing off opinions as facts, or pandering to prejudice and stereotypes?

Unfortunately, there is no shortage of speakers—and other persuaders—who are willing to take ethical shortcuts to achieve their objectives. Yet, as Martin Luther King stated years ago, it is not possible to bring about a truly beneficial result by using unethical methods. Maintaining the bond of trust with listeners is also vital to a speaker's credibility. As in other kinds of public speaking, the ideal of effective persuasion is the good person speaking well.

When you work on your persuasive speech, keep in mind the guidelines for ethical speaking discussed in Chapter 2. Make sure your goals are ethically sound and that you can defend them if they are questioned or challenged. Study the topic thoroughly so you won't mislead your audience through shoddy research or muddled thinking. Learn about all sides of an issue, seek out competing viewpoints, and get your facts right.

But knowing the facts is not enough. You also need to be honest in what you say. There is no place in ethical speechmaking for deliberately false or deceptive statements. Also be on guard against more subtle forms of dishonesty such as quoting out of context, portraying a few details as the whole story, and misrepresenting the sources of facts and figures. Take care to present statistics, testimony, and other kinds of evidence fairly and accurately.

Keep in mind as well the power of language and use it responsibly. Show respect for the rights of free speech and expression, and stay away from name-calling and other forms of abusive language. Finally, check the section of Chapter 17 that discusses the role of emotional appeal (pages 342–346). Make sure that any emotional appeal you use is appropriate to the topic and that you build your speech on a firm base of facts and logic before appealing to your audience's emotions. Aim at the highest standards and construct your speech so it will be both convincing *and* ethically sound.[3]

The Psychology of Persuasion

Persuasion is a psychological process. It occurs in a situation where two or more points of view exist. The speaker supports Social Security reform, but many listeners do not. The speaker considers cloning immoral, but some in the audience think it is justified in certain circumstances. The different points of view may be completely opposed, or they may simply be different in degree. Whichever the case, there must be a disagreement, or else there would be no need for persuasion.

THE CHALLENGE OF PERSUASIVE SPEAKING

Of all the kinds of public speaking, persuasion is the most complex and the most challenging. Your objective is more ambitious than in speaking to inform, and audience analysis and adaptation become much more demanding. In some persuasive speeches, you will deal with controversial topics that touch on your listeners' basic attitudes, values, and beliefs. This may increase their resistance to persuasion and make your task more difficult.

It is much easier, for example, to explain the history of capital punishment than to persuade an audience either that capital punishment should be abolished or that it should be reinstituted in every state. In the persuasive speech you must contend not only with your audience's knowledge of capital punishment but also with their attitudes toward crime and justice, their beliefs about the deterrent value of capital punishment, and their values about the taking of human life. Lines of argument that work with one part of the audience may fail with—or even upset—another part. What seems perfectly logical to some listeners may seem wildly irrational to others. No matter how expert you are on the topic, no matter how skillfully you prepare the speech, no matter how captivating your delivery—some listeners will not agree with you.

This does not mean persuasion is impossible. It does mean you should have a realistic sense of what you can accomplish. You can't expect a group of die-hard Democrats to become Republicans or a steak lover to turn vegetarian as a result of one speech.

In every persuasive speech, you will face some listeners who are strongly in favor of your position, some who are neutral, and some who are adamantly opposed. If listeners are neutral or only moderately committed one way or another, you can realistically hope your speech will move at least some of them toward your side. If listeners are strongly opposed to your viewpoint, you can consider your speech a success if it leads even a few to reexamine their views.

When thinking about the range of persuasive responses, you may find it helpful to visualize listeners on a scale such as that shown in Figure 16.1 below. Persuasion involves any movement by a listener from left to right on the scale, no matter where the listener begins and no matter how great or small the movement.[4]

How successful you are in any particular persuasive speech will depend above all on how well you tailor your message to the values, attitudes, and beliefs of your audience. In Chapter 6, we considered the general principles of audience analysis and adaptation. Here we emphasize two additional principles that are crucial to the psychology of persuasion. The first deals with how listeners process and respond to persuasive messages. The second pertains to the target audience for persuasive speeches.

HOW LISTENERS PROCESS PERSUASIVE MESSAGES

We often think of persuasion as something a speaker does *to* an audience. In fact, persuasion is something a speaker does *with* an audience. Listeners do not just sit passively and soak in everything the speaker has to say. Instead, they engage in a mental give-and-take with the speaker. While they listen, they assess the speaker's credibility, delivery, supporting materials,

FIGURE 16.1

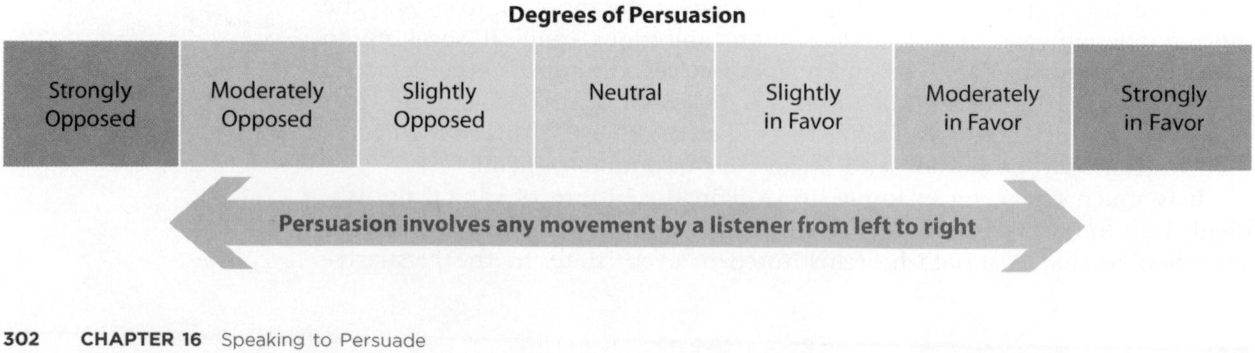

No matter what the situation, a persuasive speaker needs to adapt to the target audience. Here British Prime Minister David Cameron speaks to a local group in Flintshire, North Wales.

language, reasoning, and emotional appeals. They may respond positively at one point, negatively at another. At times they may argue, inside their own minds, with the speaker. This mental give-and-take is especially vigorous when listeners are highly involved with the topic and believe it has a direct bearing on their lives.[5]

In a sense, the psychological interaction between a speaker and audience during a persuasive speech is similar to what happens vocally during a conversation—as in this example:

Karma: It's much better to adopt a dog from a shelter than to buy a dog from a breeder. Adoption saves dogs that might otherwise be euthanized.

Robyn: It's true that adoption saves some animals' lives, but many of the dogs in shelters have behavioral problems. A person who adopts a dog like that might be seriously bitten. A person with small children doesn't want to take chances.

Karma: Most shelters today screen animals carefully before they release them for adoption. They also screen owners; for example, they allow only experienced dog owners to adopt large, active dogs.

Robyn: Still, when you adopt a dog, you don't know about its early training, health problems, or other things that would help you take the best care of it. If you go to a breeder, you know exactly what you're getting.

Karma: That's true, but to me the biggest concern is to rescue a dog that might otherwise be put to sleep, and to give a dog that's been mistreated a chance at a happy life.

Much the same kind of interaction might occur during a persuasive speech, except that the listener would respond internally rather than out loud.

mental dialogue with the audience

The mental give-and-take between speaker and listener during a persuasive speech.

What does this mean to you as a speaker? It means you must think of your persuasive speech as a kind of *mental dialogue* with your audience. You must anticipate possible objections the audience will raise to your point of view and answer them in your speech. You cannot convert skeptical listeners unless you deal directly with the reasons for their skepticism.

As you prepare your persuasive speech, put yourself in the place of your audience and imagine how they will respond. Be as tough on your speech as your audience will be. Every place they will raise a question, answer it. Every place they will have a criticism, deal with it. Every place they will see a hole in your argument, fill it. Leave nothing to chance.[6]

THE TARGET AUDIENCE

Unfortunately, no matter how carefully you plot your speech, you will seldom be able to persuade all your listeners. Like most audiences, yours will probably contain some listeners who are hostile to your position, some who favor it, some who are undecided, and some who just don't care. You would like to make your speech equally appealing to everyone, but this is rarely possible. Most often you will have a particular *part* of the whole audience that you want to reach with your speech. That part is called the *target audience*.

target audience

The portion of the whole audience that the speaker most wants to persuade.

Advertising gives us an effective model. Successful commercials are aimed at particular segments of the market. Mutual funds are now directing many of their advertisements at women. Why? Because more and more women are investing in the stock market. Beer commercials, on the other hand, are directed at men because they drink the most beer.

For your classroom speeches, you don't have the sophisticated research capability of a large advertising agency. But as we saw in Chapter 6, you can use questionnaires to find out where your classmates stand on your speech topic. This is your equivalent of market research. Once you know where your target audience stands, you can tailor your speech to fit their values and concerns—aim at the target, so to speak.

Here, for example, is how one student, Amy Shapiro, determined her target audience for a persuasive speech urging her classmates to pass on the gift of life by signing organ donor cards:

> There are 22 students in my audience. My audience-analysis questionnaires show that 3 are opposed to donating their organs under any circumstances. I can't persuade them no matter what I say. My questionnaires also show that 4 have already signed organ donor cards. I don't need to persuade them. The other 15 students could be persuaded if they knew more about the need for organ donors and about how the process works. They are my target audience.

Not only did Amy pinpoint her target audience, she also knew from her audience-analysis questionnaire the issues she would have to discuss to be convincing:

> The members of my target audience break down this way: 7 give "fear of being pronounced dead prematurely" as their main reason for not signing organ cards; 5 are concerned about their body being "cut up or disfigured"; and 3 cite religious reasons for their opposition. The questionnaires also show that 8 of the 15 don't fully understand the need for organ donors.

With all this information, Amy was able to put together a first-rate speech that focused on her classmates' attitudes and beliefs about signing organ donor cards. As a result, she was able to convince several of her classmates to sign cards.

In the next chapter, we'll discuss the methods you can use to hit the target in your persuasive speeches. In the rest of this chapter, we focus on the three major kinds of persuasive speeches and how to organize them most effectively.

Persuasive Speeches on Questions of Fact

WHAT ARE QUESTIONS OF FACT?

What college basketball team has won the most games since 1990? Who was the first African American to sit on the U.S. Supreme Court? How far is it from Los Angeles to Cairo? These questions of fact can be answered absolutely. The answers are either right or wrong.

question of fact

A question about the truth or falsity of an assertion.

But many questions of fact cannot be answered absolutely. There is a true answer, but we don't have enough information to know what it is. Some questions like this involve prediction: Will the economy be better or worse next year? Who will win the Super Bowl this season?

Other questions deal with issues on which the facts are murky or inconclusive. What will happen next in the Middle East? Is sexual orientation genetically determined? No one knows the final answers to these questions, but that doesn't stop people from speculating about them or from trying to convince other people that they have the best possible answers.

ANALYZING QUESTIONS OF FACT

In some ways, a persuasive speech on a question of fact is similar to an informative speech. But the two kinds of speeches take place in different kinds of situations and for different purposes.

The situation for an informative speech is *nonpartisan*. The speaker acts as a lecturer or a teacher. The aim is to give information as impartially as possible, not to argue for a particular point of view.

On the other hand, the situation for a persuasive speech on a question of fact is *partisan*. The speaker acts as an advocate. The aim is not to be impartial, but to present one view of the facts as persuasively as possible. The speaker may mention competing views of the facts, but only to refute them.

For example, consider the assassination of John F. Kennedy. After 50 years, there is still much debate about what really happened in Dallas on November 22, 1963. Did Lee Harvey Oswald act alone, or was he part of a conspiracy? How many shots were fired at President Kennedy and from what locations? If there was a conspiracy, who was involved in it? The informative speaker would recite the known facts on both sides of these questions without drawing a conclusion about which side is correct. The persuasive speaker, however, would draw a conclusion from the known facts and try to convert listeners to his or her point of view.

If there were no possibility of dispute on questions of fact, there would be no need for courtroom trials. In a criminal trial there is usually at least one known fact—a crime has been committed. But did the defendant commit the crime? The prosecuting attorney tries to persuade the jury that the defendant is guilty. The defense attorney tries to persuade the jury that the defendant is innocent. The jury must decide which view of the facts is more persuasive.[7]

ORGANIZING SPEECHES ON QUESTIONS OF FACT

Persuasive speeches on questions of fact are usually organized *topically*. Suppose, for example, that you want to convince your classmates that an earthquake of 9.0 or above on the Richter scale will hit California within the next ten years. Each main point in your speech will present a *reason* why someone should agree with you:

Specific Purpose: To persuade my audience that an earthquake of 9.0 or above on the Richter scale will hit California in the next ten years.

Central Idea: There are three good reasons to believe that an earthquake of 9.0 or above on the Richter scale will hit California in the next ten years.

Main Points:

I. California is long overdue for a major earthquake.

II. Many geological signs indicate that a major earthquake may happen soon.

III. Experts agree that an earthquake of 9.0 or above could strike California any day.

To take another example, suppose you are trying to persuade your classmates that the plays attributed to William Shakespeare were not actually written by him. Your specific purpose, central idea, and main points might be:

Specific Purpose: To persuade my audience that William Shakespeare did not write the plays attributed to him.

Central Idea: There is considerable evidence that the plays attributed to William Shakespeare were actually written by Francis Bacon or Edward de Vere.

Main Points:

I. Biographical and textual evidence suggest that William Shakespeare did not write the plays attributed to him.

II. Historical evidence indicates that Shakespeare's plays were probably written by either Sir Francis Bacon or Edward de Vere, 17th Earl of Oxford.

Notice in these examples that the speaker's purpose is limited to persuading the audience to accept a particular view of the facts. Sometimes, however, the dispute that gives rise to a persuasive speech will go beyond a question of fact and will turn on a question of value.

Many persuasive speeches revolve around questions of fact. Here U.S. Surgeon General Regina Benjamin discusses her report on the dangers of tobacco use.

Persuasive Speeches on Questions of Value

WHAT ARE QUESTIONS OF VALUE?

What is the best movie of all time? Is cloning morally justifiable? What are the ethical responsibilities of journalists? Such questions not only involve matters of fact, but they also demand *value judgments*—judgments based on a person's beliefs about what is right or wrong, good or bad, moral or immoral, proper or improper, fair or unfair.

question of value

A question about the worth, rightness, morality, and so forth of an idea or action.

Take the issue of cloning. It can be discussed at a purely factual level by asking such questions as "What are the scientific methods of cloning?" Or "What are the laws about cloning in different countries?" These are factual questions. The answers you reach are independent of your belief about the morality of cloning.

But suppose you ask, "Is it morally justifiable to clone human beings?" Or "Is it ethically acceptable to clone human cells in an effort to cure diseases such as AIDS and cancer?" Now you are dealing with questions of value. How you answer will depend not only on your factual knowledge about cloning, but also on your moral values.

ANALYZING QUESTIONS OF VALUE

Contrary to what many people think, questions of value are not simply matters of personal opinion or whim. If you say, "I enjoy bicycle riding," you do not have to give a reason why you enjoy it. You are making a statement about your personal taste. Even if bicycle riding were the most unpleasant activity ever invented, it could still be one of your favorites.

On the other hand, if you say, "Bicycle riding is the ideal form of land transportation," you are making a statement about a question of value. Whether bicycling is the ideal form of land transportation does not depend on your own likes and dislikes. To defend the statement, you cannot say, "Bicycle riding is the ideal form of land transportation because I like it."

Instead, you must *justify* your claim. The first step is to define what you mean by an "ideal form of land transportation." Do you mean a mode of transportation that gets people where they want to go as fast as possible? That is relatively inexpensive? That is fun? Nonpolluting? Beneficial for the user? In other words, you must establish your *standards* for an "ideal form of land transportation." Then you can show how bicycle riding measures up against those standards.

Whenever you give a speech on a question of value, be sure to give special thought to the standards for your value judgment.

ORGANIZING SPEECHES ON QUESTIONS OF VALUE

Persuasive speeches on questions of value are almost always organized *topically*. The most common approach is to devote your first main point to establishing the standards for your value judgment and your second main point to applying those standards to the subject of your speech.

Think back for a moment to the speech about bicycle riding as the ideal form of land transportation. If you organized this speech in topical order, your first main point would identify the standards for an ideal form of land transportation. Your second main point would show how biking measures up against those standards. Here is how your specific purpose, central idea, and main points might look:

Specific Purpose: To persuade my audience that bicycle riding is the ideal form of land transportation.

Central Idea: Bicycle riding is the ideal form of land transportation because it is faster than walking or running, is nonpolluting, and promotes the health of the rider.

Main Points:

I. An ideal form of land transportation should meet three major standards.
   A. It should be faster than running or walking.
   B. It should be nonpolluting.
   C. It should be beneficial for the person who uses it.

II. Bicycle riding meets all these standards for an ideal form of land transportation.
   A. Bicycle riding is faster than walking or running.
   B. Bicycle riding is not a source of air, land, water, or noise pollution.
   C. Bicycle riding is extremely beneficial for the health of the rider.

When you speak on a question of value, you must make sure to justify your judgment against some identifiable standards. In the following example, notice how the speaker devotes her first main point to judging capital punishment against moral standards and her second main point to judging it against legal standards:

Specific Purpose: To persuade my audience that capital punishment is morally and legally wrong.

Central Idea: Capital punishment violates both the Bible and the U.S. Constitution.

Main Points:

I. Capital punishment violates the biblical commandment "Thou shalt not kill."

II. Capital punishment violates the constitutional ban on "cruel and unusual punishment."

As you can see, speeches on questions of value may have strong implications for our actions. A person who is persuaded that capital punishment is morally and legally wrong is more likely to support legislation abolishing the death penalty. But speeches on questions of value do not argue directly for or against particular courses of action. Once you go beyond arguing right or wrong to arguing that something should or should not be done, you move from a question of value to a question of policy.

Persuasive Speeches on Questions of Policy

WHAT ARE QUESTIONS OF POLICY?

Questions of policy arise daily in almost everything we do. At home we debate what to do during spring vacation, whether to buy a new television, which movie to see on the weekend. At work we discuss whether to ask for a raise, what strategy to use in selling a product, how to improve communication between management and employees. As citizens we ponder whether to vote for or against a political candidate, what to do about airport security, how to promote economic growth.

All these are questions of policy because they deal with specific courses of action. Questions of policy inevitably involve questions of fact. (How can we decide whether to vote for a candidate unless we know the facts of her or his stand on the issues?) They may also involve questions of value. (The policy you favor on abortion will be affected by whether you think abortion is moral or immoral.) But questions of policy *always* go beyond questions of fact or value to decide whether something should or should not be done.

question of policy

A question about whether a specific course of action should or should not be taken.

When put formally, questions of policy usually include the word "should," as in these examples:

What measures should be taken to protect the United States against terrorist attacks?

Should the electoral college be abolished?

What steps should be taken to reduce America's dependence on foreign oil?

TYPES OF SPEECHES ON QUESTIONS OF POLICY

When you speak on a question of policy, your goal may be either to gain passive agreement or to motivate immediate action from your listeners. Deciding which goal you want to achieve will affect almost every aspect of your speech.

Speeches to Gain Passive Agreement

If your goal is passive agreement, you will try to get your audience to agree with you that a certain policy is desirable, but you will not necessarily encourage the audience to do anything to enact the policy. For example, suppose you want to persuade people that the United States should abolish the electoral college and elect the President by direct popular vote. If you seek passive agreement, you will try to get your audience to concur, but you will not urge them to take any action right now to help change presidential election procedures.

speech to gain passive agreement

A persuasive speech in which the speaker's goal is to convince the audience that a given policy is desirable without encouraging the audience to take action in support of the policy.

Here are some specific purpose statements for policy speeches that seek passive agreement:

> To persuade my audience that there should be stricter safety standards on amusement-park rides.
>
> To persuade my audience that the United States should put greater emphasis on solar power to meet the country's energy needs.
>
> To persuade my audience that a balanced-budget amendment should be added to the U.S. Constitution.

In each case, the speaker's aim is to convince listeners that the speaker's policy is necessary and practical. The speaker is not trying to get listeners to take action in support of the policy.

Speeches to Gain Immediate Action

When your goal is immediate action, you want to do more than get your listeners to nod their heads in agreement. You want to motivate them to action—to sign a petition for abolishing the electoral college, to campaign for lower tuition, to contribute to a fund drive, and so forth.

speech to gain immediate action

A persuasive speech in which the speaker's goal is to convince the audience to take action in support of a given policy.

Here are some examples of specific purpose statements for policy speeches that seek immediate action:

> To persuade my audience to give time to Big Brothers or Big Sisters.
>
> To persuade my audience to vote in the next student election.
>
> To persuade my audience to begin a regular exercise program.

Some experts say you should seek action from your audience whenever possible. Although it is much easier to evoke passive agreement than to elicit action, the listener is not making much of a commitment by thinking, "Sure, I agree with you." Within a day or two that same listener may forget entirely about your speech—and about her or his agreement with it.

Action, however, reinforces belief. A great deal of research shows that if you can persuade a listener to take some kind of action—even if it is no more than signing a petition, putting a bumper sticker on a car, or attending a meeting—you have gained a more serious commitment. Once a listener acts on behalf of a speaker's position, she or he is more likely to remain committed to it.[8]

When you call for action in a persuasive speech, you should make your recommendations as specific as possible. Don't just urge listeners to "do something." Tell them exactly what to do and how to do it.

connect

View this excerpt from "Making a Difference Through the Special Olympics" in the online Media Library for this chapter (Video 16.1).

For an excellent example, look at Video 16.1 in the online Media Library for this chapter. The speaker's aim was to convince her classmates to donate time to the Special Olympics. After talking about the mission of Special

Persuasive speeches on questions of policy are given whenever people debate specific courses of action. Such speeches can seek either passive agreement or immediate action.

Olympics, the need for volunteers, and the rewarding feelings experienced by volunteers, she explained how students can get involved for whatever amount of time they are able to commit at the moment. She also brought along brochures with additional information to pass out after her speech. When you construct your persuasive speech, remember that the more specific your instructions, the more likely it is that your call to action will succeed.[9]

ANALYZING QUESTIONS OF POLICY

Regardless of whether your aim is to elicit passive agreement or to gain immediate action, you will face three basic issues whenever you discuss a question of policy—need, plan, and practicality.

Need

There is no point in arguing for a policy unless you can show a need for it:

Is there a need for more student parking on campus?

Is there a need for the school district to institute single-sex classrooms?

Is there a need for a national ID card in the United States?

need

The first basic issue in analyzing a question of policy: Is there a serious problem or need that requires a change from current policy?

Your first step is to convince listeners that there is a serious problem with things as they are. People are not inclined to adopt a new policy unless they are convinced that the old one is not working. This is why the *burden of proof* always rests with the speaker who advocates change. (Of course, you may be defending present policy, in which case you will argue that there is *no* need to change—that things are already working as well as can be expected.)

burden of proof

The obligation facing a persuasive speaker to prove that a change from current policy is necessary.

Plan

The second basic issue of policy speeches is plan. Once you have shown that a problem exists, you must explain your plan for solving it:

What can we do to get more student parking on campus?

What topics should be taught in single-sex classrooms? Are single-sex classrooms appropriate for all grade levels?

What information should be included on a national ID card? Who will be responsible for collecting the information and creating the cards?

plan

The second basic issue in analyzing a question of policy: If there is a problem with current policy, does the speaker have a plan to solve the problem?

connect

View this excerpt from "The Horrors of Puppy Mills" in the online Media Library for this chapter (Video 16.2).

Answering such questions is especially important if you call for a new policy. It's easy to complain about problems; the real challenge is developing solutions.

In most classroom speeches, you will not have time to describe your plan in detail, but you should at least identify its major features. Look, for example, at the plan section in the speech on puppy mills in the online Media Library for this chapter. First, the speaker proposes legal measures to punish dog breeders that do not take proper care of their animals. Second, he presents four steps that individual listeners can take when buying a dog to make sure they are not supporting puppy mills. The speech would have been much less persuasive if the speaker had not spelled out the major features of his plan.

Practicality

practicality

The third basic issue in analyzing a question of policy: Will the speaker's plan solve the problem? Will it create new and more serious problems?

The third basic issue of policy speeches is practicality. Once you have presented a plan, you must show that it will work. Will it solve the problem? Or will it create new and more serious problems?

> Building a multilevel parking garage on campus would provide more student parking, but the cost would require a sharp increase in tuition.
>
> Creating single-sex classrooms would be academically beneficial for some students, but it could reinforce gender stereotypes and return education to a separate-but-equal status.
>
> A national ID card might be an easy way for people to verify their identity for security purposes, but it could also infringe on civil liberties and give the government too much personal information about individuals.

These are significant concerns. Whenever you advocate a new policy, you must be prepared to show that it is workable. No matter how serious a problem may be, listeners usually want some assurance that a speaker's plan will actually solve the problem.[10]

connect

View this excerpt from "The Most Dangerous Habit" in the online Media Library for this chapter (Video 16.3).

One way to provide this assurance is to show that a plan similar to yours has been successfully implemented elsewhere. For example, Video 16.3 in the online Media Library for this chapter shows an excerpt from a student speech calling for tougher measures to reduce smoking in the speaker's state. As you view the video, notice how the speaker points to the success of a similar plan in California as evidence that it will work in her state.

If you oppose a shift in policy, one of your major arguments will be that the change is impractical—that it will create more problems than it can solve. For example, critics of raising the federal minimum wage in the United States say it would overburden small businesses and lead to greater unemployment. Other opponents argue that a high minimum wage puts American companies at a disadvantage when competing against foreign companies. If listeners accept these arguments, they will probably decide that the United States should not raise the federal minimum wage.

How much of your speech should you devote to need, to plan, and to practicality? The answer depends on your topic and your audience. For example, if your audience is not aware of the health and environmental problems caused by the use of antibacterial chemicals in household products, you will have to give much of your time to need before covering plan and practicality. On the other hand, if your listeners already know about the problems caused by antibacterial household products, you can quickly remind them of need and then devote most of your speech to plan and practicality.

ORGANIZING SPEECHES ON QUESTIONS OF POLICY

Effective organization is crucial when you speak on a question of policy. Although any of the basic patterns of organization explained in Chapter 9 can be used, four special patterns are especially valuable for policy speeches. They are problem-solution order, problem-cause-solution order, comparative advantages order, and Monroe's motivated sequence.

Problem-Solution Order

If you advocate a change in policy, your main points often will fall naturally into problem-solution order. In the first main point you demonstrate the need for a new policy by showing the extent and seriousness of the problem. In the second main point you explain your plan for solving the problem and show its practicality. For example:

problem-solution order

A method of organizing persuasive speeches in which the first main point deals with the existence of a problem and the second main point presents a solution to the problem.

Specific Purpose: To persuade my audience that the U.S. Congress should pass legislation curbing the spread of phony pharmaceuticals.

Central Idea: Because phony pharmaceuticals are a serious problem in the United States, Congress should pass legislation ensuring that the medications we buy are safe.

Main Points:

I. The spread of phony pharmaceuticals is a serious problem.
   A. Phony pharmaceuticals are one of the most profitable areas of criminal activity in the world.
   B. The spread of phony pharmaceuticals is producing serious health risks in the United States.

II. Solving the problem of phony pharmaceuticals requires action by the federal government.
   A. Congress should pass legislation targeting the spread of phony pharmaceuticals and imposing strict penalties for violators.
   B. Experts believe that such legislation will go a long way toward solving the problem.

connect

View an excerpt from "Phony Pharmaceuticals" in the online Media Library for this chapter (Video 16.4).

You can use the problem-solution format just as easily to organize a speech opposing a change in policy. In such a speech your job is to defend the current system and to attack your opponents' proposed policy. Thus in the first main point you might argue that there is *not* a need for change. In the second main point you might show that even if there were a serious problem, the suggested new policy would *not* solve it and would create serious problems of its own. For example:

Specific Purpose: To persuade my audience that the city council should not pass legislation merging the police and fire departments.

Central Idea: Merging the police and fire departments is neither necessary nor practical.

Main Points:

I. Merging the police and fire departments is not necessary.
   A. Under the current system, the police department has developed a reputation for excellence that has made it a model for departments in other cities,
   B. The fire department is equally well-respected for doing its job quickly and efficiently.

II. Besides being unnecessary, merging the police and fire departments is highly impractical.
    A. Rather than saving the city money, merging the departments would increase costs.
    B. Merging the departments would also harm morale and reduce the high level of performance we expect from our police force and firefighters.

Problem-Cause-Solution Order

problem-cause-solution order

A method of organizing persuasive speeches in which the first main point identifies a problem, the second main point analyzes the causes of the problem, and the third main point presents a solution to the problem.

For a variation on problem-solution order, you might arrange your speech in problem-cause-solution order. This produces a speech with three main points—the first identifying a problem, the second analyzing the causes of the problem, and the third presenting a solution to the problem. For example:

Specific Purpose: To persuade my audience that action is required to deal with the problem of childhood obesity.

Central Idea: Childhood obesity is a serious problem that can be controlled by changes in diet and exercise.

Main Points:

I. Childhood obesity is a major problem in the United States.
    A. Childhood obesity continues to grow at a rapid pace.
    B. Obesity is producing serious health problems among children.

II. There are two major causes of the increase in childhood obesity.
    A. The first cause is dietary.
    B. The second cause is physical inactivity.

III. Solving the problem requires dealing with both causes.
    A. Parents and schools must make sure that children are eating healthy foods.
    B. Parents and schools must also make sure that children get enough exercise.

connect

View an excerpt from "The Epidemic of Childhood Obesity" in the online Media Library for this chapter (Video 16.5).

Some teachers prefer this method of organization because it requires a speaker to identify the causes of the problem. This in turn makes it easier to check whether the proposed solution will get at the causes of the problem.

Comparative Advantages Order

comparative advantages order

A method of organizing persuasive speeches in which each main point explains why a speaker's solution to a problem is preferable to other proposed solutions.

When your audience already agrees that a problem exists, you can devote your speech to comparing the advantages and disadvantages of competing solutions. In such a situation, you might put your speech in comparative advantages order, devoting each main point to explaining why your solution is preferable to other proposed solutions.

Suppose you want to convince your audience that automakers should put greater emphasis on developing hydrogen fuel-cell cars than gas-electric hybrid cars. Using comparative advantages order, you would compare hydrogen cars with gas-electric hybrid cars and show why the former are a better choice. Your specific purpose, central idea, and main points might look like this:

Specific Purpose: To persuade my audience that automakers should put greater emphasis on developing hydrogen fuel-cell cars than gas-electric cars.

Because it follows the process of human thinking, Monroe's motivated sequence is especially useful for persuasive speakers who seek immediate action from their listeners.

Central Idea: Unlike gas-electric cars, hydrogen cars run entirely without gasoline and do not emit air-polluting exhaust.

Main Points:

I. Unlike hybrid cars, hydrogen cars run entirely without gasoline.

II. Unlike hybrid cars, hydrogen cars do not emit any air-polluting exhaust.

Monroe's Motivated Sequence

Developed in the 1930s by Alan Monroe, a professor of speech at Purdue University, the motivated sequence is tailor-made for policy speeches that seek immediate action. The sequence has five steps that follow the psychology of persuasion:

Monroe's motivated sequence

A method of organizing persuasive speeches that seek immediate action. The five steps of the motivated sequence are attention, need, satisfaction, visualization, and action.

1. *Attention.* First, you gain the attention of your audience by using one or more of the methods described in Chapter 10: relating to the audience, showing the importance of the topic, making a startling statement, arousing curiosity or suspense, posing a question, telling a dramatic story, or using visual aids.
2. *Need.* Next, you make the audience feel a need for change. You show there is a serious problem with the existing situation. It is important to state the need clearly and to illustrate it with strong supporting materials. By the end of this step, listeners should be so concerned about the problem that they are psychologically primed to hear your solution.
3. *Satisfaction.* Having aroused a sense of need, you satisfy it by providing a solution to the problem. You present your plan and show how it will work. Be sure to offer enough details about the plan to give listeners a clear understanding of it.
4. *Visualization.* Having given your plan, you intensify desire for it by visualizing its benefits. The key to this step is using vivid imagery to show your listeners how *they* will profit from your policy. Make them *see* how much better conditions will be once your plan is adopted.

5. *Action.* Once the audience is convinced your policy is beneficial, you are ready to call for action. Say exactly what you want the audience to do—and how to do it. Then conclude with a final stirring appeal that reinforces their commitment to act.

Many speakers prefer the motivated sequence because it is more detailed than problem-solution order. It follows the process of human thinking and leads the listener step by step to the desired action. One indication of its effectiveness is that it is widely used by people who make their living by persuasion—especially advertisers. The next time you watch television, pay close attention to the commercials. You will find that many of them follow the motivated sequence.

Try using the motivated sequence when you want to spur listeners to action. You should find it easy and effective, as did one student who used it in a speech urging classmates to work for passage of a local tenants' rights bill. Here are the highlights of his speech:

Attention:	Have you ever had cockroaches running through the cupboards in your apartment? Have you shivered in the cold because the furnace was broken? Or waited months for the security deposit you never got back even though you left your apartment as clean as when you moved in?
Need:	Throughout this city students and other tenants are being victimized by unresponsive and unethical landlords. Just last year more than 200 complaints were filed with the city housing department, but no action has been taken against the landlords.
Satisfaction:	These problems could be solved by passing a strong tenants' rights bill that defines the rights of tenants, specifies the obligations of landlords, and imposes strict penalties for violators.
Visualization:	Such bills have worked in a number of college communities across the nation. If one were passed here, you would no longer have to worry about substandard conditions in your apartment. Your landlord could not violate the terms of your lease or steal your security deposit.
Action:	A tenants' rights bill has been proposed to the city council. You can help get it passed by signing the petition I will pass around after my speech. I also urge you to circulate petitions among your friends and to support the bill when it is debated in the city council next week. If we all work together, we can get this bill through the council.

Monroe's motivated sequence is perfectly compatible with the standard method of outlining discussed in Chapter 11. The following outline shows how one speaker incorporated the sequence into a speech urging her classmates to change the way they use their cell phones:

Specific Purpose: To persuade my audience to use their cell phones in a way that will protect their health.

Central Idea: You can avoid the long-term health risks of cell phone use by making some simple changes.

Introduction

Attention:

I. Your cell phone is your constant companion. You use it everywhere you go, day and night.

II. But what if your constant companion is dangerous? What if it's hazardous to your health?

III. After doing extensive research, I hope to persuade each of you to use your cell phone in a manner that will protect your health.

connect

View an excerpt from "The Dangers of Cell Phones" in the online Media Library for this chapter (Video 16.6).

Body

Need:

I. Although cell phones are safe in the short run, they pose serious long-term health risks.
   A. Using a cell phone exposes you to radiation that builds up over time.
   B. More and more scientists are warning about the long-term dangers of cell phone use.
   C. Even cell phone manufacturers warn against keeping phones too close to the body.

Satisfaction:

II. You can guard against these risks by making simple changes in the way you use your cell phone.
   A. Above all, do not press your cell phone against your head while talking.
   B. Get in the habit of using ear buds or your phone's internal speaker.

Using public speaking in your CAREER

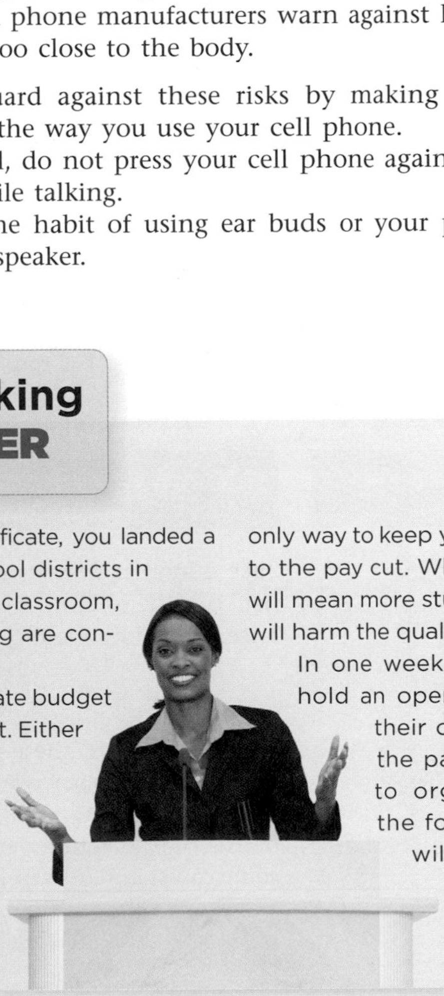

After earning your teaching certificate, you landed a job in one of the best public school districts in the state. You've excelled in the classroom, and evaluations of your teaching are consistently outstanding.

But the newly announced state budget means drastic cuts for the district. Either 100 teachers will be laid off, or every teacher will have to accept a 10 percent pay cut. Because the newest teachers are the first to be fired, and you have been on the job for only three years, you know that the only way to keep your position is if all teachers agree to the pay cut. What's more, laying off 100 teachers will mean more students in each classroom, and that will harm the quality of education.

In one week, the school superintendent will hold an open meeting for teachers to voice their opinions. You plan on arguing for the pay cut, but you're unsure of how to organize your speech. Which of the following methods of organization will be most effective, and why: problem-solution, comparative advantages, Monroe's motivated sequence?

Visualization: III. These changes will help protect your health.
A. You can use your cell phone without long-term health risks.
B. You will avoid the fate of people who have developed cancer and other conditions from prolonged cell phone use.

Conclusion

Action: I. So I encourage each of you to make these changes starting today.
II. Make sure your constant companion is not endangering your health.

Try using the motivated sequence when you seek immediate action from your listeners. Over the years it has worked for countless speakers—and it can work for you as well.

Sample Speech with Commentary

connect™

View "Phony Pharmaceuticals" in the online Media Library for this chapter (Video 16.7).

The following persuasive speech deals with a question of policy and provides an excellent example of problem-solution structure. As you read the speech, notice how the speaker deals with the issues of need, plan, and practicality. Notice also how she uses strong, well-chosen supporting materials to back up her point of view. Finally, observe how clear and uncluttered the speech is. There are few wasted words and the ideas progress cleanly and crisply. You can view the speech in the online Media Library for this chapter.

Phony Pharmaceuticals

COMMENTARY	SPEECH
The speaker captures attention by showing three PowerPoint slides and asking the audience questions about them.	Take a look at these two pills. Do you notice a difference between them? How about these two? Do you see a difference here? How about these?
Notice how the speaker uses "you" throughout her opening to relate the topic directly to her listeners.	To the naked eye, these pills are indistinguishable. But at a chemical level, they are very, very different. In each case, the pill on the left is real; it will help you get better. The pill on the right is counterfeit. It will not help you get better. In some cases, it may even kill you.

The speaker presents expert testimony to define phony pharmaceuticals and to show why they can be harmful.

Katherine Eban, author of *Dangerous Doses: How Counterfeiters Are Contaminating America's Drug Supply,* explains that phony pharmaceuticals are drugs that have been diluted, drugs in which the active ingredient has been replaced with something else, or drugs that have been relabeled to appear stronger than they truly are. Taking a phony pharmaceutical means that you do not receive the medicine you need to get better, and the results can be deadly.

The speaker establishes her credibility by stating that she has a personal connection to the topic and has done substantial research on it. She closes the introduction by stating her central idea and previewing the body of her speech.

I first became aware of this issue after my younger sister received a phony drug for her asthma last summer. Fortunately, the error was discovered before it caused her any lasting harm. But I've been concerned about the issue ever since, and I did a great deal of research on it for this speech. As a result, I am convinced that we need to take action now to combat the problem of phony pharmaceuticals. Later in my speech, I'll share with you my plan for curbing the spread of these dangerous drugs. But let's start by taking a closer look at the problem.

This speech is organized in problem-solution order. Here the speaker starts the problem main point by identifying some of the harmful ingredients found in phony pharmaceuticals.

Phony pharmaceuticals are dangerous because of the health risks they pose. According to Graham Jackson, editor of the *International Journal of Clinical Practice,* counterfeit drugs include ingredients such as boric acid, leaded road paint, floor polish, shoe polish, talcum powder, and cement powder. But that's not all. There's also brick dust, chalk, nickel, and arsenic. Ingesting too much boric acid or floor polish can make you sick; leaded road paint and arsenic can kill you.

The speaker uses an example to illustrate the dangers of phony pharmaceuticals.

In one highly publicized case, 81 people in the United States died in 2008 because they took a counterfeit version of the blood thinner heparin. As reported by CNN, the phony heparin was originally manufactured outside the United States using a cheap sulfate that proved deadly. After slipping past all regulatory checks, it ended up in the United States, with tragic results.

The speaker presents statistics and testimony to show how widespread the problem of phony pharmaceuticals is. Notice how she relates her statistics to the audience.

The U.S. government's Bureau of International Information Programs estimates that 700,000 people around the world will die this year from phony pharmaceuticals—almost three times the number of people who live here in Madison. In fact, Roger Bate, of the American Enterprise Institute, reports that "trafficking in counterfeit drugs has become one of the world's fastest-growing criminal enterprises."

Here, as elsewhere, the speaker cites recent, credible sources and identifies them clearly. The quotation from Tom Kubic is especially effective.

Phony pharmaceuticals are so widespread that they have become big business. The FDA estimates that they will bring in close to $75 billion in revenue this year alone—up from $40 billion only a few years ago. Tom Kubic, head of the Pharmaceutical Security Institute, told *USA Today* in September 2010 that criminals "can make more money in counterfeit drugs than they can in heroin."

A transition moves the speaker into the solution portion of her speech, in which she presents a concise, four-step plan to deal with phony pharmaceuticals.

Given the rewards of the counterfeit drug trade, the problem will only get worse in the coming years unless we take steps to bring it under control. The solution I propose is similar to House Resolution 2726, which is under consideration by the U.S. Congress. There are four steps to this solution.

As the speaker proceeds, she uses a signpost to introduce each part of her plan.

First, criminal penalties for drug counterfeiters should be increased from three years in prison, which is the current limit, to no limit at all. If a drug peddler kills someone with phony pharmaceuticals, the punishment should fit the crime.

As you can see from the video of this speech, the speaker highlights each point in her plan with a PowerPoint slide.

Second, the Food and Drug Administration should have the authority to recall prescription drugs. Right now, the FDA can encourage drug manufacturers to issue a recall, but it has no power to issue a recall on its own. To get phony pharmaceuticals off the street, recall authority needs to rest with a central agency that will act quickly and uniformly.

The rhetorical question at the end of this paragraph invites the audience to draw the same conclusion as the speaker.

Third, the FDA should be given the resources for spot-checking the chemical makeup of prescription medication. We have health inspectors for food, why not have inspectors for prescription drugs?

Here, as throughout the speech, the speaker uses her voice, gestures, and eye contact to help communicate her ideas and to establish a bond with the audience.

Fourth, legitimate drug manufacturers should be required to implement track-and-trace technology. As explained in the *New York Times,* this technology stamps each bottle and pill with a unique code tied to a secure, centralized database. The code allows pharmacies and distributors to determine whether drugs are legitimate or phony, plus the route the drugs took to get to store shelves.

The speaker presents a quotation to show the practicality of her plan. Establishing practicality is always important in a persuasive speech on a question of policy.

Representative Steve Israel of New York, sponsor of House Resolution 2726, says these four steps will "ensure that the domestic drug supply chain is secure for every American." It "will crack down on counterfeiting and increase the penalties for the outlaws who are compromising our health." The time has come for Congress to pass this vital legislation.

The speaker signals the beginning of her conclusion and restates her central idea.

In conclusion, phony pharmaceuticals are pervasive and dangerous. By implementing the solution I have outlined, we will be able to control this public-health menace.

In addition to using language from her introduction, the speaker returns to the PowerPoint slides with which she opened the speech. This makes for a strong ending and gives the speech a sense of psychological unity.

You have the right to know that the medication you're taking is real. You have the right to know that your next trip to the drugstore will be a safe one. And you have the right to know that what you see is what you get.

Summary

Persuasion is the process of creating, reinforcing, or changing people's beliefs or actions. When you speak to persuade, you act as an advocate. The ability to speak persuasively will benefit you in every part of your life, from personal relations to community activities to career aspirations.

How successful you are in any persuasive speech depends on how well you tailor your message to your listeners' values, attitudes, and beliefs. You should think of your speech as a mental dialogue with your audience. Identify your target audience, anticipate objections they may raise to your point of view, and answer those objections in your speech.

Persuasive speeches may center on questions of fact, value, or policy. When giving a persuasive speech about a question of fact, your role is akin to that of a lawyer in a courtroom trial. You will try to get your listeners to accept your view of the facts.

Questions of value involve a person's beliefs about what is right or wrong, good or bad, moral or immoral, ethical or unethical. When speaking about a question of value, you must justify your opinion by establishing standards for your value judgment. Speeches on questions of value do not argue directly for or against particular courses of action.

Once you go beyond arguing right or wrong to urging that something should or should not be done, you move to a question of policy. When you speak on a question of policy, your goal may be to evoke passive agreement or to spark immediate action. In either case, you will face three basic issues—need, plan, and practicality. How much of your speech you devote to each issue will depend on your topic and your audience.

There are several options for organizing speeches on questions of policy. If you advocate a change in policy, your main points will often fall naturally into problem-solution order or into problem-cause-solution order. If your audience already agrees that a problem exists, you may be able to use comparative advantages order. Whenever you seek immediate action from listeners, you should consider a more specialized organizational pattern known as Monroe's motivated sequence.

Regardless of your topic or method of organization, you need to make sure your goals are ethically sound and that you use ethical methods to persuade your audience.

Key Terms

persuasion *(300)*
mental dialogue with the audience *(304)*
target audience *(304)*
question of fact *(305)*
question of value *(307)*
question of policy *(309)*
speech to gain passive agreement *(310)*
speech to gain immediate action *(310)*
need *(311)*
burden of proof *(311)*
plan *(311)*
practicality *(312)*
problem-solution order *(313)*
problem-cause-solution order *(314)*
comparative advantages order *(314)*
Monroe's motivated sequence *(315)*

Review Questions

After reading this chapter, you should be able to answer the following questions:

1. What is the difference between an informative speech and a persuasive speech? Why is speaking to persuade more challenging than speaking to inform?
2. What does it mean to say that audiences engage in a mental dialogue with the speaker as they listen to a speech? What implications does this mental give-and-take hold for effective persuasive speaking?
3. What is the target audience for a persuasive speech?
4. What are questions of fact? How does a persuasive speech on a question of fact differ from an informative speech? Give an example of a specific purpose statement for a persuasive speech on a question of fact.
5. What are questions of value? Give an example of a specific purpose statement for a persuasive speech on a question of value.
6. What are questions of policy? Give an example of a specific purpose statement for a persuasive speech on a question of policy.
7. Explain the difference between passive agreement and immediate action as goals for persuasive speeches on questions of policy.
8. What are the three basic issues you must deal with when discussing a question of policy? What will determine the amount of attention you give to each of these issues in any particular speech?
9. What four methods of organization are used most often in persuasive speeches on questions of policy?
10. What are the five steps of Monroe's motivated sequence? Why is the motivated sequence especially useful in speeches that seek immediate action from listeners?

connect™

For further review, go to the LearnSmart study module for this chapter.

Exercises for Critical Thinking

1. Look back at the story of Ramon Trujillo at the beginning of this chapter (page 299). Like Ramon, most people do a certain amount of persuading every day in normal conversation. Keep a journal of your communication activities for an entire day, making special note of all instances in which you tried to persuade someone else to your point of view. Choose one of those instances and prepare a brief analysis of it.

   In your analysis, answer the following questions: (1) Who was the audience for your persuasive effort? (2) What were the "specific purpose" and the "central idea" of your persuasive message? (3) Did you rehearse your persuasive message ahead of time, or did it arise spontaneously from the situation? (4) Were you successful in achieving your specific purpose? (5) If you faced the same situation again, what strategic changes would you make in your persuasive effort?
2. Below are four specific purposes for persuasive speeches. In each case explain whether the speech associated with it concerns a question of fact, a question of

value, or a question of policy. Then rewrite the specific purpose statement to make it appropriate for a speech about one of the other two kinds of questions. For instance, if the original purpose statement is about a question of policy, write a new specific purpose statement that deals with the same topic as either a question of fact or a question of value.

Example:

Original statement: To persuade my audience that it is unfair for judges to favor natural parents over adoptive parents in child custody disputes. (question of value)

Rewritten statement: To persuade my audience that the courts should establish clear guidelines for settling disputes between adoptive parents and natural parents in child custody cases. (question of policy)

a. To persuade my audience that a national sales tax should be adopted to help reduce the national debt.

b. To persuade my audience that it is unethical for doctors to receive money from pharmaceutical companies to promote their products.

c. To persuade my audience that violence in video games is a major cause of violent behavior among teenagers.

d. To persuade my audience to join Teach for America.

3. Choose a topic for a persuasive speech on a question of policy. Create two specific purpose statements about that topic—one for a speech to gain passive agreement, another for a speech to motivate immediate action. Once you have the specific purpose statements, explain how the speech seeking immediate action would differ in structure and persuasive appeals from the speech seeking passive agreement. Be specific.

4. Analyze the sample speech with commentary at the end of this chapter ("Phony Pharmaceuticals," pages 318–320). Because this is a speech on a question of policy, pay special attention to how the speaker deals with the basic issues of need, plan, and practicality. Does the speaker present a convincing case that a serious problem exists? Does she offer a clear plan to solve the problem? Does she demonstrate that the plan is practical?

5. Select a television commercial that is organized according to Monroe's motivated sequence. Prepare a brief analysis in which you (a) identify the target audience for the commercial and (b) describe each step in the motivated sequence as it appears in the commercial.

SHURE

17

Methods of Persuasion

Persuasion is big business. Thousands of authors and consultants promise to teach you the one key secret to persuading people to do what you want. Dan Lok claims to reveal "forbidden psychological tactics" that will "give you an unfair advantage in dealing with people." Chris St. Hilaire offers "simple strategies to seduce audiences and win allies." Kevin Dutton claims to have discovered "a single, definitive formula" for "a mysterious, previously unidentified, superstrain of persuasion." These people all charge thousands of dollars for their seminars, hundreds for videos and motivational books. Companies and individuals flock—and pay—to read and hear what they have to say.

It sounds good, but can any of these people really have the "one key secret" to persuasion? Probably not. Persuasion is too complicated for that. Yet, as the number of books, seminars, and videos on the subject shows, there is a perpetual fascination with the strategies and tactics of effective persuasion.

What makes a speaker persuasive? Why do listeners accept one speaker's views and reject those of another? How can a speaker motivate listeners to act in support of a cause, a campaign, or a candidate? People have been trying to answer these questions for thousands of years—from the ancient Greek philosopher Aristotle to modern-day communication researchers. Although many answers have been given, we can say that listeners will be persuaded by a speaker for one or more of four reasons:

Because they perceive the speaker as having high *credibility.*

Because they are won over by the speaker's *evidence.*

Because they are convinced by the speaker's *reasoning.*

Because their *emotions* are touched by the speaker's ideas or language.

In this chapter we will look at each of these. We will not discover any magical secrets that will make you an irresistible persuasive speaker. But if you learn the principles discussed in this chapter, you will greatly increase your odds of winning the minds and hearts of your listeners.

Building Credibility

Here are two sets of imaginary statements. Which one of each pair would you be more likely to believe?

The U.S. State Department needs major changes in organization to fulfill its mission in the 21st century. (Hillary Clinton)

The State Department does not need any major organizational changes in the near future. (Johnny Depp)

The key to acting is to push your character as far as you can without making the character unbelievable. (Johnny Depp)

The key to acting is to learn your lines and hit your cues regardless of the character you are playing. (Hillary Clinton)

ethos

The name used by Aristotle for what modern students of communication refer to as credibility.

Most likely you chose the first in each pair of statements. If so, you were probably influenced by your perception of the speaker. You are more likely to respect the judgment of Clinton, Secretary of State under President Barack Obama, when she speaks about the organization of the State Department, and to respect the judgment of Depp, acclaimed for his many screen roles, when he speaks about methods of acting. Some teachers call this factor *source credibility.* Others refer to it as *ethos,* the name given by Aristotle.

FACTORS OF CREDIBILITY

Many things affect a speaker's credibility, including sociability, dynamism, physical attractiveness, and perceived similarity between speaker and audience. Above all, though, credibility is affected by two factors:

- *Competence*—how an audience regards a speaker's intelligence, expertise, and knowledge of the subject.
- *Character*—how an audience regards a speaker's sincerity, trustworthiness, and concern for the well-being of the audience.

The more favorably listeners view a speaker's competence and character, the more likely they are to accept what the speaker says. No doubt you are familiar with this from your own experience. Suppose you take a course in economics. The course is taught by a distinguished professor who has published widely in prestigious journals, who sits on a major international commission, and who has won several awards for outstanding research. In class, you hang on this professor's every word. One day the professor is absent; a colleague from the Economics Department—fully qualified but not as well known—comes to lecture instead. Possibly the fill-in instructor gives the same lecture the distinguished professor would have given, but you do not pay nearly as close attention. The other instructor does not have as high credibility as the professor.

credibility

The audience's perception of whether a speaker is qualified to speak on a given topic. The two major factors influencing a speaker's credibility are competence and character.

It is important to remember that credibility is an attitude. It exists not in the speaker, but in the mind of the audience. A speaker may have high credibility for one audience and low credibility for another. A speaker may also have high credibility on one topic and low credibility on another. Looking back to our imaginary statements, most people would more readily believe Johnny Depp speaking about acting than Johnny Depp speaking about the organization of the State Department.

TYPES OF CREDIBILITY

Not only can a speaker's credibility vary from audience to audience and topic to topic, but it can also change during the course of a speech—so much so that we can identify three types of credibility:

- *Initial credibility*—the credibility of the speaker before she or he starts to speak.
- *Derived credibility*—the credibility of the speaker produced by everything she or he says and does during the speech itself.
- *Terminal credibility*—the credibility of the speaker at the end of the speech.[1]

initial credibility

The credibility of a speaker before she or he starts to speak.

derived credibility

The credibility of a speaker produced by everything she or he says and does during the speech.

terminal credibility

The credibility of a speaker at the end of the speech.

All three are dynamic. High initial credibility is a great advantage for any speaker, but it can be destroyed during a speech, resulting in low terminal credibility. The reverse can also occur, as in the following example:

Randall Washington is the information technology manager for a major textbook publisher. Soon after taking the job, he began implementing a new content management system for the company's Web site. He assumed there would be some glitches, but they turned out to be much worse than anything he had imagined. It took nine months to get the new system working properly, and even then people continued to grumble about the confusing interface and unpredictable behavior of the Web site.

A year later, the publishing company decided to purchase new tablet computers that would allow employees to interact more efficiently with data on the internal network. The president of the company asked Randall to take charge of buying the computers and training the staff in their use.

When Randall outlined his plans at a weekly staff meeting, he had low initial credibility. Everyone remembered the content management system, and they were reluctant to go through the same problems again. But Randall realized this and was prepared.

He began by reminding everyone that the president had authorized him to purchase tablet computers that would make their jobs easier and improve office communications. He then acknowledged that he had told them the same thing about the content management system—an admission that drew a laugh and helped everyone relax. Finally, he explained that he had checked with several other companies that used the same devices, and they all reported that the computers worked flawlessly.

Throughout his presentation, Randall's approach was "I know the content management system was a disaster, and I've worked hard to make sure it doesn't happen again." By the time he finished, most staff members were eager to begin using their tablet computers. Randall had achieved high terminal credibility.

In every speech you give you will have some degree of initial credibility, which will be strengthened or weakened by your message and how you deliver it. And your terminal credibility from one speech will affect your initial credibility for the next one. If your audience sees you as sincere and competent, they will be much more receptive to your ideas.

ENHANCING YOUR CREDIBILITY

How can you build your credibility in your speeches? At one level, the answer is frustratingly general. Since everything you say and do in a speech will affect your credibility, you should say and do *everything* in a way that will make you appear capable and trustworthy. In other words—give a brilliant speech and you will achieve high credibility!

The advice is sound, but not all that helpful. There are, however, some specific ways you can boost your credibility while speaking. They include explaining your competence, establishing common ground with the audience, and speaking with genuine conviction.

Explain Your Competence

One way to enhance your credibility is to advertise your expertise on the speech topic. Did you investigate the topic thoroughly? Then say so. Do you have experience that gives you special knowledge or insight? Again, say so.

Here is how two students revealed their qualifications. The first stressed her study and research:

connect

View these excerpts from "Bursting the Antibacterial Bubble" and "Keeping the Safety Net for Those Who Need It" in the online Media Library for this chapter (Video 17.1).

Before I studied antibacterial products in my public-health class, I always used antibacterial soaps and antibacterial all-surface cleaner for my apartment. I also know from my class survey that 70 percent of you use antibacterial soaps, cleaners, or other products. But after learning about the subject in class and reading research studies for this speech, I'm here to tell you that, try as we might, we cannot build a bubble between ourselves and germs with antibacterial products and that these products actually create more problems than they solve.

The second student emphasized her background and personal experience:

Most of us have no idea what it means to be poor and hungry. But before returning to school last year, I spent three years working at local assistance centers. I can't tell you everything I have seen. But on the basis of what I can tell you, I hope you will agree with me that government help for the poor and needy must be maintained.

Both speakers greatly increased their persuasiveness by establishing their credibility.

A speaker's credibility has a powerful impact on how his or her speech is received. One way to boost your credibility is to deliver your speeches expressively and with strong eye contact.

Establish Common Ground with Your Audience

Another way to bolster your credibility is to establish common ground with your audience. You do not persuade listeners by assaulting their values and rejecting their opinions. As the old saying goes, "You catch more flies with honey than with vinegar." The same is true of persuasion. Show respect for your listeners. You can make your speech more appealing by identifying your ideas with those of your audience—by showing how your point of view is consistent with what they believe.[2]

Creating common ground is especially important at the start of a persuasive speech. Begin by identifying with your listeners. Show that you share their values, attitudes, and experiences. Get them nodding their heads in agreement, and they will be much more receptive to your ultimate proposal. Here is how a businesswoman from Massachusetts, hoping to sell her product to an audience in Colorado, began her persuasive speech:

creating common ground

A technique in which a speaker connects himself or herself with the values, attitudes, or experiences of the audience.

> I have never been in Colorado before, but I really looked forward to making this trip. A lot of my ancestors left Massachusetts and came to Colorado nearly 150 years ago. Sometimes I have wondered why they did it. They came in covered wagons, carrying all their possessions, and many of them died on the journey. The ones who got through raised their houses and raised their families. Now that I've seen Colorado, I understand why they tried so hard!

The audience laughed and applauded, and the speaker was off to a good start.

Now look at a different approach, used in a classroom speech favoring a tuition increase at the speaker's school—an unpopular point of view with his classmates. He began by saying:

connect

View this excerpt from "Let's Protect the Quality of Our Education" in the online Media Library for this chapter (Video 17.2).

> As we all know, there are many differences among the people in this class. But regardless of age, major, background, or goals, we all share one thing in common—we're all concerned about the quality of education at this school. And that quality is clearly in danger.
>
> The economic crisis has hit every aspect of life, and education is no exception. Budgets are shrinking, faculty salaries are falling, student services are disappearing,

and we are being crowded out of classes we need to take. Whether we like it or not, we have a problem—a problem that affects each of us.

There are no easy answers, but one thing that will help solve the problem is an increase in tuition. I don't like it any more than you do, but sometimes we have to do what is necessary to protect the quality of our education.

By stressing common perceptions of the problem, the student hoped to get off on the right foot with his audience. Once that was done, he moved gradually to his more controversial ideas.

Deliver Your Speeches Fluently, Expressively, and with Conviction

There is a great deal of research to show that a speaker's credibility is strongly affected by his or her delivery. Moderately fast speakers, for example, are usually seen as more intelligent and confident than slower speakers. So too are speakers who use vocal variety to communicate their ideas in a lively, animated way. On the other hand, speakers who consistently lose their place, hesitate frequently, or pepper their talk with "uh," "er," and "um" are seen as less competent than speakers who are poised and dynamic.[3]

All of this argues for practicing your persuasive speech fully ahead of time so you can deliver it fluently and expressively. In addition to being better prepared, you will take a major step toward enhancing your credibility. (Review Chapter 13 if you have questions about speech delivery.)

Speaking techniques aside, the most important way to strengthen your credibility is to deliver your speeches with genuine conviction. President Harry Truman once said that in speaking, "sincerity, honesty, and a straightforward manner are more important than special talent or polish." If you wish to convince others, you must first convince yourself. If you want others to believe and care about your ideas, you must believe and care about them yourself. Your spirit, enthusiasm, and conviction will carry over to your listeners.

Using Evidence

Evidence consists of supporting materials—examples, statistics, testimony—used to prove or disprove something. As we saw in Chapter 8, most people are skeptical. They are suspicious of unsupported generalizations. They want speakers to justify their claims. If you hope to be persuasive, you must support your views with evidence. Whenever you say something that is open to question, you should give evidence to prove you are right.

evidence

Supporting materials used to prove or disprove something.

Evidence is particularly important in classroom speeches because few students are recognized as experts on their speech topics. Research has shown that speakers with very high initial credibility do not need to use as much evidence as do speakers with lower credibility. For most speakers, though, strong evidence is absolutely necessary. It can enhance your credibility, increase both the immediate and long-term persuasiveness of your message, and help "inoculate" listeners against counterpersuasion.[4]

Evidence is also crucial whenever your target audience opposes your point of view. As we saw in Chapter 16, listeners in such a situation will mentally argue with you—asking questions, raising objections, and creating counterarguments to "answer" what you say. The success of your speech will depend partly on how well you anticipate these internal responses and give evidence to refute them.

You may want to review Chapter 8, which shows how to use supporting materials. The following case study illustrates how they work as evidence in a persuasive speech.

HOW EVIDENCE WORKS: A CASE STUDY

Let's say one of your classmates is talking about the harmful effects of repeated exposure to loud music and other noises. Instead of just telling you what she thinks, the speaker offers strong evidence to prove her point. Notice how she carries on a mental dialogue with her listeners. She imagines what they might be thinking, anticipates their questions and objections, and gives evidence to answer the questions and resolve the objections.

She begins this way:

> As college students we are exposed to loud music and other noise all the time. We go to parties, clubs, and concerts where the volume is so loud we have to shout so the person next to us can hear what we are saying. We turn our iPods so high they can be heard halfway across the room. And we seldom give it a second thought. But we should, because excessive noise can have a serious impact on our health and well-being.

How do you react? If you already know about the problems caused by noise pollution, you probably nod your head in agreement. But what if you don't know? Or don't agree? If you enjoy rock concerts and listening to your iPod at high volumes, you probably don't *want* to hear about it. Certainly you will not be persuaded by a general statement about exposure to loud music. Mentally you say to the speaker, "How do you know? Can you prove it?"

Anticipating just such a response, the speaker gives evidence to support her point:

> The American Medical Association reports that 36 million Americans have some degree of hearing loss, and that 17 million of those cases are caused by too much exposure to loud noise.

"That's unfortunate," you may think. "But everyone loses some hearing as they grow old. Why should I be concerned about it now?" The speaker answers:

> In an alarming trend, more and more victims of noise-induced deafness are adolescents and even younger children. According to the American Academy of Audiology, 12 percent of children in the United States between ages 6 and 19 have some hearing damage from amplified music and other sources. Audiologist Dean Garstecki, head of the hearing-impairment program at Northwestern University, says, "We've got 21-year-olds walking around with hearing-loss patterns of people 40 years their senior."

"These are impressive facts," you say to yourself. "Luckily, I haven't noticed any problems with my hearing. When I do, I'll just be careful until it gets better." Keeping one step ahead of you, the speaker continues:

> The problem with hearing loss is that it creeps up on you. *Sierra* magazine notes that today's hard-rock fans won't notice the effects of their hearing loss for another 15 years. And then it will be too late.

"What do you mean, too late?" you ask mentally. The speaker tells you:

> Unlike some physical conditions, hearing loss is irreversible. Loud noise damages the microscopic hairs in the inner ear that transmit sound to the auditory nerve. Once damaged, those hairs can never recover and can never be repaired.

"I didn't know that," you say to yourself. "Is there anything else?"

> One last point. Repeated exposure to loud music and other noise does more than damage your hearing. The Hearing Loss Association of America reports that excessive noise has been linked to such problems as stress, high blood pressure, chronic headaches, learning disorders, even heart disease. It's easy to see why Jill Lipoti, chief of Rutgers University's Noise Technical Assistance Center, warns that "noise affects more people than any other pollutant."

Now are you convinced? Chances are you will at least think about the possible consequences the next time you are set to pump up the volume on your iPod. Maybe you will use earplugs at a rock concert. You may even begin to reassess your whole attitude toward noise pollution. Why? Because the speaker supported each of her claims with evidence. You should try to do the same in your persuasive speeches.

TIPS FOR USING EVIDENCE

Any of the supporting materials discussed in Chapter 8—examples, statistics, testimony—can work as evidence in a persuasive speech. As we saw in that chapter, there are guidelines for using each kind of supporting material regardless of the kind of speech you are giving. Here we look at four special tips for using evidence in a persuasive speech.

Use Specific Evidence

No matter what kind of evidence you employ—statistics, examples, or testimony—it will be more persuasive if you state it in specific rather than general terms.[5] In the speech about noise pollution, for instance, the speaker did not say, "Lots of people suffer from hearing loss." That would have left the audience wondering how many "lots" amounts to. By saying "36 million Americans have some degree of hearing loss," the speaker made her point much more effectively. She also enhanced her credibility by showing she had a firm grasp of the facts.

Use Novel Evidence

Evidence is more likely to be persuasive if it is new to the audience.[6] You will gain little by citing facts and figures that are already well known to your listeners. If they have not persuaded your listeners already, they will not do so now. You must go beyond what the audience already knows and present striking new evidence that will get them to say, "Hmmm, I didn't know *that.* Maybe I should rethink the issue." Finding such evidence usually requires hard digging and resourceful research, but the rewards are worth the effort.

Use Evidence from Credible Sources

Listeners find evidence from competent, credible sources more persuasive than evidence from less qualified sources.[7] Above all, listeners are suspicious of evidence from sources that appear to be biased or self-interested. In assessing

Persuasive speeches need strong evidence to convince skeptical listeners. Finding the best evidence often takes hard digging, but it is well worth the effort.

the current state of airline safety, for example, they are more likely to be persuaded by testimony from impartial aviation experts than from the president of American Airlines. If you wish to be persuasive, rely on evidence from objective, nonpartisan sources.

Make Clear the Point of Your Evidence

When speaking to persuade, you use evidence to prove a point. Yet you would be surprised how many novice speakers present their evidence without making clear the point it is supposed to prove. A number of studies have shown that you cannot count on listeners to draw, on their own, the conclusion you want them to reach.[8] When using evidence, be sure listeners understand the point you are trying to make.

Notice, for example, how the speaker in Video 17.3 in the online Media Library for this chapter drives home the point of her evidence about the number of motor vehicle fatalities involving teenage drivers:

connect

View this excerpt from "Putting the Brakes on Teenage Driving" in the online Media Library for this chapter (Video 17.3).

> According to the National Highway Traffic Safety Administration, while teenagers make up 7 percent of the nation's licensed drivers, they represent 14 percent of all motor vehicle fatalities. The NHTSA reports that last year 3,657 drivers aged 16 to 20 were killed in automobile accidents. In addition to killing the drivers, these same accidents took the lives of 2,384 teenage passengers. But these accidents didn't affect teenagers alone. They also took the lives of 2,625 people aged 21 or older.
>
> So the total number of people killed last year in automobile accidents involving teenage drivers was 8,666—almost exactly the number of full-time students at this campus.

Evidence is one element of what Aristotle referred to as *logos*—the logical appeal of a speaker. The other major element of logos is reasoning, which works in combination with evidence to help make a speaker's claims persuasive.

logos

The name used by Aristotle for the logical appeal of a speaker. The two major elements of logos are evidence and reasoning.

checklist

Evidence

YES	NO	
☐	☐	1. Are all my major claims supported by evidence?
☐	☐	2. Do I use sufficient evidence to convince my audience of my claims?
☐	☐	3. Is my evidence stated in specific rather than general terms?
☐	☐	4. Do I use evidence that is new to my audience?
☐	☐	5. Is my evidence from credible, unbiased sources?
☐	☐	6. Do I identify the sources of my evidence?
☐	☐	7. Is my evidence clearly linked to each point that it is meant to prove?
☐	☐	8. Do I provide evidence to answer possible objections the audience may have to my position?

Reasoning

The story is told about Hack Wilson, a hard-hitting outfielder for the Brooklyn Dodgers baseball team in the 1930s.[9] Wilson was a great player, but he had a fondness for the good life. His drinking exploits were legendary. He was known to spend the entire night on the town, stagger into the team's hotel at the break of dawn, grab a couple hours sleep, and get to the ballpark just in time for the afternoon game.

This greatly distressed Max Carey, Wilson's manager. At the next team meeting, Carey spent much time explaining the evils of drink. To prove his point, he stood beside a table on which he had placed two glasses and a plate of live angleworms. One glass was filled with water, the other with gin—Wilson's favorite beverage. With a flourish Carey dropped a worm into the glass of water. It wriggled happily. Next Carey plunged the same worm into the gin. It promptly stiffened and expired.

A murmur ran through the room, and some players were obviously impressed. But not Wilson. He didn't even seem interested. Carey waited a little, hoping for some delayed reaction from his wayward slugger. When none came, he prodded, "Do you follow my reasoning, Wilson?"

"Sure, skipper," answered Wilson. "It proves that if you drink gin, you'll never get worms!"

And what does this story prove? No matter how strong your evidence, you will not be persuasive unless listeners grasp your reasoning.

Reasoning is the process of drawing a conclusion based on evidence. Sometimes we reason well—as when we conclude that ice particles forming

Reasoning is an important part of persuasive speaking. In a legal trial, for example, neither the prosecution nor the defense is likely to sway the jury unless their reasoning is clear and convincing.

on the trees may mean the roads will be slippery. Other times we reason less effectively—as when we conclude that spilling salt will bring bad luck. Most superstitions are actually no more than instances of faulty reasoning.

Reasoning in public speaking is an extension of reasoning in other aspects of life. As a public speaker, you have two major concerns with respect to reasoning. First, you must make sure your own reasoning is sound. Second, you must try to get listeners to agree with your reasoning. Let us look, then, at four basic methods of reasoning and how to use them in your speeches.

reasoning

The process of drawing a conclusion on the basis of evidence.

REASONING FROM SPECIFIC INSTANCES

When you reason from specific instances, you progress from a number of particular facts to a general conclusion.[10] For example:

reasoning from specific instances

Reasoning that moves from particular facts to a general conclusion.

Fact 1: My physical education course last term was easy.

Fact 2: My roommate's physical education course was easy.

Fact 3: My brother's physical education course was easy.

Conclusion: Physical education courses are easy.

As this example suggests, we use reasoning from specific instances daily, although we probably don't realize it. Think for a moment of all the general conclusions that arise in conversation: Politicians are corrupt. Professors are bookish. Dorm food is awful. Where do such conclusions come from? They come from observing particular politicians, professors, dormitories, and so on.

The same thing happens in public speaking. The speaker who concludes that unethical banking practices are common in the United States because several major banks have been guilty of fraud in recent years is reasoning from specific instances. So is the speaker who argues that anti-Semitism is increasing on college campuses because there have been a number of attacks on Jewish students and symbols at schools across the nation.

Such conclusions are never foolproof. No matter how many specific instances you give (and you can give only a few in a speech), it is always possible that an exception exists. Throughout the ages people observed countless white swans in Europe without seeing any of a different color. It seemed an undeniable fact that all swans were white. Then, in the 19th century, black swans were discovered in Australia![11]

When you reason from specific instances, beware of jumping to conclusions on the basis of insufficient evidence. Make sure your sample of specific instances is large enough to justify your conclusion.

Also make sure the instances you present are fair, unbiased, and representative. (Are three physical education courses *enough* to conclude that physical education courses in general are easy? Are the three courses *typical* of most physical education courses?)

Finally, reinforce your argument with statistics or testimony. Because you can never give enough specific instances in a speech to make your conclusion irrefutable, you should supplement them with testimony or statistics demonstrating that the instances are representative.

REASONING FROM PRINCIPLE

Reasoning from principle is the opposite of reasoning from specific instances. It moves from the general to the specific.[12] When you reason from principle, you progress from a general principle to a specific conclusion. We are all familiar with this kind of reasoning from statements such as the following:

1. All people are mortal.
2. Socrates is a person.
3. Therefore, Socrates is mortal.

This is a classic example of reasoning from principle. You begin with a general statement ("All people are mortal"), move to a minor premise ("Socrates is a person"), and end with a specific conclusion ("Socrates is mortal").

reasoning from principle

Reasoning that moves from a general principle to a specific conclusion.

Speakers often use reasoning from principle when trying to persuade an audience. One of the clearest examples from American history is Susan B. Anthony's famous speech "Is It a Crime for a U.S. Citizen to Vote?" Delivered on numerous occasions in 1872 and 1873, at a time when women were legally barred from voting, Anthony's speech reasoned along the following lines:

1. The United States Constitution guarantees all U.S. citizens the right to vote.
2. Women are U.S. citizens.
3. Therefore, the United States Constitution guarantees women the right to vote.

This argument progresses from a general principle ("The United States Constitution guarantees all U.S. citizens the right to vote") through a minor premise ("Women are U.S. citizens") to a conclusion ("Therefore, the United States Constitution guarantees women the right to vote").

When you use reasoning from principle in a speech, pay special attention to your general principle. Will listeners accept it without evidence? If not, give evidence to support it before moving to your minor premise. You may also need to support your minor premise with evidence. When both the general principle and the minor premise are soundly based, your audience will be much more likely to accept your conclusion.

CAUSAL REASONING

There is a patch of ice on the sidewalk. You slip, fall, and break your arm. You reason as follows: "*Because* that patch of ice was there, I fell and broke my arm." This is an example of causal reasoning, in which someone tries to establish the relationship between causes and effects.

causal reasoning

Reasoning that seeks to establish the relationship between causes and effects.

As with reasoning from specific instances, we use causal reasoning daily. Something happens and we ask what caused it to happen. We want to know the causes of chronic fatigue syndrome, of the football team's latest defeat, of our roommate's peculiar habits. We also wonder about effects. We speculate about the consequences of chronic fatigue syndrome, of the star quarterback's leg injury, of telling our roommate that a change is needed.

As any scientist (or detective) will tell you, causal reasoning can be tricky. The relationship between causes and effects is not always clear. For example, the fact that one event happens after another does not mean that the first is the cause of the second. The closeness in time of the two events may be entirely coincidental. If a black cat crosses your path and five minutes later you fall and break your arm, you needn't blame your accident on the poor cat.

You also need to beware of assuming that events have only one cause. In fact, most events have several causes. What causes the economy to boom or bust? Interest rates? Gas prices? Tax policy? Labor costs? Consumer confidence? World affairs? *All* these factors—and others—affect the economy. When you use causal reasoning, be wary of the temptation to attribute complex events to single causes.

ANALOGICAL REASONING

When arguing from analogy, a speaker compares two similar cases and infers that what is true for one case is also true for the other: For example:

analogical reasoning

Reasoning in which a speaker compares two similar cases and infers that what is true for the first case is also true for the second.

> If you're good at tennis, you will probably be good at Ping-Pong.

Although playing Ping-Pong is not exactly the same as playing tennis, the two are close enough that the speaker is on firm ground in concluding that being skilled at one significantly increases the odds of being skilled at the other.

Analogical reasoning is used frequently in persuasive speeches—especially when the speaker is dealing with a question of policy. When arguing for a new policy, you should find out whether it has been tried elsewhere. You may be able to claim that your policy will work because it has worked in like circumstances. Here is how one speaker used reasoning from analogy to support her claim that controlling handguns will reduce violent crime in the United States:

> Will my policy work? The experience of foreign countries suggests it will. In England, guns are tightly regulated; even the police are unarmed, and the murder rate is trivial by American standards. Japan has even fewer guns than England, and its crime rate is lower than England's. On the basis of these comparisons, we can conclude that restricting the ownership of guns will control crime and murder rates in America.

By the same token, if you argue against a change in policy, you should check whether the proposed policy—or something like it—has been implemented elsewhere. Here, too, you may be able to support your case by reasoning from analogy—as did one speaker who opposed gun control:

> Advocates of gun control point to foreign countries such as England and Japan to prove their case. But the key to low personal violence in these and other countries is the peaceful character of the people, not gun control laws. Switzerland, for example, has a militia system; more than 1 million automatic rifles and military pistols are sitting at this moment in Swiss homes. Yet Switzerland's murder rate is only 8 percent of ours. In other words, cultural factors are more important than gun control when it comes to violent crime.

As these examples illustrate, argument from analogy can be used on both sides of an issue. You are more likely to persuade your audience if the analogy shows a truly parallel situation.

FALLACIES

fallacy

An error in reasoning.

A fallacy is an error in reasoning. As a speaker, you need to avoid fallacies in your speeches. As a listener, you need to be alert to fallacies in the speeches you hear.

Logicians have identified more than 125 different fallacies. Here we look at 10 that you should guard against.

Hasty Generalization

hasty generalization

A fallacy in which a speaker jumps to a general conclusion on the basis of insufficient evidence.

Hasty generalization is the most common fallacy in reasoning from specific instances. It occurs when a speaker jumps to a conclusion on the basis of too few cases or on the basis of atypical cases. For example:

> Throughout American history, military leaders have always made excellent Presidents. Look at the examples of George Washington, Andrew Jackson, and Dwight Eisenhower.

Washington, Jackson, and Eisenhower are widely regarded as outstanding chief executives, but are these examples enough to conclude that military leaders *always* make excellent Presidents? In fact, they are not. James Buchanan and Ulysses S. Grant were both highly decorated military leaders during the 19th century, but they are usually rated among the nation's worst Presidents. An accurate statement would be:

> Throughout American history, military leaders have sometimes made excellent Presidents—as with Washington, Jackson, and Eisenhower.

This statement is factually correct and avoids the fallacy of hasty generalization.

False Cause

false cause

A fallacy in which a speaker mistakenly assumes that because one event follows another, the first event is the cause of the second.

The fallacy of false cause is often known by its Latin name, *post hoc, ergo propter hoc,* which means "after this, therefore because of this." In other words, the fact that one event occurs after another does not mean that the first is the cause of the second. The closeness in time of the two events may be entirely coincidental—as in this case:

In addition to using evidence to support their ideas, effective persuasive speakers rely on research to help them avoid fallacies that may undermine their credibility and persuasiveness.

> When a team from the NFC wins the Super Bowl, economic growth during the next year is stronger than when a team from the AFC wins the Super Bowl. Therefore, if we want economic growth, we should root for a team from the NFC to win this year's Super Bowl.

There may be a slight correlation between economic growth and which conference wins the Super Bowl, but there is no *causal* connection between the two events. Whether the American economy rises or falls is not dependent on who wins the Super Bowl.

Invalid Analogy

As we saw on pages 337–338, when reasoning from analogy, a speaker concludes that what is true in one case is also true in another. An invalid analogy occurs when the two cases being compared are not essentially alike. For example:

invalid analogy

An analogy in which the two cases being compared are not essentially alike.

> Employees are like nails. Just as nails must be hit on the head to get them to work, so must employees.

This statement is obviously fallacious. No one in his or her right mind can seriously think that employees, which are human beings, can be compared with inanimate objects such as nails.

But what about the following statement:

> In Great Britain, the general election campaign for Prime Minister lasts less than three weeks. Surely we can do the same with the U.S. presidential election.

At first glance, this analogy may seem perfectly sound. But are the British and American political systems enough alike to warrant the conclusion? Not really. The United States is much larger than Great Britain and its party system operates much differently. As a result, the factors that allow Great Britain to conduct campaigns for Prime Minister in less than three weeks are not present in the United States. The analogy is not valid.

As this example suggests, determining whether an analogy is valid or invalid is not always easy, but doing so is important for speakers and listeners alike.

Bandwagon

bandwagon

A fallacy which assumes that because something is popular, it is therefore good, correct, or desirable.

How often have you heard someone say, "It's a great idea—everyone agrees with it"? This is a classic example of the bandwagon fallacy, which assumes that because something is popular, it is therefore good, correct, or desirable.

Much advertising is based on the bandwagon fallacy. The fact that more people use Tylenol than Advil does not prove that Tylenol is a better painkiller. Tylenol's popularity could be due to clever marketing. The question of which product does a better job reducing pain is a medical issue that has nothing to do with popularity.

The bandwagon fallacy is also evident in political speeches. Consider the following statement:

> The governor must be correct in his approach to social policy; after all, the polls show that 60 percent of the people support him.

This statement is fallacious because popular opinion cannot be taken as proof that an idea is right or wrong. Remember, "everyone" used to believe that the world is flat and that space flight is impossible.

Red Herring

red herring

A fallacy that introduces an irrelevant issue to divert attention from the subject under discussion.

The name of this fallacy comes from an old trick used by farmers in England to keep fox hunters and their hounds from galloping through the crops. By dragging a smoked herring with a strong odor along the edge of their fields, the farmers could throw the dogs off track by destroying the scent of the fox.

A speaker who uses a red herring introduces an irrelevant issue in order to divert attention from the subject under discussion. For instance:

> How dare my opponents accuse me of political corruption at a time when we are working to improve the quality of life for all people in the United States.

What does the speaker's concern about the quality of life in the United States have to do with whether he or she is guilty of political corruption? Nothing! It is a red herring used to divert attention away from the real issue.

Ad Hominem

ad hominem

A fallacy that attacks the person rather than dealing with the real issue in dispute.

Latin for "against the man," *ad hominem* refers to the fallacy of attacking the person rather than dealing with the real issue in dispute. For instance:

> The head of the commerce commission has a number of interesting economic proposals, but let's not forget that she comes from a very wealthy family.

By impugning the commissioner's family background rather than dealing with the substance of her economic proposals, the speaker is engaging in an *ad hominem* attack.

Sometimes, of course, a person's character or integrity can be a legitimate issue—as in the case of a police chief who violates the law or a corporate president who swindles stockholders. In such cases, a speaker might well raise questions about the person without being guilty of the *ad hominem* fallacy.

Either-Or

Sometimes referred to as a false dilemma, the either-or fallacy forces listeners to choose between two alternatives when more than two alternatives exist. For example:

> The government must either raise taxes or eliminate services for the poor.

This statement oversimplifies a complex issue by reducing it to a simple either-or choice. Is it true that the only choices are to raise taxes or to eliminate services for the poor? A careful listener might ask, "What about cutting the administrative cost of government or eliminating pork-barrel projects instead?"

You will be more persuasive as a speaker and more perceptive as a listener if you are alert to the either-or fallacy.

either-or

A fallacy that forces listeners to choose between two alternatives when more than two alternatives exist.

Slippery Slope

The slippery slope fallacy takes its name from the image of a boulder rolling uncontrollably down a steep hill. Once the boulder gets started, it can't be stopped until it reaches the bottom.

A speaker who commits the slippery slope fallacy assumes that taking a first step will lead inevitably to a second step and so on down the slope to disaster—as in the following example:

> Now that the TSA is allowed to use full body scanners and invasive pat-downs before letting us through security, it's only a matter of time before they strip-search every man, woman, and child who wants to fly on a plane.

If a speaker claims that taking a first step will lead inevitably to a series of disastrous later steps, he or she needs to provide evidence or reasoning to support the claim. To assume that all the later steps will occur without proving that they will is to commit the slippery slope fallacy.

slippery slope

A fallacy which assumes that taking a first step will lead to subsequent steps that cannot be prevented.

Appeal to Tradition

Appeal to tradition is fallacious when it assumes that something old is automatically better than something new. For example:

> I don't see any reason to abolish the electoral college. It has been around since the adoption of the U.S. Constitution in 1787, and we should keep it as long as the United States continues to exist.

There are good arguments on both sides of the debate over abolishing the electoral college. However, to conclude that the electoral college should be kept forever solely because it has always been a part of the U.S. Constitution commits the fallacy of appeal to tradition.

Just because a practice, an institution, or an idea is old does not automatically make it better. Its value should be based on its contributions to society, not on its age. If tradition were the sole measure of value, we would still have slavery, women would not be able to vote, and people would undergo surgery without anesthesia.

appeal to tradition

A fallacy which assumes that something old is automatically better than something new.

Using public speaking in your CAREER

As the service manager for a local home improvement company, you have been pleased to see your company expand its size and scope, but you don't want that growth to come at the expense of customer service. In particular, you're worried about losing touch with one of the company's key demographics—women, who make up 55 percent of your customer base. To prevent this from happening, you have developed a plan for a range of personalized services targeted at women, including one-on-one teaching of do-it-yourself skills and free in-home consultations.

When you present your plan at a meeting of the company's management team, you listen as one executive argues in opposition. Among his points are the following: (1) If your plan is adopted, customers will expect more and more special services and eventually will demand free installation of flooring and carpeting; (2) Because a majority of the management team opposes your plan, it must not be a good idea; (3) One of your competitors tried a customer service plan specifically for women, but it did not succeed; therefore, your plan is doomed to failure.

In your response to the executive, you will point out the fallacy in each of his points. What are those fallacies?

Appeal to Novelty

appeal to novelty

A fallacy which assumes that something new is automatically better than something old.

The fallacy of appeal to novelty is the opposite of appeal to tradition. Appeal to novelty assumes that because something is new, it is therefore superior to something that is older. For example:

> Our church should adopt the 2011 New International Version of the Bible because it is 400 years newer than the King James Version.

The fact that the New International Version of the Bible is newer than the King James Version (completed in 1611), does not *automatically* make it better. There are many reasons why a church might prefer the New International Version, but the speaker should *explain* those reasons, rather than assuming that one version is better than another simply because it is new.

Advertisers often commit the fallacy of appeal to novelty. They tout their latest products as "new and improved," yet we know from experience that new does not always mean improved. As always, we need to look carefully at the claim and make sure it is based on sound reasoning.[13]

Appealing to Emotions

Effective persuasion often requires emotional appeal. As the Roman rhetorician Quintilian stated, "It is feeling and force of imagination that make us eloquent."[14] By adding "feeling" and the "force of imagination" to your logical arguments, you can become a more compelling persuasive speaker.

WHAT ARE EMOTIONAL APPEALS?

Emotional appeals—what Aristotle referred to as *pathos*—are intended to make listeners feel sad, angry, guilty, afraid, happy, proud, sympathetic, reverent, or the like. These are often appropriate reactions when the question is one of value or policy. As George Campbell wrote in his *Philosophy of Rhetoric,* "When persuasion is the end, passion also must be engaged."[15]

pathos

The name used by Aristotle for what modern students of communication refer to as emotional appeal.

Below is a list of some of the emotions evoked most often by public speakers. Following each emotion are a few examples of subjects that might stir that emotion:

- *Fear*—of serious illness, of natural disasters, of sexual assault, of personal rejection, of economic hardship.
- *Compassion*—for the physically disabled, for battered women, for neglected animals, for starving children, for victims of AIDS.
- *Pride*—in one's country, in one's family, in one's school, in one's ethnic heritage, in one's personal accomplishments.
- *Anger*—at terrorists and their supporters, at business leaders who act unethically, at members of Congress who abuse the public trust, at landlords who exploit student tenants, at vandals and thieves.
- *Guilt*—about not helping people less fortunate than ourselves, about not considering the rights of others, about not doing one's best.
- *Reverence*—for an admired person, for traditions and institutions, for one's deity.

There are many other emotions and many other subjects that might stir them. However, this brief sample should give you an idea of the kinds of emotional appeals you might use to enhance the message of your persuasive speech.

Emotional appeals often make a persuasive speech more compelling. Such appeals should always be used ethically and should not be substituted for facts and logic.

GENERATING EMOTIONAL APPEAL

Use Emotional Language

As we saw in Chapter 12, one way to generate emotional appeal is to use emotion-laden words. Here, for instance, is part of the conclusion from a student speech about the challenges and rewards of working as a community volunteer with young children:

> The promise of America sparkles in the eyes of every child. Their dreams are the glittering dreams of America. When those dreams are dashed, when innocent hopes are betrayed, so are the dreams and hopes of the entire nation. It is our duty—to me, it is a sacred duty—to give all children the chance to learn and grow, to share equally in the American dream of freedom, justice, and opportunity.

The underlined words and phrases have strong emotional power, and in this case they produced the desired effect. Be aware, however, that packing too many emotionally charged words into one part of a speech can call attention to the emotional language itself and undermine its impact. The emotion rests in your audience, not in your words. Even the coldest facts can touch off an emotional response if they strike the right chords in a listener.

Develop Vivid Examples

Often a better approach than relying on emotionally charged language is to let emotional appeal grow naturally out of the content of your speech. The most effective way to do this is with vivid, richly textured examples that pull listeners into the speech.

Here is how one speaker used a vivid example for emotional appeal. She was speaking about the malaria epidemic in Africa. Here is what she might have said, stripping the content of emotional appeal:

> Malaria is one of the biggest problems facing Africa. Many die from it every day. If the rest of the world doesn't help, the malaria epidemic will only get worse.

connect

View this excerpt from "The Tragedy of Malaria" in the online Media Library for this chapter (Video 17.4).

What she actually said went something like this:

> Nathan was only five years old when the fever struck him. At first, no one knew what was wrong. No one knew that parasites inside his body had infected his red blood cells. No one knew those cells were clumping together, choking the flow of blood through his body and damaging his vital organs. No one knew his kidneys would soon fail and seizures would begin. No one knew he would wind up in a coma.
>
> The parasites in Nathan's body came from a mosquito bite, a bite that gave him malaria. And Nathan is not alone. The World Health Organization tells us the horrible truth: In Africa, a child dies from malaria every 30 seconds.

People who listen to a speech like that will not soon forget it. They may well be moved to action—as the speaker intends. The first speech, however, is not nearly as compelling. Listeners may well nod their heads, think to themselves "good idea"—and then forget about it. The story of Nathan and his tragic fate gives the second speech emotional impact and brings it home to listeners in personal terms.

Speak with Sincerity and Conviction

Ronald Reagan was one of the most effective speakers in U.S. history. Even people who disagreed with his political views often found him irresistible. Why? Partly because he seemed to speak with great sincerity and conviction.

What was true for Reagan is true for you as well. The strongest source of emotional power is your conviction and sincerity. All your emotion-laden words and examples are but empty trappings unless *you* feel the emotion yourself. And if you do, your emotion will communicate itself to the audience through everything you say and do—not only through your words, but also through your tone of voice, rate of speech, gestures, and facial expressions.

ETHICS AND EMOTIONAL APPEAL

Much has been written about the ethics of emotional appeal in speechmaking. Some people have taken the extreme position that ethical speakers should avoid emotional appeal entirely. To support this view, they point to speakers who have used emotional appeal to fan the flames of hatred, bigotry, and fanaticism.

There is no question that emotional appeals can be abused by unscrupulous speakers for detestable causes. But emotional appeals can also be wielded by honorable speakers for noble causes—by Winston Churchill to rouse the world against Adolf Hitler and the forces of Nazism, by Martin Luther King to call for racial justice. Few people would question the ethics of emotional appeal in these instances.

Nor is it always possible to draw a sharp line between reason and emotional appeal. Think back to the story of Nathan, the five-year-old boy who was infected with malaria. The story certainly has strong emotional appeal. But is there anything unreasonable about it? Or is it irrational for listeners to respond to it by donating to anti-malarial causes? By the same token, is it illogical to be compassionate for victims of natural disasters? Angered by corporate wrongdoing? Fearful about cutbacks in student aid? Reason and emotion often work hand in hand.

Emotional language and vivid examples can help generate emotional appeal, but neither will be effective unless the speaker talks with genuine sincerity and conviction.

One key to using emotional appeal ethically is to make sure it is appropriate to the speech topic. If you want to move listeners to act on a question of policy, emotional appeals are not only legitimate but perhaps necessary. If you want listeners to do something as a result of your speech, you will probably need to appeal to their hearts as well as to their heads.

On the other hand, emotional appeals are usually inappropriate in a persuasive speech on a question of fact. Here you should deal only in specific information and logic. Suppose someone charges your state governor with illegal campaign activities. If you respond by saying, "I'm sure the charge is false because I have always admired the governor," or "I'm sure the charge is true because I have always disliked the governor," then you are guilty of applying emotional criteria to a purely factual question.

Even when trying to move listeners to action, you should never substitute emotional appeals for evidence and reasoning. You should *always* build your persuasive speech on a firm foundation of facts and logic. This is important not just for ethical reasons, but for practical ones as well. Unless you prove your case, careful listeners will not be stirred by your emotional appeals. You need to build a good case based on reason *and* kindle the emotions of your audience.[16]

When you use emotional appeal, keep in mind the guidelines for ethical speechmaking discussed in Chapter 2. Make sure your goals are ethically sound, that you are honest in what you say, and that you avoid name-calling and other forms of abusive language. In using emotional appeal, as in other respects, your classroom speeches will offer a good testing ground for questions of ethical responsibility.

Sample Speech with Commentary

connect

View "The Dangers of Cell Phones" in the online Media Library for this chapter (Video 17.5).

The following persuasive speech deals with a question of policy and is organized according to Monroe's motivated sequence. As you read the speech, notice how the speaker utilizes the methods of persuasion discussed in this chapter as she moves through each step of the motivated sequence. The speech also provides an excellent example of how a speaker's delivery can enhance his or her credibility and emotional appeal—as you can see by watching Video 17.5 in the online Media Library for this chapter.

The Dangers of Cell Phones

COMMENTARY

The first step in Monroe's motivated sequence is gaining attention, which the speaker does by arousing curiosity about the audience's "constant companion." The heavy use of "you" and "your" also draws the audience into the speech.

SPEECH

It's your constant companion. It's in your pocket, in your bag, in your hands, or against your head. You use it at home, in class, at the gym, before you go to sleep at night and first thing when you wake up in the morning. I'm talking, of course, about your cell phone. According to my class survey, everyone in this room has a cell phone, and all of us use it dozens of times every day.

The speaker's questions keep the audience involved while revealing the topic of the speech. The quotation from Devra Davis, an expert on cell phone radiation, underscores the importance of the topic.

But what if your constant companion is dangerous? What if it's hazardous to your health? Evidence is piling up that long-term use of cell phones can lead to tissue damage, tumors, and even brain cancer. Given that there are well over 4 billion people worldwide using cell phones, we're looking at a problem of potentially staggering magnitude. According to Devra Davis, epidemiologist and author of the 2010 book *Disconnect: The Truth About Cell Phone Radiation,* we may be watching "an epidemic in slow motion."

The speaker establishes her credibility by referring to the research she has done for the speech.

I'd never thought much about the possible perils of cell phones before I saw a CBS News report on the subject earlier this year. But doing extensive research for this speech made me realize that cell phones do in fact pose a danger to our health.

By stating that she is not arguing against cell phones in general, the speaker encourages the audience to listen with an open mind. She ends the introduction with a transition to the body of her speech.

Now, don't worry, I'm not going to try to persuade you to abandon your constant companion. I still use mine on a regular basis, and I probably always will. But I do hope to persuade you to make one simple change in the way you use your cell phone—a change that will protect your health and could even make the difference between a long life and premature death. But first, let's look more closely at the health risks posed by cell phones.

The speaker moves into the need step of Monroe's motivated sequence. She makes clear that she will focus on the long-term dangers of cell phone radiation.

Those risks stem from the fact that cell phones emit small amounts of radiation that, over time, can damage tissue. Every time you use your cell phone, you expose yourself to that radiation. The amount is miniscule in comparison to that given off by x-ray machines—about one one-billionth of the intensity. However, Ronald Herberman of the University of Pittsburgh Cancer Institute explains that the problem with cell phone radiation is not how much is emitted at a single time, but how much we are exposed to with repeated use day after day, year after year.

Because most listeners were skeptical about the dangers of cell phones, the speaker cites high-quality sources to show how harmful heavy cell phone use can be. As in other parts of the speech, she clearly identifies each source.

It's this long-term use of cell phones that has led researchers to warn about their danger. In one study, for example, the World Health Organization tracked 10,000 cell phone users over the course of 10 years. As reported in the *New York Times* on November 13, 2010, the data in this study indicated that subjects who used a cell phone 10 or more years doubled the risk of developing brain tumors.

This paragraph builds upon the previous one and presents additional evidence about the dangers of prolonged cell phone use.

Other studies have reached the same conclusion. Perhaps most important is a study in the *Journal of Occupational and Environmental Medicine* that surveyed all the previous research on cell phone use. It found "a consistent pattern of increased risk" for developing brain tumors among people who used cell phones for more than 10 years.

A vivid example reinforces the statistics and testimony cited in the previous paragraphs.

Alan Marks is one of those people. A 58-year-old real estate developer and father of three, he talked on his cell phone an hour a day for 23 years. Two years ago, doctors found a golf-ball-sized tumor in his brain. "There's no question what caused it," he says. "It was my cell phone."

The speaker cites evidence to show that the example of Alan Marks is not atypical.

And Alan Marks isn't the only person to conclude that he's sick because of his cell phone. Ann Gittleman's 2010 book *Zapped,* which deals at length with the health problems of cell phones, catalogues people who developed blinding headaches, dizziness, circulatory problems, nausea, and cancer from the kind of radiation emitted by cell phones.

By citing the usage guidelines provided by cell phone makers themselves, the speaker seeks to dispel any remaining skepticism about cell phone radiation.

Still not convinced about the potential dangers posed by your constant companion? Take a look, then, inside the thick manual that comes with your phone. You'll see that all cell phone manufacturers warn against keeping the phone right next to your body. Apple, for example, recommends keeping the iPhone five-eighths of an inch away from your body. Makers of the BlackBerry recommend that you keep their phone a full inch away. Cell phone manufacturers don't publicize this information widely, but they clearly recognize that their products are potentially hazardous.

This paragraph begins with a transition into the satisfaction section of the speech. As you can see from the video, the speaker's delivery is extemporaneous, personable, and conversational.

So what's the solution? As I said earlier, it's not to stop using cell phones altogether. I still use mine on a regular basis, and I can't imagine being without it—and I'm sure you can't imagine being without yours. You can, however, take seriously the risks of cell phones and find a way to minimize those risks. Time and again, experts point out that the single most effective way to reduce the risk is not to press your cell phone against your head while using it. Since the phone emits radiation, the closer you put it to your head, the more radiation you expose yourself to.

Here the speaker states the key element in her plan. She enhances her credibility by noting that she follows the plan when using her own phone.

At the very least, you should hold the phone one-half an inch to one full inch away from your ear. But ideally, you should get in the habit of not putting it up to your head at all. I now use my earbuds almost every time I use my phone. Another option is to use your speakerphone.

Having explained her plan, the speaker moves into the visualization section. Returning to the example of Alan Marks gives the speech a sense of unity. The quotation from Marks is highly effective.

As with breaking any habit, changing the way you talk on your cell phone may be slightly inconvenient at first but will soon become second nature. You'll be able to enjoy all the benefits of your constant companion without suffering the fate of Alan Marks. If Marks had known the dangers of prolonged cell phone use, he would have done things a lot differently. "I wouldn't have held it to my head," he says. "I would have used the headset. I would have used the speakerphone. . . . And I would not have had the problems I had."

The speaker begins the action section of her speech. Once again, she relates to the audience by using "you" and your."

So please get in the habit of keeping your cell phone away from your ear when talking, and encourage your friends and family to do the same. Start today, with your next phone call, and continue every day in the future.

As you can see from the video of this speech, the speaker ends by holding her cell phone to her head. This visually reinforces the central idea and makes for a dramatic ending.

We can avoid the slow-motion epidemic that doctors and scientists are warning us about—as long as we remember to keep this away from this.

Summary

Listeners accept a speaker's ideas for one or more of four reasons—because they perceive the speaker as having high credibility, because they are won over by the speaker's evidence, because they are convinced by the speaker's reasoning, or because they are moved by the speaker's emotional appeals.

Credibility is affected by many factors, but the two most important are competence and character. The more favorably listeners view a speaker's competence and character, the more likely they are to accept her or his ideas. Although credibility is partly a matter of reputation, you can enhance your credibility during a speech by establishing common ground with your listeners, by letting them know why you are qualified to speak on the topic, and by presenting your ideas fluently and expressively.

If you hope to be persuasive, you must also support your views with evidence—examples, statistics, and testimony. Regardless of what kind of evidence you use, it will be more persuasive if it is new to the audience, stated in specific rather than general terms, and from credible sources. Your evidence will also be more persuasive if you state explicitly the point it is supposed to prove.

No matter how strong your evidence, you will not be persuasive unless listeners agree with your reasoning. In reasoning from specific instances, you move from a number of particular facts to a general conclusion. Reasoning from principle is the reverse—you move from a general principle to a particular conclusion. When you use causal reasoning, you try to establish a relationship between causes and effects. In analogical reasoning, you compare two cases and infer that what is true for one is also true for the other.

Whatever kind of reasoning you use, avoid fallacies such as hasty generalization, false cause, invalid analogy, appeal to tradition, and appeal to novelty. You should also be on guard against the red herring, slippery slope, bandwagon, *ad hominem,* and either-or fallacies.

Finally, you can persuade your listeners by appealing to their emotions. One way to generate emotional appeal is by using emotion-laden language. Another is to develop vivid, richly textured examples. Neither, however, will be effective unless you feel the emotion yourself and communicate it by speaking with sincerity and conviction.

As with other methods of persuasion, your use of emotional appeal should be guided by a firm ethical rudder. Although emotional appeals are usually inappropriate in speeches on questions of fact, they are legitimate—and often necessary—in speeches that seek immediate action on questions of policy. Even when trying to move listeners to action, however, you should never substitute emotional appeals for evidence and reasoning.

Key Terms

ethos *(326)*
credibility *(327)*
initial credibility *(327)*
derived credibility *(327)*
terminal credibility *(327)*
creating common ground *(329)*
evidence *(330)*
logos *(333)*
reasoning *(335)*
reasoning from specific instances *(335)*
reasoning from principle *(336)*
causal reasoning *(337)*
analogical reasoning *(337)*
fallacy *(338)*
hasty generalization *(338)*
false cause *(338)*
invalid analogy *(339)*
bandwagon *(340)*
red herring *(340)*
ad hominem (340)
either-or *(341)*
slippery slope *(341)*
appeal to tradition *(341)*
appeal to novelty *(342)*
pathos *(343)*

Review Questions

After reading this chapter, you should be able to answer the following questions:

1. What is credibility? What two factors exert the most influence on an audience's perception of a speaker's credibility?
2. What are the differences among initial credibility, derived credibility, and terminal credibility?
3. What are three ways you can enhance your credibility during your speeches?
4. What is evidence? Why do persuasive speakers need to use evidence?
5. What are four tips for using evidence effectively in a persuasive speech?
6. What is reasoning from specific instances? Why is it important to supplement reasoning from specific instances with testimony or statistics?
7. What is reasoning from principle? How is it different from reasoning from specific instances?
8. What is causal reasoning? Why is the relationship between causes and effects not always clear?
9. What is analogical reasoning? Why is analogical reasoning frequently used in persuasive speeches on questions of policy?
10. What are the ten logical fallacies discussed in this chapter?
11. What is the role of emotional appeal in persuasive speaking? Identify three methods you can use to generate emotional appeal in your speeches.

connect

For further review, go to the LearnSmart study module for this chapter.

Exercises for Critical Thinking

1. Research has shown that a speaker's initial credibility can have great impact on how the speaker's ideas are received by listeners. Research has also shown that a speaker's credibility will vary from topic to topic and audience to audience. In the left-hand column below is a list of well-known public figures. In the right-hand column is a list of potential speech topics. Assume that each speaker will be addressing your speech class.

   For each speaker, identify the topic in the right-hand column on which she or he would have the highest initial credibility for your class. Then explain how the speaker's initial credibility might be affected if the speaker were discussing the topic in the right-hand column directly across from her or his name.

Speaker	**Topic**
Hillary Clinton	Life in the NFL
Jon Stewart	The Future of Social Networking
Mark Zuckerberg	Pop Music and the Cult of Celebrity
Lady Gaga	Diplomacy in the 21st Century
Peyton Manning	The Comedy of Politics

2. Identify the kind of reasoning used in each of the following statements. What weaknesses, if any, can you find in the reasoning of each?
   a. According to a study by the American Medical Association, men with bald spots have three times the risk of heart attack as men with a full head of hair. Strange as it may seem, it looks as if baldness is a cause of heart attacks.
   b. We can see from its work all around the world that Women for Women International is a worthy charitable organization. It has helped women in Rwanda operate sewing machines and make clothing. It has given women in Kosovo the skills to operate businesses in their communities. It has shown women in the Democratic Republic of Congo how to create and market ceramics.
   c. The United States Constitution guarantees all citizens the right to bear arms. Gun control legislation infringes on the right of citizens to bear arms. Therefore, gun control legislation is contrary to the Constitution.
   d. Almost every industrialized nation in the world except for the United States has a national curriculum and national tests to help ensure that schools throughout the country are meeting high standards of education. If such a system can work elsewhere, it can work in the United States.
3. Over the years there has been much debate about the role of emotional appeal in public speaking. Do you believe it is ethical for public speakers to use emotional appeals when seeking to persuade an audience? Do you feel there are certain kinds of emotions to which an ethical speaker should not appeal? Why or why not? Be prepared to explain your ideas in class.
4. Analyze "The Horrors of Puppy Mills" in the appendix of sample speeches that follows Chapter 19 (pages A7–A9). Pay special attention to the speaker's credibility, evidence, reasoning, and emotional appeal. View the video of the speech in the online Media Library for this chapter so you can also assess the speaker's delivery and use of visual aids.

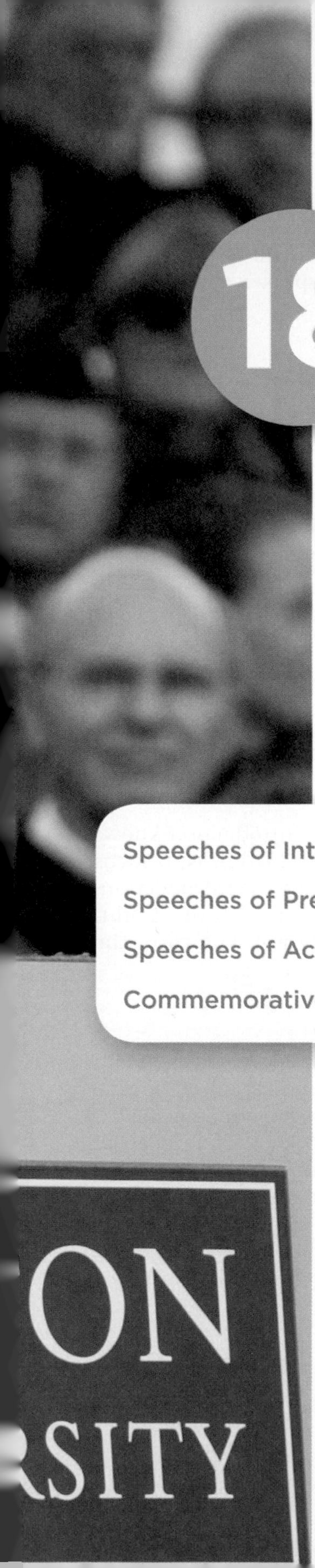

18

Speaking on Special Occasions

- Speeches of Introduction
- Speeches of Presentation
- Speeches of Acceptance
- Commemorative Speeches

Special occasions are the punctuation marks of day-to-day life, the high points that stand out above ordinary routine. Christenings, weddings, funerals, graduations, award ceremonies, inaugurals, retirement dinners—all these are occasions, and they are very special to the people who take part in them. Nearly always they are occasions for speechmaking. A close friend proposes a toast to the bride and groom; the sales manager presents an award to the sales representative of the year; a family member delivers a moving eulogy to the deceased. These speeches help give the occasion its "specialness." They are part of the ceremonial aura that marks the event.

Speeches for special occasions are different from the speeches we have considered so far in this book. They may convey information or persuade, but that is not their primary purpose. Rather, they aim to fit the special needs of a special occasion. In this chapter we look at the most common special occasions and the kinds of speeches appropriate for each.

Speeches of Introduction

speech of introduction

A speech that introduces the main speaker to the audience.

"Distinguished guests, the President of the United States." If you are ever in a situation in which you have to introduce the President, you will need no more than the eight words that begin this paragraph. The President is so well known that any further remarks would be inappropriate and almost foolish.

Most of the time, however, a speech of introduction will be neither this brief nor this ritualized. If you are introducing another speaker, you will need to accomplish three purposes in your introduction:

Build enthusiasm for the upcoming speaker.

Build enthusiasm for the speaker's topic.

Establish a welcoming climate that will boost the speaker's credibility.

A good speech of introduction can be a delight to hear and can ease the task of the main speaker. Usually you will say something about the speaker and the topic—in that order. Following are some guidelines for speeches of introduction.

Be Brief

During World War I, Lord Balfour, Great Britain's foreign secretary, was to be the main speaker at a rally in the United States. But the speaker introducing him gave a 45-minute oration on the causes of the war. Then, almost as an afterthought, he said, "Now Lord Balfour will give his address." Lord Balfour rose and said, "I'm supposed to give my address in the brief time remaining. Here it is: 10 Carleton Gardens, London, England."[1]

Everyone who has ever sat through a long-winded introduction knows how dreary it can be. The purpose of a speech of introduction is to focus attention on the main speaker, not on the person making the introduction. A speech of introduction will usually be no more than two to three minutes long, and may be shorter if the speaker is already well known to the audience.

Make Sure Your Remarks Are Completely Accurate

Many an introducer has embarrassed himself or herself, as well as the main speaker, by garbling basic facts. Always check with the speaker ahead of time to make sure your introduction is accurate in every respect.

Above all, get the speaker's name right. If the speaker's name is at all difficult—especially if it involves a foreign pronunciation—practice saying it in advance. However, don't practice so much that you frighten yourself about getting it wrong. This was the plight of an announcer whose gaffe is now a classic: "Ladies and gentlemen, the President of the United States—Hoobert Heever!"

Adapt Your Remarks to the Occasion

In preparing your introduction, you may be constrained by the nature of the occasion. Formal occasions require formal speeches of introduction. If you were presenting a guest speaker at an informal business meeting, you might be much more casual than at a formal banquet.

Adapt Your Remarks to the Main Speaker

No matter how well it is received by the audience, a speech of introduction that leaves the main speaker feeling uncomfortable has failed in part of its purpose. How can you make a main speaker uncomfortable? One way is to overpraise the person—especially for his or her speaking skills. Never say, "Our speaker will keep you on the edge of your seat from beginning to end!" You create a set of expectations that are almost impossible to fulfill.

Another way to create discomfort is by revealing embarrassing details of the speaker's personal life or by making remarks that are in poor taste. An introducer may think this line is funny: "Why, I've known Anita Fratello since she was 10 years old and so fat that everybody called her Blimpo!" To the speaker, however, the statement will probably not be a bit funny and may be painful.

Adapt Your Remarks to the Audience

Just as you adapt other speeches to particular audiences, so you need to adapt a speech of introduction to the audience you are facing. Your aim is to make *this* audience want to hear *this* speaker on *this* subject. If the speaker is not well known to the audience, you will need to establish her or his credibility by recounting some of the speaker's main achievements and explaining why she or he is qualified to speak on the topic at hand. But if the speaker is already personally known to the audience, it would be absurd to act as if the audience had never heard of the person.

Also, you will want to tell each audience what *it* wants to hear—to give the kind of information that is interesting and accessible to the members of that audience. If you were introducing the same speaker to two different groups, some of the information in the speeches of introduction might be the same, but it would be slanted differently.

Suppose, for example, that J. K. Rowling, author of the Harry Potter series, is going to address two groups—an audience of elementary-school children and an audience of educators at the International Reading Association. The introduction to the schoolchildren might go like this:

> Children, we have a very important guest today. You know her by the character she has created—Harry Potter. What you don't know is all the hard work that goes into writing the books that we all love to read. Today she is going to tell us how she came up with the idea of Harry Potter and his friends and how she goes about writing her books. Let's give a big round of applause to J. K. Rowling.

But the introduction to the International Reading Association would be along these lines:

> Ladies and gentlemen, it is my privilege to introduce to you today the world's best-selling author. We are all well acquainted with her Harry Potter series that has captured the imagination of children—and more than a few adults—around the globe.
>
> Many of us know the remarkable story of her writing life: The inspiration for Harry Potter came on a train ride from Manchester to London in 1990. Over the next few years, she compiled notes as the story took shape in her mind. The bulk of the writing took place when she was a single mother on public assistance in

Edinburgh. She was teaching French to teenagers in the mid-1990s when she heard that the first Harry Potter book had been accepted for publication. The rest is literary history.

She will be telling us this afternoon more about what inspired her fascinating story of wizardry, where she gets her ideas, and what kinds of books she wants to write next. Please give a warm welcome to J. K. Rowling.

Try to Create a Sense of Anticipation and Drama

You may have noticed one detail shared by the two speeches introducing J. K. Rowling: In both cases the speaker's name was saved for last. This is a convention in speeches of introduction. While there may occasionally be a good reason to break the convention, usually you will avoid mentioning the speaker's name until the final moment—even when the audience knows exactly whom you are discussing. By doing this you build a sense of drama, and the speaker's name comes as the climax of your introduction.

Often you will find yourself in the situation of introducing someone who is fairly well known to the audience—a classmate, a colleague at a business meeting, a neighbor in a community group. Then you should try to be creative and cast the speaker in a new light. Talk to the speaker beforehand and see if you can learn some interesting facts that are not generally known—especially facts that relate to the speaker's topic.

Above all, if you expect to be creative and dramatic, be sure to practice your speech of introduction thoroughly. You should be able to deliver it extemporaneously, with sincerity and enthusiasm.

Speeches of Presentation

Speeches of presentation are given when someone receives a gift, an award, or some other form of public recognition. Usually such speeches are brief. They may be no more than a mere announcement ("And the winner is . . .") or be up to four or five minutes in length.

speech of presentation

A speech that presents someone a gift, an award, or some other form of public recognition.

The main purpose of a speech of presentation is to tell the audience why the recipient is receiving the award. Point out his or her contributions, achievements, and so forth. Do not deal with everything the person has ever done. Focus on achievements related to the award, and discuss these achievements in a way that will make them meaningful to the audience.

Depending on the audience and the occasion, you may also need to discuss two other matters in a speech of presentation. First, if the audience is not familiar with the award, you should explain it briefly. Second, if the award was won in a public competition and the audience knows who the losers are, you might take a moment to praise the losers.

On page 357 is a sample speech of presentation. It was delivered by President Bill Clinton in presenting the Congressional Gold Medal to former South African President Nelson Mandela at a ceremony in the Rotunda of the United States Capitol in Washington, D.C. Because the Congressional Gold Medal is a special honor bestowed by the U.S. Congress, there are no public competitors for the award. Thus Clinton did not need to say anything about the "losers." His speech focused on Mandela's battle against apartheid and his efforts to promote reconciliation among the people of South Africa.

PRESENTING THE CONGRESSIONAL GOLD MEDAL

Bill Clinton

To my friend, President Mandela, Americans as one today, across all the lines that divide us, pay tribute to your struggle, to your achievement, and to the inspiration you have given us to do better. Today we offer a man who has received the Nobel Prize the highest honor within the gift of this country. . . .

Those of us who share his vision and lift him up in honor today owe it to him to build a permanent partnership between Americans and Africans—for the education of our children, for the solution of our problems, for the resolution of our differences, for the elevation of what is best about us all. . . .

In forgiving those who imprisoned him, he reminded us of the most fundamental lesson of all—that in the end apartheid was a defeat of the heart, the mind, the spirit. It was not just a structure outside and jail houses within which people were kept; it was a division of the mind and soul against itself. We owe it to Nelson Mandela not simply to give him this award, but to live by the lesson he taught us and to tear down every last vestige of apartheid in our own hearts—everything that divides us, one from another.

For those of us who have been privileged to know this remarkable man, no medal, no award, no fortune, nothing we could give him could possibly compare to the gift he has given to us and to the world. The only gift that is true recompense is to continue his mission and to live by the power of his profound and wonderful example.

Now, as prescribed by the law, it is my privilege to present the Congressional Gold Medal to President Nelson Mandela.

Speeches for special occasions are part of the ceremonial aura that makes certain events special, as in these remarks by Army Staff Sergeant Salvatore A. Giunta receiving the Congressional Medal of Honor.

Speeches of Acceptance

acceptance speech

A speech that gives thanks for a gift, an award, or some other form of public recognition.

The purpose of an acceptance speech is to give thanks for a gift or an award. When giving such a speech, you thank the people who are bestowing the award and recognize the people who helped you gain it.

The acceptance speech below is the companion piece to the speech of presentation by Bill Clinton. It was delivered by Nelson Mandela in accepting the Congressional Gold Medal, and it exemplifies the major traits of a good acceptance speech—brevity, humility, and graciousness.[2]

connect

View an excerpt from Nelson Mandela's acceptance speech in the online Media Library for this chapter (Video 18.1).

ACCEPTING THE CONGRESSIONAL GOLD MEDAL

Nelson Mandela

Thank you. President Clinton, Mr. Speaker, distinguished members of the Senate and the House, ladies and gentlemen. . . .

It has been my great privilege to serve a people whose bondage to an inhuman system evoked the solidarity of all those who love freedom and justice, a people whose triumph over the divisions of racist doctrine has given new life to humanity's hope for a world without hatred and discrimination. I am conscious that in bestowing the Congressional Gold Medal upon me you are evoking these bonds between our nations and paying tribute to the whole South African nation for its achievements in realizing our shared ideals.

It is in that spirit that I humbly accept the award, aware at the same time of the great honor you do me by using me as the vehicle of a unique distinction conferred by this hallowed institution of American democracy. As one who has dedicated his life to the pursuit of unity, I am moved by the consensus in your nation's regard for the achievements of my people. And I feel a great pride in the fact that with a few citizens of other countries who have received this high honor, the name of an African is now added. . . .

The award with which you honor me today is an expression of the common humanity that binds us, one person to another, nation to nation, and people of the north to people of the south. I receive it with pride as a symbol of partnership for peace, prosperity, and equity as we enter the new millennium. I thank you.

Commemorative Speeches

Commemorative speeches are speeches of praise or celebration. Eulogies, Fourth of July speeches, and dedications are examples of commemorative speeches. Your aim in such speeches is to pay tribute to a person, a group of people, an institution, or an idea.

As in an informative speech, you probably will have to give the audience information about your subject. After all, the audience must know *why* your subject is praiseworthy. As in other speeches, you may draw on examples, testimony, even statistics to illustrate the achievements of your subject.

Your fundamental purpose in a commemorative speech, however, is not to inform your listeners but to *inspire* them—to arouse and heighten their appreciation of or admiration for the person, institution, or idea you are praising. If you are paying tribute to a person, for example, you should not simply recount the details of the person's life. Rather, you should penetrate to the *essence* of your subject and generate in your audience a deep sense of respect.

When speaking to commemorate, you want to express feelings, to stir sentiments—joy and hope when a new building is dedicated, anticipation and good wishes at a commencement celebration, lament and consolation at a funeral, admiration and respect at a testimonial dinner. A commemorative speech is like an impressionist painting—"a picture with warm colors and texture capturing a mood or a moment."[3]

But while the painter works with brush and colors, the commemorative speaker works with language. Of all the kinds of speeches, none depends more on the creative and subtle use of language. Some of the most memorable speeches in history, including Abraham Lincoln's Gettysburg Address, have been commemorative. We continue to find such speeches meaningful and inspiring largely because of their eloquent use of language.

One of the most effective commemorative speakers in recent history was President Ronald Reagan. After the explosion of the space shuttle *Challenger* in 1986, Reagan delivered a nationally televised eulogy to the astronauts killed in the blast. Below are two versions of Reagan's closing lines. The first is what he *might* have said, stripping the text of its warm emotional content and poignant language:

> Like Francis Drake, the great explorer of the oceans, the *Challenger* astronauts gave their lives for a cause to which they were fully dedicated. We are honored by them, and we will not forget them. We will always remember seeing them for the last time this morning as they prepared for their flight.

Here is what Reagan *actually* said:

> There's a coincidence today. On this day 390 years ago, the great explorer Francis Drake died aboard ship off the coast of Panama. In his lifetime the great frontiers were the oceans, and an historian later said, "He lived by the sea, died on it, was buried in it." Well, today we can say of the *Challenger* crew: Their dedication was, like Drake's, complete.
>
> The crew of the space shuttle *Challenger* honored us by the manner in which they lived their lives. We will never forget them, nor the last time we saw them, this morning, as they prepared for their journey and waved goodbye and "slipped the surly bonds of earth" to "touch the face of God."

connect

View the ending of Ronald Reagan's eulogy to the *Challenger* astronauts in the online Media Library for this chapter (Video 18.2).

The final words—"'slipped the surly bonds of earth' to 'touch the face of God'"—are especially effective. Drawn from a sonnet called "High Flight" that many pilots keep with them, they ennoble the deaths of the astronauts and end the speech on an eloquent, moving, and poetic note.

When speaking to commemorate, your success will depend on your ability to put into language the thoughts and emotions appropriate to the occasion. It is easy—too easy—to fall back on clichés and trite sentiments. Your challenge will be to use language imaginatively to invest the occasion with dignity, meaning, and honest emotion.

commemorative speech

A speech that pays tribute to a person, a group of people, an institution, or an idea.

In doing so, you may want to utilize the special resources of language discussed in Chapter 12. Metaphor, simile, parallelism, repetition, antithesis, alliteration—all are appropriate for commemorative speeches. Some highly acclaimed commemorative speeches—including Martin Luther King's "I Have a Dream" and John Kennedy's inaugural address—are distinguished by their creative use of such devices.

Confronted with the evocative speeches of a Kennedy or a King, you may decide that the speech of commemoration is far beyond your abilities. But other students have delivered excellent commemorative speeches—not immortal, perhaps, but nonetheless dignified and moving.

Look, for example, at "My Crazy Aunt Sue" in the appendix of sample speeches that follows Chapter 19. The speaker's aim was to pay tribute to her aunt, who for years had battled rheumatoid arthritis. Although the speaker provides basic information about aunt Sue and her physical condition, the speech does not recount all the details of her life. Instead, it focuses on her courage, her sense of humor, and her refusal to complain about her fate. The speaker provides enough details to let us see why aunt Sue is so commendable, but not so many as to slow the pace of the speech.

The speaker also uses vivid language, repetition, and parallel structure to give the speech the kind of formal tone appropriate for a commemorative speech. You can see this even in the opening lines:

connect

View "My Crazy Aunt Sue" in the online Media Library for this chapter (Video 18.3).

> The strongest person I know cannot peel a potato. The strongest person I know has trouble putting on her makeup. The strongest person I know needs a special key holder to turn the key in her car's ignition.

In addition to arousing curiosity about the subject of the speech, these lines have a simple elegance that comes partly from the repetition of "The strongest person I know" at the start of each sentence. Consider, in contrast, how much less effective the opening would have been if the speaker had said:

> My aunt Sue can't peel a potato, has trouble putting on her makeup, and needs a special key holder to turn the key in her car's ignition.

These lines convey the same information, but not with the same effect.

For another example, consider the student commemorative speech printed on page 361. The subject is Elie Wiesel—humanitarian, Nobel Peace Prize winner, and tireless campaigner for international justice. Notice how the speaker uses the repetition of "A-7713" to capture attention at the beginning and to give the speech artistic unity at the end. Also notice how he tells us enough about Wiesel to know why he is praiseworthy without getting bogged down in biographical details.

ELIE WIESEL

A-7713. His new name, the graffiti stamped on his skin. A-7713, a concentration camp tattoo. At age fifteen, A-7713 was taken from his home by the Nazis and sent to Auschwitz, one of the twentieth century's most potent symbols of evil. Here A-7713 witnessed the deaths of thousands of human beings, including his mother and younger sister. Somehow, A-7713 survived, and when World War II ended, he put his pain and grief to work making sure the world did not forget the Holocaust and making sure another Holocaust did not take place.

Today, the world knows A-7713 as Elie Wiesel, noted speaker and lecturer, author of more than 40 books, and recipient of the Presidential Medal of Freedom, the Congressional Gold Medal, and the Nobel Peace Prize, among others. Elie Wiesel is an eloquent, fearless, selfless leader who took the evils of Auschwitz as motivation to improve the world.

An eloquent leader, Elie Wiesel uses the power of language to confront the problems of humanity. Through compelling prose and brutal honesty, he explains that we cannot root out evil unless we recognize it and battle it wherever it exists. In his classic book, *Night,* he says of Auschwitz: "Never shall I forget that night, the first night in camp, which turned my life into one long night, seven times cursed and seven times sealed. Never shall I forget that smoke. Never shall I forget the little faces of the children, whose bodies I saw turned into wreaths of smoke beneath a silent blue sky." Haunting words that remind us of the reality of evil.

A fearless leader no less than an eloquent one, Elie Wiesel has spent 40 years battling the evils that continue to plague our planet. To the Miskito Indians of Nicaragua, displaced from their homeland, he brought inspiring words of strength and compassion. To men and women facing apartheid in South Africa, he brought a powerful denunciation of racial segregation and violence. To Cambodian refugees suffering from starvation and disease, he brought food and the promise of a new beginning. And to those of us who follow his work, he continues to provide inspiration.

A selfless leader as much as an eloquent and fearless one, Elie Wiesel has consistently put the needs of others before his own. With every award, his modesty stands side by side with his achievements. As he stated in his Nobel Prize acceptance speech, "Neutrality helps the oppressor, never the victim. Silence encourages the tormentor, never the tormented. . . . Wherever men and women are persecuted because of their race, religion, or political views, that place must—at that moment—become the center of the universe."

Today, at 80 years of age, Elie Wiesel continues to fight against the night. Through all his trials and all his triumphs, the tattoo remains: A-7713, a constant reminder of evil, injustice, and indifference. In battling these forces, Elie Wiesel has shown the kind of moral leadership too often lacking in today's world.

There is no better way to conclude than to quote his own words: "There may be times when we are powerless to prevent injustice, but there must never be a time when we fail to protest. . . . What these victims need above all is to know that they are not alone, that we are not forgetting them, that while their freedom depends on ours, the quality of our freedom depends on theirs."

connect™

View "Elie Wiesel" in the online Media Library for this chapter (Video 18.4).

Summary

In this chapter we have considered speeches of introduction, speeches of presentation, speeches of acceptance, and commemorative speeches.

Your job in a speech of introduction is to build enthusiasm for the main speaker and to establish a welcoming climate. Keep your remarks brief, make sure they are accurate, and adapt them to the audience, the occasion, and the main speaker.

Speeches of presentation are given when someone receives a gift or an award. The main theme of such a speech is to acknowledge the achievements of the recipient. The purpose of an acceptance speech is to give thanks for a gift or an award. When delivering such a speech, you should thank the people who are bestowing the award and recognize the contributions of people who helped you gain it. Be brief, humble, and gracious.

Commemorative speeches are speeches of praise or celebration. Your aim in such a speech is to pay tribute to a person, a group of people, an institution, or an idea. A commemorative speech should inspire the audience, and its success will depend largely on how well you put into language the thoughts and feelings appropriate to the occasion.

Key Terms

speech of introduction *(354)*
speech of presentation *(356)*
acceptance speech *(358)*
commemorative speech *(360)*

Review Questions

After reading this chapter, you should be able to answer the following questions:

1. What are the three purposes of a speech of introduction? What guidelines should you follow in preparing such a speech?
2. What is the main theme of a speech of presentation? Depending on the audience and occasion, what two other themes might you include in such a speech?
3. What are the three major traits of a good acceptance speech?
4. What is the fundamental purpose of a commemorative speech? Why does a successful commemorative speech depend so much on the creative and subtle use of language?

connect

For further review, go to the LearnSmart study module for this chapter.

Exercises for Critical Thinking

1. Attend a speech on campus. Pay special attention to the speech introducing the main speaker. How well does it fit the guidelines discussed in this chapter?
2. Observe several speeches of presentation and acceptance—at a campus awards ceremony or on a television program such as the Academy Awards, Grammy Awards, Emmy Awards, or Tony Awards. Which speeches do you find most effective? Least effective? Why?
3. Analyze "Elie Wiesel" (page 361) in light of the criteria for commemorative speaking presented in this chapter.

CONSIDER
EAST
WEST
EUROPE
NORTH
SOUTH
Competition
Image
Value
PRODUCTION
Constraints
Timing
LAUNCH
Publicity

19

Speaking in Small Groups

The publisher of a national sports magazine asked Mike Lee, the new head of the human resources department, to organize an October retreat for the magazine's editorial staff. Mike went to work on setting a date, finding a place to stay, and creating an agenda for the retreat.

Mike was very pleased with his plan. He thought he had taken everyone's needs into account. But when he explained his plan at the magazine's next staff meeting, no one seemed happy.

"The date you set for the retreat is over Halloween," said the editorial manager. "I know you don't have children, but no one with kids is going to want to be away at that time."

The administrative assistant responded next. "Do you realize," she said, "that the hotel you booked is the same one we used for a retreat five years ago? It was a disaster! The food was awful, the meeting rooms were uncomfortable, and the tech support was nonexistent."

Next a member of the magazine's junior editorial staff said, "I see that all the sessions involve members of the senior editorial staff. Did you mean to exclude all the younger editors? Don't you think we're important to the magazine?"

Finally, the managing editor said, "I wish you had checked with me at some point. I could have warned you about the hotel, the conflict with Halloween, and the need to include junior staff."

What went wrong? Mike did not have enough time or resources on his own to create a successful retreat. If a group, instead of a single person, had been assigned to plan the retreat, the problems might have been averted. One person could have taken charge of looking into the best dates, another of finding accommodations, a third of coordinating with other staff members about who should be included in the retreat, and so forth. The plan would have taken *all* factors into account.

Of course, you may have heard the old saying that "a camel is a horse designed by a committee." If you have ever been part of a group that seemed to get nothing done, you may be inclined to say, "Oh, let one person decide and get it over with." The problem in such cases, however, is not that there is a group, but that the group is not functioning properly. A great deal of research shows that if members of a group work well together, they can almost always resolve a problem better than a single person.[1]

This chapter deals with speaking in a particular kind of group—the problem-solving small group.

What Is a Small Group?

dyad

A group of two people.

small group

A collection of three to twelve people who assemble for a specific purpose.

problem-solving small group

A small group formed to solve a particular problem.

As its name implies, a small group has a limited number of members. The minimum number is three. (A group of two persons is called a *dyad,* and it operates quite differently from a group of three or more.) There is some difference of opinion about the maximum number of people who constitute a small group. Most experts set the maximum number at seven or eight; some go as high as twelve. The important point is that the group must be small enough to allow free discussion among all members. In small-group communication, all participants are potentially speakers *and* listeners.

Members of a small group assemble for a specific purpose. Several shoppers milling around the clothing section of a department store are not a small group, even if they speak to one another or comment about high prices and poor service. But if those same shoppers decided to meet together and prepare a formal complaint to the store manager about high prices and poor service, they would then constitute a small group.

A *problem-solving small group* is formed to solve a particular problem. Such groups exist in every area of life. Business groups consider ways of increasing sales. Church groups discuss how to raise funds and provide for the needy. Groups of parents work on improving day-care facilities. You will almost surely be a member of many problem-solving small groups during your life.

Although speaking in a small group is not the same as public speaking, it involves similar skills. Members of a small group influence one another through communication. As a participant in a small group, you might influence your colleagues by giving them important information, by encouraging them to speak, by convincing them to change their minds, even by getting them to end a meeting of the group. All other members of the group have the same opportunity to influence you through effective communication.[2]

Leadership in Small Groups

We have said that small groups often make better decisions than do individuals. To do so, however, they need effective leadership.

KINDS OF LEADERSHIP

Sometimes there is *no specific leader.* In such a situation, members of effective groups tend to have equal influence. When a need for leadership arises, any of the members can—and one probably will—provide the necessary leadership. A typical instance might be a class project, in which you and several classmates are working together. From time to time, each of you will help the group move toward its goal by suggesting when and where to meet, by outlining the strengths and weaknesses of a certain viewpoint, by resolving disagreements among other members, and so forth.

leadership

The ability to influence group members so as to help achieve the goals of the group.

A group may have an *implied leader.* For example, if a business meeting includes one vice president and several subordinates, the vice president becomes the implied leader. The same is true if one member of the group is a specialist in the topic at hand and the others are not. Members will likely defer to the person with the highest rank or greatest expertise.

implied leader

A group member to whom other members defer because of her or his rank, expertise, or other quality.

Even when a group starts out leaderless, there may be an *emergent leader.* This is a person who, by ability or by force of personality, or just by talking the most, takes a leadership role. The emergence of a leader may or may not be desirable. If the group is stalemated or has dissolved into bickering or making jokes, an emergent leader can put it back on track. There is a danger,

Small groups require effective leadership to accomplish their goals. Some groups have a designated leader, while others have an implied leader or an emergent leader.

however, that the emergent leader may not be the most effective leader but merely the most assertive personality.

emergent leader

A group member who emerges as a leader during the group's deliberations.

Finally, there may be a *designated leader*—a person elected or appointed as leader when the group is formed. A group that meets for only one session should almost always have a designated leader who takes care of the procedural tasks and serves as spokesperson. Likewise, a formal committee will usually have a designated chairperson. The chair can perform leadership functions or delegate them, but he or she remains in charge.

designated leader

A person who is elected or appointed as leader when the group is formed.

A group may or may not need a specific leader, but it always needs *leadership*. When all members of the group are skilled communicators, they can take turns at providing leadership even if the group has a designated or implied leader. As you develop group communication skills, you should be prepared to assume a leadership role whenever necessary.[3]

FUNCTIONS OF LEADERSHIP

An effective leader helps the group reach its goals by fulfilling three overlapping sets of needs—procedural needs, task needs, and maintenance needs.

Procedural Needs

procedural needs

Routine "housekeeping" actions necessary for the efficient conduct of business in a small group.

Procedural needs can be thought of as the "housekeeping" requirements of the group. They include:

Deciding when and where the group will meet.

Reserving the room, checking the number of chairs, making sure the heat or air conditioning is turned on.

Setting the agenda of each meeting.

Starting the meeting.

Taking notes during the meeting.

Preparing and distributing any written handouts needed for the meeting.

Summarizing the group's progress at the end of the meeting.

If there is a designated leader, he or she can attend to these needs or assign one or more group members to do so. Otherwise, members of the group must split the procedural responsibilities.

Task Needs

task needs

Substantive actions necessary to help a small group complete its assigned task.

Task needs are substantive actions necessary to help the group complete the particular task it is working on. They include:

Analyzing the issues facing the group.

Distributing the workload among the members.

Collecting information.

Soliciting the views of other members.

Keeping the group from going off on a tangent.

Playing devil's advocate for unpopular ideas.

Formulating criteria for judging the most effective solution.

Helping the group reach consensus on its final recommendations.

All members should help the group satisfy its task needs. The best small groups are those in which each person contributes fully to accomplishing the group's objective.

Maintenance Needs

Maintenance needs involve interpersonal relations in the group. They include such factors as:

maintenance needs

Communicative actions necessary to maintain interpersonal relations in a small group.

How well members get along with one another.

How willing members are to contribute to the group.

Whether members are supportive of one another.

Whether members feel satisfied with the group's accomplishments.

Whether members feel good about their roles in the group.

If interpersonal problems dominate discussion, the group will have a difficult time working together and reaching a decision. A leader can do much to create and sustain supportive communication in the group. By helping group members handle conflict, by working out differences of opinion, by reducing interpersonal tension, by encouraging participation from all members, by being alert to personal feelings, and by promoting solidarity within the group, a leader can make a tremendous contribution toward helping the group achieve its goals.

Responsibilities in a Small Group

Every member of a small group must assume certain responsibilities, which can be divided into five major categories: (1) commit yourself to the goals of your group; (2) fulfill individual assignments; (3) avoid interpersonal conflicts; (4) encourage full participation; (5) keep the discussion on track. Some of these responsibilities involve leadership roles, but all five are so important that each participant should take them as personal obligations, regardless of the group's leadership.

COMMIT YOURSELF TO THE GOALS OF YOUR GROUP

For a group to succeed, members must align their personal goals with the group's goal. This sounds obvious, but it is not always easy. When you are working with other students on a class project, the group goal—and most likely the goal of each member—is to get a good grade. There is a strong incentive for members to cooperate and commit themselves to completing the task.

Problems arise when one or more members have personal goals that conflict with the group's goal. Here is the kind of situation that can occur:

Sherri Baines is a member of the committee to buy new equipment for the local newspaper's employee cafeteria. Because the budget is very tight, the committee's goal is to get the best equipment for the lowest price. But unknown to the other members of the group, Sherri's son-in-law is a salesman for a distributor of high-priced kitchen appliances. Privately, Sherri has reasoned that if she can sway the committee toward that company, her son-in-law will get a large commission. Sherri does not mention this fact to the group. Instead, she argues that quality—not price—should be the determining factor in the purchase. The group process breaks down because Sherri will not surrender her private goal.

This is an extreme example, but there can be more subtle kinds of private goals, as in the following case:

Carlos and Rachel are part of a group, and Carlos would like to be on closer terms with Rachel. To impress her, he may agree with everything she says, regardless of whether he really shares her views. Consequently, Carlos's expressed views are not his actual views. In short, Carlos has a *hidden agenda* in the group meeting. The group's agenda is to solve the problem, but Carlos's agenda is to go out with Rachel.

hidden agenda

A set of unstated individual goals that may conflict with the goals of the group as a whole.

Group members may have all sorts of hidden agendas. One may be experiencing personal problems—lowered grades, a breakup with a friend, or just a bad day. Another may have a commitment to a different group whose goals conflict with those of the present group. A third may want to take charge of the group for reasons of personal power, regardless of the group's task.

Remember that what one member of a group does affects all the other members. You should not try to advance your own interests or boost your own ego at the expense of the group and its goals. Beware of hidden agendas—whether yours or someone else's—and participate with a positive spirit.

FULFILL INDIVIDUAL ASSIGNMENTS

As mentioned earlier, one of the advantages of the group process is that it divides the workload among several people. But unless every member fulfills his or her assignments, the group's entire project may fail—as in the following example:

Several years ago, one student group decided that as a class project they would bring Easter baskets to the patients in the children's ward of a local hospital. After the project had been approved, assignments were given out. Stoya would coordinate with the hospital authorities. Corrine would handle fund-raising for the needed supplies. Jesse would supervise the egg-decorating team. Liu would be responsible for buying baskets and chocolate bunnies. Justin would arrange for transportation.

Everybody completed their assignments except Justin, who was busy writing a term paper. He asked a friend to pick up a bus schedule and assumed everything would be fine. On Easter morning, the group assembled at the bus stop, loaded down with baskets for the children. And they waited and waited. After an hour Justin called the bus company, only to discover that the buses did not run on holidays. By the time Justin had made other arrangements to get to the hospital, visiting hours were over, and the group could not get in.

No matter what other assignments they may have, *all* members of a group have one very critical assignment—listening. First, it helps you understand what is happening in the group. And unlike a public speaking situation, you can stop the speaker and ask for clarification at any point. Second, listening helps you evaluate the merits of the speaker's position. Third, listening provides support for the speaker and helps create a positive climate for discussion. Without effective listening, no group is going to make much progress.

AVOID INTERPERSONAL CONFLICTS

If groups were made up of robots, there would be no interpersonal conflicts. But groups are made up of people with likes and dislikes, animosities and prejudices, and very different personalities. It is vital to the group process that disagreements be kept on a task level, rather than on a personal level.

Suppose you disagree with another member's idea. Disagreement on the personal level could sound like this: "That's the most stupid idea I ever heard of! Do you realize how much money it would cost to do that?" But on the task level, disagreement is aimed at the *idea,* not the person: "Potentially that's a very good solution, but I'm not sure we have enough money to accomplish it."

No matter what the group, personal antagonism leaves a bad taste in everyone's mouth and harms the performance of the group. It's essential that someone take a leadership role and bring the discussion back to the relevant issues. Let's say you are part of a committee charged with setting up a speakers' series on your campus. The discussion might go like this:

Anton: We definitely should have Representative Hightower speak on campus. He has been very active in protecting the environment.

Minh: That liberal? He could care less what we pay for a gallon of gas. And forget about economic development with him.

Anton: So you support more offshore drilling? You're willing to destroy our coastlines so the oil companies can rake in more profits?

Minh: It's people like you that have made us dependent on foreign sources of oil—which threatens our prosperity and national security by making us vulnerable to economic blackmail from abroad.

Leader: Just a minute. This might make a good subject for our speakers' series. We can ask both Representative Hightower and a spokesperson for one of the oil companies to debate each other.

This is not to say that members of a group should never disagree. In fact, a serious problem occurs when members get along so well and are so concerned about maintaining the harmony of the group that they will not disagree with one another about anything. When this happens, there is no chance to reach the best decision by exploring an array of perspectives, opinions, and information. The aim is not for groups to avoid conflict but to keep it at the task level so it will not degenerate into personal feuding.[4]

ENCOURAGE FULL PARTICIPATION

If a group is to work effectively, all members must contribute fully and share their ideas with one another. Every member of a group should take responsibility for encouraging other members to participate. You can do this, first of all, by listening attentively. After all, how would you like to speak in a group where everybody else appears bored or distracted?

If there are one or two quiet members in the group, you can draw them into the discussion by asking their opinions and showing interest in their ideas. When a member speaks, you can say, "I never knew that; can you tell us more about it?" Conversely, try to avoid negative comments that will squelch a speaker before he or she has finished—comments like "Oh, no, that never works" or "What a terrible idea." Supportive comments create goodwill among group members and make everyone feel free to discuss their ideas without ridicule or embarrassment.

If you are shy or afraid your ideas will be taken too critically, you may be unwilling to participate at first. To overcome your diffidence, remember that your contribution is necessary to the group. At the very least, you can help provide a supportive environment for discussion by listening, reacting, and encouraging the free exchange of ideas.

KEEP THE DISCUSSION ON TRACK

In some groups the discussion proceeds like a stream-of-consciousness exercise. Here is a hypothetical example in which a town planning board is considering installing a new traffic light at a busy intersection:

Sharif: You know, we're going to have trouble getting cars to come to a full stop even if we do put in a traffic light.

Delany: Tell me about it! I came through there yesterday and hit my brakes, and the car just kept going. Maybe I need the brakes adjusted, though.

Mike: Get ready to pay through the nose. I had a brake job on my car last week, and it was nearly twice as much as last time.

Austin: That's nothing. Have you looked at lawnmowers lately? And if you think lawnmowers are high. . . .

Kym: Who mows lawns? I had my yard planted with ground cover and put gravel over the rest. It's . . .

Leader: Excuse me, folks, but weren't we talking about the *traffic light*?

Every member has a responsibility to keep the discussion on track and to intervene if the group wanders too far afield. There is nothing wrong with a little casual conversation, but it shouldn't be allowed to get out of hand. When working in a problem-solving group, make sure the group's ultimate goal is always in the forefront. Do your best to see that discussion proceeds in an orderly fashion from one point to the next and that the group does not get bogged down in side issues.

On the other hand, you need to guard against the tendency to progress to a solution too quickly, without thoroughly exploring the problem. If you feel your group is taking the easy way out and jumping at an easy solution, try to make the other members aware of your concern. By suggesting that they talk about the problem in more detail, you may bring out vital information or ideas.

There are systematic ways to keep the discussion on track and to avoid hasty group decisions. Research shows that if your group follows a tested method of decision making, it will have a better chance of reaching a satisfactory outcome.[5] We turn, therefore, to the most common decision-making technique for small groups—the reflective-thinking method.

In effective small groups, all members participate fully and interact with each other. They also feel that their contributions are respected and valued by the full group.

The Reflective-Thinking Method

The reflective-thinking method is derived from the writings of the American philosopher John Dewey. It offers a step-by-step process for discussion in problem-solving groups and consists of five steps: (1) defining the problem; (2) analyzing the problem; (3) establishing criteria for solving the problem; (4) generating potential solutions; (5) selecting the best solution. As we look at these steps, we'll illustrate each by following a single group through the entire reflective-thinking process.

reflective-thinking method

A five-step method for directing discussion in a problem-solving small group.

DEFINE THE PROBLEM

Before a problem-solving group can make progress, it must know exactly what problem it is trying to solve. Defining the problem for group discussion is akin to settling on a specific purpose for a speech. Unless it is done properly, everything that follows will suffer.

The best way to define the problem is to phrase it as a question of policy. As we saw in Chapter 16, questions of policy inquire about the necessity or practicality of specific courses of action. They typically include the word "should." For example:

question of policy

A question about whether a specific course of action should or should not be taken.

What measures should our school take to improve on-campus security for students?

What steps should the federal government take to deal with the federal budget deficit?

What policy should the United States adopt with respect to the exploitation of child labor in other countries around the world?

When phrasing the question for discussion, your group should follow several guidelines. First, make sure the question is as clear and specific as possible. For example:

Ineffective: What should be done about fraudulent charities?

More Effective: What should the government do to control the activities of fraudulent charities?

Second, phrase the question to allow for a wide variety of answers. Be especially wary of questions that can be answered with a simple yes or no. For example:

Ineffective: Should the city build a new elementary school?

More Effective: What steps should the city take to deal with increasing enrollment in the elementary schools?

Third, avoid biased or slanted questions. For example:

Ineffective: How can we keep the campus bookstore from ripping off students?

More Effective: What changes, if any, should be made in the pricing policies of the campus bookstore?

Fourth, make sure you pose a single question. For example:

Ineffective: What revisions should the college consider in its admissions requirements and in its graduation requirements?

More Effective: What revisions should the college consider in its admissions requirements?

More Effective: What revisions should the college consider in its graduation requirements?

To clarify this first step of the reflective-thinking method, let's see how our model problem-solving group defined the problem:

> As a class project, the group set out to discuss the problem of rising costs for attending college. Following the reflective-thinking method, they began by defining the problem. After several false starts, they phrased the problem this way: "What steps should our school take to reduce student costs for attending college?"

ANALYZE THE PROBLEM

After the problem has been defined, the group begins to analyze it. Too often, groups (like individuals) start mapping out solutions before they have a firm grasp of what is wrong. This is like a doctor prescribing treatment before fully diagnosing the patient's ailment. If your group investigates the problem as thoroughly as possible, you will be in a much better position to devise a workable solution.

In analyzing the problem, pay particular attention to two questions. First, how severe is the problem? Investigate its scope. Determine how many people it affects. Assess what might happen if it is not resolved. Second, what are the causes of the problem? Check the history of the problem and learn what factors contributed to it.

As you might imagine, analyzing the problem requires research. Effective group decisions depend on having the best information available. You can get this information in the same way you gather materials for a speech. Sometimes you can rely on your own knowledge and experience. More often, you need to get information from other sources—by looking on the Internet, by interviewing someone with expertise on the topic, or by working in the library (see Chapter 7). When meeting with your group, make sure you have done the research assigned to you so you can offer complete and unbiased information.

Let's return now to our sample group and see how it analyzed the problem of rapidly escalating student costs for attending college:

The group talked first about the severity of the problem. Tuition had risen dramatically, as had outlays for books and incidentals. One member found statistics showing that the cost of attending college had more than doubled in the past 10 years. Another provided evidence that average annual costs were now close to $15,000 for students at in-state public colleges and universities, and roughly $35,000 for students at private schools.

To determine the causes of the problem, the group researched articles about the rise in student costs for attending college across the nation. They also interviewed an economics professor and the head of the student aid program on campus. After studying the matter thoroughly, the group identified several major causes, including administrative costs, faculty salaries, the price of textbooks, and increased living expenses.

ESTABLISH CRITERIA FOR SOLUTIONS

If you planned to buy a car, how would you proceed? You would probably not just walk into a showroom and buy whatever appealed to you on the spur of the moment. You would most likely decide ahead of time what kind of car you wanted, what options it should have, and how much money you could spend. That is, you would establish *criteria* to guide you in deciding exactly which car to buy.

criteria

Standards on which a judgment or decision can be based.

You should do the same thing in group discussion. Once your group has analyzed the problem, you should not jump immediately to proposing solutions. Instead, you should establish criteria—standards—for responsible solutions. You should work out (and write down) exactly what your solutions must achieve and any factors that might limit your choice of solutions.

To get a better idea of how this stage of the reflective-thinking method works, let's look at the cost-cutting group we have been following:

After some discussion, the group established these criteria for possible solutions: (1) The solution should significantly reduce students' costs. (2) The solution should come into force at the start of the next school year. (3) The solution should not hurt the prestige of the college. (4) The cost of the solution should be minimal and should be paid by the administration. (5) The human resources needed to implement the solution should come from administrative personnel already working on the school's staff. (6) The solution should involve only actions controlled by the college—not matters controlled by outside individuals or agencies.

GENERATE POTENTIAL SOLUTIONS

Once your group has the criteria firmly in mind, you are ready to discuss solutions. Your goal at this stage is to come up with the widest possible range of potential solutions—not to judge the solutions. One member of the group should be responsible for writing down all the solutions proposed at this time.

brainstorming

A method of generating ideas by free association of words and thoughts.

Many groups find the technique of *brainstorming* helpful in this stage. In Chapter 5, we discussed how brainstorming can work for an individual in choosing a speech topic. Here brainstorming is expanded to the whole group.

The best approach is to begin by having each member of the group write down all the possible solutions he or she can think of. One person should then consolidate the individual lists into a master list. The group should discuss the master list to make sure potential solutions have not been overlooked.

At this stage, members often "piggyback" new ideas onto ideas on the master list. For example, if one suggestion is "Establish food co-ops," a group member might say, "Yes, and we could establish clothing co-ops, too." One member should write down these new ideas and add them to the master list. The brainstorming process continues until the group cannot think of any more solutions.

Brainstorming in this fashion has two advantages. First, it encourages creativity. Research shows that beginning with written lists usually produces more and higher-quality ideas than relying solely on oral discussion.[6] Second, this method of brainstorming encourages equal participation. Having each member create his or her own list makes it less likely that one or two members will dominate the process or that anyone will hold back ideas for fear of being hooted down.

Let's see how our cost-cutting group handled this stage:

By brainstorming, the group came up with the following possible solutions: (1) reduce the number of required books for each course; (2) cut some of the "fat" from the administrative staff; (3) make all professors teach more courses; (4) approach landlords about stabilizing rent and utility costs; (5) establish food

Working in a small group requires many of the skills involved in public speaking. Formal presentations may occur during a group's deliberations or when the group presents its report.

and clothing co-ops; (6) increase financial aid; (7) decrease the amount of money available for faculty research; (8) boycott businesses around the campus where price markups are highest; (9) increase out-of-state tuition; (10) decrease dormitory expenses; (11) organize fund-raising programs with the student government; (12) redirect some money from construction of new buildings to student aid. This was a good yield from a brainstorming session—12 solid suggestions.

SELECT THE BEST SOLUTION

After all potential solutions have been listed, it is time to evaluate them. The best way to proceed is to discuss each solution with regard to the criteria established earlier, then move to the next solution, and so on. This orderly process ensures that all potential solutions receive equal consideration.

As each potential solution is discussed, the group should try to reach *consensus*. A consensus decision is one that all members accept, even though the decision may not be ideal in the eyes of every member. Because it usually results in superior decisions as well as in a high degree of unity within the group, consensus is the ideal of group decision making. It comes about when members have been so cooperative that they reach a common decision through reasoning, honest exchange of ideas, and full examination of the issues.

consensus

A group decision that is acceptable to all members of the group.

checklist

Reflective-Thinking Method

YES	NO	
☐	☐	1. Did the group clearly define the problem for discussion?
☐	☐	2. Did the group phrase the question for discussion as a question of policy?
☐	☐	3. Did the group phrase the question for discussion as clearly as possible?
☐	☐	4. Did the group phrase the question for discussion so as to allow for a wide variety of answers?
☐	☐	5. Did the group phrase the question for discussion in an unbiased manner?
☐	☐	6. Did the group phrase the question for discussion as a single question?
☐	☐	7. Did the group analyze the problem thoroughly before attempting to map out solutions?
☐	☐	8. Did the group establish criteria for an ideal solution to the problem before discussing specific solutions?
☐	☐	9. Did the group brainstorm to generate a wide range of potential solutions to the problem?
☐	☐	10. Did the group evaluate each potential solution in light of the criteria for an ideal solution?
☐	☐	11. Did the group make a determined effort to reach consensus with regard to the best solution?
☐	☐	12. Did the group achieve consensus?

Like most ideals, consensus can be difficult to achieve. If there are different viewpoints, members of the group will often try to find the easiest way to resolve the differences. Sometimes a member will call for a vote, which is very agreeable to those holding a majority opinion but not so pleasant for those in the minority. Resorting to a vote does resolve the immediate conflict, but it may not result in the best solution. Moreover, it weakens unity in the group by fostering factions and perhaps by creating bitterness among the members who lose the vote. A group should vote only when it has failed in every other attempt to agree on a solution.

What kind of final decision did our model cost-cutting group reach? Let's see:

The cost-cutting group had 12 possible solutions to evaluate. Three were rejected because they violated the group's criterion that an acceptable solution must involve only actions controlled directly by the college.

Three more solutions were rejected because they were economically impractical. Increasing financial aid would hurt many students because the funds would have to come from student fees. Raising out-of-state tuition would drive away too many out-of-state students. And decreasing dorm costs would make it impossible to provide minimally acceptable services.

The proposal to reduce funds for faculty research was also rejected since most research money comes from government, corporations, and foundations. Finally, the suggestion to reduce administrative "fat" was rejected as too costly because a group would have to be established to audit all administrative duties.

After refining the suggestions, the group finally reached consensus on a solution that included the following provisions: (1) A student should not have to spend more than $200 on required books for any single course. (2) The university should authorize the student government to organize food, book, and clothing co-ops. (3) The student government should conduct five fund-raising projects each academic year. (4) Each professor should teach one more class a year.

Once consensus has been reached, the group is ready to present its findings.[7]

Presenting the Recommendations of the Group

The work of a problem-solving group does not end with the last stage of the reflective-thinking process. Once a group has agreed on its recommendations, it usually needs to present them to somebody. A business group might report to the president of the company or to the board of directors. A presidential commission reports to the President and to the nation at large. A classroom group reports to the instructor and to the rest of the class. The purpose of such reports is to present the group's recommendations clearly and convincingly.

Sometimes a group will prepare a formal written report. Often, however, the written report is supplemented with—or replaced by—an oral report, a symposium, or a panel discussion.

ORAL REPORT

An oral report is much the same in content as a written report. If the group has a designated leader, she or he will probably deliver the report. Otherwise, the group will select one person for the job.

If you are picked to present your group's report, you should approach it as you would any other speech. Your task is to explain the group's purpose, procedures, and recommendations. Your report should have three main sections. The introduction will state the purpose of the report and preview its main points. The body will spell out the problem addressed by your group, the criteria set for a solution, and the solution being recommended. The conclusion will summarize the main points and, in some cases, urge that the group's recommendations be adopted.

oral report

A speech presenting the findings, conclusions, or decisions of a small group.

As with any other speech, you should adapt your report to the audience. Use supporting materials to clarify and strengthen your ideas, and consider whether visual aids will enhance your message. Make sure your language is accurate, clear, vivid, and appropriate. Rehearse the report so you can deliver it fluently and decisively. Afterward, you—and possibly other members of the group—may be called on to answer questions from the audience.

SYMPOSIUM

A symposium consists of a moderator and several speakers seated together in front of an audience. If the group presenting the symposium has a designated leader, she or he will typically be the moderator. The moderator's job is to introduce the topic and the speakers. Each speaker delivers a prepared speech on a different aspect of the topic. After the speeches, there may be a question-and-answer session.

symposium

A public presentation in which several people present prepared speeches on different aspects of the same topic.

The symposium is often used for group reports in speech classes. One way to organize it is to have each member of the group present a brief talk sketching the group's work and decisions during one stage of the reflective-thinking process. Another way is to have each speaker deal with a major issue relating to the discussion topic. A group dealing with capital punishment, for example, might have one speaker present the group's conclusion on the issue of whether capital punishment is an effective deterrent to crime, another speaker present the group's position on the morality of capital punishment, and so forth.

All the speeches should be carefully planned. They should also be coordinated with one another to make sure the symposium reports on all important aspects of the group's project.

PANEL DISCUSSION

A panel discussion is essentially a conversation in front of an audience. The panel should have a moderator, who introduces the topic and the panelists. Once the discussion is under way, the moderator may interject questions and comments as needed to focus the discussion. The panelists speak briefly, informally, and impromptu. They talk to each other, but loudly enough for the audience to hear. As with a symposium, a panel discussion may be followed by a question-and-answer session.

panel discussion

A structured conversation on a given topic among several people in front of an audience.

Because of its spontaneity, a panel discussion can be exciting for participants and audience alike. But, unfortunately, that spontaneity inhibits systematic presentation of a group's recommendations. Thus the panel discussion is seldom used by problem-solving groups, although it can work well for information-gathering groups.

If you are a participant in a panel discussion, beware of the common fallacy that no serious preparation is required. Although you will speak impromptu, you need to study the topic ahead of time, analyze the major issues, and map out the points you want to make. An effective panel discussion also requires planning by the moderator and panelists to decide what issues will be discussed and in what order. Finally, all panelists must be willing to share talking time, so the discussion is not monopolized by one or two people.

Whatever method your group uses to present its findings, you will benefit from the public speaking guidelines given throughout this book. The techniques of effective speech remain the same whether you are one person addressing an audience, part of a small group of people working to solve a problem, or a participant in a symposium or a panel discussion.[8]

Summary

A small group consists of three to twelve people assembled for a specific purpose. A problem-solving small group is formed to solve a particular problem. When such a group has effective leadership, it usually makes better decisions than do individuals by themselves.

Most groups have a designated leader, an implied leader, or an emergent leader. Some groups have no specific leader, in which case all members of the group must assume leadership responsibilities. An effective leader helps a group reach its goals by fulfilling procedural needs, task needs, and maintenance needs.

Apart from leadership, all members of a group have five basic responsibilities. You should commit yourself to the goals of your group, fulfill your individual assignments, avoid interpersonal conflict within the group, encourage full participation by all members, and help keep the group on track.

Your group will also be more successful if it follows the reflective-thinking method, which offers a step-by-step process for decision making in problem-solving groups. The method consists of five steps: (1) defining the problem as clearly and specifically as possible; (2) analyzing the problem to determine its severity and causes; (3) establishing criteria for evaluating solutions; (4) generating a wide range of potential solutions; (5) selecting the best solution or solutions.

Once your group has agreed on its recommendations, it usually has to make an oral report or participate in a symposium or a panel discussion. Whichever kind of oral presentation your group gives will call for skills of effective speechmaking.

Key Terms

dyad *(366)*
small group *(366)*
problem-solving small group *(366)*
leadership *(367)*
implied leader *(367)*
emergent leader *(368)*
designated leader *(368)*
procedural needs *(368)*
task needs *(368)*
maintenance needs *(369)*
hidden agenda *(370)*
reflective-thinking method *(373)*
question of policy *(373)*
criteria *(375)*
brainstorming *(376)*
consensus *(377)*
oral report *(379)*
symposium *(379)*
panel discussion *(379)*

Review Questions

After reading this chapter, you should be able to answer the following questions:

1. What is a small group? What is a problem-solving small group?
2. What are the four kinds of leadership that may occur in a small group? Explain the three kinds of needs fulfilled by leadership in a small group.
3. What are the five major responsibilities of every participant in a small group?
4. What are the stages of the reflective-thinking method? Explain the major tasks of a group at each stage.
5. What are the three methods for presenting orally the recommendations of a problem-solving group?

connect™

For further review, go to the LearnSmart study module for this chapter.

Exercises for Critical Thinking

1. Identify the flaw (or flaws) in each of the following questions for a problem-solving group discussion. Rewrite each question so it conforms to the criteria discussed in the chapter for effective discussion questions.
   a. What should be done to prevent the utterly ridiculous shortage of new computers for students at this school?
   b. What should be done about child abuse?
   c. What should our state government do to reduce homelessness and to combat drunk driving?
   d. Should the federal government institute a national sales tax to help reduce the national debt?
2. If possible, arrange to observe a problem-solving small group in action. You might attend a meeting of your city council, the school board, the zoning commission, a local business, a church committee. To what extent does the discussion measure up to the criteria for effective discussion presented in this chapter? What kind of leadership does the group have, and how well does the leader (or leaders) fulfill the group's procedural needs, task needs, and maintenance needs? How do the other members meet their responsibilities? What aspects of the meeting are handled most effectively? Which are handled least effectively?
3. Identify a relatively important decision you have made in the last year or two. Try to reconstruct how you reached that decision. Now suppose you could remake the decision following the reflective-thinking method. Map out what you would do at each stage of the method. Do you still reach the same decision? If not, do you believe the reflective-thinking method would have led you to a better decision in the first place?
4. Attend a symposium or panel discussion on campus. Prepare a brief analysis of the proceedings. First, study the role of the moderator. How does she or he introduce the topic and participants? What role does the moderator play thereafter? Does she or he help guide and focus the panel discussion? Does she or he summarize and conclude the proceedings at the end?

Second, observe the participants. Are the speeches in the symposium well prepared and presented? Which speaker (or speakers) do you find most effective? Least effective? Why? Do participants in the panel discussion share talking time? Does their discussion appear well planned to cover major aspects of the topic? Which panelist (or panelists) do you find most effective? Least effective? Why?

Speeches for Analysis and Discussion

Appendix

I HAVE A DREAM

Martin Luther King, Jr.

Martin Luther King's "I Have a Dream" is widely regarded as a masterpiece. It was delivered August 28, 1963, to some 200,000 people who had come to Washington, D.C., to participate in a peaceful demonstration to further the cause of equal rights for African Americans. King spoke from the steps of the Lincoln Memorial, in the "symbolic shadow" of Abraham Lincoln, and the crowd filled the vast area between the Memorial and the Washington Monument. In addition, millions of Americans watched the speech on television or listened to it on the radio.

Like most ceremonial addresses, "I Have a Dream" is relatively short. Although it took King only 16 minutes to deliver the speech, he prepared it more carefully than any other speech in his career to that time. His purpose was to set forth as succinctly and as eloquently as possible the guiding principles of the civil rights movement, and to reinforce the commitment of his listeners to those principles.

One of the most interesting features of this speech is King's use of language to make the abstract principles of liberty and equality clear and compelling. Throughout, King relies on familiar, concrete words that create sharp, vivid images. He uses many more metaphors than do most speakers, but they are appropriate to the occasion and help to dramatize King's ideas. Finally, King makes extensive use of repetition and parallelism to reinforce his message and to enhance the momentum of the speech.

If you have heard a recording of "I Have a Dream," you know its impact was heightened by King's delivery. In his rich baritone voice, marked by the fervor of the crusader and modulated by the cadences of the Southern Baptist preacher, King gained the total involvement of his audience. As William Robert Miller says, "The crowd more than listened, it participated, and before King had reached his last phrase, a torrent of applause was already welling up."

The text of this speech is transcribed from a recording and is reprinted with permission of Joan Daves. Copyright 1963 by Martin Luther King, Jr.

1 I am happy to join with you today in what will go down in history as the greatest demonstration for freedom in the history of our nation.

2 Five score years ago, a great American, in whose symbolic shadow we stand today, signed the Emancipation Proclamation. This momentous decree came as a great beacon light of hope to millions of Negro slaves, who had been seared in the flames of withering injustice. It came as a joyous daybreak to end the long night of their captivity.

3 But one hundred years later, the Negro still is not free. One hundred years later, the life of the Negro is still sadly crippled by the manacles of segregation and the chains of discrimination. One hundred years later, the Negro lives on a lonely island of poverty in the midst of a vast ocean of material prosperity. One hundred years later, the Negro is still languished in the corners of American society and finds himself an exile in his own land. And so we've come here today to dramatize a shameful condition.

4 In a sense we've come to our nation's Capitol to cash a check. When the architects of our republic wrote the magnificent words of the Constitution and the Declaration of Independence, they were signing a promissory

note to which every American was to fall heir. This note was a promise that all men—yes, black men as well as white men—would be guaranteed the unalienable rights of life, liberty, and the pursuit of happiness.

5 It is obvious today that America has defaulted on this promissory note insofar as her citizens of color are concerned. Instead of honoring this sacred obligation, America has given the Negro people a bad check—a check which has come back marked "insufficient funds."

6 But we refuse to believe that the bank of justice is bankrupt. We refuse to believe that there are insufficient funds in the great vaults of opportunity of this nation. And so we've come to cash this check—a check that will give us upon demand the riches of freedom and the security of justice.

7 We have also come to this hallowed spot to remind America of the fierce urgency of now. This is no time to engage in the luxury of cooling off or to take the tranquilizing drug of gradualism. Now is the time to make real the promises of democracy. Now is the time to rise from the dark and desolate valley of segregation to the sunlit path of racial justice. Now is the time to lift our nation from the quicksands of racial injustice to the solid rock of brotherhood. Now is the time to make justice a reality for all of God's children.

8 It would be fatal for the nation to overlook the urgency of the moment. This sweltering summer of the Negro's legitimate discontent will not pass until there is an invigorating autumn of freedom and equality. Nineteen sixty-three is not an end, but a beginning. Those who hope that the Negro needed to blow off steam and will now be content will have a rude awakening if the nation returns to business as usual. There will be neither rest nor tranquility in America until the Negro is granted his citizenship rights. The whirlwinds of revolt will continue to shake the foundations of our nation until the bright day of justice emerges.

9 But there is something that I must say to my people, who stand on the warm threshold which leads into the palace of justice. In the process of gaining our rightful place, we must not be guilty of wrongful deeds. Let us not seek to satisfy our thirst for freedom by drinking from the cup of bitterness and hatred.

10 We must forever conduct our struggle on the high plane of dignity and discipline. We must not allow our creative protest to degenerate into physical violence. Again and again we must rise to the majestic heights of meeting physical force with soul force.

11 The marvelous new militancy which has engulfed the Negro community must not lead us to a distrust of all white people. For many of our white brothers, as evidenced by their presence here today, have come to realize that their destiny is tied up with our destiny. They have come to realize that their freedom is inextricably bound to our freedom. We cannot walk alone.

12 As we walk, we must make the pledge that we shall always march ahead. We cannot turn back. There are those who are asking the devotees of civil rights, "When will you be satisfied?" We can never be satisfied as long as the Negro is the victim of the unspeakable horrors of police brutality. We can never be satisfied as long as our bodies, heavy with the fatigue of travel, cannot gain lodging in the motels of the highways and the hotels of the cities. We cannot be satisfied as long as the Negro's basic mobility is from a smaller ghetto to a larger one. We can never be satisfied as long as our children are stripped of their selfhood and robbed of their dignity by signs stating "For Whites Only." We cannot be satisfied as long as a Negro in Mississippi

cannot vote and a Negro in New York believes he has nothing for which to vote. No, no, we are not satisfied, and we will not be satisfied until justice rolls down like waters, and righteousness like a mighty stream.

13 I am not unmindful that some of you have come here out of great trials and tribulations. Some of you have come fresh from narrow jail cells. Some of you have come from areas where your quest for freedom left you battered by the storms of persecution and staggered by the winds of police brutality. You have been the veterans of creative suffering. Continue to work with the faith that unearned suffering is redemptive.

14 Go back to Mississippi, go back to Alabama, go back to South Carolina, go back to Georgia, go back to Louisiana, go back to the slums and ghettos of our Northern cities, knowing that somehow this situation can and will be changed. Let us not wallow in the valley of despair.

15 I say to you today, my friends, so even though we face the difficulties of today and tomorrow, I still have a dream. It is a dream deeply rooted in the American dream.

16 I have a dream that one day this nation will rise up and live out the true meaning of its creed, "We hold these truths to be self-evident, that all men are created equal."

17 I have a dream that one day on the red hills of Georgia the sons of former slaves and the sons of former slaveowners will be able to sit down together at the table of brotherhood.

18 I have a dream that one day even the state of Mississippi, a state sweltering with the heat of injustice, sweltering with the heat of oppression, will be transformed into an oasis of freedom and justice.

19 I have a dream that my four little children will one day live in a nation where they will not be judged by the color of their skin but by the content of their character. I have a dream today.

20 I have a dream that one day, down in Alabama, with its vicious racists, with its governor having his lips dripping with the words of interposition and nullification, one day right there in Alabama little black boys and black girls will be able to join hands with little white boys and white girls as sisters and brothers. I have a dream today.

21 I have a dream that one day every valley shall be exalted, every hill and mountain shall be made low, the rough places will be made plane and the crooked places will be made straight, and the glory of the Lord shall be revealed, and all flesh shall see it together.

22 This is our hope. This is the faith that I go back to the South with. With this faith we will be able to hew out of the mountain of despair a stone of hope. With this faith we will be able to transform the jangling discords of our nation into a beautiful symphony of brotherhood. With this faith we will be able to work together, to pray together, to struggle together, to go to jail together, to stand up for freedom together, knowing that we will be free one day.

23 This will be the day—this will be the day when all of God's children will be able to sing with new meaning, "My country 'tis of thee, sweet land of liberty, of thee I sing. Land where my fathers died, land of the pilgrim's pride, from every mountainside, let freedom ring." And if America is to be a great nation, this must become true.

24 So let freedom ring from the prodigious hilltops of New Hampshire. Let freedom ring from the mighty mountains of New York. Let freedom ring from the heightening Alleghenies of Pennsylvania!

25 Let freedom ring from the snowcapped Rockies of Colorado! Let freedom ring from the curvaceous slopes of California!

26 But not only that. Let freedom ring from Stone Mountain of Georgia!

27 Let freedom ring from Lookout Mountain of Tennessee!

28 Let freedom ring from every hill and molehill of Mississippi. From every mountainside, let freedom ring.

29 And when this happens, when we allow freedom ring—when we let it ring from every village and every hamlet, from every state and every city—we will be able to speed up that day when all of God's children, black men and white men, Jews and Gentiles, Protestants and Catholics, will be able to join hands and sing in the words of the old Negro spiritual, "Free at last! Free at last! Thank God almighty, we are free at last!"

RAMADAN

Choosing a topic based on one's personal experience can be an excellent decision, especially when the speaker supplements her or his existing knowledge with additional research—as in the following informative presentation on the Muslim holy month of Ramadan. As you read, notice how crisply the speech is organized, how the speaker relates her topic to the audience, and how she explains each aspect of Ramadan clearly and engagingly.

The speech also provides an instructive example of extemporaneous delivery, which you can see by watching the video in the online Media Library for this appendix. The speaker maintains strong eye contact with the audience and refers to her notes only as needed. Despite her nerves, she comes across as poised and confident. Her gestures are natural and spontaneous, and her voice conveys a strong sense of communication.

connect™

View "Ramadan" in the online Media Library for this appendix (Video A.1).

1 This past month, more than one billion people around the world skipped lunch every day. They ate no food of any kind and drank no liquid of any kind from sunup to sunset. They did this every day during the month, and they do the same thing every year. I myself did it. Why? Last month was a time for tending to the mind, the body, and the spirit. Last month was the Muslim holy month of Ramadan.

2 I'm sure most of you have heard of Ramadan, but you may not know a lot about it. Ramadan refers to the ninth month in the Islamic calendar, when Muslims fast from sunrise to sunset. But Ramadan is much more than a time of fasting. As Tariq Ramadan, author of *Western Muslims and the Future of Islam,* explains, Ramadan is a time when "believers strengthen their faith and spirituality while developing their sense of social justice."

3 As a practicing Muslim, I have observed Ramadan my entire life. My parents moved to the United States from Pakistan shortly before I was born, and I remember going to the mosque as a child and breaking my fast at the end of the day with my family and friends. Nowadays, I get together with other students here on campus.

4 The goal of my speech today is to inform you about Ramadan—specifically its history and practices. In the end, I hope you'll have a better understanding of this sacred time for Muslims in the United States and around the globe. Let's begin by exploring the history of Ramadan.

5 Ramadan can be traced back 1,400 years to the Middle East and the beginnings of the Quran. As explained in Karen Armstrong's *Islam: A Short History,* in 610 A.D. the Prophet Mohammed embarked on a spiritual journey through the desert in what is now Saudi Arabia. At one point in this journey, Muslims believe, Allah spoke to Mohammed through the archangel Gabriel—the same Gabriel of the Jewish and Christian scriptures.

6 This is when the Prophet Mohammed received the first verses of the Quran. Gabriel told Mohammed to remember the revelation by observing a holy time every year. In the years after this journey, the Prophet Mohammed and his followers made the ninth month of the Muslim year the month of Ramadan.

7 The word "Ramadan" literally means "scorcher" in Arabic, because it was in the intense heat of the summer that the Prophet Mohammed encountered Gabriel. But unlike the Western calendar, the Islamic calendar follows the cycles of the moon and contains only 354 days. As a result, Ramadan always begins approximately ten days before it began the previous year. So, for example, this year Ramadan came on August 11th. Next year, it will come on August 1st.

8 Now let's take a look at what Muslims do during this holy month. The practices of Ramadan center on fasting, prayer, and charity.

9 Fasting is one of the five pillars of Islam, and it becomes especially important during Ramadan. The Ramadan fast, known as the *Sawm,* begins at sunrise and ends at sunset. Seyyed Nasr, author of *Islam: Religion, History, and Civilization,* explains that "the fast is required of all Muslims, male and female, from the age of adolescence until one no longer possesses the physical strength to undertake it." The only exceptions are for the sick, the elderly, travelers, and pregnant women.

10 At the end of daylight hours, Muslims break the fast with *Iftar*—the evening meal, during which families, friends, and communities gather. As Donna Bowen and Evelyn Early explain in their book *Everyday Life in the Muslim Middle East, Iftar* usually begins with eating a date, which is what the Prophet Mohammed is said to have done. After eating a date and drinking water, my family would eat the *Iftar* dinner my mother cooked for us. We would always marvel that even though she was fasting and couldn't taste what she was cooking, she still somehow got the spices just right.

11 Prayer is also central to Ramadan. Muslims traditionally pray five times a day, but during Ramadan prayer is encouraged even more. Ramadan prayers are often tied to oral readings of the Quran—a practice known as *Tarawih.* The goal is to read and recite the entire Quran over the course of the month.

12 In addition to fasting and prayer, charity plays a key role in Ramadan. *Iftars* are often organized and funded by the wealthy as a way of feeding the poor and the needy. Also, many Muslims increase their charitable giving during the month. At the end of Ramadan, my family donates to charity and we also exchange gifts like Christians do on Christmas.

13 If you think about it, the main purpose of Ramadan is the same as most religious holidays—spiritual development. Christians and Jews gather regularly to commemorate their histories, to enact certain rituals, and to feel closer to God. Muslims do the same thing during Ramadan.

14 Today, we've explored the history of Ramadan and its practices—fasting, prayer, and charity. I'd like to leave you with the traditional greeting that Muslims utter during this holy month: "Ramadan Kareem," which means

"Ramadan is generous." Less than a year from now, when the next Ramadan comes around, I hope you'll have a better understanding of why it is so sacred for one billion people around the world.

15 Thank you.

THE HORRORS OF PUPPY MILLS

Seventy-five million dogs are owned as pets in the United States, and 7 to 9 million puppies are purchased each year at a total cost of close to $1 billion. Most come from legitimate breeders who take good care of their animals. Two to four million, however, come from puppy mills, large-scale operations run solely for profit with no concern for the animals' physical or emotional welfare. After explaining the problem of puppy mills, the following persuasive speech presents a solution that combines legislative action with individual initiative.

In addition to reading the speech, you can watch it in the online Media Library for this appendix. As you watch, notice how the speaker uses PowerPoint to present visual evidence of the conditions animals are subjected to in puppy mills. Do you think the speech would have been as effective without this kind of evidence? All in all, does the speaker convince you that puppy mills are a serious problem? Does he present a clear and workable solution? How well does he use the methods of persuasion presented in Chapter 17?

connect

View "The Horrors of Puppy Mills" in the online Media Library for this appendix (Video A.2).

1 A cold, dark room. It smells disgusting. The creatures in front of you shake uncontrollably, packed one on top of another in tiny wire cages. To eat, they have only crumbs in front of them, and to drink, only a dirty bowl of water. Many have eye problems, ear problems, diseases, and infections. They've never been groomed. They've never been for a walk. And they've never seen the sun.

2 For too many dogs across America, this is how life begins—in a puppy mill. Puppy mills, as defined by the Humane Society of the United States, are "mass dog-breeding operations" that take place in "shockingly poor conditions." Puppy-mill breeders produce puppies for profit—only for profit—with little or no concern for the physical, social, or emotional needs of the dogs.

3 As a dog lover, I was shocked to discover the horrors of puppy mills across the country as I researched this speech. I know from my audience-analysis questionnaires that most of you had a dog or another pet while you were growing up and that you believe they should be treated humanely. Today I'll show you that puppy mills are not treating their animals humanely and I'll suggest some ways of solving the problem.

4 Puppy mills have been around for a long time, but they've grown dramatically in recent years. The Humane Society estimates that there are more than 10,000 puppy mills currently operating in the United States. According to Stephanie Shain, the Society's Director of Outreach for Companionable Animals, of the 7 to 9 million dogs sold in this country each year, 2 to 4 million come from puppy mills. That's double the number from only a decade ago.

5 Rather than producing the healthy, happy pets that millions of families dream of, puppy mills produce dogs with canine herpes, respiratory infections, parasites, seizures, and *E. coli*. Dogs that are lucky enough to escape these diseases often have rotten teeth, missing eyes or limbs, hip disorders, skin problems, and a host of other deformities.

6 In addition to suffering from physical problems, dogs in puppy mills are often emotionally unstable. Some are dangerously violent and aggressive. Others are apathetic and lack any desire to interact with people or animals. Because of the overcrowding in puppy mills, some animals literally go crazy and chew off the ears, legs, and tails of other dogs.

7 But you can see for yourself what the dogs have to endure. Here's a picture of a puppy mill provided by the U.S. Humane Society. As you can see, the cages are stacked one on top of another and the dogs are packed into the cages like sardines into a can. The dogs are not let out to go to the bathroom, so the cages are filled with waste and become breeding grounds for the diseases I mentioned earlier in my speech.

8 You can get a better sense of how disgusting puppy mills are from this photo, taken after the dogs were removed by animal protection officials. You can see how narrow the cages are and how they're crammed one against the other. You can see the filth and debris everywhere.

9 Finally, take a look at a couple individual dogs. The first one came from a puppy mill here in Wisconsin. It was so malnourished that it couldn't stand up by itself, and it had lost the fur on almost all of its body.

10 The next dog was in even worse shape. Covered with its own filth, it had a rash of infections and diseases and had lost the sight in one eye. Like other puppy-mill dogs, it never saw a veterinarian until it was rescued.

11 It's time that we stop the horrors of puppy mills and help dogs and dog owners alike. Solving the problem requires action on two fronts—legislation and individual initiative.

12 The first step is for new laws that will put puppy mills out of business. Current laws, such as the Animal Welfare Act, are ineffective at best. This law only regulates a small number of breeders, leaving countless puppy mills to operate under the radar.

13 Here's the legislation I propose. It's based on a combination of proposals that have been presented in several states. All dog breeders who produce more than 30 puppies a year should be required to register with their state's Department of Agriculture, which would inspect dog-breeding facilities just as the health department inspects restaurants.

14 Breeders with dogs in substandard conditions would be dealt with accordingly. A first offense would result in a fine of $3,000. A second offense would result in a fine of $5,000 and 30 days in jail. A third offense would result in a fine of $10,000 and 90 days in jail, plus permanent loss of the breeder's license in every state of the union.

15 But legislation alone won't do the job. You and I also have a part to play. We have to take the profit out of puppy mills by making sure we don't purchase dogs produced by puppy mills. We can do this by following guidelines laid out by the Humane Society.

16 First, consider adopting a dog from a trusted animal shelter instead of buying a new dog. The animal shelter will make sure the dog is free of physical and behavioral problems.

17 Second, if you decide to buy a new dog, visit the breeder's premises. If the breeder refuses to let you see the premises, or wants to meet you somewhere else, don't buy from that breeder.

18 Third, don't buy a dog from a pet store. The Humane Society has found that most dogs in pet stores actually come from puppy mills.

19 And fourth, don't be fooled by advertising. Just because an ad promises that a dog has been, quote, "family raised" or has a "health certificate,"

doesn't mean it's true. This is especially important when it comes to the Internet, where there is no way to verify the health of a dog or the trustworthiness of a breeder.

20 In conclusion, I'd like you to imagine your own pet—no matter what kind of animal it might be—living even one day in the conditions endured by dogs in puppy mills. Then imagine your pet living in those conditions day after day, week after week, month after month. Surely you would not want this for your own pet.

21 Yet even as we sit here, millions of dogs are suffering from the horrors of puppy mills. It's time to stop puppy-mill breeders from profiting on their cruelty. Even if, as the movie title says, all dogs go to heaven, we should not allow them to start their lives in hell.

BURSTING THE ANTIBACTERIAL BUBBLE

During the past several years, the use of household antibacterial products has grown dramatically in the United States. Today Americans spend millions of dollars on everything from antibacterial soaps and hand wipes to tissues, sponges, shampoos, and even children's toys that have been treated with antibacterial chemicals.

The following persuasive speech argues that these products do not provide the benefits they claim and may, in fact, be contributing to long-term health and environmental problems. As a solution, the speaker recommends that the U.S. Food and Drug Administration institute regulations governing the use of antibacterial products and that consumers avoid using these products.

In addition to reading this speech, you can watch the video in the online Media Library for this appendix. Study how the speaker uses examples, statistics, and testimony to support her position. Does she convince you that the heavy use of antibacterial products is a serious problem? Does she present an effective solution to the problem? How could she have made the speech more convincing?

connect

View "Bursting the Antibacterial Bubble" in the online Media Library for this appendix (Video A.3).

1 In the film *The Boy in the Plastic Bubble,* a boy born with a deficient immune system is forced to live in a germ-free environment to prevent him from contracting infections. His room is sealed against bacteria and viruses, his food is specially prepared, and his only human contact comes in the form of gloved hands.

2 Today millions of Americans are trying to build a bubble around themselves and their families to keep out germs. The bubble is not made of plastic, however, but of billions of dollars worth of antibacterial hand wipes, tissues, soaps, and sponges.

3 Before I studied antibacterial products in my public health class, I always used antibacterial hand soaps and antibacterial all-surface cleaner for my apartment. I also know from my class survey that 70 percent of you use antibacterial soaps, cleaners, and other products.

4 But after learning about the subject in class and reading research studies for this speech, I'm here to tell you that, try as we might, we cannot build a bubble between ourselves and germs with antibacterial products and that these products actually create more problems than they solve. After looking at the problems created by antibacterial products, we'll explore some solutions.

5 The place to begin is by noting that antibacterial products are popping up just about everywhere. The next time you go to the store, try to find a liquid soap that is not antibacterial. According to the Alliance for the Prudent Use of Antibiotics, 75 percent of all liquid soaps and 33 percent of all bar soaps are antibacterial.

6 In fact, there are more than 1,000 antibacterial household products on the market. In addition to all the soaps and cleaning products, there are also antibacterial cotton swabs, tons of antibacterial shampoos, and this antibacterial cutting board from Williams Sonoma. You can even get antibacterial socks, mouthwash, toothpaste, and, to protect you while away from home, this travel toothbrush with antibacterial bristles.

7 The *Boston Globe* reports that larger items such as mattresses, countertops, high chairs, and even children's toys have been coated with antibacterial chemicals. *The New York Times* calls the antibacterial craze "the biggest marketing coup since bottled water."

8 There's no doubt that antibacterial products are popular with consumers, but there is a great deal of doubt about whether they're effective in stopping the spread of germs. Elaine Larson, associate dean of the Columbia University School of Nursing, studied 238 families who used antibacterial products and found that they were just as likely to get fevers, sore throats, coughs, rashes, and stomach problems as families who used regular products. Larson's findings are echoed by Eric Kupferberg, associate director of the Harvard School for Public Health, who states: "Antimicrobial products don't significantly eliminate the number of germs you encounter on a daily basis."

9 Nor do antibacterial products prevent the transmission of diseases such as colds and flus. Why? Because these illnesses come from viruses, not from bacteria. Antibacterial products don't kill viruses. As Dr. Larson explains, "Most of the infections healthy people get are colds, flu, and diarrhea caused by viruses"—none of which can be prevented by the use of antibacterial products.

10 Not only do antibacterial products fail to deliver what they promise, but they actually increase your chances of getting sick. According to Stuart Levy, a professor of microbiology and medicine at Tufts University, excessive use of antibacterial products in the home can make children more likely to develop allergies and asthma.

11 In addition, people who use antibacterial products may become more susceptible to infections. Dr. James Chin, a research scientist in New South Wales, Australia, says: "The way we stay healthy is by low-dose exposure to bacteria and viruses. You need to exercise your immune system in the same way you need to exercise your muscles to be fit. If you don't do that, your immune system doesn't have a chance to do battle when it engages with an infection."

12 The problems caused by antibacterial products are so serious that Dr. Myron Genel, chairman of the American Medical Association's council on scientific affairs, fears one result may be the creation of antibiotic-resistant bacteria "that are largely untreatable because they are resistant to existing drugs."

13 And that's not all. Besides being ineffective at preventing diseases and being potentially dangerous to our health, antibacterial household products also appear to harm the environment. Rolf Halden of Johns Hopkins University School of Public Health reports that each year the United States releases into the water supply more than 2 million pounds of the active chemicals in antibacterial soaps.

14 The U.S. Geological Survey reports that chemicals from antibacterial products are winding up in streams and groundwater from the Denver area to remote locations in the Rocky Mountains. These chemicals are known to pollute the water supply, disrupt fish reproduction and growth, and, because they do not decompose quickly, remain active for years and years.

15 Now that we've seen the seriousness of the problem, let's look at some solutions.

16 First, we need federal legislation regulating the use of household antibacterial products. Just as the Food and Drug Administration has regulations controlling the use of antibiotics, so, too, should it institute regulations controlling the use of antibacterial products.

17 We don't let people purchase antibiotics without a doctor's prescription, and there's no reason we should allow makers of soap, tissues, hand wipes, toothbrushes, and other products to add powerful antibacterial agents without oversight from the Food and Drug Administration. Given the problems being caused by these products, it is time for the federal government to take action.

18 Second, we all need to take action as consumers. Most obviously, we need to stop buying these products. The best way to avoid germs, says the Centers for Disease Control, is to wash your hands for 10 to 15 seconds with plain soap and water.

19 In fact, a study at the University of North Carolina found that washing your hands with soap and water is more effective at getting rid of germs than using antibacterial hand wipes. Emily Sickbert-Bennett, a public epidemiologist and co-author of the study, explains that when you use soap and water, the germs go down the drain, but with waterless antibacterial hand wipes, "you never rinse your hands. You are just rubbing a chemical into your hand and letting it dry."

20 In conclusion, Americans spend millions of dollars every year on products that promise to "kill germs on contact." But as we have seen today, the antibacterial craze is a marketing coup rather than a proven way of stopping either the spread of germs or the incidence of colds, flus, and other virus-borne illnesses. Worse, these products appear to contribute to health problems, and they are creating environmental problems in the U.S. water supply. The federal government should start regulating these products and we, as consumers, should stop throwing our money away on them.

21 We need to resist the false notion that we can use these products to create a bubble around ourselves to keep out germs and disease. Instead, we can burst the bubble of marketers who are selling us a false bill of goods and then we can thoroughly wash our hands of the whole mess.

MY CRAZY AUNT SUE

The aim of a commemorative speech is to pay tribute to a person, a group of people, an institution, or an idea. In the following student speech, the speaker commemorates her aunt Sue and her heroic battle against the debilitating disease of rheumatoid arthritis.

As you read the speech, notice that it is not a biography that simply recounts the details of aunt Sue's life. Instead, it focuses on her courage, her sense of humor, and her refusal to complain about her fate. The speaker provides enough details to make clear why her aunt is so commendable, but her ultimate purpose

connect

View "My Crazy Aunt Sue" in the online Media Library for this appendix (Video A.4).

is to inspire the audience rather than to inform it. The speaker also uses vivid language, repetition, and parallel structure to give the speech the kind of formal tone appropriate for a commemorative speech.

In addition to reading this speech, you can view it in the online Media Library for this appendix.

1 The strongest person I know cannot peel a potato. The strongest person I know has trouble putting on her makeup. The strongest person I know needs a special key holder to turn the key in her car's ignition.

2 For the past 15 years, my 47-year-old aunt Sue has been living with rheumatoid arthritis, a painfully debilitating disease in which the joints of the body become intensely inflamed due to the immune system's activity. Yet despite the daily torments of this disease, my aunt Sue is stronger than any woman or man I have ever met.

3 Not a moment passes that my aunt Sue is not confronted with this demon of a disease and reminded of her disability through the pills she must take and the pain she must endure. It hurts to stand, it hurts to walk, it hurts to sit. After an infinite number of failed medications, aunt Sue is now undergoing her most aggressive treatment, which includes weekly oral chemotherapy. After half a dozen surgeries, her frail body is in need of still more.

4 And yet despite all of this, I can't recall ever hearing her complain about her fate. After all the indignities and inconveniences her illness has thrown at her, my aunt Sue still finds the energy to devote much of her time not to herself, but to those less fortunate than her. This past Thanksgiving, for example, she helped organize a dinner for more than 500 poor and homeless people. My aunt Sue, who has her medications put in non-childproof containers so she can open them, helped coordinate a dinner for those in need.

5 The picture I have painted of my aunt Sue thus far is of a kind woman, a determined woman, a warmhearted woman whose own suffering seems inconsequential when compared to that of others. This is all completely true, but there is something else about my aunt Sue that makes me admire her so. Actually, it's what makes me love her as much as I do.

6 At five feet two inches, and 105 pounds, with the spunk of a teenager, she introduces herself as "Crazy Sue"—and sometimes I'd have to agree with her. Somehow she is able to approach this demonic disease with a sense of humor. And not just any sense of humor. My aunt Sue is one of the funniest people I know.

7 Years ago, when the disease began to hit her really hard, one of the attorneys at her law firm asked why she was limping. She told him she fell off a trapeze performing her weekend hobby—and he believed her! Following an ankle sprain and further complications, her ankle became deformed and the arch of her foot completely collapsed. Whereas most people would wallow in their misery, aunt Sue calls it her "cartoon foot."

8 My aunt Sue has made a positive impression on countless people throughout her life, but I hope she knows how much of an impression she has made on me—and how much I admire her.

9 I complain about trudging through the snow to class, but I'm walking pain free. I complain about driving my friends around town, but I'm steering the wheel pain free. I complain about the final exams I'll have to write, but I have the mobility in my wrist to write pain free. I have learned from my aunt Sue that I need to do a better job about being happy for the things that I have, rather than worrying about the not-so-perfect things in my life.

10 Aunt Sue may call herself crazy, but I call her phenomenal—a joy to be around and a reminder that having a physical disability in no way diminishes a person's spirit or inner beauty.

QUESTIONS OF CULTURE

Sajjid Zahir Chinoy

Seldom does a student commencement address upstage the featured speaker—especially when that speaker is a Pulitzer Prize winner from Harvard University. Yet that is exactly what happened when Sajjid Zahir Chinoy spoke to his fellow graduates at the University of Richmond on May 12, 1996.

connect

View "Questions of Culture" in the online Media Library for this appendix (Video A.5).

Born and raised near Bombay, India, Chinoy was selected to speak as the result of a campuswide competition. After describing the jumble of emotions that filled his mind as he came to the United States to attend school, he spoke movingly of the warm reception he received in Richmond and of how cultural differences can be overcome by attempting to understand other people.

Addressing his audience of 3,000 people extemporaneously and without notes, Chinoy received thunderous applause, and his remarks were widely reported in the press. His speech was so inspiring that the main speaker, Harvard psychiatrist Robert Coles, began his address by paying tribute to Chinoy. "I've been to a number of commencements," said Coles, "but I've never heard a speech quite like that."

The text of this speech has been transcribed from a video recording and is reprinted with permission from Sajjid Zahir Chinoy and the University of Richmond. A video is available in the online Media Library for this appendix.

1 Distinguished guests, faculty, staff, students, ladies and gentlemen, and, most of all, the Class of 1996:

2 I can visualize the scene again and again: 11:30 P.M., Saturday night, the fifteenth of August, 1992, Bombay International Airport, India. I was leaving home for the University of Richmond. And as I said that final good-bye to my parents, my family, and my friends; and as I saw hope, expectation, even a tinge of sadness, in their eyes; and as I stepped aboard the Boeing 747 in front, I knew my life had changed forever.

3 The next 36 hours on board the aircraft were a time of questions, of concerns, of tremendous uncertainty.

4 Had I made the right choice in leaving home? Had I made the right choice in leaving my parents, my family, my home? Had I made the right choice in leaving my country, my culture, my background? Had I made the right choice in choosing the University of Richmond?

5 And then, of course, there was that one nagging question, that one overriding concern: As one of only three Indian students on a Richmond campus of 3,000, would I ever fit in?

6 My country was different. My culture was different. My experiences were different. My background was different. My language was different. My accent was different. Would I ever fit in?

7 And so here I was, high above the clouds, grappling with questions of culture, of interaction, of ethnicity. What I didn't know was that 30,000 feet

below, on the ground, the world was faced with these very same questions—the question of culture, the question of interaction, the question of ethnicity.

8 And so whether my aircraft took off from Bombay, where the Hindus and the Muslims lived together in a most fragile peace; or whether my aircraft was over Africa, where the Hutus and Tutsis of Rwanda and Burundi had long-standing animosity; or whether my aircraft was over Bosnia, where the Serbs, the Croats, the Muslims, and the Bosnians had broken yet another truce, the question was the same—could different cultures ever come together to reinforce one another?

9 Ladies and gentlemen, after that bumpy aircraft ride, this young Indian student had found his answer. He had been witness to the four most spectacular years of his life at the University of Richmond. The academics were great; the extracurriculars were great; his graduate plans were great.

10 But what left an indelible impact on his mind was none of this. No, instead it was those special moments, those moments of human interaction, those human relationships that can never quite be translated into words:

11 The time this young Indian student spent his first Thanksgiving dinner with his debate team coach. That Thanksgiving evening when I ate my first American turkey and saw my first American football game, not knowing the difference between a tackle and a touchdown. And yet, all of a sudden, just like that, this very different Indian student had become an inherent part of the great American tradition of giving thanks.

12 The time I spent my first Christmas Eve with my journalism professor. That Christmas evening when the relationship wasn't of a faculty member and a student anymore, but of two buddies who fought fiercely over every point in Ping-Pong.

13 The time I had a long and honest talk with an American friend on the eve of a calculus exam. I didn't learn much calculus that night, but what I did learn was that as different as we are—different countries, different cultures, different continents—inherently we are still the same.

14 The time in December 1992 when India was hit by communal riots, when violence and bloodshed were but a few hundred yards from my family and my home, and when my fantastic roommate from my freshman year sat up the entire night, giving me hope, strength, and courage at every step.

15 Yes, four years after that bumpy aircraft ride, I have found the answer to the question of culture.

16 I have found that it has taken just a little understanding, just a little sensitivity, just a little open-mindedness, just a little empathy on the part of this community—this University of Richmond community—to change my life like never before.

17 I have found that it makes no difference what culture you follow, what your background is, what your experiences are, what language you speak, what accent you have. The commonality of the human bond far transcends these superficial differences.

18 And yet look around at the world today. Look around at the very regions that were faced with the same question of culture that I was faced with four years ago.

19 Look at Bosnia, where, between 1992 and 1996, 300,000 people had been slaughtered—Bosnians, Serbs, Croats, Muslims—all because they came from a slightly different heritage or culture or history.

20 Look at Bombay, India. In one maddening week in 1992, 2,000 Indians—Hindus and Muslims—lost their lives fighting with one another. They fought

over a mosque; they fought over a structure made of brick and mortar. Two thousand human beings lost their lives.

21 Look at Africa, where, between 1992 and 1996, 1 million Hutus and Tutsis lost their lives. Just comprehend that for a moment. Between the time you were a freshman and a senior, 1 million lost their lives fighting over culture, over history, over background.

22 Yes, just look at the madness. The world has fought hard to highlight its differences. We have forgotten our inherent similarities. All because what was missing was a little understanding. Just a little sensitivity. Just a little open-mindedness. Just a little empathy.

23 Two similar questions of culture in 1992. Two diametrically opposite results in 1996.

24 And so, to the Class of 1996, I say go and distinguish yourselves like never before. Go get the best of jobs, the most rewarding of careers. Go to the best of graduate programs. And make a real difference in your communities.

25 But not for one moment, not for one moment, ever forget the memory of these four years—the memory that just a little understanding, just a little sensitivity, just a little open-mindedness, just a little empathy on your part can mean the difference between complete despair for one young boy in Bosnia and remarkable hope for another young boy at Richmond.

26 Thank you.

Notes

Chapter 1

[1]Pericles, quoted in Richard Whately, *Elements of Rhetoric,* 7th ed. (London: John W. Parker, 1846), p. 10.

[2]*Raising the Bar: Employers' Views on College Learning in the Wake of the Economic Downturn* (Washington, DC: Hart Research Associates, 2010); "Communication Tops Skills Sought by Employers," *Training,* October 11, 2010, www.training.com. May 12, 2011.

[3]Dave McGinn, "Me? Public Speaking?" *Globe and Mail,* December 1, 2009, p. L1.

[4]Quoted in Emily Driscoll, "Um, Like, Whatever: College Grads Lack Verbal Skills," Foxbusiness.com, March 4, 2011. April 6, 2011.

[5]George A. Kennedy, *Comparative Rhetoric: An Historical and Cross-Cultural Introduction* (New York: Oxford University Press, 1998).

[6]Geoffrey Brewer, "Snakes Top List of Americans' Fears," Gallup News Service, February 2001; Alex Blyth, "How to Get the Most Out of Public Speaking Training," *Training Magazine* (June 14, 2006), p. 7.

[7]A. M. Ruscio, T. A. Brown, W. T. Chiu, J. Sareen, M. B. Steain, and R. C. Kessler, "Social Fears and Social Phobia in the USA: Results from the National Comorbidity Survey Replication," *Psychological Medicine* (January 2008), pp. 15–28.

[8]Cicero, *De Oratore,* trans. E. W. Sutton (Cambridge, MA: Harvard University Press, 1942), p. xxvi.

[9]Digby Jones, "Public Speaking Tests the Nerves of Most Directors," *Birmingham Post,* August 25, 2003.

[10]Elayne Snyder, *Speak for Yourself—With Confidence* (New York: New American Library, 1983), p. 113.

[11]Sharon Aschaiek, "Conquer Your Fear of Public Speaking," *Toronto Sun,* March 16, 2005.

[12]A number of studies have shown that taking a public speaking course is effective in reducing stage fright. See Graham D. Bodie, "A Racing Heart, Rattling Knees, and Ruminative Thoughts: Defining, Explaining, and Treating Public Speaking Anxiety," *Communication Education,* 59 (2010), pp. 70–105.

[13]Lilly Walters, *Secrets of Successful Speakers* (New York: McGraw-Hill, 1993), pp. 32–36.

[14]See Steven Ungerleider, *Mental Training for Peak Performance,* rev. ed. (Emmaus, PA: Rodale Books, 2005).

[15]Joe Ayres, Tim Hopf, Michael T. Hazel, Debbie M. A. Sonandre, and Tanichya K. Wongprasert, "Visualization and Performance Visualization: Applications, Evidence, and Speculation," in John A. Daly et al. (eds.), *Avoiding Communication: Shyness, Reticence, and Communication Apprehension,* 3rd ed. (Cresskill, NJ: Hampton Press, 2009), pp. 375–394.

[16]Dick Cavett, quoted in Steve Allen, *How to Make a Speech* (New York: McGraw-Hill, 1986), p. 10.

[17]For more detail on the ideas in this paragraph, see Michael T. Motley, *Overcoming Your Fear of Public Speaking: A Proven Method* (Boston: Houghton Mifflin, 1998).

[18]Chris R. Sawyer and Ralph R. Behnke, "Reduction in Public Speaking State Anxiety During Performance as a Function of Sensitization Processes," *Communication Quarterly,* 50 (2002), pp. 110–121.

[19]For more detail on the dimensions of critical thinking, see M. Neil Browne and Stuart M. Keeley, *Asking the Right Questions: A Guide to Critical Thinking,* 9th ed. (Upper Saddle River, NJ: Pearson Education, 2010).

[20]For other models of the speech communication process, see Stephen W. Littlejohn and Karen A. Foss, *Theories of Human Communication,* 10th ed. (Long Grove, IL: Waveland Press, 2011); Em Griffin, *A First Look at Communication Theory,* 8th ed. (New York: McGraw-Hill, 2012).

[21]Herman Melville, *Redburn: His First Voyage* (New York: Harper and Brothers, 1850), p. 214.

[22]William B. Gudykunst and Young Yun Kim, *Communicating with Strangers: An Approach to Intercultural Communication,* 4th ed. (New York: McGraw-Hill, 2003), p. 4.

[23]For more detail on gestures and other aspects of intercultural communication, see Judith N. Martin and Thomas K. Nakayama, *Intercultural Communication in Contexts,* 5th ed. (New York: McGraw-Hill, 2010).

[24]Adapted from Roger E. Axtell (ed.), *Do's and Taboos Around the World,* 3rd ed. (New York: John Wiley and Sons, 1993), p. 41.

[25]Myron W. Lustig and Jolene Koester, *Intercultural Competence: Interpersonal Communication Across Cultures,* 6th ed. (Boston: Allyn and Bacon, 2010), pp. 149–152.

[26]For more on multiculturalism and communication, see Shang Liu, Zala Volčič, and Cindy Gallois, *Introducing Intercultural Communication: Global Cultures and Contexts* (Thousand Oaks, CA: Sage, 2011).

Chapter 2

[1]Richard L. Johannesen, Kathleen S. Valde, and Karen E. Whedbee, *Ethics in Human Communication,* 6th ed. (Prospect Heights, IL: Waveland Press, 2008), p. 14.

[2]Johannesen, Valde, and Whedbee, *Ethics in Human Communication,* p. 13.

[3]See, for example, Vincent Ryan Ruggiero, *Thinking Critically About Ethical Issues,* 7th ed. (New York: McGraw-Hill, 2008).

[4]Haig A. Bosmajian, *The Language of Oppression* (Lanham, MD: University Press of America, 1983), p. 5.

[5]See Steven J. Heyman, *Free Speech and Human Dignity* (New Haven, CT: Yale University Press, 2008).

[6]Thomas L. Tedford and Dale A. Herbeck, *Freedom of Speech in the United States,* 6th ed. (State College, PA: Strata Publishing, 2009), pp. 173–180.

[7]Kenneth Blanchard and Norman Vincent Peale, *The Power of Ethical Management* (New York: Ballantine Books, 1988), p. 64.

[8]For an excellent guide to ethical decision making, see Ronald A. Howard and Clinton D. Korver, *Ethics for the Real World* (Boston: Harvard Business Press, 2008).

[9]*MLA Handbook for Writers of Research Papers,* 7th ed. (New York: Modern Language Association of America, 2009), p. 52.

[10]Merry Firschein, "School Chief Calls Speech 'An Error in Judgment,'" *The Record,* June 2, 2007; "Superintendent's Speech Stirs Talk of Plagiarism," *New York Times,* June 2, 2007; Merry Firschein, "Teachers Worried About Boss's Last Year," *The Record,* June 13, 2007.

[11]Bruce Perry, *Malcolm: The Life of the Man Who Changed Black America* (Tarrytown, NY: Station Hill, 1991), p. 380.

[12]The credo is available at www.natcom.org/Default.aspx?id=134&terms=credo.

[13]See www.natcom.org/Default.aspx?id=134 & terms=credo.

Chapter 3

[1]Larry Barker and Kittie Watson, *Listen Up: What You've Never Heard About the Other Half of Every Conversation* (New York: St. Martin's, 2001), p. 5.

[2]Michael P. Nichols, *The Lost Art of Listening,* 2nd ed. (New York: Guilford, 2009).

[3]See Lyman K. Steil and Richard K. Bommelje, *Listening Leaders: The Ten Golden Rules to Listen, Lead, and Succeed* (Edina, MN: Beaver's Pond Press, 2004).

[4]Judi Brownell, *Listening: Attitudes, Principles, and Skills,* 4th ed. (Boston: Allyn and Bacon, 2010), p. 9.

[5]Jan Flynn, Tuula-Riitta Valikoski, and Jennie Grau, "Listening in the Business Context: Reviewing the State of Research," *International Journal of Listening,* 22 (2008), pp. 141–151; Laura A. Janusik, "Listening Pedagogy: Where Do We Go From Here?" in Andrew D. Wolvin (ed.), *Listening and Human Communication in the 21st Century* (West Sussex, UK: Blackwell, 2010), pp. 193–194.

[6]See, for example, Melissa L. Beall, Jennifer Gill-Rosier, Jeanine Tate, and Amy Matten, "State of the Context: Listening in Education," *International Journal of Listening,* 22 (2008), pp. 123–132.

[7]Andrew W. Wolvin and Carolyn Gwynn Coakley, *Listening,* 5th ed. (Dubuque, IA: Brown and Benchmark, 1995), pp. 223–396.

[8]Brownell, *Listening: Attitudes, Principles, and Skills,* p. 84.

[9]Louis Nizer, *My Life in Court,* repr. ed. (Whitefish, MT: 2010), pp. 297–298.

[10]Adapted from Lyman K. Steil, Larry L. Barker, and Kittie W. Watson, *Effective Listening* (Reading, MA: Addison-Wesley, 1983).

[11]George H. Putnam, *Abraham Lincoln* (New York: Putnam, 1909), pp. 44–45.

[12]M. Scott Peck, *The Road Less Traveled: A New Psychology of Love, Traditional Values, and Spiritual Growth,* 25th anniversary ed. (New York: Touchstone Books, 2003), p. 127.

[13]Jack Hayes, "Fifty Years of Meteorological Advances," *Vital Speeches,* 77 (2011), pp. 27–30.

[14]See Ralph G. Nichols and Leonard A. Stevens, *Are You Listening?* (New York: McGraw-Hill,

1957), pp. 113–114. This classic work still has much of value to say about its subject.

[15]On some of the other challenges involved in note taking, see Annie Piolat, Thierry Olive, and Ronald T. Kellogg, "Cognitive Effort During Note Taking," *Applied Cognitive Psychology,* 19 (2005), pp. 291–312.

[16]See, for example, Tamas Makany, Jonathan Kemp, and Itiel E. Dror, "Optimizing the Use of Note-Taking as an External Cognitive Aid for Increasing Learning," *British Journal of Educational Technology,* 40 (2009), pp. 619–635.

Chapter 6

[1]Seeing the speech classroom as a real audience is also important because it engages students in a form of rhetorical activity that is vital to participatory democracy. See Rosa A. Eberly, "Rhetoric and the Anti-Logos Doughball: Teaching Deliberating Bodies the Practices of Participatory Democracy," *Rhetoric and Public Affairs,* 5 (2002), p. 296.

[2]Saul Alinsky, *Rules for Radicals* (New York: Random House, 1971), p. 81.

[3]For a broader discussion of gender issues in communication, see Julia T. Wood, *Gendered Lives: Communication, Gender, and Culture,* 9th ed. (Boston: Wadsworth, 2011).

[4]Diana L. Eck, *A New Religious America* (New York: HarperCollins, 2001), p. 4.

[5]Research shows that speakers are usually more persuasive when they attempt to refute opposing arguments rather than ignoring them. See Richard M. Perloff, *The Dynamics of Persuasion: Communication and Attitudes in the 21st Century,* 4th ed. (New York: Routledge, 2010), pp. 185–186.

Chapter 7

[1]For more detail on Internet research, see Randolph Hock, *The Extreme Searcher's Internet Handbook: A Guide for the Serious Searcher,* 3rd ed. (Medford, NJ: CyberAge Books, 2010).

[2]See, for example, Adam R. Brown, "Wikipedia as a Data Source for Political Scientists: Accuracy and Completeness of Coverage," *PS: Political Science and Politics,* 44 (2011), pp. 339–343; Don Fallis, "Toward an Epistemology of Wikipedia," *Journal of the American Society for Information Science and Technology,* 59 (2008), pp. 1662–1674.

[3]These criteria are adapted from Sheridan Libraries, "Evaluating Information Found on the Internet," *Johns Hopkins University.* Web. April 14, 2011.

[4]For more information on various interview types and situations, see Charles J. Stewart and William B. Cash, Jr., *Interviewing: Principles and Practices,* 13th ed. (New York: McGraw-Hill, 2011).

[5]For an interesting study that confirms the extent to which the process of researching and developing speeches can affect the beliefs and attitudes of student speakers, see Barbara Mae Gayle, "Transformations in a Civil Discourse Public Speaking Class: Speakers' and Listeners' Attitude Change," *Communication Education,* 53 (2004), pp. 174–184.

Chapter 8

[1]See, for example, Kathryn Greene, Shelly Campo, and Smita C. Banerjee, "Comparing Normative, Anecdotal, and Statistical Risk Evidence to Discourage Tanning Bed Use," *Communication Quarterly,* 58 (2010), pp. 111–132.

[2]I would like to thank *21st Century* and *China Daily* for permission to include this excerpt from Sun Yan's speech in the online Media Library for this edition of *The Art of Public Speaking.*

[3]Elliot Aronson, *The Social Animal,* 10th ed. (New York: Worth, 2008), pp. 92–93.

[4]This point was made by James A. Winans in his classic *Speech-Making* (New York: Appleton-Century-Crofts, 1922), p. 141.

[5]Over the years, there has been much debate over whether statistics or examples have more impact on listeners. For a recent study that addresses this subject, see Hans Hoeken and Lettica Hustinx, "When Is Statistical Evidence Superior to Anecdotal Evidence in Supporting Probability Claims? The Role of Argument Type," *Human Communication Research,* 35 (2009), pp. 491–510.

[6]Joel Best, *Stat-Spotting: A Guide to Identifying Dubious Data* (Berkeley: University of California Press, 2008), provides a fascinating look at the use and misuse of statistics. For a more technical approach, see Neil J. Salkind, *Statistics for People Who (Think They) Hate Statistics,* 4th ed. (Thousand Oaks, CA: Sage, 2011).

[7]Bob Papper, "2010 Salary Survey: News Salaries Stabilize," Radio Television Digital News Association. *RTDNA.* Web. 15 April 2011.

[8]M. Allen, R. Bruflat, R. Fucilla, M. Kramer, S. McKellips, D. J. Ryan, and M. Spiegelhoff, "Testing the Persuasiveness of Evidence: Combining Narrative and Statistical Forms," *Communication Research Reports,* 17 (2000), pp. 331–336.

[9]For research confirming the importance of citing sources when presenting evidence, see Rodney A. Reynolds and J. Lynn Reynolds, "Evidence," in James Price Dillard and Michael Pfau (eds.), *The Persuasion Handbook: Developments in Theory and Practice* (Thousand Oaks, CA: Sage, 2002), pp. 429–430.

[10]Richard M. Perloff, *The Dynamics of Persuasion: Communication and Attitudes in the 21st Century,* 4th ed. (New York: Routledge, 2010), pp. 251–254.

Chapter 9

[1]Ernest C. Thompson, "An Experimental Investigation of the Relative Effectiveness of Organizational Structure in Oral Communication," *Southern Speech Journal,* 26 (1960), pp. 59–69.

[2]Harry Sharp, Jr., and Thomas McClung, "Effects of Organization on the Speaker's Ethos," *Speech Monographs,* 33 (1966), pp. 182–183.

[3]See, for example, B. Scott Titsworth, "Students' Notetaking: The Effects of Teacher Immediacy and Clarity," *Communication Education,* 53 (2004), pp. 305–320; Joseph L. Chesebro, "Effects of Teacher Clarity and Nonverbal Immediacy on Student Learning, Receiver Apprehension, and Affect," *Communication Education,* 52 (2003), pp. 135–147.

Chapter 10

[1]Judith S. Kaye, "Gathering Dreams and Giving Them Life," *Vital Speeches,* 73 (2007), pp. 239–242.

[2]Robert M. Gates, "About the Institution You Will Someday Lead," *Vital Speeches,* 77 (2011), pp. 138–142.

[3]Dorothy Sarnoff, *Speech Can Change Your Life* (Garden City, NY: Doubleday, 1970), p. 189.

[4]Sarnoff, *Speech Can Change Your Life,* p. 190.

Chapter 11

[1]Robert T. Oliver, *History of Public Speaking in America* (Boston: Allyn and Bacon, 1965), p. 143.

[2]Oliver, *History of Public Speaking,* p. 145.

Chapter 12

[1]For an authoritative exploration of the multiple functions of language, see David Crystal, *The Cambridge Encyclopedia of Language,* 3rd ed. (New York: Cambridge University Press, 2010).

[2]Dorothy Sarnoff, *Speech Can Change Your Life* (New York: Doubleday, 1970), p. 71.

[3]Annmarie Mungo, "A Child Is Born," *Winning Orations, 1980* (Mankato, MN: Interstate Oratorical Association, 1980), pp. 49–50.

[4]See Joseph Williams and Gregory G. Colomb, *Style: Lessons in Clarity and Grace,* 10th ed. (New York: Longman, 2010), for more on the principles of verbal clarity.

[5]James Geary, *I Is an Other: The Secret Life of Metaphor and How It Shapes the Way We See the World* (New York: Harper, 2011), provides a highly readable exploration of the role of metaphor in human expression.

[6]Edward Bliss, Jr. (ed.), *In Search of Light: The Broadcasts of Edward R. Murrow, 1938–1961* (New York: Knopf, 1967), p. 276.

[7]Rosalie Maggio, *Talking About People: A Guide to Fair and Accurate Language* (Phoenix, AZ: Oryx Press, 1997), p. 26.

Chapter 13

[1]Irving Bartlett, *Wendell Phillips: Boston Brahmin* (Boston: Beacon Press, 1961), p. 192.

[2]A. Craig Baird, *Rhetoric: A Philosophical Inquiry* (New York: Ronald Press, 1965), p. 207.

[3]Daniel J. O'Keefe, *Persuasion: Theory and Research,* 2nd ed. (Thousand Oaks, CA: Sage, 2002), p. 185.

[4]Dorothy Sarnoff, *Speech Can Change Your Life* (Garden City, NY: Doubleday, 1970), p. 73.

[5]See Walt Wolfram and Ben Ward (eds.), *American Voices: How Dialects Differ from Coast to Coast* (Malden, MA: Blackwell, 2006), for a collection of readings on dialects in the United States.

[6]Consult Kenneth C. Crannell, *Voice and Articulation,* 5th ed. (Boston: Wadsworth, 2012), for more detail on all aspects of voice production.

[7]Mark L. Knapp and Judith A. Hall, *Nonverbal Communication in Human Interaction,* 7th ed. (Boston: Wadsworth, 2010), pp. 12–15.

[8]Richard M. Perloff, *The Dynamics of Persuasion: Communication and Attitudes in the 21st Century,* 4th ed. (New York: Routledge, 2010), pp. 178–181.

[9]For more on delivery, plus other aspects of public speaking, see Garr Reynolds, *The Naked Presenter* (Berkeley, CA: New Riders, 2011); Scott Berkun, *Confessions of a Public Speaker* (Sebastopol, CA: O'Reilly Media, 2010).

[10]Thomas F. Calcagni, *Tough Questions—Good Answers: Taking Control of Any Interview* (Sterling, VA: Capital Books, 2008), provides many practical tips on managing question-and-answer sessions.

Chapter 14

[1]For a compendium of research on these subjects, see Richard E. Mayer (ed.), *Multimedia Learning* (New York: Cambridge University Press, 2009).

[2]See Stephen Few, *Now You See It: Simple Visualization Techniques for Quantitative Analysis* (Oakland, CA: Analytics Press, 2009), for a revealing look at the art of statistical graphics.

[3]Herbert W. Lovelace, "The Medium Is More Than the Message," *Informationweek.com* (July 16, 2001), p. 74.

[4]See, for example, Richard E. Mayer and Cheryl I. Johnson, "Revising the Redundancy Principle in Multimedia Learning," *Journal of Educational Psychology,* 100 (2008), pp. 380–386.

[5]Nancy Duarte, *Slideology: The Art and Science of Creating Great Presentations* (Sebastopol, CA: O'Reilly Books, 2008), provides a wealth of insight on designing high-impact visual aids.

[6]For more tips on the effective use of visual aids, see Garr Reynolds, *Presentation Zen: Simple Ideas on Presentation and Delivery* (Berkeley, CA: New Riders Press, 2008).

Chapter 15

[1]John R. Johnson and Nancy Szczupakiewicz, "The Public Speaking Course: Is It Preparing Students with Work-Related Public Speaking Skills?" *Communication Education,* 36 (1987), pp. 131–137; Andrew D. Wolvin and Diana Corley, "The Technical Speech Communication Course: A View from the Field," *Association for Communication Administration Bulletin,* 49 (1984), pp. 83–91.

[2]Richard E. Mayer, Sherry Fennell, Lindsay Farmer, and Julie Campbell, "A Personalization Effect in Multimedia Learning: Students Learn Better When Words Are in Conversational Style Rather Than Formal Style," *Journal of Educational Psychology,* 96 (2004), pp. 389–395.

[3]Joseph Conrad, "Youth: A Narrative," in Samuel Hynes (ed.), *Collected Stories of Joseph Conrad* (Hopewell, NJ: Ecco Press, 1991), p. 166.

[4]James Humes, *Roles Speakers Play* (New York: Harper and Row, 1976), p. 25.

Chapter 16

[1]There are many competing definitions of persuasion. Mine is drawn from Gerald R. Miller, "On Being Persuaded: Some Basic Distinctions," in James Price Dillard and Michael Pfau (eds.), *The Persuasion Handbook: Developments in Theory and Practice* (Thousand Oaks, CA: Sage, 2002), pp. 3–16.

[2]Amanda Bennett, "Economics + Meeting = A Zillion Causes and Effects," *Wall Street Journal,* January 10, 1995, B1.

[3]See Richard L. Johannesen, Kathleen S. Valde, and Karen E. Whedbee, *Ethics in Human Communication,* 6th ed. (Prospect Heights, IL: Waveland Press, 2008), for a full look at communication ethics.

[4]Adapted from Herbert W. Simons and Jean G. Jones, *Persuasion in Society,* 2nd ed. (New York: Routledge, 2011), p. 46.

[5]This view of the interaction between speaker and listener reflects cognitive processing models of persuasion in general and the Elaboration Likelihood Model in particular. For a concise explanation of the latter, see Em Griffin, *A First Look at Communication Theory,* 8th ed. (New York: McGraw-Hill, 2012), pp. 205–216.

[6]There is a great deal of research confirming the need for persuasive speakers to answer potential objections to their arguments. See John A. Banas and Stephen A. Rains, "A Meta-Analysis of Research on Inoculation Theory," *Communication Monographs,* 77 (2010), pp. 282–311.

[7]For a superb look at the research on courtroom persuasion, see John C. Reinard, "Persuasion in the Legal Setting," in Dillard and Pfau, *Persuasion Handbook,* pp. 543–602.

[8]Richard M. Perloff, *The Dynamics of Persuasion: Communication and Attitudes in the 21st Century,* 4th ed. (New York: Routledge, 2010), pp. 259–261.

[9]Daniel J. O'Keefe, *Persuasion: Theory and Research,* 2nd ed. (Thousand Oaks, CA: Sage, 2002), pp. 218–219.

[10]See, for example, Amber Marie Reinhart, Heather M. Marshall, Thomas Hugh Feeley, and Frank Tutzauer, "The Persuasive Effects of Message Framing in Organ Donation: The Mediating Role of Psychological Reactance," *Communication Monographs,* 74 (2007), pp. 229–255.

Chapter 17

[1]James C. McCroskey, *An Introduction to Rhetorical Communication,* 9th ed. (Boston: Allyn and Bacon, 2006), pp. 84–96.

[2]Rachel A. Smith and Edward L. Fink, "Compliance Dynamics Within a Simulated Friendship Network I: The Effects of Agency, Tactic, and Node Centrality," *Human Communication Research,* 36 (2010), pp. 232–260.

[3]Richard M. Perloff, *The Dynamics of Persuasion: Communication and Attitudes in the 21st Century,* 4th ed. (New York: Routledge, 2010), pp. 210–213.

[4]See John A. Banas and Stephen A. Rains, "A Meta-Analysis of Research on Inoculation Theory," *Communication Monographs,* 77 (2010), pp. 282–311.

[5]John C. Reinard, "The Empirical Study of the Persuasive Effects of Evidence: The Status After Fifty Years of Research," *Human Communication Research,* 15 (1988), pp. 37–38.

[6]See, for example, Michael T. Stephenson, "Examining Adolescents' Responses to Antimarijuana PSAs," *Human Communication Research,* 29 (2003), pp. 343–369.

[7]Rodney A. Reynolds and J. Lynn Reynolds, "Evidence," in James Price Dillard and Michael Pfau (eds.), *The Persuasion Handbook: Developments in Theory and Practice* (Thousand Oaks, CA: Sage, 2002), pp. 429–430.

[8]Daniel J. O'Keefe, *Persuasion: Theory and Research,* 2nd ed. (Thousand Oaks, CA: Sage, 2002), pp. 216–218.

[9]Adapted from James C. Humes, *A Speaker's Treasury of Anecdotes About the Famous* (New York: Harper and Row, 1978), p. 131.

[10]In classical systems of logic, reasoning from particular facts to a general conclusion was known as induction. Contemporary logicians, however, have redefined induction as any instance of reasoning in which the conclusion follows from its premises with probability, regardless of whether the reasoning moves from specific instances to a general conclusion or from a general premise to a specific conclusion. In this scheme, reasoning from specific instances is one kind of inductive argument—as are causal reasoning and analogical reasoning. See, for example, Nancy M. Cavender and Howard Kahane, *Logic and Contemporary Rhetoric: The Use of Reason in Everyday Life,* 11th ed. (Belmont, CA: Wadsworth, 2010).

[11]Lionel Ruby, *The Art of Making Sense* (Philadelphia: Lippincott, 1954), p. 261.

[12]In classical systems of logic, reasoning from a general premise to a specific conclusion was known as deduction. But just as contemporary logicians have redefined induction (see note 10), they have redefined deduction as any instance of reasoning in which the conclusion follows from its premises with certainty. Some deductive arguments move from general premises to a specific conclusion, but others move from specific premises to a general conclusion. Many speech textbooks confuse reasoning from principle, which is one form of deduction, with deductive reasoning in general.

[13]For more on fallacies and methods of reasoning, see Douglas Walton, *Informal Logic: A Pragmatic Approach,* 2nd ed. (Cambridge: Cambridge University Press, 2008).

[14]H. E. Butler (trans.), *The Institutio Oratoria of Quintilian* (Cambridge, MA: Harvard University Press, 1961), IV, p. 141.

[15]George Campbell, *The Philosophy of Rhetoric,* ed. Lloyd F. Bitzer (Carbondale, IL: Southern Illinois University Press, 1988), p. 77.

[16]Research on fear appeals, for example, has demonstrated that messages devoted exclusively to arousing fear in the audience are usually less effective than messages that combine fear appeals with reasonable explanations of how to eliminate or cope with the source of fear. For an excellent review of that research, see Perloff, *Dynamics of Persuasion,* pp. 194–207.

Chapter 18

[1]James C. Humes, *Roles Speakers Play* (New York: Harper and Row, 1976), p. 8.

[2]For both speeches, see "Remarks by President Clinton and President Nelson Mandela at Presentation of the Congressional Gold Medal to

President Nelson Mandela," September 23, 1998. (http://clinton4.nara.gov/WH/New/html/19980923-977.html) May 20, 2011.

[3]Humes, *Roles Speakers Play,* pp. 33–34, 36.

Chapter 19

[1]Gloria J. Galanes and Katherine Adams, *Effective Group Discussion: Theory and Practice,* 13th ed. (New York: McGraw-Hill, 2010), pp. 233–235.

[2]See Charlan Jeanne Nemeth and Jack A. Goncalo, "Influence and Persuasion in Small Groups," in Timothy C. Brock and Melanie C. Green (eds.), *Persuasion: Psychological Insights and Perspectives,* 2nd ed. (Thousand Oaks, CA: Sage, 2005), pp. 171–194, for a helpful review of scholarship on this subject.

[3]For more on the many dimensions of group leadership, see John W. Gastil, *The Group in Society* (Thousand Oaks, CA: Sage 2010), pp. 139–166.

[4]For more on dealing with conflict in small groups, see Scott A. Myers and Carolyn Anderson, *The Fundamentals of Small Group Communication* (Thousand Oaks, CA: Sage, 2008), pp. 199–215.

[5]Charles Pavitt and Kelly K. Johnson, "Scheidel and Crowell Revisited: A Descriptive Study of Group Proposal Sequencing," *Communication Monographs,* 69 (2002), pp. 19–32.

[6]For research on this subject, see Michele H. Jackson and Marshall Scott Poole, "Idea-Generation in Naturally Occurring Contexts: Complex Appropriation of Simple Group Procedure," *Human Communication Research,* 29 (2003), pp. 560–591.

[7]For further reading on research in small-group communication, see Marshall Scott Poole and Andrea B. Hollingshead (eds.), *Theories of Small Groups: Interdisciplinary Perspectives* (Thousand Oaks, CA: Sage, 2005).

[8]For more on small-group oral presentations, see Katherine Adams and Gloria J. Galanes, *Communicating in Groups: Applications and Skills,* 8th ed. (New York: McGraw-Hill, 2009), pp. 292–314.

Photo Credits

Chapter 1
Page 2: Courtesy of Geoffrey Canada and Harlem Children's Zone; 7: © ULTRA.F/Photodisc/Getty Images; 11: Photo by Eric Kayne/Getty Images; 14: Photo by Dan Perry, Atlanta; 17: © Image Source/Getty Images; 19: © Image Source/Getty Images; 23: © Reuters; 25: © Brand X Pictures/PunchStock

Chapter 2
Page 28: © Bryan Bedder/Getty Images; 33: © Zuma Wire World Photos/Newscom; 35: U.S. Navy photo by MC3 Travis K. Mendoza; 39: JGI/Jamie Grill/Blend Images/Getty Images; 41: Ingram Publishing; 43: © AP Photo/Joseph Kaczmarek

Chapter 3
Page 46: © Marius Becker/dpa/Corbis; 51: LWA/Dann Tardif/Blend Images/Getty Images; 55: © Terry Vine/Blend Images/Corbis; 59: © Oliver Berg/dpa/Corbis

Chapter 4
Page 65: Photo by Jemal Countess/WireImage/Getty Images

Chapter 5
Page 76: © Wolfgang Kaehler; 79: Digital Vision/Getty Images; 83: UpperCut Images/Getty Images; 85: © AP Photo/Statesman Journal, Kobbi R. Blair; 91: © Erik Isakson/Getty Images

Chapter 6
Page 96: © Kevork Djansezian/Getty Images; 101: © Ron Sachs/CNP/Corbis; 103: DESHAKALYAN CHOWDHURY/AFP/Getty Images; 109: © Reena Rose Sibayan/The Jersey Journal/Landov; 110: DreamPictures/Getty Images; 115: © AP Photo/Minnesota Daily, Mark Vancleave

Chapter 7
Page 118: © Chris Hill/National Geographic Society/Corbis; 122: PhotoAlto/Sigrid Olsson/Getty Images; 125: © Zhang Jun/XinHua/Xinhua Press/Corbis; 129: Thinkstock/Jupiterimages; 131: © Tim Pannell/Corbis; 137: moodboard/photolibrary

Chapter 8
Page 140: © Roger L. Wollenberg/UPI/Landov; 145: © Joe Skipper/Reuters; 149: Ken James/Bloomberg/Getty Images

Chapter 9
Page 164: Thomas Hawk/Flickr/Getty Images; 169: © Mike Kepka/San Francisco Chronicle/Corbis; 171: © JupiterImages/Thinkstock/Alamy; 173: © Image Source/Corbis; 179: © UPI/Kevin Dietsch /Landov

Chapter 10
Page 184: AFP Photo/Dimitar Dilkoff/Newscom; 187: © Patrick Kovarik/AFP/Getty Images; 191: Inti St Clair/Blend Images/Getty Images; 193: Diego Tuson/AFP/Getty Images; 197: Charles Eshelman/FilmMagic/Getty Images; 198: © Image Source/Corbis

Chapter 11
Page 204: © Mike Kemp/Rubberball; 205: (far right) © Rachel Epstein/PhotoEdit; 209: © Fancy/photolibrary; 214: © Dr. Billy Ingram/WireImage/Getty Images; 215: © Stockbyte

Chapter 12
Page 220: Olivier Douliery/ABACAUSA.com/Newscom; 223: © Sipa Press/Newscom; 227: © Tim Shaffer/Reuters/Landov; 229: © Mark Costantini/San Francisco Chronicle/Corbis; 231: Dave and Les Jacobs/Blend Images LLC.; 233: © Richard Langdon/Getty Images

Chapter 13
Page 238: © Michael Buckner/Getty Images; 243: © Brooks Kraft/Corbis; 245: © Jonathan Newton/The Washington Post/Getty Images; 249: © Rick Friedman/Corbis; 251: Courtesy of Southern Vermont College and Michelle Kwan; 253: Stockbyte/Getty Images; 255: © FRANCK ROBICHON/POOL/epa/Corbis

Chapter 14
Page 258: Courtesy of Kris Krüg/Flickr; 261: © Jim Zuckerman/Corbis; 265: Mannic Media/McGraw-Hill, Inc.; 266: The McGraw-Hill Companies, Inc./Andrew Resek, photographer; 271: © ZUMA Press/Newscom

Chapter 15
Page 276: © EPA/Monica M. Davey/Photolibrary; 281: © WpN/Photoshot; 285: © China Photos/Getty Images; 287: © The Star-Ledger/Jerry McCrea/The Image Works; 289: © Stockbyte; 292: © Cultura RF/Getty Images

Chapter 16

Page 298: AP Photo/Brian Lawdermilk; 303: © Mark Makela/In Pictures/Corbis; 307: © AP Photo/Cliff Owen; 311: © Matt Cardy/Getty Images; 315: © AP Photo/John Amis; 317: © Corbis

Chapter 17

Page 324: © Leigh Vogel/FilmMagic/Getty Images; 329: © AP Photo/Andrew Medichini; 333: © UPI/Kevin Dietsch/Landov; 335: Stockbyte/Getty Images; 339: © Jose Luis Pelaez, Inc./Corbis; 342: © Monty Rakusen/cultura/Corbis; 343: © Giorgio Cosulich/Getty Images; 345: © Punit Paranjpe/AFP/Getty Images

Chapter 18

Page 352: © AP Photo/The Boston Herald, Dominick Reuter; 357: © UPI/Kevin Dietsch/Newscom

Chapter 19

Page 364: © Image Source/photolibrary; 367: OJO Images/David Lees/Getty Images; 373: Jose Luis Pelaez Inc./Blend Images/Getty Images; 376: © SuperStock

Index

Q

R

S

T

U

V

W

Y

Communicating at Work

Principles and Practices for Business and the Professions

Tenth Edition

Ronald B. Adler

Jeanne Marquardt Elmhorst

2 Communication, Culture, and Work

chapter outline

chapter objectives

After reading this chapter you should be able to

1. Identify the cultures and co-cultures in a specific organization, field, or community and describe how their norms and values shape communication in the workplace.
2. Use the guidelines on pages 53–56 to describe the ways you and others can communicate most effectively in a diverse work environment.
3. Describe the culture in a specific organization or field and identify specific approaches to communicate most effectively within this culture.

Cultural Diversity and Communication

Diversity is a fact of life in today's working world. The population of Miami is two-thirds Hispanic;[1] over half of Washington, DC, residents are black; and one-third of San Franciscans are Asian Americans.[2] As Figure 2–1 on page 36 shows, the trend toward diversity will continue for the foreseeable future. According to U.S. Census Bureau, the nation's Hispanic and Asian populations will triple over the next half century, and non-Hispanic whites will represent about one-half of the total population by 2050.[3]

With the increase in international trade and immigration, the likelihood of working with people from different parts of the world is greater than ever. Over 10,000 foreign companies and their subsidiaries operate in the United States.[4] Some 300 Japanese companies operate in Michigan alone; German, British, and Dutch companies also have many U.S. sites. Immigrants accounted for over half of the growth in the U.S. labor force at the turn of the 21st century.[5] By 2016, experts predict that 2 million foreign-born workers will be moving to the United States every year.[6]

As more corporations become multi-national, Americans are moving abroad in growing numbers. Over 8 million were working overseas in 2003,[7] many for the 3,000 U.S. firms with global operations and others for over 36,000 foreign companies in more than 180 countries.[8]

Given figures like these, it's no surprise that over 80 percent of the human resources executives surveyed say that global talent will be a priority in the coming years.[9] For companies and individuals who can take advantage of the trend toward increasing cultural diversity, the opportunities are great. DuPont has a policy of hiring men and women of a variety of ages and cultures because "diversity of experience and

FIGURE 2–1
Population by Race and Ethnicity

Note: American Indian/Alaska Native not shown.

Source: J. S. Passel and D. Cohn, *U.S. Population Projections: 2005–2050* (Washington, DC: Pew Research Center, 2008).

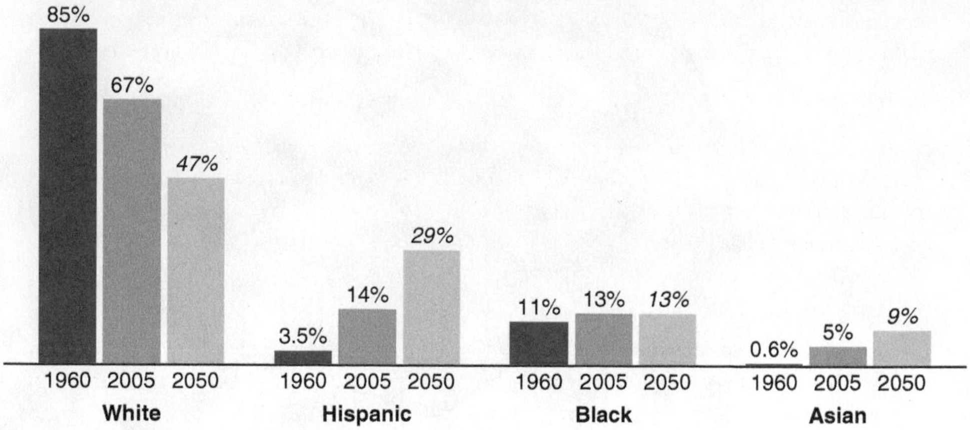

perspective gives DuPont a competitive edge."[10] Stona Fitch, vice president of manufacturing for Procter & Gamble, says, "Diversity provides a much richer environment, a variety of viewpoints, greater productivity. And, not unimportantly, it makes work more fun and interesting."[11] A spokesperson for the American Society of Civil Engineers states, "Without embracing diversity, the engineering profession will be unable to compete effectively in the global marketplace."[12] Whether you are working abroad, for or with foreign nationals at home, or with native-born people from different backgrounds, understanding cultural differences is an essential part of being an effective communicator.

The Nature of Culture

When most people use the word *culture,* they think of people from different national backgrounds. National cultures certainly do exist, and they play an important role in shaping the way people communicate. Other factors that define a culture and shape the way people communicate include race, ethnicity, age, socioeconomic status, gender identity, and language. Taking all these factors into account, we can define **culture** as a learned set of shared interpretations about beliefs, values, and norms, which affect the behaviors of a relatively large group of people.[13]

It's important to realize that culture is learned, not innate. A Korean-born infant adopted soon after birth by non-Korean parents and raised in the United States will think and act differently from his or her cousins who grew up in Seoul. An African American may view the world differently depending on whether he or she was raised in a small town, an inner city, or a middle-class suburb—or in a country like France or Zaire, where African heritage has a different significance from that in the United States. The overwhelming influence of culture on communication led famous anthropologist Edward Hall to assert that "culture is communication and communication is culture."[14]

Cultures are invisible to the people who are used to inhabiting them. But to people from different backgrounds, the power of dominant norms is obvious. One account of a corporate training session illustrates this point:

> *[The trainer] would run a little experiment when she was talking to corporate audiences that were mixed—including white men, women, and minorities. She would ask the audience to do a simple task: "Please list," she would request, "the rules needed to be successful in a white male society." Immediately the women and the minorities would begin to write down all the things*

> *they had to do to "fit in." Meanwhile, the white males in the audience just sat there, doing nothing, looking around at the women and the minorities writing for all they were worth.*[15]

The author describing this experiment explains the important truth it reveals:

> *[Cultural] paradigms are like water to fish. They are invisible in many situations because it is "just the way we do things." Often they operate at an unconscious level. Yet they determine, to a large extent, our behavior. As a white male, I cannot write down all those rules. My wife can. My minority friends can.*[16]

Cultural Differences in Doing Business

Some cultural differences in customs and behavior are obvious. For example, your work life will be simpler once you understand that punctuality is important in Switzerland and Germany but less important in most parts of Africa. Other differences, though, are much more subtle. We begin this section by looking at the more obvious differences in customs and behavior that distinguish cultures. Next we explore some fundamental dimensions of diversity that are less obvious but at least as important.

Differences in Customs and Behavior

Browse the travel and business sections of any decent bookstore and you're likely to find many volumes detailing the cultures and business practices around the world. The following categories are not an exhaustive list of differences between countries, but they suggest the importance of learning rules of the cultures in which you will operate.

Before going on, though, it is important to keep a sense of perspective about cultural influences on communication. Along with important differences, people from varied backgrounds also share many similarities. For example, computer engineers from Singapore, Lima, Tel Aviv, and Vancouver would find plenty of mutual interests and perspectives due to their shared occupational and socioeconomic backgrounds. Even when we acknowledge cultural variation, the fact remains that not everyone in a culture behaves identically. Figure 2–2 shows both the overlap in communication practices and the range of behavior within each one. Furthermore, within every culture, members display a wide range of communication styles. Ignoring cross-cultural similarities and intracultural variation can lead to stereotyping people from different backgrounds.

Formality U.S. Americans take pleasure in their informality and their quickness in getting on a first-name basis with others. With the exception of a few countries, including Thailand and Australia, business exchanges with persons from other countries

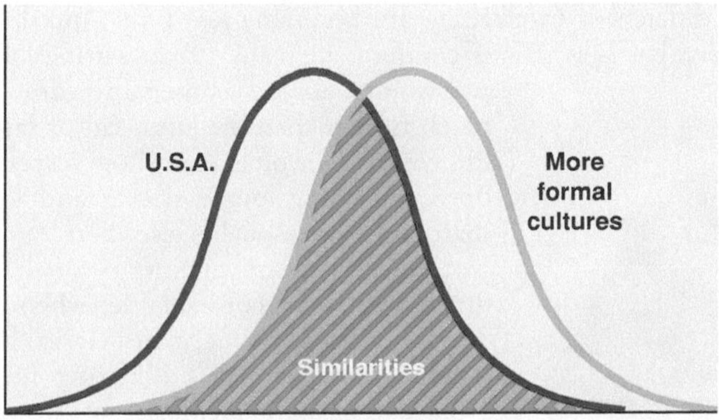

FIGURE 2–2
Differences and Similarities within and between Cultures

Sources: Adapted from M. H. Bond, *Beyond the Chinese Face* (New York: Oxford University Press, 1991), p. 3, and F. Trompenaars, *Riding the Waves of Culture* (New York: McGraw-Hill/Irwin, 1994), p. 28.

tend to be much more formal, especially toward the beginning of a relationship.[17] In the United States and Canada, first names are seen as friendly and indicative of fondness and attachment. In many other countries—Mexico, Germany, and Egypt, for example—titles are an important way of showing respect, and it's best to use them until you are invited to move to a first-name basis.[18]

Names and titles aren't the only way to express degrees of formality. The way people do—or don't—converse with strangers varies from one culture to another. In North America, it's not uncommon to strike up a conversation with a stranger; but this custom isn't universal. The U.S. retailing giant Wal-Mart made the strategic decision not to hire greeters at its German stores for reasons expressed by a public relations expert from that country: "As a German, I find the idea of being greeted at the door uncomfortable. I would feel astonished if someone I didn't know started talking to me."[19]

Social customs Cultural differences begin as soon as communicators encounter one another. Greetings range from the bow (lower is more respectful) in Japan, to the *wai* (pressed palms with a head bow) in Thailand, to the handshake in Europe and South America.

In many countries, exchanging business cards is an important ritual. In Japan, especially, cards are given and received with care: The recipient should use two hands and study the card carefully, treating it with the same respect he or she would give its owner.[20] One U.S. businessperson lost a deal in Japan because his inattention to the Japanese businessmen's cards was taken as a measure of the lack of attention he would give to their business.[21]

In many cultures, gift giving is a part of business protocol. Knowing the details of a specific culture can be important. For example, in India, where cows are sacred, gifts of leather are to be avoided. In China, avoid giving white flowers (associated with death) or gifts in sets of four since the sound of that number is the same as the word for "death." Lavish gifts may put your host in an awkward position, so learn cultural specifics and choose carefully.

Another variable is the degree of overlap between doing business and socializing. While entertaining is part of business in virtually all cultures, in many parts of the world socializing after business hours is a central part of building a working relationship. In much of eastern Asia, drinking is regarded as a way of building bonds that carry over into working relationships. One consultant alerts travelers to be prepared for a turn singing in the karaoke bars that are part of the scene in China, Japan, and other countries in the region.[22]

Styles of dress As travel and communication make the world feel like a smaller place, regional differences in clothing are becoming less pronounced. For men, the standard Western business suit is common in many urban settings. For both men and women abroad, conservative dress will take you much further than the latest fad or fashion. In Muslim countries, women can show respect with modest dress, including longer sleeves and lower hemlines than may be fashionable elsewhere.

Even in an era of international business, local differences exist. For example, when United Parcel Service entered the German market, it belatedly discovered that the firm's signature brown uniforms evoked unpleasant memories of brown-shirted Nazi storm troopers. In Indonesia, the company had to modify its usual business suit dress rule, and allow executives to wear more casual attire that is common in that hot and humid climate.[23]

Time In international business, the first shock for travelers from the United States may be the way members of other cultures understand and use time. North Americans, like most northern Europeans, have what anthropologists term a **monochronic** view of time, seeing it as an almost tangible substance. American speech reflects this attitude when people talk about saving time, making time, having time, wasting time, using time, and taking time. In U.S. culture, time is money, so it is rationed carefully. Appointments are scheduled and rigidly adhered to. Tasks are performed in a scheduled order, one at a time.

This monochronic orientation is not universal. Cultures with a **polychronic** orientation see time as taking a backseat to personal relationships. Meetings go on for as long as they take; they don't abruptly end because "it's time." Most Latin American cultures, as well as southern European and Middle Eastern cultures, have a polychronic orientation. In Mexico, for example, "you make friends first and do business later," according to R. C. Schrader, who heads California's trade office in Mexico City.[24]

Members of polychronic cultures are less concerned with punctuality than those raised with monochronic standards. It is not that being punctual is unimportant; it is just that other relational factors may take priority. This fact helps explain why the notion of being "on time" varies. Extremely monochronic cultures view even small delays as an offense. In polychronic cultures, varying degrees of lateness are acceptable—from roughly 15 minutes in southern Europe to part, or sometimes even all, of the day in the Middle East and Africa.[25]

Tolerance for conflict In some cultures, each person is responsible for helping to maintain harmony of a group and of society. The maintenance and pursuit of harmony is expressed in the Japanese term *wa*. In Chinese, a similar term is *zhong he*.[26] In other places—the Middle East and southern Europe, for example—harmony takes a backseat to emotional expression. Figure 2–3 illustrates how the rules for expressing emotions vary around the world.

The cultural avoidance of conflict means most Asian businesspersons will probably not say "no" directly to you, fearing that you will lose face and suffer embarrassment. To help you maintain harmony and save face, they might spare you unpleasant news or

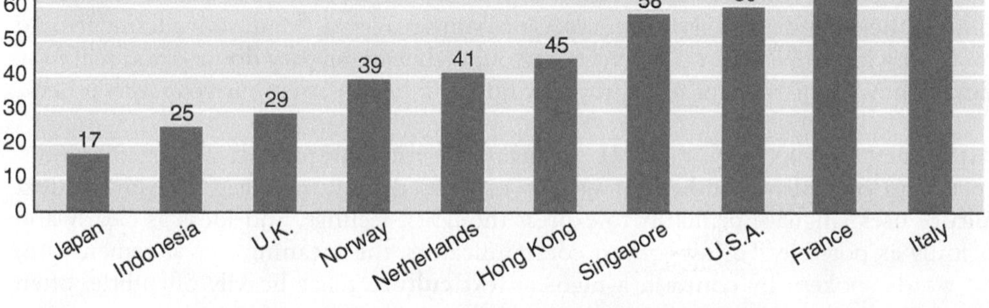

FIGURE 2–3
Percentage of Employees Who Would Openly Express Feeling Upset at Work

Source: F. Trompenaars, *Riding the Waves of Culture* (New York: McGraw-Hill/Irwin, 1994), p. 70.

information; it will be softened so that you don't suffer disgrace or shame, especially in front of others. You may be told that they will consider the matter or that it would be very difficult. Mexican business culture also values harmony and discourages confrontation. This attitude creates problems when it clashes with more aggressive standards that U.S. businesspeople usually bring to transactions. As president of Black & Decker Latin America, José Maria Gonzales is used to working with colleagues and suppliers from north of the border. Despite that fact, he says that coping with the difference between U.S. and Mexican approaches to conflict doesn't come easily:

> *In a meeting Americans can argue, hit the table and leave as if nothing happened, while a Mexican might not forgive you for three months. I have to make sure not to personalize things sometimes.*[27]

This sort of accommodation works both ways. People from cultures that seek harmony can learn to adapt to and accept conflict, and communicators from more aggressive societies like the United States can learn to appreciate the importance of harmony when communicating cross-culturally. Once communicators learn to appreciate different sets of rules about how to express and handle disagreements, conducting business becomes much easier.

Gender roles Women from North America, western Europe, and Australia/New Zealand who travel internationally are likely to be astonished and chagrined by the way they are regarded in some overseas cultures, where ideas of appropriate feminine behavior can be quite different. In some countries, a woman who outranks a man may not be treated that way by hosts; they may still speak to and prefer to negotiate with the male, assuming he is her superior. In Asian countries and Muslim countries women may find they are omitted from substantive conversation or overlooked in negotiations because of designated gender roles. Sometimes, a woman can establish greater credibility by clarifying her title, role, and responsibilities in writing before a personal visit, but even this step won't guarantee the desired effect.

The kinds of differences described here can present challenges when workers from different cultures work together. Table 2–1 illustrates some of these challenges by listing differences between Chinese and Western businesspeople in both concerns and communication styles.

Fundamental Dimensions of Cultural Diversity

So far we have discussed obvious differences between cultures. As important as customs and norms are, they are only the tip of the cultural iceberg. Underlying what might appear to be idiosyncrasies in behavior are a number of fundamental values that shape the way members of a culture think, feel, and act. In the following pages, we look at some of these fundamental differences. Once you appreciate them, you will understand how and why people from different backgrounds behave as they do, and you will have ideas of how you can adapt to improve the quality of your communication with others.

High versus Low-Context Anthropologist Edward Hall identified two distinct ways in which members of various cultures deliver messages.[28] A **low-context culture** uses language primarily to express thoughts, feelings, and ideas as clearly and logically as possible. To low-context communicators, the meaning of a statement is in the words spoken. By contrast, a **high-context culture** relies heavily on subtle, often

Table 2–1 Contrasting Chinese–Western Concerns and Communication Practices

	Chinese	Western
Concerns	Saving face	Frankness, "honesty"
	Respect, politeness	Assertiveness
	Compromise, flexibility	Self-assurance
	General feeling, "spirit"	Specific terms
	Social status	Task at hand
	Patience	Time efficiency
Communication practices	Reserved	Extroverted
	Tentative	Firm
	Personal	Less personal
	No body contact	Hugging, backslapping acceptable
	No pointing	Index finger used to point

Source: Ming-Jer Chen, *Inside Chinese Business: A Guide for Managers Worldwide* (Boston: Harvard Business School Press, 2001), p. 136.

nonverbal cues to convey meaning, save face, and maintain social harmony. Communicators in these societies learn to discover meaning from the context in which a message is delivered: the nonverbal behaviors of the speaker, the history of the relationship, and the general social rules that govern interaction between people. When delivering difficult or awkward messages, high-context speakers often convey meaning through context rather than plainly stated words to avoid upsetting their listeners. Consider a few differences between how a low-context Westerner and a high-context Chinese might express the same idea:[29]

Western	Chinese
Do you understand? *(Responsibility placed on other.)*	Am I being clear? *(Speaker takes responsibility for understanding.)*
Is the project acceptable? *(Requires direct "yes" or "no" answer.)*	What do you think of the project? *(Gives respondent latitude to reply diplomatically.)*
We can't do that. *(Clear refusal could be perceived as harsh.)*	This may be a little difficult for us to do. *(Context makes it clear that the answer is still "no.")*

Mainstream culture in the United States and Canada falls toward the low-context end of the scale. Longtime residents generally value straight talk and grow impatient with "beating around the bush." By contrast, most Middle Eastern and Asian cultures fit the high-context pattern. In many Asian societies, for example, maintaining harmony is important, so communicators avoid speaking directly if that would threaten another person's dignity. One U.S. project manager describes how her insensitivity to high-context communication almost derailed an international team in developing a Japanese-language version of an Internet search service:

> *As an American project manager, I was expecting that if I was proposing something stupid, I would hear it from the people on the team. In reality, I had a plan with a fatal flaw, and the Japanese team members knew it, but it was not their style of communication to embarrass me by telling me.*[30]

Even within a single country, co-cultures can have different notions about the value of direct speech. For example, Puerto Rican language style resembles high-context Japanese or Korean more than low-context English. As a group, Puerto Ricans value social harmony and avoid confrontation, which leads them to systematically speak in indirect ways to avoid giving offense.[31] The same holds true for Mexican Americans, as communication researcher Don Locke explains:

> *Whereas members of the dominant culture of the United States are taught to value openness, frankness, and directness, the traditional Mexican-American approach requires the use of much diplomacy and tact when communicating with another individual. Concern and respect for the feelings of others dictate that a screen be provided behind which an individual may preserve dignity. . . . The manner of expression is likely to be elaborate and indirect, since the aim is to make the personal relationship at least appear harmonious, to show respect for the other's individuality. To the Mexican-American, direct argument or contradiction appears rude and disrespectful.*[32]

A preference for high- or low-context communication isn't the only factor that distinguishes one culture from another. One survey of 160,000 employees in 60 countries revealed several other ways in which the worldviews of one national culture can differ from those of another.[33] Table 2–2 lists those dimensions and the styles that are most common in some countries. We will look at those differences now.

Individualism and Collectivism Members of **individualistic cultures** are inclined to put their own interests and those of their immediate family ahead of social concerns. Individualistic cultures offer their members a great deal of freedom, the belief being that this freedom makes it possible for each person to achieve personal success. **Collectivist cultures,** however, have tight social frameworks in which members of a group (such as an organization) feel primary loyalty toward one another and the group to which they belong. China, like most East Asian cultures, is highly collective.

In collectivist societies, members are expected to believe that the welfare of the organization is as important as their own.[34] Workers are less likely to strive to become organizational "stars," since that approach would dishonor other members of the team. "You seldom see an individual

Table 2–2 Cultural Values in Selected Countries

Long-Term Orientation	Short-Term Orientation
China	Pakistan
Hong Kong	Philippines
Taiwan	Norway
Japan	Canada
South Korea	East Africa*
Individualistic	**Collectivistic**
U.S.	Guatamala
Australia	Ecuador
United Kingdom (England)	Panama
Canada	Venezuela
New Zealand	Pakistan, Indonesia
Avoid Uncertainty	**Tolerate Uncertainty**
Greece	Singapore
Portugal	Jamaica
Uraguay	Denmark
Guatemala	Sweden
Belgium and El Salvador	Hong Kong
High Power Distance	**Low Power Distance**
Malaysia	Austria
Philippines	Israel
Mexico	Denmark
Arab world**	New Zealand
China	Ireland
Task Oriented	**Socially Oriented**
Japan	Sweden
Hungary	Norway
Austria	Netherlands
Italy	Denmark
Switzerland	Costa Rica

**Ethiopia, Kenya, Tanzania, Zambia.*
***Egypt, Iraq, Kuwait, Lebanon, Libya, Saudi Arabia, United Arab Emirates.*
Source: Adapted from *Cultures and Organizations: Software of the Mind* by G. Hofstede (New York: McGraw-Hill, 1997). Accessed from **http://www.geert-hofstede.com/hofstede-dimensions.php?culture1=95&culture2=14.**

Japanese executive who stands above the rest until he is the most senior individual in the company," says international corporate recruiter Richard M. Ferry.[35] The power of collectivist beliefs was illustrated when PepsiCo rewarded one of its managers in China with a sizable cash bonus that he divided equally among his subordinates.[36]

Power Distance The term **power distance** refers to attitudes toward differences in authority. Cultures with high power distance, such as Mexico and the Philippines, accept the fact that power is distributed unequally—that some members have greater resources and influence than others. In these cultures, differences in organizational status and rank are expected, routine, and clear-cut. Employees respect those in high positions. Other cultures, such as the U.S., downplay differences in power. Employees are more comfortable approaching—and even challenging—their superiors and may expect to gain greater power.

Colleagues with different notions of power distance might find it difficult to work together. Imagine, for example, how a young business school graduate from a U.S. firm might grow frustrated after being transferred to the Guadalajara branch office, where the same relentless questioning that marked her as a free thinker in school is regarded as overly aggressive troublemaking.

Uncertainty Avoidance The world is an uncertain place. International politics, economic trends, and the forces of nature make it impossible to predict the future with accuracy. **Uncertainty avoidance** is a measure of how accepting a culture is of a lack of predictability. Some cultures (e.g., Singapore and Hong Kong) are comfortable with this fact. Their acceptance of uncertainty allows them to take risks, and they are relatively tolerant of behavior that differs from the norm. Other cultures (e.g., Japan, Greece, and Portugal) are less comfortable with change. They value tradition and formal rules, and show less tolerance for different ideas.

Task versus Social Orientation* Groups in societies with a strong **task orientation** (e.g., Japan, Austria, and Switzerland) focus heavily on getting the job done. By contrast, groups in cultures with a high degree of **social orientation** (Scandinavian countries, Chile, Portugal, and Thailand, and much of Latin America) are more likely to be concerned about the feelings of members and their smooth functioning as a team. When compared to other countries, the U.S. falls slightly toward the task-oriented end of the spectrum and Canada is almost exactly in the middle, balanced between task and social concerns.[37] For many Latinos in the U.S., *personalismo,* the interpersonal relationship between managers and employees, is of utmost importance.[38]

Task-oriented societies focus on making the team more competent through training and use of up-to-date methods and are highly concerned with individual success: advancing to more responsible jobs, better training, and so on. By contrast, groups in socially oriented societies focus more on collective concerns: cooperative problem solving, maintaining a friendly atmosphere, and good physical working conditions.

**These categories were originally labeled "masculine" and "feminine," based on traditional views that men are assertive and results-oriented, while women are nurturing. In an era of increasingly flexible sex roles these terms are considered sexist and misleading, so we have substituted different labels.*

career tip

Difference as Advantage

Historically, being different from the norm was a disadvantage for many career-minded people. For that reason, job-seekers often tried to downplay differences such as being born abroad, speaking differently, or appearing visibly different from the mainstream. But as society becomes more diverse, tolerance grows, and world trade expands, diversity can be a career-enhancer.

Here are some tips that can help you use your unique background in your career:

1. If you are skilled at speaking other languages, feature that information in your resume. Being bi- or multilingual can make you a very attractive candidate. If you are already employed, show your bosses how fluency can help the organization.
2. If English isn't your first language, make sure your literacy skills and accent reduction are up to par. Most communities offer classes in English, public speaking, and writing where you can sharpen these skills.
3. Identify ways your cultural background will help you be an asset in marketing, sales, client support, management, and other areas. Make sure your bosses understand these advantages.
4. Don't overplay your unique identity and risk being pigeonholed as a "token minority employee." Career success depends on a variety of factors, including your personal background, but performance is the best measure of your value.

Source: C. Prasad, "Difference as Advantage: Maximize the Benefits of Your Cultural Identity on the Job," retrieved May 3, 2009, from **www.imdiversity.com/Villages/Careers/articles/careerjournal_languages_105.asp.**

Short-versus Long-Term Orientation Cultures with a **short-term orientation** look for quick payoffs, while people with **long-term orientations** defer gratification in pursuit of long-range goals. The willingness to work hard today for a future payoff is especially common in East Asian cultures, while Western industrialized cultures are much more focused on short-term results.

As long as employees and employers share the same orientation toward payoffs, the chances for harmony are good. When some people push for a quick fix while others urge patience, conflicts are likely to arise.

It's easy to see how a society's task or social orientation, attitudes toward uncertainty, individuality, power distance, and short- or long-term results can make a tremendous difference in how work situations evolve. Cultural values shape what persons communicate about and how they interact. Cultural differences don't account for every aspect of workplace functioning, of course, but they do provide a set of assumptions that exert a subtle yet powerful effect on each person's workplace communication.

Co-cultural Dimensions of a Diverse Society

It isn't necessary to travel abroad to find cultural differences. Diversity at home exerts a powerful effect on communication at work. Society is made up of a variety of **co-cultures**—groups that have a clear identity within the majority culture.

Language As society becomes more diverse, the mix of languages spoken and heard in the workplace increases. As the Case Study on page 46 shows, this trend presents real challenges: To what degree are non-native speakers obliged to learn the dominant language? How many accommodations are organizations and workers obliged to make

case study

A $48 Million Misunderstanding?

Jockey Jose Santos filed a libel claim against the Miami *Herald*, seeking $48 million in damages over a reporter's misunderstanding of his accented English. The *Herald* published a photograph showing Santos apparently holding an object in his hand as he rode thoroughbred Funny Cide across the finish line in the 2003 Kentucky Derby. In the accompanying story, reporter Frank Carlson misquoted the jockey as stating the object was an illegal "cue ring." The item turned out to be a Q-Ray, an ionized bracelet the jockey wore to help with his arthritis. As a result of the story, the Kentucky Racing Commission launched an investigation into what one official called "very suspicious" behavior.

The newspaper later printed a correction, but jockey Santos maintained that the story caused him emotional distress. The horse's owners were co-parties in the lawsuit, alleging that the article's allegation of underhanded racing tactics cost them potential business.

Santos' attorney said that the misunderstanding would never have happened if the *Herald* had chosen a Spanish-speaking reporter. In the same vein, the editor of Miami's alternative paper *New Times* commented: "Let me get this straight: In Miami, the most Hispanic city in the country, the newspaper of record screwed up because someone misunderstood a Spanish speaker?"

CRITICAL ANALYSIS: Answer the following questions as you consider this case.

1. What parties might have been harmed as a result of this misunderstanding?
2. How might the misunderstanding have been significantly reduced if the reporter and interviewee had been more familiar with each other's first language?
3. Describe at least one situation from your experience where misunderstandings could occur due to language differences. How could the chances of the misunderstanding(s) be reduced?

Sources: Based on "Santos, Sackatoga Sue Miami Herald for Libel," *Thoroughbred Times,* May 9, 2004; Richard Prince, "Latino Jockey's Case against Herald to Proceed," February 11, 2005, **www.maynardije.org/columns/dickprince/050211_prince/**, retrieved May 3, 2009; and "Photo of Kentucky Derby Winner Leads to Investigation," *Sports Illustrated.com* **http://sportsillustrated.cnn.com/horse_racing/news/2003/05/10/derby_photo_ap/**, retrieved May 3, 2009.

to help non-native speakers? Regardless of how you answer these difficult questions, it's indisputable that the ability to speak more than one language is an asset in virtually every career.

Even when communicators all speak the same language, accent can have a strong effect on how they are perceived. In the U.S., for example, a variety of accents can be heard in the workplace. Besides the standard dialect (think of speech by newscasters), regional and ethnic accents are common. Research suggests that speech differences are powerful. Speakers of standard dialect are rated higher than nonstandard speakers in a variety of ways: They are perceived as more competent and more self-confident, and the content of their messages is rated more favorably.[39] In one experiment, human resource directors listened to identical recorded passages of text spoken in different U.S. regional accents—and then recommended the best type of job for the speaker. Job-seekers with identifiable accents, such as a heavy southern drawl, were more often recommended for lower-level jobs that offer little client or customer contact, while those with a less identifiable accent were more likely to be recommended for higher-contact, higher-profile—and often higher-paying—jobs with more public contact.[40]

Regional Differences Beyond accent, regional differences in communication can be significant. In the United States, for example, the unwritten rules about smiling differ from one part of the country to another. Communication researcher Ray Birdwhistell found that midwesterners from Ohio, Indiana, and Illinois smiled more than New Englanders from Massachusetts, New Hampshire, and Maine. None of those people smiled as much as people from southern and border states like Georgia, Kentucky, and Tennessee.[41] Given these differences, it is easy to imagine how a manufacturer from Memphis might regard a banker from Boston as unfriendly, and how the New Englander might view the southerner as overly demonstrative.

Ethnicity It is an oversimplification to describe a single "Hispanic," "Asian," "white," or "black" style of communication, just as it is dangerous to claim that all Arabs, baby boomers, Israelis, or women are alike. Each person's communication style is a combination of individual and cultural traits. Keeping in mind the risks of overgeneralizing, scholars have found some patterns of communication that are common for many members of various groups. Understanding how communication is affected by cultural conditioning can help prevent jumping to mistaken conclusions about what a certain kind of behavior means.

The amount of talk and silence that is appropriate can differ from one co-culture to another. For example, most Native American and many Asian American cultures value silence more than mainstream U.S. culture does. By contrast, African American and Euro-American cultures place a high value on verbal skills, and their members tend to speak more. It is easy to imagine how the silence of, say, a Japanese American or Native American employee could be viewed by an African American or Euro-American colleague as a sign of dislike.

Attitudes toward conflict also differ from one ethnic co-culture to another. Because Asian cultures place a high value on saving face, some Asian Americans can display a preference for not disagreeing assertively and directly. Native Americans may prefer to deal with conflict through silence rather than direct confrontation. By contrast, many (though certainly not all) people with a Greek, Israeli, Italian, French, or South American background may prefer a direct, open conflict style.[42]

Even when communicators from different backgrounds speak roughly the same amount, the degree of personal information they reveal can differ dramatically. For example, Euro-Americans disclose more than African Americans or Puerto Ricans, who in turn reveal more than Mexican Americans.[43] (Of course, varying social and cultural contexts may create different disclosure patterns.)

Nonverbal standards also vary by co-culture. Most communicators unconsciously assume that their rules for behaviors such as eye contact are universal. Researchers, however, have found that eye behavior can vary significantly. One study found that widely opened eyes are often interpreted in mainstream U.S. culture as a sign of surprise or wonder and in Hispanic culture as a call for help, signifying "I don't understand." To some African Americans, the same kind of gaze is often regarded as a measure of innocence.[44] Chapter 4 has more to say about cultural differences in nonverbal behavior.

Since Euro-Americans often associate eye contact with honesty and respect, it is easy to misjudge others for whom steady eye contact would be a sign of disrespect. There are many cases where attempts by Puerto Ricans and Native Americans to show respect to persons in authority by not looking at them have been interpreted as dishonesty or disrespect by those accustomed to greater eye contact. Traditionally, Hopi and Navajo people generally avoid steady eye contact, as it is considered offensive, disrespectful, and rude. Blacks tend to make more eye contact when speaking but will not have such a steady gaze at someone they are listening to. Whites tend to make more continuous eye contact while listening to someone.[45]

technology tip

Generational Preferences in Communication Technology

Age often matters when choosing the best technology for exchanging messages on the job. The channels that communicators prefer are often a function of the era in which they came of age.

When boomers entered the workforce, typewriters and telephones were the principal communication technologies. Over 80 percent now use the Internet in one way or another, and most have embraced e-mail. But they are less likely than younger communicators to use or appreciate the value of text messaging, blogging, social networking, or instant messaging. Differences even exist between Gen X-ers and their Gen Y counterparts. For example, about half of the Y's in one survey reported sending or receiving at least one text message within the past day—roughly double the proportion of those in Gen X.

Beyond technology, generational differences also arise in communication style. Gen Y workers are used to the speed and brevity of texting and IM-ing. As a consequence, they often aren't sticklers for correct spelling and syntax. By contrast, matures, boomers, and even Gen X-ers grew up learning that accuracy is essential. They are likely to regard careless writing as a sign of incompetence.

Keeping differences like these in mind can help you choose the communication channel and style that best suits the people you are trying to reach. As always, generalizations don't apply to every person: Some boomers are avid users of all technologies, and some members of Generation Y resemble their grandparents when it comes to using digital media. Despite exceptions to the rule, it often pays to be mindful of generational differences when communicating strategically.

Sources: T. Erickson, "'Where Are My Corduroy Pants?' Is Gen Y's Texting Obsession Headed for the Workplace?" *Harvard Business Online,* May 29, 2007. Retrieved **http://discussionleader.hbsp.com/erickson/2007/05/where_are_my_corduroy_pants_is.html**. S. Fox and M. Madden, *Generations Online* (Washington, DC: Pew Internet and American Life Project, 2006).

Generational Differences Along with factors like ethnicity and regional differences, the era in which people have been raised can shape the way they communicate. Demographers, marketers, and social scientists often categorize people born in the Western world in the 20th century into four groups: "matures," "boomers," "Generation X," and "Generation Y." While generalizing can be risky, awareness of fundamental differences can make intergenerational communication more effective.[46]

Matures (born 1900–1945) have been called "The Greatest Generation." Their formative experiences included the Depression, World Wars I and II, and the dawn of the atomic era. These events led to a strong sense of self-control and self-sacrifice. Matures commonly have a strong respect for authority. In the workplace, they have traditionally been loyal to the organizations for which they work. They follow the rules, which they assume exist for good reason. Their work ethic includes timeliness and productivity.

Boomers (born 1946–1964) benefited from growing up in the post–World War II era of prosperity. They witnessed and participated in an era of social reform and upheaval that included the Civil Rights revolution. Social upheaval surrounding the Vietnam War and the degradation of the environment led many boomers to question the claims of authority figures—an ironic position now that they have become the authorities. Boomers have an optimistic, can-do belief in themselves and in the potential for society and organizations to change for the better. As a group, boomers have grown used to getting their way.

Generation X (born 1965–1982) has accepted technological advances as a fact of life. During their youth, gender roles for women became more flexible, contributing to the notion that anything is possible. Because of their many options, Generation X-ers

characteristically explore what is desirable for themselves as individuals. They are adept with technology, skeptical, and independent, seeking a good balance between work and the rest of life. They don't accept orders uncritically, and they expect work and life to be meaningful. They respect performance over tenure and are loyal to people, not organizations.

Generation Y (born 1982–1991) also goes by a number of descriptive labels: the Why Generation, Net Generation, The First Globals, and Digital Natives. When compared to the preceding generation, they are hopeful and determined. They have an international worldview; over half have passports and one quarter expect to work outside the U.S.[47] They are technologically adept, and they like to learn by doing. They have high—sometimes unrealistic—expectations for salary, job, and duties. They are remarkably able to shift attention rapidly from one task to another. As a result, they are excellent at multitasking. On the other hand, they may ignore what doesn't interest them—at their own expense and that of their work.

Disabilities Belonging to a co-culture based on ethnicity or nationality requires years of immersion. By contrast, says columnist Karen Stone, "Disability is a club anyone can join, anytime. It's very easy. Have a stroke and be paralyzed. . . . Be in a car wreck and never walk again."[48] The Americans with Disabilities Act of 1990 (ADA) seeks to guarantee that people with disabilities receive reasonable accommodations and equal access to employment, buildings, transportation, and services. These legal guarantees are important, but they don't change the fact that, in many ways, having a disability may change how one is regarded. Typical language habits reflect this fact. The tendency is to use labels like "blind," "wheelchair-bound," or "deaf" to describe a person, putting him or her in a category that emphasizes physical condition over all other attributes.

Advocates urge terms that treat a disability as one feature, not as a defining characteristic. Describing Mike as "a person who is blind" is both more accurate and less constricting than calling him a "blind person." The difference between "deaf person" and "person who is deaf" might seem subtle—until you imagine which label you would prefer if you lost your hearing.

There are no hard-and-fast rules about communicating with people who have disabilities. After 11 years of research, communication researcher Dawn Braithwaite found that strategies preferred by some were rejected by others.[49] This variability showed up in situations in which an able-bodied person might appropriately offer help. About half of the survey respondents were open to offers of assistance, while others preferred that able-bodied persons wait until they receive a request for help. In either case, though, one message came through clearly: It is important for the self-esteem and safety of a person with a disability to maintain control over if, when, and how help is given. If your offer of help is turned down, accept that fact. If it is accepted, either ask "How can I help?" or ask whether your intentions are acceptable: "Would you like me to open the door?"

Despite the lack of specific overall rules, there are some guidelines for interacting with people who have disabilities:

1. Speak directly to people with disabilities, rather than looking at and talking to their companion or sign language interpreter.
2. When introduced to a person with a disability, offer to shake hands. People with limited hand use or who wear an artificial limb can usually shake hands. (Shaking hands with the left hand is an acceptable greeting.)
3. When meeting a person who is visually impaired, identify yourself and others who may be with you. When conversing in a group, remember to identify the person to whom you are speaking. If you are leaving a group, tell the other person.
4. If you offer assistance, wait until your offer is accepted. Then listen to or ask for instructions.
5. Treat adults as adults. Address people who have disabilities by their first names only when extending the same familiarity to all others. Never patronize people who use wheelchairs by patting them on the head or shoulder.
6. Leaning on or hanging on to a person's wheelchair is similar to leaning or hanging on to a person and is generally considered annoying. The chair is part of the personal body space of the person who uses it.
7. Listen attentively when you're talking with a person who has difficulty speaking. Be patient and wait for the person to finish, rather than correcting or speaking for the person. If necessary, ask short questions that require short answers, a nod, or shake of the head. Never pretend to understand if you are having difficulty doing so. Instead, repeat what you have understood and allow the person to respond. The response will clue you in and guide your understanding.
8. When speaking with a person who uses a wheelchair or a person who uses crutches, place yourself at eye level in front of the person to facilitate the conversation.
9. To get the attention of a person who is deaf, tap the person on the shoulder or wave your hand. Look directly at the person and speak clearly, slowly, and expressively to determine whether the person can read your lips. Not all people who are deaf can read lips. For those who do lip read, be sensitive to their needs by placing yourself so that you face the light source and keep hands, cigarettes, and food away from your mouth when speaking.
10. Relax. Don't be embarrassed if you happen to use accepted, common expressions such as "See you later" or "Did you hear about that?" that seem to relate to a person's disability. Don't be afraid to ask questions when you're unsure of what to do.[50]

So far we have focused on guidelines for able-bodied communicators. People with disabilities also can take steps to improve communication. Braithwaite identified several strategies, including the following, that can minimize the impact of the disability and help put able-bodied people at ease:

- *Initiating a transaction:* "Excuse me. Would you mind looking up a phone number?"
- *Modeling behavior:* "If you move your lips more like this, I can understand you better."
- *Establishing normalcy:* "Don't you hate waiting in lines like this?"

Self-Assessment | Diagnosing Your Cultural Intelligence

These statements reflect different facets of cultural intelligence. For each set, add up your scores and divide by four to produce an average. Our work with large groups of managers shows that for purposes of your own development, it is most useful to think about your three scores in comparison to one another. Generally, an average of less than 3 would indicate an area calling for improvement, while an average of greater than 4–5 reflects a true CQ strength.

Rate the extent to which you agree with each statement, using the scale:
1 = strongly disagree, 2 = disagree, 3 = neutral, 4 = agree, 5 = strongly agree.

______ Before I interact with people from a new culture, I ask myself what I hope to achieve.

______ If I encounter something unexpected while working in a new culture, I use this experience to figure out new ways to approach *other* cultures in the future.

______ I plan how I'm going to relate to people from a different culture before I meet them.

\+ ______ When I come into a new cultural situation, I can immediately sense whether something is going well or something is wrong.

Total ______ **÷ 4 =** [ ] **Cognitive CQ**

______ It's easy for me to change my body language (for example, eye contact or posture) to suit people from a different culture.

______ I can alter my expression when a cultural encounter requires it.

______ I modify my speech style (for example, accent or tone) to suit people from a different culture.

\+ ______ I easily change the way I act when a cross-cultural encounter seems to require it.

Total ______ **÷ 4 =** [ ] **Physical CQ**

______ I have confidence that I can deal well with people from a different culture.

______ I am certain that I can befriend people whose cultural backgrounds are different from mine.

______ I can adapt to the lifestyle of a different culture with relative ease.

\+ ______ I am confident that I can deal with a cultural situation that's unfamiliar.

Total ______ **÷ 4 =** [ ] **Emotional/ motivational CQ**

Source: P.C. Earley and E. Mosakowski, "Cultural Intelligence," *Harvard Business Review,* October 2004, pp. 139–146.

- *Confronting the issue:* "I may have trouble speaking, but I can understand just fine!"
- *Using humor:* "Tony, they tell me your singing is so awful that even a guy like me who can't hear would hate it!"

Diversity and Ethical Issues

Some cultural differences may challenge your sense of what is normal or proper behavior without raising ethical questions. For example, you probably could readjust your sense of promptness or what to wear to a business meeting without facing any sort of moral dilemma. In other cases, though, doing business in an unfamiliar culture might challenge your fundamental sense of right and wrong. You might be offended by differing notions of gender equality. You could be shocked to learn that bribes or payoffs are considered a normal part of doing business. You could encounter favoritism toward friends and family members that offends your sense of fair play. You might see a profound disregard for the environment.

There is growing recognition that businesses that operate in a worldwide economy need a universal code of business ethics. Toward that end, a collaboration of business leaders in Japan, Europe, and the United States have developed a code of ethics based on ideals from both East Asia and the West. Called the Caux Round Table Principles for Business, this code includes many communication-related principles, such as treating all employees with honesty and dignity, listening to employee suggestions, avoiding discriminatory practices, dealing with all customers fairly, and avoiding industrial espionage and other dishonest means of acquiring commercial information.[51]

Despite this admirable effort, you may encounter ethical challenges arising out of cultural differences. In cases like these, you can respond in a variety of ways:

Avoiding: You might refuse to do business in cultures which operate according to ethical principles that are different from yours.

Accommodating: You could accept the different ethical system and conform to practices that are fundamentally different from yours.

Forcing: You could insist on doing business in a way that you believe is ethically proper.

Educating–Persuading: You could try to convince the people with whom you want to do business why your set of ethical principles is more appropriate.

Negotiating–Compromising: Both parties could give up something to negotiate a settlement.

Collaboration–Problem Solving: The parties could confront the conflict directly and work together to develop a mutually satisfying solution.[52]

All of these approaches have obvious drawbacks. It's easy to imagine a situation in which you may have to choose between compromising your principles to please your bosses and customers or being true to yourself and risking your career.

Facing ethical dilemmas you never anticipated can be especially hard. You can begin to prepare yourself by grounding yourself in ethical principles and learning about the ethical practices of a new culture. When you do encounter new situations, ask yourself the following questions to help you make the best possible decision:

- *How morally significant is this situation?* Not all ethical conflicts have the same moral significance. For example, while giving contracts to friends or family members may offend the sensibilities of a businessperson used to awarding jobs on the basis of merit, the practice may not be as morally offensive as one exploiting child labor or irreparably damaging the environment.[53]

- *Is there home culture consensus regarding the issue?* If there is not widespread agreement in your home culture about the ethical principle, you justifiably may have more latitude about how to act. For example, since corporations in the United States have a wide range of policies about supporting the families of employees, there might be less obligation for a company to provide family benefits in a host country.[54]

Communicating across Diversity

By now it should be clear that communicating with others from different backgrounds isn't always easy. Matters including culture, ethnicity, and gender may have made others' experiences quite different from yours.[55] Some of the responsibility for building bridges rests with management, and a growing number of businesses are taking this job seriously. But you don't need to join a corporate training program to benefit from cultural diversity. Figure 2–4 shows the range of attitudes about cultural differences, and Table 2–3 lists attitudes and behaviors that can promote more satisfying, productive relationships among members of different cultures. These principles can be summarized in the five categories on pages 53–56. Adopting a more perceptive attitude can go a long way toward opening the door to more rewarding and productive communication.

Become Culturally Literate Many cultural problems are caused not by malice but by a lack of knowledge. Trainers in cultural sensitivity cite examples of how mistaken assumptions can lead to trouble.[56] In one West Coast bank, officials were dismayed when Filipino female employees didn't cooperate with the new "friendly teller" program. Management failed to realize that in Filipino culture overtly friendly women can be taken for prostitutes. A Taiwanese executive who was transferred to the midwestern offices of a large company was viewed as aloof and autocratic by his peers, who did not understand that Asian culture encourages a more distant managerial style.

Misunderstandings like these are less likely to cause problems when mainstream workers understand each other's cultural backgrounds. As Paulette Williams, former senior manager at Weyerhauser's nurseries in Southern California, put it, "If you don't learn how other people feel, you can hurt them unintentionally."[57]

Timothy Weiss, a U.S. professor who spent a year teaching at the Chinese University of Hong Kong, illustrates the kind of open-minded, inquiring attitude that can make communicators more effective when they encounter different cultural practices.

> *Why, in a culture that so dearly values every second and minute saved, will meetings and conversations last for what Americans would consider such inordinately long periods? . . . In these departmental meetings–which I find excruciating–I suspect that something else is going*

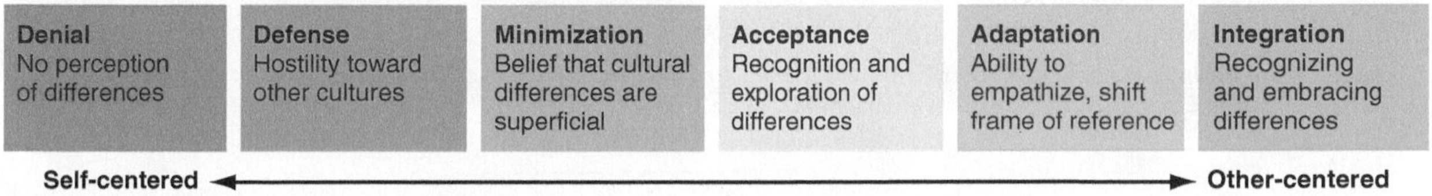

FIGURE 2–4
Stages of Intercultural Sensitivity

Table 2–3 Attitudes and Behaviors That Block or Promote Intercultural Relations

Assumptions That Block Authentic Relations

Assumptions Majority Makes	Assumptions Minorities Make
• Differences should not affect performance.	• All members of the majority have the same attitudes about minorities.
• Minorities will always welcome inclusion in the majority culture.	• There are no majority members who understand minorities.
• Open recognition of differences may embarrass minorities.	• Majority members are not really trying to understand minorities.
• Minorities are using their situation to take advantage of the majority.	• The only way to change the situation is by confrontation and force.
• "Liberal" members of the majority are free of discriminatory attitudes.	• All majority members will let you down in a "crunch."
• Minorities are oversensitive.	

Behaviors That Block Authentic Relations

Behaviors of Majority Cultures	Behaviors of Minority Cultures
• Interruptions.	• Confronting too early and too harshly.
• Condescending behavior.	• Rejecting offers of help and friendship.
• Expressions of too-easy acceptance and friendship.	• Giving answers majority members want to hear.
• Talking about, rather than to, minorities who are present.	• Isolationism.

Assumptions and Behaviors That Promote Authentic Relations

• Treating people as individuals as well as members of a culture.	• Staying with and working through difficult confrontations.
• Demonstrating interest in learning about other cultures.	• Acknowledging sincere attempts (even clumsy ones).
• Listening without interrupting.	• Dealing with others as they are, instead of expecting them to be perfect.
• Taking risks (e.g., being first to confront needed differences).	• Recognizing that interdependence is needed between members of majority and minority cultures.
• Expressing concerns directly and constructively.	

Source: From Philip R. Harris and Robert T. Moran, *Managing Cultural Differences: Global Leadership Strategies for the 21st Century.* (Boston: Elsevier/Butterworth-Heinemann, 2004), pp. 245–247.

on that a Westerner such as myself will understand sooner or later. Although I certainly am not ready to abandon my American sense of how departmental meetings should be conducted, in allowing myself to remain open-minded about other ways of conducting these meetings, I begin to learn something about other ways of approaching departmental issues and of communicating messages within a group.[58]

View Diversity as an Opportunity It is easy to think of cultural differences as an annoyance that makes it harder to take care of business. Dealing with others who have different attitudes or customs takes patience and time—both scarce commodities in a busy work schedule. But with the right attitude, cultural diversity can stop being just a necessary cost of doing business and can become an opportunity.[59]

People with differing backgrounds can bring new strengths to a business. Women, for instance, are generally more skilled than men at reading nonverbal cues.[60] This makes them ideal members of a negotiating team, where they may be especially skilled at interpreting how the other people are feeling. Workers from diverse ethnic groups can offer new insights into how customers or other workers with similar backgrounds can be reached. A Hispanic supervisor, for example, may be especially effective at motivating and training other Hispanics, and a Korean team member can give new insights into how a Korean-managed competitor operates.

Avoid Ethnocentrism **Ethnocentrism** is the inclination to see all events from the perspective of your own culture and to evaluate your own culture as superior. Ethnocentrism is evident when you judge someone to be less intelligent or less important because he or she doesn't keep up with your national teams, critique others as less sophisticated because their dress doesn't match your culture's notion of fashion, or assume others have less business acumen because they use different software programs. Taking advantage of intercultural communication training and opportunities for multicultural interactions may help reduce your ethnocentrism.[61]

Don't Condescend It's easy to view people who are different as unequal. Your first reaction to a physically challenged colleague might be sympathy or pity. Immigrants who are learning English as a second language might sound less intelligent than native speakers. Even white males, members of the traditional majority, might seem like members of the "good old boy" club, undeserving of respect since their success seemingly owes more to personal connections than to merit.

Even excessive efforts to demonstrate an attitude of equality can come across as condescending. One African American woman listed three statements that white women who want to treat black women with respect and friendship should never utter: (1) "I never even notice that you're black"; (2) "You're different from most black people"; (3) "I understand what you're going through as a black woman, because I'm (Jewish, Italian, etc.)."[62]

Create Dialogue Intercultural communication experts Judith Martin and Thomas Nakayama advise that an important first step toward intercultural competence is to enter into dialogue.[63] Dialogue occurs when persons acknowledge each other's common humanity and engage with each other authentically and spontaneously. Dialogue requires an attitude of mutual respect in which each person is listening to the other without preplanned agendas or past prejudices and distortions.

When people from differing backgrounds don't listen to and talk with one another constructively, misperceptions can take root. In a study of American corporations,

"After the merger, you may notice a few changes in our corporate culture."

Charles Kelly found that blacks perceived whites as being reserved and ambitious and having an attitude of superiority. He found that whites perceived blacks as being easygoing and ambitious and feeling as if they are owed something.[64] Without understanding each other's concerns, attitudes like these are less likely to disappear.

Not all talk about diversity is constructive: The way people talk about differences can determine whether relationships improve or suffer. Journalist Ellis Cose describes two nonproductive styles:

> *Discussions tend to be conducted at one of two levels—either in shouts or whispers. The shouters are generally so twisted by pain or ignorance that spectators tune them out. The whisperers are so afraid of the sting of truth that they avoid saying much of anything at all.*[65]

Experts agree with Cose that ignoring differences can be just as dangerous as emphasizing them. The challenge, then, is to discuss differences openly without using the kinds of inflammatory language described in Chapter 4. If you approach others with a constructive attitude, the odds of positive outcomes increase.

Organizational Culture and Communication

So far we have explored culture as a matter of geography, ethnicity, and physical condition. But even people with identical personal backgrounds can find themselves in very different cultures, depending on the organizations to which they belong. Just like individuals, organizations have personalities. Some are casual, energetic, even zany; others are formal, slow-moving, and serious. Social scientists call this personality an **organizational culture**—a relatively stable, shared set of rules about how to behave and set of values about what is important. In everyday language, culture is the insiders' view of "the way things are around here." Founder and former CEO of Southwest Airlines, Herb Kelleher, defined culture as "what people do when no one is looking."[66]

Like human personalities, organizational cultures that appeal to one kind of person repel others. Many people abhor bureaucracies, with their clearly defined job hierarchies and voluminous rules; others feel most comfortable in that sort of setting. Some people welcome the chaotic disorganization and constant change that often characterize new companies in emerging fields; others feel more at home in organizations with clearly defined jobs and products. Some people like a working environment in which employees are one big family; others prefer to keep their working and personal lives separate.

Belonging to an organizational culture means choosing a way of life. Consider one example of how cultures—and their effects—can differ.

> *Tattoos, piercings, long hair and good books. It's an odd combination that helps bookselling superstore Borders distinguish itself from the competition. Borders goes for funky, edgy employees who use their personality and passion to sell the products. Barnes & Noble, its closest competitor, prefers clean-cut employees in pressed shirts who smile brightly while helping customers find whatever they're looking for.*[67]

A Great Place to Work: Griffin Hospital

For eight consecutive years, *Fortune* magazine has honored Connecticut-based Griffin Hospital as one of the best companies to work for in the United States. The most important factor in choosing award winners is what employees themselves say about their organization.

Employees report that salary and benefits are important; but they are looking for something more basic. They want to have a voice in how the organization operates. They want to be told the truth, especially if the news is bad.

Griffin's culture of openness was tested in the dark days of 2001, when a rash of anthrax poisonings had the entire country on edge. A patient had become the nation's fifth victim of the deadly bacterium. The hospital's lab confirmed the diagnosis, and word was sure to leak out via the organizational grapevine. Despite pressure from the state's governor and the FBI to withhold the information, Griffin's administration felt obligated to honor its policy of openness and keep its workforce informed. The hospital held a briefing for 400 of its day-shift employees.

In light of Griffin's commitment to openness, a representative of the American Hospital Association endorsed the decision, saying, "If you do not follow the open and honest culture you have created at Griffin, you will destroy in one day what has taken you 10 years to build." Local opinion also supported the hospital. Griffin received an award from the New London newspaper for its commitment to keeping employees informed, calling the hospital's decision "nothing short of heroic."

Most organizations claim a commitment to a culture of open communication, but the real test is in what they do when faced with challenges. When choosing where to work, prospective employees would be wise to explore whether a company's deeds match its words.

CRITICAL ANALYSIS: Explore the importance of organizational culture by answering these questions:

1. How might the culture at Griffin have changed if administrators had been less open with employees in the anthrax case?
2. Why would a commitment to truth-telling and openness be at least as important as salary and benefits to employees at Griffin and elsewhere?
3. What elements of an organizational culture are most important to you? To what degree have these been present in organizations where you have worked and studied?
4. How can you use the guidelines on pages 61–62 ("Organizational Culture and Career Planning") to identify organizations with cultures that match your values and goals?

Sources: Carmine Gallo, "Creating a Great Place to Work," *Business Week*, February 4, 2008, p. 28, and "Changing the Face of Healthcare" **www.griffinhealth.org/Performance/FortuneSurvey.aspx**.

Cultures aren't limited to large corporations. Every organization has its own way of doing business and treating people. Anyone who has worked for more than one restaurant or retail store, attended more than one college or university, belonged to more than one team, or volunteered for more than one worthy cause knows that even when the same job is being performed, the way of doing business can be radically different. Furthermore, a person's "fit" with the culture of an organization can make all the difference between a satisfying and a disappointing job. Research shows that employees are more satisfied and committed to their jobs when their values match those of their supervisors and the organization.[68] They are also more successful. Harvard Business School professors John Kotter and James Heskett flatly claim that people who conform to the norms of their organization's culture will be rewarded, while those who do not will be penalized.[69]

Some of the rules for communicating in organizational settings are spelled out: "Customers come first" is one example. But in other cases, rules aren't made explicit. For instance, "don't complain" or "document *everything*" can be powerful rules, even though they aren't ever discussed.[70] One study revealed that the costs of employees not understanding the unspoken rules of an organization can be high—running into millions of dollars in lost time, reduced productivity, quality problems, and ill will.[71] Another study suggests that it is mid-level managers who best know, understand, and transmit company culture, perhaps making them the best source of information for new hires.[72]

The Importance of Organizational Culture

It's hard to overstate the importance of organizational culture. The cost of having a workforce that doesn't understand and play by the rules can be staggering. In one survey, respondents reported that the annual cost of workers not "knowing the ropes" ranged from less than $100 to as much as $10 million.[73] When employees didn't understand or accept their organization's culture, the results included lost time, lowered productivity, bad publicity for the firm, lowered morale and trust, lost customers, and lost opportunity. Poor fit between cultures may even cause organizational mergers to fail.[74]

Organizational culture can affect you in a variety of ways, both large and small. Among other things, the culture of your organization can determine where and how long you work, including options such as flextime and telecommuting. It can shape the emotional environment, including the degree of cooperation or competition, and notions of how much and what kinds of fun are appropriate. Culture will surely influence the way you and others dress and the space in which you work: its size, degree of privacy (or lack thereof), and decoration. Organizational culture will govern the amount and type of interaction you have (both on and off the job) with other employees, both co-workers and management.[75]

Dimensions of Organizational Culture

What elements distinguish one culture from another? In his well-known management book *The Human Side of Enterprise*, Douglas McGregor proposed two theories that shape organizational cultures. He referred to these opposing motivational theories as **Theory X** and **Theory Y.**[76] As Table 2–4 shows, the assumptions behind each theory are different. It's easy to imagine how the top-down, authoritarian structure in a Theory X organization would differ from the more optimistic, supportive culture in a Theory Y operation.

Several dimensions distinguish organizations, even those doing the same kind of work.

1. *Sociability.* Are employees involved with one another on a personal level, or do they limit interaction to job-related tasks? A "one big family" culture isn't necessarily superior to a less personal one, but shared notions about how much sociability is appropriate is an important ingredient of job satisfaction.
2. *Power distribution and job autonomy.* What is the degree of power distance between people at different levels within the organization? What are the demands to report and justify actions to higher management? How much freedom do employees have

on your feet

Describing Organizational Cultures

The culture of an organization can be a powerful influence on the experience members have in it and the public has with it.

In 2 minutes or less, brief your class on the culture of an organization (e.g., a place where you have worked or an organization you have belonged to) or a field (e.g., construction, software design) that you are familiar with.

Begin with a brief description of the organization or field and your experience with it. Then use the qualities listed on pages 58–60 that best describe the kinds of communication that shape this culture and how the culture shapes the way communication operates in the organization or field. Include at least one example of an incident or practice that illustrates the culture you are describing.

Table 2–4 Theory X and Theory Y Organizational Cultures

Theory X Organizations	Theory Y Organizations
• Work is inherently distasteful to most people, and they will attempt to avoid work whenever possible. • Most people are not ambitious, have little desire for responsibility, and prefer to be directed. • Most people have little aptitude for creativity in solving organizational problems. • Most people are self-centered. As a result, they must be closely controlled and often coerced to achieve organizational objectives. • Most people resist change. • Most people are gullible and unintelligent.	• Work can be as natural as play, if the conditions are favorable. • People will be self-directed and creative to meet their work and organizational objectives if they are committed to them. • The capacity for creativity spreads throughout organizations. • Most people can handle responsibility because creativity and ingenuity are common in the population. • Under these conditions, people will seek responsibility.

to make decisions themselves? Some workers are most comfortable when they have both limited authority and responsibility; others prefer more freedom.

3. *Degree of structure.* Are job roles highly defined, with people operating within their own area of responsibility, or is it considered acceptable to get involved in other areas of the organization's work? Does the organization have a large number of policies and procedures, or are issues handled less formally?
4. *Achievement rewards.* How (if at all) are the accomplishments of employees acknowledged and rewarded? Are praise and other types of reinforcement commonplace or infrequent? Is recognition based on true ability or other, less fair reasons? Is the level of reinforcement suitable to meet your personal needs?
5. *Opportunities for growth.* Does the company encourage workers to develop their skills and take on new responsibilities, or does it focus exclusively on employees' handling their present jobs competently? Does it encourage education and training? Are you satisfied with the opportunities for growth provided by the organization?

ethical challenge

Corporate Culture Supports Ethical Behavior

Electronics manufacturer Texas Instruments wants employees to ask themselves the following questions whenever they have a concern about whether a business action is ethical. This information is provided to TI employees on a business-card-size mini-pamphlet to carry with them. Note how these questions and statements reflect an organizational culture of integrity.

Is the action legal?

Does it comply with our values?

If you do it, will you feel bad?

How will it look in the newspaper?

If you know it's wrong, don't do it!

If you're not sure, ask.

Keep asking until you get an answer.

Source: Texas Instruments, Inc. Retrieved May 3, 2009, from **www.ti.com/corp/docs/company/citizen/ethics/quicktest.shtml**.

6. *Tolerance for risk and change.* Does management encourage employees to take well-reasoned chances, or is avoiding risk a high priority? Is change expected and welcomed, or are tradition, predictability, and stability highly valued?
7. *Conflict tolerance.* Does the company believe that disagreement is not necessarily a sign of disloyalty, or is harmony stressed? Are the organizational norms for managing conflict compatible with your personal style?
8. *Emotional support.* Does management show a genuine interest in the well-being of employees by seeking out and responding to their concerns? Do you feel like you are receiving the emotional support you want and deserve?[77]

Creating and Maintaining Organizational Cultures

Whether the culture is created deliberately or evolves without a grand design, the earliest phase of an organization's life is the best time to set the tone for its lifelong culture. Early events are enshrined in stories that can take on the quality of legends.[78] One of the most famous of these tales is told at IBM about former chairman of the board Thomas Watson Jr. Watson was barred from entering a high-security area of one of the company's plants because he was not wearing the proper identification badge. Rather than firing the assertive guard who blocked his entry, Watson acknowledged the policy and waited at the gate until the proper identification was found. The story confirms a policy central to IBM's culture: Everybody at the company obeys the rules.

An organization's culture takes on a life of its own. Customs and rituals develop that perpetuate a company's values.[79]

- The "work hard, play hard" culture of the Los Angeles Dodgers baseball club is apparent by a long history of practical jokes which included locking former manager Tommy Lasorda in his office, stealing the clothes of rookies while they are showering, and smearing shoe polish inside an unwitting player's cap in order to give him a black "halo." Players who have misconstrued these pranks as personal insults have overreacted until they understood the team's culture.[80]
- At Tupperware, the president and senior managers spend fully 1 month per year at celebrations honoring top salespersons and managers.[81]

- Some cultural practices involve changing labels. Employees are called crew members at McDonald's, hosts at Disney Productions, and associates at JCPenney, reflecting those companies' shared belief that every worker plays an important role in the corporation's success.

Practices like these both reflect a company's culture and continue to shape it, but they are nothing more than gimmicks unless they are backed up by day-to-day activities.

Not all cultural traditions are so positive. Supervisors often try to prod unproductive workers by issuing more and more rules, feeding the flames of unhappiness that they are trying to extinguish. In some organizations, negative customs perpetuate an unhappy state of affairs. Complaining can become a part of a company's culture: Bitter employees may spend time over coffee ridiculing management and criticizing the company. Unavailability is sometimes an organizational trait as well: Managers who dislike and fear subordinates often barricade themselves in offices, cutting off communication with the rank-and-file employees, who, in turn, feel increasingly alienated. One observer pointed out how corporate downsizing can be the ultimate measure of management's attitude toward employees.

> *Perhaps the most dramatic and egregious gestures companies make are layoffs. On one level, it looks as though the corporation has just gone feral and is chewing off its right leg because its left leg is in a trap. But when layoffs are particularly callous, an additional message is sent, one that speaks of arrogance, omnipotence and impunity. It's as if a gang of executives, clad in navy suits, were walking down a city sidewalk four abreast, bumping hapless strangers into gutters or shop windows. Downsizing's subtext is this: "We have the power and the money. We can do what we like, and there's not much you can do about it except whine."*[82]

Organizational Culture and Career Planning

As a prospective employee, you might be tempted to select a company on the basis of its most obvious characteristics. What is the starting salary? How are the working conditions? What are the chances for promotion? If you consider only these factors, you could wind up with an impressive title and income—but miserable.

When you are thinking about going to work for an organization, make an effort to pin down its personality, just as you would if you were choosing a mate. After all, you are likely to spend more hours per year at work than you will with a spouse. You can get a sense of a company's culture in five ways.[83]

Study the Physical Setting An organization's physical plant and architecture says something about its personality. Even though most organizations don't make statements by building their environment, they do say something about themselves by choosing the space in which they operate. For example, choosing to locate in a high-rent or low-rent district might say something about the prosperity of the organization, its concern with controlling costs, the public it wants to serve, or even its competence. Likewise, the physical condition of the facilities makes a statement. Is the workplace clean or dirty? Are workers' areas personalized or standardized?

Read What the Company Says about Itself Press releases, annual reports, and advertisements can all be revealing. Companies with strong values are proud to publicize them. An emphasis on only profit and loss raises doubts about the company's concern for its personnel. Pride about innovation, service to customers, and commitment to the community–all are clues about an organization's culture. Of course, noble statements may be only lip service to praiseworthy values. Use the other suggestions in this section to see whether a company practices what it preaches.

Observe Communication Practices How are you treated when you visit a company or deal with its employees? Do e-mails and other written correspondence suggest a welcoming culture?[84] A walking tour of the working areas can help give a feel for the organization's personality. "Vibrations" may not be a scientific term, but companies do have them.

Interview Company People Communication scholar J. Kevin Barge talks about the importance of learning about an organization's culture from the people who know it best: "Corporate cultures come from the way people talk about their organization, the way they construct what values are important, what rituals are important, what standards for performance are important, and what it means to be a member of this organization."[85]

An employment interview probably isn't the best place to explore how a company treats its employees. Talking with employees off the record can provide valuable insights about the way the company operates. See what they say about the company. Even rehearsed answers can be revealing: The apparent enthusiasm and sincerity with which they are delivered offer a clue about whether employees believe in the company line. Even if you don't learn much about the organization as a whole, you'll get a good picture of the kind of people you will be working with.

Learn How People Spend Their Time During your interview and observations, find out how employees spend their time at work. A surprising amount of effort might go into activities that are only remotely related to getting the job done: dealing with paperwork, playing office politics, struggling with balky equipment, or attending one unproductive meeting after another.

Check out the parking lot or garage on evenings and weekends: Lots of vehicles can be a tip-off that you will be expected to work long hours. Decide whether you are willing to accept this lifestyle. The way a company goes about its business reveals more about its culture than the kind of work it does.

review points

- U.S. society is increasingly diverse and communicating with many cultures (race, nationality, physical ability, gender identity, socioeconomics) and co-cultures (language, region, ethnicity, age) is a business necessity.
- Culture consists of learned beliefs, values, and norms of a group.
- Astute business communicators are aware of differences in formality, social customs, dress, time, tolerance for conflict, and gender roles as well as more "hidden" cultural dimensions of high/low context, individualism/collectivism, power distance, uncertainty avoidance, task/social orientation, and long-/short-term focus.
- Business communicators must consider the greater complexity of multicultural ethical issues.

- Employees must continuously update their cultural knowledge, view diversity as an opportunity, avoid ethnocentrism, treat everyone with equal respect, and develop dialogue.
- Prospective employees can understand organizational cultures (Theory X or Y, rules, customs, rituals, leaders, and history) by observation and interview and then evaluate the cultural "fit."

key terms

Test your understanding of these key terms by visiting the Online Learning Center Web site at www.mhhe.com/adler10e.

boomers 48
co-cultures 45
collectivist cultures 42
culture 36
ethnocentrism 55
Generation X 48
Generation Y 49
high-context culture 40
individualistic cultures 42
long-term orientation 45
low-context culture 40
matures 48
monochronic time orientation 39
organizational culture 56
polychronic time orientation 39
power distance 44
short-term orientation 45
social orientation 44
task orientation 44
Theory X 58
Theory Y 58
uncertainty avoidance 44

activities

Go to the self-quizzes at the Online Learning Center at www.mhhe.com/adler10e to test your knowledge of chapter concepts.

1. Invitation to Insight

a. Either through personal interviews or research, identify several differences in communication practices between your own culture and another culture that interests you.

b. If you were interacting with a person from that culture, how would you bridge the differences?

2. Invitation to Insight

Choose one set of cultural values summarized on pages 40–45 and identify the characteristic that is not representative of your own culture. For example, if you are used to a low-context culture, you might focus on high-context communication. Now consider both the advantages and the disadvantages of working in an environment in which this unfamiliar norm is the dominant one. For instance, how might interaction be more effective or otherwise desirable if most people communicated in a high-context manner?

3. Skill Builder

Select one form of disability. Collaborate with several of your classmates to create two role plays, illustrating effective and ineffective communication with a person who is challenged by the disability. Act out your role plays in front of the class.

4. Skill Builder

Develop your ability to identify and communicate effectively within an organization's culture. Choose an organization in a field that interests you, or focus on an organization to which you already belong. By analyzing the organization's physical setting and literature, interviewing others, and making your own observations, construct a description of the organizational culture that addresses the dimensions listed on pages 53–60. On the basis of your findings, describe an optimal way to communicate in the following areas:

a. Introducing new ideas.
b. Interacting with superiors.
c. Dealing with conflict.
d. Managing time.
e. Socializing with fellow workers.
f. Using preferred methods of exchanging information (e.g., telephone, e-mail, face-to-face interaction).

5. Skill Builder

Choose three cultures around the world with which you are likely to interact in the course of your career. To discover the keys to effective intercultural communication in your three chosen cultures, use the Internet sites listed in On the Web, World Cultures, on the Online Learning Center Web site at **www.mhhe.com/adler10e**. For each of the three cultures describe

a. The culture in general.
b. Business protocol for that culture.
c. The language(s).
d. Sources you could go to for additional training and/or e-mail contacts.

6. Skill Builder

Representatives from Japan, the United States, and European nations collaborated in an attempt to create an international code of business ethics. Read about the Caux Round Table by using a search engine to find articles on this process begun in 1994. Read the document at **http://www.cauxroundtable.org** and then

a. List the seven principles found in the document.
b. Describe how these seven principles relate to the ethical standards on page 12 of Chapter 1.
c. Write a short essay describing how your own personal sense of ethics corresponds to each of the seven principles.

7. Invitation to Insight

Choose one of the following options to better understand the importance of organizational culture. In each case, use the most relevant dimensions of communication described on pages 58–60 to structure your analysis and description.

a. Interview someone familiar with an organization or field that interests you to learn about its culture. Identify the kinds of communication that shape this culture and how the culture shapes the way communication operates in the organization or field.

b. Assume the administration of your college or university has asked you to brief newly hired faculty members about the academic culture of your school from an undergraduate student's perspective. Describe how communication practices at your school both shape and reflect its culture. You can make your remarks more clear and interesting by including one or more brief examples to illustrate how the culture operates.

resources

➔ For extensive readings and Web sites on cultural diversity and organizational communication, see the Online Learning Center Web site at **www.mhhe.com/adler10e.**

4 Verbal and Nonverbal Messages

chapter outline

chapter objectives

After reading this chapter you should be able to

1. Describe business situations in which ambiguous or specific language is preferable and create each type of statement.
2. Define, identify, and remedy examples of inflammatory language described in these pages.
3. Compare and contrast characteristically male and female speech and describe the potential benefits and problems arising from differences.
4. Describe how you can apply the information on nonverbal behavior in these pages in your own career.
5. Define and give examples of eight types of nonverbal behavior and summarize the importance of each in a specific organization or career field.
6. Predict the outcomes of various verbal and nonverbal behaviors with regard to sexual harassment and explain communication options for targets of harassment.

Although they are neighbors and see each other almost every day, Bob and Carolyn rarely speak to each other. Ever since their partnership broke up, the hard feelings have made even casual conversation painful.

"We both should have known better," Bob lamented. "It was such a simple misunderstanding. We went into the partnership agreeing that we would be 'equal partners,' but now I can see that we had different ideas about what being 'equals' meant. I saw each of us taking charge of the areas that we did best: I'm good at marketing and sales, and Carolyn knows product design and production backward and forward. So it made sense to me that, while we were each equally responsible for the business and deserving an equal share of the profits, we would each make the final decisions in the areas where we were experts."

"That's not what I meant by 'equal partners,'" stated Carolyn flatly. "Bob wasn't willing to take responsibility for the hard work of production. He kept saying, 'That's where you're the expert.' And he didn't have any faith in my ideas about sales and marketing. He wanted to make those decisions himself, whether or not I agreed. To me, being equal means you have just as much say as the other person in every part of the business."

In hindsight, both Bob and Carolyn realize that there had been signs of trouble from the beginning of their partnership. "Even before we opened for business, I could tell that Carolyn was unhappy," sighs Bob. "I always saw the venture as a chance to make a fortune. But whenever I'd get excited and talk about how much money we could make, Carolyn would clam up and get this grim look on her face."

Carolyn also remembers early, unspoken signs of trouble. "I've always wanted to have a business that my kids could be proud of," she said. "But when I'd talk about that, Bob wouldn't have much to say. Even though he never said so, at times I got the feeling that he was laughing at my high ideals."

This story illustrates the importance of paying close attention to verbal and nonverbal messages. The ill-fated partnership between Bob and Carolyn could have been

technology tip

Online Translation Services

In the age of global business, sooner or later you will need to communicate with someone who speaks an unfamiliar language. If you type "online translation" into your Internet search engine, you will find a variety of services available to help you bridge the language gap. One excellent—and free—option is Google Translate (**www.translate.google.com**).

A good test of a computerized translation is to convert a message from one language to another, and then back to the original one. Because idioms don't rely on word-for-word meanings, they provide an especially tough challenge. Google Translate did a surprisingly effective job at this task. It flawlessly retained the meanings of expressions such as "cross your fingers," "start from scratch," and "blessing in disguise" when those phrases were translated from English to Arabic and back again.

Even Google Translate wasn't perfect, though: It translated the phrase "from rags to riches" into "of the flags of wealth," and it mistakenly converted the idiom "go for broke" to "broken leg."

While computerized services can't match the talents of a skilled human translator, the better ones are surprisingly accurate for basic messages and are useful tools in the global village.

avoided if they had paid more attention to the unspoken but powerful nonverbal clues that warned of trouble. Examining more carefully just what an equal partnership meant also could have helped them avoid the clash that finally led to their breakup.

This chapter looks at the two channels by which you communicate: your words and your nonverbal behavior. By the time you have finished it, you will recognize that significant problems can lurk in even the simplest statements, and you will have discovered some ways to avoid or overcome such problems. You will also become more aware of the wordless messages that each of us constantly sends and receives.

Verbal Messages

As the case study on page 66 and the story that opened this chapter suggest, misunderstandings are a fact of life. In fact, most people vastly overestimate how well their explanations get through, and how well they understand others.[1] Linguistic theorists C. K. Ogden and I. A. Richards constructed a simple but profound model that explains the nature of many misunderstandings.[2] The broken line in their famous **triangle of meaning** model (Figure 4–1) shows that there is no direct relationship between an object, idea, process, or other referent and the word (or other symbol) used to represent it. Rather, the pathway to understanding—or misunderstanding—passes through

FIGURE 4–1
Ogden and Richards's Triangle of Meaning

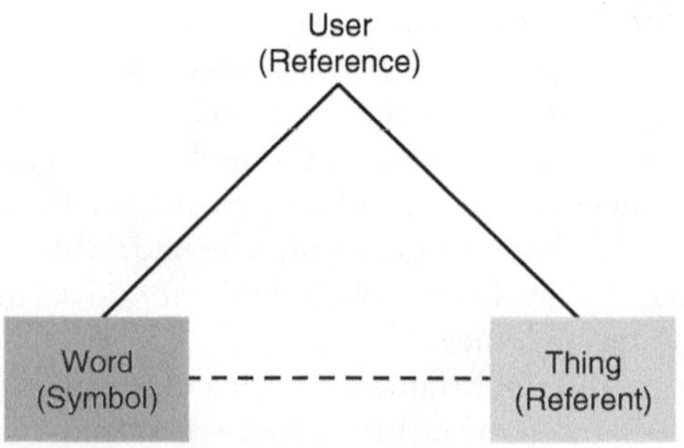

Table 4–1 Even Simple Messages Can Be Misunderstood

What the Manager Said	What the Manager Meant	What the Subordinate Heard
I'll look into hiring another person for your department as soon as I complete my budget review.	We'll start interviewing for that job in about 3 weeks.	I'm tied up with more important things. Let's forget about hiring for the indefinite future.
Your performance was below par last quarter. I really expected more out of you.	You're going to have to try harder, but I know you can do it.	If you screw up one more time, you're out.
I'd like that report as soon as you can get to it.	I need that report within the week.	Drop that rush order you're working on and fill out that report today.
I talked to the boss, but at the present time, due to budget problems, we'll be unable to fully match your competitive salary offer.	We can give you 95 percent of that offer, and I know we'll be able to do even more for you next year.	If I were you, I'd take that competitive offer. We're certainly not going to pay that kind of salary to a person with your credentials.
We have a job opening in Los Angeles that we think would be just your cup of tea. We'd like you to go out there and look it over.	If you'd like the job, it's yours. If not, of course you can stay here in Denver. You be the judge.	You don't have to go out to L.A. if you don't want to. However, if you don't you can kiss good-bye to your career with this firm.
Your people seem to be having some problems getting their work out on time. I want you to look into this situation and straighten it out.	Talk to your people and find out what the problem is. Then get together with them and jointly solve it.	I don't care how many heads you bust, just get me that output. I've got enough problems around here without you screwing things up too.

Source: From Steven Altman, Enzo Valenzi, and Richard M. Hodgetts, *Organizational Behavior: Theory and Practice* (Academic Press, Inc., 1985).

the mind of the sender or receiver. As Table 4–1 shows, the listener can understand the meaning of every word perfectly and still interpret a message in a way that is completely different from its intended meaning.

Clarity and Ambiguity

Since the most basic language problems involve misunderstandings, we begin our study of language by examining how to prevent this sort of miscommunication. We also look at times when a lack of clarity can actually be desirable.

Use Unequivocal Terms to Avoid Misunderstandings

Equivocal terms are those with two different, but equally acceptable or common, meanings:

A shipment ordered for Portland goes to Oregon instead of Maine.

A client asks a contractor for a mid-project change: "Can you move that door from here to there?" The contractor replies, "No problem." Later, the client is astonished to find that she has been charged for the change order.

You agree to call on a client at home at "dinner time" in a part of the country where "dinner" is midday and "supper" is in the evening. When you appear at 6:00 P.M., the client asks why you didn't arrive at the promised time.

Most equivocal misunderstandings arise in casual conversation, where statements seem perfectly clear until you discover that others can interpret them differently.[3] Sometimes equivocal problems arise because communicators from different fields use the same term in specialized ways. Hollywood agent Jerry Katzman describes just such a situation. In a meeting with representatives of a Silicon Valley software publisher, he used the phrase "in development" to mean a project that was at the rough-idea stage. By contrast, the software people were used to using that phrase to describe a project that had been funded and was being created. Katzman reported, "It was like when the Japanese first came to Hollywood. They had to use interpreters, and we did too."[4]

Equivocation sometimes comes from different cultural values. Compared with U.S. businesspeople, Mexicans are less inclined to express conflict and are more polychronic and relaxed about managing time. The Spanish word *ahorita* means "right now" or "immediately" in English. Despite its dictionary meaning, North Americans have found that their Mexican counterparts use the term quite differently:

When are those photocopies going to be ready?

"*Ahorita,*" answers the secretary who knows the copy machine is broken.

When will that delivery be made?

"*Ahorita,*" answers the salesman who has no truck.

One U.S. financial officer sheepishly admits he finally prohibited his Mexican staff from giving him *ahorita* as an answer.[5]

At least some equivocation problems can be avoided if you double-check your understanding of terms that might be interpreted in more than one way. When you agree to meet "Wednesday" with someone, mention the date to be sure that you're both thinking of the same week. When your supervisor says that your ideas are "OK," make sure that the term means "well done" and not just "adequate."

Use Lower-Level Abstractions When Clarity Is Essential Any object or idea can be described at various levels, some very general and others quite specific. **Low-level abstractions** are specific, concrete statements that refer directly to objects or events that can be observed. By contrast, **high-level abstractions** cover a broader range of possible objects or events without describing them in much detail. High-level abstractions can create problems because they are often subject to a wide variety of interpretations, such as the following examples:

Statement	Clarification
The job will take a little longer.	How much longer: Hours? Days? Weeks?
Straighten up the area.	A quick cleanup or a spit-and-polish job?
We need some market research.	A short questionnaire for a few customers or lengthy personal interviews and detailed surveys?
Give me your honest opinion.	Be diplomatic or blunt?

Since both abstract language and specific language have their advantages, it is often best to use both. One way to achieve maximum clarity is to begin explaining your proposal, problem, request, or appreciation with an abstract statement, which you then qualify with specifics:

> "I'm worried about the amount of time we seem to be spending on relatively unimportant matters [abstract]. In our last meeting, for instance, we talked for 20 minutes about when to schedule the company picnic and then had only 15 minutes to discuss our hiring needs [specific]."

> "I'd like to take on more responsibility [abstract]. Until now, the only decisions I've been involved in are about small matters [still abstract], such as daily schedules and customer refunds [more specific]. I'd like a chance to help decide issues such as buying and advertising [specific requests]."

Another type of ambiguous language that causes problems is the use of **relative words** such as *soon, often, large,* and *short* that have meaning only in relationship to other (unspecified) terms. Telling your supervisor that you'll have the memo done *soon* or agreeing to do a *short* report can cause problems. If *soon* means "in a few weeks" to you, but it means "in a few days" to your boss, a conflict is brewing. Replacing relative words with numeric words can eliminate most of these problems. Use "in 2 days" rather than *soon* and "two paragraphs" rather than *short,* for example.

Use Slang with Caution Casual, slang-laden speech may be fine off the job, but it can create the wrong impression with bosses, clients, and even colleagues. Some slang simply won't be understandable to others. For example, the British term "gobsmacked" is likely to draw a blank stare when used in conversation with someone outside the U.K. ("I was gobsmacked when they gave me that assignment"). Other terms are also likely to cast you in an unprofessional light. You may call your friends "dude" and label anything that's positive as "the bomb," but it's smart to talk more professionally in professional settings.

Use Jargon Judiciously Every profession has its own specialized vocabulary, often termed **jargon.** People who order office supplies talk about "NCR paper" and "three-up labels." Computer users talk about "64-bit architecture" and "image-compression boards."

In many cases, jargon serves a useful purpose. For one thing, it can save time. It's quicker for an accountant to use the term *liquidity* than to say "the degree to which an asset can be converted into cash." A specialized vocabulary is particularly vital when the subject matter is technical and complex. The phrase "sleeping pill" is unacceptable to health professionals because it says nothing about the dosage or the particular drug. Similarly, geologists can't discuss their findings by talking about "rocks."

A certain amount of jargon has its value for outsiders as well. Speakers who sprinkle their comments with jargon will

"O.K. What part of 'malignant regression and pathogenic reintrojection as a defense against psychic decompensation' don't you understand?"

ethical challenge

Strategic Ambiguity

a. Develop strategically ambiguous ways to rephrase each of the following statements:
   i. You've done a sloppy job here.
   ii. I can't understand what you're trying to say in this letter.
   iii. Nobody likes your idea.
   iv. Would you hurry up and get to the point?

b. On the basis of your responses here, decide how honest strategically ambiguous statements are. If they are not completely honest, can they be considered ethical?

appear more credible to some listeners.[6] While incomprehensible language may *impress* listeners, it doesn't help them to *understand* an idea. Thus, if your goal is to explain yourself (and not merely to build your image), the ideal mixture may be a combination of clear language sprinkled with a bit of professional jargon.

Problems arise when insiders use their specialized vocabulary without explaining it to the uninitiated. According to one survey, people in computer support industries are the worst offenders when it comes to jargon.[7] A customer shopping for a computer might be mystified by a dealer's talk about bus speed, onboard circuitry, and data transfer rates. When the same information is translated into language the buyer can understand—the length of time it takes to download a file, for example—a sale is more likely.[8]

Certain words are used so often that they become clichés.[9] As one communication expert says, they "are brief and snappy, roll off the tongue easily, and can fool us into thinking that we know what we're talking about."[10] If you overuse buzzwords like "mission focused," "paradigm shift," and "at the end of the day," you run the risk of not clarifying your ideas in your own mind and not being clear to others.[11]

Use Ambiguous Language When It Is Strategically Desirable

In low-context cultures like the U.S. and Canada, speaking directly is valued. "Don't beat around the bush" is a common phrase. Vague language can be seen as a sign of deliberate deception, as an old joke shows: A reporter warned a state senator, "Sir, your constituents were confused by today's speech." "Good," the senator replied. "It took me two days to write it that way."

Despite its bad reputation, ambiguous language does have its place. High-context cultures have made an art of strategic ambiguity, finding ways to express difficult messages indirectly. One U.S. author describes how indirectness works:

> *Instead of criticizing a report, the manager asks for more information. . . . When they say "I'd like to reflect on your proposal a while," when the decision must be [made] soon, it means "You are dead wrong, and you'd better come up with a better idea very soon. But I don't tell you so, because you should know that yourself!"*
>
> *It seems to me that such indirectness in interpersonal communication is a virtue; it is just as efficient, and it is certainly more mature and polite than the affront, "You are dead wrong." We need not talk to one another as if we were children (or characters out of the pages of pulp fiction)—yes, children need clarity—but adults can deal with indirectness and multiple meanings.*[12]

Even in the normally low-context cultures like the U.S., Canada, Israel, and Germany, there are many times when indirect speech helps communicators achieve two useful goals.[13] The first is *to promote harmony*. A group of workers who have been feuding over everything from next year's budget to funding the office coffee supply can at least reach consensus on an abstraction like "the need to reduce waste," a small but important start toward more cooperation.

A second function of ambiguous speech is *to soften the blow of difficult messages.* Business communicators face the constant challenge of delivering difficult messages: "This work isn't good enough." "We don't want to do business with you anymore." While statements like these may be honest, they can also be brutal. Ambiguous language provides a way to deliver difficult messages that softens their blow and makes it possible to work smoothly with the recipients in the future. For example:

Brute Honesty	Strategic Ambiguity
This work isn't good enough.	I think the boss will want us to back up these predictions with some figures.
I don't want to work with you.	Right now I don't see any projects on the horizon.

A final function of strategic ambiguity is to make a *point indirectly that can't be expressed overtly.* In the current litigation-prone environment, business communicators often use strategic ambiguity to communicate critical messages without exposing themselves to lawsuits.[14] For example, consider this humorous letter of reference "endorsing" a former employee who was fired for being a slow, lazy, unmotivated worker with an inflated ego and who lacked qualifications, causing the company to lose money:

> *I am pleased to say John Doe is a former colleague of mine. John left this job the same way he came, fired with enthusiasm. We are deeply indebted for the services he has given our firm over the years.*
>
> *John will do nothing which will lower your high regard for him. His job requires few skills which he lacks. I honestly don't think he could have done a better job for us if he had tried. I most enthusiastically recommend John Doe with no qualifications whatsoever. It will not take John long to get up to speed. No salary would be too much for him. You won't find many people like John.*[15]

One problem with strategic ambiguity, of course, is that it can easily be misunderstood. This problem can be especially acute in medical settings, when health care providers try to deliver bad news to patients in a way that softens its impact. For example,

> *[A surgeon] took one look at a patient's badly infected foot and recognized that it would have to be amputated. "I don't think we're going to be able to deal with this with local treatments," he told the patient.*
>
> *When the surgeon left the examining room, the woman turned to the doctor and asked: "Does that mean I'm going to have to go to Los Angeles for treatment?"*[16]

Even when misunderstandings aren't a problem, strategic ambiguity works only when both sender and receiver are willing to tolerate a deliberate lack of clarity. Without that understanding, the result can be confusion, and often feelings of being betrayed or manipulated.[17]

Choose the Optimal Degree of Powerful Language Some types of language make a speaker sound less powerful, while other types create an air of power and confidence.

Less Powerful Speech	More Powerful Speech
Tag questions	
"This report is good, *isn't it?*"	"This report is good."
Hesitations	
"I, *uh,* think we should, *um,* use the newer format."	"I think we should use the newer format."
Qualifiers	
"*I don't know if you'll like this idea, but* we could hire an outside consultant."	"We could hire an outside consultant."
Intensifiers	
"That was *such* a good job!"	"That was a good job!"
Questions	
"*Do you think we* should shorten the report?"	"I think we should shorten the report."

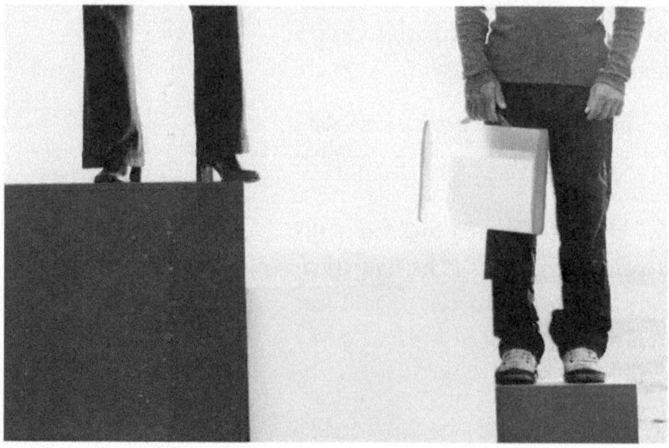

Speakers who use more powerful speech are rated as more competent, dynamic, and attractive than speakers who sound powerless.[18] One study revealed that even a single type of powerless speech mannerism can make a person appear less authoritative.[19] So, when your goal is to create an impression of power and conviction, it's best to avoid less powerful speech.

On the other hand, there are times when powerful individuals might intentionally use less powerful language to avoid throwing their weight around. In some situations less powerful forms of speech can even enhance a speaker's effectiveness.[20] For example, a boss might say to her assistant, "Would you mind making copies of these files before you go home?" Both the boss and the assistant know this is an order and not a request, but the questioning form is more considerate and leaves the assistant feeling better about the boss.[21] The importance of achieving both content and relational goals helps explain why a mixture of powerful and polite speech is usually most effective.[22]

Inflammatory Language

Language has the power to stir intense emotions. It can motivate, inspire, and amuse audiences. Unfortunately, it can also generate negative feelings: antagonism, defensiveness, and prejudice. You can prevent these negative outcomes by following two guidelines.

Avoid Biased Language

Emotional problems arise when speakers intentionally or unintentionally use **biased language**—terms that seem to be objective but actually conceal an emotional bias. Consider, for example, the range of words you could use to refer to a 25-year-old man who disagrees with your proposal: *gentleman, fellow, guy, young man,* or *dude.* Each one paints a different picture in the listener's mind. None of them is neutral.

When faced with biased language, it's wise to recognize that the speaker is editorializing. Tactfully restate the term in language that doesn't contain an evaluation, paraphrase with neutral language, or use terms that quantify:

Speaker Biased Language	Listener's Restatement
It's a *gamble.*	So you don't think the idea is a reasonable risk. Is that it? (paraphrase)
He's *long-winded.*	Bill *has* been talking for a half hour. (quantify)
She's so *wishy-washy.*	You think Susan isn't willing to make a decision? (rephrase in nonbiased language)

Beware of Trigger Words

Some terms have such strong emotional associations that they act almost like a trigger, setting off an intense emotional reaction in certain listeners. These **trigger words** can refer to specific people (your boss, the president), groups or categories of individuals (union stewards, the Human Resources department, customers with complaints), issues (affirmative action, flexible scheduling), or other topics (imports, downsizing).

What is the best way to deal with trigger words? The first thing to realize is that, like others, you almost certainly have your own trigger words. You, therefore, ought to begin by recognizing them, so that when one comes up you'll at least be aware of your sensitivity and, thus, avoid overreacting. If, for example, your parents are farmers and you are sensitive about people speaking condescendingly about farmers, you might catch yourself before you overreact when a co-worker refers to someone on Casual Friday as "dressed like a farmer." It could be an innocent or uninformed remark.

Sometimes, however, you will discover too late that a term that seems innocuous to you is a trigger word for others. After the other person vents his or her strong feelings, you can acknowledge the misunderstanding, apologize, choose a more agreeable term and proceed with the discussion.

"Sorry, Chief, but of course I didn't mean 'bimbo' in the pejorative sense."

Masculine and Feminine Language Use

Chapter 2 described how culture affects communication. Some social scientists have suggested that conversation between men and women is a kind of cross-cultural communication in which members of each sex are not speaking different dialects but **"genderlects."**[23]

They have argued that these different approaches affect the way men and women interact with one another in ways that are powerful but usually unnoticed.

As you read about differences in male and female speech, understand that the descriptions don't characterize all men and women. The relationship between gender and language is like the one between gender and height: Men are generally taller than women, but some women are taller than some men. In fact, the difference between the tallest man and the shortest man (or the tallest woman and the shortest woman) is greater than the difference between the average man and the average woman. For this reason, the words "masculine" and "feminine" are actually better adjectives to describe language differences, since they refer to traits characteristically linked to each gender and not to biological sex. Remember also that gender isn't the only factor that influences conversational style. Cultural, geographical, and occupational influences also play a role. Finally, understand that the differences outlined in this section reflect past communication patterns. As the roles of men and women in society evolve, speech styles may change as well.

Feminine Speech From childhood, females learn to use speech for what some researchers refer to as **rapport talk:** to create connections, establish goodwill, show support, and build community.

For many women an important part of building rapport is using language as an *expressive tool:* to articulate emotions ("I'm worried about finishing those reports today"; "I'm glad everybody had a chance to speak") and clarify relationships ("We don't seem to be working well together").

Characteristically feminine speech often goes beyond just expressing emotions; it also is *supportive.* Women are most likely to listen and respond to spoken and unspoken conversational clues about the other person's feelings. A characteristically feminine reply to a description of difficulties at work is "I know what that's like. Last year I had so much trouble with a client on the Bustos case. . . ." This response lets the speaker know that she is not alone, that she is understood.

Another characteristic of feminine conversational style is its *tentative* nature. This is reflected in questioning forms ("Could we go now?" "Would you type that for me?"), hedges and disclaimers ("I'm not sure about these figures . . ."; "This might not be a good time to bring this up, but . . ."), and tag questions ("The report is due today, isn't it?"). While these forms exhibit the less powerful characteristics described earlier in this chapter on pages 97–98, linguist Deborah Tannen describes them more as a bid for solidarity than a sign of weakness:

> *Many women are frequently told, "Don't apologize" or "You're always apologizing." The reason "apologizing" is seen as something they should stop doing is that it seems synonymous with putting oneself down. But for many women, and a fair number of men, saying "I'm sorry" isn't literally an apology; it is a ritual way of restoring balance to a conversation. "I'm sorry," spoken in this spirit, if it has any literal meaning at all, does not mean "I apologize," which would be tantamount to accepting blame, but rather "I'm sorry that happened.".*[24]

Speech forms like apologizing, especially when used by women, can create the impression of less authority, status, certainty, accuracy, or credibility. However, tentative speech doesn't have to be regarded as weak.[25] Another interpretation is that it builds rapport by avoiding dogmatism and suggesting equality.

Conversational initiation and maintenance are also characteristic of feminine speech. Women have long been taught to ask questions to get a conversation going, to find out what others are interested in, and to show interest in a conversational partner. So, many women ask questions to start and maintain conversations: "Did you hear about . . . ?" "Are you going to . . . ?" "Did you know that . . . ?" In addition, women use "listening noises" ("Uh, huh." "Oh really?" "Is that right?") to show interest. If women do interrupt, it is often to support or affirm the speaker, not to challenge or threaten.

Masculine Speech Whereas women use talk to build rapport, men are more comfortable with what linguists have labeled **report talk**—speech that focuses less on feelings and relationships and more on information, facts, knowledge, and competence. Men are more inclined to use language to claim attention, assert a position, establish status, and show independence. Research shows that men need to be just as sensitive as women, but they may use that awareness differently: In one study, male managers who were more accurate at emotion perception received higher satisfaction ratings if they used the information to be more persuasive, whereas more emotionally perceptive female managers received higher satisfaction ratings when they demonstrated more supportiveness.[26]

Characteristically masculine speech uses language *instrumentally* (as opposed to expressively) to get things done: report information, solve visible problems, achieve, accomplish, attain, execute, perform. The results are often tangible and the reward is visible: "Fax these reports to accounting"; "I'll make reservations at Sara's"; "Finish that proposal by Monday." Language is often used by men to define status.

When dealing with personal problems, a characteristically masculine approach is to offer *advice* that will lead to a solution. Empathizing to show sympathy and establish solidarity just doesn't seem helpful or appropriate to many men.

Characteristically masculine speech is more *assertive, certain, direct,* and *authoritative.* Men often use statements of fact rather than opinion: "That deduction belongs on Schedule C" rather than "I think that's a Schedule C deduction." Declarative sentences and dropped pitch at the end create a sense of sureness and authority. Men are more likely to speak directly, giving clear and unambiguous commands or directions rather than couching requests in the form of questions.

Men's speech style typically includes several characteristics of conversational *dominance* or *control:* verbosity, topic control, and interruptions. Most research supports the statement that in public conversations between men and women, men talk at greater length.[27] Often in response to questions from women, men decide which topic of conversation to pursue and talk longer than the women in the same conversation. Research on interruptions is mixed as to who interrupts more, but it appears that the purpose of men's interruptions is often to gain control of the conversational topic or the conversation itself. Table 4–2 on page 102 summarizes research findings on characteristics of feminine and masculine speech styles.

Meeting Gender-Related Language Challenges Problems can arise when stereotypically masculine and feminine language styles clash on the job—often without anyone knowing exactly why. For instance, a woman who says, "I'm having difficulty with the Garcia account," may want to hear her concerns acknowledged and know that others have experienced similar problems. Her goal may be to gain support, establish connection, and seek rapport. Or she may just want to talk about the situation. A man, conditioned to use speech to solve problems, might respond with advice: "Here's one way you could handle it . . ." If the woman wanted support and connection, being given advice might produce an effect that is just the opposite of the rapport she

Table 4–2 Characteristics of Feminine and Masculine Speech Styles

Characteristically Feminine Speech	Characteristically Masculine Speech
Builds rapport	Reports facts
Is expressive	Is instrumental
Offers support	Offers advice
Sounds tentative	Sounds certain
Initiates and maintains conversation	Controls conversation

was looking for: The woman might feel that her male colleague was trying to appear "one-up," coming across as a superior. From his frame of reference, the man *was* being helpful: He offered useful information at the request of someone in need.

Another gender-related problem can arise when a man pays attention to the content of a message while a woman focuses on the relational dimension of the words. If a male supervisor says, "I can't do anything about your hours; the boss says they're set and can't be changed," a woman may hear a relational message of "I don't care" or "I don't want to be bothered." The man, used to dealing with communication at the content level, isn't being unsympathetic; he is just responding to a request.

Both masculine and feminine language styles work well—as long as listeners use the the same rules. Frustrations result when people expect others to use the same style as theirs.[28] The following suggestions can help communicators understand and adapt to one another's differing uses of language:

- *Be aware of different styles.* Once you are aware that men and women have been taught to use language differently, there's less likelihood of being dismayed at a style that doesn't match yours. The cultural analogy is apt here: If you were traveling in another country, you wouldn't be offended by the customs of its inhabitants, even if they were different from yours. In the same way, accepting gender differences can lead to smoother relationships—even if members of the other sex behave differently from you.
- *Switch styles, when appropriate.* Being bilingual is an obvious advantage in a multicultural world. In the same way, using a communication style that isn't characteristic of you can be useful. If you routinely focus on the content of others' remarks, consider paying more attention to the unstated relational messages behind their words. If you generally focus on the unexpressed-feelings part of a message, consider being more task-oriented. If your first instinct is to be supportive, consider the value of offering advice; and if advice is your reflexive way of responding, think about whether offering support and understanding might sometimes be more helpful.
- *Combine styles.* Effective communication may not be an either–or matter of choosing one style. In many situations, you may get the best results by combining typically masculine and feminine approaches. Research confirms what common sense suggests: A "mixed-gender strategy" that balances the traditionally masculine, task-oriented approach with the characteristically feminine, relationship-oriented approach is

rated most highly by both male and female respondents.[29] Choosing the approach that is right for the other communicator and the situation can create satisfaction far greater than that which comes from using a single stereotypical style.

Nonverbal Communication

Words are not the only way we communicate. You can appreciate this fact by imagining the following scenes:

> Your boss has told the staff that she welcomes any suggestions about how to improve the organization. You take her at her word and schedule an appointment to discuss some ideas you have had. As you begin to outline your proposed changes, she focuses her gaze directly on you, folds her arms across her chest, clenches her jaw muscles, and begins to frown. At the end of your remarks, she rises abruptly from her chair, says "Thank you for your ideas" in a monotone, and gives you a curt handshake.
>
> Despite the expense, you have decided to have a highly regarded CPA handle your tax matters. While waiting for the accountant to appear, you scan the impressive display of diplomas from prestigious universities and professional associations. The accountant enters, and as the conversation proceeds, he yawns repeatedly.

Most people would find these situations odd and disturbing. This reaction would have nothing to do with the verbal behavior of the people involved. In each case, nonverbal behavior sends messages above and beyond the words being spoken: The boss doesn't really seem to want to hear your suggestions, and you wonder whether the accountant is capable or caring with regard to your taxes.

In the following pages we examine the role of nonverbal communication in the working world. For our purposes, **nonverbal communication** involves messages expressed by other than linguistic means.

Characteristics of Nonverbal Communication

Now that we have defined nonverbal communication and discussed its importance, we need to take a look at some of its characteristics. Nonverbal communication resembles verbal communication in some ways and is quite different in others.

Nonverbal Behavior Always Has Communicative Value

You may not always *intend* to send nonverbal messages, but everything about your appearance, every movement, every facial expression, every nuance of your voice has the potential to convey meaning.[30] You can demonstrate this fact by imagining that your boss has "called you on the carpet," claiming that you haven't been working hard enough. How could you not send a nonverbal message? Nodding gravely would be a response; so would blushing, avoiding or making direct eye contact, or shaking your head affirmatively or negatively. While you can shut off your linguistic channels of communication by refusing to speak or write, it is impossible to avoid behaving nonverbally.

One writer learned this fact from movie producer Sam Goldwyn while presenting his proposal for a new film. "Mr. Goldwyn," the writer implored, "I'm telling you a sensational story. I'm only asking for your opinion, and you fall asleep." Goldwyn's reply: "Isn't sleeping an opinion?"

Nonverbal communication operates even in mediated communication. Some nonverbal elements are obvious: The use of emoticons, an abundance of exclamation points, and the impression of shouting when a message is typed in ALL CAPITAL LETTERS, are clear examples. But even *not* responding to an e-mail, IM, or text message can suggest a put-down.[31]

Nonverbal Communication Is Powerful Despite folk sayings like "you can't judge a book from its cover," we form impressions of others mostly from nonverbal observations—about physical appearance and behavior. Once we form these impressions, they influence our subsequent impressions and judgments. Canadian communication consultant Lee McCoy gives an example:

> *If I meet Susan and initially perceive her to be professional, attractive and intelligent, I'm also likely to begin to attribute other positive characteristics to her. I might see her as organized, successful and warm. This is not to suggest that I'll ignore negative characteristics, but it will take me longer to become aware of something negative if my initial perceptions of her are very positive. If, on the other hand, Susan presents herself to me as sloppily dressed, with bitten fingernails and a lack of eye contact, I may begin to attribute equally negative characteristics to her—insecurity, lack of knowledge, coldness.*[32]

Even after first impressions have been made, the impact of nonverbal behavior is powerful. In fact, when nonverbal behavior seems to contradict a verbal message, the spoken words carry less weight than the nonverbal cues.[33]

Nonverbal Behavior Is Ambiguous While nonverbal communication can create powerful impressions, the messages it conveys are ambiguous.[34] You don't have to be as clueless as the boss in the cartoon below to misinterpret nonverbal cues. Does a customer's yawn signal boredom or fatigue? Are your co-workers laughing with or at you? Does your boss's frown reflect disapproval or preoccupation? Most nonverbal behaviors have a multitude of possible meanings, and it is a serious mistake to assume that you can decide which is true in any given case.

Nonverbal Communication Primarily Expresses Attitudes While it is relatively easy to infer general interest, liking, disagreement, amusement, and so on, from another's actions, messages about ideas or concepts don't lend themselves to nonverbal channels. How, for instance, would you express the following messages nonverbally?

Dilbert: © Scott Adams/Dist. by United Feature Syndicate, Inc. Reprinted by permission.

Sales are running 16 percent above last year's.

Management decided to cancel the sales meeting after all.

Let's meet at two to plan the agenda for tomorrow's meeting.

It's apparent that such thoughts are best expressed in speech and writing. It's also apparent, though, that nonverbal behavior will imply how the speaker *feels* about these statements: whether the speaker is pleased that sales are up or worried that they're not as high as expected, how urgently the cashier at checkstand 2 needs change, and so on.

Nonverbal Communication Affects Career Success

Not surprisingly, the ability to effectively manage your nonverbal behavior plays a strong role in communicative success. For example, salespeople who were better at reading nonverbal cues of potential clients make more sales and earn higher income than less astute colleagues.[35] Likewise, successful entrepreneurs owe a great measure of their success to social skills including the ability to manage their own nonverbal behavior and read those of others.[36] Managers who were good at reading and responding to nonverbal cues received higher performance ratings from both their bosses and their subordinates.[37]

Much Nonverbal Behavior Is Culture-Bound

Certain types of nonverbal behavior seem to be universal. For example, there is strong agreement among members of most literate cultures about which facial expressions represent happiness, fear, surprise, sadness, anger, and disgust or contempt.[38] On the other hand, many nonverbal expressions do vary from culture to culture, however. (See Table 4–3 on page 106 for a few examples.)

In this age of international communication in business, it is especially important to understand that there are cultural differences in the meaning assigned to nonverbal behaviors. Consider the different rules about what distance is appropriate between speakers. One study revealed that the "proper" space between two speakers varied considerably from one culture to another: To Japanese, a comfortable space was 40.2 inches; for a U.S. resident, 35.4 inches; and to Venezuelans, 32.2 inches.[39] It's easy to see how this could lead to problems for a U.S. native doing business overseas.

Types of Nonverbal Communication

We have already mentioned several types of nonverbal messages. We now discuss each in more detail.

Voice

Your own experience shows that the voice communicates in ways that have nothing to do with the words a speaker utters. You may recall, for instance, overhearing two people arguing in an adjoining room or apartment; even though you couldn't make out their words, their emotions and the fact that they were arguing were apparent from the sound of their voices. Similarly, you have probably overheard people talking in a language you didn't understand; yet the speakers' feelings—excitement, delight, exhaustion, boredom, grief—were conveyed by their voices.

Social scientists use the term **paralanguage** to describe a wide range of vocal characteristics, each of which helps express an attitude: pitch (high-low), resonance (resonant-thin), range (spread-narrow), tempo (rapid-slow), articulation (precise-imprecise), dysfluencies (*um, er,* etc.), rhythm (smooth-jerky), pauses (frequency and duration), and volume (loud-soft).

Not surprisingly, voice contributes dramatically to the success or failure of business and professional communicators. For example, surgeons with harsh, impatient voices

Table 4–3 Co-cultural Differences Can Lead to Misunderstandings

Behaviors that have one meaning for members of the same culture or co-culture can be interpreted differently by members of other groups.

Behavior (in Traditional Co-culture)	Probable In-Group Perception	Possible Out-Group Perception
Avoidance of direct eye contact (Latino/a)	Used to communicate attentiveness or respect.	A sign of inattentiveness; direct eye contact is preferred.
Aggressively challenging a point with which one disagrees (African American)	Acceptable means of dialogue; not regarded as verbal abuse, or a precursor to violence.	Arguments are viewed as inappropriate and a sign of potential imminent violence.
Use of finger gestures to beckon others (Asian American)	Appropriate if used by adults for children, but highly offensive if directed at adults.	Appropriate gesture to use with both children and adults.
Silence (Native American)	A sign of respect, thoughtfulness, and/or uncertainty/ambiguity.	Interpreted as boredom, disagreement, or refusal to participate/respond.
Touch (Latino/a)	Normal and appropriate for interpersonal interactions.	Deemed appropriate for some intimate or friendly interactions; otherwise perceived as a violation of personal space.
Public display of intense emotions (African American)	Accepted and valued as measure of expressiveness. Appropriate in most settings.	Violates expectations for self-controlled public behaviors; inappropriate in most public settings.
Touching or holding hands of same-sex friends (Asian American)	Acceptable behavior that signifies closeness in platonic relationships.	Perceived as inappropriate, especially for male friends.

Source: Adapted from M. P. Orbe and T. M. Harris, *Interracial Communication: Theory into Practice* (Belmont, CA: Wadsworth, 2001), p. 65.

were more likely to be sued by patients for malpractice than were those with more friendly speech mannerisms.[40] One distinctive vocal trait is "uptalk"—the tendency to end sentences on a rising pitch. This vocal pattern makes assertions sound like questions: "Mr. Chen? It's Eliza Palmer? From Accounts Receivable?" Since uptalk is more common among women, it's easy to imagine how this trait can contribute to perceptions of female unassertiviness. "If women always sound like they're asking for approval or agreement, they seem less sure of themselves," says communication consultant Mary-Ellen Drummond.[41]

Appearance Appearance plays a tremendous role in determining how a communicator's messages will be received in business and elsewhere.[42] As a rule, people who *look* attractive are considered to be likable and persuasive, and they generally have successful careers.[43] For example, research suggests that beginning salaries increase about $2,000 for every 1-point increase on a 5-point attractiveness scale and that more attractive men

Models of Nonverbal Effectiveness

Think of an especially effective communicator you have encountered in business or professional settings. This may be someone you know (e.g., a boss, colleague, instructor) or a person you don't know personally but have dealt with (e.g., a medical professional, salesperson, public safety official). The person you choose may even be a character in a film.

Describe to your audience

1. Who this person is and the context in which you encountered him or her.
2. The nonverbal behaviors and attitudes that contribute to his or her effectiveness. Be as specific as possible: Give examples of how the person you are describing has used the types of behaviors described in this chapter: facial expression, voice, attire, etc.
3. What lessons you have learned from the person you've chosen, and how you can apply them in your life.

If time and the facilities permit, you may even share a photo of the person you are describing with your audience.

(but not more attractive women) are given higher starting salaries than their less handsome counterparts.

A number of factors contribute to how attractive a person seems. For instance, potential employers, customers, and co-workers are usually impressed by people who are trim, muscular, and in good shape. One study, in fact, shows that people who are overweight have more trouble getting job offers.[44] Some aspects of physical appearance cannot be changed very easily. One very significant factor in appearance, though—and one over which you may have the most control—is clothing.

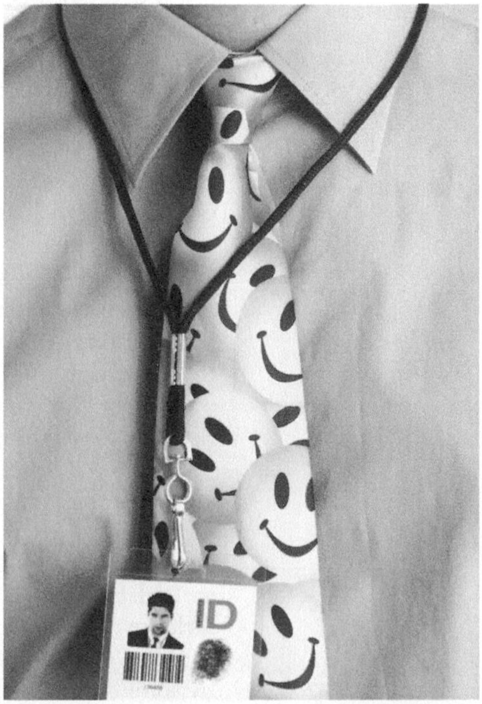

The kind of clothing one wears can influence how people react. Boeing Aircraft CEO Philip Condit is aware of this fact. Having discovered that discussions were hard to get going when he appeared in a business suit and tie, Condit routinely dressed down when making trips to the shop floor to talk with the men and women who build Boeing aircraft.[45]

Attitudes about what clothing is acceptable keep changing. By the mid-1990s, even conservative IBM abandoned its decades-long policy of requiring employees to wear a dark business suit, even allowing male workers in some jobs to show up for work without a suit and tie. A spokesperson for IBM explained, "You try to dress like your customers do."[46] But the casual dress trends brought on by the 1990 dot-coms seem to be in decline.[47]

Whether to dress up or dress down depends on several factors, including the industry or field of work. California's outdoor gear clothing manufacturer Patagonia, Inc., may have one of the most liberal dress codes: Even shoes aren't required.[48] By contrast, financial services and public administration businesses have some of the most conservative dress standards, while high-tech, utilities, and natural resources tend to be the most informal.[49]

Geography also makes a difference in determining an appropriate working wardrobe. In one survey, Washington, DC, proved to have the most conservative attire, with New York and Philadelphia close behind. California and New England—the location of many high-tech companies—had more liberal standards.[50] Knowing an office has a "business casual" dress code isn't enough. As business etiquette expert Dana Casperson notes, business casual "means one thing on the West Coast, another thing on the East Coast, and no one knows in the middle."[51] The culture of an individual organization also makes a difference in how to dress. Two companies in the same field might have quite different appearance codes.

When choosing your wardrobe, consider the following tips:

- *Look around.* The best guide to an appropriate wardrobe is right in front of you. Look at key people in the industry and country where you work. Wearing a conservative, dark business suit in a freewheeling start-up company where everyone else comes to work in jeans would look just as odd as wearing wrinkled Levis in a Wall Street stock brokerage.
- *Be flexible.* Within your company's dress code, choose an outfit that fits your daily activities. If you are seeing an important client, a business suit may be the best look. If you will be working all day at your desk, more casual dress may be fine.
- *Don't confuse "casual" with "sloppy."* A T-shirt and grubby denims send a different message than well-fitting khakis and a sharp shirt or sweater. Looking good in casual dress can be at least as challenging (and expensive) as a more formal look.
- *Never risk offending.* Your definition of appropriate attire may not match those of people whose approval you need. For example, only a slight majority of respondents in one survey thought exposed underwear is inappropriate, although this is a look that would jeopardize success in most fields.[52]
- *Dress for the job you want.* If you are seeking advancement, consider dressing in a way that makes it easy for the people who have the power to promote you to visualize you in a position of more responsibility.

The Face and Eyes On an obvious level, a person's face communicates emotions clearly: a subordinate's confused expression indicates the need to continue with an explanation; a customer's smile and nodding signal the time to close a sale; and a colleague's frown indicates that your request for help has come at a bad time. Facial expressions, like other nonverbal signals, are ambiguous (a co-worker's frown could come from a headache rather than the timing of your request). Nonetheless, researchers have found that accurate judgments of facial expressions can be made.[53]

The eyes themselves communicate a great deal. A skilled nonverbal communicator, for example, can control an interaction by knowing when and where to look to produce the desired results. Since visual contact is an invitation to speak, a speaker who does not want to be interrupted can avoid looking directly at people until it is time to field questions or get reactions.

Eye contact can be a good indicator of how involved a person is in a situation, although the advice to always look people straight in the eye has been partially contradicted by research. In most two-person conversations, people seem to look at their partners somewhere between 50 and 60 percent of the time, often alternating short gazes with glances away. Still, a person who makes little or no eye contact may seem to have little involvement in the situation.

The rules for eye contact and facial expressions vary from one culture to another. In some cultures—Diné (Navajo), for example—lack of eye contact may indicate respect for elders, not a lack of interest. In Japan, smiling is less common than in North America, which can confuse visitors who mistakenly perceive formality for unfriendliness. Clerks greet customers with a simple "Irasshaimase"—"Welcome"—but typically don't accompany the greeting with a smile.[54] Some foreign companies, including McDonald's Corp., have created "smile schools" to teach employees how to greet customers in a manner that seems more friendly.

"You have until he rolls his eyes and looks at his watch."

Even among communicators who follow the rules of Euro-American culture, eye contact can be deceptive; some people *can* lie while looking you right in the eye. And even barely perceptible changes in eye contact can send messages that may or may not be accurate. The following story illustrates how eye contact can be misleading—with serious repercussions:

> *Discussing his corporation's financial future in front of television cameras, the chief executive officer of a Fortune 500 company lowered his eyes just as he began to mention projected earnings. His downcast eyes gave the impression—on television—that the executive wasn't on the level. Wall Street observers discounted the CEO's optimistic forecast, and the company's stock price dropped four points over the next few trading days. It took two years to build it up again—even though the projection had proved to be accurate.*[55]

Posture and Movement A person's body communicates messages in several ways. The first is through posture. The way you sit at your desk when you're working can reflect your attitude toward your job or how hard you're working to anyone who cares to look. A less obvious set of bodily clues comes from the small gestures and mannerisms that every communicator exhibits at one time or another. While most people pay reasonably close attention to their facial expression, they are less aware of hand, leg, and foot motions. Thus, fidgeting hands might betray nervousness; a tapping foot, impatience; and clenched fists or white knuckles, restrained anger. Table 4–4 describes the way others may be likely to interpret some of your gestures.

A study on privacy in the workplace by GF Business Equipment Company describes ways in which such gestures can be used to discourage visits from co-workers. In addition to avoiding eye contact with your visitor, the company suggests that you shuffle papers or make notes to indicate a desire to return to work . . . keep pen or pencil poised—that communicates an aversion to engage in conversation . . . and if interrupted when dialing a call, don't hang up the receiver.[56]

Good communicators are sensitive to small cues like this and tailor their behavior accordingly. They will notice a forward-leaning position as an indication that their remarks are being well received and will capitalize upon the point that led to this reaction. When a remark results in a pulling back, a smart communicator will uncover the damage and try to remedy it. Awareness of such subtle messages can make the difference between success and failure in a variety of business settings: interviews, presentations, group meetings, and one-to-one interactions.

Table 4–4 Common Gestures and Their Possible Perceived Meanings

Gesture	In Moderate Form	When Exaggerated
Forward lean	Friendly feelings	Hostile feelings
Direct eye contact	Friendly feelings	Hostile feelings
Unique dress and hairstyle	Creativity	Rebelliousness
Upright posture	Expertise; self-confidence	Uprightness; hostility
Variability in voice pitch, rate, and loudness	Lively mind	Nervousness; anxiety; insecurity
Smiling	Friendliness; relaxed and secure composure	Masking hostility; submissiveness
Averting gaze	Shyness; modesty	Guilt; unreliability
Knitted brow	Involvement	Hostility
Nodding and reaching out the hands while talking	Self-confidence	Uncertainty

Source: Adapted from University of Northern Iowa College of Business Administration. Accessed from **http://www.cba.unl.edu/buscomm/nonverbal/body%20Language.htm.**

Body relaxation or tension is a strong indicator of who has the power in one-to-one relationships. As a rule, the more relaxed person in a given situation has the greater status.[57] This is most obvious in job interviews and high-stake situations in which subordinates meet with their superiors—requesting a raise or describing a problem, for example. The person in control can afford to relax, while the supplicant must be watchful and on guard. While excessive tension does little good for either the sender or receiver, total relaxation can be inappropriate for a subordinate. A job candidate who matched the interviewer's casual sprawl would probably create a poor impression. In superior–subordinate interactions, the best posture for the one-down person is probably one that is slightly more rigid than the powerholder's.

Height also affects perceptions of power: Tallness usually equates with dominance. Standing up tall can help you appear more authoritative, whereas slumped posture or slouched shoulders create an appearance of submissive or passive demeanor. Getting your body at the same level as others is a way of nonverbally diminishing status whether speaking with a colleague in a wheelchair or with others shorter than you. To literally have to look up to someone may make the shorter person feel like a subordinate. Sitting down with someone could signal your desire for collegiality rather than status, while standing over or behind someone signals power or status. Since women and persons from some minority co-cultures may not be as tall as the average American male, and since persons in wheelchairs interact at a shorter height, your relative height is a factor worth considering in professional interactions. If you are taller than others or are standing when others are sitting, they may be seeing you as an authority figure or higher-status individual, even if you don't wish to appear as one.[58]

Personal Space and Distance The distance we put between ourselves and others also reflects feelings and attitudes, and thus it affects communication. Anthropologist

Edward Hall has identified four distance zones used by middle-class Americans: intimate (ranging from physical contact to about 18 inches), casual–personal (18 inches to 4 feet), social–consultative (4 to 12 feet), and public (12 feet and beyond).[59]

In some cases the distance zones don't apply at all—or at least the distances aren't flexible enough to reflect the attitudes of the parties. Dentists and barbers, for instance, work within intimate distance—actual physical contact; yet the relationship between dentist and patient or barber and client may be rather impersonal.

In other cases, though, the distance that people put between themselves and others is significant. For example, distance can reflect the attitude of the person who does the positioning. Research shows that a person who expects an unpleasant message or views the speaker as unfriendly takes a more distant position than does someone expecting good news or viewing the speaker as friendly.[60] An observant communicator can thus use the distance others choose with respect to him or her as a basis for hunches about their feelings. ("I get the feeling you're worried about something, Harry. Is there anything wrong?")

Besides reflecting attitudes, distance also creates feelings. In one study, subjects rated people who communicated at a greater distance as less friendly and understanding than those who positioned themselves closer.[61] (Closeness has its limits, of course. Intimate distance is rarely appropriate for business dealings.) Thus, an effective communicator will usually choose to operate at a casual–personal distance when a friendly atmosphere is the goal.

Interpersonal distance is another nonverbal indicator of power. One unspoken cultural rule is that the person with higher status generally controls the degree of approach. As Mehrabian puts it, "It is easy enough to picture an older person in this culture encouraging a younger business partner by patting him or her on the back; but it is very difficult to visualize this situation reversed; that is, with the younger person patting the older and more senior partner."[62] This principle of distance explains why subordinates rarely question the boss's right to drop in to their work area without invitation but are reluctant to approach their superior's office even when told the door is always open.

When a subordinate does wind up in the office of a superior, both tension and distance show who is in charge. The less powerful person usually stands until invited to take a seat and, when given the choice, will be reluctant to sit close to the boss. Wise managers often try to minimize the inhibiting factor of this status gap by including a table or comfortable easy chairs in their offices so that they can meet with subordinates on a more equal level.

Some managers try to promote informal communication by visiting employees in the employees' own offices. David Ogilvy, head of one of the largest advertising agencies in the country, says, "Do not summon people to your office—it frightens them. Instead, go to see them in *their* offices."[63]

Physical Environment So far we have discussed how personal behavior sends nonverbal messages. The physical environment in which we operate also suggests how we feel and shapes how we communicate.

Consider the way space is allocated in an organization. Power locations become apparent when we look at the amount and location of existing space given to various employees and groups. In many organizations, for instance, an employee's status may be measured by whether his or her office is next to the boss's or is in a dark alcove. An office with a window or an office on the corner often indicates higher status than an inside office with no window, and any office usually signals higher status than a cubicle.

Another way in which environments shape communication is proximity. The distance that separates people is perhaps the most important factor in shaping who talks with whom. Other things being equal, officemates will talk with one another more than with the people next door, and workers in the same area deal with one another more than with similarly employed people in another area. Researcher Thomas J. Allen studied workers in research facilities, medical laboratories, and business schools. He found that the frequency with which a person spoke to colleagues was a direct function of the distance between their desks.[64]

Furniture arrangement also plays a big role in the way people communicate. For example, in one study of a medical office, only 10 percent of the patients were "at ease" when conversing with a doctor seated behind a desk, while the figure rose to 55 percent when the desk was removed.[65] Even when the location of furniture is fixed, choices about seating can influence interaction. Dominant, high-status persons often select the position at a table where they can see and be seen. This allows more interaction and more influence over the interactions at the table. Not surprisingly, the person who is seated at the head of a table is more often perceived as a leader. Persons who want to diminish their potential for interaction and leadership often seat themselves in less visible spots along the sides of a table.[66]

This sort of information can be useful on the job. You may be able to relocate your work to an area that will give you the interaction you want. Beyond this, realize that several places in your working environment will probably allow you to interact informally with desirable communication partners. Employee lounges, elevators, and dining areas are a few examples. If you are interested in making your bosses more aware of your work, it's important to be visible to them. On the other hand, if you would just as soon be left alone, the old axiom "Out of sight, out of mind" applies here.

If you are a manager, think about arranging your subordinates' working areas to increase communication between people who should interact and to separate those who don't need to talk to one another. You can encourage communication between groups of workers by arranging gathering spots where congregation is easy. A good setting for informal contact needs to meet three criteria.[67] First, it ought to be centrally located so that people have to pass through it on their way to other places. Second, it should contain places to sit or rest, to be comfortable. Finally, it must be large enough so that the people gathered there won't interfere with others passing through or working nearby. Of course, if you want to discourage contact at a central spot (the copying machine, for example), simply change one or more of these conditions.

When it comes to managing interaction between members of an organization and its public, you can create the most desirable degree of accessibility by use of space and barriers. Proximity and visibility encourage contact, while distance and closure discourage it.

Time The way we use time provides a number of silent messages.[68] Leonard Berlin, senior financial analyst at ExxonMobil, attributes his reputation as a hard worker to the fact that he routinely arrives at work half an hour early. "That's a big thing to my boss," he says.

Many business advisers recommend that you be particularly scrupulous about your use of time during the first few months you are on the job:

> *If . . . in that first ninety days, you're late or absent frequently, or seen as a clock watcher, you may earn yourself . . . negative scrutiny for a long time thereafter by your superiors. Rather than excusing any "infractions" of the rules, they'll be looking for slip-ups and a reason potentially to discharge you.*[69]

career tip

Cubicle Etiquette

As the comic character Dilbert has shown the world, daily life in a cubicle (or cube) has its challenges. These tips can help you manage the communication dynamics of cubicle life.

Privacy

Treat others' cubicles as if they were private offices. Knock gently to avoid startling occupants. Don't enter without verbal invitation or eye-contact permission—act as if there were a door. Never read the occupant's computer screens or borrow items from their desks just because you have access. Let others know when you aren't available by a "Do Not Disturb" sign or by your lack of eye contact. Resist the urge to shout out an answer to another cube dweller's question just because you overheard it. Avoid popping up over the top of cubicles to talk to others; instead, walk over or send an e-mail or instant message. Remember that whatever you say can be heard by others, so conduct meetings and personal conversations elsewhere. Keep conversations with your banker, family, doctor, and/or sweetheart out of the cubicle. Be polite enough to not listen to others' conversations, and certainly don't repeat anything overheard. Don't use a speaker phone in a cubicle; it is rude to the person on the other end and to your colleagues.

Noise

Don't add to the noise of a cube farm. Keep your voice on the low side. Set your phone ringer on low and turn it off when you are away from your desk. Don't let your cell phone ring when you are on another call. Use headphones for radios or CDs, and use a screen saver without sounds.

Odors

Your favorite scent (whether perfume, lotion, aftershave, or hair product) may be someone else's allergen, so think about its effect on others. Think about eating in lunch areas, not at your desk as your colleagues may not appreciate the odor of your food.

Children

In most organizations, children (especially if they are too young for school) are best kept away from work except on special occasions. No matter how well behaved, children may not be welcome or allowed by company policy to a shared cubicle.

Illness

Your determination to work when sick may be commendable, but you aren't doing any favors if you infect everybody in the office. If you wouldn't want someone in your state of health coming to work, try to stay away yourself.

Note: For more information see G. M. Smith, "Cubicle Etiquette" *Intercom,* November 2000, pp. 12–13, retrieved June 23, 2006, from **http://www.stc.org/intercom/PDFs/2000/200011_12-13.pdf**; J. Bremmer, "Cubicle Etiquette," at **www.bremercommunications.com/Cubicle_Etiquette.htm**; and "Cube and Cubicle Etiquette," at **http://papa.essortment.com/cubicleetiquett_ppb.htm**.

Rules and customs about time vary widely from one culture to another. Whereas most North Americans and northern Europeans value punctuality, other cultures value taking time for important relationships more highly than routine appointments and deadlines. Chris Pagliaro, an American football coach, learned this lesson the hard way when he spent a season leading Milan's team in the Italian league. His realization that time is treated differently began to dawn on him when he arrived for the first practice sessions, scheduled for 8:30 P.M.:

> *We got out there at 8:30 P.M. I'm dressed, I've got my whistle, my (American) assistant coach is there, the two American players are there. And there's no Italians. It's ten 'til nine and I don't see anybody: [not] the owner, nobody. Around 9 o'clock, a couple of them start trickling in.*

Self-Assessment Your Nonverbal Immediacy

Indicate in the space at the left of each item the degree to which you believe the statement applies to you, using the following five-point scale:

1 = Never
2 = Rarely
3 = Occasionally
4 = Often
5 = Very often

____ 1. I use my hands and arms to gesture while talking to people.
____ 2. I touch others on the shoulder or arm while talking to them.
____ 3. I use a monotone or dull voice while talking to people.
____ 4. I look over or away from others while talking to them.
____ 5. I move away from others when they touch me while we are talking.
____ 6. I have a relaxed body position when I talk to people.
____ 7. I frown while talking to people.
____ 8. I avoid eye contact while talking to people.
____ 9. I have a tense body position while talking to people.
____ 10. I sit close or stand close to people while talking with them.
____ 11. My voice is monotonous or dull when I talk to people.
____ 12. I use a variety of vocal expressions when I talk to people.
____ 13. I gesture when I talk to people.
____ 14. I am animated when I talk to people.
____ 15. I have a bland facial expression when I talk to people.
____ 16. I move closer to people when I talk to them.
____ 17. I look directly at people while talking to them.
____ 18. I am stiff when I talk to people.
____ 19. I have a lot of vocal variety when I talk to people.

I had made a practice schedule–typical American coach: at 8:30 we do this, at 8:35 this, at 8:50 this. You might as well throw that one out the window. We got started around 9:20 or 9:30.[70]

The coach was smart and flexible enough to realize that he couldn't fight against a lifetime of cultural conditioning. He developed a compromise between the American need for punctuality and the casual Italian attitude about time:

By Friday, I knew it was useless. So what I did, I made a schedule and waited around. While the team ran laps, we set our watches back to 8:30. That's the only way I could do it. So we were always starting at 8:30, regardless of what time it was.

_____ 20. I avoid gesturing while I am talking to people.

_____ 21. I lean toward people when I talk to them.

_____ 22. I maintain eye contact with people when I talk to them.

_____ 23. I try not to sit or stand close to people when I talk with them.

_____ 24. I lean away from people when I talk to them.

_____ 25. I smile when I talk to people.

_____ 26. I avoid touching people when I talk to them.

Scoring Procedure:

1. Start with a score of 78. Add to that the scores from the following items: 1, 2, 6, 10, 12, 13, 14, 16, 17, 19, 21, 22, and 25.
2. Add only the scores from the following items: 3, 4, 5, 7, 8, 9, 11, 15, 18, 20, 23, 24, and 26.
3. Subtract your total score in step 2 from your total score in step 1. This is your final score.

When using this instrument it is important to recognize that the difference in these self-reports between females and males is statistically significant and socially significant (that is, substantial variance in the scores on this instrument can be attributed to biological sex). Whether these differences are "real" (that is, females may actually be more nonverbally immediate than males) or a function of social desirability (that is, females think they should be more immediate than males think they should be) or a function of actual behavior has not yet been determined.

Scoring Norms:

Females	Mean = 96.7	S.D. = 16.1	High = >112	Low = <81
Males	Mean = 91.6	S.D. = 15.0	High = >106	Low = <77
Combined	Mean = 94.2	S.D. = 15.6	High = >109	Low = <79

Sources: Adapted from V. P. Richmond, J. C. McCroskey, and A. D. Johnson, "Development of the Nonverbal Immediacy Scale (NIS): Measures of Self- and Other-Reported Nonverbal Immediacy," *Communication Quarterly* 51 (2003), pp. 505–517; and J. C. McCroskey, Nonverbal Immediacy Scale-Observer Report. Retrieved May 12, 2009, from **www.jamescmccroskey.com/measures.**

In monochronic cultures, speaking within the allotted time generally shows good planning and concern for the audience. Speaking longer inconveniences the listeners and communicates lack of regard for their schedules. But in some polychronic cultures, speaking only for the allotted time would indicate lack of excitement or actual indifference toward the audience or the issue. Getting down to business quickly can be seen as a rude and insulting move on the part of a potential business associate. In many polychronic cultures, the relationship is an important part of the business at hand. If the personal relationship is not established by taking time for dialogue and discussion, the business relationship will be at risk.

ethical challenge

Consideration vs. Candor

Part of being professional is acting politely and showing interest even when you may not feel like doing so. What obligation do you have to present yourself as being interested and respectful when you're bored or dislike another person? How do you balance honesty and professionalism?

Improving Nonverbal Effectiveness

Now that you understand the elements of nonverbal communication, you can use the following guidelines to help achieve your professional goals.

Monitor Your Nonverbal Behavior If you have ever asked yourself "how am I doing?" you know something about **self-monitoring**—the process of paying close attention to your behavior and using these observations to shape the way you behave.

High self-monitors are good at knowing when to adapt their nonverbal behavior to suit the situation.[71] By contrast, low self-monitors don't even recognize the negative impact of some of their behaviors. One study found low self-monitors were blissfully ignorant of their shortcomings and more likely to overestimate their skill than were better communicators.[72] For example, experimental subjects who scored in the lowest quartile on joke-telling skills were more likely than their funnier counterparts to grossly overestimate their sense of humor.

It's easy to see how self-monitoring can help you manage your nonverbal behavior. In a meeting or delivering a presentation, you might catch yourself droning on and losing your audience. When dealing with a difficult situation, your mental alarm will go off if you are losing your patience and showing irritation. Dealing with an unhappy client or customer, you can monitor and control your defensiveness.

While too much self-monitoring can make you overly self-conscious, keeping an eye on how you may look and sound to others is likely to enhance your image as a professional.

Demonstrate Interest in Others Social scientists use the term **immediacy** to describe verbal and nonverbal behaviors that indicate closeness and liking. Among the nonverbal cues are closer proximity (within social conventions, of course), more direct eye gaze, more forward lean, more relaxed posture, positive facial expression, and warmer vocal qualities.[73]

There's a strong link between high immediacy and career success.[74] For example, supervisors perceived as having high immediacy are regarded by their subordinates as more competent, credible, and attractive than less immediate bosses, and the subordinates are more cooperative. By contrast, low immediacy cues can be a put-off. Recall from your own experience how you reacted when you encountered someone with an unfriendly expression, a flat or hostile voice, and lack of animation.

Immediacy cues are especially important in the beginning states of a relationship. First impressions are powerful, particularly when strangers don't have much other information available to form opinions of you. Even after you know someone well, there are times when immediacy is especially important.[75]

With practice and self-monitoring, you can manage your nonverbal immediacy most effectively. You can begin by evaluating your current level of immediacy using the Self-Assessment inventory on pages 114–115.

Be Positive Emotions can be contagious. As one writer put it, "We catch feelings from one another as though they were some kind of social virus."[76] Psychologists use the term *emotional contagion* to describe this phenomenon. They have discovered that we can "infect" one another with our moods in as little as 2 minutes.[77] Given this fact, a professional identity that reflects calmness, confidence, and goodwill will serve you well.

Just as others might "catch" an emotional state from you, you can be infected by the tone of others' nonverbal behavior. That's not a problem when you are around positive communicators, but sometimes you will need to struggle not to be overcome by the attitude of negative people.

Observe Conventions As you read in Chapter 2, some conventions are cultural. For example, in northern Europe you can expect to greet associates with a handshake, while in Mediterranean countries and Latin America, a hug and even a ritual kiss might be more appropriate. Likewise, an American woman traveling in an Islamic country probably would dress more conservatively and be more likely to wear a head covering than she would at home.

Some nonverbal conventions are just as strong within certain fields or organizations. The style of dress worn by personal trainers or Web page designers would look out of place at a meeting of investment bankers, and the way you would dress or act at a company picnic or weekend retreat would probably differ from the clothes you would wear or the way you would act back in the office on Monday morning.

Actually, violating others' expectations can be effective, as long as your unexpected behavior is judged positively.[78] Dressing better, and being more enthusiastic can all generate positive reactions—as long as you don't overdo it so that your violation is regarded as negative or phony.

Sexual Harassment

Verbal and nonverbal sexual harassment on the job has always existed, but in recent decades it has been identified as a problem requiring governmental response. The Civil Rights Act of 1964 and subsequent legislation and court decisions have identified two types of sexual harassment:

- **Quid pro quo** (a Latin term meaning "this for that"). Examples of this form of harassment include directly or indirectly threatening not to promote someone who won't date you or implying that employment depends on the giving of sexual favors.

- **Hostile work environment.** This category includes any verbal or nonverbal behavior that has the intention or effect of interfering with someone's work or creating an environment that is intimidating, offensive, or hostile. Unwelcome remarks ("babe," "hunk"), humor, stares ("elevator eyes"), hand or body signs, and invasions of physical space all can create a hostile work environment.

Of the two types of harassment, there is less confusion about blatant quid pro quo propositions, and most people agree on what constitutes blatant harassment.[79] There is less agreement, though, on what kinds of behavior create a hostile working environment. One person's harmless joke can be deeply offensive to someone else, and what seems like a sincere compliment to the person who offers it can sound like a come-on to the receiver.

Sexual harassment can occur in a variety of circumstances. It may arise between members of the same sex or between men and women. The harasser can be the target's supervisor, an agent of the employer, a supervisor in another area, or a co-worker. Even behavior by non-employees (e.g., customers or people from other organizations) can be grounds for a harassment claim. The target does not have to be the person harassed but could be anyone affected by the offensive conduct. (Situations like this are termed "third-party harassment.") Unlawful sexual harassment may occur without economic injury to or discharge of the target.[80]

Reports of harassment are widespread. In fiscal year 2000, a total of 15,836 complaints were filed in the United States.[81] For example, in addition to a $7.75 million cash settlement in a suit against Ford Motor Company by 900 female employees, sensitivity training must now be given at Ford plants across the nation, at an estimated cost of $10 million.[82] Furthermore, sensitivity training is now provided at every organizational level of every federal government agency.[83] In Los Angeles, harassment was so widespread that the mayor ordered training programs for every city worker.

Avoiding Sexual Harassment Problems

Beyond the normal precautions and courtesy, it is smart to be especially sensitive in situations where others might take offense at your words or behaviors. Look at the situation from the other person's point of view. Could your language be considered offensive? Could your actions lead to discomfort? Read your company's sexual harassment policies carefully, know what the EEOC guidelines are, and be very familiar with any training and other information provided by your Human Resources professionals. If you wonder whether a behavior might be construed as harassment, not engaging in it is probably the safest course of action.

Responding to Sexual Harassment

Most organizations have written policies prohibiting sexual harassment and procedures for people who believe they are being harassed. Options may include hotlines and Human Resources representatives. If you believe you have been the target of harassment, be sure you understand the policies and resources that are available to you.

In addition to company policy, targets of sexual harassment are entitled to legal protection. The EEOC, state and local agencies, and the court system all enforce civil rights acts relating to harassment.

Despite the determination of government to protect employees, fighting sexual harassment through legal channels can take stamina. The process can be time-consuming, and targets sometimes experience depression, ridicule, isolation, and reprisal.[84] For these reasons, taking care of harassment at the lowest, most informal level possible may solve the problem in a way that doesn't punish the target. Listed below are several options, in escalating order. They aren't meant as a step-by-step guide for how to respond, but they will help you decide which options may best suit a given situation.

1. *Consider dismissing the incident.* This approach is appropriate only if you truly believe that the remark or behavior isn't worth worrying about. Pretending to dismiss

case study

Sexual Harassment: Speak Up or Keep Quiet?

Susan Carter was one of the few female partners in a New York consulting firm. During an out-of-town planning meeting in her hotel room, the client made a clumsy pass, knocking her over. He later apologized, but Susan was unable to forget the incident. The next day, Susan's boss, Justin Peale, called to ask how her meeting went. She knew from the office grapevine that Justin only put her on this key account with reluctance, thinking that the clients would feel more comfortable working with a male account representative. Susan feared that telling her boss about the incident could prejudice him against giving her future assignments. On the other hand, she knew that keeping quiet compromises her dignity and that not reporting the incident could result in the client's firm being exposed to future lawsuits.

CRITICAL ANALYSIS: As you consider this situation, answer the following questions:

1. How can Susan balance her career advancement with her knowledge of what happened? Feelings of being treated badly?
2. Imagine that the incident described above happened to you, or to a female colleague who seeks your advice. Decide which of the seven alternatives listed on pages 118–119 is the most effective and appropriate response.

For a more detailed account of this incident and commentary by several executives, see J. Margetta, "Will She Fit In?" *Harvard Business Review*, March/April 1997, pp. 18–32.

incidents that you believe are important can lead to repetition of the offensive behavior, self-blame, and diminished self-esteem.

2. *Tell the harasser to stop.* Inform the harasser early that the behavior is unwelcome, and tell him or her to cease immediately. Your statement should be firm, but it doesn't have to be angry. Remember that many words or deeds that make you uncomfortable may not be deliberately hostile remarks. (See Chapter 5 for details on how to be assertive without being aggressive.)
3. *Keep notes.* Keep a record of every incident. Detail the date, time, place, witnesses, and exactly what happened in specific, concrete language. Describe how you responded and how you felt.
4. *Write a personal letter to the harasser.* A written statement may help the harasser to understand what behavior you find offensive. Just as important, it can show that you take the problem seriously. Put the letter in a sealed envelope (keeping a copy for yourself). Use information from your diary to detail specifics about what happened, what behavior you want stopped, and how you felt. You may want to include a copy of your organization's sexual harassment policy. Keep a record of when you delivered the letter. If you want to be certain that the delivery of the letter will be acknowledged, take a friend along when you present it or send it via certified mail. [See sample letters at **www.colorado.edu/Ombuds/InformalStrategies.pdf**.
5. *Ask a trusted third party to intervene.* Perhaps a mutual acquaintance can persuade the harasser to stop. The person you choose should be someone who you are convinced understands your discomfort and supports your opinion. Be sure this intermediary is also someone the harasser respects and trusts.
6. *Use company channels.* Report the situation to your supervisor, Human Resources office, or a committee that has been set up to consider harassment complaints.
7. *File a legal complaint.* You may file a complaint with the federal EEOC or with your state agency. You have the right to obtain the services of an attorney regarding your legal options. (See **www.eeoc.gov** for detailed explanations of this procedure.)

review points

- Verbal messages are clearest when they use unequivocal and nonabstract language, an appropriate level of power, with few relative words, slang and jargon. Strategically ambiguous messages are occasionally useful to promote harmony, facilitate change, and soften difficult messages.
- Stay effective by avoiding inflammatory language (biased terms and trigger words that convey speaker attitudes and generate strong listener emotions) and monitoring your own responses to others' inflammatory words.
- Masculine and feminine language differ in some significant ways. Feminine language emphasizes rapport and relationships, while masculine speech focuses on reporting, accomplishing tasks, and controling situations. Meet gender challenges by being aware of style differences and switching or combining styles to suit the situation.
- Nonverbal behavior is a part of every communication exchange. It expresses attitudes and emotions more than ideas, and needs to be interpreted with caution, because it tends to be ambiguous and culture-bound.
- Nonverbal messages can be expressed vocally, through appearance (physical stature and clothing), and through the face, eyes, posture, gesture, distance, physical environment, and time.
- Achieve your workplace goals by monitoring your nonverbal behavior, demonstrating interest in others through immediacy, remaining positive, being aware of emotional contagion, and observing nonverbal cultural and organizational conventions.
- Minimize problems of sexual harassment by understanding verbal and nonverbal behaviors that are inappropriate and illegal in the workplace and staying aware of others' perceptions of and reactions to your behaviors.
- People who perceive themselves as targets of harassment in the workplace have a number of options available, ranging from informal to formal.

key terms

Test your understanding of these key terms by visiting the Online Learning Center Web site at www.mhhe.com/adler10e.

activities

➔ Go to the self-quizzes at the Online Learning Center at www.mhhe.com/adler10e to test your knowledge of chapter concepts.

1. Skill Builder

Practice your skill at using unequivocal language by describing how each of the following sentences is likely to be misunderstood (or not understood at all). Then improve the clarity of each message by introducing your message with a high-level abstraction and qualifying it with low-level abstractions. To invent meaningful low-level abstractions, you will have to imagine a specific scenario.

a. You did a heck of a job on that proposal.
b. There are just a few small problems to clear up.
c. I just need a little more time to finish the job.
d. Your job performance hasn't been good this year.

2. Skill Builder

Practice clarifying your understanding of another person's ambiguous messages. For each sentence below, construct a polite question you could ask the speaker to help clarify the meaning.

a. I need this report right away.
b. This presentation needs to be perfect.
c. Whenever I leave to go to a meeting, nothing gets done in this office.
d. I'm on my own around here!

3. Invitation to Insight

Identify jargon in your own line of work, or interview a worker in a field that interests you and identify jargon that he or she uses. Then answer the following questions:

a. How does each term make communication more efficient?
b. What confusion might arise from the use of each term with certain listeners?
c. In cases where confusion or misunderstandings might arise, suggest alternative words or phrases that could convey the meaning more clearly.

4. Skill Builder

Describe a former co-worker three times. In your first account, use positively biased terms. In the second description, discuss the same person, using words with negative connotations. Finally, describe the co-worker in low-level abstractions without using biased language of any sort.

5. Invitation to Insight

Become more aware of your own emotional triggers by following these instructions:

a. In each category shown, identify two words that trigger positive reactions for you and two other words you react to negatively:
   1. A person's name.
   2. The label for a category of people (e.g., "fanatic").
   3. A rule, policy, or issue (e.g., gay marriage).

b. How do you react, both internally and observably, when you hear these terms? Ponder the source of your reactions (the way you were raised? past experiences?). How might your reactions impact your communication?
c. Use the same categories to identify words that trigger positive and negative reactions in a person you work with. What are the consequences of using these emotion-laden words with that person? Suggest neutral words you could use to replace the trigger words.

6. Invitation to Insight

Explore the characteristics of nonverbal communication as communicative yet ambiguous.

a. Observe the nonverbal behaviors of a person you work with. What interpretations do you attach to your observations? Describe an alternative interpretation for each nonverbal behavior you have noticed. Speculate on which of your interpretations might be more accurate. Verify your perceptions by asking your co-worker what the behavior means.

b. Ask a co-worker to observe you during a meeting. After the meeting, have your co-worker describe some of your nonverbal behaviors and speculate what meanings you intended. Did your co-worker's perceptions match your intentions?

7. Skill Builder

Demonstrate the impact of nonverbal communication by describing effective and ineffective examples of behaviors in each of the following categories.

a. Voice.
b. Dress.
c. Face and eyes.
d. Posture and movement.
e. Personal space and use of distance.

8. Skill Builder

Using the Web sites in Nonverbal Communication around the World (go to the Online Learning Center at **www.mhhe.com/adler10e**), choose two countries that are likely to be a part of a specific career field or organization you may work for. Find two or more gestures that have different meanings in those countries. Categorize the gestures into those that appear similar to a gesture in your culture but have a different meaning, those that appear unlike any gesture that would be recognized in your culture, and those that are very different from the gestures with the same meaning in your culture.

9. Invitation to Insight

Visit the Indiana University Human Resource Web site at **http://www.indiana.edu/~uhrs/policies/uwide/sexual_harass.html.** Scroll down to Appendix A. Choose one of the examples of behavior that could lead to allegations of sexual harassment and answer the following questions.

a. Do you agree that this situation could lead to allegations of sexual harassment? If so, identify whether this behavior would be classified as quid pro quo or hostile work environment.

b. Use the guidelines in the text on pages 118–119 to decide how you would respond if you were the recipient of the harassment.

10. Invitation to Insight

Explore your present level of nonverbal effectiveness and how you might improve it.

a. Using the format on the next page, identify an important business or professional context from your life (e.g., in meetings, with customers, on the phone). If you are not currently working, choose a context from school (e.g., in class discussions, meeting with professors).

b. Using the information in this chapter, describe in the format on the next page both the aspects of your nonverbal behavior that are effective and also those you could improve.

c. Interview someone who has seen you operate in the context you are analyzing (e.g., a colleague, supervisor, professor, fellow student). Explain the types of nonverbal behavior described on pages 105–115. Then learn your interviewee's opinion of your effective nonverbal communication in this context, and how you could communicate more effectively.

d. Based on the information you have compiled, develop an action plan that describes how you can improve your nonverbal effectiveness in the context you are analyzing.

Context ____

	Effective	Could Do Better (Describe How)
Self-appraisal		
Other's appraisal		
Action plan	1.	
	2.	
	etc.	

resources

For extensive readings and Web sites on verbal and nonverbal communication, see the Online Learning Center Web site at **www.mhhe.com/adler10e.**

5 Interpersonal Skills

chapter outline

chapter objectives

After reading this chapter you should be able to

1. Describe the communication climate in a working environment, identify the messages that have helped create it, and suggest ways of communicating that can improve that climate.
2. Use the guidelines in this chapter to give effective praise and constructive feedback.
3. Use the guidelines in this chapter to respond to criticism in a nondefensive manner.
4. Identify various approaches to conflict and steps to conflict management.
5. Describe four styles of negotiating solutions in work-related conflicts and predict likely consequences of using each style.
6. Demonstrate how to seek a win–win solution in a work-related negotiation.

What does it take to succeed in your career? Talent, good ideas, a good education, technical expertise, skills, hard work, motivation, initiative—all of these are important. In addition, because all jobs require you to get things done with other people—co-workers, customers, managers, people in other companies—career success also depends on your ability to communicate effectively. That ability, often called people skills, is the ability to work with other people, contribute to a positive climate, give and receive feedback, and handle conflicts so that you can do your job effectively.

Building Positive Relationships

Numerous studies have revealed just how important communication skills are in a career. In one survey, 1,000 personnel directors in the United States were asked to describe the "ideal management profile." The number-one characteristic was "ability to work well with others one-on-one."[1] Even CEOs who manage technical workers need people skills to succeed, and poor interpersonal skills are often blamed for "derailed" CEOs.[2]

The ability to work well with others is just as important for newcomers as it is for managers. A survey of chief executive officers and human resource managers from leading organizations rated the ability to work cooperatively with others as a most desirable quality in college graduates.[3] Good interpersonal communication skills are important in careers as diverse as medicine, engineering, real estate, and franchise management.[4]

Everyone can tell stories about co-workers, bosses, and customers whose communication style made life unpleasant. Table 5-1 on page 126 details some types of communication that surveys have found are especially unpleasant. You can probably recognize at least some of these behaviors in people you have worked with, and possibly even in yourself.

Former Chrysler chairman Lee Iacocca summed up the importance of maintaining good interpersonal working relationships when he said,

Table 5–1 Some Communication Traits of Unpleasant Co-workers

Busybody

- Butts in to conversations
- Butts in to others' business
- Expresses opinion on matters that don't concern him/her

Controlling/Bossy

- Tries to control, boss others around
- Gives orders without having the proper authority
- Is condescending/talks down to others
- Wants his/her own way

Self-promotion

- Competitive, wants to be number one
- Tries to promote him/herself
- Is self-centered
- Tries to make him/herself look good

Unprofessional Behavior

- Is rude
- Gossips and bad-mouths others to a third party
- Criticizes others
- Yells or screams

Unprofessional Focus of Attention

- Talks about personal problems at work
- Brings personal problems to work
- Talks about non-work-related issues

Distracting

- Distracts others from work
- Behaves in irritating ways

Defensive and Judgmental

- Sees others as a threat to his/her job
- Attacks others' behavior and judgments
- Critical, rather than constructive

Source: After J. M. H. Fritz, "How Do I Dislike Thee? Let Me Count the Ways: Constructing Impressions of Troublesome Others at Work," *Management Communication Quarterly* 15 (2003), pp. 410–38.

There's one phrase I hate to see on any executive's evaluation, no matter how talented he may be, and that's the line: "He has trouble getting along with other people." To me that's the kiss of death.[5]

Some social scientists have coined the terms **emotional intelligence** (**EQ**) and **social intelligence** to describe the ability and skills of interacting well with others.[6] According to emerging research, cognitive IQ takes a backseat to emotional intelligence in determining outstanding job performance.[7] Across the world and across the job spectrum, from copier repair technicians to scientists, IQ accounts for no more than 25 percent of entrepreneurial failure and success. The more difficult the job and the higher it is in an organization's hierarchy, the more important emotional intelligence becomes. Consultant Robert Dilenschneider contrasts emotional intelligence with intellectual aptitude:

Your cognitive IQ could be 145, and you could get a doctorate in business, but you'll never break away from the pack unless your interpersonal skills are top-drawer.[8]

Boss's Angry E-mail Sends Shares Plunging

A chief executive who sent his staff an email accusing them of being lazy and threatening them with the sack has seen the share price of his company plummet after his message was posted on the Internet.

In the three days after publication of his outburst—which gave managers a two-week ultimatum to shape up—stock in the American health care company dropped by 22 per cent over concerns about staff morale. It is now trading at more than a third less than it was before the email was sent. Neal Patterson, head of the Cerner Corporation, based in Kansas City, has spent the past three weeks trying to assuage investors.

His email to managers read: "We are getting less than 40 hours of work from a large number of our EMPLOYEES. The parking lot is sparsely used at 8am; likewise at 5pm. As managers, you either do not know what your EMPLOYEES are doing or you do not CARE. In either case, you have a problem and you will fix it or I will replace you."

His email read: "NEVER in my career have I allowed a team which worked for me to think they had a 40-hour job. I have allowed YOU to create a culture which is permitting this. NO LONGER." He added that "hell will freeze over" before he increased employee benefits. He wanted to see the car park nearly full by 7.30am and half full at weekends. He wrote: "You have two weeks. Tick, tock."

A week later, the email appeared on a Yahoo financial message board and Wall Street analysts began receiving calls from worried shareholders. Stephen Davas of Goldman Sachs said: "It raised two real questions for investors. Has anything changed at Cerner to cause such a seemingly violent reaction? And is this a chief executive that investors are comfortable with?"

CRITICAL ANALYSIS: As you think about this case, consider the following questions:

1. Which of the types of disconfirming communication described on page 128 does this memo exhibit? How would you expect employees who read this memo to react?
2. Construct an alternate memo expressing the same concerns, but using more confirming language.
3. Describe how a situation in your experience could have been handled using either confirming or disconfirming communication.

Source: Daily Telegraph of London, April 6, 2001.

Communication Climate

Social scientists use the term **communication climate** to describe the quality of personal relationships in an organization. Do people feel respected? Do they trust one another? Do they believe that they are appreciated? Organizations create an overall climate, which can be healthy or polluted, but within that environment individual relationships have their own microclimates. For example, your interactions with one colleague might be described as icy, while you and another person enjoy a warm relationship. There's no question that communication climate is a key factor in job satisfaction and commitment to the organization.[9] For this reason, communicators need to understand how to create positive climates.

The climate of an organization comes not so much from the specific tasks that members perform as from the feelings they have about those tasks and one another. In fact, a positive climate can exist under the worst working conditions: in a cramped, poorly furnished, understaffed office; during the graveyard shift of an urban newspaper; or even in a road gang cleaning up trash by the highway. Conversely, the most comfortable, prestigious settings can be polluted by a hostile climate. (See the Case Study above for an example of a hostile organizational climate.)

While communication climates are created by a variety of messages, they do share a common denominator. Positive climates result when people believe they are valued, and negative climates occur when people don't believe they are appreciated. Scholars have labeled messages that express feelings of value as **confirming** and those that fail to express value—or that explicitly show a lack of value—as **disconfirming.**[10] Psychologist Jack Gibb described six kinds of messages that are likely to promote a supportive, confirming climate and six types of disconfirming messages that are likely to generate a defensive climate (see Table 5–2). Gibb's supportive categories provide a list of ways to promote positive, confirming relationships.

Use Descriptive "I" Language

Many communicators unnecessarily attack the other person when delivering a message:

"Your report is too sloppy. You'll have to clean it up."

"You're always late."

"That was a dumb promise you made. We can never have the job done by the end of the month."

Statements like these are often called **"you" language** because they point a verbal finger of accusation at the receiver: "You're lazy." "You're wrong." By contrast, **descriptive statements** are often termed **"I" language** since they focus on the speaker instead of judging the other person. Notice how each of the evaluative statements above can be rephrased in descriptive "I" language:

"I'll take the blame if we turn in a report with this many errors. We'll get a better reaction if it's retyped."

"Since you've been coming in late, I've made a lot of excuses when people call asking for you. That's why I need you to start showing up on time."

"I'm worried about the promise you made. I don't see how we can get the job done by the end of the month."

Statements like these show that it's possible to be nonjudgmental and still say what you want without landing any verbal punches. In fact, descriptive statements like the

Table 5–2 Confirming and Disconfirming Message Identifiers

Supportive, Confirming Messages Are	Defense-Arousing, Disconfirming Messages Are
Descriptive (Use "I" language)	Evaluative
Focused on solving the problem	Controlling
Honest	Manipulative
Concerned with another's position	Indifferent
Equal	Superior
Open-minded, provisional	Dogmatic, certain

ethical challenge

Is Total Honesty Always the Best Policy?

In principle, few people would dispute the ethical principle that honesty is the best policy. At the same time, it is hard to imagine a world in which everyone told the whole truth all the time.

Explore how you can reconcile the need to be honest with other goals by re-creating a list of all the opportunities you had to tell the truth during a typical day. Identify each occasion when you chose to either:

1. Tell even a partial lie (e.g., saying "Nothing's wrong" when you are bothered).
2. Hedge the truth by equivocating (e.g., saying "That's an unusual idea" instead of saying "I don't think that idea will work").
3. Keep quiet instead of volunteering the truth.

Based on your self-analysis, construct a principled yet pragmatic code of ethics involving honesty.

ones you just read are *more* complete than are typical everyday complaints since they express both the speaker's feelings and the reason for bringing up the matter—things most evaluative remarks don't do.

Focus on Solving Problems, Not Controlling Others Even if you're in charge, others can get defensive if you force them to accept an idea they don't agree with or understand. If you're up against a tight deadline it's easy to say, "Just do it my way." Because control shows a lack of regard for the other person's needs, interests, or opinions, it can cause problems in the relationship even if it gets you what you want now.

In contrast, **problem-oriented messages** aim at solving both persons' needs. The goal isn't to solve a problem my way or your way but rather to develop a solution that meets everyone's needs. You will learn more about how to achieve problem-oriented solutions when we discuss win–win negotiating strategies later in this chapter.

Be Honest: Don't Manipulate Once people discover that they have been manipulated, a defensive reaction is almost guaranteed. As Roger Fisher and Scott Brown explain, "If one statement of mine in a hundred is false, you may choose not to rely on me at all. Unless you can develop a theory of when I am honest and when I am not, your discovery of a small dishonesty will cast doubt over everything I say and do."[11]

By contrast, simple honesty is less likely to generate defensiveness, even when the news isn't welcome. Even though others might sometimes dislike what you have to say, your reputation for candor can earn you the respect of subordinates, co-workers, and management. (See the Case Study on page 57 in Chapter 2 for an example of how honesty in a difficult situation can produce good results.)

Show Concern for Others Indifference—lack of acknowledgment or concern for others—is a strong disconfirming message. By contrast, a genuine message

"I'll take care of it impersonally."

on your feet

Best and Worst Communication Climates

Be prepared to describe to your group two organizations to which you have belonged:

- One with the most positive, confirming climate
- One with the most negative, disconfirming climate

The organizations you describe may be a work group, team, class, volunteer group, or any other group of people formed with the purpose of accomplishing a task.

Make sure your account of each group includes

- A description of how the communication qualities listed on pages 128–130 (or the absence of these qualities) helped create the climate you are describing.
- One or more specific examples that captures the kinds of communication that created the positive or negative climate.
- The lessons you've learned about communication from the experiences you have described.

of interest can make a tremendous difference. A simple apology for making you wait can do wonders. The customer support agent who takes the time to find the right person to answer your questions can leave you feeling grateful and worthwhile, encouraging you to do business with that company again. The manager who seems genuinely concerned with your opinions—even if she doesn't agree with them—is easier to work with than one who brushes your concerns aside.

Demonstrate an Attitude of Equality Neither talents nor job titles justify arrogance. Al Neuharth, founder of *USA Today*, earned a reputation as a tough, abrasive boss. His superior, evaluative comments like the following one suggest why: "When I criticize a female or when I criticize a grossly overweight person or anybody else, it's because, damn it, I think they ought to do better, just as I do."[12]

The essence of a more positive attitude is *respect*. Communication expert Kerry Patterson explains that respect is essential, just like the air we breathe: "If you take it away, it's all people can think about. At that point, the conversation is all about defending dignity."[13] Respect often comes from how we construct messages. Consider, for example, the difference between saying "Could you get me the files?" and demanding, "Get me the files." As this example illustrates, *how* we speak and act can be more important than the words themselves. Pay close attention not only to what you say but also to your nonverbal behavior, including your vocal tone and facial expression, when expressing yourself.

Keep an Open Mind Listening with an open mind makes good sense. Whether the people you're dealing with are in your department or another, subordinates or customers, they probably have knowledge that you don't. Hearing them out may teach you something useful. Besides providing useful information, listening open-mindedly can promote good relationships. Take a moment and reflect on how much more you value people who consider your ideas carefully than those who dismiss them.

A tentative approach also works well when you are bringing up ideas. Paradoxically, you may get a better hearing if you present them as ideas, not facts. As one business

career tip

Respecting Spirituality in the Workplace

Research shows that spiritual practices can increase integrity and purposefulness, while decreasing stress and burnout. The challenge, of course, is to respect the rights and sensibilities of all employees and customers.

Here are some guidelines:

1. **Treat all faiths equally.** If an organization creates opportunity for any spiritual practices by its employees, it must welcome all equally. Some organizations create "quiet rooms" that can be used for prayers or meditation by people of all persuasions.
2. **Draw clear boundaries.** Personal practices and conversations are private matters. It isn't appropriate to make your beliefs an overt part of work. Open proselytizing is never acceptable. Neither is pressuring fellow workers to use any practice (such as prayer or meditation), even if it has been shown to be useful. Religious symbols, art, or sayings in public areas can create discomfort. In personal work spaces, discretion is the best principle.
3. **Don't be judgmental.** Sooner or later you will encounter beliefs that are contrary to yours. If you can't listen respectfully to beliefs that are different than yours, the best approach is to remove yourself from the situation as soon as possible.
4. **Defuse hot-button issues promptly.** Controversies are bound to arise. One person's idea of what is or isn't appropriate can offend someone else. If possible, the best way to resolve matters is via direct problem-solving among the people involved. (See the tips on pages 146–149 of this chapter for ideas.) If necessary, bringing in management or some other third party to help work out a constructive solution is far better than letting hostility escalate.

Source: P. M. Sullivan, "Spiritual Etiquette at Work," *Workforce Management*. Online at **http://www.workforce.com/section/09/feature/25/96/27/index.html.**

newsletter put it, "There's a certain irony here—the more forceful we are, the less influential we're likely to be."[14]

Giving Praise

There's truth to the old saying, You can catch more flies with honey than with vinegar. Sincere praise, delivered skillfully, can work wonders. The following tips can help make sure praise gets the desired results.

Praise Promptly The more quickly you can provide positive feedback, the more meaningful it will be. It doesn't take much time to praise positive behavior, and the results will most likely be well worth the investment.

Make Praise Specific Almost any sincere praise will be appreciated, but describing exactly *what* you appreciate makes it easier for the other person to continue that behavior. Notice how the following specific compliments add clarity:

Broad	Specific
Good job on handling that complaint.	You really kept your voice soft and spoke slowly when the customer complained.
I appreciate the support you've given me lately.	Thanks for being so flexible with my schedule while I was sick.
You've really been on top of your work lately.	You've finished every job this month within 2 days.

Being specific doesn't mean you have to avoid giving broad comments like the ones above. But along with giving general praise, consider the value of adding enough particulars to help the other person understand exactly what you appreciate.

Praise Progress, Not Just Perfection You might wonder whether some people do much of anything that deserves sincere praise. If you look for outstanding performance, the answer may be no; but you can still deliver genuine compliments by looking for progress. Consider a few examples:

> "This draft of the report is a lot clearer. Adding a detailed budget really helps explain where the money will go. I think the same kind of detail would help make the schedule clearer."

> "I know we still see things differently, but I'm glad we were able to work so well together on the Baretti job."

Praise Intermittently Too much praise can become as uncomfortable as too much rich food or too many jokes. Constant praise is also likely to sound insincere. In addition, social scientists have discovered that it isn't even as effective as occasional compliments. Praise others from time to time, when your remarks will have the best effect, but don't go overboard.

Relay Praise If you already believe that complimenting someone sincerely can improve the communication climate in your relationship, wait until you see the benefits of singing their praises to others who deserve to know. You will win the gratitude of the person you are complimenting; you will show your own sense of security and team spirit; and you will be informing others about information they will probably find valuable. Praising others takes little time, and it benefits everyone.

You can also become a "praise messenger" by letting people know that you've heard others saying complimentary things about them. They will be more likely to continue the behavior, and they will feel better both about the person who praised them and about you for delivering the good news.

Praise Sincerely Insincere praise is worse than no praise at all. It casts doubt on all your other compliments. It suggests that you can't think of anything the other person has done that deserves genuine acknowledgment, and it suggests that you think the recipient is naive enough to believe in your phony compliments.

ethical challenge

When You Can't Think of Praise

The value of praise is clear, and the guidelines in this section offer advice for when and how to compliment others. But what can you do when you cannot think of anything about another person's performance to praise?

As you consider when and how to praise, it is important to be aware of the cultural rules that may influence both the person receiving compliments and the audience to whom you are delivering them. In some collectivist cultures, it can be embarrassing to be singled out for praise, especially in front of others. In such cases, giving private reinforcement is probably wiser than lavishing compliments publicly.

Dealing with Criticism

Praise is a pleasure to give and receive, but it isn't always possible. In the real world of work, criticism is a fact of life. Sometimes you have to deliver a complaint, and other times you are on the receiving end of others' gripes. Either way, criticism can start a cycle of defensiveness that pollutes the communication climate between people or working groups. Despite their risks, critical messages don't have to create problems. With enough skill, you can learn to both deliver and respond to them in ways that can maintain—or even improve—working relationships.

Offering Constructive Feedback

Despite its faultfinding nature, criticism doesn't have to trigger a defensive reaction. As Table 5-3 on page 134 illustrates, the way you present your comments can make the difference between their being accepted and considered or being disputed and rejected.[15] You can maximize the chances of your comments being understood and accepted by carefully considering how they can be expressed.

Consider the Content The first concern is to edit your remarks so that they follow some important guidelines:

- *Limit the criticism to one topic.* You may have several complaints, but it is smart to focus on only one at a time. Your respondent may be able to handle a single problem, but he or she could grow understandably defensive if you pile on one gripe after another.
- *Make sure the criticism is accurate.* Be absolutely sure you get the facts straight before speaking out. If even a small detail is out of line, the other person can argue about that, sidetracking the discussion from the real problem at hand.
- *Define the problem clearly.* List the facts in enough detail that the recipient knows exactly what you are talking about. Be prepared to give some examples to back up your point, but don't overwhelm the other person with an avalanche of examples.
- *Show how your criticism can benefit the recipient.* Whenever possible, describe the payoffs for responding to your remarks. At the very least, the other person will get you off his or her back by heeding your complaints!

Table 5–3 Characteristics of Constructive Feedback

1. **It is descriptive . . .**

   Tim, I like your report. The style was clear and concise and your ideas were organized logically. The documentation you used made the problem credible and vivid.

   . . . not evaluative.

   Tim, that was a terrific report.

2. **It focuses on behavior . . .**

   Tim, slow down a little bit, and I think you can reduce the number of errors.

   . . . not on personal characteristics.

   Tim, you could be a lot faster on that machine if you were better coordinated.

3. **It is specific . . .**

   Tim, I couldn't hear you from where I was sitting.

   . . . not general.

   Tim, your voice isn't effective.

4. **It is timed appropriately . . .**

   Tim, let's get together around 2:00 p.m. and talk about your progress on the AMF.

   . . . not delayed or left to chance.

   Let's get together sometime.

5. **It is offered . . .**

   Tim, perhaps my reactions to your report would help you in preparing for next week's meeting. Would you like to get together sometime this afternoon?

   . . . not imposed.

   Tim, I've got talk with you about that report before you give it at our meeting next week.

Source: J. Brownell, *Listening: Attitudes, Principles, and Skills,* 3rd ed. (Boston: Pearson Education, Inc., 2006), p. 23.

Consider the Sender Who delivers the criticism can be as important as the content of the remarks. Two guidelines will help you in this area:

- *Choose the most credible critic.* Sometimes the recipient will be more receptive to one person than to another. If a choice is available, make sure that the message comes from whoever can deliver it most effectively.
- *Make sure the criticism is appropriate to the critic's role.* Even accurate criticism is likely to be rejected if you have no business delivering it. For example, most comments about someone's personal life are out of place unless they affect a working relationship. Job-related comments should be appropriate for your relationship to the other person.

Consider the Relational Climate The framework in which your remarks are delivered can have an important impact on how they are received. Paying attention to three context-related factors can boost the odds of getting the desired reaction:

- *Deliver remarks as part of a positive relationship.* Let the other person know that your specific criticism doesn't diminish your respect or appreciation for the person in other areas. Sincerely acknowledging the positives can make the negatives easier to accept.
- *Accept partial responsibility for the problem.* If possible, show that you may have contributed in some degree to the issue. If nothing else, you might be able to say, "I probably should have brought this up sooner."
- *Accompany your criticism with an offer to help.* You can earn the goodwill of the other person by offering to play a role in solving the problem at hand.

Consider the Delivery

How you express a criticism can make a big difference in the way it is received. Two delivery-related guidelines can help:

- *Deliver criticism in a face-saving manner.* Probably the most important consideration is to make sure your remarks are delivered privately. Criticizing someone in front of others is likely to trigger resentment and embarrassment.
- *Avoid sounding and looking judgmental.* Avoid using the kind of emotive language described in Chapter 4. Don't call names or use inflammatory labels, and don't attribute motives to the other person. Try to use the kind of descriptive "I" language described earlier in this chapter instead of defense-arousing "you" statements. Avoid condescending nonverbal behaviors such as shaking your finger, raising your voice, or rolling your eyes.

Responding to Criticism

When people are faced with criticism, the two most common responses are "fight" and "flight." Fighters react by counterattacking and blaming others: "I'm not the only one who's at fault here." Your own experience probably shows that fighting with your critics seldom persuades them to back down.

Most businesspeople are too mature to actually run away from a critic, but there are other ways of evading negative remarks. Sometimes you *can* physically avoid critics—steering clear of their offices or not returning their phone calls, for example. Even when you can't escape unpleasant remarks, you can mentally disengage by refusing to listen thoughtfully to the criticism. While keeping quiet can seem to work in the short run, it is seldom a satisfying way to deal with an ongoing relationship in which you are constantly under attack.

Since neither fighting nor fleeing is likely to satisfy your critics or help you understand legitimate criticism, you need alternatives that allow you to listen nondefensively without losing face. Fortunately, two such alternatives exist.

Seek More Information

Asking your critic to explain the problem gives you a constructive option to fighting or fleeing. By asking your critic for more information, you are showing that you take the criticism seriously, but at the same time, you aren't accepting blame for the problem. There are several ways to seek more information:

- *Ask for examples or clarification.* "You've said I'm not presenting a good attitude to customers. Can you describe exactly what I'm doing?"
- *Guess about details of the criticism.* Even if the critic isn't willing or able to offer specifics, you can guess: "Was it the way I handled Mr. Tyson when the bank sent back his check for insufficient funds?"
- *Paraphrase the critic.* "When you say I have a bad attitude toward customers, it sounds like you think I'm not giving them the service they deserve."
- *Ask what the critic wants.* "How do you think I should behave differently around customers?"

It can be hard to listen sincerely when you are being criticized. But it's easier to keep your cool if you realize that trying to understand the objections doesn't mean you have to agree with them—at least not at this point. You may find that keeping notes of your critic's comments can give you something to do besides defend yourself. In addtion, this approach will show your critic that you take his or her comments seriously.

career tip

The Art of the Apology

When you have made a mistake, nothing is as honest and potentially effective as a genuine apology. Besides being the right thing to do, apologizing can be a smart business strategy. Research suggests that sincerely acknowledging mistakes can drastically reduce both resentment and legal actions by offended parties.[16]

A complete apology contains several elements:

- ***Sincere regret.*** The fundamental part of an apology is a genuine expression of regret. "I feel bad about not showing up for yesterday's shift. I'm really sorry I let you down."
- ***Understanding that the person suffered harm.*** Show that you recognize how the other person was affected and that you're sorry. "I know it was busy, and it must have been a nightmare."
- ***An explanation of what happened.*** Without offering excuses, consider explaining how the offending behavior came to happen. "I got a panicky call from my grandmother, and felt like I had to get over there and see what the matter was. It turned out to be nothing, but by the time I got her calmed down it was too late to call you."
- ***Corrective action.*** Show that you intend to prevent future problems. "I've asked her to call my sister if anything like this happens again, so unless there's a real emergency there shouldn't be any more problems like this."
- ***Restoration.*** Do what you can to compensate the other person for the misdeed. "If it would help, I'm happy to cover tomorrow's shift, even though I'm not scheduled."

Source: After Patrick J. Kiger, "The Art of the Apology," *Workforce Management*, October 2004, pp. 57–62.

Agree with the Criticism An obvious but often overlooked way of responding is to agree with the criticism. Although this approach might seem like a form of self-punishment, it can be extremely effective. There are three ways to agree with a critic:

- *Agree with the facts.* Sometimes you are confronted with facts that can't be disputed. In these cases, your best approach is probably to face up to the truth: "You're right. I *have* been late three times this week." Notice that agreeing with the facts doesn't mean that you are accepting responsibility for every imaginable fault. In the case of being late to work, you might go on to point out that your lateness is a fluke in an otherwise spotless work record; but arguing with indisputable information isn't likely to satisfy your critic, and it will probably make you look bad.
- *Agree with the critic's right to his or her own perception.* Sometimes you can't honestly agree with the criticism. For example, a customer might unjustly accuse you of not caring about good service. After asking for more information to find out the basis of the criticism (a shipment didn't arrive on time, for example), you can acknowledge how the other person might view you as being at fault: "I can understand why it might seem that I don't care about your needs. After all, you did tell me that you absolutely had to have that shipment by last

Friday, and I told you that it would be there. I'd be mad too if I were you." Notice that agreeing with the perception doesn't require you to *accept* your critic's evaluation as accurate, although you might indeed find that it does have some merit. What you are doing is acknowledging the other person's right to view the issue in a way that may differ from yours; you are agreeing that you can see how their perception makes sense to them, whether or not you see it the same way.

- *Emphasize areas of common ground.* As much as possible, point out areas where you and the other person share the same point of view. For example:

  Critic: The customers will never go for this idea!

  Response: We *do* have to keep the customers satisfied. What if we test market the idea? If they hate it, of course I'll drop the suggestion.

  Even when the criticism is extreme, you can probably find something in the other person's position to agree with:

  Hysterical Critic: You're going to ruin the whole job!

  Response: I know how important it is to you. (Then let the critic talk about the job's importance, reinforcing your agreement.)

Work for a Cooperative Solution Once your critic believes that you've understood his or her position and acknowledged at least some parts of it, he or she will be as ready as possible to hear your point of view. A few strategies can maximize the chances for a constructive solution.[17]

- *Ask for the chance to state your point of view.* If you push ahead and state your position before the critic is ready to listen, your words probably won't get through. It's far more productive to give your critic a thorough hearing, agree with whatever points you can, and then ask, "May I tell you my perspective?" Doing so won't guarantee that you'll get a respectful hearing, but it gives you the best chance of one.
- *Focus on a solution, not on finding fault.* Your own experience will show that playing the blame game rarely works. A far more productive approach is to focus on finding a solution that will work for both you and the critic by asking, "What would make this situation better?" or "How can we handle this situation in a way that both of us can accept?"

Managing Conflict

Like it or not, conflict is part of every job. In one study, human resource managers reported spending up to 60 percent of their time dealing with employee disputes, and over half of the workers said they lost time at work worrying about past confrontations or fretting about future conflicts.[18]

To most people, the fewer conflicts, the better. But since conflict is unavoidable, an inability or refusal to face problems can lead to job-hopping. Brenda Richard, director of human resources for the Radisson Hotel New Orleans, describes people who fit this pattern: "They don't want to solve problems, they don't want conflict."[19] The problem isn't conflict itself, but rather *the way in which it is handled.* With the right approach, conflict can produce good results. Management consultant and Harvard Medical School psychologist Steven Berglos argues flatly that constructive conflict is an essential ingredient in organizational success:

> *If you're not looking for ways to promote healthful conflict between people of different backgrounds who cannot possibly see the world the same way, don't be surprised if anarchy ensues or if the best and the brightest abandon you.*[20]

In Chinese, the ideogram for the word *crisis* is made up of two characters: danger and opportunity. A poorly handled organizational conflict can certainly be dangerous; relationships suffer and productivity declines. On the other hand, a skillfully handled conflict can result in several benefits.[21] It can function as a safety valve, letting people ventilate frustrations that are blocking their effective functioning, and it can lead to solving troublesome problems.

What Are Conflicts About?

Conflicts fall into several categories.[22] To understand them all, take another look at the dispute between business partners Marissa and Tran described in the "Computer Solutions" case study on page 66.

The Topic at Hand The most obvious source of conflicts is the subject at hand. Topic-related disagreements are a fact of life in the workplace. They involve issues including

pay and other compensation
resources
scheduling and job assignments
level of autonomy
the quality of products and services
budgeting

The Process Some disputes are more about *how* to do something than what to do. For example,

> A project team might all agree that the work at hand needs to be divided up, but they could disagree on how to decide who does what.
>
> Members of a community nonprofit group might decide to hold a fundraiser, but disagree on how to choose the type of event.

In the Computer Solutions case study, Tran and Marissa know they need to resolve their feelings about each other's contributions to the partnership, but each has trouble deciding how to proceed. Marissa wants to bring in an outside expert to mediate the problem, whereas Tran thinks they could work out the problems without any outsiders getting involved. So, the process has become a second area of conflict.

Relational Issues As you read in Chapter 1, along with substantive content issues are *relational* disputes that center on how parties want to be treated by one another. Relational issues can involve control, affinity, and respect.

> Are we a big family, or are we a group of professionals who keep our personal lives separate from work? (affinity)

Should the company allow employees to book their own hotels and flights on business trips as long as costs are within the organization's cost guidelines? (respect, control)

Does management really welcome ideas from rank-and-file employees, or is the suggestion box just a prop? (respect, control)

In the Computer Solutions case, Marissa and Tran aren't just disagreeing about who is working harder. As the conflict escalates, each is probably feeling disrespected and resentful. Unless they can address and resolve these feelings, equalizing the workload won't resolve their conflict.

Ego/Identity Issues

Social scientists use the term "face" to describe the identity each of us strives to present. In a work context, most people try to present a face of

competence	honesty
commitment	reasonableness
fairness	professionalism

Relationships do well when others acknowledge our presenting face, and conflicts intensify when others communicate in face-threatening ways.[23] Marissa's calling Tran a "sexist nerd" is an obvious face-threatening attack. Such accusations open a whole new front in the dispute, in addition to the original disagreement about equalizing the workload.

Even though the four types of conflicts are listed separately here, most disputes involve a combination of issues. As the preceding paragraphs show, Tran and Marissa have conflicts in each area. When you deal with a conflict, it's important to explore all of the dimensions on which it operates.

Approaches to Conflict

When faced with a conflict, you have several choices about how to respond. Each of these approaches has different results.[24]

Avoiding

One way to deal with conflict is to avoid it whenever possible and withdraw when confronted. In some cases, avoidance is physical: refusing to take phone calls, staying barricaded in the office, and so on. In other cases, however, avoidance can be psychological: denying that a problem exists or that it is serious, repressing emotional reactions, and so on. In the workplace, a communicator who avoids conflicts might accept constant schedule delays or poor-quality work from a supplier to avoid a confrontation or might pretend not to see a co-worker's dishonest behavior. As these examples suggest, avoidance may have the short-term benefit of preventing a confrontation, but there are usually long-term costs, especially in ongoing relationships. "I think it's better to face whatever the conflict is head on and deal with the situation as it comes up and not side-step it or go to someone else about the problem," advises Jean Stefani, a senior operations analyst at Comcast Communication.[25]

Despite its drawbacks, avoidance may sometimes be a wise choice. Table 5-4 on page 141 lists some circumstances in which keeping quiet may be the most appropriate course of action. For example, when standing up for your rights would be hopeless, silence might be the best policy. You might simply tolerate a superior's unreasonable demands while you look for a new job, or you might steer clear of an angry co-worker who is out to get you. In many cases, however, avoidance has unacceptable costs: You lose self-respect, you become frustrated, and the problem may only get worse.

Accommodating

Whereas avoiders stay away from conflicts, accommodators give ground as a way of maintaining harmony. It can be equivalent to appeasement, sacrificing one's principles, and putting harmony above dealing with important issues. In her fascinating book *Talking from 9 to 5,* sociolinguist Deborah Tannen describes an extreme case in which accommodating led to disaster.[26] On January 13, 1982, Air Florida flight 90 crashed shortly after takeoff from Ronald Reagan National Airport in Washington, DC; 69 passengers were killed. The cause of the disaster was excessive ice on the airplane's wings. An analysis of cockpit recordings made on the heavily armored black box recovered after the accident revealed that the co-pilot had hinted about excessive ice several times to the pilot before takeoff but that his suggestions went unheeded. The command structure of aircraft operations dictates that the pilot has the final word on whether a plane is fit to fly. It is easy to imagine that a less accommodating approach might have caused the pilot to recheck the situation before making what turned out to be a catastrophic decision.

"It's not enough that we succeed, Cats must also fail."

Though it has obvious drawbacks, accommodating does have merit in some circumstances (see Table 5-4). If you are clearly wrong, then giving up your original position can be a sign of strength, not weakness. If harmony is more important than the issue at hand—especially if the issue is a minor one—then accommodating is probably justified. For example, if you don't care strongly whether the new stationery is printed on cream or gray paper and fighting for one color might be a big concern for others, then giving in is probably smart. Finally, you might accommodate if satisfying the other person is important enough to your welfare. You might, for example, put up with an overly demanding customer to make an important sale.

Competing A competitive approach to conflicts is based on the assumption that the only way for one party to reach its goals is to overcome the other. This zero-sum approach is common in many negotiations, as you will see later in this chapter. Sometimes a power-based approach to conflict is based on simply disregarding the other person's concerns. Unsympathetic management might turn a deaf ear to the request of employees to make provisions for on-site exercise facilities, implying—or even stating outright—that the physical condition of employees is not the concern of the employer and that providing easy access to exercise would require a cash outlay and reduce time spent on the job.

In many cases, a competitive attitude is unnecessary. As the section of this chapter on win-win negotiating shows, it often *is* possible for both sides in a conflict to reach their goals (see pages 149–151). For instance, an employer might find that the cost of providing on-site exercise equipment is more than offset by reduced absenteeism and greater appeal when recruiting new employees. Furthermore, a competitive orientation

Table 5–4 Factors Governing Choice of a Conflict Style

Consider Avoiding

1. When an issue is genuinely trivial, or when more important issues are pressing.
2. When you have no chance of winning.
3. When the potential for disruption outweighs the benefits of resolution.
4. To let others cool down and regain perspective.
5. When the long-term costs of winning may outweigh short-term gains.
6. When others can resolve the conflict more effectively.

Consider Accommodating

1. When you find you are wrong.
2. When the issue is important to the other party and not important to you.
3. To build social credits for later issues.
4. To minimize loss when you are outmatched and losing.
5. When harmony and stability are more important than the subject at hand.
6. To allow others to learn by making their own mistakes.

Consider Competing

1. When quick, decisive action is vital (e.g., emergencies).
2. On important issues where unpopular actions need implementing (e.g., cost cutting, enforcing unpopular rules).
3. When others will take advantage of your noncompetitive behavior.

Consider Collaborating

1. To find solutions when both parties' concerns are too important to be compromised.
2. When a long-term relationship between the parties is important.
3. To gain commitment of all parties by building consensus.
4. When the other party is willing to take a collaborative approach.

Consider Compromising

1. When goals are important but not worth the effort or potential disruption of more assertive modes.
2. When opponents with equal power are committed to mutually exclusive goals.
3. To achieve temporary settlements of complex issues.
4. To arrive at expedient solutions under time pressure.
5. As a backup, when collaboration is unsuccessful.

Source: Kenneth W. Thomas, "Toward Multi-Dimensional Values in Teaching: The Example of Conflict Behavior," *Academy of Management Review* 2, no. 3 (1987), p. 487.

can generate ill will that is both costly and unpleasant. In our physical-fitness example, workers whose needs are ignored are likely to resent their employer and act in ways that ultimately wind up costing the company a great deal.

Despite its drawbacks, competition isn't always a bad approach. In some cases, an issue isn't important enough to spend time working it out. In other instances, there isn't time to collaborate on solutions. Finally, if others are determined to gain advantage at your expense, you might compete out of self-defense.

Self-Assessment — Your Conflict Management Style

Instructions: Below are 15 statements that describe possible strategies for dealing with a conflict. Use the following scale to describe how you typically behave in conflicts.

1 = Always **2 = Usually** **3 = Sometimes** **4 = Not very often** **5 = Rarely, if ever**

___ a. I argue the merits of my position forcefully.
___ b. I try to work out compromises between my position and others.
___ c. I try to meet others' expectations as much as possible.
___ d. I try to explore differences with others in order to find solutions that are mutually acceptable.
___ e. I am firm in resolve when it comes to defending my side of the issue.
___ f. I prefer to avoid conflict, keeping disagreements to myself as much as possible.
___ g. I defend my solutions to problems.
___ h. I'm willing to compromise in order to reach solutions.
___ i. I like to exchange important information with others so our problems can be solved together.
___ j. I avoid discussing my differences with others.
___ k. I try to accommodate the wishes of my peers and colleagues.
___ l. I prefer to bring everyone's concerns out into the open in order to resolve disputes in the best possible way.
___ m. I advocate middle positions in efforts to break deadlocks.
___ n. I accept the recommendations of others about how to resolve conflicts.
___ o. I avoid hard feelings by keeping my feelings and ideas to myself.

Scoring

The 15 statements you just read are listed below under five categories. Each category contains the letters of 3 statements. Record the number you placed next to each statement. Calculate the total under each category.

Style				**Total**
Competing	a. ______	e. ______	g. ______	______
Collaborating	d. ______	i. ______	l. ______	______
Avoiding	f. ______	j. ______	o. ______	______
Accommodating	c. ______	k. ______	n. ______	______
Compromising	b. ______	h. ______	m. ______	______

Results

My dominant style is ____ (your **LOWEST** score)
and my back-up style is ______________________________________ (your second-lowest score).

Sources: Adapted from A. Falikowski, *Mastering Human Relations,* 4th ed. (Don Mills, Ontario, Canada: Pearson Education, 2007), and K. Hamilton, "What's Your Conflict Style?" **http://webhome.idirect.com/~kehamilt/ipsyconstyle.html.**

career tip

How to Say No

There are times when even the most cooperative communicators feel compelled to decline the requests of a customer, a colleague, or even a boss. Following these steps can help soften the blow when you choose to say no.

1. Acknowledge that the request is important to the person making it: "I can understand why you need help to meet the deadline. . . ."
2. Decline the request: "I won't be able to help you out on this one."
3. Give your reasons, if appropriate: "I'm using every minute of my time to finish the XYZ report."
4. Offer help in finding a solution: "I could show you the report format I used last year. It might help you figure out how to approach this job."

Collaborating Rather than taking a competitive approach, collaborative communicators are committed to working together to resolve conflicts. Collaboration is based on the assumption that it is possible to meet one's own needs and those of the other person. This approach is reflected in Rabbi Hillel's statement, "If I am not for myself, who will be? If I am only for myself, what am I? If not now, when?"

Whereas avoiding and accommodating are based on the assumption that conflict should be avoided, and competing is based on the belief that conflict is a struggle, collaboration assumes that conflict is a natural part of life and that working with the other person will produce the best possible solution. The benefits of collaboration are clear: Not only can the issue at hand be resolved, but the relationship between the parties can also be improved.

Despite its advantages, collaborative communication isn't a panacea. It takes time to work with others, and a mutually satisfactory outcome isn't always possible. Furthermore, collaboration requires the cooperation of everyone involved. If the other party isn't disposed to work with you, then you may be setting yourself up for exploitation by communicating openly and offering to work cooperatively.

Compromising In a **compromise,** each party sacrifices something he or she is seeking to gain an agreement. On one hand, this approach is cooperative, recognizing that both parties must agree to resolve a conflict. On the other, compromise is self-centered, since the parties act in their self-interest to get the best possible deal.

Compromise is a middle-range approach. It is more assertive than avoiding and accommodating yet less aggressive than competing. It is cooperative yet less so than collaboration. While it does not give any one of the parties in a dispute everything he or she seeks, it provides an outcome that, by definition, everyone involved can live with. As Table 5–4 shows, compromise may not be the perfect approach, but under many circumstances it produces the best possible outcome.

Handling Conflicts Constructively

When you avoid a conflict or accommodate another's demand, few communication skills are necessary. But if you decide to address an issue directly—either to collaborate, to compete, or to seek a compromise—you will need to negotiate.

Negotiation occurs when two or more parties—either individuals or groups—discuss specific proposals to find a mutually acceptable agreement. Although we don't always

technology tip

Managing Conflicts in Cyberspace

In a world where communicators are dispersed around the globe, conflicts often unfold online. The following tips can help you avoid unnecessary disagreements in cyberspace, and deal with them constructively when they arise.

1. **Reread the troublesome message, and share it with someone you trust.** Your first reaction to a message may be colored by how you're feeling at the time. Rereading it later may give you a different perspective. Sharing a troublesome message with someone whose judgment you trust can bring a new perspective. If you do share the message, use a printed version rather than forwarding any e-mails. This will reduce the chances of the message being forwarded electronically.
2. **Decide whether or not to respond.** The best response to some messages is no response at all. If the message directed at you is accusatory or inflammatory and the sender's style tends to be aggressive or bullying, the best strategy may be to ignore it.
3. **Don't respond right away.** When you are hurt or angry, it's tempting to respond immediately. Since you can't un-send a regrettable message, it's wise to hold on to a draft of your reply for at least 24 hours. The next day, see whether your message needs rewriting before sending.
4. **Compose your reply offline.** If you use the "Reply" function of your e-mail program to compose your response, you risk hitting the "Send" button before your message is complete. You can avoid this problem by composing your reply offline in a word processing program. When you are sure it's ready to send, copy and paste it into an e-mail.

Sources: Adapted from K. Monroe, "Conflict in Cyberspace," **www.kalimunro.com/article_conflict_online.html,** and J. Suler, "The Online Disinhibition Effect," *CyberPsychology and Behavior* 7 (2004), pp. 321–26.

use the term, we negotiate every day. As one consultant explains, "Negotiations are seldom formal, sit-around-the-table affairs. In fact, almost any form of business problem or disagreement—from scheduling work shifts to 'Who's going to pay this $500 expense?'—is resolved by some form of negotiation."[27]

There's nothing magical about negotiation. When poorly handled, it can leave a problem still unsolved and perhaps worse than before. ("I tried to work things out, but he just tried to railroad me. I'm going to file a lawsuit this time.") When negotiation is handled skillfully, though, it can improve the position of one or even both parties. The remainder of this chapter will introduce communication strategies that can produce the best possible outcomes to your negotiations.

Negotiation Strategies and Outcomes

A common negotiating strategy is the competitive **win–lose** approach. It is based on the assumption that only one side can reach its goals and that any victory by that party will be matched by the other's loss. As Table 5-4 shows, you probably will need to take a competitive win–lose approach to protect your interests if others insist on gaining at your expense or when resources are truly scarce. For example, your company and another might compete for the same customers, and you might compete with another candidate for the same once-in-a-lifetime job.

Nobody seeks out **lose–lose** outcomes, but they can arise when competitors try to gain an advantage at one another's expense. Like armies that take mortal losses while trying to defeat their enemies, disputants who go for a competitive victory often find that they have hurt themselves as much as their opponents. For example, if you push for an unrealistically low price, you might antagonize the seller so much that you don't get the product you're seeking and the seller doesn't make the sale. On the job, feuding parties may ruin their own careers by gaining reputations as difficult employees or as poor team players.

Sometimes it seems better to *compromise* than to fight battles in a competitive manner and risk a lose–lose outcome. There certainly are cases in which compromise is the best obtainable outcome—usually when disputed resources are limited or scarce. If two managers each need a full-time assistant but budget restrictions make this impossible, they may have to compromise by sharing the services of one employee. While compromises may be necessary, they are less than ideal because both parties lose at least some of what they were seeking. Buyers, for instance, may pay more than they can afford, while sellers receive less than they need.

When negotiators collaborate, they can often—though not always—achieve a **win–win** outcome, in which everybody involved is satisfied. Win–win solutions are easiest when the needs of each party aren't incompatible, as in the following examples:

- *Shorter working hours.* Even though they were paid overtime, teachers at a preschool resented working weekends to keep school equipment clean and organized. A brainstorming session between the teachers and director produced a solution that satisfied everyone's needs: Substitutes covered for the teachers during some school hours while the teachers sorted and cleaned equipment. This approach had several benefits: Teachers' weekends were free, and teachers got a weekly change-of-pace from child care. Furthermore, the director welcomed the chance to observe the substitutes who were seeking full-time teaching jobs. She was also happy because the substitutes' pay was lower than the teachers' overtime.
- *Increasing employee compensation.* A contractor's employees wanted a raise. The contractor recognized that the employees deserved more, but couldn't afford to increase his payroll. After considering alternatives together, the boss and employees came up with a plan that pleased everyone. Workers were allowed to use company vehicles during nonworking hours, saving them the expense of an extra car or truck. The owner rented his vacation home to employees at a bargain rate. Finally, the boss negotiated lower prices for his employees on home furnishings and appliances at local merchants. These changes increased the employees' buying power—at little cost to the boss.
- *Blending business goals and community beauty.* A cellular phone company wanted to install a tower in the middle of a town, but residents didn't want an eyesore. The company agreed to build a long-needed new steeple for a local church, with the transmitter concealed inside. Furthermore, it paid the church $2,000 monthly rent. The result was a triple win: Expanded phone service, maintenance of the community's beauty, and both a new steeple and income for the church.[28]

As these few examples illustrate, the specific solutions that will work for a problem differ in each case. The important point is that parties working together *can* often find no-lose solutions to their problems. And, not surprisingly, research shows that a win–win approach is preferred to other problem-solving styles.[29] In one study, researchers compared the problem-solving styles used in six organizations. They found that the two highest-performing organizations used a win–win approach to a greater degree than did the less effective companies, while the lowest-performing organizations used that style less than the others.[30]

Win–win outcomes are ideal, but they aren't always realistic. Table 5–5 offers guidelines about when the chances are best for using this approach, as well as others.

Preparing to Negotiate Successful negotiations begin before you say a word to the other person. You can take several steps to think out your position and approach your negotiating partners in a way that boosts the odds of getting your message across and getting a constructive response.

Clarify your interests and needs Communicators can doom negotiations by prematurely focusing on means instead of ends. *Ends* are the goals you want, and *means* are ways of achieving those goals. In their best-selling book *Getting to Yes,* Roger Fisher and William Ury show that win-win results come from focusing on means instead of ends.[31] To illustrate the difference, we can adapt a story they tell.

Imagine a dispute between two office workers. John wants to open a window and Mary wants it closed. (This issue may seem trivial, but long-standing feuds have developed over smaller issues.) At this point the issue seems irreconcilable; but imagine that a colleague asks each worker what he wants. John replies, "To get some fresh air." To the same question, Mary replies, "To avoid a draft." "I have an idea," the mediating colleague suggests: "What if we open a window in the next room? That would give John the fresh air he needs and prevent the draft that Mary wants to avoid."

This simple example illustrates the difference between means and ends:

Issue	Ends	Means
John	Fresh air	Open window
		or
		Open window in adjoining room
Mary	No draft	Keep window closed
		or
		Open window in adjoining room

If Mary and John stayed focused on the first means that occurred to them, the issue would never be resolved to their satisfaction. But once they identified the ends each was seeking, the pathway to a mutually acceptable means was perfectly clear.

It's far better to identify the real end you are seeking and leave a discussion of means for later.

Consider the best time to raise the issue Raising a difficult issue when the other person is tired, grumpy, or distracted by other business is likely to threaten the odds of getting the results you are seeking. Review the variables about chronological communication contexts in Chapter 1 (page 9) when you consider when to raise an issue.

Table 5–5 When to Use Competitive and Win-Win Negotiating Styles

Consider a Competitive Approach	Consider a Win–Win Approach
When your interests and the other party's clearly conflict.	When you and the other party have common interests.
When the other party insists on taking a win-lose approach.	When the other party is willing to consider a win–win approach.
When you do not need a long-term harmonious relationship.	When a continuing, harmonious relationship is important.
When you are powerful enough to prevail.	When you are weaker or power is approximately equal.
When short-term goals are more important.	When long-term goals are more important.

Table 5–6 Chinese and Western Negotiating Styles

Chinese	Western
Less direct communication (high context)	More direct communication (low context)
Incremental gains	Winner-takes-all
Finesse	Overt power
Avoidance of confrontation	Head-to-head disagreement expressed
Niche and local context focused	Broad-based and overall market dominance
Risk-averse	Prone to take bigger risks
Privacy valued	Transparent flow of information valued

Source: Adapted from M-J Chen, *Inside Chinese Business: A Guide for Managers Worldwide* (Boston: Harvard Business School Press, 2001), p. 119.

Consider cultural differences As you plan your approach, consider the cultural sensibilities of your negotiating partners. As Chapter 2 explained in detail, the approach that seems comfortable to you may be quite alien to someone from a different background. Table 5–6 illustrates some of the differences that could distinguish the approaches of Western and Chinese negotiators.

Prepare your statement Think over how you can best express yourself, following the advice for offering constructive feedback on pages 133–135 in this chapter. Practicing your message can help make your point quickly and clearly, and it will prevent you from blurting out an angry statement you'll regret later. When planning your remarks, be sure to think about how you can use "I" language instead of delivering defense-arousing "you" messages.

Rehearsing your statement doesn't mean you should memorize your remarks word for word; this approach would sound canned and insincere. Think about your general ideas and perhaps a few key phrases you'll use to make your ideas clear.

Conducting the Negotiation

The win–win approach is most successful when it follows the steps described below.

Identify the ends both parties are seeking As you read earlier, seemingly irreconcilable conflicts can be resolved if negotiators focus on their needs, and not on positions. Consider the example of a parent who has found that the traditional work schedule isn't compatible with his child care responsibilities. Here are the ends that the employee and the boss identified:

Employee:	Make sure the children are cared for after school.
Boss:	Make sure employee's productivity doesn't drop.
Both:	Keep the employee on the job. Keep a positive relationship.

Brainstorm a list of possible solutions Once both parties have identified the ends they are seeking, the next step is to develop a list of solutions that might satisfy each party's needs. Recall the problem-oriented approach introduced earlier in this chapter: Instead of working against one another (How can I defeat you?), the parties work together against the problem (How can we beat the problem?).

Consider again the case of the employee trying to have his child cared for after school. In this case, a number of potential win–win solutions are worth exploring:

- The employee could do some work at home during nonbusiness hours.
- The company could offer flexible work hours, so employees can get their jobs done when children are at school or being cared for by others.
- The employee could share his full-time position with another worker, giving the boss the coverage the boss needs and the employee the free time. If the employee needs additional income, he could take part-time work that could be done at home at his convenience.
- The boss could subsidize after-school child care, on the assumption that productivity would rise and absenteeism decline as children of employees are being cared for.

While not all of the above options are likely to be workable, the key to successful brainstorming is to avoid judging any possible solutions for the time being. Nothing deflates creativity and increases defensiveness as much as saying, "That won't work." You can judge the quality of each idea later; but for now, the key is quantity. Perhaps one person's unworkable idea will spark a productive suggestion.

Evaluate the alternative solutions After brainstorming as many ideas as possible, decide which ones are most promising. During this stage, it is still critical to work for an answer that meets the important needs of all the parties. Cooperation will come only if everyone feels satisfied with the solution.

Implement and follow up on the solution Once the best plan is chosen, make sure everyone understands it; then give it a try. Even the most appealing plans may need revision when put into action. After a reasonable amount of time, plan to meet

career tip

Ethical Communication Gets Positive Results

Stephen Covey, author of *The Seven Habits of Highly Effective People*, *Principle-Centered Leadership*, and *First Things First*, offers these guidelines for principled communication. Covey argues that, besides being ethical, this approach can increase your influence with others.

- *Refrain from saying the unkind or negative things.* When you are provoked or fatigued, the temptation to lash out at others is strong. Being kind under pressure will earn you the respect of others.
- *Distinguish between the person and the behavior or performance.* You may disapprove of bad behavior and poor performance, but separate your judgment of the work from the person who has done it.
- *Keep your promises.* Never make agreements unless you are prepared to keep them. Being known as a dependable person will generate trust that makes your word a powerful thing.
- *Reward open, honest expressions or questions.* Too often we punish honest, open expressions or questions. As a result others learn to hide their ideas, opinions, and feelings. You may not agree with someone, but you can always say, "Thank you for being honest with me."
- *Admit your mistakes.* Everyone makes mistakes. When you do, apologize. When personal problems occur, consider whether you are at least partly to blame. Resist the urge to offer excuses, explanations, or defenses: They rarely convince or impress anyone.
- *Accept the other person.* Nothing reinforces defensive behavior more than judgment, comparison, or rejection. Accepting others as they are frees them from the need to defend themselves. Acceptance doesn't necessarily require you to agree with the other person's opinion. Rather, it means accepting his or her right to hold a position, even when it is different from yours.

Source: Stephen Covey, "Seven Methods of Influence," *Incentive* 17 (October 1996), p. 22.

with the other parties to discuss how the solution is working out. If necessary, identify the needs that are still unmet, and then repeat the problem-solving procedure.

Win–Win Problem Solving in Action

The case of Marta, a senior manager, and Kurt, her assistant, shows how win–win problem solving can work. Kurt has learned that his department is about to launch a particularly ambitious project. He feels ready to take on more responsibility and thinks this could be a good chance to show what he can do. Kurt is disappointed that Marta hasn't offered him the chance to lead the effort, but he wisely has thought about how to approach her instead of unassertively nursing his grudge or aggressively attacking her. Knowing from experience that Marta is most receptive when not distracted by other matters, he makes an appointment to talk with her. They agree to meet at the end of the workday, after most employees have gone home and the office is quiet.

Identify the needs of both parties

Marta: What's up?

Kurt: I'm really excited about the KDM project, and I'd like a shot at taking the lead on managing it.

Marta: Kurt, that's a major project. I need someone with more experience, especially in public relations, to handle that job. I've asked Greta to handle it. *(Marta explains her need—to have the job managed by someone with more experience.)*

Kurt: Well, I guess I understand. But I'd really like to take on more responsibility. This is the second time a big job went to somebody else. I'd like to find some way of proving myself and showing what I can do for this company. *(Kurt wisely avoids arguing about the specific project and instead focuses on his real goal—to get a chance to show he can handle more responsibility.)*

Marta: Fair enough. Let's try to figure out a way that you can have the responsibility and recognition you want and I can feel confident that the job is the right size. *(Like Kurt, Marta focuses on ends—Kurt growing in his job—instead of means.)*

Brainstorm a list of possible solutions

Kurt: Great. What if you put me in charge of a major project—one not quite as big as this one, and I could just check everything with you along the way?

Marta: Or I might be able to team you up with someone who has experience in areas where you're weak, and you could run the project together. Or I could get you to assist Greta on this project, so you could get some experience under her supervision and see how the aspects all fit together.

Kurt: I'd really like to show I can take the lead. What if I took on a less important project—one that called for me to figure out problems in these areas? Or maybe I could manage just the public relations part of a bigger project, to show you that I can handle that. *(Notice that Kurt and Marta have brainstormed five options to consider, without judging any at this point.)*

Evaluate the alternative solutions

Marta: All of these are possibilities. Let's see which of them will best suit us both. I could put you in charge of a major project, I guess, but you would need a lot of support, and I'm afraid I don't have enough time to give it to you.

Kurt: Plus it would drive us both crazy if I had to check every detail with you. And I don't really want to team up with someone, either. The whole idea is for me to get some experience where I need it, and a person who has that experience will just handle those concerns—which gets me nowhere.

Marta: On the other hand, I don't want to just put you on your own. How would you feel about handling the public relations on Greta's project? She could use some extra help, and having that help would give her time to train you. It would also help you get a sense of the whole project—not just part of it.

Implement the solution Kurt agreed to the idea of handling Greta's public relations:

Kurt: Just one thing. I want Greta to know that my job is to be responsible for that part of the project—not just be her assistant.

Marta: Sounds fair to me. I'll talk to Greta and make sure she's agreeable. I do think she has a lot of good advice to offer, though. You'd be foolish not to consider her opinions. And, of course, both she and I will have to support your decisions. But I'll be sure both of us give you the freedom to come up with your own plan—and the responsibility that goes with the freedom.

Follow up on the solution Marta, Kurt, and Greta met several weeks after developing their plan to check its progress:

Kurt: I'm feeling pretty good about the arrangement. I appreciate the chance to be responsible for one part of such a big project. Just one thing, Greta. When we agree on the way I'll do a job, I feel uncomfortable when you keep checking on how I'm doing. It makes me wonder whether you think I'll mess it up.

Greta: Not at all, Kurt. I thought you'd want to know that I'm available for support. Of course, I do want to keep posted, but I don't have any intention of being a snoop. What do you suggest?

Kurt: How about letting me come to you. I promise to keep you on top of things, and I do appreciate your advice. I'd just like to have a little more operating room.

Marta: Sounds like a good arrangement. Let's give it a try and get together next week at this time to see how it works.

review points

- A positive communication climate is an important element in successful working relationships. Such a climate comes from messages that convey respect for others, even during conflicts.
- Confirming messages use descriptive "I" language rather than "you" language. They focus on solving problems, not imposing solutions. They are honest, not manipulative. They show concern for the other party and reflect attitudes of equality and open-mindedness.
- Effective praise creates and maintains positive communication climates when it follows these guidelines: Praise progress; praise specifically, promptly, and sincerely; and relay praise from others.
- Even criticism can enhance a relationship if offered constructively: (1) Frame the content so it is limited, accurate, clearly defined, and benefits the recipient. (2) Choose a sender who is credible, is in a legitimate position to deliver criticism, and can maximize criticism's beneficial effects. (3) Deliver remarks as part of a positive relationship, accept partial responsibility for the problem, and add an offer of help. (4) Deliver criticism in a face-saving, nonjudgmental manner.
- When receiving criticism, prevent defensiveness by (1) seeking more information: ask for examples or clarification, guess about details if necessary, paraphrase the critic, or

ask what the critic wants; and (2) agreeing with facts or with a critic's right to his/her perception. (3) Work for cooperative solutions by asking to state your view and focusing on solutions, not fault.

- Handle the inevitable on-the-job conflicts constructively: (1) Explore whether the conflict is about a topic, a process, the relationship, or one's ego. (2) Choose the best conflict strategy (avoiding, accommodating, competing, collaborating, or compromising) for this situation. (3) Consider the best format (competitive, lose–lose, compromise, and win–win) to negotiate a mutually acceptable agreement.
- Successful negotiating includes these steps: Clarify your interests and needs by distinguishing between ends and means; pay attention to timing, culture, and nondefensiveness; and use a win–win approach (identify each party's needs, brainstorm then evaluate possible solutions, implement and follow up on a solution).

key terms

Test your understanding of these key terms by visiting the Online Learning Center Web site at www.mhhe.com/adler10e.

communication climate 127
compromise 143
confirming messages 128
descriptive statements 128
disconfirming messages 128
emotional intelligence (EQ) 126
"I" language 128
lose–lose orientation 144
negotiation 143
problem-oriented messages 129
social intelligence 126
win–lose orientation 144
win–win orientation 145
"you" language 128

activities

Go to the self-quizzes at the Online Learning Center at www.mhhe.com/adler10e to test your knowledge of chapter concepts.

1. Invitation to Insight

Recall two or three instances in which you have enacted troublesome communicative behaviors (see Table 5–1).

a. Identify which types of behaviors you enacted. What circumstances led you to enact these behaviors?
b. What were the results of these behaviors for you and the other people involved?
c. Describe specifically how you could have behaved in a more confirming manner.

2. Skill Builder

Convert each of the following disconfirming messages into a confirming message. In your messages, use descriptive "I" language (pp. 128–129) and unequivocal terms (pp. 93–94). Invent details about the situation as necessary.

a. "I sure wish I had someone to help me with this project."
b. "Look . . . stop asking questions and just get it done."
c. "You may think you know how to handle the situation, but you really don't have

enough experience. I'm the boss and I know when an assignment is over your head."

d. "What a tacky idea. A formal reception with paper plates! I can't believe you'd even suggest that."

e. "If you want to keep your job, you had better round up 10 new accounts by Monday."

3. Invitation to Insight

Familiarize yourself with effective praise by completing the following exercise:

a. Recall three situations in which someone has praised you. Using the guidelines on pages 131–133, evaluate the praise you received. Was it specific? Sincere? How did the praise impact you?

b. Think of three co-workers or acquaintances you could praise sincerely. How could you deliver the praise effectively? For each, write a short statement or paragraph expressing your praise.

4. Skill Builder

Practice your ability to manage criticism constructively by creating a brief role play with a partner based on one of the scenarios below (or use any critical message you are likely to receive on the job).

A co-worker accuses you of trying to ingratiate yourself with (kiss up to) the boss.

A hard-to-please client snaps at you about not returning his phone calls in a timely manner.

You forgot to proofread the budget committee's minutes before you distributed them; you accidentally mistyped several of the budget figures and the boss is upset.

You walk through a co-worker's work area on the way to the drinking fountain. She barks, "Can't you give me some space to do my job?"

At a meeting, you present a proposal that angers one of your co-workers. He attacks you verbally, claiming that you don't have your facts right.

Your supervisor criticizes you for taking too long to finish a job.

Enact the role play three times as follows:

a. The sender of the message uses judgmental language and the receiver responds defensively.

b. The sender uses judgmental language. The receiver responds nondefensively, using the skills described on pages 136–137.

c. The sender delivers the criticism as constructive feedback, using the guidelines on pages 135–137. The receiver responds nondefensively.

Discuss the impact that each approach is likely to have (1) on the relational climate and (2) on future interactions between these employees. Explain your answer by using the communication model in Chapter 1, pp. 7–9.

5. Invitation to Insight

Recall two conflicts you've been involved in recently.

a. For each, identify the primary source of conflict described on pages 138–139 (topic, process, relational, ego/identity). Do you think the other party(ies) would agree about the primary source of the conflict? Why or why not?

b. Next, identify any secondary sources of each conflict.

c. How did each dimension affect the way the participants approached the conflict?

6. Skill Builder

Describe an avoiding, accommodating, competing, collaborating, and compromising response to each of the following situations. Then decide which approach you would recommend. Because the meaning of a message varies with the context, you will need to decide on the specifics of the situation in order to make an informed choice. Explain your choice, using the information on pages 139–143.

a. At 4:30 P.M. a boss asks her assistant to work late to retype a 25-page report due the next morning. The assistant has already purchased nonrefundable tickets to attend a concert that evening.

b. The co-worker with whom you share a small cubicle habitually leaves papers, files, and books strewn all over her desk. The litter bugs you. Besides, you are concerned that it gives your clients a bad impression.

c. The assistant manager of a bookstore is faced with a customer demanding a refund for a book he claims was a gift. The book has several crumpled pages and a torn cover.

d. You are facilitator of a student group that is writing a research report worth half of your grade for the term. One group member misses two meetings without contacting you. When he returns, he explains that he had a family emergency and asks what he can do to make up the work.

7. Skill Builder

Sharpen your skill at knowing when and how to communicate assertively by following these steps:

a. Develop an assertive message for each of the following situations in your professional life:
   1. Making a request.
   2. Describing a problem involving the recipient of your message.
   3. Offering a suggestion.

b. Practice each message with a partner until you are confident that it is organized and delivered as effectively as possible. Recording your rehearsal can provide valuable feedback.

c. Now discuss with your partner the potential benefits and drawbacks of delivering each assertive message.

8. Skill Builder

In the following conflicts, identify the type(s) of conflict (topic, process, relational, ego/identity) and the ends desired by each party. For each situation, identify solutions (means to the end) that can satisfy the needs of everyone involved.

a. A landlord and tenant disagree about who should pay for an obviously necessary paint job for the office space.

b. Two co-workers contributed equally to developing a proposal for an important client. They both want to be the one who delivers the final proposal.

c. A sales manager and sales representatives disagree over the quota necessary to earn bonuses.

d. In a company with limited resources to spend on a new project, the marketing manager wants more money to be spent on advertising, while the product development manager wants a greater budget for researching new product lines.

9. Skill Builder

With a partner, select one of the following situations. Plan how you would prepare for and conduct the negotiation, working through each step on pages 146–149. Provide details as necessary to explain the situation.

a. You want to ask for a raise.

b. You and your co-workers would like your boss to hire an additional worker so you can accomplish all the necessary work in a timely fashion, without burnout.

c. You want to rent office space for your small business at a rate that is 5 to 10 percent less than the advertised price.

d. You need an extra week to complete a long, complex assignment.

resources

For extensive readings and Web sites on the interpersonal skills discussed in this chapter (climate, criticism, conflict), see the Online Learning Center Web site at **www.mhhe.com/adler10e.**©

7

Types of Interviews

chapter outline

chapter objectives

After reading this chapter you should be able to

1. Plan and conduct an information-gathering or career research interview that will help you clarify and/or achieve your career-related goals.
2. Identify and demonstrate the steps to prepare for, participate in, and follow up after an employment interview.
3. List various types of employment interviews and describe how you can prepare for each one.
4. Distinguish between legal and illegal employment interview questions and identify several methods of responding to illegal ones.
5. Describe how you can prepare for and effectively participate in a performance appraisal.

Of all the interview types described in Chapter 6, four are essential in almost every occupation: information-gathering, career research, employment, and performance appraisal. This chapter outlines the skills required for each of these important types of interview.

The Information-Gathering Interview

Information-gathering interviews come in many forms. For example, **investigative interviews** help answer the question, "What happened?" **Survey interviews** are used for various types of research to sample large groups of people. **Diagnostic interviews** are used by professionals in health care, law, counseling, and other areas to assess and treat clients. **Research interviews** turn up information that can help individuals and organizations perform more effectively. Finally, **exit interviews** help an organization learn why employees are leaving.

Many businesspeople owe their success in great part to the lessons they learned in information-gathering interviews. Sam Walton, founder of the Wal-Mart empire, explains how he used this approach early in his career to interview executives who had information that would help him:

> *I would just show up and say, "Hi, I'm Sam Walton from Bentonville, Arkansas. We've got a few stores out there, and I'd like to speak with Mr. So-and-So"—whoever the head of the company was—"about his business." And as often as not, they'd let me in, maybe out of curiosity, and I'd ask lots of questions about pricing and distribution, whatever. I learned a lot that way.*[1]

Another start-up tale reinforces the value of informational interviews. Three years out of college and jobless, entrepreneur Michael Mellinger created a thriving computer programming business in Barbados, where a staff of talented workers from second- and third-world Asian countries develop software for clients from wealthy, industrialized economies. He developed this idea by interviewing executives of Fortune 500 companies, whom he asked what services they needed. Despite his inexperience, Mellinger's approach captured the interest of top-level people. Before long, his mentors included the chief information officers of Pepsi, Merrill Lynch, and Chase Bank.[2]

Whatever their form, all types of information-gathering interviews follow the same general approach described in the following pages.

Collect Background Information

In many cases, pre-interview research is well worth the effort. Suppose, for instance, that you are interested in proposing a job-sharing plan—a system in which two people would share the responsibilities and salary of one full-time job. You decide you need to interview several people in your company before presenting your idea formally. Before conducting these interviews, however, you need to research the answers to some basic questions: How common is job sharing? In what industries does it occur? What forms does it take? Has it been tried by any firms in your field? What have the results of such arrangements been? Until you know at least the rough answers to these questions, you won't be ready to bring up the idea in your company.

Besides conducting traditional library research, you can get answers to questions like these by interviewing knowledgeable people. In this sense, talking about a single information-gathering interview is really an oversimplification, for you will usually conduct several during various stages of a task. You might, indeed, collect some fundamental background information during your first round of interviews. Perhaps you know someone who worked for a company that already has a job-sharing policy. An acquaintance might have mentioned a recent newspaper article on the subject, and you can get the reference that will help you locate it. During this phase, your questions will necessarily be vague, similar to the request you might make of a reference librarian: "I'm looking for information about job sharing. How do you think I ought to go about it?"

Once you have collected the necessary background information, you can use this knowledge to plan an intelligent approach to your second round of interviews—perhaps with people suggested by your earlier research or with the key decision makers who are your ultimate target.

Define Interview Goals and Questions

Defining the specific goal of your interview is always a key step. Your goal ought to be as specific as possible and be worded in a way that will tell you whether you have the answers you were seeking. Here are examples of how you might define a goal for an information-gathering interview:

Vague	Specific
I want to learn about tax-free municipal bonds.	Will tax-free municipal bonds give me liquidity, appreciation, safety, and tax shelter better than my present investments?
What happened at the accident yesterday?	What caused the accident, and could it have been prevented?
Should I buy a database management system?	Will a database management system improve my efficiency enough to justify the purchase?

Once you have identified your purpose, you must develop questions that will help you achieve it. For example:

Purpose: To learn what steps I need to take to have a job-sharing arrangement approved by management.

Questions:

Whom should I approach first?

Who will be the key decision maker on this issue?

Should I present my formal proposal first, or should I start by mentioning the subject informally?

What objections might management have to the proposal?

Is anyone else in the company (nonmanagement personnel) likely to oppose or support the idea?

What arguments (such as precedent, cost savings, employee morale) will most impress management?

What influential people might support this idea?

As you develop your questions, use the guidelines in Chapter 6. Make sure you gather both facts and opinions—and recognize which is which. Be prepared to follow up your primary questions with secondary queries as necessary.

Choose the Right Interviewee

The ideal respondent within an organization will be part of an informal communication network and may have no official relationship with you on the organizational chart. It might be naive to talk with your boss about the job-sharing proposal until you have consulted other sources who could suggest how to broach the subject: Perhaps a politically astute co-worker, someone who has experience making proposals to management, or even the boss's administrative assistant, if you are friends, will be helpful.

After you have established the purpose and the appropriate person to interview, follow the guidelines in Chapter 6 to plan and conduct the interview.

The Career Research Interview

The **career research interview** is a special type of informational interview in which you meet with someone who can provide information that will help you define and achieve your career goals. It is based on the principle that speaking with the right people can give you valuable ideas and contacts that you simply can't find from books, magazines, the Internet, or any other source.

The Value of Personal Contacts

The old phrase "It isn't what you know, it's who you know" is certainly true when it comes to getting a job. Over 30 years of research confirm that the vast majority of people don't find jobs from advertisements, headhunters, or other "formal" means.[3] Like these traditional sources, Web-based services like Monster.com aren't as useful as they might seem: Job-finding expert Richard Bolles cites research suggesting that less than 10 percent at best of job seekers find employment by using the Internet.[4] Other research backs up the value of personal contacts. A study of over 150,000 jobs found that more people were hired by referrals than by any other source.[5] Other research confirms this fact. A survey conducted by global resources company DBM revealed that 75 percent of job-seekers obtained their current positions through personal networking.[6]

Instead of using impersonal means, the majority of new hires get offers for employment through personal contacts. The reverse is also true: Most employers find good employees through their personal networks.[7] One corporate recruiter explained why networking is superior to Web-based employment sites:

> *. . . in the rare instances where I actually post a position online, I get résumés from all over the world. Many of them bear no relationship to the job I am trying to fill. It's as though people just "point and shoot."*
>
> *The last professional position I posted–with extremely explicit qualifications laid out in the posting–received almost 1,000 responses, of whom only 25 or so even met the technical and educational qualifications for the position. My time is much better spent networking personally with people to find good candidates than reviewing and responding to these résumés.*[8]

Finding a job is only one goal of career research interviews. These conversations can serve three purposes:

To conduct research that helps you learn more about the field and specific organizations that interest you.

To be remembered by making contacts who will recall you at an appropriate time and either offer you a position, inform you of employment opportunities, or suggest you to a potential employer.

To gain referrals to other people whom you might contact for help in your job search. These referrals can easily lead to meetings with more useful contacts, all of whom might mention you to *their* friends and associates.

Choosing Interviewees

The key to finding the wealth of unadvertised positions is to cultivate a network of contacts who can let you know about job opportunities and pass along your name to potential employers. Chapter 1 (pages 19–23) offered tips on how to build and nurture a personal network.

career tip

Getting Through Gatekeepers

Many potential career research interviewees are guarded by **gatekeepers**—personal assistants, receptionists, secretaries, etc. Even your most carefully crafted request for help may not gain you an interview if the gatekeeper is zealously guarding his or her boss's precious time. Here are some strategies for getting in touch with the person you want to interview.

Make your first request in writing

Your letter or e-mail has a much better chance of getting through to your target than an introductory phone call. Be sure your message follows the approach outlined in these pages, and that it is impeccably correct. Be sure to include your e-mail address and phone number so your target can reply.

Phone early or late

If you need to follow your introductory letter or e-mail with a phone call, the best time to reach your potential interviewee may be before or after regular business hours—when the gatekeeper isn't around to screen the boss's phone calls. If you are greeted by voice mail, be prepared to leave a fluent and concise reply: "Hi Ms. Allen. This is Daniel Mosher [phone number], following up on my letter to you from last week. I'm hoping to arrange a time when we can meet so I can get your advice about the best ways to prepare myself for breaking into the field of ________. My professor, Dr. Joy Chen, says you've been very helpful to other graduating seniors, and I would be very grateful for any ideas you're willing to share. I can be very flexible about when and where to meet. Again, my phone number is ________. I'll look forward to hearing from you at your earliest convenience."

Enlist gatekeepers as allies

If you find yourself speaking to the gatekeeper, begin by confidently asking to be put through to your prospective interviewee: "This is Daniel Mosher calling for Ms. Allen." If the reply is something like "She's in a meeting now. May I help?" your best approach may be to enlist the gatekeeper's assistance: "Certainly. I'd appreciate your advice. I'm following up on a letter I sent to Ms. Allen last week, and would like to set up a meeting with her. Could you suggest a time for an appointment, or maybe a time when I could call back and talk to her?" Be sure you get the gatekeeper's name, and address him/her personally from this point on.

Be flexible

Since you are asking for a favor, make yourself available for a meeting whenever it's convenient for your interviewee. Consider offering to conduct your interview over a meal or cup of coffee. One ambitious student even offered to chauffer his interviewee to the airport—a 90-minute drive. He argued that the chance to have an uninterrupted conversation made the effort well worthwhile.

There's no doubt that the people in your immediate networks can be helpful; but surprisingly, you can benefit even more from more-distant connections. In his classic study "The Strength of Weak Ties," Mark Granovetter surveyed over 280 residents of a Boston suburb who had taken a new job within the past year. While only 17 percent of the people surveyed found their jobs through close friends or relatives, the majority learned about their new positions from people who were only distant associates—old college friends, former colleagues, parents of a child's playmate, and so on.[9] Weak ties are often more useful than close acquaintances in finding jobs because your close associates rarely know more than you do about career opportunities. Distant acquaintances, however, are connected to other, less familiar communication networks, networks that often contain valuable information about new jobs.[10]

You might wonder why the kind of important person you would like to interview would be willing to meet with you. There are actually several reasons. First, if you have made contact through a referral, your subject will probably see you in deference to your mutual acquaintance. If you can gain a referral, you are most likely to get a friendly reception. Second, interviewees might be willing to see you for ego gratification. It is flattering to have someone say "I respect your accomplishments and ideas" and difficult for even a busy person to say no to a request that accompanies such a comment. A third reason is simple altruism. Most successful people realize they received help somewhere along the line, and many are willing to do for you what others did for them. Finally, you may get an interview because the person recognizes you as ambitious, someone who might have something to offer his or her organization.

Contacting Prospective Interviewees

When you approach a career research interviewee—especially one you don't know well—it can be smart to make your first contact in writing. A telephone call runs the risk of not getting through; and even if you do reach the interviewee, your call may come at a bad time. While e-mail can be quick and efficient, a traditional letter can make a strong, positive first impression. Your first message, like the one in Figure 7–1, should introduce yourself, explain your reason for the interview (stressing that you are *not* seeking employment), state your availability for a meeting, and promise a follow-up telephone call.

Unless you'll be conducting the interview within a day or two of the time your interviewee agrees to meet with you, a second letter, e-mail, or phone call should precede the interview and confirm its date, place, and time. This sort of follow-up can save you the

FIGURE 7–1
Request for an Informational Interview

From: Emily Park <eprk112@sunnet.net>
Sent: Tuesday, May 25, 2010 12:51 PM
To: Vanessa J. Yoder <v.yoder@DGHattysatlaw.com>
Subject: Seeking your advice

Dear Ms. Yoder:

I am currently a junior at the University of New Mexico, majoring in political science and communication. After graduating from UNM, I plan to attend law school and focus my studies on immigration law.

From several news accounts and also from several of my professors, I've learned that you are an expert in immigration law and have a stellar reputation for representing women when the cases involve both domestic violence and immigration issues. I also heard of your work during my internship at the Women's Workforce Training Center.

I would appreciate the opportunity to meet with you to discuss how I might best prepare myself for an eventual career in immigration law. I would also like to know which law schools you would recommend and hear about the challenges and rewards of this type of practice.

Let me stress that I am not seeking employment at this time. Your advice would be invaluable as I prepare myself for a career in law. I will call your office next week hoping to schedule an appointment. I know you are a busy person and I would be grateful for 30-45 minutes of your time.

I look forward to benefiting from your insights and recommendations.

Sincerely,
Emily Park
9971 Washoe St., NE
Albuquerque, NM 87112
(505) 793-3510

frustration of being stood up by a forgetful interviewee. Just as important, it shows that you know how to handle business engagements in a professional manner.

Giving your interviewee an advance list of topic areas and questions you hope to cover will distinguish you as a serious person, worth the interviewee's time and effort. Also, supplying this list will give your interviewee a chance to think about the areas you want to discuss and ideally come to your meeting best prepared to help you. Figure 7–2 illustrates a confirming e-mail with list of questions.

Following Up

In a post-interview letter or e-mail, express thanks for the interviewee's time and mention how helpful the information was. Besides demonstrating common courtesy, these messages become a tangible reminder of you and provide a record of your name and address that will be useful if the interviewee wants to contact you in the future.

FIGURE 7–2
Confirming E-mail with List of Questions

Subject: Interview confirmation and questions
Date: Fri, 11 June 2010, 8:26 a.m. (MDT)
From: Emily Park <eprk112@sunnet.net>
To: Vanessa J. Yoder <v.yoder@DGHattysatlaw.com>

Dear Ms. Yoder:

Thank you again for agreeing to speak with me about how I can best prepare myself for a career in immigration law. I am looking forward to our meeting at your office this coming Thursday, June 17, at 2:00 p.m. I know how busy you must be, and I'm grateful for your giving me 45 minutes of your time.

In order to use our time together most efficiently, here is a list of some questions I hope we can discuss at our meeting:

TRENDS IN IMMIGRATION AND LAW
- What trends do you anticipate in immigration patterns?
- How do you view the field of immigration law changing to reflect these conditions?

EDUCATION
- What law schools do you recommend for someone interested in practicing immigration law?
- Do you recommend any courses I should take in my senior year at the university?

EXPERIENCE
- What types of work experience (paid or volunteer) could help prepare me for law school and eventual employment?
- Can you recommend ways I might pursue positions in these areas?

EMPLOYMENT
- What types of jobs are there for attorneys who specialize in immigration law?
- How easy/difficult do you anticipate it will be to secure employment in these sorts of jobs?
- What, if any, are the pros and cons I might expect as a woman practicing law in this area?

LIFESTYLE
- How would you describe the benefits and challenges of working in the field of immigration law?
- How compatible is a career in this area with being a parent?

OTHER CONTACTS
- Can you recommend other people who might be willing to talk with me about preparing for a career in immigration law?

Of course, all correspondence should be typed neatly with impeccable format, spelling, and grammar: Your letters are a reflection of you.

The Employment Interview

An **employment interview** is designed to explore how well a candidate might fit a job. The exploration of fit works both ways: Employers certainly measure prospective candidates during this conversation, and prospective employees can decide whether the job in question is right for them. The Bureau of Labor Statistics reports that the typical American worker holds nearly nine different jobs before age 32, so the probability of facing at least one employment interview in the near future is high.[11]

The short time spent in an employment interview can have major consequences. Consider the stakes: Most workers spend the greatest part of their adult lives on the job—roughly 2,000 hours per year or upward of 80,000 hours during a career. The financial difference between a well-paid position and an unrewarding one can also be staggering. Even without considering the effects of inflation, a gap of only $200 per month can amount to almost $100,000 over the course of a career. Finally, the emotional results of having the right job are considerable. A frustrating job not only makes for unhappiness at work but these dissatisfactions also have a way of leaking into nonworking hours as well.

How important is an interview in getting the right job? The Bureau of National Affairs, a private research firm that serves both government and industry, conducted a survey to answer this question. It polled 196 personnel executives, seeking the factors that were most important in hiring applicants. The results showed that the employment interview is the single most important factor in landing a job.[12] Further research revealed that the most important factor during these critically decisive interviews was communication skills. Employers identified the ability to communicate effectively as more important in shaping a hiring decision than grade-point average, work experience, extracurricular activities, appearance, and preference for job location.[13]

Even though interviews can play an important role in hiring, research shows that potential employers—at least those who aren't trained in employment interviewing—are not very good at using interviews to choose the best applicant for a job.[14] They fail to recognize the potential in some candidates who would make fine employees, and they are impressed by others who prove to be less than satisfactory as workers. In other words, the best candidate does not necessarily get the job offer.

"You don't look like a Dave."

In many situations, the person who knows the most about getting hired gets the desired position. "Chemistry is the paramount factor in hiring," states Wilhelmus B. Bryan III, executive vice president of William H. Clark Associates, a New York recruiting firm.[15] While job-getting skills are no guarantee of qualifications once the actual work begins, they are necessary to get hired in the first place.

Pre-Interview Steps

Scanning the newspaper for openings and then filing an application with the company's personnel or human resources department is one way of looking for a job but often not the most effective. Many employers never advertise jobs, and depending on the salary sought, only 5 to 24 percent of job seekers find a job solely through local newspaper ads.[16] Employment expert Richard Bolles explains:

> *I know too many stories about people who have been turned down by a particular company's personnel department, who then went back to square one, found out who, in that very same company, had the power to hire for the position they wanted, went to that woman or man, and got hired–ten floors up from the personnel department that had just rejected them.*[17]

Even when a company does advertise, the odds don't favor an applicant who replies with an application and résumé. Since most job announcements attract many more applicants than an employer needs, the job of the personnel department becomes *elimination,* not selection. The goal is to reduce the pool of job seekers to a manageable number by rejecting as many applicants as possible. Given this process of elimination, any shortcoming becomes welcome grounds for rejecting the application and the applicant. Many consultants, therefore, suggest identifying and contacting the person who has the power to hire you *before* an opening exists. The process has several steps.

Conduct Background Research The first step is to explore the types of work and specific organizations that sound appealing to you. This involves doing Internet research, reading magazines and newspaper articles, taking classes, and simply fantasizing about jobs you might find interesting. The result of your research should be a list of organizations and names of people who can tell you more about your chosen field.

Besides helping you find organizations where you want to work, your knowledge of a company will distinguish you as a candidate worth considering for a job. Desiree Crips of Salus Media in Carpinteria, California, reflects the view of most potential employers: "If someone walks in here and doesn't know anything about our company, that's a real negative. There's just no excuse for not being up to speed on any company you're applying to these days."[18] Doing your homework is just as important in the workforce as in school.

Contact Potential Employers At some point, your research and networking will uncover one or more job leads. You might read a newspaper story about the need of a local employer for people with interests or training like yours. Perhaps a career research interview subject will say, "I know someone over at ________ who is looking for a person like you." You might learn through a friendly contact that a desirable firm is about to expand its operations. In such a case, it is time to approach the person who has the power to hire you and explore how you can help meet the company's needs.

Whether the job lead comes from a formal announcement or a contact from your personal network, your first step is to let the organization know about your interest in a job. In most cases, the best way to do this is with written correspondence, usually a cover letter and a copy of your résumé. The Appendix of this book has advice on constructing and formatting résumés. A cover letter like the one in Figure 7–3 on page 196 that takes the following approach will serve you well.

In the first paragraph, introduce yourself to the reader. Clearly state your purpose for writing (e.g., in response to an advertisement, at the suggestion of a mutual acquaintance, as a result of your research) and describe your ability to meet the company's needs. When appropriate, mention any mutual acquaintances that the addressee will recognize. If you are writing to the human resources department of a medium- or large-sized

FIGURE 7–3

Sample Message Requesting an Employment Interview

The writer identifies her reason for writing, and makes reference to a mutual acquaintance, who presumably can vouch for her.

This paragraph links the writer's experience to the job being sought.

This paragraph details professional accomplishments that are relevant to the job being advertised.

The applicant closes by clearly expressing her desire to meet and discuss the job, indicating when she will be available.

The applicant includes her mailing address and phone number, in case the employer wishes to contact her in one of these ways.

From: Krista Dudley [krista.dudley@rockycast.net]
Sent: Friday, April 16, 2010 5:41 PM
To: John Waldmann [john.waldmann@boulderarts.org]
Subject: Events Coordinator application

Attached: K Dudley Resume.doc

Dear Mr. Waldmann:

Our mutual friend Marcia Sherwood recently alerted me to the open position of Events Coordinator for the Boulder Arts Council, and I am writing to express my interest in that position.

I would welcome the chance to use skills acquired over the past 12 years planning events for a variety of community organizations in the Denver area to help the Council extend its reach in the community. The attached resume will help you gain a sense of my experience.

As a person who has coordinated a wide range of community events for nonprofit organizations, I can bring the Arts Council demonstrated ability to motivate and coordinate the work of volunteers and to generate widespread publicity for events on a limited budget. Most recently, I was chairperson for Aurora's Earth Day festival, and I was the public information coordinator for last year's Halloween auction and dance to benefit Denver's Shelter Services for Women. The enclosed résumé details a variety of other activities that have helped prepare me for the position of Events coordinator.

I would welcome the chance to discuss how I might help the Boulder Arts Council. I will be available any time in the next month, except for the weekend of April 23–24.

I look forward to hearing from you soon.

Sincerely,
Kristina Dudley
387 Blythe St.
Aurora, CO 80017
(303) 654-7909

organization, be sure to give the job number if there is one; a company that has many job openings won't know which one you're applying for unless you identify it.

In the next paragraph or two, highlight one or two of your most impressive accomplishments that are *relevant to the job at hand.* Don't just say you can help the organization: Offer some objective evidence that backs up your claim.

In the closing paragraph, describe the next step you hope to take—usually requesting an interview. Detail any information about limits on your availability (though you should keep these to an absolute minimum). Supply any other information that the prospective employer may have requested. Finally, close with a cordial expression of gratitude.

Most career counselors recommend directing your request for an interview to the person who has the ability to hire you, rather than to the company's human resources department. We have already discussed why personnel departments aren't the best avenue for getting hired: Employees there are usually screening large numbers of applicants, so they are looking for reasons to reject as many as possible to arrive at a manageable number of finalists to interview. Also, personnel screeners are usually not familiar with the position, so they may reject candidates for superficial or mistaken reasons.

The mechanical nature of this screening process is best illustrated by the growing use of **scannable résumés.** These documents are "read" by document scanning devices, not humans. The software searches for keywords and phrases that describe the skills and education required for the position. Applications that contain these words are passed on to a human who evaluates them further. The Appendix of this book offers tips on creating effective scannable résumés; but even the best document may not capture the unique traits you can offer an employer. For this reason, you will maximize your chances at being recognized by developing a relationship with people who know both your talents and the characteristics of the job.

Another screening technique are job interviews by computer. Retailers such as Target, Macy's, and Hollywood Video are replacing paper applications and in-person interviews with computer kiosks in the initial screening of applicants.[19]

Prepare for Possible Interview Formats The standard one-on-one, question-and-answer interview format isn't the only one you may encounter. Employers use a variety of interview formats. If you are prepared for all of them, you aren't likely to be surprised.

In a **panel interview** (sometimes called a *team* or *group interview*), the candidate is questioned by several people. Panel interviews save the company time and provide the people with whom you may work an opportunity to compare their perceptions of you. When setting up an interview, it is appropriate to ask whether you will be facing a team of questioners. If you are, do your best to learn and use the names of each person. When you answer questions, make sure you look at everyone in the group. Some employers use a **stress interview** to evaluate your behavior under pressure; you can find tips to prepare for this at the Online Learning Center at **www.mhhe.com/adler10e**.

In an **audition interview** you will be asked to demonstrate whatever skills the employer is looking for. You might be asked to create a project, solve a problem, or respond to a typical scenario in the job, such as dealing with a difficult client. The audition shows the potential employer how you are likely to do on the job. The prospect of an audition can be especially helpful if you will be competing against candidates with more experience or stronger credentials. For that reason, you might even volunteer for an audition if you are confident you can handle the job well.[20]

A **behavioral interview** is based on the assumption that past experience is the best predictor of future performance. In this approach interviewers explore specifics about the candidate's past accomplishments. John Madigan, a vice president at The Hartford Financial Services Group, explains the way behavioral interviews work: "We actually ask what you did in specific situations. Concrete examples will demonstrate a person's preferred way of dealing with those situations and give you a better idea of that person and how they're likely to act on the job."[21]

Here are some questions you might hear in a behavioral interview:

- Give me a specific example of when you sold your supervisor or professor on an idea or concept. What was the result?
- Tell me about a time when you came up with an innovative solution to a challenge you or your company was facing. What was the challenge? What role did others play?
- Describe a situation where you faced multiple projects. How did you handle it?[22]

Preparing for Behavioral Interviews

Interviewers often ask questions about your past behavior in order to judge the way you are likely to handle a job if hired.

Each answer to a behavioral question should include (1) one or more specific examples of what you did and (2) what the example(s) you've chosen say about you as a prospective employee. Choose examples that showcase some of your best qualities. If it is a question about something you did wrong or a mistake you made, show how you learned something or how something positive resulted from the experience. For example, if asked to describe a time when you were faced with a stressful situation that demonstrated your coping skills, you might answer: "In the middle of my last semester as a senior, my father had emergency surgery. That put a big load on my family, and I moved back home for about 2 months to lend a hand. During that time I managed to finish all my classes with As and Bs, and I also covered every shift on my job after the first week. It wasn't fun, but that experience taught me that I can handle a lot of demands."

Practice your skill at behavioral interviews by answering the questions below in a group:

- Describe a time that you needed to work as part of a team.
- Tell about a time that you had to use creativity and problem-solving skills to solve an important problem.
- Explain how you handled a situation when you had to make an important ethical decision.
- Describe a time when you didn't succeed at something you were trying to accomplish.
- Give an example of a time when you took on a greater share of responsibility or decision making than was required by your job.

For more examples of behavioral interview questions, see **www.quintcareers.com/sample_behavioral.html.**

If you have a proven record of accomplishments that will clearly work well in the job you are seeking, a behavioral interview should sound ideal. If you don't have work experience that is clearly relevant to the new position, find ways to demonstrate how things you have done in other contexts apply to the job you are seeking. For example, you might be able to show how experience in retail sales taught you how to deal with difficult customers you'll encounter in a customer service job, or how being a volunteer for a nonprofit charity gave you an appreciation for working with limited resources—an attitude most employers will welcome.

Think Constructively The way you think about an upcoming interview can affect how you feel and act during the session. A research team at Washington State University interviewed both highly anxious and more confident students to discover what causes some people to become especially apprehensive during the process of meeting prospective employers.[23] The differences between the groups were startling. Anxious students avoided thinking about an interview in advance, so they did little in the way of research or preparation. When they did think about an upcoming interview, they dwelled on negative self-talk: "I won't do well" or "I don't know why I'm doing this." It's no surprise that thoughts like these created negative self-fulfilling prophecies that led to poor interview performances. Students who handled interviews better weren't anxiety-free, but they thought about the upcoming challenge in more productive ways. We can imagine them thinking, "The interviewer isn't trying to trick me or trip me up" and "I'll do a lot better if I prepare."

case study

Recovering from Interview Blunders

Most job seekers plan carefully for employment interviews. But occasionally an applicant blunders so spectacularly that his or her performance earns a place in the Communication Hall of Fame. The following true stories were reported by employment interviewers.

> "A man who forgot dark socks to wear with his suit colored in his ankles with a black felt-tip marker."
>
> "The candidate said that by crossing the Maryland state line he was in violation of his probation but felt the interview was worth risking possible jail time."
>
> "A candidate was asked what person they would most like to meet, living or dead, and their response was the living one."
>
> "I was interviewing someone who took a cell-phone call and asked me to leave my office while they talked."
>
> "When a candidate was asked about his greatest accomplishment, he replied that it was writing a short novel. When the interviewer said, 'No, I mean something you did while at work,' the candidate replied, 'But I did write it while at work!'"

No employer would hire an applicant who behaved so poorly in an interview. But job candidates do make less serious, though egregious, mistakes. According to experts in the field, some of the most common blunders are

arriving late

being rude to other employees

calling someone by the wrong name

an error in résumé or cover letter

referencing a potential employer's competitor

CRITICAL ANALYSIS: One way to avoid bungling an interview is to anticipate—and thereby avoid mindless errors. You can prepare yourself for an error-free interview by considering the following points.

1. What other kinds of careless mistakes might an otherwise prepared job candidate make in an interview situation?
2. How could you guard against making each of the mistakes you listed in the question above?
3. Devise a strategy for recovering from each of the five mistakes above and those that you have identified. Compare your strategies with those suggested by experts at **http://m.cnn.com/cnn/ne/living/detail/217858/full;jsessionid=F6AA61F989728D95410C0E6E9C5BD7E1.live4ib.**

Sources: "Great Places to Work: Interview Horror Stories," *Washingtonian*, November 1, 2005, retrieved January 3, 2009, from **www.washingtonian.com/articles/businesscareers/2159.html;** and "Job Search Mistakes," CNN.com, December 24, 2008, retrieved December 30, 2008, from **http://m.cnn.com/cnn/ne/living/detail/217858/full;jsessionid=F6AA61F989728D95410C0E6E9C5BD7E1.live4ib.**

Dress Appropriately and Act Professionally Looking good when you meet a potential employer is vitally important. In one survey, recruiters ranked clothing as the leading factor in shaping their initial impressions of applicants (ahead of physical attractiveness and résumé). Furthermore, 79 percent of the recruiters stated that their initial impressions influenced the rest of the interview.[24] The best attire to wear will depend on the job you are seeking: The professional business suit that would be appropriate for a banking job would almost certainly look out of place if you were interviewing for a job in the construction industry, and it might look overly formal at many software companies. When in doubt, it is always safest to dress on the conservative side. Of course, cleanliness and personal hygiene are essential.

Be sure to arrive at the interview 5 to 10 minutes early. Be polite to everyone in the office. While you wait, choose reading material about the business or company, not about current TV personalities. When introduced, shake hands firmly, no more than three shakes, avoiding a limp or hand-crushing grip. Smile, make eye contact, and take your lead from the interviewer about how to proceed.

During the Interview

If your fate in the selection process were determined by a skilled, objective interviewer, the need for strategic communication might not be essential. Research shows, however, that the rating you are likely to receive from an interviewer can be influenced by a variety of factors as varied as the time of day, the sex of the interviewer and interviewee, whether the candidates before you did well or poorly, and the employer's mood.[25] Since the interview is not a scientific measure of your skills, it is especially important to do everything possible to make the best impression. Interviewing expert Anthony Medley describes one memorable job candidate who illustrates the importance of first impressions:

> *She was attractive, presentable, and had good references. But after showing up ten minutes late, she called me "Mr. Melody" throughout the interview.*
>
> *The two things I remembered about her were that she had kept me waiting and constantly mispronounced my name. I finally offered the position to someone whose . . . skills were not nearly so good.*[26]

Your background research will pay dividends during the employment interview. One criterion most interviewers use in rating applicants is "knowledge of the position," and a lack of information in this area can be damaging. One example illustrates the advantages that come from knowing even a small amount about a position:

> *When I first took a job as a young attorney for Litton Industries, I was interviewing for the position as an assistant division counsel for their Guidance Control Systems Division. That name alone was enough to boggle my mind. A scientist I was not. After a little research, I found that they made something called an inertial navigation system. That was worse than the name of the division. What was an inertial navigation system?*
>
> *Finally I went to a fraternity brother who had majored in engineering and asked him if he knew what it was all about. He explained to me that inertial navigation was a method of navigating whereby the system allows you, if you know your starting point, to measure speed and distance and therefore know where you are at all times. He also explained the components of the system.*
>
> *When I went into my interview with the division counsel, I astounded him by my ability to talk the jargon of inertial navigation . . .*
>
> *He later told me that I was the first person he had interviewed for the job to whom he did not have to explain inertial navigation. Since he didn't understand it any better than I did, his being relieved of this obligation was a big plus in my favor. Also he said that he knew that it was not an easy task for me to find someone who could explain the subject and understand it well enough to have the confidence to discuss it. My initiative and interest in going to this extent to prepare for the interview had impressed him.*[27]

Table 7–1 lists common interviewer complaints about interviewees.

Anticipate Key Questions Most employment interviewers ask questions in five areas:

Educational background. Does the candidate possess adequate training for a successful career? Do the candidate's grades and other activities predict success in this organization?

Work experience. Do any previous jobs prepare the candidate for this position? What does the candidate's employment history suggest about his or her work habits and ability to work well with others?

Table 7–1 Most Frequent Interviewer Complaints about Interviewees

1. Poor personality, manners; lack of poise, confidence; arrogant; egotistical; conceited
2. Poor appearance, lack of neatness, careless dress
3. Lack of enthusiasm, shows little interest, no evidence of initiative, lack of drive
4. Lack of goals and objectives, lack of ambition, poorly motivated, does not know interests, uncertain, indecisive, poor planning
5. Inability to express self well, poor oral expression, poor habits of speech
6. Unrealistic salary demands, overemphasis on money, more interested in salary than opportunity, unrealistic concerning promotion to top jobs
7. Lack of maturity, no leadership potential
8. Lack of extracurricular activities, inadequate reasons for not participating in activities
9. Failure to get information about our company, lack of preparation for the interview, inability to ask intelligent questions
10. Excessive interest in security and benefits, "what can you do for me" attitude
11. Objects to travel, unwilling to relocate

Source: Victor R. Lindquest, *The Northwestern Endicott Report 1988* (Evanston, IL.: The placement Center, Northwestern University, 1988).

Career goals. Does the candidate have clear goals? Are they compatible with a career in this organization?

Personal traits. Do the actions and attitudes of the candidate predict good work habits and good interpersonal skills?

Knowledge of organization and job. Does the candidate know the job and organization well enough to be certain that he or she will feel happy in them?

While the specifics of each job are different, many questions are the same for any position. Table 7-2 on page 202 lists the most common questions asked by interviewers. In addition, knowledge of the company and job should suggest other specific questions to you.

There's a good chance you will be asked at least some of the common questions listed below. Here are some tips about how to approach them, keeping the focus on what you can do for the organization.

Question	What to Emphasize
Why should we hire you?	Don't give a generic answer: Nearly everyone says they are hardworking and motivated. Briefly list your unique strengths and qualifications, showing how they **will help you perform the job in question.**
Why do you want to work here?	If you have researched the organization, this question gives you an opportunity to explain how your experience and qualifications match the **company's needs.**

Table 7–2 Commonly Asked Questions in Employment Interviews

Educational Background

How has your education prepared you for a career?
Why did you choose your college or university?
Describe your greatest success (biggest problem) in college.
What subjects in school did you like best? Why?
What subjects did you like least? Why?
What was your most rewarding college experience?

Work Experience

Tell me about your past jobs. (What did you do in each?)
Which of your past jobs did you enjoy most? Why?
Why did you leave your past jobs?
Describe your greatest accomplishments in your past jobs.
What were your biggest failures? What did you learn from them?
How have your past jobs prepared you for this position?
What were the good and bad features of your last job?
This job requires initiative and hard work. What in your experience demonstrates these qualities?
Have you supervised people in the past? In what capacities? How did you do?
How do you think your present boss (subordinates, co-workers) would describe you?
How do you feel about the way your present company (past companies) is (were) managed?

Career Goals

Why are you interested in this position?
Where do you see yourself in 5 years? 10 years?
What is your eventual career goal?
Why did you choose the career you are now pursuing?

Tell me about yourself.	Keep your answer focused on parts of your life that relate to the job. Pick a couple of points that show how you possess skills and/or experiences that show **what you can contribute to this organization.**

You can't anticipate every question a prospective employer will ask. Still, if you go into the interview with a clear sense of yourself—both strengths and limitations—and the nature of the job you are seeking, you can probably handle almost any question. Consider a few examples of unusual questions, and what the interviewers who asked them were seeking.

What are your financial goals?
How would you describe the ideal job?
How would you define success?
What things are most important to you in a career?

Self-Assessment

In your own words, how would you describe yourself?
How have you grown in the last years?
What are your greatest strengths? Your greatest weaknesses?
What things give you the greatest satisfaction?
How do you feel about your career up to this point?
What is the biggest mistake you have made in your career?
Do you prefer working alone or with others?
How do you work under pressure?
What are the most important features of your personality?
Are you a leader? (a creative person? a problem solver?) Give examples.

Knowledge of the Job

Why are you interested in this particular job? Our company?
What can you contribute to this job? Our company?
Why should we hire you? What qualifies you for this position?
What do you think about ___________ (job-related topic)?
What part of this job do you think would be most difficult?

Other Topics

Do you have any geographical preferences? Why?
Would you be willing to travel? To relocate?
Do you have any questions for me?

Question	What the Interviewer Was Seeking
What's the biggest career mistake you've made so far?	Have you learned from your errors? What mistakes are you not likely to make if you work for us?
If I asked your previous co-workers what I'd better watch out for from you, what would they say?	How aware are you of your own strengths and weaknesses?
Who else are you interviewing with, and how close are you to accepting an offer?	How committed are you to our organization? How do others view your potential as an employee?[28]

"Will my office be near an ice machine?"

Since most employers are untrained in interviewing, you can't expect them to ask every important question.[29] If your interviewer doesn't touch on an important area, look for ways of volunteering information that he or she probably would want to have. For instance, you could show your knowledge of the industry and the company when you respond to a question about your past work experience: "As my résumé shows, I've been working in this field for 5 years, first at Marston-Keenan and then with Evergreen. In both jobs we were constantly trying to keep up with the pace you set here. For example, the VT-17 was our biggest competitor at Evergreen. . . ."

Respond to the Employer's Needs and Concerns While you may need a job to repay a college loan or finance your new Porsche, these concerns won't impress a potential employer. Companies hire employees to satisfy *their* needs, not yours. Although employers will rarely say so outright, the fundamental question that is *always* being asked in an employment interview is, *"Are you a person who can help this organization?"* That is, *"What can you do for us?"* One career guidance book makes the point clearly:

> *It is easy to get the impression during an interview that the subject of the interview, the star (so to speak) of the interview is, well, you. After all, you're the one in the hot seat. You're the one whose life is being dissected. Don't be too flattered. The real subject of the interview is the company. The company is what the interviewer ultimately thinks is important.*
>
> *Of course, you will be very concerned about what opportunities and skills the company has to offer you, but if you're smart, you'll keep that to yourself. It's not that it isn't proper to be interested in advancement and money—in fact, that's a given. What is not a given is your ability to put the interests of your company ahead of your own from time to time; to make personal sacrifices for the good of an important project. The interviewer will be extremely interested in these things if you can find a way to communicate them.*[30]

Your approach in an interview, then, should be to show your potential employer how your skills match the company's concerns. Background research will pay off here, too: If you have spent time learning about what the employer needs, you will be in a good position to show how you can satisfy company needs and concerns. Consider an example:

Interviewer: What was your major in college?

Poor Answer: I was a communication major.

Better Answer: I was a communication major. I'm really glad I studied that subject, because the skills I learned in school could help me in this job in so many ways: dealing with customers, working with you and the other people in the department, and also with all the external contractors who are part of the job. . . .

Interviewer: Tell me about your last job as a sales rep.

Poor Answer: I handled outside sales. I called on about 35 customers. My job was to keep them supplied and show them new products.

Better Answer: (elaborating on previous answer) I learned how important it is to provide outstanding customer service. Even though the products I sold in my last job are different from the ones I'd be selling here, I know that the competitive edge comes from making sure the customers get what they want, when they need it. I know that this company has a reputation for good service, so I'm really excited about working here.

Just because you respond to the employer's needs doesn't mean you should ignore your own goals; but as you are in an interview, keep in mind that you need to demonstrate how you can help the organization or you won't have a job offer to consider.

Because most employers have had bad experiences with some of the people they have hired, they are likely to be concerned about what might go wrong if they hire you. In Richard Bolles's words, employers worry that

> *you won't be able to do the job, you lack the skills, you won't work full days, regularly, you'll quit unexpectedly, it will take you a long time to master the job, you won't get along with others, you'll do the minimum, you'll need constant supervision, you'll be dishonest, irresponsible, negative, substance abuser, incompetent, you'll discredit the organization or cost them a lot of money.*[31]

You can allay these fears without ever addressing them directly by answering questions in a way that showcases your good work habits:

Interviewer: What were the biggest challenges in your last job?

Answer: The work always seemed to come in spurts. When it was busy, we had to work especially hard to stay caught up. I can remember some weeks when we never seemed to leave the office. It was hard, but we did whatever it took to get the job done.

Interviewer: How did you get along with your last boss?

Answer: My last manager had a very hands-off approach. That was a little scary at times, but it taught me that I can solve problems without a lot of supervision. I was always glad to get guidance, but when it didn't come, I learned that I can figure out things for myself.

Be Honest Whatever else an employer may be seeking, honesty is a mandatory job requirement. If an interviewer finds out that you have misrepresented yourself by lying or exaggerating about even one answer, then everything else you say will be suspect.[32]

Being honest doesn't mean you have to confess to every self-doubt and shortcoming. As in almost every type of situation, both parties in an employment interview try to create desirable impressions. In fact, some ethicists have noted that the ability to "sell" yourself honestly but persuasively is a desirable attribute, since it shows that you can represent an employer well after being hired.[33] So, highlight your strengths and downplay your weaknesses, but always be honest.

career tip

Negotiating a Salary

It is usually best to save a discussion of salary until you have been offered a job. Compensation is almost always negotiable to some degree. It becomes increasingly so for positions that require more expertise and experience. The way you handle this issue can make a significant difference in the pay and benefits you receive. The following tips can help you negotiate the best possible compensation package.

Find Out the Prevailing Compensation for Your Type of Job

Discover what others are paid for the kind of work you do. Begin by exploring compensation levels in your field or industry. Several strategies will help you come up with realistic figures:

- *Online information:* Glassdoor.com, Payscale.com, Jobstar.org, and Careerbuilder.com provide useful ways to compare salaries. You can also use a search engine like MetaCrawler (**www.metacrawler.com**) to seek out compensation. Combine terms like "wages" or "salary" with the name of your field (e.g., "sales" or "programming") to find the numbers you are seeking. The Salary Calculator (**www.homefair.com/calc/salcalc.html**) and Salary.com (**www.salary.com**) provide additional salary comparisons and information.
- *Personal contacts:* Your personal network can provide very useful information on prevailing salaries and benefits. Career counselors, recruiters, and outplacement counselors can be useful sources of information. An informational interview with people like this can be extremely useful. Contacts within a specific geographical area or company where you hope to work can be especially helpful. Rather than embarrassing people by asking for personal information ("How much do you earn?") or proprietary data ("What's the top salary the company would pay for a job like this?"), it's better to ask questions like, "What is the salary range in this company for a job like mine?" A good follow-up is, "What might lead an employer to offer a salary at the top end of this scale?"

Learn How Much the Company Wants You

Your leverage will be greatest under two conditions: first if the company needs to hire someone quickly, and if it is specifically interested in you. Your personal network is, again, the ideal way to determine whether these conditions exist. You can also determine how motivated the company is to hire you from your knowledge of the job market—both nationally and locally—for positions like the one you are seeking.

Consider Negotiating for Nonsalary Compensation

Even if the salary offer isn't everything you hope for, you may be able to get benefits such as the following that improve the overall compensation package:

- Nonsalary financial gains: commissions, bonuses (for signing or future performance), money in lieu of unneeded benefits (e.g., health insurance when you already have coverage), profit sharing, stock options.
- Time: personal leave days, extra vacation, flexible scheduling of work hours, telecommuting, job sharing.
- Educational benefits: tuition reimbursement, training programs.
- Perquisites: better office, expense account, company car, reserved or paid parking.
- Relocation expenses: house-hunting trips, moving costs, realty fees for home purchase/sale.
- Support: free on-site child care, company time for volunteering in your child's school.
- Lifestyle: use of company apartment, upgraded business travel (hotel, air), company tickets to sporting events and theaters, health club membership.

ethical challenge

Promoting Yourself with Honesty

Think of a job that you are probably capable of handling well but for which you would most likely not be the candidate hired. Develop a list of questions you would probably be asked in an interview for this position. Then develop a list of answers that show you in the best possible light while being honest.

Emphasize the Positive Although you should always be honest, it is also wise to phrase your answers in a way that casts you in the most positive light. Consider the difference between positive and negative responses to this question:

Interviewer: I notice you've held several jobs, but you haven't had any experience in the field you've applied for.

Negative Answer: Uh, that's right. I only decided that I wanted to go into this field last year. I wish I had known that earlier.

Positive Answer: That's right. I've worked in a number of fields, and I've been successful in learning each one quickly. I'd like to think that this kind of adaptability will help me learn this job and grow with it as technology changes the way the company does business.

Notice how the second answer converted a potential negative into a positive answer. If you anticipate questions that have the ability to harm you, you can compose honest answers that present you in a favorable manner.

Even if you are confronted with comments that cast you in a negative light, you can recast yourself more positively. Notice how each negative trait below could be reframed as a positive attribute:[34]

Negative Trait	Positive Attribute
Overly detailed	Thorough, reliable
Cautious	Careful, accurate
Intense	Focused
Slow	Methodical, careful
Naive	Open, honest
Aggressive	Assertive

Don't misunderstand: Arguing with the interviewer or claiming that you have no faults isn't likely to win you a job offer. Still, reframing shortcomings as strengths can shift the employer's view of you:

Employer: If I were to ask your colleagues to describe your biggest weaknesses, what do you think they'd say?

Candidate: Well, some might say that I could work faster, especially when things get frantic. On the other hand, I think they would agree that I'm very careful about my work and that I don't make careless errors. In the long run, I think that saves the company and our customers a lot of grief. I want to work faster, but never at the cost of making mistakes.

Another important rule is to avoid criticizing others in an employment interview. Consider the difference between the answers below:

Interviewer: From your transcript, I notice that you graduated with a 2.3 grade-point average. Isn't that a little low?

Negative Answer: Sure, but it wasn't my fault. I had some terrible teachers during my first 2 years of college. We had to memorize a lot of useless information that didn't have anything to do with the real world. Besides, professors give you high grades if they like you. If you don't play their game, they grade you down.

Positive Answer: My low grade-point average came mostly from very bad freshman and sophomore years. I wasn't serious about school then, but you can see that my later grades are much higher. I've grown a lot in the past few years, and I'd like to think that I can use what I've learned in this job.

Most job candidates have been raised to regard modesty as a virtue, which makes it hard to toot their own horns. Excessive boasting certainly is likely to put off an interviewer, but experts flatly state that showcasing your strengths is essential. Florida State University management professor Michele Kacmar found that job seekers who talked about their good qualities were rated higher than those who focused on the interviewer.[35] Pre-interview rehearsals will help you find ways of saying positive things about yourself in a confident, nonboastful manner.

Back Up Your Answers with Evidence As you read a few pages ago, behavioral interviewers figure that the best predictor of a potential employee's performance is what he or she has done in the past. Even if you aren't in a behavioral interview, it is usually effective to back up any claims you make with evidence of your performance.

One good framework for answering questions is the "PAR" approach. These initials stand for the three parts of a good answer: Identifying the *problem,* describing the *action* you took, and stating the *results* that your actions produced. You can see the value of this approach by comparing the two answers below:

Interviewer: What strengths would you bring to this job?

Weak Answer: I'm a self-starter who can work without close supervision [unsupported claim].

Stronger Answer: I'm a self-starter who can work without close supervision [claim]. For example, in my last job, my immediate supervisor was away from the office off and on for 3 months because of some health issues [problem]. We were switching over to a new accounting system during that time, and I worked with the software company to make the change [action]. We made the changeover without losing a single day's work, and without any loss of data [results].

technology tip

Creating a Digital Portfolio

Showing a prospective employer what you can do is much more effective than simply talking about your qualifications. This is especially true for jobs that involve tangible products like graphic design, commercial art, journalism, and technical writing.

Portfolios can also work in less obvious fields. You might, for example, demonstrate your ability to do solid work by sharing a report you helped create, a training you devised, or a collection of letters from satisfied customers praising your work.

The nature of your work may lend itself to a digital portfolio that can be posted online. You can include links to this site in your print material, as well as in any electronic correspondence with potential employers and references. To keep a professional appearance, make sure your digital portfolio has its own Web address: Don't embed it in any social networking sites that include personal information. If you are applying for different types of positions, such as training and marketing, consider creating two different electronic portfolios that showcase your work for each type of position.

You can find extensive guides to constructing portfolios at the career centers of many colleges and universities, including

- Ball State University **http://www.bsu.edu/art/article/0,25305~,00.html** and **http://www.bsu.edu/commstudies/article/0,,16720~,00.html**
- University of Wisconsin–River Falls **www.uwrf.edu/ccs/portfolio-steps.htm**

For specific tips on creating a digital portfolio, see

- EFolio Minnesota: **www.efoliomn.com**
- Eduscapes: **http://eduscapes.com/tap/topic82.htm**
- E-portfolios at Penn State: **www.portfolio.psu.edu/**
- EIFEL: **www.eifel.org/publications/eportfolio/proceedings2/ep2008/presentations**
- Quintcareers: **www.quintcareers.com/QuintZine/archives/20021014.html**

Keep Your Answers Brief It is easy to rattle on in an interview out of enthusiasm, a desire to show off your knowledge, or nervousness, but in most cases highly detailed answers are not a good idea. The interviewer probably has a lot of ground to cover, and long-winded answers won't help. A general rule is to keep your responses under 2 minutes. An interviewer who wants additional information can always ask for it.

Be Enthusiastic If you are applying for jobs that genuinely excite you, the challenge isn't to manufacture enthusiasm, but to show it. This can be difficult when you are nervous during what feels like a make-or-break session. Just remember that the interviewer wants to know how you really feel about the job and organization, so all you have to do is share your enthusiasm. Sharing your interest and excitement in the job and company can give you a competitive edge. Career Center director Gregory D. Hayes says, "If I talk to five deadbeat people and have one who is upbeat, that's the one I'm going to hire."[36]

Have Your Own Questions Answered Any good employer will recognize that you have your own concerns about the job. After you have answered the interviewer's questions, you should be prepared to ask a few of your own. Realize that your questions make indirect statements about you just as your answers to the interviewer's inquiries did. Be sure your questions aren't all greedy ones that focus on salary, vacation time, benefits, and so on. Table 7-3 on page 210 lists some questions to consider asking when you are invited to do so.

Table 7–3 Questions to Consider Asking the Interviewer during an Employment Interview

Why is this position open?
How often has it been filled during the past 5 years?
What have been the reasons for people leaving in the past?
Why did the person who most recently held this position leave?
What would you like the next person who holds this job to do differently?
What are the most pressing issues and problems in this position?
What support does this position have (people, budget, equipment, etc.)?
What are the criteria for success in this position?
What might be the next career steps for a person who does well in this position?
What do you see as the future of this position? This organization?
What are the most important qualities you will look for in the person who will occupy this position?

Rehearsing an Interview No athlete would expect to win without practicing, and no performer would face an audience without practicing long and hard. The same principle holds when you are facing an important employment interview: You should practice enough to be your very best when facing a prospective employer.

Effective practicing involves several steps:

1. Use your pre-interview research to identify the nature of the job you are seeking. What skills are required? What personal qualities are most desirable for this position? What kind of person will fit best with the culture of the organization?
2. Draft a series of questions that explore the job description you have created; use the lists in Table 7–2 as a guide. Be sure to include questions in each key area: educational background, work experience, career goals, personal traits, and knowledge of the organization and job.
3. Think about how you can answer each question. Each answer should contain a *claim* ("I have experience making presentations using Microsoft PowerPoint") and *evidence* to back it up ("I learned PowerPoint in a college business communications course and used it to train customer service reps in my last job"). In every case, make sure your answer shows how you can satisfy the employer's needs.
4. Role-play the interview several times with the help of a friend. Be sure you include the orientation and conclusion phases of the interview, as well as practice the questions you plan to ask the interviewer. If possible, videotape and review your performance twice: once to evaluate the content of your answers and again to check your appearance and the image you are projecting.

Many colleges have student job placement centers that have tremendous print resources on interviewing as well as a way of scheduling and recording a mock interview with a professional job counselor who will go over your video with you and give you constructive advice. Alternatively, use interview simulators listed at the end of the chapter to practice your answers to interview questions and to get feedback about a variety of responses.

Self-Assessment — Your IQ (Interview Quotient)

Assess how ready you are to handle employment interviews skillfully by answering the questions below, using the following scale:

5 = strongly agree; 4 = agree; 3 = maybe, not certain; 2 = disagree; 1 = definitely not.

Pre-Interview Planning

1. I have conducted background research and understand the organization and the field. 5 4 3 2 1
2. I know the nature of the job (responsibilities, skills, how it fits in the company). 5 4 3 2 1
3. When possible and appropriate, I have asked members of my personal network to give the prospective employer favorable information about me. 5 4 3 2 1
4. I am prepared for any interview format. 5 4 3 2 1
5. I think constructively about the upcoming interview, rather than dwell on negative thoughts. 5 4 3 2 1
6. I will dress and groom in a way that is appropriate for this company and position. 5 4 3 2 1
7. I know how to arrive at the interview site. 5 4 3 2 1

During the Interview

8. I can handle the small talk that arises in the opening phase of the interview. 5 4 3 2 1
9. I nonverbally communicate my interest and enthusiasm for the job. 5 4 3 2 1
10. I am prepared to answer the kinds of questions likely to be asked (see Table 7-3) in a way that shows how I can meet the employer's needs. 5 4 3 2 1
11. I back up all my answers with examples that help clarify and prove what I'm saying. 5 4 3 2 1
12. I give concise answers to the interviewer's questions. 5 4 3 2 1
13. I present myself confidently and with enthusiasm. 5 4 3 2 1
14. I am prepared to respond to illegal questions the interviewer might ask. 5 4 3 2 1
15. I know when and how to deal with salary questions. 5 4 3 2 1
16. I have prepared a list of references. 5 4 3 2 1
17. I am prepared to ask questions of my own about the job and organization. 5 4 3 2 1
18. I practiced asking and answering questions until I am comfortable and articulate. 5 4 3 2 1

After the Interview

19. I know how to write an effective thank-you letter. 5 4 3 2 1
20. I am prepared to follow up with the interviewer to determine my status, if necessary. 5 4 3 2 1

Scoring

Total the numbers you have circled. If your score is between 80 and 100, you appear to be well-prepared for interviews. If your score is between 60 and 80, you are moderately prepared. If your score is below 60, you would do well to make additional preparations before any employment interviews.

Source: After Ron and Caryl Krannich, *Interview for Success: A Practical Guide to Increasing Job Interviews, Offers, and Salaries,* 8th ed. (Manassas Park, VA: Impact Publications, 2003), pp. 12–17.

Post-Interview Follow-up

Without exception, every employment interview should be followed immediately by a thank-you letter to the person who interviewed you. As Figure 7–4 shows, this letter serves several purposes:

- It demonstrates common courtesy.
- It reminds the employer of you.
- It gives you a chance to remind the interviewer of important information about you that came up in the interview and to provide facts you may have omitted then.
- It can tactfully remind the interviewer of promises made, such as a second interview or a response by a certain date.
- It can correct any misunderstandings that may have occurred during the interview.[37]

If you don't get the job, consider contacting the person who interviewed you and asking what shortcomings kept you from being chosen. Even if the interviewer isn't comfortable sharing this information with you (it might not have anything to do with your personal qualifications), your sincere desire to improve yourself can leave a positive impression that could help you in the future.

Unlike most business correspondence, a thank-you letter doesn't have to be typewritten. Because it is a personal expression of gratitude, handwriting is considered acceptable. Depending on the formality of your relationship and the image you want to create, you may still choose to use a regular business-letter format. Whatever style you choose, the letter should be neat, error-free, and carefully composed.

FIGURE 7–4
Sample Thank-You Message

From: Susan Mineta [stm@comnet.net]
Sent: Tuesday, March 30, 2010 9:14 AM
To: Leslie Thoresen [lesthor@blogsite.com]
Subject: Thank you!
Attached: S Mineta articles.pdf

Dear Mr. Thoresen:

I left our meeting yesterday full of excitement. Your remarks about the value of my experience as a student journalist and blogger were very encouraging. I also appreciate your suggestion that I speak with Mr. Leo Benadides. Thank you for promising to tell him that I'll be calling within the next week.

Since you expressed interest in the series I wrote on how Asian women are breaking cultural stereotypes, I am attaching copies to this e-mail. I hope you find them interesting.

Your remarks about the dangers of being typecast exclusively as a writer on women's issues were very helpful. Just after we spoke I received an assignment to write a series on identity theft and the elderly. I'll be sure to let you know when these articles appear online.

Thank you again for taking time from your busy day. I will look forward to hearing from you when the job we discussed is officially created.

Sincerely,

Susan Mineta
8975 Santa Clarita Lane
Glendale, CA 90099
(818) 214-0987

Interviewing and the Law

Many laws govern which questions are and are not legal in employment interviews, but the general principle that underlies them all is simple: Questions may not be asked for the purpose of discriminating on the basis of race, color, religion, sex, disabilities, national origin, or age. Employers may still ask about these areas, but the U.S. government's Equal Employment Opportunity Commission (EEOC) permits only questions that investigate a **bona fide occupational qualification (BFOQ** in bureaucratic jargon) for a particular job. This means any question asked should be job-related. The Supreme Court has said that "the touchstone is business necessity."[38] Table 7-4 on pages 214–215 lists questions that are generally not considered BFOQs as well as those that are legitimate.

The Americans with Disabilities Act of 1990 (ADA) requires equal access to employment and provision of "reasonable accommodations" for persons with disabilities. It defines *disability* as a "physical" or "mental impairment" that "substantially limits" one or more "major life activities." As with any other job-related issue, the key question is what is "reasonable." The law clearly states, however, that disabled candidates can be questioned only about their ability to perform "essential functions" of a job and that employers are obligated to provide accommodations for disabled candidates and employees. If a person indicates a need for reasonable accommodation during the application process, the company is required to provide it. For example, a person who is deaf can request an interpreter at company expense for the interview.[39]

There are several ways to answer an unlawful question:[40]

1. *Answer without objection.* Answer the question, even though you know it is probably unlawful: "I'm 47."
2. *Seek explanation.* Ask the interviewer firmly and respectfully to explain why this question is a BFOQ: "I'm having a hard time seeing how my age relates to my ability to do this job. Can you explain?"
3. *Redirection.* Shift the focus of the interview away from a question that isn't job-related and toward the requirements of the position itself: "What you've said so far suggests that age is not as important for this position as is willingness to travel. Can you tell me more about the travel requirement?"
4. *Refusal.* Explain politely but firmly that you will not provide the information requested: "I'd rather not talk about my religion. That's a personal matter for me." If you are sure you aren't interested in the job, you could even end the interview immediately: "I'm very uncomfortable with these questions about my personal life, and I don't see a good fit between me and this organization."

Choosing the best response style depends on several factors.[41] First, it is important to consider the probable intent of the interviewer. The question may indeed be aimed at collecting information that will allow the employer to discriminate, but it may just as well be a naive inquiry with no harm intended. Some interviewers are unsophisticated at their job. A study reported in *The Wall Street Journal* revealed that over 70 percent of 200 interviewers in Fortune 500 corporations thought that at least 5 of 12 unlawful questions were safe to ask.[42] In another survey, employers at 100 small businesses were presented with five illegal interview questions. All of the respondents said they either would ask or had asked at least one of them.[43] Results like these suggest that an illegal question may be the result of ignorance rather than malice. The interviewer who discusses family, nationality, or religion may simply be trying to make conversation. Be careful not to introduce these topics yourself as it may open the door to conversations and questions you would rather not deal with.

Table 7–4 Questions Interviewers Can and Cannot Legally Ask

Federal law restricts employer interviewer questions and other practices to areas clearly related to job requirements. The following are some questions and practices that are generally considered legitimate and others that are not.

Subject	Unacceptable	Acceptable
Name	What is your maiden name? Have you ever changed your name?	Name "Is there another name I'd need to check on your work and education record?"
Residence	"Do you own or rent your home?"	Place of residence
Age	Age Birth date Dates of attendance or completion of elementry or high school Questions that tend to identify applicants over age 40	Statement that hire is subject to verification that applicant meets legal age requirements "If hired, can you show proof of age?" "Are you over 18 years of age?" "If under 18, can you, after employment, submit a work permit?"
Birthplace, citizenship	Birthplace of applicant, applicant's parents, spouse, or other relatives "Are you a U.S. citizen?" *or* citizenship of applicant, applicant's parents, spouse, or other relatives Requirement that applicant produce naturalization, first papers, or alien card *prior to employment*	"Can you, after employment, submit verification of your legal right to work in the United States?" *or* statement that such proof may be required after employment
National origin	Questions as to nationality, lineage, ancestry, national origin, descent, or parentage of applicant, applicant's parents, or spouse "What is your mother tongue?" *or* language commonly used by applicant How applicant acquired ability to read, write, or speak a foreign language	Languages applicant reads, speaks, or writes, if use of a language other than English is relevant to the job for which applicant is applying
Sex, marital status, family	Questions that indicate applicant's sex Questions that indicate applicant's marital status Number and/or ages of children or dependents Provisions for child care Questions regarding pregnancy, childbearing, or birth control Name or address of relative, spouse, or children of adult applicant "With whom do you reside?" or "Do you live with your parents?"	Name and address of parent or guardian if applicant is a minor, statement of company policy regarding work assignment of employees who are related
Race, color	Questions as to applicant's race or color Questions regarding applicant's complexion or color of skin, eyes, hair	

Subject	Unacceptable	Acceptable
Religion	Questions regarding applicant's religion Religious days observed *or* "Does your religion prevent you from working weekends or holidays?"	Statement by employer of regular days, hours, or shifts to be worked
Arrest, criminal record	Arrest record *or* "Have you ever been arrested?"	"Have you ever been convicted of a felony?" Such a question must be accompanied by a statement that a conviction will not necessarily disqualify an applicant from employment
Military service	General questions regarding military service such as dates and type of discharge Questions regarding service in a foreign military	Questions regarding relevant skills acquired during applicant's U.S. military service
Organizations	"List all organizations, clubs, societies to which you belong."	"Please list job-related organizations or professional associations to which you belong that you believe enhance your job performance."
References	Questions of applicant's former employers or acquaintances that elicit information specifying the applicant's race, color, religious creed, national origin, ancestry, physical handicap, medical condition, marital status, age, or sex	"By whom were you referred for a position here?" Names of persons willing to provide professional and/or character references for applicant
Physical description, photograph	Questions as to applicant's height and weight Requirement that applicant affix a photograph to application Request that asks applicant, at his or her option, to submit a photograph Requirement that calls for a photograph after interview but before employment	Statement that photograph may be required after employment
Physical condition, handicap	Questions regarding applicant's general medical condition, state of health, or illnesses Questions regarding receipt of workers' compensation "Do you have any physical disabilities or handicaps?"	Statement by employer that offer may be made contingent on applicant's passing a job-related physical examination "Do you have any physical condition or handicap that may limit your ability to perform the job applied for? If yes, what can be done to accommodate your limitation?"

For further information about illegal questions consult these online sources:
http://jobsearchtech.about.com/od/interview/l/aa022403_2.htm
www.collegegrad.com/ezine/23illega.shtml
www.usatoday.com/careers/resources/interviewillegal.htm

A second factor when considering how to respond to an illegal question is your desire for the job at hand. You may be more willing to challenge the interviewer when a position isn't critical to your future. On the other hand, if your career rides on succeeding in a particular interview, you may be willing to swallow your objections. A third factor to consider is your feeling of comfort with the interviewer. For example, a female candidate with school-age children might welcome the chance to discuss child care issues with an interviewer who has identified herself as a single mother who faces the same challenges. A fourth item to consider is your own personal style. If you are comfortable asserting yourself, you may be willing to address an illegal question head-on. If you are less comfortable speaking up, especially to authority figures, you may prefer to respond less directly.

Being interviewed does not mean you are at the mercy of the interviewer; laws do govern your rights as a candidate. If you choose to take a more assertive approach to illegal questioning that you believe resulted in discrimination, you have the right to file a charge with the EEOC and your state Fair Employment Practices Commission within 180 days of the interview. In practice, the EEOC will withhold its investigation until the state commission has completed its inquiry. Federal and state agencies have a backlog of cases, however, so it may take years to complete an investigation. The commission may mediate the case, file a suit, or issue you a letter to sue.[44] Keep in mind that just because you can file a lawsuit doesn't mean this will always be the best course of action: A suit can take many months, or even years, to be settled and a ruling in your favor may not result in a large settlement. Furthermore, knowledge that you've filed a suit is not likely to make you an attractive candidate to other employers who hear of your action. Seeking professional counsel can help you make a decision that balances your personal values and practical considerations.

Sample Employment Interview

The following transcript is based on a real interview. As you read it, pay attention to both the interviewer's questions and the applicant's responses. In both cases, notice the strengths and the areas needing improvement. What parts of this interview would you like to incorporate in your style? What parts would you handle differently?

[The interview begins with an exchange of pleasantries]	**Interviewer:**	Monica Hansen? I'm Chris Van Dyke. Welcome.
	Applicant:	It's good to meet you.
[. . . and small talk.]	**Interviewer:**	Did you have any trouble finding us?
	Applicant:	The directions were perfect. And thanks for the parking pass.
[The interviewer briefly previews the approach of the interview and the anticipated amount of time.]	**Interviewer:**	Oh, yes. That's a necessity. The garage costs $12 per day if you don't have one. We'll have about a half-hour this morning to talk about the personnel administrator's position you've applied for. I'd like to learn about you. And, of course, I want to answer any questions you have about us.
	Applicant:	Great. I'm looking forward to it.

technology tip

Cleaning Up Your Digital Dirt

In spite of your best efforts to create a résumé and present yourself as a qualified job applicant, prospective employers have other ways of forming impressions of you, including all of the information available online. To discover what others can easily see about you, try these options:

1. Google yourself by typing your name into the search engine at **www.google.com.** Employers do it and so can you. The only hits may be advice you gave about training your Jack Russell terrier or a review you wrote about a great restaurant. On the other hand, you may find comments you made at meetings you attended, information about you in newspaper articles, public hearings, or court actions. You may be able to get site owners to remove things you would rather not have on record. Learn how to "un-Google" yourself at **www.wikihow.com/Ungoogle-Yourself.**
2. Review your profile on Web sites like Facebook (**www.facebook.com**) or MySpace (**www.myspace.com**), and/or Web sites you have created. Imagine the impression your profiles would make on prospective employers and consider editing references and photos you no longer want to share with the world—or at least change your privacy settings. The photo of you from the Halloween party your sophomore year or the comments others wrote about you might not create the best impression.

Source: Mike Hargis, "Social Networking Dos and Don'ts," available at **www.careerbuilder.com/Article/CB-964-The-Workplace-Social-Networking-Dos-and-Donts/?ArticleID=964&cbRecursionCnt=1&cbsid=316e44f43ea14225975e2c4d365bc009-283878043-JA-5&ns_siteid=ns_us_g_Mike_Hargis%2C_%E2%80.** Retrieved on December 29, 2008.

[Body of interview begins with an open question about employment history.]	**Interviewer:**	Good. Let's begin by having you tell me about your most recent position. Your résumé says you were at ITC in Springfield. Is that right?
[Interviewee uses question to showcase the skills acquired in past job that could help in the one being offered here.]	**Applicant:**	That's right. My official job title was personnel assistant, but that really doesn't describe very well the work I did. I recruited nonexempt employees, processed the payroll, oriented new employees, and maintained the files.
[Follow-up questions explore areas of interest in the new job.]	**Interviewer:**	Were you involved with insurance?
[The applicant uses this answer to point out another skill that she brings to the job.]	**Applicant:**	Yes. I processed workers' compensation claims and maintained the insurance reports for our health care plans. I learned a lot about dealing with government regulations.
	Interviewer:	And you said you were involved in hiring?
	Applicant:	Yes. I was responsible for recruiting and interviewing all clerical and administrative support people.
[Another open question, this time exploring the applicant's ability to analyze her own performance.]	**Interviewer:**	How did that go?

[The applicant fails to use this answer to showcase her abilities . . .]	**Applicant:**	It was tough in Springfield. There's actually a shortage of talented support people there. It's an expensive town to live in, and there aren't a lot of people who can afford living there on an administrative assistant's salary. It's not like Atlanta, where there's plenty of good help.
[so the interviewer follows up with another question.]	**Interviewer:**	What did you learn about hiring from your experiences at ITC?
[This answer is better, since it describes insights and skills the applicant brings to this job.]	**Applicant:**	I learned to look further than the résumé. Some people seem great on paper, but you find there's something wrong when you hire them. Other people don't have much experience on paper, but they have a lot of potential.
	Interviewer:	How did you get beyond paper screening?
	Applicant:	Well, if someone looked at all promising, I would phone the former employers and talk to the people the applicant actually worked for. Of course a lot of former employers are pretty noncommittal, but they usually would give clues about what they really thought about the person I was investigating—giving an indirect opinion without saying it outright.
	Interviewer:	What would you do if this was the person's first job?
[The applicant demonstrates resourcefulness here, spelling out her skill in the last sentence of her answer.]	**Applicant:**	I found that almost everyone had done some kind of work—part-time or vacation. And I could check up on that. Or I would even ask for the names of a few teachers and phone them up, if the person was just graduating. I learned that there's almost always a way to find what you're looking for, if you get creative.
	Interviewer:	Didn't that take a lot of time?
[This is a subtle way of saying, "I have good judgment."]	**Applicant:**	Yes, it did. But it was worth it in the long run, since we got much better employees that way. We almost never had to dismiss someone whom we'd done a phone check on.
	Interviewer:	You were promoted after a year. Why?
[Again, the applicant's answer introduces a trait that would be valuable in the new job: The desire for self-improvement.]	**Applicant:**	I was lucky to be in the right place. The company was growing, and we were very busy. I tried to take advantage of the situation by offering to do more and by taking classes at night.

	Interviewer:	What classes did you take?
[Presumably the skills acquired in these courses would be useful if the applicant is hired. In any case, she demonstrates the desire to learn skills useful in the business world.]	**Applicant:**	I took an applied human relations class last spring. And before that, a couple of computer classes: one in database management and one in desktop publishing. Our department was thinking about starting an employee newsletter, and I wanted to see if we could produce it in-house.
	Interviewer:	It sounds like you've done very well at ITC. Why do you want to leave?
[The response begins with a provocative statement, and then goes on to supply a solid reason for seeking a new job.]	**Applicant:**	In some ways I *don't* want to leave. The people are great—most of them—and I've enjoyed the work. But I'm looking for more challenges, and there isn't much chance for me to take on more responsibility there.
	Interviewer:	Why not?
	Applicant:	Well, my boss, the personnel director, is very happy in her job and has no plans to leave. She's young, and there's very little chance I'll be able to advance.
[The interviewer seeks specifics to elaborate on the broad statement "I'm looking for more challenges"]	**Interviewer:**	I see. Well, that is a problem. And what kind of responsibilities are you looking for?
[. . . and the candidate supplies answers.]	**Applicant:**	I'd say the biggest one is the chance to help make policy. In my past jobs, I've been carrying out policies that other people—management—have made. That's been fine, but I'd like to be involved in setting some policies myself.
[Again, the interviewer follows up by seeking more specifics]	**Interviewer:**	What kinds of policies?
[. . . and the candidate is prepared with detailed responses.]	**Applicant:**	Oh, there are several. Designing benefits packages. Coming up with a performance review system that people will take seriously. Teaching our supervisors how to interview and hire more systematically.
[The interviewer makes a smooth transition to a new topic.]	**Interviewer:**	I see. Well, the position you've applied for certainly does have those sorts of responsibilities. Let me ask you another question. What do you enjoy most about personnel work?
[The stock answer "I like to work with people" is so broad that it has little meaning]	**Applicant:**	Well, I really enjoy the chance to work so much with people. Of course, there's a lot of paperwork, too, but I especially like the chance to work with people.

[. . . so the interviewer seeks clarification.]

Interviewer: When you say "people," what kinds of work are you thinking of?

Applicant: I guess the common denominator is making people happy. Lots of employees get involved with the personnel department—once they've been hired, that is—because they have problems. Maybe it's an insurance claim or a problem with their performance review. It makes me feel good to see them leave feeling satisfied, or at least feeling better after they've come in so upset.

Interviewer: Are you always able to help them?

Applicant: No, of course not. Sometimes a person will want the impossible, and sometimes there just won't be any answer.

[Again, the interviewer uses a situational approach, seeking specifics.]

Interviewer: Can you give examples of these times?

[The applicant does a good job of describing a situation that illustrates her previous answer.]

Applicant: Well, one example of an impossible request comes up a lot with health insurance. At ITC we could choose from two plans. With one plan you could use any doctor you wanted. You had to make a co-payment with that one. With the other plan, you had to choose a doctor from a list of preferred providers, but there was no co-payment. If an employee chose the preferred-provider plan and later decided he or she wanted to use a doctor that wasn't on the list, we just couldn't do anything about it.

Interviewer: We've had that problem here, too. How did you handle it?

Applicant: Being sympathetic helped a little. Even if I couldn't give them what they wanted, at least saying I was sorry might have made it seem less like a total rejection. I also pointed out that they *could* switch plans during the open-enrollment period, which comes every year. I've also suggested to my boss that we do a better job of informing people about the restrictions of the preferred-provider plan before they sign up and maybe even get them to sign a statement that says they understand them. I think that would reduce the surprises that come up later.

[With this new topic, the interviewer shifts from fact to opinion questions.]	**Interviewer:**	That's a good idea. Monica, what qualities do you think are important for a personnel officer?
	Applicant:	Knowing the job is definitely important, but I'd say getting along with people might be even more important.
	Interviewer:	And how would you describe your ability to get along?
	Applicant:	Sometimes I think I deserve an Academy Award for acting the opposite of the way I feel.
	Interviewer:	Really? Tell me about it.
[The applicant offers a specific example to illustrate her provocative statement about acting the opposite of the way she feels.]	**Applicant:**	Every so often people will come in with an attitude problem, and I try to calm them down by acting more pleasant than I feel. For example, we've had people who think they're entitled to take 6 months off for a workers' compensation claim, when the doctor has said they're ready to come back after a few weeks. They come in and yell at us, and it's tough to be pleasant at times like those. But I don't think there's any point in being blunt or rude. It just makes them more angry.
[This indirect question really asks, "What kind of manager might you be?"]	**Interviewer:**	I see what you mean. Let's shift gears, Monica. If you were to pick a boss, what are the important traits that he or she should have?
	Applicant:	Let me see . . . certainly lots of follow-up—letting people know where they stand. The ability to give criticism constructively and to compliment good work. Giving people a task and then leaving them alone, without nagging.
	Interviewer:	But still being there to help if it's needed, right?
	Applicant:	Sure. But also giving me the space to finish a job without staying *too* close.
	Interviewer:	Anything else?
	Applicant:	Being available for help, as you said. Being consistent. And being willing to train employees in new jobs, letting them grow. And considering the personal goals of employees.
[The interviewer turns to a new topic area.]	**Interviewer:**	In personnel work, there's a need for confidentiality. What does that mean to you?

Applicant: That's an important area. You see lots of personal information, and it's easy to make offhand remarks that could upset someone.

Interviewer: What kinds of things do you have to be careful about?

Applicant: Oh, even something as simple as a person's birthday. Most people wouldn't care, but some people might be offended if their birthdays got out. I've learned to be constantly on guard, to watch what I say. I'm a private person anyway, so that helps.

[This question explores the candidate's personal attitudes.]

Interviewer: Monica, I've been asking you a lot of questions. Let me ask just one more; then it can be your turn. What are the factors that motivate you?

Applicant: Well, I like to be busy. If things aren't busy, I still work, but I like to be stimulated. I seem to get more work done when I'm busy than when there's plenty of time. It's crazy, but true. I'm also motivated by the chance to grow and take on as much responsibility as I can handle.

[Almost every employment interview includes a chance for the interviewee to ask questions.]

Interviewer: Monica, what questions do you have for me? What can I tell you about the job or the company?

[The applicant wisely begins by asking about the company, not focusing on personal questions such as compensations.]

Applicant: What kind of growth do you see for the company?

Interviewer: Well, we have 155 employees now. As I think you know, we're 5 years old, and we started with five employees. Our sales were up 14 percent last year, and it looks like we'll be expanding more.

Applicant: How many employees do you think will be added?

Interviewer: Well, we hired 20 new people last year, and we expect to hire almost the same number this year.

Applicant: And what's the turnover like?

Interviewer: That's a good question for a personnel person to ask! We've been growing so much, and people have been able to move into more responsible jobs, so they've been satisfied for the most part. Our turnover has been pretty low—about 15 percent annually.

[This question focuses on responsibilities of the job.]	**Applicant:**	Will the person you hire be involved in making policy?
	Interviewer:	Yes, definitely. We're still trying to catch up with ourselves after growing so fast. A big project for this year is to put together an employee handbook. Too many of our policies are verbal now, and that's not good. Developing that handbook would mean working directly with the president of the company, and that definitely involves developing policy.
[Finally, the applicant asks about compensation and benefits.]	**Applicant:**	Of course, I'm interested in learning about the benefits and salary.
[The interviewer appropriately defers a complete answer until the company has a clearer idea of the candidate's desirability.]	**Interviewer:**	Of course. Here's a copy of our benefits summary for you to study. We can talk about salary later. Right now I'd like you to meet a couple of our managers. After you've spoken with them, we can get back together to discuss salary and other matters.
[The interviewer wraps up the conversation by describing when the hiring decision will be made.]		We will definitely be making our decision within the next 10 days, so I promise you you'll have an answer before the first of next month. It's been a real pleasure talking to you, Monica. You certainly express yourself well. I'll talk with you again soon.
	Applicant:	Thanks. I've enjoyed the talk, too. I'll look forward to hearing from you.

The Performance Appraisal Interview

A working group is like an athletic team: Even the best players need the guidance of a coach to help them do their individual best and work with other members. Managers are the coaches in most organizations, and the performance appraisal interview is one way they help their team members.

Definition and Importance

Performance appraisal interviews are scheduled regularly between superior and subordinate to discuss the quality of the subordinate's performance. More specifically, these interviews have several functions, including the following:

- *Letting the employee know where he or she stands.* This kind of feedback includes praising good work, communicating areas that need improvement, and conveying to the employee his or her prospects for advancement.
- *Developing employee skills.* The review can be a chance for the employee to learn new skills. Among their other roles, managers and supervisors should be teachers. The performance appraisal interview can be a chance to show an employee how to do a better job.

- *Improving employment relationship.* Performance reviews should improve superior–subordinate relationships and give employees a sense of participation in the job. Ideally, employees will leave the interview feeling better about themselves and the organization.
- *Helping management learn the employee's point of view.* A performance appraisal should include upward as well as downward communication. It provides a chance for subordinates to explain their perspective to managers.
- *Counseling the employee.* An appraisal interview provides the chance for managers to learn about personal problems that may be affecting an employee's performance and to offer advice and support.
- *Setting goals for the future.* One result of every performance appraisal interview should be a clear idea of how both the superior and the subordinate will behave in the future.

Some bosses and employees complain that performance reviews are a nuisance. Management guru Robert Townsend agrees—to a point. "Printed forms for performance appraisal and MBOs are used by incompetent bosses in badly managed companies," he claims.[45] Performance appraisals appear to be increasingly unpopular and a recent survey of human resources professionals found that 32 percent were unsatisfied with their company's process.[46] Despite criticisms of this sort, authorities on communication agree that most managers and supervisors need to give employees *more* feedback, not less. "Day-to-day coaching is the most overlooked step of the performance process," says *One Minute Manager* co-author Kenneth Blanchard.[47] Townsend agrees. "Real managers manage by frequent eyeball contact," he insists, quoting one good boss's description of the process: "Half our meetings are held in the hall, the other half in the washroom."

Perhaps these management experts have a point. If bosses spent more time giving employees informal feedback and setting goals on a day-to-day basis, there might be less

Dilbert: © Scott Adams/Dist. by United Feature Syndicate, Inc. Reprinted by permission.

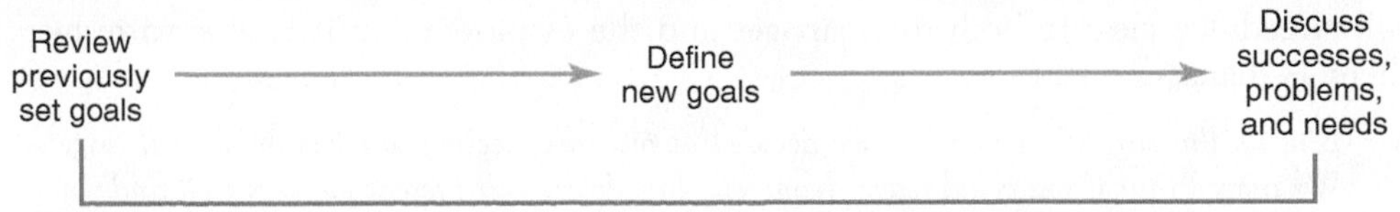

FIGURE 7–5 The Performance Appraisal Process

need for quarterly or semiannual formal meetings. But one way or the other, performance review is one of the most important responsibilities a manager has.

Despite the potential threat of being evaluated, performance appraisals can be welcomed by employees. One of the greatest hungers that workers have is to know where they stand with management. Researchers have found that receiving personal feedback correlates highly with job satisfaction,[48] and appraisal interviews offer a periodic session dedicated to providing just that feedback. Despite this fact, 40 percent of all employees report that they don't receive a regular performance review.[49]

Just because employees want feedback doesn't mean that they are always satisfied with the performance appraisals they do receive. Sometimes performance reviews can be contaminated by organizational politics, generating resentment and undermining morale.[50] This sort of bias isn't new: Over 18 centuries ago in 3rd-century China, a member of the Wei dynasty's court complained about a manager: "The Imperial Rater of Nine Grades seldom rates men according to their merits but always according to his likes and dislikes."[51] Intentionally or not, many unskilled managers turn appraisal sessions into criticisms of past shortcomings that do little besides arouse resentment and defensiveness in employees. The interviewing skills outlined in this section can help make sure that a performance review meets the needs of both management and employees.

Performance review should be an ongoing process, not something that happens only at infrequent intervals during a scheduled interview.[52] The functions of performance appraisal listed on pages 223–224 can and should be performed constantly in the kind of process pictured in Figure 7–5. This doesn't mean that formal interviews are useless, for they provide a chance to focus on how well the ongoing job of judging and improving performance is proceeding. The value of a formal review is captured by former Chrysler chairman Lee Iacocca, who describes how the procedure works in his company:

> *Every three months, each manager sits down with his immediate superior to review the manager's past accomplishments and to chart his goals for the next term. Once there is agreement on these goals, the manager puts them in writing and the supervisor signs off on it. . . . The discipline of writing something down is the first step toward making it happen. In conversation, you can get away with all kinds of vagueness and nonsense, often without even realizing it. But there's something about putting your thoughts on paper that forces you to get down to specifics. That way, it's harder to deceive yourself–or anybody else.*[53]

Steps in the Appraisal Process

After an initial exchange of pleasantries–usually brief–the manager should provide a rationale for the interview, an outline of what information will be covered and how it will be used, and a preview of the interview's probable length. After the preliminaries, the body of an appraisal interview should go on to cover three areas: a review of the criteria established in past meetings, a discussion of the employee's performance, and a setting of goals for the future.

Review Progress The first step in the body of any appraisal interview should be to identify the criteria by which the employee is being evaluated. Ideally, these criteria will already be clear to both the manager and the employee, but it is wise to restate them. A manager might say,

> *Bill, as I'm sure you remember, we decided at our last meeting to focus on several targets. We agreed that if you could reach them, you'd be doing your present job very well and you'd be setting yourself up for an assistant sales manager's position. Here's the list of targets we developed last time [shows employee list]. So these are the areas we need to look at today.*

Discuss Successes, Problems, and Needs After the criteria have been defined, the discussion can focus on how well the employee has satisfied them. Discussion will be easiest when the goals are measurable: Are sales up 15 percent? Have jobs been completed on time? If the employee has explanations for why targets were not reached, it is the manager's job to consider these fairly. Some goals are subjective, so the evaluation of their performance will be a matter of judgment as well. Even seemingly vague goals like "being more patient with customers" can be at least partially clarified by turning them into simple behavioral descriptions such as "letting customers talk without interrupting them."

When evaluating past performance, it is important to maintain a balance among the points under consideration. Without meaning to let it happen, a manager and employee can become involved in discussing (or debating) a relatively unimportant point at length, throwing the overall look at the employee's performance out of perspective. A skillful interviewer will focus only on the most important criteria, usually dealing with no more than three areas that need work. Even the most demanding manager will realize upon reflection that changing old habits is difficult and that it is unrealistic to expect dramatic improvement in too many areas within a short time.

Even when an appraisal is conducted with the best of intentions, its evaluative nature raises the odds of a defensive response. Feedback will be best received when it meets several criteria. Observing these guidelines can boost the chances of keeping the interview's tone constructive:

- *Feedback should be accurate.* Perhaps the worst mistake an evaluator can make is to get the facts wrong. Before you judge an employee, be sure you have an accurate picture of his or her performance and all the factors that affected it. A tell-and-listen approach can help the manager understand an employee's performance more fully.
- *Feedback should be relevant to the job.* For example, it may be legitimate to comment on an employee's appearance in a job that involves contact with the public, but it is out of line to be critical about the way he or she handles personal matters after business hours.

The best chances of success occur when the review offers a balance of praise and constructive suggestions for improvement. Both everyday experience and research have demonstrated the power of positive reinforcement. One study revealed that the commitment level of employees dropped when their behavior was identified as only "satisfactory."[54] A manager who uses praise in appraisal interviews should remember the tips for praising outlined in Chapter 5 (pages 131–133).

Sooner or later, even the most outstanding employee will need to hear criticism about his or her work. Delivering negative information is one of the biggest challenges a manager or supervisor can face. The guidelines in Chapter 5 (pages 133–135) offer tips on how to offer negative feedback supportively. Handling critical situations well isn't just the boss's responsibility; the subordinate needs to behave responsibly too. The guidelines for coping nondefensively with criticism outlined on pages 135–137 should

Table 7–5 Checklist for Performance Appraisal Interviewing

a. Interview covers key areas
   i. Orients employee
   ii. Establishes positive climate
   iii. Reviews past achievement of goals
   iv. Identifies successes, problems, and needs in employee's area of responsibility
   v. Establishes new goals with employee
b. Feedback delivered constructively
   i. Information accurate
   ii. Feedback appropriate to critic's role
   iii. Balance of praise and constructive criticism
c. Praise delivered effectively
   i. Praise sincere
   ii. Specific behaviors identified
   iii. Emphasis on progress, not perfection
   iv. Praise communicated by deeds as well as by words
d. Criticism expressed constructively
   i. Criticism limited to key areas
   ii. Criticism delivered in face-saving manner
   iii. Criticism accompanied by offer to help
   iv. Benefits of cooperating emphasized
e. Interview accomplishes all necessary functions
   i. Lets employee know where he or she stands
   ii. Develops employee skills
   iii. Improves communication climate, boosts morale
   iv. Helps management understand employee's point of view
   v. Counsels employee as appropriate
   vi. Sets goals for future

be helpful when it is your turn to receive critical messages. While following these guidelines won't guarantee a successful performance review, it can increase the chances that the meeting will be genuinely constructive and serve the interests of both the superior and the subordinate.

Set Goals Once the employee and manager have discussed past successes, problems, and needs, the task becomes defining goals for the future. The goals should meet several criteria:

- They should focus on the most important aspects of the job. The tried-and-true 80:20 rule applies here: Changing 20 percent of a worker's behavior will usually solve 80 percent of the problems.
- They should be described as specifically as possible so that both manager and employee will know what actions constitute the target.

- A time period should be stated for each target. People often work best when faced with a deadline, and setting dates lets both parties know when the results are due.
- The targets ought to provide some challenge to the worker, requiring effort yet being attainable. A manageable challenge will produce the greatest growth and leave workers and managers feeling pleased with the changes that occur.

Review and Respond to the Written Record The appraisal process commonly has a written dimension in addition to the interview itself. Before the meeting, the manager often completes an evaluation form listing characteristics or behaviors important to the job. Ideally, the information on this form is taken from the goals set at the previous interview. In some organizations, the subordinate also fills out a self-rating form covering similar areas. In most companies, a performance review is summarized and documented with a written evaluation. In most cases, the manager completes a final report that summarizes the results of the session. The employee usually has the option of adding his or her own response to the manager's report. This document then becomes part of the employee's records and is used as a basis for future evaluations and as a source of information for decisions about promotions. (See Table 7–5.)

review points

- Information-gathering interviews conduct research by collecting background information to define goals and create specific questions and to identify the best interviewee.
- A career research interview helps the interviewer research a career field, be remembered by the interviewee, and gain referrals to assist in beginning and shaping one's career.
- Personal contacts are vital to choosing interviewees and professionalism in written and oral communication are essential while contacting an interviewee, conducting the interview, and following up after the interview.
- Performing well in an employment interview is usually necessary for being hired. Many positions are never advertised, so job-seekers must begin long before an interview to conduct background research, then contact potential employers appropriately, usually with a cover letter and résumé.
- Candidates should rehearse for panel, behavioral, and audition interview formats and in all cases, think constructively, make contact professionally, and dress appropriately. Interviewees need to be prepared for key questions and constantly focus on how they can help the organization reach its goals by responding to the employer's needs and concerns. Answers should be honest, positive, brief, and enthusiastic. Support answers with evidence and ask pertinent questions. Always follow up with a letter of thanks to the interviewer(s).
- Federal and state laws restrict interviewers from asking questions that are not related to the bona fide occupational qualifications of a job. Interviewees can know what questions are acceptable and unacceptable and be prepared with several strategies for responding to illegal questions.

- Performance appraisal interviews are a structured way for superiors and their subordinates to look at the quality of the subordinate's performance and how employees are viewed by management, and to jointly set goals.
- Appraisal interviews begin with a clear statement of criteria and a review of the employee's performance, citing successes and problems, and conclude with both the manager and employee setting goals for the next evaluation period.

key terms

Test your understanding of these key terms by visiting the Online Learning Center Web site at www.mhhe.com/adler10e.

activities

Go to the self-quizzes at the Online Learning Center at **www.mhhe.com/adler10e** to test your knowledge of chapter concepts.

1. Invitation to Insight

Consider the four types of interviews common to most occupations. For each type:

a. Identify a specific interview you have taken part in or will encounter.
b. Describe the goal of the interviewee and the interviewer in each situation. Is it similar or conflicting? If conflicting, what extra preparations would be advisable?
c. For the past interviews, describe how satisfied you were with your behavior. For future interviews, predict how satisfied you expect to be with your behavior, given your present level of interviewing skill.
d. Use concepts you have learned in this chapter to suggest at least two improvements you can enact in your next interview.

2. Invitation to Insight

Select a person in your chosen career who plays a role in hiring new employees. Conduct an information-gathering interview to discover the following:

a. What methods are used to identify job candidates?
b. What format is used to interview applicants?
c. What formal and informal criteria are used to hire applicants?
d. What personal qualities of applicants make a positive or negative impression?

3. Invitation to Insight

Brainstorm 5 to 10 specific actions you have taken (in classes, on the job, or in volunteer activities) that demonstrate your ability to perform well. Include specific evidence for each. Recall the positive results of your actions.

For added practice, team up with a classmate. Use the PAR approach (see p. 208) to role-play asking and answering interview questions. As your classmate asks questions, answer with actions and results. Then switch roles.

4. Skill Builder

For each of the following topics identify at least two people you could interview to gather information and write one or more specific objectives for each interview:

a. Learning more about a potential employer. (Name a specific organization.)
b. Deciding whether to enroll in a specific class. (You choose which one.)
c. Deciding which type of personal computer or software application to purchase.
d. Exploring career opportunities in a city of your choice.
e. Determining the best savings or investment vehicle for you at this time.
f. Comparing health insurance plans available to students.

5. Skill Builder

You can develop your skill and gain appreciation for the value of the informational interview by doing one of the following activities:

a. Conducting an informational interview with a professional in a career field that interests you. Possible goals are to learn more about the field, to learn how to advance in your current job, or to learn what it would take to switch fields. Follow these steps:

1. Identify a promising interviewee.
2. Write a letter requesting an interview.
3. Follow up your letter with a phone call to arrange a date.
4. Develop a list of questions that will achieve your stated purpose. Be sure that these questions follow the guidelines in Chapter 6.
5. Conduct the interview and report your results. Analyze how well you performed and suggest how you could improve in conducting future interviews.
6. Write a thank-you letter to your interviewee.

b. Identifying a specific organization you would like to work for, and completing the following pre-interview steps:
   1. Identify the person—by title and name, if possible—who has the power to hire you.
   2. Using research and the results of informational interviews, analyze the requirements for the position you would like to hold.
   3. Develop a list of questions a potential boss might ask in a selection interview.
   4. Prepare answers to those questions.

c. Role-playing an actual interview, with a companion filling the role of your potential employer.

6. Skill Builder

Imagine that a supervisor or instructor is preparing an evaluation of your performance. Four areas will be covered:

a. Quality of work.
b. Productivity.
c. Communication skill.
d. Attitude.
   1. For each area, write one or two measurable objectives that could be used as assessments in your area of work.
   2. Based on your actual behavior on the job, prepare a verbal explanation describing how well you have met these assessments during the last month.
   3. Identify several areas in which you could improve. From this information compose several measurable behavioral objectives for the coming month.

resources

For extensive readings and Web sites on types of interviews, see the Online Learning Center Web site at **www.mhhe.com/adler10e.**FIGURE 7–3